Loudoun County Virginia
Death Register
1853-1896

Elizabeth R. Frain and *Marty Hiatt, CGRS*

HERITAGE BOOKS
2007

HERITAGE BOOKS
AN IMPRINT OF HERITAGE BOOKS, INC.

Books, CDs, and more—Worldwide

For our listing of thousands of titles see our website at
www.HeritageBooks.com

Published 2007 by
HERITAGE BOOKS, INC.
Publishing Division
65 East Main Street
Westminster, Maryland 21157-5026

Copyright © 1998 Elizabeth R. Frain and Marty Hiatt

All rights reserved. No part of this book may be reproduced or transmitted in any form or by any means, electronic or mechanical, including photocopying, recording or by any information storage and retrieval system without written permission from the author, except for the inclusion of brief quotations in a review.

International Standard Book Number: 978-1-888265-62-0

Table of Contents

INTRODUCTION V

DEATHS BY YEAR AND DISTRICT VII

ABBREVIATIONS USED VIII

SLAVES LISTED BY OWNERS 1

NON-SLAVE DEATHS 27

INDEX 285

Introduction

On April 11, 1853, the General Assembly of the State of Virginia passed an Act requiring that each county clerk keep marriage, birth and death records for his county, beginning January 1, 1854. One copy was to be kept in the clerk's office, the other submitted to the State Auditors. The death records for Loudoun County are included in this book. The records as filed with the state are available on the Virginia Department of Health, Bureau of Vital Statistics, Deaths, Microfilm Reel #17. The county copies are available in a large bound volume at the courthouse in Leesburg, Loudoun County, Virginia.

The death information was to be recorded by each commissioner of revenue when he collected the information regarding personal property subject to taxation in his district. The information required was place and date of death, full name, sex, age, condition (married or not), color of deceased (white or colored), if colored whether free or slave; if slave, name of owner, the occupation of the deceased, place of birth, name of husband or wife, and cause of death.[1] All this information was to be collected for the year ending the previous December 31. Usually the commissioners gathered this information sometime between May and July. It is important to remember this six to eighteen month delay when judging the accuracy of these records.

Loudoun County's records are fairly complete. The years 1853 and 1854 were filed together with the state, all as 1854 deaths. Luckily, the county records are available and we have corrected those dates. The deaths filed for 1860 are actually duplicates of 1859. There are no 1860 deaths in the county records. The years 1861, 1862, 1863, 1867, 1868, 1870, and 1895 are missing completely from both sets of records. 1869 includes only 48 deaths, far less than would be expected. There are also many instances where pages have been duplicated. We have tried to combine these into one entry, but have shown all information and references. Where there are two possible entries, the information is separated by a "/" as in 1859/60. All state records of deaths stop in 1896.

Beginning about 1870 the pages began to indicate the taxing district. That information has been included to help identify the area of residence. The commissioner was collecting

---

[1] For a more complete discussion of the Act and it's requirements, see *Alexandria, Virginia Death Records*, by Wesley E. Pippenger, p. xix

death information for previous residents of his taxing district. The deaths did not necessarily take place in the district of residence. The districts are Broad Run, Jefferson, Leesburg, Lovettsville, Mercer and Mount Gilead. In several years the districts were listed as the 1st District which included Broad Run and Mercer, the 2nd District which included Leesburg and Lovettsville, and the 3rd District which included Jefferson and Mount Gilead. Several years use a combination of the above. A chart is included on page vii which indicates the number of deaths in each district for each year. These numbers will not be absolute because of the entry duplications. They do indicate which districts or areas are entirely missing.

We have organized the book into two sections. The first section lists all slave deaths by the names of the owners. This was done to give some connection to possible family groups. The form of the listing under the owner's name is as follows: Given name, LAST NAME, sex, date of death (d.), place of death, cause, age (years-months-days), parents (p.), place of birth (b.), occupation, consort of (c/o), source (sc), microfilm reference (BVS: year: page #), county reference (LC: page #). Those items of information that were not listed in the records are not indicated in any way.

The second section, non-slaves, is alphabetical. These listings are as follows: LAST NAME, given name, color, sex, date of death (d.), place of death, cause, age (years-months-days), parents (p.), place of birth (b.), occupation, consort (c/o:), source (sc:), district, microfilm reference (BVS: year: page #), county reference(LC: page #). Again, items not included in the registers are simply skipped.

Because most names are already alphabetized, only those names within a listing which differ from the last name of the deceased are included in the index, such as slaves with last names, parents of married women, and the informant. Slaves are also indexed by their given name under the heading "Slaves".

Deaths by Year and District

Year	Total	None	1st	2nd	3rd	BR	JF	LE	LV	MC	MT
1854	642	642									
1855	260	260									
1856	224	224									
1857	231	231									
1858	233	233									
1859	191	191									
1860	192	192									
1864	88	88									
1865	191	139	52								
1866	126	126									
1869	48	48									
1871	97					28	17	17		27	8
1872	149					32	12	56	14	23	12
1873	144					30		26	15	48	25
1874	132					34	32	22	16	28	
1875	163					29	22	61	17		34
1876	195					21	18	60	31	46	19
1877	189					32	17	60	18	45	17
1878	170					24	14	55	22	45	10
1879	82			52	30						
1880	228		99	86	43						
1881	222		88	82	52						
1882	108		68		40						
1883	234		52	156	26						
1884	192		79	70	43						
1885	187		90	57	40						
1886	166		77	66	23						
1887	197		88	56	53						
1888	205		64	87	54						
1889	127		37	54	36						
1890	195		65	77	53						
1891	152		67				19	19	17		30
1892	202		116				19	26	18		23
1893	131		55				18	25	15		18
1894	119		56		39			14	10		
1896	189					34	32	36	20	51	16

Abbreviations Used

0-0-0	age: 0 years-0 months-0 days
B	non-white
b.	place of birth
BR	Broad Run (District)
BVS	Bureau of Vital Statistics
c/o	consort of
d.	death date
F	female
(f)	free non-white
FN or F.N.	free negro (used in records)
JF	Jefferson (District)
LC	Loudoun County
LE	Leesburg (District)
LV	Lovettsville (District)
M	male
MC	Mercer (District)
MT	Mount Gilead (District)
nr	near
sc	source
unk	unknown
unm	unmarried
W	white
[ ]	added from other parts of the listing, or a comment by the authors

Loudoun County, Virginia, Death Register, 1853-1896

Slaves Listed by Owners

No Owner Given:
Emma, F, d. Oct 1857, typhoid, 14-0-0, sc: Edward L. Carter, neighbor, BVS 1857:7, LC:29
Frank, M, d. 1855 , consumption, 1-0-0, p. Harriet, b. Hope & Try, sc: Jos. Helm, BVS 1855:6, LC:17
John, M, d. Nov 1857, typhoid, 3-0-0, sc: Edward L. Carter, neighbor, BVS 1857:7, LC:29
Martha, F, d. Oct 1855, unk, 0-10-0, b. LC, sc: N.J. Skinner, head of family, BVS 1855:8, LC:19
Martin, M, d. 3 May 1858, Res. of master, suddenly, 0-8-0, p. Mary, b. Res. of parents, sc: E.S. Hirst, overseer, BVS 1858:4, LC:31
Mary, F, d. 22 Aug 1855, Jonah Osburn's, typhoid fever, 11-0-0, p. Ellen, b. Jane Osburn's, sc: Jonah Osburn, BVS 1855:7, LC:18
Nat, F, d. Nov 1857, typhoid, 8-0-0, sc: Edward L. Carter, neighbor, BVS 1857:7, LC:29
no name, M, d. Jun 1855, Res. of master, unk, p. Jane, b. Res. of master, sc: Jno. B. Butcher, BVS 1855:5, LC:17
Rebecca, F, d. Oct 1857, typhoid, 15-0-0, sc: Edward L. Carter, neighbor, BVS 1857:7, LC:29
Sally, F, d. Oct 1857, old age, 70-0-0, sc: R.M. Bentley, friend, BVS 1857:7, LC:29
Thomas, M, d. Sep 1857, unk, 60-0-0, sc: Edward L. Carter, neighbor, BVS 1857:7, LC:29
Thomas, M, d. 15 Apr 1864, Grisley Reeder's, small pox, 18-0-0, p. Rachel, sc: Wm. A. Reeder, BVS 1864:1, LC:38

Abel, Geo:
Jane, F, d. 30 Aug 1854, LC, dysentery, 10-10-4, p. Matilda, (s), b. LC, sc: Geo. Abel, owner, BVS 1854:9, LC: 8

Adam, Francis' heirs:
Patty WEB, F, d. Jul 1854, unk, 19-0-0, sc: Charles B. Adams, part owner, BVS 1854:14, LC:14

Adams, Geo W.:
Charlotte, F, d. 9 Sep 1859, LC, typhoid fever, 14-0-0, b. LC, sc: Francis Chinn, friend, BVS 1859:6, LC:36

Adams, Wm. F.:
Mary, F, d. Jul 1859, Res. of master, summer complaint, 1-0-0, p. Margaret, b. Place of Death, sc: Wm. F. Adams, master, BVS 1859:3, LC:34

Adie, Mary E.:
Alsey, F, d. 29 May 1859, Leesburg, unk, 60-0-0, p. unk, b. unk, sc: Mary E. Adie, owner, BVS 1859:2, LC:38

Aldridge, John:
Henry PARKER, M, d. 24 Dec 1853, Glebe, smothered, 0-8-0, p. Stephen & Millie Parker, b. Glebe, sc: master, BVS 1854:1, LC: 4
Ary SWENEY, F, d. May 1853, Glebe, heart disease, 60-0-0, p. Nace & Bet Tilman, b. Maryland, sc: master, BVS 1854:1, LC: 4

Ambler, Susan:
Fanny, F, d. 10 Dec 1858, LC, burnt, 65-0-0, b. LC, sc: Susan Ambler, owner, BVS 1858:6, LC:33

Anderson, Elijah's Estate:
no name, M, d. 4 Jan 1859, Washington Beavers, destroyed by its mother, 0-0-1, p. Margaret, b. Washington Beaver's, sc: W. Beavers, BVS 1859:4, LC:35

Anderson, Mrs. E.:
no name, F, d. 15 Aug 1855, John A. Beaver's, stillborn, p. Margaret, b. Jno. A. Beavers', sc: Jno. A. Beavers, BVS 1855:5, LC:17

Ayre, Geo:
Eli, M, d. Jun 1853, nr Upperville, dysentery, 1-6-0, p. Lucinda Summers, sc: master, BVS 1854:7, LC: 6

Ayre, Geo. S.:
Jane, F, d. Jul 1859, master's, sackpan ?, 13-0-0, p. Lucinda, b. At place of

death, sc: G. S. Ayre, master, BVS 1859:3, LC:34

Baldwin, Mahlon:
George, M, d. 15 Apr 1854, Trap, dis. of head, 1-1-0, p. Ellen, b. Trap, sc: Mahlon Baldwin, BVS 1854:11, LC:11
no name, M, d. Mar 1855, Trap, unk, p. Ellen, b. Trap, sc: Mahlon Baldwin, BVS 1855:4, LC:16

Ball, Charles B.:
Benjamin, M, d. 15 Mar 1858, LC, quinsy, 70-0-0, p. unk, b. Lancaster, sc: Charles B. Ball, owner, BVS 1858:2, LC:30

Ball, Geo. W.:
Delpha, F, d. 15 Jun 1854, LC, abscess on liver, 60-0-0, p. unk, b. unk, sc: Geo. W. Ball, owner, BVS 1854:10, LC: 9
Martena, F, d. 1 Sep 1853, LC, unk, 21-3-7, p. Milly (s), b. LC, house servant, unm, sc: Geo T. Rust, head of family, BVS 1854:4, LC: 2
Nannie, F, d. 9 Jun 1855, Leesburg, consumption, 7-4-13, p. Lucy, b. LC, sc: Mary Turner, head of family, BVS 1855:3, LC:15

Ball, Lucy T.:
Fanny, F, d. 4 Aug 1853, Leesburg, diarrhea, 1-10-2, p. Mary, (s), b. Leesburg, sc: Lucy Ball, owner, BVS 1854:5, LC: 3
Mary, F, d. 7 Nov 1854, LC, consumption, 28-0-0, p. unk, b. unk, sc: Lucy T. Ball, owner, BVS 1854:10, LC:10
Parris, M, d. 25 Dec 1853, Leesburg, old age, 100-0-0, p. unk, b. Leesburg, sc: Lucy Ball, owner, BVS 1854:5, LC: 3

Bartlett, Burgess D.:
Sarah Margaret, F, d. 20 Jul 1858, Middleburg, measles, 10-0-0, p. Margaret, b. Middleburg, sc: Julia Bartlett, aunt, BVS 1858:3, LC:30

Beard, Jonathan:
Betty, F, d. Mar 16 1855, old age, 91-0-0, b. Stafford Co., VA, sc: Jonathan Beard, owner, BVS 1855:8, LC:19
Jane, F, d. Aug 1854, LC, scalded, 1-10-0, sc: Jonathan Beard, owner, BVS 1854:14, LC:14

Jerry, M, d. Oct 1853, LC, unk, 65-0-0, p. unk, b. LC, sc: J. Beard, owner, BVS 1854:2, LC: 7

Beavers, John:
Dinah, F, d. Jan 1855, Foot B. Ridge, suddenly, 55-0-0, p. Sarah, b. Clarke Co., sc: M. Waltman, BVS 1855:6, LC:18
Dinah, F, d. 1 Jan 1856, Res. of master, suddenly, 50-0-0, p. Sarah, b. Clark Co., sc: James Beavers, master, BVS 1856:5, LC:22

Belt, Alfred:
no name, M, d. 2 Dec 1858, Maryland, burned to death, 1-3-0, p. Mary (s), b. Maryland, sc: Alfred Belt, owner, BVS 1858:2, LC:30

Bennett, Martha:
no name, M, d. 20 Sep 1854, LC, dysentery, 0-5-0, p. Mary (s), b. LC, sc: Geo. W. Bennett, one of the family, BVS 1854:8, LC: 8

Bennett, Nancy:
Harriett or Hammat, F, d. 9 Aug 1854, LC, dysentery, 1-7-8, p. Nelly (s), b. LC, sc: Geo. W. Bennett, one of the family, BVS 1854:8, LC: 8

Bentley, E.L.:
[no name], F, d. Dec 1858, LC, unk, unk, b. LC, sc: E.L. Bentley, owner, BVS 1858:6, LC:34
Mary, F, d. 17 Dec 1856, Leesburg, unk, 20-0-0, b. LC, BVS 1856:1, LC:19
Mary, F, d. 19 Dec 1856, LC, consumption, 22-0-0, p. unk, b. Leesburg, sc: E.L. Bentley, owner, BVS 1856:2, LC:21
no name, F, d. 30 Jun 1854, LC, dysentery, unk, p. Eliza(s), b. Leesburg, sc: A. R. Mott, family physician, BVS 1854:10, LC:10

Benton, William:
Charles Henry, M, d. 15 May 1857, Joseph Baldwin's, pneumonia, 0-6-0, p. Elizabeth, b. Eli Chinn's, sc: Eliza Baldwin, BVS 1857:4, LC:27
Henson, M, d. 18 Dec 1858, Res. of master, pneumonia, 0-9-0, p. Vermelia, b. Wm. Benton's, sc: W.H. Benton, BVS 1858:3, LC:30

Loudoun County, Virginia, Death Register, 1853-1896   3

Berkley, Francis C.:
Alfred, M, d. 1 Sep 1854, Aldie, typhoid fever, 8-0-0, p. John & Frankey, b. Aldie, sc: Mrs. F. C. Berkley, BVS 1854:10, LC:10
Jane, F, d. 11 Aug 1854, Aldie, consumption, 24-0-0, p. Mike & Nelly, b. Aldie, farm hand, c/o: Bob, sc: Mrs. F. C. Berkley, BVS 1854:10, LC:10
Juno, F, d. 15 Jun 1855, Aldie, old age, 90-0-0, b. Middlesex Co., sc: Wm. Berkley, BVS 1855:4, LC:16
Kitty, F, d. 15 Oct 1855, Aldie, old age, 100-0-0, b. Middlesex Co., sc: Wm. Berkley, BVS 1855:4, LC:16
Mensor, M, d. 1 Sep 1854, Aldie, typhoid fever, 0-9-0, p. Simon & Louisa, b. Aldie, sc: Mrs. F. C. Berkley, BVS 1854:10, LC:10
Nelson, M, d. 11 Aug 1854, Aldie, typhoid fever, 40-0-0, p. John & Nancy, b. Caroline Co., farm hand, married, sc: Mrs. F. C. Berkley, BVS 1854:10, LC:10
Squire, M, d. 15 Sep 1854, Aldie, typhoid fever, 0-9-0, p. Bob & Jane, b. Aldie, sc: Mrs. F. C. Berkley, BVS 1854:10, LC:10
Tera, F, d. 1 Aug 1855, Aldie, dropsy, 70-0-0, b. Middlesex Co., sc: Wm. Berkley, BVS 1855:4, LC:16

Berkley, Lewis:
two negro children, m/f, d. 1853, in Aldie, dysentery, 1 & 8-0-0, b. Aldie, sc: master, BVS 1854:6, LC: 6

Berkley, Nobourne:
Arthur, M, d. Jul 1853, nr Aldie, bronchitis, 1-0-0, p. Mima, b. nr Aldie, sc: master, BVS 1854:6, LC: 6

Berkley, Wm. N.:
Jackson, M, d. Sep 1858/59, Res. of master, accident, 6-0-0, p. Adaline. b. Aldie, sc: Wm. N. Berkley, master, BVS 1858:4, 1859:5, LC:31/36
Julia Ann, F, d. 1859, Res. of master, typhoid fever, 14-0-0, p. Betsy, b. Aldie, sc: Wm. N. Berkley, master, BVS 1859:5, LC:36
Lot, M, d. 1859, Res. of master, disease of lungs, 35-0-0, p. Nelly, b. Aldie, sc: Wm. N. Berkley, master, BVS 1859:5, LC:35

no name, F, d. 1859, Res. of master, 0-6-0, p. Adaline, b. Aldie, sc: Wm. N. Berkley, master, BVS 1859:5, LC:36
no name, F, d. 1859, Res. of master, 0-6-0, p. Hannah, b. Aldie, sc: Wm. N. Berkley, master, BVS 1859:5, LC:36

Best, Amanda A.:
Eliza, F, d. Jun 1859, Mrs. White's, unk, 14-0-0, p. Elizabeth, b. nr Snickersville, sc: Mrs. White, BVS 1859:4, LC:35

Binns, Ann A.:
no name, M, d. 10 May 1856, Leesburg, whooping cough, 0-0-7, p. Lavenia (s), b. Leesburg, sc: Ann A. Binns, owner, BVS 1856:3, LC:21

Binns, Miss:
no name,F, d. Sep 1858, N. R. Heaton, burn, 0-8-0, p. Livinia, b. Leesburg, sc: N.R. Heaton, BVS 1858:5, LC:33

Birkby:
Molly, F, d. 4 Dec 1854, Poor House, old age, 75-0-0, p. Moses & Ruth Arnett, b. Res. of father, sc: Wm. Furr, BVS 1854:11, LC:11

Bitzer, George L.:
no name,F, d. Spring 1857, unk, p. Eliza, b. Res. of master, sc: George L. Bitzer, master, BVS 1857:6, LC:28
Violet, F, d. Nov 1858, Res. of master, 55-0-0, b. Fauquier, sc: George L. Bitzer, master, BVS 1858:5, LC:33

Bolen, Ezra:
Armistead, M, d. 15 May 1859, LC, consumption, 17-0-0, b. LC, sc: Isaac M. Rice, head of family, BVS 1859:1, LC:36

Bowman, Catharine:
Joseph, M, d. 1 Jan 1856, Philomont, pneumonia, 25-0-0, p. Emily, b. LC, sc: G.W. Bowman, BVS 1856:6, LC:23

Bowman, Robert C.:
Amelia, F, d. Feb 1856, F. T. Grady's, poison, 19-0-0, sc: F.T. Grady, BVS 1856:5, LC:22
no name, M, d. Sep 1856, Res. of master, unk, p. Maria, b. Res. of master, sc: R.C. Bowman, master, BVS 1856:5, LC:23

Braden, Noble S.:
Charles, M, d. 30 Aug 1853, LC, dysentery, 1-6-0, p. Martha Jane (s), b. LC, sc: Noble S. Braden, owner, BVS 1854:4, LC: 2

Bronaugh, Sally:
George, M, d. Jun 1859, LC, unk, 2-6-0, p. Violet GASKINS, b. LC, sc: Sally Bronaugh, owner, BVS 1859:6, LC:36
Mary, F, d. 15 Aug 1853, LC, unk, 27-0-0, p. unk, b. LC, sc: Sally Bronaugh, owner, BVS 1854:2, LC: 7
Mary, F, d. 7 Mar 1856, LC, unk, 0-25-0, b. LC, sc: Sally Bronaugh, owner, BVS 1856:7, LC:24
Richard, M, d. Feb 1853, LC, unk, 0-1-0, p. unk, b. LC, sc: Sally Bronaugh, owner, BVS 1854:2, LC: 7

Brown, E.C.:
Levina, F, d. Apr 1857, Middleburg, heart affection, 40-0-0, p. Esther, b. LC, sc: master, BVS 1857:3, LC:25
no name, F, d. Sep 1854, Middleburg, 0-3-0, p. Sally, b. Middleburg, house servant, sc: R. Smith, BVS 1854:11, LC:10
Peter, M, d. Jun 1857, Middleburg, old age, 60-0-0, p. Eve, b. LC, sc: master, BVS 1857:3, LC:25
Sarah, F, d. 1 Mar 1858, Middleburg, consumption, 25-0-0, p. Vermelia, b. Middleburg, sc: E.C. Brown, master, BVS 1858:3, LC:30

Brown, John V.:
no name, M, d. 2 Jan 1854, LC, unk, 0-0-1, p. Delila (s), b. LC, sc: John V. Brown, owner, BVS 1854:8, LC: 8

Brown, Mrs.:
Milly NOURSE, F, d. 15 Jun 1859, LC, old age, 85-0-0, p. unk, b. LC, sc: Harriet Wright, daughter, BVS 1859:2, LC:37

Buckner, Lucy:
Mary Ann, F, d. Jul 1853, LC, 0-3-0, p. unk, b. LC, sc: S. A. Buckner, owner, BVS 1854:2, LC: 6
Stephen, M, d. Jul 1853, LC, 0-7-0, p. unk, b. LC, sc: S. A. Buckner, owner, BVS 1854:2, LC: 6
Dinah BOOKER, F, d. Jun 1853, LC, old age, 75-0-0, p. unk, b. LC, sc: S. A. Buckner, owner, BVS 1854:2, LC: 6

Jas. BOOKER, M, d. May 1853, LC, old age, 100-0-0, p. unk, b. LC, sc: S. A. Buckner, owner, BVS 1854:2, LC: 6

Buckner, S. Ariss:
[no name], M, d. Sep 1857, unk, 0-8-0, sc: S. Ariss Buckner, owner, BVS 1857:7, LC:29
[no name], M, d. Aug 1858, LC, unk, unk, b. LC, sc: S. Ariss Buckner, owner, BVS 1858:6, LC:34
George, M, d. Aug 1857, unk, 22-0-0, sc: S. Ariss Buckner, owner, BVS 1857:7, LC:29
Harriet, F, d. Jun 1859, LC, unk, 1-0-0, p. Maria, b. LC, sc: S. Ariss Buckner, owner, BVS 1859:6, LC:36

Burwell, Susan:
no name, M, d. 5 Apr 1858, A.B. Carter, unk, p. Billy, b. A.B. Carter, sc: A.B. Carter, BVS 1858:4, LC:32

Butcher, John H.:
Albert, M, d. 6 Nov 1858, Res. of master, found dead in bed, 0-5-4, p. Harriet, b. Res. of master, sc: J.H. Butcher, master, BVS 1858:3, LC:31
Alice, F, d. Nov 1857, Res. of master, pneumonia, 3-5-0, p. Cidnah, b. Res. of master, sc: J.H. Butcher, master, BVS 1857:4, LC:27
Laura, F, d. Fall 1857, Jefferson C. Thomas', croup, 2-6-0, p. Cidney, b. Prince Wm., sc: J.C. Thomas, BVS 1857:5, LC:28
no name, M, d. 22 Feb 1857, Res. of master, 0-0-7, p. Cidnah, b. Res. of master, sc: J.H. Butcher, master, BVS 1857:4, LC:27
no name, M, d. 26 Mar 1858, Res. of master, unk, 0-0-10, p. Eliza, b. Res. of master, sc: J.H. Butcher, master, BVS 1858:3, LC:31

Butcher, Martin & Ann:
no name, M, d. Feb 1854, White Hall, 0-0-7, p. Fanny, b. White Hall, sc: mistress, BVS 1854:12, LC:12

Carr, David:
Clara, F, d. 1 Apr 1855, Leesburg, pneumonia, 51-0-0, b. Leesburg, sc: Wm. A. Powell, head of family, BVS 1855:3, LC:15

Loudoun County, Virginia, Death Register, 1853-1896   5

Carr, Joseph:
no name, M, d. 15 Jul 1855, nr Union, unk, 0-0-10, p. Anica Berry, b. Union, sc: master, BVS 1855:4, LC:16

Carr, Wm. J.:
no name, F, d. 16 Jan 1856, Res. of master, 0-0-1, p. Jane Pinkett, b. master's Res., sc: W.J. Carr, master, BVS 1856:5, LC:23

Carter, A.B:
Louis, M, d. 1 Mar 1854, Meadow View, apoplexy, 45-0-0, b. Probably Fauquier, sc: A. B. Carter, BVS 1854:11, LC:11

Carter, B.F.:
Charles, M, d. Jun 1853, nr Mountville, pneumonia, 26-0-0, p. Sylvia, b. nr Leesburg, sc: father, BVS 1854:7, LC: 6
Lizzie, F, d. 27 Jul 1858, Res. of master, congestion of brain, 0-6-0, p. Frances, b. Res. of master, sc: Miss Carter, BVS 1858:5, LC:32
Martha, F, d. Oct 1857, Res. of master, 0-8-0, p. Maria, b. Res. of master, sc: Mrs. B.F. Carter, mistress, BVS 1857:5, LC:27
no name,F, d. Apr 1857, Res. of master, 0-1-0, p. Annett, b. Res. of master, sc: Mrs. B.F. Carter, mistress, BVS 1857:5, LC:27

Carter, Charlotte:
Sarah, F, d. Aug 1854, LC, old age, 90-0-0, sc: E. L. Carter, neighbor, BVS 1854:14, LC:13

Carter, Elizabeth O.:
Bushrod, M, d. Dec 1858, Oatlands, croup, 0-6-0, p. Susan, b. Oatlands, sc: Miss Grayson, BVS 1858:5, LC:33
George, M, d. 27 Dec 1854, nr Oatlands, dropsy, 60-0-0, p. Abby, b. Oatlands, sc: E.O. Carter, BVS 1854:12, LC:12
no name, M, d. Aug 1857, Oatlands, unk, 0-0-3, p. Dinah, b. Oatlands, sc: E.O. Carter, mistress, BVS 1857:4, LC:26
no name, M, d. Dec 1856, Res. of mistress, spasms, 7-0-0, p. Sophia, b. Res. of mistress, sc: E.O. Carter, mistress, BVS 1856:5, LC:23
no name, F, d. Dec 1856, Res. of mistress, 7-0-0, p. Mary, b. Res. of mistress, sc: E.O. Carter, mistress, BVS 1856:5, LC:23
Phebe, F, d. 8 Dec 1853, Oatlands, scarlet fever, 27-0-0, b. LC, sc: mistress, BVS 1854:6, LC: 5
Philip, M, d. Mar 1857, Oatlands, dropsy of brain, 0-3-0, p. Louisa, b. Oatlands, sc: E.O. Carter, mistress, BVS 1857:4, LC:26
Scott, M, d. 2 Dec 1853, Oatlands, sf, 0-8-0, sc: mistress, BVS 1854:6, LC: 5
Solomon, M, d. 9 Dec 1855, Oatlands, dropsy, 60-0-0, p. Cela, b. Oatlands, sc: E.O. Carter, BVS 1855:5, LC:17
Tascar, M, d. Jul 1855, Oatlands, dysentery, 2-0-0, p. Louisa, b. Oatlands, sc: E.O. Carter, BVS 1855:5, LC:17
Walter, M, d. 15 Nov 1856, LC, unk, 0-3-0, b. LC, sc: Peyton Powell, head of family, BVS 1856:1, LC:20
George RUSS, M, d. 31 Dec 1855, Oatlands Farm, dyspepsia, 65-0-0, p. Abby Russ, b. Westmoreland Co., c/o: Patsy Russ, sc: Patsy Russ, BVS 1855:6, LC:17

Carter, Jas:
no name, M, d. Dec 1853, Millsville, unk, 0-0-1, p. Mary, b. nr Clifton, sc: master, BVS 1854:7, LC: 6

Carter, John A.:
no name, M, d. Apr 1859, master's, unk, 0-0-4, p. Bella, b. Res. of master, sc: J.H. Carter, master, BVS 1859:3, LC:34

Carter, John R.:
Betty, F, d. Mar 1857, putrid sore throat, 1-8-0, p. Jane, b. At place of death, sc: J.R. Carter, master, BVS 1857:5, LC:27

Carter, Landon:
Emanuel, M, d. Oct 1854, LC, paralyzed, 85-0-0, sc: Landon Carter, owner, BVS 1854:14, LC:13

Cassaday, Wm. H:
Eliza, F, d. 28 Apr 1855, LC, consumption, 1-5-2, p. Frances (s), b. LC, sc: Mary J. Cassaday, mistress, BVS 1855:1, LC:14

Loudoun County, Virginia, Death Register, 1853-1896

Catlett, Erskine:
George, M, d. 15 Nov 1854, LC, accidental, 14-1-11, p. Ellen (s), b. LC, sc: Alfred C. Belt, head of family, BVS 1854:9, LC: 9

Chancellor, S.A.:
Charles, M, d. Jan 1859, Rappahannock, pneumonia, 20-0-0, p. Jane, b. Fauquier, sc: S. A. C. Chancellor, master, BVS 1859:4, LC:35

Chin, Frances A.:
Hager, F, d. 15 Dec 1854, LC, dropsy, 80-0-0, sc: Frances A. Chinn, owner, BVS 1854:14, LC:14

Chinn, Lemuel:
Westwood, M, d. Aug 1853, Middleburg, consumption, 2-0-0, p. Jack & Mary Hamilton, b. Middleburg, sc: R.S. Chinn, young master, BVS 1854:1, LC: 4

Clagett, Thomas N.:
Alice, F, d. 13 Aug 1859, LC, unk, 0-3-0, p. Elizabeth, b. LC, sc: Thomas N. Clagett, owner, BVS 1859:2, LC:38
Elizabeth, F, d. 15 Jul 1859, LC, consumption, 35-0-0, b. Pr George, sc: Thomas N. Clagett, owner, BVS 1859:2, LC:38

Clendening, Ruth:
Joseph, M, d. 8 Jan 1856, LC, whooping cough, 1-2-0, p. Mary (s), b. LC, sc: Ruth Clendening, owner, BVS 1856:2, LC:21

Clendening, Wm:
Albert, M, d. 23 Dec 1855, LC, typhoid fever, 25-0-0, p. unk, b. LC, sc: Wm. Clendening, owner, BVS 1855:2, LC:15
Alfred, M, d. 10 Jul 1855, LC, unk, 25-0-0, p. unk, b. LC, sc: Wm. Clendening, owner, BVS 1855:2, LC:15

Cockran, Emily & Amanda:
Caroline, F, d. 2 Aug 1854, Asa Janney's, typhoid fever, 16-0-0, sc: Asa Janney, BVS 1854:13, LC:12

Coe, Robert:
Samuel, M, d. Mar 1854, Res. of master, consumption, 25-0-0, p. Maria, b. Coe's Mill, sc: master, BVS 1854:12, LC:12

Coleman, John J.:
Emma, M, d. Jun 1853, LC, whooping cough, 0-0-1, p. unk, b. LC, sc: John J. Coleman, owner, BVS 1854:2, LC: 7
no name, F, d. 15 Apr 1854, croup, 0-3-0, sc: R. H. Presgraves, head of family, BVS 1854:14, LC:14
Peggy, F, d. Feb 1856, LC, unk, 32-0-0, b. LC, sc: J.J. Coleman, owner, BVS 1856:7, LC:24
John RILEY, M, d. Oct 1858, LC, unk, 70-0-0, b. LC, sc: John J. Coleman, owner, BVS 1858:6, LC:33

Compher, John:
Emily, F, d. 7 Oct 1857, LC, unk, 0-2-25, p. Frances (s), b. LC, sc: John Compher, owner, BVS 1857:1, LC:24
no name, M, d. 15 Aug 1857, LC, unk, 0-0-3, p. Nancy (s), b. LC, sc: John Compher, head of family, BVS 1857:1, LC:24

Compher, Peter:
Wm. WEST, M, d. 1 May 1853, LC, palsy, 54-0-0, p. unk, b. Maryland, farm hand, c/o: Mary West (s), sc: Peter Compher, owner, BVS 1854:2, LC: 1

Conard, Abner:
Catharine, F, d. 20 Mar 1858, LC, unk, 0-0-7, p. Henrietta (s), b. LC, sc: Abner Conard, owner, BVS 1858:2, LC:30
Jonathan, M, d. 3 Apr 1856, LC, unk, 0-6-0, p. Henrietta (s), b. LC, sc: Abner Conard, owner, BVS 1856:3, LC:21

Corbin, James M.:
no name, F, d. 19 Feb 1853, LC, unk, 0-0-1, p. Geo. & Angelina, slaves, b. LC, sc: James N. Corbin, head of family, BVS 1854:3, LC: 1

Corbin, Nelson:
Charles, M, d. Nov 1858, Levi James', found dead in bed, 0-6-0, p. Theadosia, b. Levi James', sc: Levi James, BVS 1858:5, LC:32
Jonah, M, d. Aug 1858, Levi James', found dead in bed, 2-14-0,

Loudoun County, Virginia, Death Register, 1853-1896

p. Theadosia, b. Levi James', sc: Levi James, BVS 1858:5, LC:32

Cox, Samuel:
Betty, F, d. Aug 1859, Res. of master, typhoid fever, 65-0-0, sc: John Cox, BVS 1859:5, LC:36
Elizabeth, F, d. Sep 1859, Res. of master, typhoid fever, 60-0-0, b. Fauquier, sc: John Cox, BVS 1859:4, LC:35
John, M, d. Oct 1859, Res. of master, typhoid fever, 18-0-0, p. Lina, b. LC, sc: John Cox, BVS 1859:4, LC:35
John, M, d. Sep 1859, Res. of master, typhoid fever, 17-0-0, p. Lina, sc: John Cox, BVS 1859:5, LC:36

Crane, Warner:
Amanda CARTER, F, d. Feb 1855, P. R. Crane, child bed, 18-0-0, p. Mary, b. LC, sc: Phila B. Crane, BVS 1855:3, LC:16
no name, M, d. Feb 1855, P. R. Crane, 0-1-0, p. Amanda Carter, b. LC, sc: Phila B. Crane, BVS 1855:3, LC:16

Crims, John's Estate:
Susan, F, d. 15 Jul 1859, LC, paralysis, 70-0-0, b. LC, sc: Philip Vincell, head of family, BVS 1859:1, LC:37

Currell, Mrs.:
Madison JAMES, M, d. Nov 1855, Middleburg, inflammatory rheumatism, 70-0-0, sc: Lorman Chancellor, BVS 1855:3, LC:16

Darne, Catharine:
C. H. SMITH, M, d. March 1853, LC, unk, 19-0-0, p. unk, b. LC, sc: Catharine Darne, owner, BVS 1854:2, LC: 6

Dawson, Sarah A.:
Emily, F, d. 22 Aug 1855, LC, worms, 3-2-1, p. Maria (s), b. LC, sc: Sarah A. Dawson, owner, BVS 1855:2, LC:15

Dennis, Wm. A.:
Lucy, F, d. Apr 1856, LC, unk, 35-0-0, b. LC, sc: W.A. Dennis, owner, BVS 1856:7, LC:24
no name, F, d. Dec 1854, unk, 1-1-0, sc: Wm. A. Dennis, owner, BVS 1854:14, LC:14

Dishman, Marcus:
Fanny, F, d. Aug 1853, Millsville, lock jaw, 18-0-0, p. Sylvia, b. LC, sc: master, BVS 1854:7, LC: 6

Dodd, Samuel:
James, M, d. 28 May 1856, Waterford, dropsy, 13-7-0, b. LC, sc: Samuel Dodd, owner, BVS 1856:2, LC:20

Dowell, C. R.:
Virginia, F, d. Jun 1855, Res. of master, typhoid fever, 15-0-0, p. Mary Jane, b. nr Waterford, sc: C.R. Dowell, BVS 1855:6, LC:17

Dowell, C.R.'s Estate:
Flavius, M, d. Apr 1858, Mrs. Dowell's, measles, 11-0-0, p. Mary Jane, b. Dr. Edwards', sc: John Dowell, BVS 1858:5, LC:32
Flavius, M, d. 15 Apr 1857, Res. of mistress, consumption, 11-0-0, p. Mary, b. Waterford, sc: John Dowell, BVS 1857:5, LC:28
Lewis WARNER, M, d. Jun 1858, Mrs. Dowell's, gangrene, 65-0-0, sc: John Dowell, BVS 1858:5, LC:32

Dowell, Malinda:
Maria, F, d. Jul 1859, Res. of mistress, consumption, 50-0-0, b. Middleburg, sc: Mrs. Dowell, mistress, BVS 1859:4, LC:35

Drake, Francis T.:
John, M, d. 18 Dec 1855, Leesburg, overlayed, 0-3-13, p. Matilda (s), b. Leesburg, sc: Francis F. Drake, owner, BVS 1855:1, LC:14

Drish, Wm. D.:
Mitty, F, d. 28 Jul 1854, LC, dysentery, 2-2-1, p. Maria (s), b. Leesburg, sc: Wm. D. Drish, owner, BVS 1854:10, LC:10

Dulany, R.H.:
Nancy, F, d. Nov 1858, Res. of master, consumption, 13-0-0, p. Arianna, b. Clifton, sc: R.H. Delaney, master, BVS 1858:3, LC:31
no name, F, d. 4 Nov 1854, Wellbourn, 0-0-2, p. Arianna, b. Welbourn, sc: R. H. Dulany, BVS 1854:11, LC:11
no name, , d. Dec 1855, Wellbourn, unk, 0-0-1, p. Arianna, b. Wellbourn, sc: R.H. Dulany, BVS 1855:4, LC:16

Pompy, M, d. Oct 1856, Welbourn, 0-9-0, p. Ellen, b. Welbourn, sc: R.H. Dulaney, master, BVS 1856:4, LC:22

Duncan, Charles:
Josephine, F, d. Jul 1854, Clifton, croup, 1-0-0, p. Susan, b. Clifton, sc: James R. Slack, BVS 1854:12, LC:11

Edwards, Richard H.:
Henrietta, F, d. 10 Mar 1853:54, Waterford, worms, 4-0-0, p. Margaret (s), b. LC, sc: Chas Williams, head of family, BVS 1854:3, LC: 1
no name, F, d. 1 Jun 1854, LC, unk, 0-0-20, p. Margaret (s), b. LC, sc: Chas. Williams, head of family, BVS 1854:9, LC: 9
Samuel, M, d. 25 Jul 1853, Waterford, dysentery, 4-10-3, p. Margaret (s), b. LC, sc: R.H. Edwards, owner, BVS 1854:3, LC: 1

Eidson, Joseph:
Annie, F, d. Aug 1859, Jeff Berryman's, pneumonia, 9-0-0, p. Maria, b. Joseph Eidson's, sc: Joseph Eidson, master, BVS 1859:4, LC:35
George, M, d. Oct 1859, Res. of parents, pneumonia, 58-0-0, p. Jemima, b. LC, sc: Joseph Eidson, master, BVS 1859:4, LC:35
Maria, F, d. Apr 1859, J. H. Berryman's, child bed, 40-0-0, p. Permelia, b. LC, sc: Joseph Eidson, master, BVS 1859:4, LC:35
no name, M, d. 15 Oct 1855, Jno. Triplett's farm, 0-4-0, p. Maria, b. Jno. Triplett's farm, sc: Jeffrey Berryman, FN, father, BVS 1855:7, LC:18
no name, M, d. Apr 1859, J. H. Berryman's, 0-0-1, p. Maria, b. Joseph Eidson's, sc: Joseph Eidson, master, BVS 1859:4, LC:35
Permelia, F, d. May 1859, G. H. Hutchison's, pneumonia, 60-0-0, sc: Joseph Eidson, master, BVS 1859:4, LC:35

Elgin, Francis:
Mildred, F, d. 7 Aug 1855, Res. of master, cholera infantum, 0-3-0, p. Patsey, b. Francis Elgin's, sc: Francis Elgin, BVS 1855:5, LC:17
no name, M, d. 15 Jun 1855, LC, unk, 0-1-5, p. Eliza (s), b. LC, sc: Alfred C. Belt, head of family, BVS 1855:1, LC:14
Patsey, F, d. 15 Aug 1855, Res. of master, dropsy. 36-11-5, p. Amy, b. Prince William, sc: Francis Elgin, BVS 1855:5, LC:17

Elgin, Ignatius:
Elizabeth, F, d. 15 Oct 1856, Res. of master, dropsy, 4-7-0, p. Julia, b. nr Ball's Mill, sc: Ignatius Elgin, master, BVS 1856:5, LC:23

Elgin, Mary:
Mary Ellen, F, d. Apr 1856, Aldie, 2-0-0, p. Matilda, b. Aldie, sc: Mary Elgin, mistress, BVS 1856:4, LC:22
George THOMPSON, M, d. 10 Sep 1854, Aldie, consumption, 16-0-0, p. Matilda, b. Aldie, farm hand, sc: mistress, BVS 1854:10, LC:10

Elgin, Mrs. Gustavus:
Mahala, F, d. Feb 1857, S.P. Rogers', croup, 1-9-0, p. Mahala, b. S.P. Rogers, sc: S.P. Rogers, BVS 1857:5, LC:28

Elgin, Robert:
Harriet Ann, F, d. Aug 1856, Res. of master, whooping cough, 2-0-0, p. Mary Jane, b. Res. of master, sc: R. Elgin, master, BVS 1856:5, LC:23
Harrison, M, d. 11 Apr 1854, Peach Grove, pneumonia, 9-0-0, p. Mary Jane, b. nr Aldie, sc: mistress, BVS 1854:12, LC:11
no name, F, d. Feb 1858, Robt Elgin's, unk, 0-0-7, p. Mary Jane, b. Place of death, sc: Robert Elgin, master, BVS 1858:4, LC:32

Ellzey, Lucy E.:
no name, M, d. 5 Aug 1858, LC, unk, 0-3-0, p. Caroline (s), b. LC, sc: John George Jr., head of family, BVS 1858:1, LC:29

Fadeley, Charles F.:
no name, M, d. 15 Aug 1858, LC, unk, 0-1-1, p. Matilda (s), b. LC, sc: Charles F. Fadeley, owner, BVS 1858:1, LC:29

Fitzhugh's Estate:
no name, M, d. 1 Oct 1855, Mrs. Fitzhugh's, smothered, 0-3-0,

Loudoun County, Virginia, Death Register, 1853-1896   9

p. Cidney, b. Mrs. Fitzhugh's, sc: Fitzhugh, BVS 1855:6, LC:17

Fitzhugh, Matilda:
Andrew, M, d. Feb 1857, Res. of mistress, smothered, 0-1-7, p. Alla, b. Res. of mistress, sc: Matilda Fitzhugh, mistress, BVS 1857:5, LC:27
Anna, F, d. Nov 1854, The Grove, consumption, 3-0-0, p. Harriet, b. Middleburg, sc: mistress, BVS 1854:12, LC:11
Eliza Maria, F, d. Nov 1857, Res. of mistress, dropsy of brain, 0-0-5, p. Sidney, b. Res. of mistress, sc: Matilda Fitzhugh, mistress, BVS 1857:5, LC:27

Fletcher, Joshua:
Burr, M, d. Mar 1855, Res. of master, typhoid fever, 24-0-0, p. Harriet, b. LC, sc: Joshua Fletcher, BVS 1855:5, LC:17
Harriet, F, d. 31 Aug 1854, Capitol Hill, suddenly, 50-0-0, p. unk, b. Fauquier Co., sc: master, BVS 1854:12, LC:11
John, M, d. 1 May 1853, nr Upperville, pneumonia, 30-0-0, p. unk, b. Rappahannock, sc: master, BVS 1854:7, LC: 6

Florence, Silas:
Jonah, M, d. 19 Oct 1858, Res. of master, typhoid fever, 25-0-0, p. Elizabeth Florence, b. James Love's, sc: Miss Nichols, BVS 1858:5, LC:32

Foley, Wm:
Clarissa, F, d. Jul 1853, LC, dysentery, 6-0-0, p. unk, b. LC, sc: Wm. Foley, owner, BVS 1854:2, LC: 6

Fouch, Elizabeth J.:
Cordelia, F, d. 5 Nov 1857, Middleburg, whooping cough, 0-4-5, p. Lucy, b. Middleburg, sc: mistress, BVS 1857:3, LC:25
John Henry, M, d. 11 Feb 1856, Middleburg, dropsy of brain, 0-8-0, p. Lucy, b. Middleburg, sc: E.J. Fouch, mistress, BVS 1856:4, LC:21

Francis, John:
no name,F, d. Nov 1858, Francis Quarry, violence of mother, 0-0-1, p. Marietta, b. Francis' Quarry, sc: John Francis, master, BVS 1858:3, LC:30

Francis, Thos:
Monarchy, F, d. Feb 1853, nr Mountvilee, old age, 90-0-0, b. LC, sc: master, BVS 1854:2, LC: 4

Frazier, Saml H.'s Estate:
Shem, M, d. 28 Jun 1858, LC, diarrhea, 0-5-0, p. Maria (s), b. LC, sc: Samuel H. Frazier, young master, BVS 1858:1, LC:29

Frazier, Townsend:
no name, F, d. Nov 1854, Res. of master, 0-0-2, p. Susan, b. Res. of master, sc: master, BVS 1854:12, LC:11
Thomas, M, d. Jun 1856, Res. of master, 0-11-0, p. Ellen, b. master's Res., sc: Mrs. Frazier, mistress, BVS 1856:4, LC:22

Fred, Thos:
Sarah GASKINS, F, d. 8 Sep 1854, Frederick, disease of hart, 8-0-0, p. Amanda, b. Frederick, sc: master, BVS 1854:11, LC:11

Freeman, Garret C.:
Lucky JETT, F, d. 28 May 1854, paralyzed, 54-0-0, sc: G. C. Freeman, owner, BVS 1854:14, LC:14

Freeman, H.C.:
[no name], F, d. Nov 1859, LC, 0-0-1, p. Ann, b. LC, sc: H.C. Freeman, owner, BVS 1859:6, LC:36

Freeman, N. C.:
Jane Susan, F, d. 25 Apr 1853, LC, consumption, 11-0-0, p. Wm. & Emily, b. Fairfax, sc: Garret C. Freeman, head of family, BVS 1854:2, LC: 7

Freeman, Sophia:
George, M, d. Jun 1855, consumption, 19-0-0, b. LC, sc: G.C. Freeman, head of family, BVS 1855:8, LC:19

French, Elizabeth:
no name, F, d. Jul 1854, unk, 0-0-18, sc: Harriet Haris, mother, BVS 1854:14, LC:14
no name, M, d. Jul 1854, unk, 0-0-6, sc: Harriet Haris, mother, BVS 1854:14, LC:14

Furr, Fenton:
no name,F, d. 1 Apr 1855, master's Res., unk, p. Delilah, b. nr Ebenezer

Church, sc: Fenton Furr, BVS 1855:5, LC:17
Sarah, F, d. Apr 1854, master's Res., 2-6-0, p. Delila, b. masters, sc: master, BVS 1854:13, LC:13

Garrett, Enoch:
Howard, M, d. Jan 1858, Res. of master, whooping cough, 0-10-0, p. Zina, b. E. Garrett, sc: E. Garrett, master, BVS 1858:5, LC:33
no name, M, d. Jul 1855, Res. of master, 0-0-1, p. Zina, b. master's Res., sc: Enoch Garrett, BVS 1855:7, LC:18

Garrett, Silas' Estate:
Harrison GASKINS, M, d. 11 Sep 1854, nr Philomont, heart affection, 32-6-29, p. Judith Ghaskins, b. Jos. Garret decd., blacksmith, sc: mistress, BVS 1854:11, LC:11

George, John:
Nelly, F, d. 29 Oct 1855, LC, dropsy, 82-0-0, b. LC, sc: John George, owner, BVS 1855:2, LC:15
no name, M, d. 13 Sep 1858, LC, unk, 0-0-3, p. Mary (s), b. LC, sc: Samuel W. George, young master, BVS 1858:1, LC:30

Gibson, Alpheus:
Judith, F, d. Feb 1855, Res. of master, typhoid fever, 19-0-0, p. Dorothy, b. Res. of master, sc: Alpheus Gibson, BVS 1855:7, LC:18

Gibson, George:
Amanda, F, d. Sep 1855, S. Triplett's, typhoid fever, 28-0-0, p. Hannah, sc: Joseph Gibson, BVS 1855:6, LC:18

Giddings, Wm:
John, M, d. 15 Apr 1854, LC, consumption, 20-0-0, p. unk, b. LC, farm hand, sc: Wm Giddings, owner, BVS 1854:8, LC: 7
Louisa, F, d. 15 May 1856, LC, fever, 11-0-0, p. unk, b. LC, sc: Wm. Giddings, owner, BVS 1856:2, LC:20
Sarah, F, d. 16 May 1854, LC, croup, 2-1-3, p. Martena (s), b. LC, sc: Wm Giddings, owner, BVS 1854:8, LC: 7
Tena, F, d. 10 Aug 1853, LC, bilious fever, 18-0-0, p. unk, b. unk, house servant, sc: Wm. Giddings, owner, BVS 1854:3, LC: 2

Glasscock, Thomas:
Alfred, M, d. Apr 1857, Fauquier Co., typhoid fever, 26-0-0, b. LC, sc: master, BVS 1857:3, LC:26
Edith, F, d. Sep 1856, Fauquier., brain affected, 6-0-0, p. Frances, b. Fauquier., sc: Mrs. Glasscock, mistress, BVS 1856:4, LC:22
John, M, d. Apr 1857, Fauquier Co., typhoid fever, 20-0-0, b. Fauquier. Co., sc: master, BVS 1857:3, LC:26
Robert, M, d. Apr 1857, Fauquier Co., typhoid fever, 9-0-0, p. Frances, b. Fauquier Co., sc: master, BVS 1857:3, LC:26
Stephen, M, d. Aug 1858, Res. of master, inflammation of bowels, 13-0-0, p. Mary, b. Fauquier, sc: Mrs. Glasscock, mistress, BVS 1858:3, LC:31

Gochenaur, Jas:
Charles, M, d. Dec 1859, master's, abortion, 0-0-1, p. Mary Jane, b. Res. of master, sc: Jos. Gochenaur, master, BVS 1859:3, LC:34

Gochnauer, Jos:
Cordelia, F, d. 6 Sep 1854, Southern View, supposed to have been smothered, 0-0-7, p. Hannah, b. Southern View, sc: Jos. Gochnaeur, BVS 1854:11, LC:10
Cornelia, F, d. 29 Dec 1854, Southern View, supposed to have been smothered, 0-4-0, p. Hannah, b. Southern View, sc: Jos. Gochnaeur, BVS 1854:11, LC:10

Gore, Tilghman:
Alfred, M, d. 2 Feb 1857, LC, pneumonia, 1-0-0, b. LC, sc: Tilghman Gore, owner, BVS 1857:1, LC:24
Amelia, F, d. 10 Mar 1856, LC, pneumonia, 0-9-0, p. unk, b. LC, sc: Tilghman Gore, master, BVS 1856:1, LC:20
Armistead, M, d. 9 Oct 1857, LC, accidental, 7-0-0, b. LC, sc: Tilghman Gore, owner, BVS 1857:1, LC:24
Caroline, F, d. 17 Feb 1857, LC, pneumonia, 1-3-0, b. LC, sc: Tilghman Gore, owner, BVS 1857:1, LC:24

Loudoun County, Virginia, Death Register, 1853-1896　　　11

Eliza, F, d. 3 Jan 1854, LC, unk, 0-1-25, p. Jane (s), b. LC, sc: Tilghman Gore, owner, BVS 1854:8, LC: 8

Letty, F, d. 10 Sep 1857, LC, pneumonia, 18-0-0, b. LC, sc: Tilghman Gore, owner, BVS 1857:1, LC:24

Mary Jane, F, d. 15 Dec 1857, LC, pneumonia, 1-2-0, b. LC, sc: Tilghman Gore, owner, BVS 1857:1, LC:24

Milly, F, d. 12 Jun 1857, LC, pneumonia, 13-0-0, b. LC, sc: Tilghman Gore, owner, BVS 1857:1, LC:24

Rebecca, F, d. 12 Feb 1857, LC, pneumonia, 19-0-0, b. LC, sc: Tilghman Gore, owner, BVS 1857:1, LC:24

Gouchnauer, David:
Clara, F, d. Oct 1857, Res. of master, chronic, 40-0-0, p. Hannah, b. Fauquier Co., sc: David Gochnauer, master, BVS 1857:5, LC:27

Gover, John W.:
no name, F, d. 25 Jan 1854, Leesburg, unk, 0-4-0, p. Harriet (s), b. Leesburg, sc: John W. Gover, owner, BVS 1854:8, LC: 7

Sarah, F, d. 30 Jan 1853, LC, unk, 30-0-0, p. unk, b. Leesburg, sc: John W. Gover, owner, BVS 1854:5, LC: 3

Grady, Sarah:
Cela, F, d. Oct 1857, Res. of mistress, Typhoid pneumonia, 55-0-0, sc: Sarah Grady, mistress, BVS 1857:3, LC:26

Gray, Abert W.:
George, M, d. 3 Jun 1853, LC, by lightning, 33-1-0, p. unk, b. unk, farm hand, sc: Joseph Mead, head of family, BVS 1854:3, LC: 2

Gray, Dr. Jos. G.:
Randolph, M, d. Jun 1854, Llangolon, croup, 5-0-0, p. Lina, b. Frederick; sc: Dr. Jos. G. Gray, BVS 1854:12, LC:11

Gray, Joseph G.:
Richard, M, d. Oct 1858, Res. of master, unk, p. Susan, b. Res. of parents, sc: E.S. Hirst, overseer, BVS 1858:4, LC:31

Gray, Robert W.:
Irena, F, d. 9 Dec 1858, Leesburg, affection of womb, 58-0-0, p. unk, b. LC, sc: R.W. Gray, owner, BVS 1858:2, LC:30

Jesse, M, d. 12 Dec 1858, Leesburg, paralysis, 60-0-0, p. unk, b. LC, sc: R.W. Gray, owner, BVS 1858:2, LC:30

Mary, F, d. 15 Jul 1853, Leesburg, unk, 0-0-7, p. Sarah (s), b. unk, sc: Robert W. Grey, owner, BVS 1854:5, LC: 3

Grayson, Ann L.:
Harry, M, d. 11 Nov 1857, Res. of mistress, dropsy, 50-0-0, b. Fauquier Co., sc: Alexr L. Grayson, BVS 1857:4, LC:27

Greeman, Garret C.:
Hiram, M, d. Feb 1855, dropsy, 50-0-0, b. LC, sc: G.C. Freeman, owner, BVS 1855:8, LC:19

Gregg, Gibson:
Shadrac LEE, M, d. Apr 1858, Res. of master, unk, 0-4-0, p. Maria Lee, b. Res. of master, sc: Mrs. Gregg, mistress, BVS 1858:3, LC:31

Gregg, Peter:
Eliza, F, d. Apr 1855, LC, typhoid fever, 25-3-0, p. Lucy, b. LC, sc: Emily J. Gregg, BVS 1855:3, LC:16

John, M, d. 12 Feb 1855, LC, croup, 0-10-0, p. Eliza, b. LC, sc: Emily J. Gregg, BVS 1855:4, LC:16

Greyson, Mary D.:
Jenny, F, d. 31 Jan 1854, Mrs. Mary D. Greyson's, ulcerated stomach, 49-0-0, p. Clara, b. Belmont, sc: Mary D. Greyson, BVS 1854:11, LC:11

Grubb, Benjn:
James, M, d. 10 Oct 1856, LC, typhoid fever, 18-6-0, p. Maria, b. LC, sc: Benj.n Grubb, owner, BVS 1856:2, LC:20

Grubb, Ebenezer:
Harrison, M, d. 27 Apr 1854, LC, accidental, 13-4-20, p. Ann (s), b. LC, sc: Ebenezer Grubb, owner, BVS 1854:9, LC: 9

Joshua, M, d. 1 Dec 1855, LC, unk, 0-5-0, p. Sarah (s), b. LC, sc: Ebenezer Grubb, owner, BVS 1855:1, LC:14

Harrison, Burr W.:
Anna, F, d. 1 Sep 1853, Leesburg, diarrhea, 52-3-7, p. unk, b. unk, c/o: Abraham (s), sc: Burr W. Harrison, owner, BVS 1854:5, LC: 3

Harrison, Jno. M.:
Milly, F, d. 16 Aug 1855, Unison, dropsy, 70-0-0, b. Westmoreland Co., sc: Mrs. Jno. M. Harrison, BVS 1855:4, LC:16
Newman, M, d. 22 Aug 1855, Unison, accident, 70-0-0, p. Euphemia, b. LC, sc: Mrs. Jno. M. Harrison, BVS 1855:4, LC:16

Hatcher, Joshua:
Lafayette DAVIS, M, d. May 1858, Res. of master, abscess, 28-0-0, b. Jos. Garrett's Est., sc: J. Hatcher, master, BVS 1858:5, LC:33

Hawling, Isaac:
Laura, F, d. Dec 1853, on Sycolin, phthisic, 7-0-0, p. Mary, b. on Sycolin, sc: master, BVS 1854:5, LC: 5

Hawling, Isaac W.:
Daniel, M, d. Spring 1854, White Hall, scrofula, 18-0-0, p. Mary, b. White Hall, sc: Miss Jemima Hawling, BVS 1854:12, LC:12
Hannah, F, d. Summer 1854, White Hall, croup, 0-0-1, p. Harriet, b. White Hall, sc: Miss Jemima Hawling, BVS 1854:12, LC:12
Lewis, M, d. Summer 1854, White Hall, fall, 3-0-0, p. Harriet, b. White Hall, sc: Miss Jemima Hawling, BVS 1854:12, LC:12

Heaton, J.D.:
Jupitor, M, d. May 1857, Res. of master, typhoid fever, 70-0-0, p. Agnes, b. Waterford, sc: C.M. Heaton, mistress, BVS 1857:5, LC:28
Mars, M, d. Mar 1857, Res. of master, 5-0-0, p. Catharine, b. At place of death, sc: C.M. Heaton, mistress, BVS 1857:5, LC:28

Heaton, James D.'s Estate:
Flora, F, d. Apr 1859, His Res. Exedra, scarlet fever, 0-9-0, p. Agnes, b. Res. of master, sc: C.M. Heaton, mistress, BVS 1859:4, LC:35

Hempstone, C. T.:
Noah, M, d. 10 Sep 1854, LC, consumption, 24-0-0, p. unk, b. unk, sc: C. T. Hempstone, owner, BVS 1854:10, LC:10

Hempstone, Cephas:
Mary, F, d. 15 Aug 1856, LC, whooping cough, 0-3-0, b. LC, sc: Cephas Hempstone, owner, BVS 1856:2, LC:21

Hepburn, Martha:
Letty, F, d. 20 May 1856, LC, unk, 55-0-0, b. LC, sc: Hugh S. Thompson. Friend, BVS 1856:2, LC:21

Hicks, Kimble G.:
George, M, d. 15 Apr 1854, Amon Dale, diarrhea, 29-0-0, p. Emily, b. Warren Co., sc: master, BVS 1854:12, LC:11
Meshack, d. Nov 1855, nr Paris, typhoid fever, 46-0-0, p. Betty, sc: Mrs. Hicks, mistress, BVS 1855:6, LC:18
Stephen, M, d. Dec 1854, Amon Dale, typhoid fever, 1-6-0, p. Maria, b. Annandale, sc: master, BVS 1854:12, LC:11
Thornton, M, d. Oct 1855, nr Paris, consumption, 21-0-0, p. Frances, b. Fauquier, sc: Mrs. Hicks, mistress, BVS 1855:6, LC:18

Hixon, Elizabeth:
no name, F, d. Spring 1856, nr Dover, 0-9-0, p. Mary Virginia, b. Landmark, Fauquier Co., sc: Rufus Smith, father, BVS 1856:4, LC:21

Hixson, Abner:
no name, F, d. Feb 1853, nr Philomont, spasms, 0-2-0, p. Daniel & Catharine Dorcas, b. LC, unk, unm, sc: Jonathan Tavenner, employer, BVS 1854:1, LC: 3

Hodgson, Sidney L.:
no name, M, d. 2 Oct 1854, LC, unk, 8-0-0, sc: S. L. Hodgson, owner, BVS 1854:14, LC:13

Hoffman, Elizabeth:
no name, M, d. 3 Dec 1854, LC, unk, 0-0-3, p. Eliza (s), b. LC, sc: Sally Hoffman, one of the family, BVS 1854:10, LC: 9

Loudoun County, Virginia, Death Register, 1853-1896   13

Hummer, Washington:
Lewis THOMAS, M, d. 11 Jun 1853, LC, suicide, 20-0-0, p. unk, b. LC, sc: Washington Hummer, owner, BVS 1854:2, LC: 7

Hunter, Nathaniel C.:
Henry, M, d. 4 Sep 1853, Leesburg, unk, 35-0-0, p. unk, b. Fairfax, sc: Chas G. Eskridge, head of family, BVS 1854:5, LC: 3

Hutchison:
Harriett FOX, F, d. Jun 1853, LC, dropsy, 65-0-0, p. unk, b. LC, sc: H.B. Hutchison, son of owner, BVS 1854:2, LC: 7

Hutchison, Elizabeth:
[no name], M, d. Feb 1857, unk, 0-0-7, sc: Elizabeth Hutchison, owner, BVS 1857:7, LC:29
Infants, F, d. Aug 1859, Jos. H. Hutchison's, unk, 0-0-12, p. Matilda, b. Jos. A. Hutchison, sc: Jos. A. Hutchison, father, BVS 1859:3, LC:34
no name, M, d. Feb 1856, S. W. McCarty's, ulcerated throat, 0-5-0, p. Caroline, b. Res. of master, sc: L.W. McCarty, master, BVS 1856:5, LC:23

Hutchison, Lemuel:
no name, M, d. Nov 1856, Charles Lucius, 2-0-0, p. Sarah, b. on Blue Ridge, sc: Charles Lucius, BVS 1856:4, LC:22

Hutchison, Mary:
Franklin PIERCE, M, d. Aug 1853, LC, unk, 0-2-0, p. unk, b. LC, sc: M. B. Hutchison, neighbor, BVS 1854:2, LC: 6

Hutchison, Sampson:
Fanny CARTER, F, d. Oct 1853, LC, old age, 80-0-0, p. unk, b. LC, sc: Samson Hutchison, owner, BVS 1854:2, LC: 7

Ish, Robert A.:
no name, F, d. Apr 1854, LC, unk, 0-2-0, sc: R. A. Ish, owner, BVS 1854:14, LC:14
Winefred, F, d. Apr 1854, LC, unk, 18-0-0, sc: R. A. Ish, owner, BVS 1854:14, LC:14

Jackson, Giles:
Eliza Jane, F, d. 19 May 1856, Leesburg, whooping cough, 3-0-0, p. Lucy, b. Leesburg, sc: S.E. Jackson, mistress, BVS 1856:4, LC:22
Thomas, M, d. May 1856, Leesburg, accident from fall, 23-0-0, p. Milly, b. nr Leesburg, sc: S.E. Jackson, mistress, BVS 1856:4, LC:21

Jackson, Mary:
no name, F, d. 24 Dec 1854, LC, unk, 0-0-1, p. Lucy (s), b. Leesburg, sc: A. R. Mott, head of family, BVS 1854:10, LC:10

James, David B:
Angelina, F, d. 1 Sep 1858, LC, unk, 3-0-0, b. LC, sc: David B. James, owner, BVS 1858:6, LC:33
Mary Jane, F, d. 15 Sep 1858, LC, unk, 0-4-0, b. LC, sc: David B. James, owner, BVS 1858:6, LC:33
Jesse DEAN, M, d. Aug 1855, congestive fever, 2-0-0, p. unk, b. Fairfax Co, VA, sc: D.B. James, owner, BVS 1855:8, LC:19

Janney, George W:
Amos, M, d. 10 Jul 1856, LC, unk, 19-0-0, p. Harriett, a slave, b. LC, sc: George W. Janney, owner, BVS 1856:1, LC:20

Johnson, A.W.:
James POLK, M, d. 7 Sep 1854, dysentery, 10-0-0, sc: A. W. Johnson, owner, BVS 1854:14, LC:14

Johnson, Edward:
John, M, d. 10 Sep 1858, LC, typhoid fever, 21-0-0, p. unk, b. Fairfax, unm, sc: Alfred C. Belt, head of family, BVS 1858:1, LC:29

Johnson, Peter W.:
Sally, F, d. 16 Nov 1853, Leesburg, scarlet fever, 4-5-17, p. Kitty (s), b. Leesburg, sc: Peter W. Johnson, owner, BVS 1854:5, LC: 3

Jones, John Jr:
Clinton, M, d. 12 Oct 1855, LC, accidental, 7-0-0, sc: John Jones Jr., owner, BVS 1855:2, LC:15

Kephart, George:
no name, M, d. Sep 1856, LC, unk, 2-0-0, b. LC, sc: George Kephart, owner, BVS 1856:7, LC:24

Kincheloe, Mary:
Sandy BERRY, M, d. 25 Nov 1858, LC, unk, 80-0-0, p. unk, b. Prince Wm., sc: Wilson C. Sanders, head of family, BVS 1858:2, LC:30

Lee, A.D.:
Richard PETERSON, M, d. Oct 1853, LC, unk, 65-0-0, p. unk, b. LC, sc: Alexr. D. Lee, owner, BVS 1854:2, LC: 7

Lee, John:
George NEWMAN, M, d. Dec 1857, croup, 3-0-0, sc: John Lee, owner, BVS 1857:7, LC:29

Lee, Matthew P.:
Susan STEWARD, F, d. May 1854, LC, premature birth, 19-0-0, b. LC, sc: M. P. Lee, owner, BVS 1854:14, LC:13

Leith, Dr. Theoderick:
Alice, F, d. Jul 1858, Res. of master, measles, 0-8-0, p. Rebecca, b. Union, sc: Theodrick Leith, master, BVS 1858:5, LC:32
Harriet, F, d. May 1855, Union, typhoid fever, 19-0-0, b. nr Pothouse, sc: Thoedrick Leith, BVS 1855:5, LC:17
John, M, d. Oct 1854, Union, 2-0-0, p. Milly Jones, b. Union, sc: master, BVS 1854:13, LC:13

Leith, Margaret:
Josephine, F, d. Feb 1859, Union, drowned, 13-0-0, p. Winny, b. nr Lisbon, sc: Dr. T. Leith, BVS 1859:3, LC:34
Susan, F, d. Jun 1855, Union, typhoid fever, 12-0-0, p. Winney, b. nr Pothouse, sc: Thoedrick Leith, BVS 1855:5, LC:17

Leith, Wm.:
John BRISCOE, M, d. Jan 1853, nr Newtesbow, scrofula, 11-0-0, p. Adam & Winney Briscoe, b. nr Lisbon, sc: master in law, BVS 1854:1, LC: 4

Leslie, John:
Ann, F, d. 15 Jan 1853, LC, consumption, 30-6-2, p. unk, unm, sc: John Leslie, owner, BVS 1854:4, LC: 2

Lewis, Martha J.:
no name, F, d. Oct 1856, LC, unk, 0-0-7, b. LC, sc: Martha I. Lewis, owner, BVS 1856:7, LC:24
Ida NEIL, F, d. Aug. 1855, LC, unk, 0-0-20, b. LC, sc: Martha J. Lewis, head of family, BVS 1855:8, LC:19

Lewis, Susan:
John WALKER, M, d. Mar 1854, LC, unk, 18-6-0, p. John & Malinda Walker, b. LC, sc: Martha J. Lewis, head of family, BVS 1854:14, LC:13

Lickey, Wm:
Nancy, F, d. 22 Dec 1855, master's Res., consumption, 22-0-0, p. Emily, b. nr Mount Gilead, sc: Wm. Lickey, BVS 1855:7, LC:18

Lindsey, Hulda C.:
no name, M, d. 12 Feb 1855, Leesburg, smothered, 0-1-15, p. Kitty (s), b. Fauquier, sc: L. J. Lindsey, head of family, BVS 1855:1, LC:14

Lindsey, S.J.:
Toney, M, d. 10 Dec 1857, Leesburg, inflammation brain, 1-0-14, p. Eliza (s), b. Clarke Co., sc: Hannah E. Lindsey, mistress, BVS 1857:2, LC:25

Littleton, Bush:
Welby LEWIS, M, d. Aug 1853, Trap, inflammation lungs, 1-6-0, p. Addison & Mariah Lewis, b. Trap, sc: master, BVS 1854:1, LC: 4

Littleton, Hannah:
Allice, F, d. Aug 1855, Trap, smothered, 0-2-0, p. Amanda, b. Trap, sc: Hannah Littleton, BVS 1855:4, LC:16

Littleton, John:
no name,F, d. Aug 1855, Isaac G. Nichols', thrush, 0-3-3, p. Mahala Harvy, b. Isaac G. Nichols', sc: Isaac G. Nichols, BVS 1855:6, LC:18
no name, M, d. 7 Sep 1854, LC, unk, 0-0-1, p. Mahala (s), b. LC, sc: Levi W. Nixon, head of family, BVS 1854:9, LC: 9

Loudoun County, Virginia, Death Register, 1853-1896   15

Littleton, Martha J.:
no name,M, d. 15 Jun 1857, Foot Blue Ridge, spasms, 0-0-4, p. Eliza Clark, b. Foot Blue Ridge, sc: Martha J. Littleton, mistress, BVS 1857:4, LC:27

Love, Mrs.:
Esther, F, d. 9 Dec 1853, LC, old age, 95-0-0, p. unk, b. unk, washer, unm, sc: Esther Selma, friend, BVS 1854:5, LC: 3

Lovett, Tazwell:
Jennie, F, d. 1 Oct 1858, Res. of master, whooping cough, 0-4-0, p. Jane, b. Res. of master, sc: C. Lovett, mistress, BVS 1858:4, LC:32

Luck, John M.:
Edgar, M, d. 25 Aug 1859, B. F. Skinner's, accidental shooting, 19-0-0, p. Easther, b. LC, sc: J. M. Moran, BVS 1859:3, LC:34

Luck, Jordan B.:
Emily, F, d. May 1853, on Goose Creek, scarlet fever, 1-0-0, p. Eve, b. Caroline Co., sc: young master, BVS 1854:6, LC: 5
Eve, F, d. Aug 1853, on Goose Creek, dysentery, 25-0-0, b. Caroline Co., sc: young master, BVS 1854:6, LC: 5

Luckett, Horace:
no name, F, d. Feb 1856, Res. of master, 0-1-1, sc: H. Luckett, master, BVS 1856:4, LC:21
Julus MASSEY, M, d. 16 May 1854, Res. of master, old age, 90-0-0, b. Goochland Co., carpenter, sc: master & mistress, BVS 1854:10, LC:10

Luckett, Ludwl:
Betsy, F, d. 25 Jun 1855, Montpelier, typhoid fever, 50-0-0, sc: Geo. W. Bronaugh, BVS 1855:5, LC:17

Lynn, John T.:
Harriet Ann, F, d. 8 Sep 1855, Mount Prominent, typhoid fever, 19-8-0, p. Harriett, b. Mt. Prominent, sc: John T. Lynn, BVS 1855:6, LC:18

Lynn, Parmelia:
Dundinah, F, d. Mar 1853, LC, dropsy, 2-0-0, p. unk, b. LC, sc: John G.C., son of owner, BVS 1854:2, LC: 7

Louisa, F, d. Apr 1853, nr Aldie, 16-0-0, p. Amanda, b. nr Aldie, sc: J. Lynn, young master, BVS 1854:6, LC: 6

Lynn, Wm:
Mariah, F, d. 3 Jul 1853, nr Dover, consumption, 27-0-0, p. Levinia Mason, b. Dumphries, sc: mistress, BVS 1854:6, LC: 6

Marlow, Geo:
Mahala, F, d. 3 Apr 1853, LC, typhoid pneumonia, 11-11-1, p. Nancy (s), b. Maryland, sc: Geo Marlow, owner, BVS 1854:3, LC: 1
no name, M, d. 6 Jun 1853, LC, croup, 0-0-6, p. Nancy (s), b. Maryland, sc: Geo Marlow, owner, BVS 1854:3, LC: 1

Mason, John F.:
Billy, M, d. 14 Nov 1856, LC, old age, 65-0-0, p. unk (s), b. LC, sc: J.F. Mason, owner, BVS 1856:2, LC:20
Harriet, F, d. 25 Oct 1856, LC, inflammation bowels, 5-6-0, p. Harriet (s), b. LC, sc: J.F. Mason, owner, BVS 1856:2, LC:20
Maria, F, d. 6 May 1856, LC, paralysis, 47-0-0, p. unk (s), b. LC, sc: J.F. Mason, owner, BVS 1856:2, LC:20

Mason, Wm. T. T.:
no name, F, d. Nov 1854, unk, 0-1-15, sc: John C. Tippett, head of family, BVS 1854:14, LC:14
no name, M, d. 21 Sep 1854, smothered, 0-0-10, sc: Wm. L. H. Kendrick, head of family, BVS 1854:14, LC:14
Samuel, M, d. 26 Dec 1854, LC, dropsy, 65-0-0, b. Anne Arundle Co. MD, sc: Wm. T. T. Mason, Jr., head of family, BVS 1854:10, LC:10

Matthews, Squire:
Mary Catharine, F, d. Jun 1855, Fauquier Co., cola ?, 1-0-0, p. Angelina, b. Fauquier Co., sc: Squire Matthews, BVS 1855:4, LC:16

Matthews, Squire E.:
Kesiah, F, d. Sep 1857, pneumonia, 75-0-0, p. Dinah, b. LC, sc: S.E. Matthews, master, BVS 1857:4, LC:26

McCarty, G. W.:
Elizabeth, F, d. Aug 1854, Res. of master, dysentery, 8-0-0, p. Sarah, b. master, sc: G. B. McCarty, BVS 1854:13, LC:13
Harriet, F, d. Aug 1854, Res. of master, dysentery, 8-0-0, p. Lutitia, b. master, sc: G. B. McCarty, BVS 1854:13, LC:13
Nancy, F, d. Apr 1854, Res. of master, consumption, 18-0-0, p. Tilly, b. master, sc: G. B. McCarty, BVS 1854:13, LC:12
no name, F, d. Jul 1854, Res. of master, dysentery, 0-0-21, p. Frances, b. master, sc: G. B. McCarty, BVS 1854:13, LC:13

McCarty, George B.:
Dink, M, d. Jun 1859, Res. of master, cold, 1-0-0, p. Frances, b. Res. of master, sc: G. B. McCarty, master, BVS 1859:3, LC:34

McCarty, Margaret:
no name, M, d. 25 Aug 1854, Res. of Mrs. McCarty's unk, unk, 0-0-3, p. Nancy, b. nr G.C.B.B.L.T.P., sc: Billington McCarty, BVS 1854:12, LC:12

McCarty, S.W.:
Burr, M, d. Jun 1857, Res. of master, bronchitis, 23-0-0, p. Rachel, b. Poor House, sc: S.W. McCarty, master, BVS 1857:5, LC:27
no name, M, d. 1 May 1857, Res. of master, inflammation bowel, 0-2-0, p. Henry, b. Res. of master, sc: S.W. McCarty, master, BVS 1857:5, LC:27
James, M, d. May 1857, Res. of master, pneumonia, 3-0-0, p. Cela, b. Res. of master, sc: S.W. McCarty, master, BVS 1857:5, LC:27

McCarty, Washington:
Harriet, F, d. Sep 1853, nr Middleburg, dysentery, 8-0-0, p. Lititia, b. nr Aldie, sc: master, BVS 1854:7, LC: 6
Lizzy, F, d. Sep 1853, nr Middleburg, dysentery, 8-0-0, p. Sarah, b. nr Aldie, sc: master, BVS 1854:7, LC: 6
no name, F, d. Oct 1853, Fauquier, croup, 1-3-0, p. Littitia, b. nr Gilead, sc: master, BVS 1854:7, LC: 6

McCray, Wm:
no name, M, d. Dec 1856, Res. of master, 0-1-0, p. Margaret, b. Res. of master, sc: Wm. McCray, master, BVS 1856:6, LC:23

McDaniel, Archibald:
no name, F, d. Nov 1858, Res. of master, unk, p. Martha Washington, b. Res. of master, sc: A. McDaniel, master, BVS 1858:5, LC:32
Eugene WASHINGTON, F, d. Mar 1853, nr Wheatland, croup, 0-9-0, p. A & Martha Washington, b. nr Wheatland, sc: master, BVS 1854:1, LC: 4

McDaniel, James:
Albert, M, d. Feb 1858, Res. of master, scrofula, 7-0-0, p. Percella, b. Res. of master, sc: James McDaniel, master, BVS 1858:4, LC:32
no name, , d. Fall 1854, Res. of master, 0-0-2, p. Priscilla, b. master's residence, sc: master, BVS 1854:12, LC:12

McDowell, Elijah:
Richard, M, d. 16 Sep 1858, LC, stomach affection, 58-0-0, p. unk, b. LC, sc: Eli S. Schooley, friend, BVS 1858:1, LC:29

McIlhany, James:
Marcus, M, d. 9 Jan 1856, James McIlhany's, old age, 75-0-0, b. Prince William, sc: James McIlhany, master, BVS 1856:5, LC:22
no name, F, d. 18 May 1856, Res. of master, 0-0-5, p. Sarah, b. Res. of master, sc: James McIlhany, master, BVS 1856:5, LC:22

McNealy, Mrs.:
Mary, F, d. Aug 1859, Middleburg, typhoid fever, 25-0-0, p. Ellen, b. LC, sc: J. M. Moran, BVS 1859:3, LC:34

McNealy, Sarah:
Addison JACKSON, M, d. 20 Apr 1853, Middleburg, congestion of blood, 0-9-0, p. Mary Jackson, b. unk, sc: John M. Moran, employer, BVS 1854:1, LC: 4
no name, F, d. 5 Oct 1855, Middleburg, unk, 0-0-5, p. Mary Frances, b. Middleburg, sc: John M. Moran, BVS 1855:3, LC:16

Loudoun County, Virginia, Death Register, 1853-1896   17

McPherson, Wesley:
Ann GANT, F, d. 19 Mar 1853, nr Leesburg, pneumonia, 36-0-0, p. unk, b. Fairfax Co., sc: master, BVS 1854:5, LC: 5

McVeigh, Jesse:
Eliz. THORNTON, F, d. 10 Jul 1855, Res. of master, paralyses, 60-0-0, p. Rachel Randal, b. Fauquier, sc: Milton McVeigh, BVS 1855:3, LC:16

McVeigh, Townsend:
Esther, F, d. Jul 1856, S. W. McCarty's, teething, 0-5-0, p. Amanda, b. Res. of master, sc: T.M. McVeigh, master, BVS 1856:5, LC:23
Richard Henry, M, d. Aug 1857, Res. of master, cold, 0-10-0, p. Martha, b. Res. of Mast, sc: T. McVeigh, master, BVS 1857:4, LC:26
Robert, M, d. Nov 1858, Res. of master, heart affection, 55-0-0, p. Sarah, b. Fairfax, sc: Townsend McVeigh, master, BVS 1858:4, LC:31

Mead, Joseph:
Eliza Ann, F, d. 12 Jul 1856, LC, unk, 0-1-0, p. Caroline (s), b. LC, sc: Joshua White, head of family, BVS 1856:2, LC:21
no name, F, d. 5 Aug 1857, LC, unk, 0-3-3, p. Caroline, b. LC, sc: Joseph Mead, owner, BVS 1857:2, LC:25

Megeath, Alfred:
Franklin, M, d. 13 Apr 1856, Res. of master, 3-0-0, p. Jemima, b. Bladensburg, MD, sc: A. Megeath, master, BVS 1856:6, LC:23

Minor, John W.:
Samuel, M, d. 28 Dec 1856, LC, old age, 90-0-0, p. unk, b. Charles Co., MD, sc: John W. Minor, owner, BVS 1856:2, LC:20

Miskell, George W.:
George, M, d. Feb 1854, unk, 0-1-0, sc: G. W. Miskell, owner, BVS 1854:14, LC:14

Moore, A. M.:
Emily, F, d. Sep 1859, Snickersville, cancer, 53-0-0, b. Jefferson, sc: A. M. Moore, master, BVS 1859:3, LC:34

Moore, John:
Arch, M, d. 1853, Aldie, unk, 4-0-0, p. Amanda, b. Aldie, sc: master, BVS 1854:2, LC: 4
Bob, M, d. Mar 1855, Aldie, hemorrhage lungs, 19-0-0, p. Lucy, b. Aldie, sc: John Moore, BVS 1855:4, LC:16
Henry, M, d. 1853, Aldie, unk, 2-0-0, p. Amanda, b. Aldie, sc: master, BVS 1854:2, LC: 4
Livenia, F, d. Apr 1854, Aldie, bronchitis, 2-0-0, p. Lucinda, b. Aldie, sc: John Moore, BVS 1854:10, LC:10
Lucy, F, d. Apr 1854, Aldie, consumption, 55-0-0, p. unk, b. LC, cook, sc: John Moore, BVS 1854:10, LC:10
William, M, d. Fall 1858, Aldie, measles, 2-0-0, p. Lucinda, b. Aldie, sc: John Moore, master, BVS 1858:3, LC:30

Moran, Elizabeth:
Charles, M, d. 25 Aug 1859, B. F. Skinner's, suicide, 19-0-0, p. Judith, b. LC, sc: J. M. Moran, BVS 1859:3, LC:34
no name, M, d. Feb 1858, Peter Etcher, dropsy of brain, 0-4-0, p. Lucy, b. Elizabeth Moran's, sc: Mrs. Etcher, BVS 1858:4, LC:32

Morgan, Jane C.:
Violet, F, d. 12 Mar 1853, Leesburg, consumption, 33-4-15, p. unk, b. LC, house servant, sc: Jane C. Morgan, owner, BVS 1854:5, LC: 3

Morgan, Mrs. Mary:
Washington, M, d. 2 Aug 1854, Jos. Worthington, suddenly, 25-0-0, sc: Jas Worthington, BVS 1854:13, LC:12

Mount, James:
Frank, M, d. Dec 1857, Mountsville, putrid sore throat, 0-5-0, p. Elizabeth, b. Mountsville, sc: master, BVS 1857:3, LC:25

Murrey, Dr:
Julia, F, d. 1 Feb 1854, Middleburg, consumption, 16-0-0, p. Luckey, b. Middleburg, house servant, sc: John M. Thomson, BVS 1854:11, LC:10

Neal, Nancy's estate:
Judith NELSON, F, d. Dec 1858, Jonah Orrison's, old age, 70-0-0, sc: Charles W. Orrison, BVS 1858:5, LC 32

Newman, James T.:
Charles Edwin, M, d. 15 Jul 1856, LC, unk, 1-3-0, p. Winny (s), sc: James T. Newman, owner, BVS 1856:1, LC:20

Newman, Theorem W.:
Huldah, F, d. 13 Sep 1854, dysentery, 2-6-0, sc: A. W. Johnson, head of family, BVS 1854:14, LC:14

Newton, E.J.:
Patience, F, d. Oct 1856, LC, typhoid fever, 40-0-0, b. LC, sc: E.J. Newton, owner, BVS 1856:7, LC:24

Nichols, Jonah:
Clara, F, d. Jul 1854, Res. of masters, pulmonary, 0-10-0, p. Juliet, b. Res. of master, sc: Miss Nichols, BVS 1854:13, LC:12
Harriet, F, d. Nov 1853, nr Purcelville, teething, 0-6-0, p. Catherine, b. nr Purcellville, sc: master, BVS 1854:6, LC: 5

Noland, Sarah C.:
Flora, F, d. 5 Jun 1856, Jonah W. Nixon, heart disease, 65-0-0, b. Lower Virginia, sc: J.W. Nixon, BVS 1856:5, LC:23

Oden, James S.:
Bob, M, d. Aug 1858, LC, killed, 53-0-0, b. LC, sc: James S. Oden, owner, BVS 1858:6, LC:33
Peter, M, d. Sep 1858, LC, unk, 4-4-0, b. LC, sc: James S. Oden, owner, BVS 1858:6, LC:33

Oden, N. S.:
Margaret, F, d. 26 Apr 1853, LC, affections of spine, 0-9-0, p. unk, b. LC, sc: N. S. Oden, owner, BVS 1854:2, LC: 7

Osburn, Ann:
Ellen, F, d. 9 Sep 1854, LC, dysentery, 0-5-3, p. Matilda (s), b. LC, sc: Bushrod Osburn, head of family, BVS 1854:9, LC: 8
no name, F, d. 30 Nov 1855, LC, unk, 0-1-14, p. unk, b. LC, sc: Ann Osburn, owner, BVS 1855:2, LC:15

no name, F, d. 22 Apr 1859, LC, unk, 0-0-1, p. Catharine (s), sc: Annie Osburn, mistress, BVS 1859:1, LC:36

Osburn, Joel:
Ben, M, d. 10 Dec 1858, Res. of master, suddenly, unk, BVS 1858:5, LC:33

Osburn, Jonah:
Nancy, F, d. Nov 1857, Res. of master, influenza, 0-1-14, p. Nancy, b. Res. of master, sc: Jonah Osburn, master, BVS 1857:5, LC:27

Osburn, Nicholas:
Margaret, F, d. 12 Oct 1855, Leesburg, unk, 16-0-0, p. Charlotte, b. LC, sc: Nicholas Osburn, owner, BVS 1855:3, LC:15

Osburn, Patsy:
Hannah, F, d. 15 Feb 1859, Res. of mistress, child bed, 41-0-0, p. Jane, b. Clarke, sc: P. Osburn, mistress, BVS 1859:4, LC:35

Osburn, Thompson:
Edith, F, d. 28 Sep 1859, Res. of master, cholera infantum, 0-11-0, p. Huldah, b. Res. of master, sc: T. Osburn, master, BVS 1859:4, LC:35
Logan, M, d. 20 Sep 1859, Res. of master, cholera infantum, 0-11-0, p. Huldah, b. Res. of master, sc: T. Osburn, master, BVS 1859:4, LC:35

Overfield, Mrs.:
Agie JONES, F, d. 5 Jun 1859, poorhouse, old age, 80-0-0, sc: steward, BVS 1859:4, LC:35
Wm. JONES, M, d. 3 Apr 1859, poorhouse, old age, 80-0-0, sc: steward, BVS 1859:4, LC:35

Pancost, Joseph:
Allice HUNTER, F, d. Oct 1853, foot of Blue Ridge, croup, 2-0-0, p. Sarah Hunter, b. foot of Blue Ridge, sc: Jonah Purcell, employer, BVS 1854:1, LC: 4

Paxson, John C.:
[no name], M, d. Feb 1857, unk, 0-2-0, sc: John C. Paxson, owner, BVS 1857:7, LC:29

Loudoun County, Virginia, Death Register, 1853-1896

Peacock, Noble B.:
no name, F, d. 17 Jun 1854, LC, unk, 0-0-1, p. Kitty (s), b. LC, sc: C. M. Vandevanter, head of family, BVS 1854:10, LC: 9
no name, M, d. 17 Jun 1854, LC, unk, 0-0-1, p. Kitty(s), b. LC, sc: C. M. Vandevanter, head of family, BVS 1854:10, LC: 9

Peck, Patience:
Wesley, M, d. 3 Jun 1853, LC, by lightning, 55-2-16, p. unk, b. unk, farm hand, sc: Joseph Mead, head of family, BVS 1854:3, LC: 2

Perry, Verlinda:
Olivia Jane, F, d. 16 Jul 1853, Leesburg, diarrhea, 7-2-7, p. Mary West (s), b. LC, sc: Verlinda Perry, owner, BVS 1854:5, LC: 3

Peugh, Mary:
Emily, F, d. 16 Apr 1855, Pugh's Mill, consumption, 40-0-0, p. Hannah, b. nr Woodgrove, sc: Mary Peugh, BVS 1855:6, LC:17

Powell, H. B.:
Dolly, F, d. Feb 1856, Res. of master, cholera morbus, 12-0-0, p. Lucy, b. Middleburg, sc: H.B. Powell, master, BVS 1856:5, LC:22
no name, M, d. Nov 1853, Middleburg, unk, 1-6-0, p. Chloe, b. Middleburg, sc: master, BVS 1854:1, LC: 4
no name, F, d. [1855], Middleburg, 1-0-0, p. Lucy, b. Middleburg, sc: H.B. Powell, BVS 1855:7, LC:18
no name, M, d. Jan 1856, Res. of master, 0-0-6, p. Jane, b. Middleburg, sc: H.B. Powell, master, BVS 1856:5, LC:22

Powell, Marietta:
Ellen, F, d. 15 Jul 1855, Middleburg, typhoid fever, 21-0-0, p. Judith, b. Middleburg, sc: Marietta Powell, BVS 1855:4, LC:16
Eve, F, d. Aug 1855, Middleburg, unk, 59-0-0, p. Julia, b. Middleburg, sc: Marietta Powell, BVS 1855:4, LC:16
Mary, F, d. Aug 1855, Middleburg, brain affection, 3-10-0, p. Ellen, b. Middleburg, sc: Marietta Powell, BVS 1855:4, LC:16
Rosetta, F, d. Jun 1856, S. W. McCarty's, consumption, 41-0-0, p.

Gooley, b. Kinlock Fauquier Co., sc: Mrs. M. Powell, mistress, BVS 1856:5, LC:23

Presgraves, Wm. W.:
Arthur, M, d. Sep 1858, LC, dysentery, 2-0-0, p. Armena, b. LC, sc: Wm. W. Presgraves, owner, BVS 1858:6, LC:33

Purcell, Enos:
no name, --, d. Dec 1854, Enos Purcell's, 0-0-20, p. Delilah Jenkins, sc: master, BVS 1854:13, LC:12

Purcell, James H.:
Samuel, M, d. Jul 1858, Res. of master, whooping cough, 1-6-0, p. Huldah, b. Res. of master, sc: J.H. Purcell, master, BVS 1858:5, LC:32

Purcell, Samuel:
Amanda, F, d. Mar 1859, Res. of master, typhoid fever, 14-0-0, p. Maria, sc: Samuel Pursel, master, BVS 1859:5, LC:35
Annabella, F, d. 7 Aug 1857, Res. of master, dysentery, 2-0-0, p. Emily, sc: Samuel Purcell, master, BVS 1857:5, LC:28
Mariah, F, d. Nov 1853, R. B. Factory, child bed, 45-0-0, b. unk, sc: master, BVS 1854:6, LC: 5

Pusey, Joshua:
Henrietta, F, d. 15 Nov 1853, LC, accidental, 0-1-0, p. Martha (s), b. LC, sc: Noble S. Braden, head of family, BVS 1854:4, LC: 2
Martha, F, d. 1 Nov 1856, LC, congestive fever, 30-0-0, p. Nancy (s), b. LC, sc: C.F. Anderson, head of family, BVS 1856:1, LC:20
no name, F, d. 21 Sep 1853, LC, unk, 0-1-3, p. Martha (s), b. LC, sc: Joshua Pusey, owner, BVS 1854:3, LC: 1
no name, F, d. 1 May 1855, LC, congestion of brain, 0-1-15, p. Martha (s), b. LC, sc: C. F. Anderson, head of family, BVS 1855:1, LC:14

Ramey, Mr.:
no name, F, d. May 1853, nr Waterford, unk, 0-0-12, p. Amanda, b. nr Waterford, sc: Dennis Winters, FN., friend, BVS 1854:6, LC: 5

Ramey, Sanford J.:
Adam, M, d. 2 Jan 1853, LC, unk, 1-6-0, p. Helen, b. LC, sc: Sanford J. Ramey, owner, BVS 1854:5, LC: 3
Charles, M, d. 19 Feb 1854, LC, unk, 2-0-0, p. Letitia (s), b. LC, sc: Sanford J. Ramey, owner, BVS 1854:10, LC: 9
Frank, M, d. 11 Sep 1854, LC, unk, 1-0-0, p. Winny (s), b. LC, sc: Sanford J. Ramey, owner, BVS 1854:10, LC: 9
Mary, F, d. 12 Aug 1856, LC, unk, 0-0-10, p. Luticia, b. LC, sc: Levi W. Nixon, friend, BVS 1856:2, LC:21
no name, M, d. 13 Feb 1853, LC, unk, 1-0-0, p. Amanda, b. LC, sc: Sanford J. Ramey, owner, BVS 1854:5, LC: 3
no name, M, d. 10 Apr 1853, LC, unk, 1-2-0, p. Amanda, b. LC, sc: Sanford J. Ramey, owner, BVS 1854:5, LC: 3
Sally, F, d. 17 May 1854, LC, unk, 9-0-0, p. Amanda (s), b. LC, sc: Sanford J. Ramey, owner, BVS 1854:10, LC: 9

Rawlings, John M.:
no name, M, d. 28 Feb 1858, Res. of master, unk, 0-7-0, p. Maria, b. Res. of master, sc: Mrs. Rawlings, mistress, BVS 1858:3, LC:31

Rhodes, George:
Charles, M, d. 17 Mar 1859, LC, typhoid fever, 32-0-0, b. LC, sc: George Rhodes, owner, BVS 1859:1, LC:37

Rhodes, Randolph:
Mary BROWN, F, d. 12 Mar 1856, Res. of master, consumption, 14-0-0, p. Lucy, b. Foot Blue Ridge, sc: Samuel Harrison, BVS 1856:4, LC:22
Fanny LEWIS, F, d. 1 Jul 1854, Res. of master, typhoid fever, 22-0-0, p. Hanna P., b. Foot of Blue Ridge, sc: master, BVS 1854:12, LC:11

Riticor, Charles:
Amanda, F, d. Sep 1859, LC, unk, 0-0-6, p. Kitty, b. LC, sc: Charles Riticor, owner, BVS 1859:6, LC:36
Mann, M, d. 1 Apr 1859, LC, typhoid fever, 10-0-0, p. Lucinda, b. LC, sc: Charles Riticor, owner, BVS 1859:6, LC:36

Riticor, Zilpha:
Frances, F, d. 3 Mar 1854, LC, bronchitis, 30-0-0, sc: Zilpha Riticor, owner, BVS 1854:14, LC:14
no name, M, d. 3 Mar 1854, unk, 0-0-1, sc: Zilpha Riticor, owner, BVS 1854:14, LC:14

Rogers, Asa:
no name, M, d. Jul 1854, Middleburg, dysentery, 0-8-0, p. Lucinda, b. Middleburg, sc: A. O. Kinsolving, BVS 1854:13, LC:13

Rogers, Elizabeth:
Toby, F, d. Feb 1859, Isaiah B. Beans', suddenly, 0-10-0, p. Louisa, b. J. B. Beans', sc: J. B. Beans, BVS 1859:4, LC:35

Rogers, Sanford:
Gabriel, M, d. Mar 1859, Res. of parents, unk, 55-0-0, sc: S. Rogers, master, BVS 1859:4, LC:35

Ross, John:
John Richard, M, d. 10 Jan 1854, Willow Creek, dysentery, 1-10-2, p. Cela, b. Willow Creek, sc: master, BVS 1854:11, LC:11

Ross, Samuel:
Daniel, M, d. 15 Aug 1859, LC, remittent fever, 40-0-0, p. unk, b. LC, sc: Samuel Ross, owner, BVS 1859:1, LC:37

Russell, Sally A.:
Florabell, F, d. 16 Apr 1859, Leesburg, consumption bowels, 10-0-0, p. Hester, b. Leesburg, sc: Sally A. Russell, owner, BVS 1859:2, LC:37
Mana, F, d. 2 Jul 1853, Leesburg, scarlet rash, 1-0-10, p. Hester (s), b. LC, sc: Sally A. Russell, owner, BVS 1854:5, LC: 3

Russell, Wm.:
no name, F, d. 15 Aug 1854, LC, unk, 0-0-1, p. Mary (s), b. LC, sc: Wm H. Russell, head of family, BVS 1854:10, LC: 9
Sarah, F, d. 1 Oct 1856, LC, unk, 0-3-0, p. Mahala (s), b. LC, sc: William Russell, owner, BVS 1856:2, LC:20
Craven A. KING, M, d. 1 Mar 1854, LC, accidental, 14-6-15, p. Malinda (s), b. LC, sc: Wm. Russell, owner, BVS 1854:8, LC: 8

Rust, George:
James, M, d. 25 Aug 1853, LC, dysentery, 9-3-12, p. Milly (s), b. LC,

Loudoun County, Virginia, Death Register, 1853-1896 21

sc: George Rust, owner, BVS 1854:3, LC: 1
Rebecca, F, d. 27 Aug 1853, LC, dysentery, 0-6-0, p. Lydia (s), b. LC, sc: George Rust, owner, BVS 1854:3, LC: 1
Sanford, M, d. 20 May 1853, LC, pneumonia, 25-9-2, p. unk, b. LC, sc: George Rust, owner, BVS 1854:3, LC: 1

Samsell, Henry G.:
Lydia, F, d. Dec 1859, Fauquier, lion's complt ?, 64-0-0, b. Fauquier, sc: H.B. Samsell, master, BVS 1859:3, LC:34

Sanders, Wilson C.:
Bettie, F, d. 10 Jul 1858, LC, unk, 0-1-15, p. Lucinda (s), b. LC, sc: Wilson C. Sanders, owner, BVS 1858:2, LC:30

Saunders, Aaron R.:
no name, 2m:1f, d. 20 Dec 1854, LC, unk, 0-0-10, p. Alsey (s), b. LC, sc: Aaron R. Saunders, owner, BVS 1854:9, LC: 8

Saunders, Edith:
Ruth, F, d. 30 Sep 1855, LC, overlayed, 0-0-20, p. Jenny (s), b. Leesburg, sc: Edith Saunders, owner, BVS 1855:3, LC:16

Saunders, Thos:
Amey, F, d. 18 Feb 1855, LC, consumption, 59-0-0, p. unk, b. LC, sc: Thos. M. Saunders, young master, BVS 1855:3, LC:16

Scott, John M.:
no name, M, d. Feb 1856, Res. of master, 0-7-0, p. Eliza, b. nr Upperville, sc: J.M. Scott, master, BVS 1856:4, LC:22
no name,M, d. 23 Oct 1857, Res. of master, 0-0-1, p. Nancy, b. nr Upperville, sc: master, BVS 1857:3, LC:26

Seaton, Nancy:
no name, F, d. 12 Jan 1854, Res. of Mrs. Seaton, 0-0-14, p. Rachel, b. Mrs. Nancy Seaton, sc: Mrs. Nancy Seaton, BVS 1854:11, LC:11

Seaton, William:
Benjamin, M, d. Feb 1856, William Seaton's, 21-0-0, p. Sarah, b. Fauquier Co., sc: W. Seaton, master, BVS 1856:4, LC:22
no name, M, d. Aug 1854, Wm. Seaton, 0-1-0, p. Sarah, b. Wm. Seaton, sc: Wm. Seaton, BVS 1854:11, LC:11
no name, M, d. 28 Sep 1857, Res. of master, thrush, 0-1-0, p. Sarah, b. Res. of master, sc: master, BVS 1857:3, LC:26
Sarah, F, d. Aug 1853, Clifton, summer complaint, 0-2-0, p. Sarah, b. nr Clifton, sc: master, BVS 1854:7, LC: 6

Shepherd, Humphrey:
Albert, M, d. Apr 1853, nr Philomont, enlargement of head, 1-6-0, p. Becca, b. LC, sc: master, BVS 1854:1, LC: 3

Shepherd, Nancy:
Fanny, F, d. Spring 1857, Res. of mistress, dropsy, 35-0-0, b. LC, sc: F.C. Shepherd, physician, BVS 1857:3, LC:26

Shreve, Daniel:
Laura Virginia, F, d. 10 Jul 1856, LC, whooping cough, 1-6-0, p. Mary (s), b. LC, sc: Daniel Shreve, owner, BVS 1856:1, LC:20
Maria, F, d. 29 Jan 1854, LC, pneumonia, 20-3-7, p. unk, b. LC, sc: Daniel Shreve, owner, BVS 1854:9, LC: 9
Mary, F, d. 15 Jul 1856, LC, whooping cough, 20-0-0, p. Mary (s), b. LC, sc: Daniel Shreve, owner, BVS 1856:1, LC:20
no name, F, d. 10 Jun 1853, LC, unk, 0-0-4, p. Maria (s), b. LC, sc: Daniel Shreve, owner, BVS 1854:3, LC: 1
Samuel, M, d. 26 Dec 1855, LC, appoplexy, 22-0-0, p. unk, b. Fairfax, farm hand, sc: Danl. Shreve, owner, BVS 1855:1, LC:14
Nancy PAYNE, F, d. 10 Nov 1853, LC, unk, 45-0-0, p. unk, b. LC, unm, sc: Lemuel L. Beall, friend, BVS 1854:3, LC: 1

Silcott, Meshack:
Charity, F, d. May 1859, Snickersville, consumption, 1-6-0, p. Maria, b. Snickersville, sc: M. Silcott, master, BVS 1859:3, LC:34

Maria, F, d. May 1859, Snickersville, consumption, 23-0-0, b. LC, sc: M. Silcott, master, BVS 1859:3, LC:34

Simpson, Henson:
Henry, M, d. May 1858, Res. of master, cancer in the eyes, 6-0-0, p. Percella, b. Res. of master, sc: Mrs. Simpson, mistress, BVS 1858:5, LC:32

Simpson, Louisa:
Emily, F, d. May 1859, R. H. Turner's, heart affection, 18-0-0, p. Helen, b. Place of Death, sc: R. H. Turner, BVS 1859:3, LC:34
Hagerty, M, d. Jun 1859, R. H. Turner's, pneumonia, 80-0-0, b. nr Leesburg, sc: R. H. Turner, BVS 1859:3, LC:34

Simpson, Samuel:
Edith, F, d. Sep 1858, Res. of master, cancer, 30-0-0, p. Judith, b. LC, sc: S. Simpson, master, BVS 1858:4, LC:31
Hannah Elizabeth, F, d. Mar 1854, Res. of master, consumption, 1-0-0, p. Alcinda, b. At. res. of master, sc: master, BVS 1854:12, LC:12
no name, F, d. May 1858, Res. of master, whooping cough, 0-5-0, p. Alcinda, b. Res. of master, sc: S. Simpson, master, BVS 1858:4, LC:31
no name, F, d. May 1858, Res. of master, 0-0-7, p. Edith, b. Place of birth, sc: S. Simpson, master, BVS 1858:4, LC:31

Skillman, Abraham:
Benjamin, M, d. Jun 1857, Res. of master, 0-11-0, p. Silvy, b. At place of death, sc: Abraham Skillman, master, BVS 1857:5, LC:27

Skinner, Gabriel's Estate:
Bartley, M, d. Dec 1858, Benjn Skinner's, disease of brain, 60-0-0, b. LC, blacksmith, sc: B. Skinner, master, BVS 1858:5, LC:33
Lucy, F, d. Sep 1858, Benjn Skinner's, consumption, 55-0-0, b. Frederick Co., sc: B. Skinner, BVS 1858:5, LC:33

Skinner, Peter:
Charles, M, d. Aug 1853, nr Drymill, dysentery, 1-6-0, p. Tyna, b. Drymill, sc: master, BVS 1854:5, LC: 5

Smart, John P.:
Martin, M, d. 15 Jan 1858, Leesburg, dropsy, 66-0-0, p. unk, b. unk, sc: John P. Smart, owner, BVS 1858:2, LC:30

Smith, A.G.:
Herbert, M, d. Jun 1859, Middleburg, scrofula, 8-0-0, p. Elizabeth, b. Middleburg, sc: A. G. Smith, master, BVS 1859:3, LC:34
Mary, F, d. Nov 1858, LC, bilious fever, 17-0-0, b. LC, sc: A.G. Smith, owner, BVS 1858:6, LC:33

Smith, Geo. D.:
Benjamin, M, d. 10 Mar 1856, LC, spinal affection, 4-3-0, p. Amy Ann (s), b. LC, sc: George D. Smith, owner, BVS 1856:2, LC:21
Mary, F, d. 10 Oct 1853, LC, unk, 1-6-2, p. Nancy (s), b. LC, sc: Geo D. Smith, owner, BVS 1854:4, LC: 2
Rosanna, F, d. 20 Jul 1855, LC, unk, 30-0-0, b. LC, sc: Geo. D. Smith, owner, BVS 1855:2, LC:15

Smith, George:
Ely, F, d. 22 Dec 1853, nr Wheatland, worms, 1-3-0, p. Rose Ellen, b. nr Hillsborough, sc: Levi James, employer, BVS 1854:1, LC: 3

Smith, Hugh:
Bushrod, M, d. Jun 1857, Middleburg, pneumonia, 1-0-0, p. Alice, b. Middleburg, sc: master, BVS 1857:3, LC:25
Elizabeth, F, d. Aug 1856, Middleburg, consumption, 22-0-0, p. Ellen, b. Middleburg, sc: Hugh Smith, master, BVS 1856:4, LC:21
Thomas, M, d. Feb 1854, Middleburg, 0-9-0, p. Henry & Frances, b. Middleburg, sc: Hugh Smith, BVS 1854:11, LC:10
Henry BAILEY, M, d. Aug 1858, Middleburg, pneumonia, 1-0-0, p. Alice, b. Middleburg, sc: Hugh Smith, master, BVS 1858:3, LC:30
Martha Jane JOHNSON, F, d. Sep 1855, Middleburg, consumption, 20-0-0, p. Ellen Johnson, b. Hill Farm, sc: Lorman Chancellor, BVS 1855:3, LC:16
Cornelia MORTON, F, d. Jul 1858, Middleburg, consumption, 15-0-0,

Loudoun County, Virginia, Death Register, 1853-1896   23

p. Mary, b. Hill Farm, sc: Hugh Smith, master, BVS 1858:3, LC:30

Smith, Job:
Patsy, F, d. 20 Oct 1859, LC, paralysis, 55-0-0, b. LC, sc: Job Smith, owner, BVS 1859:1, LC:37

Stone, Samuel S.:
Sarah DAY, F, d. 23 Feb 1858, LC, dropsy, 60-0-0, b. LC, sc: Samuel S. Stone, owner, BVS 1858:1, LC:29

Stringfellow, Benjn:
no name, F, d. Oct 1856, Res. of master, suddenly, 0-2-0, p. Margaret, b. Res. of master, sc: Mrs. Stringfellow, mistress, BVS 1856:4, LC:22

Sullivan, Wm. B.:
no name, F, d. 15 Jun 1856, Res. of master, 0-0-1, p. Mary Hamilton, b. Res. of master, sc: Wm B. Sullivan, master, BVS 1856:4, LC:21

Swann, Wilson C.:
John, M, d. 12 Jun 1856, LC, burnt, 2-0-0, b. LC, sc: Richard S. Mercer, friend, BVS 1856:3, LC:21
Maria, F, d. 11 Jan 1855, LC, unk, 47-6-9, p. unk, b. LC, c/o: Jas. Bowman (col), sc: Jas. Bowman, husband, BVS 1855:1, LC:14

Swart, C.F.:
Geo. STEWART, M, d. 20 Mar 1853, in Aldie, cancer, 18-0-0, p. Alfred & Milly, b. Prince Wm. Co., sc: master, BVS 1854:6, LC: 6

Swart, Charles J.:
[no name], M, d. Feb 1858, LC, unk, 3-6-0, b. LC, sc: Charles J. Swart, owner, BVS 1858:6, LC:34

Swart, Mersa:
John COMBS, M, d. 25 Sep 1853, LC, unk, 22-0-0, p. unk, b. LC, sc: Mersa Swart, owner, BVS 1854:2, LC: 7

Taylor, James W.:
Caroline, M[sic], d. 5 Aug 1853, nr Aldie, whooping cough, 0-5-0, p. Ann, b. nr Aldie, sc: master, BVS 1854:6, LC: 5
Milly, F, d. 15 Dec 1857, Res. of master, old age, 100-0-0, b. Lower Virginia, sc: James W. Taylor, master, BVS 1857:4, LC:26

Taylor, Jesse:
Jno., M, d. Sep 1853, nr Dover, dysentery, 6-1-0, p. Mary, b. Dover, sc: master, BVS 1854:6, LC: 6

Thomas, Herod:
Caroline, F, d. 15 Nov 1857, Res. of master, heart disease, 45-0-0, sc: H. Thomas, master, BVS 1857:4, LC:27
no name, M, d. Dec 1855, LC, unk, 0-0-1, p. Caroline, b. LC, sc: Herod Thomas, BVS 1855:4, LC:16

Thomas, James:
Maria, F, d. 26 Oct 1858, LC, consumption, 15-9-3, b. LC, sc: James Thomas, owner, BVS 1858:1, LC:29

Thomas, Jefferson:
Henry, M, d. 25 Nov 1854, master Res. Scotland, typhoid fever, 13-9-18, p. Alcinda, b. Res. of master, sc: master, BVS 1854:13, LC:12

Thompson, James:
Charity, F, d. 15 May 1859, LC, dropsy in chest, 58-0-0, b. LC, sc: John C. Thompson, young master, BVS 1859:1, LC:36

Thompson, John H.:
Florinda, F, d. 1 Jun 1853, LC, child bed, 29-5-0, p. Jas. & Charity, slaves, b. LC, house servant, sc: Jno. H. Thompson, owner, BVS 1854:3, LC: 1

Thrift, Sanderson:
no name,M, d. 4 Nov 1857, Res. of master, 0-0-1, p. Mary, b. Res. of master, sc: master, BVS 1857:3, LC:25
Mary, F, d. 10 Nov 1857, Res. of master, pneumonia, 19-0-0, p. Nancy, b. Littleton Farm, sc: master, BVS 1857:3, LC:25

Throckmorton, H.W.:
Sarah FORD, F, d. 1 Jul 1853, nr Snickersville, dropsy, 90-0-0, p. unk, b. VA, sc: master, BVS 1854:1, LC: 4

Throckmorton, James B.:
Ralphney, M, d. Sep 1856, Res. of master, old age, 90-0-0, b. Prince

Wm., sc: Jas. B. Throckmorton, master, BVS 1856:4, LC:22

Tillett, John:
William STRINGER, M, d. 13 Mar 1856, Jane Tillett's, dropsy, 80-0-0, sc: T.R. Tillett, BVS 1856:5, LC:23

Trundle, Hezekiah:
Frank, M, d. 10 Mar 1858, LC, consumption, 55-0-0, p. unk, b. unk, sc: H. Trundle, owner, BVS 1858:2, LC:30

Tyler, Misses:
Cyrus, M, d. Dec 1855, unk, 80-0-0, b. LC, sc: Misses Tylers, owners, BVS 1855:8, LC:19
George, M, d. Jun 1859, LC, unk, 1-1-0, p. Mary, b. LC, sc: Miss Tyler, owner, BVS 1859:6, LC:36
Nelly, F, d. 4 Feb 1855, pneumonia, 50-0-0, b. LC, sc: Misses Tylers, owners, BVS 1855:8, LC:19

Upp, Sarah:
Oscar, M, d. 30 May 1855, Middleburg, unk, 2-0-0, p. Rocksaline, b. Middleburg, sc: Sarah Upp, BVS 1855:4, LC:16
Rocksalina, F, d. 20 May 1855, Middleburg, unk, 20-0-0, p. Maria Melville, b. Middleburg, sc: Sarah Upp, BVS 1855:4, LC:16

Vandevanter, Cornelius:
Frances, F, d. 15 Aug 1854, LC, convulsions, 2-0-0, p. Maria (s), b. LC, sc: Cornelius Vandevanter, owner, BVS 1854:10, LC:10

Vandevanter, Gabriel:
Edward, M, d. 30 Oct 1853, LC, unk, 10-1-2, p. Matilda (s), b. LC, sc: Gabriel Vandevanter, owner, BVS 1854:4, LC: 2
Harriet, F, d. 15 Sep 1857, LC, scrofula, 2-0-0, p. Maria (s), b. LC, sc: Gabriel Vandevanter, owner, BVS 1857:1, LC:25

Vandevanter, Washington:
no name, F, d. 15 Sep 1854, LC, unk, 0-3-2, p. Kitty (s), b. LC, sc: Sydney Hawling, BVS 1854:9, LC: 8

Vansickler, Wm:
Silas, M, d. 3 Jan 1853, LC, unk, 1-0-0, p. Sarah (s), sc: Wm. Vansickler, owner, BVS 1854:5, LC: 3

Veale, Estate of John:
no name, M, d. May 1856, LC, whooping cough, 0-6-0, b. LC, sc: William Veale, owner, BVS 1856:7, LC:24

Virts, Henry:
no name, F, d. 17 Apr 1856, LC, unk, 0-1-15, p. Margaret (s), b. LC, sc: Henry Virts, owner, BVS 1856:1, LC:20

Virts, William:
Thomas, M, d. 25 Aug 1856, LC, quinsy, 2-0-0, p. Maria (s), b. LC, sc: William Virts, owner, BVS 1856:1, LC:20

Walker, G.B.:
[no name], F, d. Jun 1858, LC, unk, 0-3-0, b. LC, sc: G.B. Walker, owner, BVS 1858:6, LC:34

Walker, J. G.:
John, M, d. Jan 1856, LC, typhoid fever, 10-0-0, b. LC, sc: J.G. Walker, owner, BVS 1856:7, LC:23

Walker, Jas. J.:
Mensor, M, d. Mar 1853, LC, dropsy, 8-0-0, p. unk, b. LC, sc: Jas J. Wilkins, owner, BVS 1854:2, LC: 7

Walker, Mrs.'s Estate:
Nancy, F, d. May 1856, C. F. Swart's, consumption, 33-0-0, p. Cinthia, b. James Swart's, sc: C.F. Swart, BVS 1856:5, LC:23

Warnal, Charlotte:
Sarah, F, d. Jan 1853, Millsville, croup, 0-3-0, p. Mary, b. nr Millsville, sc: mistress, BVS 1854:7, LC: 6

Watt, Duanna's Estate:
John, M, d. 5 Nov 1858, LC, unk, 0-8-0, p. Mary Ann (s), sc: Sydnor Bennett, head of family, BVS 1858:1, LC:30

Waugh, Mary:
John, M, d. Nov 1857, Res. of mistress, consumption, 25-0-0, p.

Peggy, b. LC, sc: Mary Waugh, mistress, BVS 1857:6, LC:28

Violet, F, d. 14 Dec 1854, Rural Villa, old age, 80-0-0, b. Alexandria, sc: mistress, BVS 1854:12, LC:11

Violett, F, d. 8 Dec 1855, nr Middleburg, old age, 80-0-0, b. Pennsylvania, sc: Mary Waugh, BVS 1855:5, LC:17

Weadon, Ashford:
Isaac TURNER, M, d. Oct 1853, Bunkers Hill, measles, 1-6-0, p. George & Arcaner Turner, b. Bunkers Hill, sc: master, BVS 1854:1, LC: 4

Whaley, Mary A:
Betty, F, d. Nov 1859, LC, rheumatism, unk, b. LC, sc: Mary A. Whaley, owner, BVS 1859:6, LC:36
no name, M, d. Nov 1853, LC, unk, 0-0-7, p. unk, b. LC, sc: Mary Whaley, owner, BVS 1854:2, LC: 6

Whaley, William:
Henry, M, d. Aug 1856, LC, unk, 30-0-0, b. LC, sc: Charles A. Whaley, head of family, BVS 1856:7, LC:24

White, Joshua:
Ellen, F, d. 30 May 1856, LC, consumption, 25-0-0, b. LC, sc: Joshua White, owner, BVS 1856:2, LC:21

White, R. J. T.:
Hannah, F, d. 15 Nov 1855, LC, old age, 85-0-0, p. unk, b. LC, sc: R. J. T. White, owner, BVS 1855:2, LC:15

Whitmore, Jno. H.:
Richard NELSON, M, d. 1 Jul 1853, LC, old age, 85-0-0, p. unk, b. unk, sc: John H. Whitmore, owner, BVS 1854:3, LC: 1

Wildman, Jane D.:
Lucinda, F, d. 15 Nov 1857, Leesburg, erysipelas, 15-0-0, b. Leesburg, sc: John W. Wildman, young master, BVS 1857:2, LC:25
no name, F, d. 20 Jul 1854, LC, unk, 0-3-0, p. Joanna (s), b. LC, sc: John W. Wildman, one of the family, BVS 1854:10, LC:10

Wilkinson, William:
Jenny Linn, F, d. 23 Mar 1855, LC, quinsy, 0-7-0, p. Matilda Boss, b. Res. of master, sc: Wm. Wilkinson, BVS 1855:4, LC:16

Wilkison, Sarah:
Ann, F, d. 31 Dec 1854, Res. of mistress, rheumatism, 13-0-0, p. Laura, sc: L. L. Wilkison, BVS 1854:13, LC:12

Williams, John:
Ralph, M, d. 16 Mar 1854, LC, dropsy, 13-1-21, p. unk, b. LC, sc: John Williams, owner, BVS 1854:9, LC: 9

Williams, Mary C.:
Ann, F, d. 23 Dec 1859, LC, dropsy, 45-0-0, b. LC, sc: Mary C. Williams, mistress, BVS 1859:1, LC:36

Williams, Syddnah:
no name, M, d. 30 Apr 1854, LC, unk, 0-0-21, p. Martha (s), b. LC, sc: Syddnah Williams, owner, BVS 1854:8, LC: 7

Wilson, John A.:
James, M, d. 6 Dec 1858, Res. of master, scarlet fever, 4-0-0, p. Clara, b. Res. of master, sc: John A. Wilson, master, BVS 1858:3, LC:30
John, M, d. 10 Nov 1858, Res. of master, scarlet fever, 5-0-0, p. Clara, b. Res. of master, sc: John A. Wilson, master, BVS 1858:3, LC:30

Wornal, Charlotte:
Amanda R., F, d. Aug 1857, Res. of mistress, croup, 0-1-15, p. Milly, b. Mrs. Wornal's, sc: mistress, BVS 1857:3, LC:26

Wright, Robert L.:
no name, M, d. 30 Jan 1854, LC, unk, 0-0-4, p. Sandy & Ann, (s), b. LC, sc: Robert L. Wright, owner, BVS 1854:9, LC: 8
no name, F, d. 18 Mar 1857, LC, unk, 0-0-3, p. Kitty (s), b. LC, sc: Robert L. Wright, owner, BVS 1857:1, LC:24

Loudoun County, Virginia, Death Register, 1853-1896   27

Non-Slave Deaths

NO SURNAME GIVEN:
Charlotte, (f), F, d. 15 Dec 1856, LC, dropsy, 65-0-0, p. Jane (s), b. LC, sc: C.B. Ball, friend, BVS:1856:3, LC:21
Elick, (f), M, d. 16 Nov 1859/60, Poor House, old age, 80-0-0, sc: steward, BVS:1859:4, 1860:2, LC:35
Elizabeth, B, F, d. 1865, LC, typhoid fever, 16-0-0, b. LC, cook, unm, sc: Saml Carr, employer, 1st Dist., BVS:1865:2/4
Frank, (f), M, d. 30 Oct 1855, LC, old age, 85-0-0, b. LC, sc: J.S. Look, head of family, BVS:1855:8, LC:19
Henry, W, M, d. 1875, Lovettsville Dist, unk, b. Foreign, stranger who came to the house and died, LV Dist., BVS:1875:4
[no name], (f), F, d. 18 Jan 1857, Bloomfield, frozen, 14-0-0, b. Fauquier Co., sc: Ulysses Monroe, employer, BVS:1857:4, LC:27
[no name], W, F, d. Nov 1860, res of parents, scarlet fever, 0-0-25, BVS:1860:2
no name, B, F, d. 1865, nr Mt. Zion, unk, 0-0-8, p. Betty, b. nr Mt. Zion, unm, sc: Jno J. Tyler, head of family, BVS:1865:2
no name, B, M, d. 20 Aug 1865, nr Wheatland, croup, unk, p. unk, b. LC, sc: George S. Moore, employer, 1st Dist., BVS:1865:3/4
no name, B, M, d. 1875, Lovettsville Dist, run over by wagon, 10-0-0, LV Dist., BVS:1875:4
no name, B, M, d. 1 Sep 1882, LC, unk, unk, p. unk, sc: Jno R. Carter, superintendent, 1st Dist., BVS:1882:2
Walter, B, M, d. Dec 1855, Aldie, dropsy, 2-0-0, p. Frankey, b. Aldie, sc: Wm. Berkley, BVS:1855:4, LC:16
William, B, M, d. 2 Mar 1869, LC, heart disease, unk, b. Albemarle Co., laborer, sc: employer, BVS:1869:1

ABBOTT, Charles Davis, W, M, d. 25 Nov 1876, Leesburg, diphtheria, 3-4-1, p. Joseph & Mary E. Abbott, b. Leesburg, sc: Joseph Abbott, father, LE Dist., BVS:1876:6
ABBOTT, Richard T., W, M, d. 7 Jun 1876, Leesburg, heart disease, 0-4-1, p. Joseph & Mary E. Abbott, b. Leesburg, sc: Joseph Abbott, father, LE Dist., BVS:1876:6
ABEL, Nellie, W, F, d. 25 Jul 1886, cholera infantum, 0-3-24, p. Wm. M. & Annie, sc: Wm. M. Abel, father, 2nd Dist., BVS:1886:5
ABEL, William M., W, M, d. 28 Apr 1896, Neersville, inflammation of bones, 42-0-0, p. George & Sarah Abel, b. Neersville, farmer, c/o: Annie Abel, sc: Annie Abel, consort, LV Dist., BVS:1896:7
ABLE, Catherine, W, F, d. 16 Apr 1888, LC, dropsy, 62-0-0, p. George & Nancy Abel, b. LC, none, unm, sc: William Abel, nephew, 2nd Dist., BVS:1888:5
ADAMS, Ana, W, F, d. 3 May 1874, LC, fever, 21-0-0, p. Wm. H. & Mahala Adams, b. LC, unm, sc: Wm. H. Adams, father, JF Dist., BVS:1874:2
ADAMS, Anna, W, F, d. 29 Jun 1857, her res, unk, 72-0-0, p. Annacretis Dier, b. Maryland, c/o: Richard Adams, sc: R. Adams, widower, BVS:1857:4, LC:27
ADAMS, Anna, W, F, d. 29 Jan 1858, her res, 74-0-0, p. Annacretus & Ellen Dier, b. Prince George, c/o: Richard Adams, sc: Richard Adams, companion, BVS:1858:5, LC:33
ADAMS, Benj. F., W, M, d. 15 Mar 1871, consumption, 72-0-0, farmer, married, BR Dist., BVS:1871:3
ADAMS, Benjamin, W, M, d. 27 Sep 1883, nr Leesburg, accident, 9-0-0, p. Jas. & Sarah C. Adams, b. LC, sc: Wm. B. Adams, brother, 2nd Dist., BVS:1883:3
ADAMS, Caroline J., W, F, d. Jun 1865, Middleburg, diarrhea, 0-10-0, p. Geo Wm & Ann M. Adams, b. Middleburg, sc: father, BVS:1865:1
ADAMS, Charles, W, M, d. 17 Jul 1874, Broad Run Dist., typhoid fever, 17-11-16, p. Chas. B. & Julia Adams, b. LC, farmer, sc: Chas. B.

Adams, father, BR Dist., BVS:1874:3

ADAMS, Charles T., W, M, d. 19 Aug 1886, Bloomfield, consumption, 25-0-0, p. John H. & Mary Adams, b. LC, laborer, unm, sc: Lydia V. Adams, sister-in-law, 1st Dist., BVS:1886:1

[ADAMS], Cornelia Virginia, W, F, d. Nov 1854, Cherry Grove, convulsions, 0-1-0, p. Robert E. & Helen L. Adams, b. Cherry Grove, sc: father, BVS:1854:13, LC:12

ADAMS, Daniel, W, M, d. 5 Dec 1889, LC, dropsy, 79-0-0, p. James & Abigal Adams, b. LC, laborer, c/o: Susan Adams, sc: Henry Snoots, friend, 3rd Dist., BVS:1889:5

ADAMS, Francis, W, M, d. 15 Dec 1896, Middleburg, cholera infantum, 0-10-0, p. R. L. & Mattie Adams, b. Middleburg, none, unm, sc: R.L. Adams, father, MC Dist., BVS:1896:1

ADAMS, Francis Littleton, W, M, d. 6 Feb 1854, Middleburg, unk, 2-4-0, p. George W. & Ann Maria Adams, b. Middleburg, sc: G. W. Adams, BVS:1854:11, LC:10

ADAMS, George ., W, M, d. 3 Mar 1885, Middleburg, paralysis, 66-7-29, p. Francis & Chloe Adams, b. Fauquier Co., merchant, unk, sc: ___ Adams, 1st Dist., BVS:1885:3

ADAMS, Gertrude, W, F, d. 17 Nov 1887, LC, cholera infantum, 0-8-0, p. James & Gertrude Adams, b. LC, farmer, sc: James Adams, father, 2nd Dist., BVS:1887:4

ADAMS, Henry, B, M, d. 4 Jul 1883, Leesburg, inflammation bowels, 0-6-4, p. Harriet Adams, b. LC, sc: Leroy Veirs, grandfather, 2nd Dist., BVS:1883:6

ADAMS, Henry, B, M, d. 7 Jun 1877, Leesburg, consumption, 1-11-0, p. Noble & Fannie Adams, b. Leesburg, sc: Lucinda Harris, friend, LE Dist., BVS:1877:8

ADAMS, John R., (f), M, d. 2 Jul 1859/60, Waterford, water on brain, 1-7-10, p. Elizabeth Adams, b. Waterford, sc: Elizabeth Adams, mother, BVS:1859:1, 1860:3, LC:36

ADAMS, John T., W, M, d. 15 Dec 1854, LC, water on brain, 0-3-2, p.

Wm. H. & Mahala Adams, b. LC, sc: Wm. H. Adams, father, BVS:1854:8, LC:8

ADAMS, Joseph A., W, M, d. 14 May 1885, Bloomfield, consumption, 38-0-0, p. Henry & Mary Adams, b. LC, farmer, c/o: Lydia V. Adams, sc: Lydia V. Adams, wife, 1st Dist., BVS:1885:3

ADAMS, Katie, W, F, d. 31 Mar 1871, Bloomfield, diphtheria, 12-0-0, p. Mary & J.H. Adams, MC Dist., BVS:1871:2

ADAMS, Lucy B., W, F, d. 26 Dec 1890, nr Lenah, consumption, 35-0-0, p. Alfred & Rachel Adams, b. Illinois, unm, sc: Joseph W. Adams, brother, 1st Dist., BVS:1890:1

ADAMS, Mrs. Martha N., W, F, d. 3 Jul 1854, Middleburg, consumption, 58-0-0, p. Thos. & Joanna Wren, b. Centerville, Pr. W., c/o: Frances Adams, decd, sc: G. W. Adams, BVS:1854:11, LC:10

ADAMS, Matilda, W, F, d. 10 Mar 1875, paralysis, 68-0-0, p. Wm. & Elizabeth Adams, b. LC, unm, sc: Elizabeth Adams, MT Dist., BVS:1875:8

[ADAMS], no name,W, M, d. 26 Dec 1855, nr North Fork Church, unk, unk, p. David & Emily J. Adams, b. nr North Fork Church, sc: David Adams, father, BVS:1855:6, LC:17

ADAMS, no name, B, F, d. 24 Apr 1883, Leesburg, unk, 0-0-5, p. Harriet Adams, b. LC, sc: Mary Vena, grandmother, 2nd Dist., BVS:1883:3

ADAMS, no name, B, F, d. 1 Jun 1884, Leesburg, unk, 0-1-0, p. Harriet Adams (unm), b. LC, sc: Leroy Vena, grandfather, 2nd Dist., BVS:1884:4

ADAMS, S. C., W, M, d. 4 Jun 1877, LC, sun stroke, 40-0-0, p. unk, b. unk, farmer, c/o: Sarah E. Adams, sc: Sarah E. Adams, wife, LE Dist., BVS:1877:8

ADAMS, Sarah J., W, F, d. 10 Mar 1880, LC, consumption, 24-0-0, p. J. H. & Mary J. Adams, b. LC, unm, sc: J.H. Adams, father, 1st Dist., BVS:1880:1

ADAMS, Susan, W, F, d. Apr 1876, nr Bolington, dropsy, 73-0-0, c/o:

Loudoun County, Virginia, Death Register, 1853-1896   29

Daniel Adams, sc: Daniel Adams, husband, LV Dist., BVS:1876:3

ADAMS, Susan, B, F, d. 15 Feb 1883, Harrisonburg, PA, consumption, 25-0-0, p. Chas. & Celia Venay, b. LC, c/o: Charles Adams, sc: Charles Venay, father, 1St Dist., BVS:1883:1

ADAMS, Susan V., W, F, d. Sep 1853, Bloomfield, bronchial affection, 9-3-0, p. John & Mary P. Adams, b. LC, unk, unm, sc: John H. Adams, father, BVS:1854:1, LC:3

[ADAMS], Susan Virginia, W, F, d. Jun 1854, Bloomfield, scrofula, 7-0-0, p. J. H. & Mary J. Adams, sc: father, BVS:1854:11, LC:11

ADAMS, William H., W, M, d. 6 Oct 1889, LC, disease of stomach, 74-0-0, p. James & Abigal Adams, b. LC, farmer, c/o: Mahalah Adams, sc: Mahalah Adams, wife, 3rd Dist., BVS:1889:5

ADIE, Gustavia B., W, F, d. 22 Oct 1875, nr Leesburg, general debility, 57-0-0, MT Dist., BVS:1875:8

ADIE, Mary J, W, F, d. 27 Feb 1892, Sterling, consumption, 53-0-0, p. Jas & Mary Whaley, b. LC, c/o: Jas O. Adie, sc: Alice Adie, daughter, 1st Dist., BVS:1892:1

ADRIAN, Claudine, W, F, d. 14 Mar 1880, LC, unk, 5-0-0, p. Jas. A. & Olivia Adrian, b. LC, unm, sc: Olivia Adrian, mother, 1St Dist., BVS:1880:1

[AHALT], no name, W, F, d. Oct 1873, LC, children's complaint, 0-1-0, p. C. E. & L. E. Ahalt, b. LC, unm, sc: C.E. Ahalt, father, LE Dist., BVS:1873:2

AHALT, Sarah E., W, F, d. 25 Sep 1888, LC, heart trouble, 41-0-0, p. Henson & Hadley Orshman, b. Frederick Co. MD, none, c/o: C.E. Ahalt, sc: C.E. Ahalt, husband, 2nd Dist., BVS:1888:5

AKERS, Sallie, W, F, d. 13 Jul 1872, nr Broad Run, consumption, 61-0-0, p. unk, b. LC, c/o: John Akers, sc: John Akers, husband, BR Dist., BVS:1872:6

AKIN, no name,B, F, d. 3 Sep 1878, nr Aldie, unk, 0-0-7, p. Henry & Georgiana Akin, b. LC, sc: Henry Akin, father, MC Dist., BVS:1878:6

[ALDEN], no name, B, M, d. 25 Aug 1882, LC, convulsions, 0-0-5, p.

Saml. & Nancy Alden, sc: Samuel Alden, father, 1St Dist., BVS:1882:2

ALDER, Amanda E., W, F, d. 29 Nov 1885, Snickersville, heart disease, 66-0-0, p. Ruei & Ellen Marshal, b. LC, sc: Archie H. Alder, son, 3rd Dist., BVS:1885:6

ALDER, Carrie M., W, F, d. 23 Aug 1880, nr Lovettsville, unk, 1-2-0, p. Geo. W. & Hannah A. Alder, b. LC, unm, sc: Geo. W. Alder, father, 2nd Dist., BVS:1880:6

ALDER, Hannah A., W, F, d. 20 Nov 1888, LC, heart trouble, 50-0-0, p. Israel & Mary Myers, b. LC, none, c/o: Geo Alder, sc: Geo Alder, husband, 2nd Dist., BVS:1888:5

ALDER, James, W, M, d. 17 May 1859/60, his res, gravel, 79-9-2, p. George & Lucy Alder, b. Maryland, farmer, c/o: Hester Alder, sc: Latimore Alder, widow, BVS:1859:4, 1860:1, LC:35

ALDER, Jane, W, F, d. 25 Dec 1854, her res, cancer, 54-3-9, p. Nathan & Jane Nichols, b. Old homestead, foot of Blue Ridge, c/o: Hawkins Alder, sc: husband of dec'd, BVS:1854:12, LC:12

ALDER, John Isaac, W, M, d. 10 Dec 1859/60, res of parents, scarlet fever, 2-8-10, p. James & Mary J. Alder, b. place of death, sc: Jas Alder, father, BVS:1859:4, 1860:2, LC:35

ALDER, John Wynn, W, M, d. 5 Sep 1859/60, res of parents, unk, 0-1-7, p. Geo H. & Sallie A. Alder, b. Snickersville, sc: Geo. H. Alder, father, BVS:1859:3, BVS:1860:1, LC:34

ALDER, Mary C., W, F, d. 1 Jun 1887, LC, heart disease, 66-0-0, p. unk, none, c/o: George Alder, sc: Frank E. Alder, son, 2nd Dist., BVS:1887:4

ALDER, Raymond, W, M, d. 15 Dec 1894, Hillsboro, croup, 0-1-12, p. Jno E. & Agnes Alder, b. nr Hillsboro, sc: Jno E. Alder, father, 3rd Dist., BVS:1894:5

ALDER, Sallie, W, F, d. 17 Dec 1859, res of parents, scarlet fever, 7-7-17, p. James & Mary J. Alder, b. place of death, sc: Jas Alder, father, BVS:1859:4, LC:35

ALDRIDGE, Adam, B, M, d. 11 Dec 1887, nr Philomont, consumption, 75-0-0, p. unk, b. LC, laborer, unk, sc: F.E. Robey, superintendent of poor, 1st Dist., BVS:1887:2

ALDRIDGE, John, W, M, d. 13 Aug 1864, Glebe LC, inflammation of bowels, 13-0-0, p. Jno & Mary Aldridge, b. LC, sc: John Aldridge, father, BVS:1864:2, LC:39

ALDRIDGE, Mary E., W, F, d. 15 Mar 1876, nr Mount Gilead, rheumatism, unk, p. Robet. & Ellen Mead Moffett, b. LC, c/o: John Aldridge, sc: John Adridge, husband, MT Dist., BVS:1876:1

ALDRIDGE, Robt M., W, M, d. 15 Aug 1864, Glebe LC, pneumonia, 19-6-0, p. Jno & Mary Aldridge, b. LC, farmer, sc: John Aldridge, father, BVS:1864:2, LC:39

ALDRIDGE, Rose A., W, F, d. 8 Feb 1885, Baltimore, MD, meningitis, 22-0-0, p. John & Mary Aldridge, b. LC, unm, sc: John Aldridge, father, 3rd Dist., BVS:1885:6

ALEXANDER, Basil, W, M, d. 6 Aug 1864, Point Lookout Prison, heart disease, 25-0-0, p. Wm. & Eliz Alexander, b. Fauquier Co., soldier, sc: Wm. Alexander, father, BVS:1864:1, LC:38

ALEXANDER, David, W, M, d. 14 May 1873, Middleburg, dropsy of heart, 38-0-0, p. Wm. & Elizabeth Alexander, b. LC, mechanic, unm, sc: William Alexander, father, MC Dist., BVS:1873:5

ALEXANDER, Ella V., W, F, d. 28 Dec 1889, Sterling, consumption, 24-0-0, p. G. W. & Frances Thayer, b. Fauquier Co., c/o: Edgar W. Alexander, sc: Edgar W. Alexander, husband, 1st Dist., BVS:1889:1

ALEXANDER, Jane E., (f), F, d. Oct 1853, Hillsboro, consumption, 23-0-0, p. George & Elizabeth Alexander, b. LC, unm, sc: father, BVS:1854:1, LC:3

ALEXANDER, Lydia Jane, W, F, d. 14 Dec 1878, nr Trappe, consumption, 43-0-0, b. LC, c/o: James F. Alexander, sc: Jas F. Alexander, husband, MC Dist., BVS:1878:6

ALEXANDER, Martha E., W, F, d. 25 Feb 1878, nr Mt. Hope Church, child birth, 24-0-0, p. Bassill & Rachel Havener, b. nr Mt. Hope Church, c/o: R.W. Alexander, sc: Robt. W. Alexander, husband, BR Dist., BVS:1878:4

ALEXANDER, Mary J., W, F, d. 28 Dec 1878, nr Evergreen Mills, typhoid fever, 14-0-0, p. John T. & Mary Alexander, b. nr Mt. Hope Church, unm, sc: John T. Alexander, father, BR Dist., BVS:1878:4

ALEXANDER, Mary W., W, F, d. 5 Jul 1889, Waxpool, consumption, 0-6-0, p. Burr T. & Melvina Alexander, b. Waxpool, sc: Burr T. Alexander, father, 1st Dist., BVS:1889:1

ALEXANDER, Willie W., W, M, d. 8 Oct 1889, Sterling, scrofula, 4-0-0, p. Edgar W. & Ella V. Alexander, b. LC, sc: Edgar W. Alexander, father, 1st Dist., BVS:1889:1

ALEXANDER, Wm., W, M, d. 15 Aug 1864, Point Lookout Prison, chronic diarrhea, 23-0-0, p. Wm. & Eliz Alexander, b. LC, soldier, sc: Wm. Alexander, father, BVS:1864:1, LC:38

ALISON, Grace, W, F, d. 15 Jul 1896, Fauquier Co, cholera infantum, 0-5-0, p. O. B. & Mollie Alison, b. Fauquier Co., none, unm, sc: Mollie Alison, mother, MC Dist., BVS:1896:1

ALLDER, Carl Elliott, W, M, d. 28 Aug 1893, Round Hill, unk, 1-1-0, p. Jno. E. & Agnes L. Allder, b. LC, sc: father, JF Dist., BVS:1893:3

ALLDER, Emma C., W, F, d. 9 Sep 1855, nr Woodgrove, pneumonia, 2-7-10, p. Jas. W. & Lucy Allder, b. nr Woodgrove, sc: Jas. W. Allder, father, BVS:1855:7, LC:18

ALLDER, James, W, M, d. 11 Mar 1877, nr Snickersville, jaundice, 63-4-0, p. James & Mary Hester Allder, b. LC, farmer, c/o: Amanda Allder, sc: Jas. Allder, Jr., son, MT Dist., BVS:1877:2

ALLDER, James, W, M, d. 12 Oct 1891, Philomont, internal injury, 55-0-0, p. George & Margaret Allder, b. LC, farmer, consort, sc: Jno H. Allder, MT Dist., BVS:1891:6

ALLDER, James, W, M, d. 5 Aug 1893, Purcellville, cancer stomach, 73-0-0, p. Jno & Mary Allder, b. LC,

Loudoun County, Virginia, Death Register, 1853-1896 31

husband, sc: wife, JF Dist., BVS:1893:3

ALLDER, Marcus, W, M, d. 7 Aug 1891, Snickersville, old age, 85-0-0, p. James & Hester Allder, b. Snickersville, farmer, unm, sc: Latimer Allder, MT Dist., BVS:1891:6

ALLDER, Margaret, W, F, d. 26 Jan 1885, Waterford, inflammation bowels, 76-4-0, b. LC, c/o: Geo Allder, sc: James L. Allder, son, 3rd Dist., BVS:1885:6

ALLDER, Mary, W, F, d. 18 Sep 1858, res of parents, 0-0-3, p. Sanford M. & Mary A. Allder, b. Snickersville, sc: S.M. Allder, father, BVS:1858:4, LC:32

ALLDER, Sallie, W, F, d. 17 Dec 1860, res of parents, scarlet fever, 7-7-17, p. Jas & Mary J. Allder, b. place of death, sc: Jas Allder, father, BVS:1860:2

ALLDER, Sarah, W, F, d. 24 Sep 1858, res of parents, 0-0-9, p. Sanford M. & Mary A. Allder, b. Snickersville, sc: S.M. Allder, father, BVS:1858:4, LC:32

ALLEN, Ada, B, F, d. 7 May 1884, nr Hamilton, scrofula, 8-1-4, p. Arch & Sarah Allen, b. LC, unm, sc: Arch Allen, parent, 3rd Dist., BVS:1884:6

ALLEN, Annie S., B, F, d. 11 Mar 1892, Aldie, la grippe, 16-4-17, p. Ben & Annie Allen, b. Aldie, laborer, unm, sc: Annie Allen, mother, 1st Dist., BVS:1892:4

ALLEN, Asa, B, M, d. 16 Sep 1882, LC, unk, 0-0-14, p. Stuart & Annie Allen, b. LC, sc: Stuart Allen, parent, 3rd Dist., BVS:1882:3

ALLEN, Clay, B, M, d. 25 May 1891, nr Aldie, membranous croup, 0-6-0, p. John & Fannie Allen, b. LC, laborer, unm, sc: John Allen, head of family, 1st Dist., BVS:1891:1

ALLEN, Fannie, W, F, d. 20 Dec 1889, LC, unk, 0-0-1, p. Geo. W. & Albina Allen, b. LC, none, unm, sc: G.W. Allen, head of family, 2nd Dist., BVS:1889:3

ALLEN, James H., B, M, d. 20 Apr 1890, Waterford, heart disease, 33-0-0, p. John & Caroline Allen, b. LC, laborer, unm, sc: Henson Young, friend, 3rd Dist., BVS:1890:6

ALLEN, Joseph, B, M, d. 10 Aug 1880, LC, typhoid fever, 15-0-0, p. John W. Allen, b. LC, unm, sc: Jno. W. Allen, father, 1st Dist., BVS:1880:1

ALLEN, Joshua, B, M, d. 28 May 1880, LC, typhoid fever, 22-0-0, p. John W. Allen, b. LC, farmer, unm, sc: Jno. W. Allen, father, 1st Dist., BVS:1880:1

ALLEN, Lizzie, B, F, d. 20 Feb 1888, Farmwell, insanity, 22-0-0, p. John & Catharine Allen. b. LC, unm, sc: John Allen, father, 1st Dist., BVS:1888:3

ALLEN, Mary, B, F, d. 1 May 1894, Philomont, cholera infantum, 0-5-0, p. Spencer & Sallie Allen, b. Philomont, sc: Spencer Allen, father, 3rd Dist., BVS:1894:5

ALLEN, May Virginia, B, F, d. Feb 1892, Philomont, spinal meningitis, 6-0-0, p. Spencer & Sallie Allen, b. LC, sc: Spencer Allen, father, MT Dist., BVS:1892:8

[ALLEN], no name, B, M, d. 16 Apr 1866, nr Snickersville, unk, 0-0-1/2, p. Isaiah Allen, b. nr Snickersville, sc: father, BVS:1866:1

[ALLEN], no name, B, M, d. 10 Mar 1872, nr Corner Hall, unk, 0-0-7, p. Mary Allen, b. LC, sc: Mary Allen, BR Dist., BVS:1872:6

ALLEN, no name, B, F, d. 2 Mar 1891, nr Farmwell, premature, 0-0-1, p. Nimrod & Maria Allen, b. LC, laborer, unm, sc: Nimrod Allen, head of family, 1st Dist., BVS:1891:1

ALLEN, Richard N., B, M, d. 22 Dec 1888, LC, consumption, 5-0-0, p. Alfred & Eliza Allen, b. LC, none, unm, sc: Eliza Allen, mother, 2nd Dist., BVS:1888:5

ALLEN, Sarah, W, F, d. 11 Sep 1890, LC, unk, 0-0-1, p. Geo. W. & Albina Allen, b. LC, none, unm, sc: Geo W. Allen, father, 2nd Dist., BVS:1890:3

ALLEN, Wilson, B, M, d. 30 Sep 1887, nr Farmwell, cancer, 66-0-0, p. Alfred & Susan Allen, b. Fairfax Co., laborer, unk, sc: Henry Craven, son-in-law, 1st Dist., BVS:1887:2

ALLENDER, Susan, W, F, d. 29 Jan 1896, Morrisonville, heart trouble, 54-0-0, p. unk, b. unk, c/o: John Allender, sc: John Allender, consort, LV Dist., BVS:1896:7

ALLNUTT, James, W, M, d. 5 Oct 1887, nr Daysville, consumption, 83-0-0, p. Thomas D. & Elizabeth Allnutt, b. Maryland, farmer, unm, sc: Robert G. Allnutt, son, 1st Dist., BVS:1887:2

ALNUTT, Elizabeth, W, F, d. 28 Jun 1854, LC, pneumonia, 72-0-0, p. Richard & Ellen Gott, b. Maryland, sc: Ellen J. Allnutt, daughter, BVS:1854:14, LC:13

AMBLER, Elizabeth, W, F, d. 15 Apr 1875, nr Gum Spring, consumption, 62-0-0, p. William & Susan Ambler, b. nr Gum Spring, LC, unm, sc: Wm. Ambler, brother, BR Dist., BVS:1875:5

AMBLER, Jno. H., W, M, d. 22 Apr 1855, dysentery, 1-1-14, p. Vincent L. & Mary Ambler, b. LC, sc: Julia Ann Wrenn, neighbor, BVS:1855:8, LC:19

AMBLER, Wm., W, M, d. 12 Sep 1858, LC, unk, 76-6-0, p. Wm. & Jemima Ambler, b. LC, sc: Susan Ambler, wife, BVS:1858:6, LC:33

AMBROSE, Sally Ann, W, F, d. 13 Aug 1866, Potomac Furnace, cancer, 66-0-0, p. unk, b. LC, laborer, c/o: Robt. Ambrose, sc: Robt. Ambrose, husband, BVS:1866:1

AMICK, George, W, M, d. 5 Jul 1887, LC, old age, 80-0-0, p. unk, farmer, unm, sc: Chas T. Williams, friend, 2nd Dist., BVS:1887:4

ANDERSON, Bushrod, W, M, d. 4 Jul 1859/60, res, cholera morbus, 57-4-22, p. Elijah & Eleanor Anderson, b. nr New Lisbon, farmer, c/o: Nancy Anderson, sc: Alfred Anderson, brother, BVS:1859:3, BVS:1860:1, LC:34

ANDERSON, Geo. W., W, M, d. 26 Apr 1853, LC, convulsions, 0-0-14, p. Chas. F. & Mary F. Anderson, b. LC, sc: Chas Anderson, father, BVS:1854:3, LC:1

ANDERSON, Geo. W., W, M, d. 24 Apr 1854, LC, unk, 0-0-15, p. Chas. F. & Mary F. Anderson, b. LC, sc: Charles F. Anderson, father, BVS:1854:8, LC:7

ANDERSON, Henry, B, M, d. 29 May 1873, nr Mountville, brain fever, 2-0-0, p. George & Bettie Anderson, b. Mountville, sc: George W. Anderson, father, MC Dist., BVS:1873:5

ANDERSON, Jane, B, F, d. 6 Jan 1892, Lovettsville, pneumonia, 33-0-0, p. unk, b. LC, consort, sc: Geo. Anderson, LV Dist., BVS:1892:6

ANDERSON, Mary, W, F, d. 31 Jan 1881, LC, gangrene, 74-6-17, p. James & Elizabeth Hefling, b. Stafford Co., farmer, c/o: Wm. Anderson, sc: Jas A. Anderson, son, 2nd Dist., BVS:1881:6

ANDERSON, Mary, B, F, d. 1 Apr 1882, LC, pneumonia, 2-5-0, p. Thomas & Charlotte Anderson, b. LC, unm, sc: Thomas Anderson, parent, 3rd Dist., BVS:1882:3

ANDERSON, Nancy, W, F, d. 28 Jul 1872, Wornal's Store, dropsy, 70-0-0, c/o: Bushrod Anderson, sc: Bushrod Anderson, husband, MC Dist., BVS:1872:7

ANDERSON, Sarah A., W, F, d. 21 Feb 1896, Leesburg, paralysis, 71-0-0, b. Stafford, housewife, wife, sc: husband, LE Dist., BVS:1896:5

ANKERS, Harriet M., W, F, d. 20 Oct 1880, nr Guilford, unk, 70-0-0, p. unk, b. LC, married, sc: A.T. Ankers, son, 1st Dist., BVS:1880:1

ANKERS, Jas. S., W, M, d. 9 Apr 1853, LC, unk, 0-5-0, p. Saml & Henrietta Ankers, b. LC, sc: Saml Ankers, father, BVS:1854:2, LC:7

ANKERS, Mary J., W, F, d. 18 Jun 1887, nr Sterling, paralysis, 56-0-0, p. John & Harriet Ankers, b. LC, unm, sc: C.W. Ankers, brother, 1st Dist., BVS:1887:2

APEL, Thomas, W, M, d. 24 Dec 1888, LC, gravel, 75-0-0, p. unk, b. Germany, miller, widower, sc: Rosallie, daughter, 2nd Dist., BVS:1888:5

APPEL, Henry Wilson, W, M, d. 1 May 1872, LC, stabbed in an affray, 21-0-0, p. Thomas & Mary Appel, b. Maryland, farmer, unm, sc: Thos. Appel, father, LE Dist., BVS:1872:3

APPEL, Mary C., W, F, d. 28 Aug 1879, nr Leesburg, paralysis, 57-5-5, p. Sebastian Heilbach, b. Germany, c/o: Thomas Appel, sc: Thomas Appel, husband, 2nd Dist., BVS:1879:1

Loudoun County, Virginia, Death Register, 1853-1896				33

APPLE, Chas H., W, M, d. 28 Oct 1865, nr Point of Rocks Furnace, typhoid fever, 17-0-0, p. Thos & Mary Apple, b. Germany, miller, unm, sc: Thos Apple, father, 1st Dist. BVS:1865:2/4

APPLE, Mary, W, F, d. Sep 1871, LC, 28-0-0, p. Thos. & Mary Apple, b. Maryland, unm, LE Dist., BVS:1871:4

APPLE, Thomas A., W, M, d. 28 Dec 1865, Point of Rocks Furnace, croup, 4-0-0, p. Thoms & Mary Apple, b. Germany, miller, unm, sc: Thos Apple, father, 1st Dist. BVS:1865:2/4

ARKINS, Sarah Jane, W, F, d. 10 Apr 1877, LC, hemorrhage of lungs, 35-0-0, p. Isaac Virts, b. Shenandoah Co., c/o: John W. Arkins, sc: John W. Arkins, husband, LV Dist., BVS:1877:4/7

ARMES, Martena, B, F, d. 20 Mar 1883, Leesburg, pneumonia, 62-0-0, p. Millie Armes, b. LC, laborer, unm, sc: Wm. A. Jones, friend, 2nd Dist., BVS:1883:6

ARNETT, Anna, W, F, d. 18 Nov 1872, nr Hamilton, old age, 87-9-3, p. unk, b. LC, c/o: Wm. Arnett, sc: Samuel Arnett, son, JF Dist., BVS:1872:1

ARNETT, Daisy, W, F, d. 2 Jan 1885, Hamilton, paralysis, 2-4-20, p. Mahlon T. & Mollie Arnett, b. LC, sc: Mahlon T. Arnett, father, 3rd Dist., BVS:1885:6

ARNETT, George, W, M, d. Sep 1856, LC, typhoid fever, 14-0-0, p. Thomas M. & Emily Arnett, b. Westmoreland, sc: Edward L. Carter, friend, BVS:1856:7, LC:24

ARNETT, Hannah, W, F, d. 9 Aug 1872, nr Hamilton, unk, 0-3-0, sc: Samuel Arnett, son, JF Dist., BVS:1872:1

ARNETT, Henry C., W, M, d. 1 Aug 1853, Wheatland, dysentery, 2-10-0, p. Henry & Mary Arnett, b. nr Wheatland, sc: father, BVS:1854:6, LC:5

ARNETT, Louisa, W, F, d. 23 Apr 1869, LC, consumption, 64-0-0, p. Peter & Hannah Moore, b. LC, married, sc: William Arnett, husband, BVS:1869:1

ARNETT, Mary Ann, W, F, d. 8 Jan 1866, nr Snickersville, consumption, 24-0-0, p. Wm. & Louisa Arnett, b. Snickersville, Seamstress, sc: father, BVS:1866:1

ARNETT, Mary E., W, F, d. 8 Sep 1890, Hamilton, unk, 0-0-7, p. Samuel R. & Mary E. Arnett, b. LC, none, unm, sc: Samuel Arnett, father, 3rd Dist., BVS:1890:6

ARNETT, Mary E., W, F, d. 10 Nov 1884, nr Hamilton, typhoid fever, 14-0-7, p. Samuel & Mary Arnett, b. LC, unm, sc: Samuel Arnett, parent, 3rd Dist., BVS:1884:6

ARNETT, Moses, W, M, d. 13 Jun 1864, Bloomfield, dysentery, 50-5-0, p. Nathe Arnett, farmer, sc: Ruth Arnett, widow, BVS:1864:1, LC:38

[ARNETT], no name, W, M, d. 29 May 1853, Wheatland, unk, 0-0-4, p. Henry & Mary Arnett, b. nr Wheatland, sc: father, BVS:1854:6, LC:5

ARNETT, Ruth Hannah, W, F, d. 24 Jul 1893, Purcellville, old age, 80-0-0, p. Solomon Gibson, b. LC, wife, sc: husband, JF Dist., BVS:1893:3

ARNETT, Walter, W, M, d. 15 Aug 1875, nr Bunkers Hill, water on brain, 0-2-0, p. Wm. N. & Mollie Arnett, b. nr Bunker Hill, unm, sc: Wm. N. Arnett, father, MT Dist., BVS:1875:8

ARNOLD, Almeta, W, F, d. 9 Oct 1890, LC, unk, 5-9-0, p. E. S. & Bettie Arnold, b. LC, none, unm, sc: E.S. Arnold, father, 2nd Dist., BVS:1890:3

ARNOLD, Catharine, W, F, d. 14 Apr 1893, Lovettsville, heart trouble, 73-0-0, p. unk, b. Lovettsville, consort, sc: Samuel S. Arnold, LV Dist., BVS:1893:5

ARNOLD, Charles W., W, M, d. 5 Aug 1883, nr Lovettsville, hemorrhage, 27-0-18, p. Jno. & Elizabeth Arnold, b. LC, farmer, c/o: Mary Arnold, sc: John Arnold, father, 2nd Dist., BVS:1883:6

ARNOLD, Elizabeth P., W, F, d. 26 Apr 1859/60, LC, convulsions, 38-11-8, p. John & Christina Case, b. LC, c/o: John Arnold, sc: John Arnold, husband, BVS:1859:1,1860:4, LC:37

ARNOLD, James T., W, M, d. 23 May 1893, Lucketts, drowned, 21-0-0, p.

John & Sarah, b. Leesburg, unm, sc: John Arnold, LE Dist., BVS:1893:6

ARNOLD, Martha A., W, F, d. 26 Jun 1880, nr Lovettsville, rheumatism, 74-0-0, p. Martha Oswald, b. LC, sc: Anne S. Arnold, neice, 2nd Dist., BVS:1880:6

ARNOLD, Martha S., W, F, d. 13 Feb 1853, Lovettsville, rupture, 32-5-3, p. Michael & Mary Arnold, b. Lovettsville, saddler, sc: Jacob Smith, father-in-law, BVS:1854:3, LC:2

ARNOLD, no name, W, M, d. 22 Jul 1881, LC, summer complaint, 0-1-18, p. Jno & Sarah J. Arnold, b. LC, sc: Jno. Arnold, father, 2nd Dist., BVS:1881:6

ARNOLD, Nora, W, F, d. 5 Jan 1890, LC, unk, 0-0-1, p. Mahlon D. & Emma Arnold, b. LC, none, unm, sc: M.D. Arnold, father, 2nd Dist., BVS:1890:3

ARNOLD, Sarah E., W, F, d. 30 Oct 1855, LC, child bed, 24-13-0, p. David & Elizbt. Wire, b. LC, c/o: Jacob Arnold, sc: Jacob Arnold, husband, BVS:1855:2, LC:15

ARUNDELL, Honour, W, F, d. 13 Feb 1872, nr Farmwell Station, pneumonia, 59-0-0, p. William Lefever & wife, b. LC, c/o: Joseph Arundell, sc: Joseph Arundell, BR Dist., BVS:1872:6

ARUNDELL, Joseph, W, M, d. 13 Mar 1881, Farmwell, old age, 73-0-0, b. LC, farmer, c/o: Mariah Arundell, sc: Mrs. Arundell, wife, 1st Dist., BVS:1881:1

ASH, James Clifford, W, M, d. 11 Nov 1875, Round Hill, unk, 0-2-14, p. N. B. & Lucy Ash, b. LC, sc: N.B. Ash, father, JF Dist., BVS:1875:3

ASH, Martha C., B, F, d. 19 Mar 1883, Leesburg, teething, 1-7-0, p. Butler C. & Theresa Ash, b. LC, sc: Butler Ash, father, 2nd Dist., BVS:1883:6

[ASH], no name, B, F, d. 13 Aug 1875, Leesburg, strangulation birth, unk, p. Scott & Nancy Ash, b. Leesburg, sc: Scott Ash, father, LE Dist., BVS:1875:1

ASH, Pamelia A., B, F, d. 30 Aug 1885, nr Mount Gilead, cholera infantum, 0-9-0, p. Albert & Kittie Ash, b. LC, sc: Albert Ash, father, 1st Dist., BVS:1885:3

ASHBY, Montie, W, M, d. 26 Sep 1893, Trappe, whooping cough, 3-3-0, p. Jos. A. & Annie Ashby, b. Trappe, laborer, sc: Jas A. Ashby, father, 1st Dist., BVS:1893:1

ASHBY, Thomas, B, M, d. 15 Sep 1890, Maxville, consumption, 76-0-0, p. unk, b. LC, laborer, unk, sc: Geo W. Mason, son-in-law, 1st Dist., BVS:1890:1

ASHTON, Lillie E., B, F, d. 9 Oct 1887, nr Mountville, dysentery, 5-0-0, p. Lee & Emily Ashton, b. nr Mountville, sc: Lee Ashton, father, 1st Dist., BVS:1887:2

ASHTON, Mary, B, F, d. 11 Nov 1885, nr Mountville, old age, 72-0-0, p. Joseph & Mary Ethern, b. LC, c/o: John Ashton, sc: Lee Ashton, son, 1st Dist., BVS:1885:3

ASHTON, Nancy, B, F, d. 23 Jan 1892, Pleasant Valley, la grippe & pneumonia, 59-0-0, p. Thos. & Mary Crankins, b. Fauquier Co., laborer, c/o: Kenna Ashton, sc: Kenna Ashton, husband, 1st Dist., BVS:1892:4

ASHTON, Sarah F., B, F, d. 7 Oct 1887, nr Mountville, dysentery, 11-0-0, p. Lee & Emily Ashton, b. nr Mountville, sc: Lee Ashton, father, 1st Dist., BVS:1887:2

ASKINS, Henrietta, B, F, d. Aug 1873, LC, dropsy, 75-0-0, b. Maryland, Servant, unm, sc: W.B. Jackson, former master, LE Dist., BVS:1873:2

ATHEY, Charles E., W, M, d. 1 Feb 1858, Leesburg, scarlet fever, 0-11-3, p. John M. & Sarah E. Athey, b. Leesburg, sc: John M. Athey, father, BVS:1858:1, LC:29

ATHEY, Gracie R., F, d. 12 Feb 1896, LC, croup, 11-0-0, p. Jno. & M. Athey, b. LC, farmer, sc: father, LE Dist., BVS:1896:5

ATHEY, Virginia, W, F, d. 8 Feb 1858, Leesburg, scarlet fever, 4-11-0, p. John M. & Sarah E. Athey, b. Leesburg, sc: John M. Athey, father, BVS:1858:1, LC:29

ATTWELL, Harriet, W, F, d. 25 Nov 1876, LC, paralysis, 60-0-0, b. LC, c/o: William R. Attwell, sc: Thomas

Loudoun County, Virginia, Death Register, 1853-1896   35

H. Attwell, son, LE Dist., BVS:1876:6
ATTWOOD, Wm., W, M, d. 4 Sep 1853, LC, consumption, 59-7-11, p. Jas. & Mary Attwood, b. St. Mary's Co., MD, unk, c/o: Prisilla Attwood, sc: Prisilla Attwood, wife, BVS:1854:4, LC:2
ATWELL, Harriet E., W, F, d. 9 Feb 1879, Lovettsville, diphtheria, 5-7-0, p. R.M.J. & Carre V. Atwelll, b. LC, sc: R.M.J. Atwell, father, 2nd Dist., BVS:1879:1
ATWELL, Mary J., W, F, d. 20 Aug 1887, LC, cancer, 44-0-0, p. Christopher & Emily Head, b. LC, none, c/o: Ewell B. Atwell, sc: Ewell B. Atwell, husband, 2nd Dist., BVS:1887:4
ATWELL, William R., W, M, d. 1 Aug 1887, LC, old age, 84-0-0, p. unk, b. Clarke Co., Va., farmer, unm, sc: Sarah Benjamin, friend, 2nd Dist., BVS:1887:4
AULT, Charles E., W, M, d. 30 Nov 1854, LC, unk, 4-9-7, p. John & Mahala Ault, b. LC, sc: John Ault, father, BVS:1854:10, LC:9
AULT, Clara, W, F, d. 19 Jun 1877, nr Frankville, consumption, 26-0-0, p. Nancy Ault, name of father unk, b. nr Frankville, unm, sc: John W. Downs, friend, BR Dist., BVS:1877:1
AULT, Estella, W, F, d. 11 Sep 1872, LC, cholera infantum, 1-5-24, p. Fenton & Mary J. Ault, b. LC, sc: Fenton Ault, father, LE Dist., BVS:1872:3
AULT, George R., W, M, d. 1865, LC, typhoid fever, 19-0-0, p. John & Mahala Ault, b. LC, farmer, unm, sc: John Ault, father, 1st Dist., BVS:1865:2/4
AULT, John Z., W, M, d. Nov 1879, nr Leesburg, tumor, 10-0-0, p. John W. & Susan A. Ault, b. LC, sc: John W. Ault, father, 2nd Dist., BVS:1879:1
AULT, Martha S., W, F, d. 1865, LC, typhoid fever, 13-0-0, p. John & Mahala Ault, b. LC, farmer, unm, sc: John Ault, father, 1st Dist., BVS:1865:2/4
AULT, Millie M., W, F, d. 22 Feb 1883, nr Leesburg, scrofula, 7-0-0, p. John W. & Susan A. Ault, b. LC, sc: John

W. Ault, father, 2nd Dist., BVS:1883:6
AULT, Richard, W, M, d. 1865, LC, typhoid fever, 17-0-0, p. John & Mahala Ault, b. LC, farmer, unm, sc: John Ault, father, 1st Dist., BVS:1865:2/4
AULT, Rozetta, W, F, d. 25 Dec 1866, Goose Creek, pneumonia, 1-4-21, p. J.W. & S.A. Ault, b. Maryland, sc: S. Ann Ault, mother, BVS:1866:3
AULT, Wm., W, M, d. 4 Jan 1853, LC, pneumonia, 68-3-10, p. Jacob & Rachel Ault, b. LC, farmer, c/o: Ann Ault, sc: Ann Ault, wife, BVS:1854:3, LC:2
AUSTIN, Carrie, B, F, d. 17 Jan 1878, Middleburg, disease of lungs, 28-0-0, b. Fairfax Co., c/o: Wm. Austin, sc: Wm Austin, husband, MC Dist., BVS:1878:6
AUSTIN, Jane O., W, F, d. Oct 1877, nr Daysville, congestive chills, 78-0-0, p. unk, b. unk, c/o: Dr. John Austin, sc: P.W. Cooper, son-in-law, BR Dist., BVS:1877:1
AXLINE, Charles T., W, M, d. 28 Dec 1891, Lovettsville, diphtheria, 7-0-0, p. David & Martha, b. nr Lovettsville, farmer, sc: parents, LV Dist., BVS:1891:5
AXLINE, Margaret C., W, F, d. 15 Sep 1886, LC, cholera infantum, 0-6-5, p. David E.& Ellen, b. LC, sc: David Axline, grandfather, 2nd Dist., BVS:1886:5
AYERS, Grace M., W, F, d. 29 Dec 1886, LC, diphtheria, 3-1-0, p. Daniel W. & Mary Ayers, b. LC, unm, sc: D.W. Ayers, father, 3rd Dist., BVS:1886:4
AYERS, no name, W, F, d. 9 Oct 1883, nr Leesburg, unk, 0-7-0, p. David W. & Mary A. Ayers, b. LC, sc: Daniel W. Ayers, father, 2nd Dist., BVS:1883:6
AYERS, Orra C., W, F, d. 30 Dec 1886, LC, diphtheria, 1-0-6, p. Daniel W. & Mary Ayers, b. LC, unm, sc: D.W. Ayers, father, 3rd Dist., BVS:1886:4
AYRE, Ada, W, F, d. 15 Oct 1888, LC, diphtheria, 4-0-0, p. George & Sarah Ayre, b. LC, unm, sc: George Ayre, father, 1st Dist., BVS:1888:3

AYRE, Alies, W, M, d. 15 Aug 1896, Waterford, unk, 0-10-0, p. E.V. & Martha, b. Waterford, unm, sc: E.V. Ayre, LV Dist., BVS:1896:7

AYRES, Saml., W, M, d. 6 Oct 1855, unk, 76-0-0, p. unk, b. LC, sc: Sam'l Ayers, son, BVS:1855:8, LC:19

AYRES, Thomas W., W, M, d. 19 Jan 1890, nr Oatlands, bright's disease, 69-0-0, p. Samuel & Mary Ayres, b. Fauquier Co., farmer, c/o: Emiline Ayers, sc: Elija V. Riticor, son-in-law, 1st Dist., BVS:1890:1

AYRES, Virginia, W, F, d. 22 Jun 1866, Red Hill, consumption, 22-3-0, p. C.W. & M.J. Ayres, b. Kentucky, unm, sc: Saml J. Carter, head of family, BVS:1866:3

BAGEANT, James W. F., W, M, d. 6 Oct 1886, brain fever, 2-1-0, p. Daniel & Betty, sc: Bettie Bageant, mother, 2nd Dist., BVS:1886:5

BAGEANT, Lydia C., W, F, d. 12 Sep 1881, LC, diphtheria, 4-0-0, p. Wm. & Sarah E. Bageant, sc: Wm. Bageant, father, 2nd Dist., BVS:1881:6

BAGEANT, Martha A., W, F, d. 22 Dec 1883, nr Lovettsville, unk, 49-0-0, p. Jas. & Elizabeth Stevens, b. LC, c/o: Geo. W. Bageant, sc: Geo W. Bageant, husband, 2nd Dist., BVS:1883:6

BAGEANT, Mary A., W, F, d. 10 Oct 1886, malarial fever, 46-0-0, p. John & Maria Mobberly, c/o: Joseph D. Bageant, sc: Joseph D. Bageant, husband, 2nd Dist., BVS:1886:5

[BAGEANT], no name, W, M, d. 1 Jun 1889, LC, unk, 0-0-1, p. Geo. W. & Fannie Bageant, b. LC, none, unm, sc: G.W. Bagent, head of family, 2nd Dist., BVS:1889:3

BAGEANT, William O., W, M, d. 25 Mar 1890, LC, croup, 1-6-0, p. Ada Bageant, b. LC, none, unm, sc: W. Bageant, grandfather, 2nd Dist., BVS:1890:3

BAGENT, Joseph Samuel, W, M, d. 24 Oct 1878, nr Harpers Ferry, croup, 5-11-24, p. George W. & Martha Bagent, b. LC, sc: George W. Bagent, father, LV Dist., BVS:1878:1/5

[BAGENT], no name, W, M, d. 17 Oct 1858, LC, unk, 0-0-2, p. Wm. & Elizth Bagent, b. LC, sc: Wm. Bagent, father, BVS:1858:2, LC:30

[BAGLEY], no name, W, M, d. 18 Jul 1855, Gum Spring, still born, unk, p. Patrick & Mary Bagley, b. Gum Spring, sc: Patrick Bagley, father, BVS:1855:8, LC:19

BAILEY, Eddie, B, M, d. 10 Feb 1884, LC, measles, 0-5-0, p. James & Lucy Bailey, b. LC, unm, 1st Dist., BVS:1884:1

BAILEY, Robert, W, M, d. 10 Feb 1875, Little River Church, consumption, 88-0-0, p. Pierce & Mary Bailey, b. L. E. Church, LC, farmer, unm, sc: H.B. Hutchison, nephew, BR Dist., BVS:1875:5

BAILY, James, B, M, d. 25 May 1885, nr Arcola, pneumonia, 39-0-0, p. Stephen & Sydney Bailey, b. nr Arcola, c/o: Lucy Baily, sc: Lucy Baily, wife, 1st Dist., BVS:1885:3

BAKER, Calvin Elwood, W, M, d. 12 Jun 1876, nr Short Hill, cholera infantum, 0-5-1, p. John S. & Sarah A. Baker, b. nr Short Hill, sc: John S. Baker, father, LV Dist., BVS:1876:3

BAKER, Carl, W, M, d. 24 Dec 1874, fever, 4-0-0, p. John S. & Sarah Baker, LV Dist., BVS:1874:6

BAKER, Claud B., W, M, d. Jan 1883, nr Lovettsville, unk, 0-3-0, p. Chas. W. & Kate E. Baker, b. LC, sc: Chas W. Baker, father, 2nd Dist., BVS:1883:6

BAKER, Daniel C., W, M, d. 17 Mar 1887, LC, unk, 1-3-0, p. Curtis J. & Mary Baker, b. LC, none, unm, sc: Curtis J. Baker, father, 2nd Dist., BVS:1887:4

BAKER, Edmund, W, M, d. 11 Jun 1880, LC, unk, 70-0-0, p. unk, b. LC, unm, sc: Jno. F. Allen, friend, 1st Dist., BVS:1880:1

BAKER, Hannah E., W, F, d. 13 Apr 1882, LC, pneumonia, 68-0-0, b. Delaware, c/o: Harlen Baker, sc: ? Baker, son, 3rd Dist., BVS:1882:3

BAKER, Harriet, W, F, d. 4 Aug 1880, LC, typhoid fever, 57-0-0, p. unk, b. LC, unm, sc: Jno. F. Allen, friend, 1st Dist., BVS:1880:1

BAKER, Harry O., W, M, d. 30 Dec 1889, LC, gun shot wound, 16-0-0,

p. Chas. W. & Kate Baker, b. LC, none, unm, sc: C.W. Baker, head of family, 2nd Dist., BVS:1889:3

BAKER, John S., W, M, d. 13 Mar 1893, Britain, paralysis of throat, 58-0-0, p. unk, b. Britain, farmer, consort, sc: Sarah A. Baker, LV Dist., BVS:1893:5

BAKER, Kirby W., W, M, d. 25 Mar 1883, nr Lovettsville, affection of brain, 3-9-8, p. Jno. W. & Sarah A. Baker, b. LC, sc: Sarah W. Baker, mother, 2nd Dist., BVS:1883:6

BAKER, Mary, W, F, d. 1886, dropsy, 60-0-0, p. George & ---, unm, sc: Annie V. Baker, niece, 2nd Dist., BVS:1886:5

BAKER, Mary E., W, F, d. 17 Aug 1883, Hamilton, heart disease, 24-0-0, b. Maryland, c/o: John R. Baker, sc: Jno R. Baker, husband, 3rd Dist., BVS:1883:5

BAKER, Max, W, M, d. 9 Apr 1888, LC, measles & bronchitis, 7-10-28, p. John S. & Sarah Baker, b. LC, none, unm, sc: John S. Baker, father, 2nd Dist., BVS:1888:5

[BAKER], no name, W, M, d. 2 Nov 1854, LC, unk, 0-0-1, p. Saml. & Elizabeth Baker, b. LC, sc: Samuel Baker, father, BVS:1854:8, LC:8

BAKER, Robert L., W, M, d. 2 Mar 1888, LC, unk, 1-0-15, p. Geo. D. & Ida Baker, b. LC, none, unm, sc: Geo D. Baker, father, 2nd Dist., BVS:1888:5

BAKER, Sarah, W, F, d. 21 Oct 1891, Unison, heart failure, 75-1-6, p. unk, b. LC, farmer, c/o: Thomas A. Baker, sc: Thos A. Baker, husband, 1st Dist., BVS:1891:2

BAKER, Sarah A., W, F, d. 25 Jan 1896, Morrisonville, heart disease, 52-0-0, p. unk, b. unk, c/o: William Baker, sc: William Baker, consort, LV Dist., BVS:1896:7

BALDWIN, Eleanor, W, F, d. 29 Nov 1892, North Fork, diphtheria, 2-0-0, p. Adrian & Elizabeth Baldwin, b. North Fork, physician, sc: Adrian Baldwin, father, MT Dist., BVS:1892:8

BALDWIN, Joseph, W, M, d. 18 Dec 1896, nr Welbourne, old age, 81-0-0, p. unk, b. nr Welbourne, farmer, consort, sc: J.D. Pratt, head of house, MC Dist., BVS:1896:1

BALDWIN, Mahlon, W, M, d. 11 Oct 1858, Powell's Shop, erysipelas, unk, p. Stacy & Margaret Baldwin, b. nr Middleburg, blacksmith, BVS:1858:4, LC:32

BALDWIN, Mary, W, F, d. 2 Nov 1892, North Fork, diphtheria, 9-10-0, p. Adrian & Elizabeth Baldwin, b. North Fork, physician, sc: Adrian Baldwin, father, MT Dist., BVS:1892:8

BALDWIN, Ruth, W, F, d. 20 Nov 1891, Philomont, old age, 98-0-0, p. Isaac & Sarah Brown, b. Philomont, wife, sc: Jno M. Chamblin, MT Dist., BVS:1891:6

BALENGER, Clynton C., W, M, d. 22 Dec 1888, LC, pneumonia, 12-3-0, p. Edger & Darcus Balenger, b. LC, none, unm, sc: Edger Balenger, father, 3rd Dist., BVS:1888:1

BALES, Ann E., (f), F, d. 6 Mar 1854, Leesburg, inflammation of brain, 7-6-2, p. Wm. F. & Eliza Bales, b. Leesburg, sc: Wm. F. Bales, father, BVS:1854:8, LC:7

BALES, Ernest W, M, d. Oct 1874, Leesburg, cancer of stomach, 50-0-0, p. Rodney & Annie T. Bales, sc: Rodney Bales, father, LE Dist., BVS:1874:5

BALES, John H., W, M, d. 30 Jul 1854, LC, pleurisy, 8-11-3, p. Thos. & Catherine Bales, b. LC, sc: Catherine Bales, mother, BVS:1854:9, LC:9

BALES, Mary A., W, F, d. 11 Feb 1853, LC, pneumonia, 25-0-0, p. Catharine Harper, b. LC, unm, sc: Joshua C. Bales, husband, BVS:1854:2, LC:1

[BALES], no name, W, F, d. 8 Oct 1856, LC, unk, 0-6-0, p. Thomas & Catharine Bales, b. LC, sc: Thomas Bales, father, BVS:1856:2, LC:20

BALL, Catharine, (f), F, d. 2 Apr 1853, Poor House, heart disease, 60-0-0, p. unk, b. unk, sc: Wm. Furr, keeper of poor house, BVS:1854:6, LC:6

BALL, Elizabeth A., W, F, d. 9 Aug 1866, Temple Hall, consumption, 51-0-0, p. Chas. & Nancy Thrift, b. LC, farmer, c/o: H. Ball, sc: Henry A. Ball, husband, BVS:1866:1

BALL, Ella J., W, F, d. 16 Jun 1881, LC, croup, 1-4-0, p. Chas. H. & Jane Ball, b. LC, sc: Chas H. Ball, father, 3rd Dist., BVS:1881:4

BALL, Ellen Rose, W, F, d. 5 Sep 1893, Woodburn, cholera infantum, 0-2-0, p. Notley & Gertrude Ball, b. LC, farmer, sc: father, MT Dist., BVS:1893:4

BALL, James, B, M, d. 15 Oct 1888, LC, heart disease, 56-0-0, p. unk, b. LC, school teacher, c/o: Allison Ball, sc: Oscar Cary, friend, 3rd Dist., BVS:1888:1

[BALL], no name, W, M, d. Jan 1854, Evergreen, 0-0-1/2, p. Henry H. & Elizabeth Ann Ball, b. Evergreen, sc: father, BVS:1854:12, LC:12

[BALL], no name, W, F, d. 4 Apr 1874, Broad Run Dist., unk, 0-0-10, p. John & Kate Ball, carpenter, sc: John Ball, father, BR Dist., BVS:1874:3

[BALL], no name, B, F, d. 15 Sep 1885, nr Bloomfield, croup, 0-0-8, p. Amanda Ball, b. Bloomfield, sc: Amanda Ball, mother, 1st Dist., BVS:1885:3

BALL, Sarah Ellen, W, F, d. 14 Apr 1893, North Fork, la grippe, 76-0-0, p. Lee Family, b. LC, wife, sc: son-in-law, MT Dist., BVS:1893:4

BALL, Wm., W, M, d. 4 Nov 1891, Woodburn, paralysis, 79-0-0, p. Jno A. Lynn[sic], b. Woodburn, farmer, husband, unm, sc: J.A. Lynn, MT Dist., BVS:1891:6

BALLENGER, Mollie May, W, F, d. 7 Aug 1891, Jefferson Co. WV, cholera infantum, 0-4-0, p. Ewd & Kate Ballenger, b. Hillsboro, sc: Edwd Ballenger, head of family, JF Dist., BVS:1891:7

BALLENGER, Sarah, W, F, d. 18 Nov 1866, nr Tanyard, diphtheria, 20-0-0, b. Philomont, unm, sc: Aquila Mead, friend, BVS:1866:1

BANISTER, Andrew, B, M, d. 15 Dec 1888, Middleburg, unk, 55-0-0, p. John & Alsey Banister, b. Petersburg, Va., unm, sc: Peter Banister, brother, 1st Dist., BVS:1888:3

BANKS, Ailsey, B, F, d. 30 Jun 1882, LC, dropsy, 85-0-0, p. unk, b. LC, unm, sc: S.E. Palmer, friend, 3rd Dist., BVS:1882:3

BANTZ, John, W, M, d. 1 Feb 1888, LC, gravel, 79-6-0, p. unk, b. LC, shoemaker, c/o: Mary Bantz, sc: G.M. Wrightman, friend, 3rd Dist., BVS:1888:1

BARBOUR, no name, B, M, d. 1 Apr 1887, LC, croup, 0-1-0, p. William & Dinah Barbour, b. LC, none, unm, sc: William Barbour, father, 2nd Dist., BVS:1887:4

BAREFORD, James, W, M, d. 1 Jan 1856, Poor House, old age, 70-0-0, b. LC, sc: steward, BVS:1856:4, LC:22

BARKER, No name,W, F, d. 13 Feb 1878, nr Gum Spring, pneumonia, 0-0-1, p. Jno M. & Marion H. Barker, b. LC, sc: Jno M. Barker, father, MC Dist., BVS:1878:6

BARKER, M. Janette, W, F, d. 15 Sep 1880, LC, diphtheria, 1-0-0, p. Jno. M. & Marian Barker, b. LC, unm, sc: Jno. M. Barker, father, 1st Dist., BVS:1880:1

[BARKER], Martha Frances, W, F, d. 19 Feb 1854, Middleburg, measles, 1-11-0, p. Samuel B. & Rebecca Barker, b. Middleburg, sc: Samuel B. Barker, BVS:1854:11, LC:10

BARNES, Artlinda, B, F, d. 13 Jun 1894, nr Arcola, old age, 100-0-0, p. unk, b. unk, c/o: Reuben Barnes, sc: John Barnes, son, 1st Dist., BVS:1894:2

BARNES, Carolina, B, M, d. 26 Aug 1889, LC, unk, 55-0-0, b. LC, none, c/o: John Barnes, sc: John Barnes, head of family, 2nd Dist., BVS:1889:3

BARNES, Eva L., B, F, d. 10 Jun 1896, LC, 1-5-0, p. Wash. & Martha Barnes, b. LC, sc: Washn Barnes, father, LE Dist., BVS:1896:5

BARNES, Kate, B, F, d. 25 Dec 1883, nr Arcola, burned to death, 14-0-0, p. James & Harriet Barnes, b. nr Arcola, unm, sc: James Barnes, father, 1st Dist., BVS:1883:1

BARNES, Louisa, B, F, d. 1 Nov 1889, LC, unk, 0-1-15, p. Walter & Martha Barnes, b. LC, none, unm, sc: Wash Barnes, head of family, 2nd Dist., BVS:1889:3

BARNES, Peter, B, M, d. 13 Feb 1896, LC, 0-1-14, p. Wash. & Martha

Barnes, b. LC, sc: Washn Barnes, father, LE Dist., BVS:1896:5

BARNES, Susan R., B, F, d. 17 Jul 1896, LC, 2-5-0, p. Wash. & Martha Barnes, b. LC, sc: Washn Barnes, father, LE Dist., BVS:1896:5

BARNETT, Fannie, B, F, d. 2 Jun 1880, LC, croup, 0-1-0, p. John & Rosie Barnett, b. LC, unm, sc: John Barnett, father, 1st Dist., BVS:1880:1

BARNETT, John, B, M, d. 30 Aug 1888, nr Aldie, dysentery, 36-0-0, p. Harry & Frances Barnett, b. nr Aldie, c/o: Rose Barnett, sc: Rose Barnett, wife, 1st Dist., BVS:1888:3

BARNETT, Rose B., B, F, d. 5 Jul 1888, nr Aldie, dysentery, 2-0-0, p. John & Rose Barnett, b. nr Aldie, unm, sc: Rose Barnett, mother, 1st Dist., BVS:1888:3

BARNEY, Addison, B, M, d. 9 Aug 1880, LC, paralysis, 78-0-0, p. unk, unm, sc: Henry Hibbs, friend, 1st Dist., BVS:1880:3

BARNHOUSE, Christopher, W, M, d. 4 Jul 1881, LC, spasms, 2-7-0, p. Geo. W. & Christie Barnhouse, sc: Christie Barnhouse, mother, 2nd Dist., BVS:1881:6

BARNHOUSE, Elizabeth A., W, F, d. 25 Sep 1866, nr Lovettsville, dysentery, 70-0-0, p. unk, b. LC, sc: Eleanora Hickman, friend, BVS:1866:1

BARNHOUSE, Elizth. R., W, F, d. 11 Aug 1855, LC, unk, 0-1-11, p. John & Sarah M. Barnhouse, b. LC, sc: John Barnhouse, father, BVS:1855:2, LC:15

BARNHOUSE, Frances E., W, F, d. 28 Jun 1854, LC, pneumonia, 1-5-3, p. Randolph & Elisth. Barnhouse, b. LC, sc: Randolph Barnhouse, father, BVS:1854:9, LC:9

BARNHOUSE, Jno., W, M, d. 18 Jan 1896, LC, dropsy, 76-0-0, p. R. & V. Barnhouse, b. LC, farmer, husband, sc: Richd Harns, son-in-law, LE Dist., BVS:1896:5

BARNHOUSE, Joseph T., W, M, d. 25 Jul 1856, LC, scrofula, 4-2-0, p. John & Sarah M. Barnhouse, b. LC, sc: John Barnhouse, father, BVS:1856:2, LC:20

BARNHOUSE, O. P., W, M, d. 6 Apr 1883, nr Leesburg, unk, 1-9-2, p.

Geo. W. & Alberta Barnhous, b. LC, sc: Alberta Barnhouse, mother, 2nd Dist., BVS:1883:6

BARR, Laura A., W, F, d. 1 Mar 1853, on Goose Creek, consumption, 0-5-20, p. Geo. & Mary Barr, b. on Goose Creek, sc: mother, BVS:1854:6, LC:5

BARRETT, Alexander, B, M, d. 10 Dec 1883, nr Middleburg, unk, 70-0-0, p. unk, b. unk, laborer, c/o: Jane Barrett, sc: Jane Barrett, wife, 1st Dist., BVS:1883:1

BARRETT, Caroline M. E., W, F, d. 18 Dec 1877, Leesburg, cancer, 68-0-0, c/o: James F. Barrett, sc: W. F. Barrett, son, MT Dist., BVS:1877:2

BARRETT, Matilda, B, F, d. 10 Dec 1878, Middleburg, old age, 73-0-0, b. Albemarle Co., c/o: Alexander Barrett, sc: Edith Barrett, daughter, MC Dist., BVS:1878:6

BARRETT, Minnie T., B, F, d. 15 Feb 1883, nr Middleburg, dropsy, 2-0-0, p. Kate T. Barrett, b. nr Middleburg, unm, sc: Kate T. Barrett, mother, 1st Dist., BVS:1883:1

BARRETT, William F., W, M, d. 9 Jun 1885, nr Leesburg, consumption, 49-0-0, p. John & Caroline Barrett, b. LC, farmer, c/o: Lizzie A. Barrett, sc: Lizzie A. Barrett, wife, 3rd Dist., BVS:1885:6

BARTLETT, Caroline, W, F, d. Mar 1896, Hillsboro, heart disease, 80-0-0, JF Dist., BVS:1896:8

BARTLETT, Daisy, W, F, d. 1 Nov 1881, LC, croup, 5-2-0, p. Jno. W. & E. P. Bartlett, sc: Jno. H. Bartlett, father, 2nd Dist., BVS:1881:6

BARTLETT, Eliza H., W, F, d. 20 Jan 1872, nr Hoysville, heart disease, 36-7-23, p. Wm. & Eliza Hern, b. Ohio, farmer, married, sc: Jno W. Bartlett, husband, LV Dist., BVS:1872:5

BARTLETT, Guley E., W, F, d. 24 Jun 1865, Middleburg, inflammation bowels, 60-0-0, p. Sanford & Nancy Bartlett, b. Harrison Co., VA, unm, sc: brother, BVS:1865:1

BARTLETT, James L., W, M, d. 23 May 1854, LC, pneumonia, 4-10-19, p. Minor & Car Bartlett, b. LC, sc: Minor Bartlett, father, BVS:1854:13, LC:13

BARTLETT, John, W, M, d. 16 Jan 1892, Lovettsville, old age, 82-0-0, p. unk, b. unk, farmer, consort, sc: N. H. Bartlett, friend, LV Dist., BVS:1892:6

BARTLETT, Minor, W, M, d. 27 Mar 1855, drowned, 40-0-0, p. Jas. & Mary Bartlett, b. LC, sc: A.M. Taylor, friend, BVS:1855:8, LC:19

BARTLETT, N.H., W, M, d. 19 Dec 1896, Lovettsville, typhoid fever, 22-0-0, p. Howard & Maggie, b. Lovettsville, farmer, unm, sc: Howard Bartlett, LV Dist., BVS:1896:7

BARTLETT, Paul C., W, F, d. 5 May 1885, nr Lovettsville, Bright's disease, 8-5-12, p. N. H. & Margaret V. Bartlett, sc: A. H. Bartlett, father, 2nd Dist., BVS:1885:1

BARTLETT, Sanford H., W, M, d. 16 Jul 1858, Middleburg, cholera infantum, 11-6-28, p. Burgess D. & Armenia Bartlett, b. Middleburg, sc: Julia Bartlett, aunt, BVS:1858:3, LC:30

BARTLETT, Sarah, W, F, d. 28 Dec 1887, LC, old age, 77-0-0, p. John L. & Sarah Bartlett, b. LC, none, unm, sc: John W. Bartlett, nephew, 2nd Dist., BVS:1887:4

BARTON, Baily, W, M, d. 28 Aug 1877, nr Millville, injuries from a fall, 70-0-0, b. LC, farmer, c/o: Sarah A. Barton, sc: Chas. H. Barton, son, MC Dist., BVS:1877:5

BARTON, Benj F., W, M, d. 19 Apr 1864, Waterford, killed in battle, 19-0-17, p. B.R. & Sarah Barton, b. Trappe, soldier, sc: B.R. Barton, father, BVS:1864:1, LC:38

BARTON, Jas Bailey, W, M, d. 13 Jul 1864, father's res, consumption, 24-4-0, p. B.R. & Sarah Barton, b. nr Millville, sc: B.R. Barton, father, BVS:1864:1, LC:38

BARTON, Sally A., W, F, d. 31 Aug 1883, nr Unison, consumption, 45-0-0, p. John & Elizabeth Crain, b. nr Unison, c/o: Charles Barton, sc: Chas Barton, husband, 1st Dist., BVS:1883:1

BARTON, Saml. A., W, M, d. 19 Mar 1855, Jas. Heskett's, typhoid pneumonia, 49-0-0, p. Thos. & Sarah Barton, b. nr Bloomfield, huckster, sc: James Heskett, brother-in-law, BVS:1855:7, LC:18

BARTON, Simon, W, M, d. 19 May 1880, LC, pneumonia, 40-0-0, p. John & Sarah Barton, b. LC, carpenter, unm, sc: George Barton, friend, 3rd Dist., BVS:1880:4

BASCUE, Charles, W, M, d. 14 Jul 1880, Hillsboro, natural decay, 92-0-0, b. LC, laborer, c/o: Rachel Bascue, sc: Nathaniel Bascue, friend, 3rd Dist., BVS:1880:4

BASCUE, Joseph, W, M, d. Jun 1858, res of parents, whooping cough, 0-1-14, p. James S. & Sarah C. Bascue, b. nr Ketoctin, sc: James S. Bascue, father, BVS:1858:5, LC:32

BASELL, Josephine, B, F, d. 24 Jun 1880, LC, consumption, 27-0-0, p. Jerry & Josephine Bassell, b. LC, unm, sc: Jerry Bassell, father, 1st Dist., BVS:1880:1

BASIL, Bessie, B, F, d. 14 Jan 1894, Bloomfield, consumption, 18-0-0, p. Thos. & Eliza Basil, b. LC, unm, sc: Thos Basil, father, 1st Dist., BVS:1894:2

BASSELL, Ferrand T., W, M, d. 7 Nov 1883, Leesburg, diphtheria croup, 1-8-0, p. Jno Y. & Rebecca G. Bassell, b. LC, sc: Jno Y. Bassell, father, 2nd Dist., BVS:1883:6

BATEMAN, Thomas, B, M, d. 9 Nov 1876, nr Neersville, gravel, 70-0-0, b. LC, laborer, unm, sc: Amos C. ?, head of family, LV Dist., BVS:1876:3

BAXTER, Nellie, W, F, d. 8 Aug 1885, nr Trappe, brain fever, 0-3-0, p. Wm.& Sarah Baxter, b. Trappe, sc: Wm. Baxter, father, 1st Dist., BVS:1885:3

[BAXTER], no name, W, M, d. 31 Aug 1881, LC, unk, 0-2-1, p. Wm. & Sarah C. Baxter, b. LC, sc: S.C. Baxter, mother, 1st Dist., BVS:1881:1

BAYLOR, Beatrice, B, F, d. 10 Apr 1894, nr Sterling, unk, 1-0-0, p. Sarah Baylor, b. nr Sterling, sc: Robt Baylor, grandfather, 1st Dist., BVS:1894:2

BAZZEL, John, W, M, d. 23 Nov 1855, Aldie, suddenly, 74-0-0, p. Jno. & Ruth Bazzel, b. Annapolis, shoemaker/toll gatherer, c/o: Eliz.

Loudoun County, Virginia, Death Register, 1853-1896   41

Bazzell, sc: Eliz. Bazzell, widow & daughter, BVS:1855:4, LC:16
BAZZELL, Jerry, B, M, d. 19 Oct 1890, Bloomfield, dropsy, 77-0-0, p. Benjamin & Harriet Bazzell, b. LC, laborer, unk, sc: Benjamin Bazzel, son, 1st Dist., BVS:1890:1
BAZZLE, Clarence, B, M, d. 10 Dec 1877, LC, spasms, 1-6-0, p. Emma B. Bazzle, sc: B.B. Martin, friend, LE Dist., BVS:1877:8
BAZZLE, no name, B, M, d. 19 May 1896, nr Bloomfield, unk, 0-2-5, p. Willis & Amanda Bazzle, b. nr Bloomfield, none, unm, sc: Amanda Bazzle, mother, MC Dist., BVS:1896:1
BEACH, Ann H., W, F, d. 27 Jul 1853, LC, dysentery, 4-9-0, p. Lyol T. & Charlotte E. Beach, b. LC, sc: Lyol T. Beach, father, BVS:1854:4, LC:2
BEACH, Armistead M., W, M, d. 26 Jul 1853, LC, dysentery, 7-5-8, p. Lyol T. & Charlotte E. Beach, b. LC, sc: Lyol T. Beach, father, BVS:1854:4, LC:2
BEACH, Barbara, W, F, d. 13 May 1892, Farmwell, measles & bronchitis, 17-0-0, p. A. J. & Sarah E. Beach, b. Waxpool, unm, sc: A.J. Beach, father, 1st Dist., BVS:1892:1
BEACH, Commodore B., W, M, d. 26 Nov 1854, nr Harmony, 0-0-21, p. Presley & Frances A. Beach, b. nr Harmony, sc: father, BVS:1854:12, LC:12
BEACH, Cornelius, W, M, d. 1 Apr 1887, LC, pneumonia, 2-1-0, p. Cornelius & Susan Beach, b. LC, none, unm, sc: Cornelius Beach, father, 2nd Dist., BVS:1887:4
BEACH, Jane, W, F, d. 12 Nov 1887, nr Philomont, paralysis, 70-0-0, p. unk, b. LC, unk, sc: F.E. Robey, superintendent of poor, 1st Dist., BVS:1887:2
BEACH, no name, W, M, d. 17 Aug 1881, LC, unk, 1-0-4, p. Chas. W. & Annie M. Beach, sc: Charles W. Beach, father, 2nd Dist., BVS:1881:6
BEALES, Addie, W, F, d. 4 Jul 1893, Woodburn, dropsy, 32-0-0, p. Thomas & Elizabeth Wynkoop, b. LC, MT Dist., BVS:1893:4
BEALES, Benjamin R., W, M, d. 12 Aug 1881, LC, diphtheria, 1-3-17, p. David & Rebeca Beales, b. LC, sc: Rebecca Beales, mother, 3rd Dist., BVS:1881:4
BEALES, Earnest E., W, M, d. 5 Oct 1880, nr Leesburg, unk, 5-1-0, p. Richard A. & Mary E. Beales, b. LC, unm, sc: Richard A. Beales, father, 2nd Dist., BVS:1880:6
BEALES, Edgar T., W, M, d. 10 Aug 1881, LC, diphtheria, 9-10-0, p. David & Rebeca Beales, b. LC, sc: Rebecca Beales, mother, 3rd Dist., BVS:1881:4
BEALES, John L., W, M, d. 17 Aug 1881, LC, diphtheria, 7-8-3, p. David & Rebeca Beales, b. LC, sc: Rebecca Beales, mother, 3rd Dist., BVS:1881:4
BEALES, Joseph T., W, M, d. 23 Dec 1853, LC, croup, 4-5-0, p. Mortimer J. & Sarah L. Beales, b. LC, sc: Sarah L. Beales, mother, BVS:1854:4, LC:2
BEALES, Lorenzo A. W., W, M, d. 10 Sep 1859/60, LC, fever, 0-6-0, p. Mortimor J. & Sarah L. Beales, b. LC, sc: Mortimor J. Beales, father, BVS:1859:2, 1860:4, LC:37
BEALES, Luther, W, M, d. 2 Oct 1882, LC, diphtheria, 11-0-0, p. Mort & Lizzie Beales, b. LC, unm, sc: Mort J. Beales, parent, 3rd Dist., BVS:1882:3
BEALES, Sarah E., W, F, d. 23 Jul 1890, Hamilton, typhoid fever, 27-0-0, p. Mort & Sarah Beales, b. LC, none, c/o: J.E. Beales, sc: J.E. Beales, husband, 3rd Dist., BVS:1890:6
BEALES, Willie Carruthers, W, M, d. 26 Feb 1875, nr Lincoln, scarlet fever, 2-0-0, p. Joel E. & Mattie. b. Lincoln, laborer, unm, sc: Joel E. Beales, father, MT Dist., BVS:1875:8
BEALES, Willie R., W, M, d. 10 Aug 1881, LC, diphtheria, 4-2-12, p. David & Rebeca Beales, b. LC, sc: Rebecca Beales, mother, 3rd Dist., BVS:1881:4
BEALL, no name, W, F, d. 26 Nov 1888, Daysville, unk, 0-0-1, p. Geo. A. & Eliza Beall, b. Daysville, sc: George A. Beall, father, 1st Dist., BVS:1888:3

BEALS, Eliza, B, F, d. 17 Mar 1878, LC, pneumonia, 59-0-0, p. unk, b. LC, c/o: Wm. F. Beales, sc: Virginia Jones, daughter, LE Dist., BVS:1878:8

BEAMER, Adam Alonzo, B, M, d. 24 Jul 1877, Pleasant Valley, unk, 0-4-0, p. Adam & Lucinda Beamer, b. LC, sc: A. Beamer, father, MT Dist., BVS:1877:2

BEAMER, Carrie, W, F, d. 19 Apr 1883, nr Leesburg, unk, 40-0-0, p. Wm. & --- Palmer, b. Maryland, c/o: Nelson Beamer, sc: Nelson Beamer, husband, 2nd Dist., BVS:1883:3

BEAMER, Elizth., W, F, d. 6 Jun 1881, LC, paralysis, 76-0-0, p. --- Dixon, c/o: George Beamer, sc: Wm. F. McKimmey, son-in-law, 2nd Dist., BVS:1881:6

BEAMER, George, W, M, d. 15 Mar 1859/60, LC, unk, 9-2-4, p. Mary Beamer, b. LC, sc: Caroline Underwood, neighbor, BVS:1859:1, 1860:4, LC:37

BEAMER, George, W, M, d. 17 Jul 1877, LC, old age, 90-0-0, farmer, married, sc: George Beamer Jr., son, LV Dist., BVS:1877:4/7

BEAMER, Hannah, B, F, d. 20 Jun 1891, Bolington, child birth, 34-0-0, b. nr Bolington, c/o: Robt. Beamer, sc: husband, LV Dist., BVS:1891:5

BEAMER, Mary E., W, F, d. 1 Nov 1853, LC, child bed, 22-2-5, p. Henry & Elizabeth Goodhart, b. LC, c/o: Jas W. Beamer, sc: Geo Beamer, father-in-law, BVS:1854:3, LC:1

[BEAMER], no name, W, M, d. 20 Oct 1853, LC, unk, 0-2-2, p. James W. & Mary E. Beamer, b. LC, sc: Geo Beamer, grandfather, BVS:1854:3, LC:1

BEAMERDAFFER, Elizabeth I., W, , d. 16 Sep 1853, nr Bloomfield, putrid sore throat, 5-0-0, p. Jno. & Nancy Beamerdaffer, b. nr Bloomfield, sc: father, BVS:1854:7, LC:6

[BEAMERDAFFER], no name,W, F, d. 17 Nov 1857, res of parents, unk, 0-4-0, p. John & Mary A. Beamerdaffer, b. nr Bellfield, sc: John Beamerdaffer, father, BVS:1857:4, LC:27

BEAMERSDAFFER, Nancy Adelaide, W, F, d. 5 Aug 1859/60, nr Bellfield, unk, 0-3-16, p. John & Nancy J. Beamersdaffer, b. nr Bellfield, sc: Jno Beamersdaffer, father, BVS:1859:3,1860:1, LC:34

BEAMERSDAFFER, Nancy J., W, F, d. 28 Jul 1859/60, nr Bellfield, consumption, 32-7-19, p. James & Jane Alexander, b. nr Powell's Shop, c/o: Jno. Beamersdaffer, sc: Jno Beamersdaffer, husband, BVS:1859:3, 1860:1, LC:34

BEANS, A. H., W, M, d. 10 Apl 1879, Woodgrove, pneumonia, 52-9-0, p. Isaiah & Hannah Beans, b. LC, farmer, c/o: Sarah Beans, sc: Sarah Beans, wife, 3rd Dist., BVS:1879:3

BEANS, Amie Ann, W, F, d. 12 Aug 1890, Purcellville, typhoid fever, 66-0-0, p. Mahlon & Sallie Beans, b. LC, none, unm, sc: Isaiah Beans, brother, 3rd Dist., BVS:1890:6

BEANS, Charles W., W, M, d. 28 Dec 1857, res of parents, consumption, 33-2-26, p. Samuel & Pleasant Beans, b. nr Peugh's Mill, farmer, sc: Samuel Beans, father, BVS:1857:4, LC:26

BEANS, Elizabeth, W, F, d. Jun 1865, nr Woodgrove, paralyzed, 72-0-0, p. Thos & Emily Moss, married, sc: husband, BVS:1865:1

BEANS, Hannah, W, F, d. 12 Oct 1887, LC, spinal affection, 84-0-0, b. LC, c/o: Samuel Beans, sc: Jonathan Beans, son, 3rd Dist., BVS:1887:6

BEANS, Henry H., W, M, d. 2 Nov 1876, LC, unk, 0-0-5, p. Wm. H. & Henrietta Beans, b. LC, sc: Henrietta Beans, mother, JF Dist., BVS:1876:8

[BEANS], no name, W, F, d. Jul 1855, nr Woodgrove, 0-0-1, p. A. H. & Sarah C. Beans, b. nr Woodgrove, sc: A.H. Beans, father, BVS:1855:7, LC:18

BEANS, Isaiah B., W, M, d. 23 Nov 1883, Woodgrove, general debility, 92-0-0, p. Wm. & Hannah Beans, b. LC, farmer, sc: Nancy Beans, daughter, 3rd Dist., BVS:1883:5

BEANS, Janette R., W, F, d. 28 May 1853, Hillsboro, summer complaint, 0-10-20, p. Isaiah & Saphronia

Loudoun County, Virginia, Death Register, 1853-1896   43

Beans, b. LC, sc: father, BVS:1854:1, LC:3

BEANS, Mahlon, W, M, d. 22 Jul 1875, LC, dropsy, 76-6-4, p. Mahlon & Hannah Beans, b. LC, farmer, sc: ? Beans, ?, JF Dist., BVS:1875:3

BEANS, Maria, W, F, d. 7 Jan 1854, her res, typhoid fever, 49-0-0, p. David & Anna Goodwin, b. nr Purcellville, c/o: Absolom Beans, sc: Husband, BVS:1854:13, LC:12

BEANS, Sallie, W, F, d. 12 Jun 1879, Davis Mill, consumption, 32-0-0, p. Mahlon & Sallie Beans, b. LC, unm, sc: Burr Beans, brother, 3rd Dist., BVS:1879:3

BEANS, Sarah L., W, F, d. 9 Sep 1854, Old Hough Farm, typhoid, 50-0-0, p. Jas. & Anna Hyott, c/o: Mahlon Beans, sc: husband, BVS:1854:13, LC:13

BEANS, Thomas H., W, M, d. 25 Jul 1869, LC, heart disease, 24-0-0, p. Mahlon & Sarah L. Beans, b. LC, sc: Mahlon Beans, father, BVS:1869:1

BEARD, Frances E., W, F, d. Apr 1854, bilious fever, 38-0-0, p. Stephen & Orpha Beard, b. LC, sc: Jonathan Beard, brother, BVS:1854:13, LC:13

BEATTY, Julia A., W, F, d. 29 Mar 1858, res of parents, consumption, 15-0-0, p. Wm. & Rebecca Beatty, b. Beatty's Mill, sc: W. Beatty, father, BVS:1858:4, LC:32

BEATTY, William, W, M, d. 6 Jul 1883, nr Lovettsville, gravel, 72-0-0, unk, b. LC, farmer, c/o: Eliza & Lydia J. Beatty, sc: Lydia J. Beatty, wife, 2nd Dist., BVS:1883:3

BEAVERS, Barney, W, M, d. 30 Jun 1881, Farmwell, dropsy, 70-0-0, b. LC, laborer, sc: Dr. Warner, physician, 1st Dist., BVS:1881:1

BEAVERS, Eliza Ann, W, F, d. Dec 1855, burned, 4-0-0, p. Jno. W. & M. A. Beavers, b. LC, sc: Jno. Beavers, father, BVS:1855:8, LC:19

BEAVERS, Janette, W, F, d. Oct 1855, unk, 0-9-0, p. Jno. W. & M. A. Beavers, b. LC, farmer, sc: Jno. Beavers, father, BVS:1855:8, LC:19

BEAVERS, John, W, M, d. 29 Jan 1859/60, res, pneumonia, 87-0-0, p. John & Mary Beavers, b. LC, farmer, c/o: Margaret Beavers, sc: M.V. Waltman, nephew, BVS:1859:3, 1860:1, LC:34

BEAVERS, John D., W, M, d. 2 Aug 1858, his res, consumption, 43-5-1, p. Samuel & Sarah Beavers, b. nr Isaac Piggott's res., farmer, c/o: Christina Beavers, sc: Washington Beavers, brother, BVS:1858:3, LC:31

BEAVERS, Margaret, W, F, d. 27 Nov 1859/60, res, pneumonia, 72-2-11, p. Abram & Ann Buskirk, b. Clark, c/o: John Beavers decd, sc: M.V. Waltman, nephew, BVS:1859:3, 1860:1, LC:34

BEAVERS, Margaret, W, F, d. 23 Apr 1887, LC, consumption, 41-0-0, p. Lewis & Donohoe, b. LC, none, c/o: Morgan Beavers, sc: Morgan Beavers, husband, 3rd Dist., BVS:1887:6

[BEAVERS], no name, W, M, d. 24 Oct 1875, nr Mt. Hope Church, unk, 0-0-2 hrs, p. Jas. T. & Ann C. Beavers, b. nr Mt. Hope, unm, sc: Jas. T. Beavers, father, BR Dist., BVS:1875:5

BEAVERS, Samuel, W, M, d. 23 Dec 1891, nr Arcola, pneumonia, 74-0-0, p. Wm. & Lavinia Beavers, b. Fairfax, farmer, c/o: Mary Beavers, decd, sc: Saml A. Beavers, son, 1st Dist., BVS:1891:2

BEAVERS, Thomas, W, M, d. 30 Jan 1881, LC, consumption, 76-0-0, b. LC, farmer, c/o: Delilah Beavers, sc: D. Beavers, wife, 1st Dist., BVS:1881:1

BEAVERS, Thos J., W, M, d. 28 Aug 1864, Philomont, typhoid fever, 21-5-8, p. Thos & Delila Beavers, b. LC, soldier, sc: Thos Beavers, father, BVS:1864:1, LC:38

BEAVERS, Viney, W, F, d. 5 Jun 1881, Guilford, consumption, 22-0-0, p. Saml & Marianne Beavers, b. LC, sc: Dr. Warner, physician, 1st Dist., BVS:1881:1

BEAVERS, William, W, M, d. 7 Mar 1859/60, LC, consumption, 72-0-0, p. Gabriel Beavers, b. LC, sc: Jno W Beavers, son, BVS:1859:6, 1860:3, LC:36

BELL, Annie L., W, F, d. 21 Dec 1892, Lincoln, abscess, 23-0-0, p. Edwin & Amanda Bell, b. LC, teacher, unm, sc: Edwin Bell, head of family, MT Dist., BVS:1892:8

BELL, Chs. A., W, M, d. 25 Nov 1888, LC, diphtheria, 6-0-0, p. Albert B. & Julia Bell, b. LC, none, unm, sc: A.B. Bell, father, 3rd Dist., BVS:1888:1

BELL, Decatur, W, M, d. 7 Nov 1881, LC, diphtheria, 0-3-0, p. Albert & Julia Bell, b. LC, sc: Albert W. Bell, father, 3rd Dist., BVS:1881:4

BELL, Elizabeth, B, F, d. 1 May 1880, Leesburg, consumption, 22-0-0, p. Frank & Amanda Parkinson, b. LC, c/o: Louis Bell, sc: Mary Newman, sister, 2nd Dist., BVS:1880:6

BELL, Janie, W, F, d. 23 Aug 1896, Snickersville, unk, 0-1-0, p. Chas. & Sarah Bell, b. Snickersville, mechanic, sc: Chas Bell, father, MT Dist., BVS:1896:9

BELL, Jas, B, , d. Sep 1874, LC, 12-0-0, sc: Wm. Bell, father, LE Dist., BVS:1874:5

BELL, John, W, M, d. 24 May 1884, nr Hillsboro, consumption, 73-0-0, p. Arch & Sarah Allen, b. LC, farmer, c/o: Mary C. Bell, sc: Chas C. Bell, son, 3rd Dist., BVS:1884:6

BELL, Nancy, W, F, d. 15 Nov 1871, dropsy, 70-0-0, married, BR Dist., BVS:1871:3

[BELL], no name, W, F, d. 2 Mar 1896, Waxpool, premature, 0-0-1, p. Jno. W. & Emma Bell, b. Waxpool, sc: Jno W. Bell, father, BR Dist., BVS:1896:3

[BELL], no name, W, F, d. 24 Apr 1896, Waxpool, unk, 0-1-3, p. Jno. W. & Emma Bell, b. Waxpool, sc: Jno W. Bell, father, BR Dist., BVS:1896:3

BELL, Susan, B, F, d. 15 Jan 1866, Alpheus Gibson's, inflammation brain, 1-0-0, p. Sarah Bell, b. nr Snickersville, sc: Alpheus Gibson, former master, BVS:1866:1

BELT, Alfred, W, M, d. 1 Jul 1872, Rock Hill, unk, 84-0-0, p. unk, b. Maryland, farmer, unk, sc: A.C. Belt, son, LE Dist., BVS:1872:3

BELT, Maria, W, F, d. Sep 1873, nr Leesburg, consumption, 52-0-0, p. John & Delia Murphee, b. Maryland, c/o: Geo. Belt, sc: Townsend Belt, son, MC Dist., BVS:1873:5

[BELT], no name, W, F, d. 7 Jan 1853, LC, unk, 0-0-1, p. Alfred C. & Mary R. Belt, b. LC, sc: Alfred C. Belt, father, BVS:1854:4, LC:2

BELT, Randolph, W, M, d. 22 May 1866, nr Middleburg, pneumonia, 2-9-0, p. G. J. P. & Leanna Belt, b. Prince William Co., sc: father, BVS:1866:2

BENEDICT, Henrietta, W, F, d. 1 May 1890, LC, old age, 73-0-0, p. unk, b. LC, none, unm, sc: Rebecca Bassell, daughter, 2nd Dist., BVS:1890:3

BENEDUM, Charles E., W, M, d. 1 Sep 1886, LC, pistol shot, 13-8-0, p. Jno. E. & Eliza Benedum, b. LC, sc: Jno E. Benedum, father, 3rd Dist., BVS:1886:4

BENEDUM, John E., W, M, d. 4 Apr 1880, Purcellville, pneumonia, 0-4-6, p. Jno. & Eliza Benedum, b. LC, sc: Jno. Benedum, father, 3rd Dist., BVS:1880:4

BENJAMIN, James H., W, M, d. 15 Sep 1874, infantile, 0-0-7, p. G.W. & Irene Benjamin, laborer, LV Dist., BVS:1874:6

BENJAMIN, Lela R., W, F, d. 2 Feb 1877, LC, pneumonia, 2-6-0, p. Wm. H. & Susan Benjamin, sc: Wm. H. Benjamin, father, LE Dist., BVS:1877:8

BENJAMIN, Lucretia, W, F, d. 13 Aug 1876, nr nr Funkville, typhoid fever, 28-0-0, p. John & Harriet Benjamin, b. LC, unm, sc: John Benjamin, father, BR Dist., BVS:1876:2

BENJAMIN, W. H., W, M, d. 16 Aug 1893, Leesburg, chronic diarrhea, 53-0-0, p. unk, b. Leesburg, merchant, consort, sc: L.L. Benjamin, LE Dist., BVS:1893:6

BENJAMIN, Warren, W, M, d. 27 May 1856, James Benjamin's, consumption, 23-0-0, p. Wm. & Sarah Benjamin, b. Fauquier Co., laborer, sc: James Benjamin, brother, BVS:1856:5, LC:23

BENNETT, Addison, B, M, d. 10 Apr 1885, nr Arcola, old age, 82-0-0, p. John & Mary A. Bennett, b. nr Arcola, laborer, c/o: Millie Bennett, sc: Louis W. Lee, grandson, 1st Dist., BVS:1885:3

BENNETT, Jno. S., W, M, d. 23 Mar 1893, Clarkes Gap, pneumonia, 0-0-18, p. E.L. & R. H. Bennett, b. LC, sc: father, JF Dist., BVS:1893:3

BENNETT, Mary E., W, F, d. 8 Sep 1885, nr Lovettsville, paralysis, 55-0-0, p. Jonas P. & Sarah A. Schooley, c/o: Sydnor Bennett, sc: Sydnor Bennett, husband, 2nd Dist., BVS:1885:1

BENT, Gertie, B, F, d. 18 Nov 1887, LC, brain fever, 3-0-0, b. LC, unm, sc: George W. Bent, father, 3rd Dist., BVS:1887:6

BENTLEY, Catharine, W, F, d. May 1856, LC, whooping cough, 0-1-0, p. R. M. & Catharine Bentley, b. LC, sc: R. M. Bentley, father, BVS:1856:7, LC:24

BENTLEY, James A, B, M, d. 6 Aug 1866, nr Hamilton, dysentery, 1-6-0, p. Adaline Bentley, b. nr Hamilton, sc: Mary H. Love, former mistress, BVS:1866:1

BENTLEY, R. Montgomery, W, M, d. 18 May 1872, Leesburg, typhoid fever, 44-10-18, p. Robt. & Catharine Bentley, b. Leesburg, agent, c/o: Catherine A. Bentley, sc: Catherine Bentley, consort, LE Dist., BVS:1872:3

BENTLEY, Robert, W, M, d. 9 Nov 1880, LC, asthma, 58-0-0, p. Robert & Virginia Bentley, b. LC, farmer, c/o: Elizabeth Bentley, sc: Elizabeth Bentley, wife, 1st Dist., BVS:1880:1

BENTLEY, Robt. Sr., W, M, d. 2 Sep 1872, Leesburg, old age, 80-0-0, p. unk, b. Leesburg, farmer, c/o: Kate L. Bentley, sc: A.R. Mott, son-in-law, LE Dist., BVS:1872:3

BENTLEY, Wm., B, M, d. 3 Jun 1892, Aldie, old age, 78-0-0, p. unk, b. Aldie, laborer, c/o: Ann Bentley, sc: Ann Bentley, wife, 1st Dist., BVS:1892:4

BENTLY, Arthur B., B, M, d. 15 Jun 1887, LC, brain fever, 0-3-0, p. Arthur & Jane Bently, b. LC, unm, sc: Arthur Bently, father, 3rd Dist., BVS:1887:6

BENTON, Cathrn., W, F, d. 9 Dec 1855, Springhill, croup, 50-0-0, p. Washington Cocke, b. Fauquier Co., c/o: Wm. Benton, sc: Wm. H. Benton, son, BVS:1855:6, LC:17

BENTON, Sarah, W, F, d. Feb 1854, Spring Hill, pneumonia, 60-0-0, p. Daniel & Sarah Hyde, b. Spotsylvania, c/o: Wm. Benton Sen., sc: Wm. Benton Jr., son, BVS:1854:11, LC:10

BERKELY, Frances C., W, F, d. 12 Aug 1855, Aldie, h., 56-0-0, p. Wm. & Catharine Noland, b. nr Noland's Ferry, c/o: Lewis Berkeley, dec'd, sc: Wm. Berkley, son, BVS:1855:4, LC:16

BERKLEY, Lewis, W, M, d. 13 Apr 1853, Aldie, liver disease, 63-0-0, p. Edmund & Mary Berkley, b. Middlesex Co., farmer, c/o: Francis Berkley, sc: Wm. Berkley, son, BVS:1854:6, LC:6

BERN, Katie, W, F, d. 9 Sep 1896, Ashburn, killed by r r train, 2-0-10, p. Jas. H. & Belle Bern, b. Ashburn, sc: Jas H. Bern, father, BR Dist., BVS:1896:3

BERRY, Estella, W, F], d. 9 Oct 1865, Waterford, croup, 0-3-23, p. Newton & Ida E. Berry, b. Waterford, clerk, unm, sc: Newton Berry, father, 1st Dist., BVS:1865:3/4

BERRY, Fannie, B, F, d. 27 Apr 1887, LC, child birth, 30-0-0, p. unk, b. LC, none, unm, sc: W.H. Benjamin, friend, 2nd Dist., BVS:1887:4

BERRY, Frances, B, F, d. 2 Apr 1885, nr Mountville, consumption, 23-0-0, p. Sherlock & Betsy Davis, b. nr Mountville, c/o: Philip Berry, sc: Daniel Berry, father-in-law, 1st Dist., BVS:1885:3

BERRY, George Gibson, W, M, d. Oct 1871, Waterford, unk, 0-2-0, p. Newton & Jane Berry, b. Waterford, sc: Newton Berry, father, JF Dist., BVS:1871:1

BERRY, Mary, W, F, d. 2 Jan 1866, Hamilton, b. colic, 66-0-0, p. Jas. & Phebe Marlow, b. Shenandoah Co., unm, sc: Wm. Berry, son, BVS:1866:2

BERRY, Sintha, B, F, d. 15 Dec 1882, Mountville, old age, 86-0-0, p. unk, b. Leesburg, unm, sc: Daniel Berry, brother, 1st Dist., BVS:1886:1

BERRY, Virginia Ellen, W, F, d. 25 Aug 1856, res of parents, dysentery, 1-11-25, p. Wm. & Elizabeth Berry, b.

res of parents, sc: W. Berry, father, BVS:1856:5, LC:22

BERRY, William, W, M, d. 10 Oct 1884, nr Hamilton, gun shot wound, 65-5-0, p. Wm. & Mary Berry, b. Virginia, laborer, c/o: Jane Berry, sc: John N. Berry, son, 3rd Dist., BVS:1884:6

BERRYMAN, Amelia, B, F, d. 12 Nov 1896, nr Mountville, diphtheria, 10-0-0, p. George & F. Berryman, b. Mountville, none, unm, sc: George Berryman, father, MC Dist., BVS:1896:1

BERRYMAN, Jefferson, B, M, d. 10 Mar 1891, Mountville, old age, 90-0-0, p. unk, b. unk, unk, unm, sc: Geo Berryman, head of family, 1st Dist., BVS:1891:1

BESSY, Charles, B, M, d. 29 Oct 1883, nr Leesburg, unk, unk, p. unk, b. LC, laborer, unk, sc: Chas T. Birkby, undertaker, 2nd Dist., BVS:1883:3

BEST, Albert J., W, M, d. 4 Oct 1885, Hillsboro, paralysis, 74-4-0, b. LC, farmer, c/o: Amanda Best, sc: Amanda Best, wife, 3rd Dist., BVS:1885:6

BEST, Arabella, W, F, d. 29 Jul 1882, LC, consumption, 27-0-0, p. Enos & Permelia Best, b. LC, unm, sc: Enos F. Best, parent, 3rd Dist., BVS:1882:3

BEST, Ella M., W, F, d. 15 May 1885, Hillsboro, heart disease, 21-11-4, p. Albert & Amanda Best, b. LC, unm, sc: Amanda Best, mother, 3rd Dist., BVS:1885:6

[BEST], no name, W, M, d. 26 Feb 1853, LC, not given, 3-1-0, p. Albert & Elizth. Best, b. LC, sc: Albert Best, father, BVS:1854:2, LC:1

[BEST], no name, W, M, d. 15 Jul 1855, res of parents, 0-3-0, p. Jonas & Nancy Best, b. Lovett farm, sc: Jonas Best, father, BVS:1855:7, LC:18

[BEST], no name, W, M, d. 29 Jul 1856, res of parents, 0-0-15, p. Jonas & Nancy Best, b. res of parents, sc: Nancy Best, mother, BVS:1856:6, LC:23

BEST, Uriah, W, M, d. 10 Jun 1878, LC, brain fever, 0-9-0, p. Robt. & Mary E. Best, b. LC, unm, sc: R.H. Best, father, LE Dist., BVS:1878:8

BETTIS, Freddie, W, M, d. 17 Dec 1892, Vernon Mills, membranous croup, 2-6-0, p. Ham & Mary F. Bettis, b. Vernon Mills, sc: Ham Bettis, father, 1st Dist., BVS:1892:1

BEUCHLER, Bell, W, F, d. 15 May 1891, Leesburg, diphtheria, 6-0-0, p. John R. & Ella Beuchler, b. Leesburg, Dairyman, unm, sc: father, LE Dist., BVS:1891:4

BEUCHLER, Eva, W, F, d. 10 May 1891, Leesburg, diphtheria, 3-0-0, p. John R. & Ella Beuchler, b. Leesburg, Dairyman, unm, sc: father, LE Dist., BVS:1891:4

BEUCHLER, Gertrude A., W, F, d. 2 Jul 1880, Leesburg, unk, 0-2-4, p. Georg T. & Allice V. Beuchler, b. LC, sc: George Beuchler, father, 2nd Dist., BVS:1880:6

BEUCHLER, James C., W, M, d. 11 Jul 1877, Leesburg, thrush, 0-4-0, p. G. T. & Alice V. Beuchler, b. Leesburg, sc: G.T. Beuchler, father, LE Dist., BVS:1877:8

[BEUCHLER], no name, W, F, d. Sep 1871, LC, 0-6-0, p. J.R. & Mollie Beuchler, b. Leesburg, unm, LE Dist., BVS:1871:4

BEUCHLER, no name, W, F, d. 26 May 1887, LC, blood poison, 0-7-0, p. John R. & Mary Beuchler, b. LC, none, unm, sc: John R. Beuchler, father, 2nd Dist., BVS:1887:4

BEVERLY, Frances W., W, F, d. 6 Jul 1880, Leesburg, unk, 50-0-0, p. William H. & Frances Gray, b. LC, c/o: William Beverly, sc: James B. Beverly, son, 2nd Dist., BVS:1880:6

BEVERLY, Robert W., W, M, d. 2 Apr 1883, nr Leesburg, unk, 0-0-5, p. Jas. B. & Annie D. Beverly, b. LC, sc: J.B. Beverley, father, 2nd Dist., BVS:1883:3

BEVERLY, William, W, M, d. 10 Jan 1879, nr Upperville, pneumonia, 50-0-10, p. James B. & ___ Beverly, b. Fauquier Co., farmer, c/o: Frances W. Beverley, sc: John Gray, friend, 2nd Dist., BVS:1879:1

[BEVERS], no name, W, M, d. May 1874, LC, child complaint, 0-2-0, p. John & Martha Bevers, sc: John W. Bevers, father, LE Dist., BVS:1874:5

BIAS, Hannah J., B, F, d. 25 May 1876, nr Guilford, consumption, 26-

0-0, p. Ellen Jackson, b. LC, married, sc: Benj. Bias, husband, BR Dist., BVS:1876:2

BIGGS, Annie, W, F, d. 9 Mar 1886, nr Farmwell, liver disease, 27-0-0, p. Peter L. & Margaret E. Biggs, b. New Jersey, unm, sc: John O. Biggs, brother, 1st Dist., BVS:1886:1

BIGGS, Joanna, W, F, d. 6 Mar 1886, nr Farmwell, pneumonia, 24-0-0, p. Peter L. & Margaret E. Biggs, b. New Jersey, unm, sc: John O. Biggs, brother, 1st Dist., BVS:1886:1

BIGSBEE, Ann B., B, F, d. 5 Dec 1881, LC, whooping cough, 6-0-0, p. Geo L. & Fanny F. Bigsbee, b. LC, sc: Fanny F. Bigsbee, mother, 1st Dist., BVS:1881:1

BIGSBY, Jesse, B, M, d. 1 Dec 1872, nr Gum Spring, intemperance, 68-0-0, p. unk, b. LC, laborer, married, sc: Jane Bigsby, wife, BR Dist., BVS:1872:6

BIGSBY, Maurice F., B, M, d. 10 Jan 1885, nr Farmwell, pneumonia, 0-6-0, p. Louis & Nancy Bigsby, b. nr Farmwell, sc: Louis Bigsby, father, 1st Dist., BVS:1885:3

[BIGSBY], no name, B, F, d. 13 Jul 1873, nr Gum Spring, whooping cough, 0-0-19, p. George & Fanniel Bigsby, b. nr Gum Spring, sc: Geo. Bigsby, head of family, BR Dist., BVS:1873:1

BIGSBY, no name, B, M, d. 20 Aug 1887, Farmwell, unk, 0-0-9, p. Louis & Nancy Bigsby, b. Farmwell, unm, sc: Louis Bigsby, father, 1st Dist., BVS:1887:2

BINNS, Emily, B, F, d. 19 Apr 1880, Leesburg, consumption, 31-11-22, p. Hester & Harriet Spriggs, b. LC, sc: Mary Harris, sister, 2nd Dist., BVS:1880:6

BINNS, Lewis, B, M, d. 27 Dec 1876, Leesburg, unk, 1-2-0, p. Edward & Emily Binns, b. Leesburg, sc: Emily Binns, mother, LE Dist., BVS:1876:6

BINNS, Lorinda, B, F, d. 10 Mar 1886, Guilford, pneumonia, 70-0-0, p. Charles & Mary Adams, b. LC, c/o: Charles Binns, sc: George Dean, son-in-law, 1st Dist., BVS:1886:1

BIRDSALL, Amasa H., W, M, d. 5 Sep 1864, LC, dysentery, 1-10-1, p.

Berry Birdsall, b. LC, sc: Benj Birdsall, father, BVS:1864:1, LC:38

BIRDSALL, Hannah, W, F, d. 24 Apr 1857, Benjn Birdsall's, cancer of mouth, 58-0-0, p. Wilson & Rachel Birdsall, b. Pennsylvania, sc: Benjamin Birdsall, brother, BVS:1857:3, LC:26

BIRDSALL, Herbert, W, M, d. 28 Jan 1882, LC, brain fever, 3-0-2, p. Eli & Maria Birdsall, b. LC, unm, sc: Eli Birdsall, parent, 3rd Dist., BVS:1882:3

BIRDSALL, Mary, W, F, d. 11 Mar 1859, her res, dyspepsia, 65-0-0, p. John & Ann Brown, b. nr Hamilton, c/o: John Birdsall decd, sc: Benj Birdsall, son, BVS:1859:4, LC:35

BIRDSALL, Mary, W, F, d. 11 Nov 1860, res, dyspepsia, 45-0-0, p. John & Ann Brown, b. nr Hamilton, c/o: Mr. Birdsall decd, sc: Benj Birdsall, son, BVS:1860:2

BIRDSALL, Sarah, W, F, d. 5 Mar 1893, Lincoln, unk, 74-0-0, p. Israel & Mary Birdsall, b. LC, wife, MT Dist., BVS:1893:4

BIRKBY, Anna S., W, F, d. 10 Apr 1859/60, Leesburg, inflammation of stomach, 1-2-0, p. Thomas W. & Susan Birkby, b. Leesburg, sc: Thomas W. Birkby, father, BVS:1859:2, 1860:5, LC:37

BIRKBY, Maria, B, F, d. 16 Dec 1885, nr Guilford, heart disease, 57-0-0, p. Thomas & Emeline Smith, b. nr Guilford, c/o: Chas Birkby, sc: Chas Birkby, husband, 1st Dist., BVS:1885:3

BIRKBY, Mary, W, F, d. 14 Jun 1883, Leesburg, heart disease, 70-0-0, p. John & Mary Major, b. England, c/o: Joseph Birkby, sc: Chas T. Birkby, son, 2nd Dist., BVS:1883:6

BIRKBY, Mollie, W, F, d. 27 Jun 1887, LC, unk, 28-0-0, p. Thomas W. & Susan Birkby, b. LC, none, unm, sc: Susan Birkby, mother, 2nd Dist., BVS:1887:4

BIRKBY, Samuel R., W, M, d. 20 Mar 1857, Leesburg, croup, 2-10-0, p. Thomas W. & Susan Birkby, b. Leesburg, sc: Thomas W. Birkby, father, BVS:1857:2, LC:25

BIRKBY, Thomas W., W, M, d. 7 Apr 1885, Leesburg, paralysis, 62-0-0, p.

Thomas & --- Birkby, mechanic, c/o: Susan Birkby, sc: Edgar W. Birkby, son, 2nd Dist., BVS:1885:1

BITZER, Alcinda, W, F, d. 9 Nov 1857, White Hall, pneumonia, 40-0-2, p. John & Ellen Cochran, b. Fauquier Co., c/o: George L. Bitzer, sc: George L. Bitzer, widower, BVS:1857:6, LC:28

BITZER, George L., W, M, d. 29 Oct 1871, White Hall, pneumonia & paralysis, 71-0-0, widower, MC Dist., BVS:1871:2

BITZER, Jefferson D., W, M, d. 18 Aug 1869, LC, dysentery, 10-0-0, p. John & Amanda Bitzer, b. LC, sc: John Bitzer, father, BVS:1869:1

[BITZER], John David, W, M, d. 26 Jul 1855, res of parents, dysentery, 1-0-5, p. Jno. & Amanda G. Bitzer, b. nr Chamblin's Mill, sc: Jno. Bitzer, father, BVS:1855:7, LC:18

BITZER, Maggie M., W, F, d. 19 Feb 1878, nr Mt. Hope Church, typhoid pneumonia, 0-9-21, p. John W. & Laura M. Bitzer, b. nr Mt. Hope Church, unm, sc: Jas. Maffett, grandfather, BR Dist., BVS:1878:4

BLACK, George, B, M, d. 1 Nov 1864, Wm. McCray's, typhoid fever, 14-0-0, sc: Wm. McCray, BVS:1864:2, LC:39

[BLACK], no name, B, F, d. 22 Aug 1872, LC, unk, 0-0-7, p. Emeline Black, b. LC, sc: Emeline Black, mother, LE Dist., BVS:1872:3

BLADEN, Betsy, W, F, d. 12 Jul 1892, Belmont, old age, 82-0-0, p. unk, b. Fairfax, c/o: Wesley Bladen, sc: Jas Bladen, son, 1st Dist., BVS:1892:1

BLADEN, Wesley, W, M, d. 1 Apr 1892, Ryan, old age, 88-0-0, p. Gustav & Elizabeth Bladen, b. Fairfax, laborer, c/o: Betsy Bladen, sc: Jas Bladen, son, 1st Dist., BVS:1892:1

BLAKELY, Letitia, W, F, d. 15 Jun 1858, Charles Blakeley's, dropsy of heart, 79-11-6, p. Robt & Mary Russell, b. foot of Blue Ridge, c/o: Wm. Blakeley decd, sc: Charles Blakeley, son, BVS:1858:3, LC:31

[BLAND], no name, B, F, d. Sep 1866, Pleasant Valley, born dead, p. Crede & Caroline Bland, b. LC, sc: Crede Bland, father, BVS:1866:3

BLAY, Helen, B, F, d. 30 Mar 1883, Leesburg, pneumonia, 64-0-0, p. Millie Armes, b. LC, laborer, c/o: --- Blay, sc: Wm. A. Jones, friend, 2nd Dist., BVS:1883:6

BLINCOE, Adaline, W, F, d. 18 Jul 1881, nr Guilford, consumption, 25-0-0, p. Albert G. & Mary E. Blincoe, b. LC, sc: Dr. Day, physician, 1st Dist., BVS:1881:1

BLINCOE, Albert T., W, M, d. 5 Jul 1888, Sterling, paralysis, 84-0-0, p. Joseph Blincoe, b. Sterling, c/o: Mary Blincoe, sc: John T. Blincoe, brother, 1st Dist., BVS:1888:3

BLINCOE, Chas. H., W, M, d. 27 Aug 1892, Arcola, a falling tree, 22-1-0, p. Chas. & Mary Blincoe, b. Sterling, laborer, unm, sc: Martha Blincoe, cousin, 1st Dist., BVS:1892:1

BLINCOE, Henrietta E., W, F, d. 2 Oct 1885, nr Guilford, consumption, 45-0-0, p. Henry & Mary A. Blincoe, b. LC, unm, sc: Martha Blincoe, sister, 1st Dist., BVS:1885:3

BLINCOE, Joseph, W, M, d. 22 Mar 1857, pneumonia, 43-0-0, p. Jos. & Eliza Blincoe, b. LC, sc: Mary E. Blincoe, wife, BVS:1857:7, LC:28

BLINCOE, Mary E., W, F, d. 2 Apr 1883, nr Guilford, unk, 70-0-0, p. unk, b. unk, c/o: Albert Blincoe, sc: Albert Blincoe, husband, 1st Dist., BVS:1883:1

BLINCOE, Mary E., W, F, d. 17 Oct 1893, nr Waxpool, congestion, 74-0-0, p. unk, b. LC, laborer, c/o: Jos A. Blincoe, sc: S.W. Ankers, son-in-law, 1st Dist., BVS:1893:1

BLINCOE, Sarah F., W, F, d. 6 Nov 1854, LC, dysentery, 17-11-18, p. Henry & M. Blincoe, b. LC, sc: H. Blincoe, father, BVS:1854:14, LC:13

BLINCOE, Thomas J., W, M, d. 13 Novv 1882, LC, consumption, 26-0-0, p. Thos. J. & M. E. Blincoe, clerk, unm, sc: Thomas J. Blincoe, father, 1st Dist., BVS:1882:1

BLUNDELL, Mary E., W, F, d. 27 Nov 1859/60, LC, confinement, 32-0-0, p. James W. & Jane Jones, b. LC, c/o: Daniel W. Blundell, sc: Daniel W. Blundell, husband, BVS:1859:6, 1860:3, LC:36

BODINE, Alishia, W, F, d. 29 Nov 1877, Waterford, pneumonia, 70-0-

Loudoun County, Virginia, Death Register, 1853-1896 49

0, p. Henry & Jane Bodine, b. LC, unm, sc: Harriet Russell, daughter, JF Dist., BVS:1877:3

BODINE, Andrew J., W, M, d. 25 Aug 1859/60, LC, unk, 3-3-0, p. Isaac/Jacob & Mary E. Bodine, b. LC, sc: Isaiah/Jacob Bodine, father, BVS:1859:6, 1860:3, LC:36

BODINE, Charles A., W, M, d. 9 Apr 1887, nr Farmwell, rheumatism, 7-0-0, p. Henry H. & Caroline Bodine, b. LC, unm, sc: H.H. Bodine, father, 1st Dist., BVS:1887:2

BODINE, Henry, W, M, d. 18 Aug 1856, Waterford, dropsy, 76-6-2, p. unk, b. LC, c/o: Jane Bodine, sc: Jane Lemon, daughter, BVS:1856:1, LC:20

BODINE, John, W, M, d. 20 Nov 1876, nr Gum Spring, dropsy, 54-0-0, p. Robt Bodine & wife, b. LC, farmer, married, sc: Robert Power, son-in-law, BR Dist., BVS:1876:2

BODINE, John W., W, M, d. 20 Mar 1855, LC, croup, 0-8-2, p. Jno. & Margt. A. Bodine, b. LC, sc: Margt. A. Bodine, mother, BVS:1855:1, LC:14

BODINE, Mary C., W, F, d. 10 Feb 1884, LC, consumption, 18-0-0, p. Harrison & Caroline E. Bodine, unm, 1st Dist., BVS:1884:1

[BODINE], no name, W, M, d. 25 Dec 1882, Farmwell, premature, 0-0-1, p. Harrison H. & Caroline E. Bodine, b. Farmwell, unm, sc: Harrison H. Bodine, father, 1st Dist., BVS:1886:1

BODINE, Sarah E., W, F, d. 15 Sep 1856, LC, whooping count, 0-4-13, p. John W. & Margaret A. Bodine, b. LC, sc: Margaret A. Bodine, mother, BVS:1856:2, LC:21

BODINE, Wm. A., W, M, d. 21 Oct 1892, Belmont, consumption, 22-0-0, p. H. H. & Jane Bodine, b. Farmwell, laborer, unm, sc: H.H. Bodine, father, 1st Dist., BVS:1892:1

BODMER, Jacob B., W, M, d. 28 Nov 1890, Middleburg, membranous croup, 1-9-28, p. Jacob & Carra M. Bodmer, b. Middleburg, sc: Jacob Bodmer, father, 1st Dist., BVS:1890:1

BODMER, Mary M., W, F, d. 29 Oct 1884, LC, consumption, 34-0-0, p. John W. & Elizabeth Davis, c/o:

Geo. W. Bodmer, 1st Dist., BVS:1884:1

BODMER, Minnie, W, F, d. 4 Sep 1894, Middleburg, dysentery, 0-9-0, p. Geo. W. & Louiza Bodmer, b. Middleburg, sc: Geo W. Bodmer, father, 1st Dist., BVS:1894:1

BOGER, Joseph H., W, M, d. 16 Dec 1883, nr Lovettsville, erysipelas, 23-0-0, p. Wm. H. & Eliza Boger, b. LC, laborer, unm, sc: W.H. Boger, father, 2nd Dist., BVS:1883:6

BOGER, Mary E. R., W, F, d. 1 Aug 1857, LC, dysentery, 3-0-10, p. Samuel & Mary A. Boger, b. LC, sc: Samuel Boger, father, BVS:1857:1, LC:24

BOGER, Rachel, W, F, d. 28 Aug 1856, LC, liver complaint, 28-0-1, p. John & Margaret Boger, b. LC, unm, sc: John Boger, father, BVS:1856:2, LC:21

BOGER, Sarah C., W, F, d. 13 Oct 1873, nr Lovettsville, unk, 12-11-0, p. Saml & Mary A. Boger, b. nr Lovettsville, farmer, married, sc: Mary A. Boger, mother, LV Dist., BVS:1873:4

BOGER, William H., W, M, d. 9 May 1885, nr Lovettsville, paralysis, 62-0-0, p. John & Margaret Boger, farmer, c/o: Eliza A. Boger, sc: Eliza A. Boger, wife, 2nd Dist., BVS:1885:1

BOLDEN, Millie, B, F, d. 12 Apr 1894, Middleburg, unk, 30-0-0, p. unk, b. LC, c/o: Shed Bolden, sc: Shed Bolden, husband, 1st Dist., BVS:1894:2

BOLDEN, Wm., B, M, d. 10 Feb 1892, Middleburg, pneumonia, 1-6-0, p. Chas. & Nellie Bolden, b. Middleburg, sc: Chas Bolden, father, 1st Dist., BVS:1892:4

BOLEN, Caroline, B, F, d. 3 Jun 1877, nr Middleburg, brain fever, 0-11-0, p. Jno & Bettie Bolen, b. LC, sc: Betty Bolen, mother, MC Dist., BVS:1877:5

BOLEN, Lamon, W, M, d. 14 Jan 1893, nr Bloomfield, whooping cough, 2-0-0, p. Jos & Mary Bolen, b. nr Bloomfield, sc: Jos Bolen, father, 1st Dist., BVS:1893:1

BOLEY, Margie, W, F, d. 2 Feb 1896, nr Bloomfield, spinal meningitis, 1-4-0, p. Jas & Jane Boley, b. nr

Bloomfield, none, unm, sc: Jno F. Walkman, friend, MC Dist., BVS:1896:1

BOLIN, Josiah, B, M, d. 12 Jun 1874, Middleburg, cramp, 48-0-0, p. Joseph & Massie Bolin, b. LC, laborer, c/o: Kesiah Bolin, sc: Jno. Bolin, brother, MC Dist., BVS:1874:4

BOLLS, Bertie, B, F, d. 16 Sep 1888, nr Aldie, pneumonia, 5-0-0, p. Mary Bolls, b. LC, sc: Daniel Bolls, grandfather, 1st Dist., BVS:1888:3

BOLLS, George, B, M, d. 17 Aug 1888, nr Aldie, pneumonia, 1-8-0, p. Ginnie Bolls, b. LC, sc: Ginnie Bolls, mother, 1st Dist., BVS:1888:3

BOLLS, Ginnie, B, F, d. 25 Aug 1888, nr Aldie, unk, 25-0-0, p. Daniel & Lucy Bolls, b. LC, unm, sc: Daniel Bolls, father, 1st Dist., BVS:1888:3

BOLLS, no name, B, M, d. 15 Jul 1888, nr Aldie, pneumonia, 0-3-0, p. Ginnie Bolls, b. LC, sc: Ginnie Bolls, mother, 1st Dist., BVS:1888:3

BOLON, Lydia, W, F, d. 26 Mar 1858, Purcellville, apoplexy, 62-0-0, p. Nathaniel & Letitia Barker, b. Fairfax Co., c/o: Eli Bolon, sc: John W. Bolon, son, BVS:1858:5, LC:32

BOLON, Robert, W, M, d. 17 Jan 1854, res of mother, typhoid fever, 19-1-5, p. Wm. & Mary Ann Bolon, b. res, nr Goose Creek Meeting House, Clerk, sc: mother & T. Whitacre, BVS:1854:12, LC:12

BOLYN, Elsie, W, F, d. 3 Apr 1885, Philomont, bright's disease, 76-0-0, b. LC, unm, sc: F.L. Tavenner, friend, 3rd Dist., BVS:1885:6

BOLYN, Mary A., W, F, d. 15 Aug 1880, Lincoln, typhoid fever, 4-0-0, p. Somerfield & Sarah Bolyn, b. LC, sc: Somerfield Bolyn, father, 3rd Dist., BVS:1880:4

BOND, Asa M., W, M, d. 11 Nov 1878, Waterford, consumption, 73-10-0, p. Joseph & Elizabeth Bond, b. LC, farmer, c/o: Mary A. Bond, sc: T.H. Bond, son, JF Dist., BVS:1878:10

BOND, Sarah A., W, F, d. 28 Dec 1886, LC, general debility, 77-0-0, b. LC, c/o: Asa M. Bond, sc: Alice Bond, daughter, 3rd Dist., BVS:1886:4

BONDA, Roberta, B, F, d. 15 Apr 1896, LC, 5-0-0, sc: Noble Adams, no kin, LE Dist., BVS:1896:5

BOOTH, Millard F., W, M, d. 29 Jul 1853, LC, water on brain, 1-3-0, p. James & Sarah Booth, b. LC, sc: Jas Booth, father, BVS:1854:4, LC:2

BOOTH, Sarah, W, F, d. 29 Jun 1881, LC, paralysis, 68-9-27, p. Adam & --- Arnold, c/o: James Booth, sc: Wm. H. Booth, son, 2nd Dist., BVS:1881:6

BOSS, Josephine, B, F, d. Aor 1873, nr Paris, Fauq. Co., pneumonia, 0-1-0, p. James & Catherine Boss, b. nr Paris, sc: James Boss, father, MC Dist., BVS:1873:5

BOSS, Samuel M., W, M, d. 24 Aug 1872, Leesburg, dysentery, 74-4-20, p. Peter & Mary Boss, b. Pennsylvania, merchant, c/o: Elizabeth Boss, sc: Elizabeth Boss, consort, LE Dist., BVS:1872:3

BOSZELL, Elizabeth, W, F, d. 22 Aug 1856, Aldie, congestion of brain, 72-0-0, sc: T.M. Boyle, physician, BVS:1856:5, LC:23

BOWIE, Robert G., W, M, d. 11 Apr 1881, LC, congestion brain, 73-0-0, b. LC, farmer, c/o: Julia H. Bowie, sc: Allen W. Bowie, son, 3rd Dist., BVS:1881:4

BOWMAN, Flora, B, F, d. 15 Sep 1877, Middleburg, paralysis, 47-0-0, b. Frederick Co. VA, c/o: Henry J. Bowman, sc: Henry J. Bowman, husband, MC Dist., BVS:1877:5

BOWMAN, James, B, M, d. 22 Feb 1892, Aldie, la grippe, 78-0-0, p. unk, b. LC, laborer, c/o: Janine Bowman, sc: Janine Bowman, wife, 1st Dist., BVS:1892:4

BOWMAN, Lutie, B, F, d. 27 Mar 1892, Aldie, whooping cough, 1-0-10, p. Frank & Lavinia Bowman, b. Welbourne, unm, sc: Lavinia Bowman, mother, 1st Dist., BVS:1892:4

BOWMAN, Mary, B, F, d. 1 Nov 1874, res, Short Hill, consumption, 13-0-0, p. Ann Bowman (father dead), LV Dist., BVS:1874:6

[BOWMAN], no name, B, F, d. 14 Apr 1882, LC, unk, 0-0-21, p. James & Frankie Bowman, b. LC, sc: James Bowman, father, 1st Dist., BVS:1882:1

Loudoun County, Virginia, Death Register, 1853-1896   51

BOYD, Henry, (f), M, d. 24 Jul 1858, LC, intermittent fever, 18-10-13, p. Samuel & Eliza Boyd, b. LC, sc: Samuel Boyd, father, BVS:1858:1, LC:29

BOYD, Jonathan, B, M, d. Feb 1896, Paeonian Springs, tree fell on him, 68-0-0, farmer, consort, sc: Will Boyd, son, JF Dist., BVS:1896:10

BOYL, T. M., W, M, d. 1 Sep 1872, Aldie, dysentery, 63-0-0, physician, unm, MC Dist., BVS:1872:7

BOZELL, John W., W, M, d. 17 Oct 1856, Dover, putrid sore throat, 8-0-0, p. James & Mary F. Bozell, b. Goose Creek Meeting House, sc: James Bozell, father, BVS:1856:4, LC:22

BRABHAM, Elizabeth M., W, F, d. 1 Aug 1858, res of parents, dysentery, 1-6-0, p. Francis & Mary E. Brabham, b. Sycolin, sc: F. Brabham, father, BVS:1858:5, LC:32

BRABHAM, Mary T., W, F, d. 15 Jul 1853, on Goose Creek, dysentery, 0-11-3, p. Frank & Mary Brabham, b. LC, sc: father, BVS:1854:5, LC:5

[BRABHAM], no name, W, M, d. 23 Apr 1872, Mount Gilead Twp., unk, 0-0-25, p. F. M. & Mary E. Brabham, b. Mount Gilead Town, unm, sc: F.M. Brabham, father, MT Dist., BVS:1872:2

BRADEN, Carrie E., W, F, d. 16 Jul 1880, LC, inflammation womb, 36-0-0, p. R.G. & E.A. Braden, b. LC, c/o: Gabriel V. Braden, sc: G.V. Braden, husband, 3rd Dist., BVS:1880:4

BRADEN, Eliza A., W, F, d. 28 Dec 1878, nr Waterford, erysipelas, 62-11-0, p. Joseph & Elizabeth Braden, b. LC, c/o: Rodney Braden, sc: Gabriel Braden, son, JF Dist., BVS:1878:10

BRADEN, Noble S., W, M, d. 21 Aug 1853, LC, dysentery, 2-0-0, p. Noble S. & Mary A. Braden, b. LC, sc: Noble S. Braden, father, BVS:1854:3, LC:2

BRADFIELD, Elizabeth, W, F, d. 11 May 1859/60, Snickersville, consumption, 29-1-16, p. James & Mary Keen, b. Clarke, c/o: Francis M. Bradfield, sc: Francis M. Bradfield, husband, BVS:1859:3, 1860:1, LC:34

BRADFIELD, John K., W, M, d. 7 May 1859/60, Snickersville, 0-0-2, p. Francis M. & Elizabeth Bradfield, b. Snickersville, sc: Francis M. Bradfield, father, BVS:1859:3, 1860:1, LC:34

BRADFIELD, Lucinda, W, F, d. 10 Jan 1857, res of father, consumption, 40-0-0, p. Wm. & Elizth L. Bradfield, b. Snickersville, sc: William Bradfield, father, BVS:1857:4, LC:26

BRADFORD, Charles E., W, M, d. 7 Nov 1877, nr Daysville, burned to death, 3-0-21, p. Webster & Mary E. Bradford, b. nr Daysville, sc: Webster Bradford, father, BR Dist., BVS:1877:1

[BRADLEY], Cora Bell, W, F, d. 26 Aug 1865, Fauquier Co, 0-0-25, p. Geo W. & Sarah A. Bradley, b. Fauquier Co., sc: father, BVS:1865:1

BRADLEY, George W., W, M, d. 24 Sep 1886, tumor in throat, 62-0-0, p. J.H. & Mary Bradley, laborer, c/o: Sarah A. Bradley, sc: Sarah A. Bradley, wife, 2nd Dist., BVS:1886:5

BRADSHAW, Lydia J., W, F, d. 5 Mar 1885, nr Farmwell, old age, 85-0-0, p. Louis & Ann French, b. nr Farmwell, c/o: Louis Bradshaw, sc: Geo Bradshaw, son, 1st Dist., BVS:1885:3

[BRADSHAW], no name, W, , d. 15 Jul 1878, LC, fever, 0-6-5, p. Lewis F. & E. J. Bradshaw, b. LC, unm, sc: E.J. Bradshaw, mother, LE Dist., BVS:1878:9

BRADY, Daniel, B, M, d. Feb 1877, Hughes Mill, unk, p. Willie & Emily Brady, sc: Wm. Humphrey, friend, MT Dist., BVS:1877:2

BRADY, Lutie, W, F, d. Aug 1894, Round Hill, brain fever, 0-4-0, p. Thos. E. & Mattie Brady, b. Round Hill, sc: Thomas Brady, father, 3rd Dist., BVS:1894:5

BRADY, Mary E., W, F, d. Mar 1896, Paeonian Springs, unk, 36-0-0, p. Oscar Braden, JF Dist., BVS:1896:8

BRADY, no name, W, M, d. 24 Dec 1880, nr Leesburg, 0-0-3, p. Robert & Mary Brady, b. LC, unm, sc: Robert Brady, father, 2nd Dist., BVS:1880:6

BRAMHALL, Rebecca J., W, F, d. 15 Oct 1865, nr Lovettsville, bilious dysentery, 2-0-0, p. B.W. & R.J. Bramhall, b. nr Lovettsville, stone mason, unm, sc: Blanco Bramhall, father, BVS:1865:2/4

BRAMHALL, Viola R., W, F, d. 26 Nov 1879, nr Lovettsville, pneumonia, 1-2-0, p. Blanco W. & Rebecca Bramhall, b. LC, sc: Blanco W. Bamhall, father, 2nd Dist., BVS:1879:1

BRANCH, Henry, W, M, d. 18 Jul 1874, nr Waterford, cholera infantum, 0-4-22, p. H. & Melissa Branch, b. LC, sc: Rev. Henry Branch, father, JF Dist., BVS:1874:2

BRANDON, Louisa M., W, F, d. 14 Jul 1858, Union, unk, 42-0-0, p. James & Elizth Brandon, b. Nichols Old Mill, sc: Rebecca Brandon, sister, BVS:1858:3, LC:31

BRAWNER, Geo R., W, M, d. 24 Jan 1865, Aldie, consumption, 26-11-1, p. J.W. & Sarah Brawner, b. Aldie, teacher, unm, sc: Jas. W. Brawner, father, BVS:1865:2

BRAWNER, James W., W, M, d. 24 Jul 1877, Aldie, paralysis, 73-0-0, b. Georgetown, DC, saddler, c/o: Sarah Brawner, sc: B.P. Brawner, son, MC Dist., BVS:1877:5

BRAWNER, Mary Julia, W, F, d. 11 Nov 1876, Bloomfield, affection of the brain, 0-2-10, p. Wm. A. & Laura P. Brawner, b. LC, sc: Wm. A. Brawner, father, MC Dist., BVS:1876:4

BRAWNER, Willie Strother, W, M, d. 5 Aug 1878, nr Bloomfield, blood rupture, 0-0-10, p. Wm A. & Laura P. Brawner, b. Bloomfield, sc: Wm A. Brawner, father, MC Dist., BVS:1878:6

BRECKENRIDGE, Anna, W, F, d. 12 May 1879, Woodburn, unk, 0-0-3, p. Anna Breckenridge, b. LC, unm, sc: Anna Breckenridge, mother, 3rd Dist., BVS:1879:3

BRECKENRIDGE, Bessie L., W, F, d. 10 Sep 1886, LC, unk, 0-0-1, p. Saml. T. & Julia Breckenridge, b. LC, unm, sc: S.T. Breckenridge, father, 3rd Dist., BVS:1886:4

BRECKENRIDGE, Chas., W, M, d. 25 Dec 1893, Lucketts, unk, 4-0-0, p. Lemuel & Alberta, b. Lucketts, unm, sc: Lemuel Breckinridge, LE Dist., BVS:1893:6

BRECKINRIDGE, Russell, W, M, d. 1896, LC, marasmus, 0-5-0, p. S. K. & K. Breckinridge, b. Leesburg, sc: father, LE Dist., BVS:1896:5

BRENT, Ada, B, F, d. 10 Aug 1885, Lincoln, unk, 11-6-0, p. Washn. & Matilda Brent, b. LC, sc: Wash Brent, father, 3rd Dist., BVS:1885:6

BRENT, Barbara, B, F, d. 2 Apr 1880, LC, paralysis, 65-0-0, p. unk, b. LC, unm, sc: Benj. F. Hibbs, friend, 1st Dist., BVS:1880:1

BRENT, Fannie, B, F, d. 10 Apr 1886, nr Unison, pneumonia, 10-0-0, p. Grace Brent (unm), b. Mountville, laborer, unm, sc: Humphrey Thornton, uncle, 1st Dist., BVS:1886:1

BRENT, Howard, B, M, d. 30 Oct 1880, LC, consumption, 22-0-0, p. Jas. & Susan Brent, b. LC, farmer, unm, sc: James Brent, father, 1st Dist., BVS:1880:1

BRENT, Maria, B, F, d. 20 Mar 1871, pneumonia, 80-0-0, married, BR Dist., BVS:1871:3

BRENT, Martha, B, F, d. 2 Apr 1878, nr Bloomfield, scrofula, 13-0-0, p. Henry & Lucy Brent, b. Fauquier Co., sc: Henry Brent, father, MC Dist., BVS:1878:6

[BRENT], no name, B, M, d. 30 Oct 1866, Aldie, unk, 0-0-22, p. Nelly Brent, b. LC, sc: A.G. Davis, head of family, BVS:1866:3

BRENT, Oliver, B, M, d. 23 Dec 1871, 76-0-0, MC Dist., BVS:1871:2

BRENT, Rosetta, B, F, d. 1 Jan 1877, nr Clifton, scrofula, 16-0-0, p. Henry & Lucy Brent, b. Fauquier Co., unm, sc: Henry Brent, father, MC Dist., BVS:1877:5

BREUNER, child, W, F, d. 10 Jul 1873, Middleburg, still born, unk, p. J. E. & Fannie C. Breuner, b. Middleburg, sc: J.E. Breuner, father, MC Dist., BVS:1873:5

BREUNER, Frances C., W, F, d. 12 Jul 1873, Middleburg, inflammation of womb, 29-0-0, p. F. P. Crissey, b. Leesburg, c/o: J.E. Breuner, sc: J.E. Breuner, husband, MC Dist., BVS:1873:5

Loudoun County, Virginia, Death Register, 1853-1896   53

BREUNER, Lillian, W, M, d. 22 Feb 1880, LC, croup, 0-9-0, p. Jno. E. & J. M. Breuner, b. LC, unm, sc: Jno. E. Breuner, father, 1st Dist., BVS:1880:1

BREUT, Charity, B, F, d. Jun 1873, Middleburg, heart disease, 50-0-0, p. unk, b. unk, married, sc: Robert Bruet, son, MC Dist., BVS:1873:5

BREUT, Harriet, B, F, d. 17 Jan 1876, nr Clifton, scrofula, 21-0-0, p. Henry & Lucy Breut, b. LC, laborer, unm, sc: Henry Breut, father, MC Dist., BVS:1876:4

BREWER, Hampton R., W, M, d. 20 Dec 1884, LC, old age, 84-0-0, p. Geo. & Mary Brewer, b. Virginia, farmer, unm, 1st Dist., BVS:1884:1

BREWERD, George W., W, M, d. 20 Apr 1857, LC, consumption, 41-0-0, p. Edwd & Martha Brewerd, b. LC, laborer, c/o: Jane E. Brewerd, sc: John H. Brewerd, brother, BVS:1857:1, LC:25

BREWERD, Jane E., W, F, d. 15 Mar 1856, LC, consumption, 28-9-0, p. Wm. & Pleasant Stream, b. LC, c/o: George W. Brewerd, sc: Martha Brewerd, mother-in-law, BVS:1856:1, LC:20

BREWERD, Margaret P., W, F, d. 5 Oct 1856, LC, croup, 0-10-0, p. George W. & Jane E. Brewerd, b. LC, sc: Martha Brewerd, grandmother, BVS:1856:1, LC:20

BRICE, John, B, M, d. 15 Aug 1865, Geo L. Moore's, nr Wheatland, consumption, 35-0-0, p. Saml Brice, b. LC, laborer, unm, sc: Geo S. Moore, employer, BVS:1865:3/4

BRIDGES, Edna, W, F, d. 10 Sep 1883, nr Guilford, inflammatory rheumatism, 2-6-0, p. Benja. & Alice Bridges, b. nr Guilford, unm, sc: Benja Bridges, father, 1st Dist., BVS:1883:1

BRIDGES, Lucy E., W, F, d. 26 Oct 1892, nr Leesburg, whooping cough, 4-6-0, p. R. D. & M. E. Bridges, b. Leesburg, unm, sc: R.D. Bridges, LE Dist., BVS:1892:5

BRIDGES, Margaret A., W, F, d. 23 May 1857, consumption, 32-6-0, p. A.D. & Alice Lee, b. LC, sc: Hardage Bridges, husband, BVS:1857:7, LC:28

[BRIDGES], no name, W, M, d. 2 Dec 1855, unk, 0-0-8, p. Benj. & Lucy A. Bridges, b. LC, sc: B. Bridges, father, BVS:1855:8, LC:19

BRIDGES, William, W, M, d. 1857, unk, unk, BVS:1857:7, LC:28

BRISCO, William, B, M, d. 7 Apr 1888, LC, typhoid fever, 17-0-0, p. James & Charity Brisco, b. LC, laborer, unm, sc: James Briscoe, father, 3rd Dist., BVS:1888:1

BRISCOE, Virginia, B, F, d. 1 Mar 1872, Mount Gilead Twp., unk, 0-2-0, p. Jerry & Mary Brisco, b. Mount Gilead Town, unm, sc: Jerry Briscoe, father, MT Dist., BVS:1872:2

BRISCOE, Winnie, B, F, d. 22 Dec 1887, nr Mountville, old age, 74-0-0, p. Thomas & Nancy Swan, b. Fauquier Co., c/o: Adam Briscoe, sc: Harry Hunt, son-in-law, 1st Dist., BVS:1887:2

BRONAUGH, George W., W, M, d. 31 Oct 1857, Ludwell Luckett's, pneumonia, 52-0-0, p. Wm. & Jane Bronaugh, b. place of death, sc: G.F. Luckett, nephew, BVS:1857:5, LC:27

BRONAUGH, Henry, W, M, d. 10 Mar 1887, LC, consumption, 43-0-0, p. P. H. W. & Ella Bronaugh, b. LC, bank clerk, unm, sc: Ella Bronaugh, mother, 2nd Dist., BVS:1887:4

BROOK, Emily, B, F, d. 2 Oct 1891, Leesburg, inflammation, 34-0-0, p. unk, b. unk, c/o: John Brook, sc: husband, LE Dist., BVS:1891:4

BROOK, Sarah, W, F, d. 2 May 1878, Poor House, chronic diarrhea, 30-0-0, unm, sc: Wm. H. Hibbs, superintendant of poorhouse, MC Dist., BVS:1878:6

BROOKINS, Eliza, B, F, d. 2 Dec 1873, nr Corner Hall, consumption, 30-0-0, p. Caroline Manly, b. LC, c/o: John Brookins, sc: Thos. Manly, uncle, BR Dist., BVS:1873:1

BROOKS, Amada, B, F, d. 12 Aug 1874, nr Middleburg, spasms, 0-0-6, p. Philip & Lydia Brooks, b. LC, laborer, sc: Philip Brooks, father, MC Dist., BVS:1874:4

BROOKS, Catharine, B, F, d. 25 Feb 1896, Daysville, consumption, 28-0-0, b. LC, c/o: Wm. Brooks, sc: Wm.

Brooks, husband, BR Dist., BVS:1896:4

BROOKS, Charles T., W, M, d. 1 Aug 1887, LC, unk, 0-8-0, p. James & Mary Brooks, b. LC, none, unm, sc: James Brooks, father, 2nd Dist., BVS:1887:4

BROOKS, Frances, W, F, d. 25 Jun 1885, nr Goresville, dropsy, 59-0-0, p. --- & Nancy Brooks, b. LC, unm, sc: Columbus Brooks, brother, 2nd Dist., BVS:1885:1

BROOKS, Jas. H. Alexander, W, M, d. 7 Oct 1854, Broad Run, unk, 0-2-0, p. Mary Ann Brooks, b. on Broad Run, sc: mother, BVS:1854:12, LC:11

BROOKS, Lillian, W, F, d. 8 Sep 1883, Leesburg, intermittent fever, 1-0-13, p. Phillip & Annie E. Brooks, b. LC, sc: Philip Brooks, father, 2nd Dist., BVS:1883:6

BROOKS, Mary, W, F, d. 12 Oct 1865, old age, 90-0-0, widow, BVS:1865:1

BROOKS, Mary A. V., W, F, d. 24 Jul 1854, Waterford, water on brain, 0-1-2, p. Philip & Mary Brooks, b. Waterford, sc: Philip Brooks, father, BVS:1854:10, LC:9

BROOKS, Nancy, W, F, d. 10 Apr 1883, nr Leesburg, heart disease, 77-0-0, p. Elijah & Mary Brooks, b. LC, laborer, unm, sc: Frances Newman, daughter, 2nd Dist., BVS:1883:3

BROOKS, Philip, W, M, d. 1 Jul 1887, LC, consumption, 66-0-0, p. unk, b. LC, merchant, sc: William Brooks, son, 2nd Dist., BVS:1887:4

BROOKS, Phillip, B, M, d. 15 Sep 1876, Middleburg, pneumonia, 50-0-0, b. Maryland, laborer, c/o: Lydia Brooks, sc: Lydia Brooks, wife, MC Dist., BVS:1876:4

BROOKS, Wesley, W, M, d. 15 Oct 1881, LC, lock jaw, 74-0-0, p. Mary Brooks, laborer, unm, sc: B.F. Mathers, nephew, 2nd Dist., BVS:1881:6

BROSIUS, Hinton, B, , d. [1869], LC, old age, unk, b. LC, married, sc: wife, BVS:1869:1

BROWN, Abner, W, M, d. Oct 1858, res of parents, croup, 4-0-0, p. George N. & Juliet A. Brown, b. Wm. Seaton's Farm, sc: George N. Brown, father, BVS:1858:3, LC:31

BROWN, Ann, W, F, d. 10 Nov 1872, Woodgrove, typhoid fever, 12-7-2, p. Saml. & Permelia Brown, b. Woodgrove, sc: Samuel Brown, father, JF Dist., BVS:1872:1

BROWN, Ann, B, F, d. 4 Dec1875, Leesburg, dropsy, 72-0-0, c/o: Alfred Brown, sc: Mariah P?, daughter, LE Dist., BVS:1875:1

BROWN, Annett, B, F, d. 25 March 1875, Leesburg, cholera infantum, 0-3-0, p. Horace & Rose Brown, sc: Annett Elgin, grandmother, LE Dist., BVS:1875:1

BROWN, Annie, B, F, d. [1877], Hughesville, unk, sc: Washington Carter, friend, MT Dist., BVS:1877:2

BROWN, Asa, W, M, d. 15 Oct 1872, Waterford, consumption, 78-0-16, p. James Brown, b. LC, saddler, c/o: Jane Brown, sc: Jane Brown, wife, JF Dist., BVS:1872:1

BROWN, Benjamin, W, M, d. 6 Jul 1859/60, LC, affection of head, 74-0-0, p. unk, b. Berkley Co., c/o: Anna Brown, sc: Fielding Brown, son, BVS:1859:2, 1860:4, LC:37

BROWN, Benjamin, B, M, d. 23 Jan 1887, LC, spasms, 0-6-0, p. Horace & Amelia Brown, b. LC, none, unm, sc: Horace Brown, father, 2nd Dist., BVS:1887:4

BROWN, Bertha Lee, W, F, d. 20 Apr 1892, Hamilton, whooping cough, 0-19-0, p. J. Edwin & Gertrude A. Brown, b. Hamilton, sc: J.E. Brown, JF Dist., BVS:1892:7

BROWN, Catharine, W, F, d. 27 Apr 1874, Clifton, pneumonia, 2-0-20, p. Jas. W. & Martha J. Brown, b. LC, sc: James W. Brown, father, MC Dist., BVS:1874:4

BROWN, Easter, B, F, d. 1875, pneumonia, unk, b. Shenandoah Co., laborer, married, MT Dist., BVS:1875:8

BROWN, Edgar M., W, M, d. 19 Feb 1888, LC, typhoid fever, 31-0-0, p. Burr & Mary E. Brown, b. LC, farmer, c/o: Maggie Brown, sc: Maggie Brown, wife, 3rd Dist., BVS:1888:1

BROWN, Elizabeth C., W, F, d. 29 Jun 1857, Snickersville, cramp colic, 7-0-

Loudoun County, Virginia, Death Register, 1853-1896   55

0, p. Wm. & Rosetta Brown, b. Snickersville, sc: William Brown, father, BVS:1857:4, LC:26

BROWN, Emanuel, W, M, d. 9 Aug 1853, LC, unk, 46-10-0, p. David & Mary Brown, b. Warren Co., none, unm, sc: Wm. B. Steer, brother-in-law, BVS:1854:3, LC:2

BROWN, Emily, B, F, d. 3 Oct 1877, LC, dropsy, 50-0-0, p. Emly Cook, b. unk, sc: Ida Brown, friend, JF Dist., BVS:1877:3

BROWN, Ernest G., B, M, d. 25 May 1876, LC, consumption, 8-0-0, p. Jacob & Eliza Brown, b. LC, sc: Samuel Cheek, friend, LE Dist., BVS:1876:6

BROWN, J. Isaac, W, M, d. 11 Apr 1893, Falls Church, Fairfax Co., pneumonia, 45-0-0, p. Jonah & Alice Brown, b. LC, teacher, consort, sc: Sallie Brown, wife, MT Dist., BVS:1893:4

BROWN, James, W, M, d. 27 Feb 1857, Snickersville, consumption, 29-0-0, p. Wm. & Elizabeth Brown, b. Ireland, saddler, sc: William Brown, brother, BVS:1857:4, LC:26

BROWN, Janie, B, F, d. May 1896, Silcott Springs, consumption, 0-19-0, p. Lewis & Edith Brown, b. Silcott Springs, sc: Lewis Brown, father, MT Dist., BVS:1896:9

BROWN, John, B, M, d. 28 Oct 1878, LC, kicked by horse, 55-0-0, p. unk, b. LC, c/o: Matilda Brown, sc: Matilda Brown, wife, LE Dist., BVS:1878:8

BROWN, John V., W, M, d. 14 Mar 1892, Lucketts, old age, 87-0-0, p. unk, b. unk, farmer, consort, LE Dist., BVS:1892:5

BROWN, Jonah, W, M, d. 22 Aug 1853, Goose Creek Meeting House, cholera, 29-1-0, p. Isaac & Mariah Brown, b. LC, plasterer, c/o: Alice Brown, sc: mother, BVS:1854:2, LC:4

BROWN, Jonathan, W, M, d. 1 May 1882, LC, pneumonia, 60-1-11, p. Wm. & Sarah Brown, b. LC, farmer, unm, sc: ? Brown, brother, 3rd Dist., BVS:1882:3

BROWN, Julia A., B, F, d. 15 Dec 1880, LC, pneumonia, 68-0-0, p. unk, b. unk, unm, sc: Wm. Williams, friend, 3rd Dist., BVS:1880:4

BROWN, Katherine, W, F, d. 14 Dec 1896, Middleburg, diphtheria, 4-0-0, p. E. L. & Louise Brown, b. Middleburg, none, unm, sc: E.L. Brown, father, MC Dist., BVS:1896:1

BROWN, Larina, B, F, d. 8 Mar 1890, Hillsboro, unk, 0-3-0, p. W. & Jane Brown, b. LC, none, unm, sc: W. Brown, father, 3rd Dist., BVS:1890:6

BROWN, Latitia, B, F, d. Jun 1893, Falls Church, blood poison, 20-0-0, p. Allen & Mary J. Brown, b. LC, c/o: daughter, MT Dist., BVS:1893:4

BROWN, Laura, B, F, d. 16 Mar 1879, Silcott Springs, cholera infantum, 0-6-0, p. Allen & Sarah Brown, b. Silcott Springs, laborer, sc: Allen Brown, father, 3rd Dist., BVS:1879:3

BROWN, Maggie, B, F, d. 6 Sep 1885, nr Leesburg, summer complaint, 1-1-0, p. Horace & Amelia Brown, sc: Horace Brown, wife, 2nd Dist., BVS:1885:1

BROWN, Martha, W, F, d. 26 Mar 1872, Mount Gilead Twp., consumption, 50-0-0, p. Benjamin & Sarah Brown, b. Mount Gilead Town, unm, sc: J.B. Nixon, friend, MT Dist., BVS:1872:2

BROWN, Mary Ann, W, F, d. 5 Nov 1871, Circleville, consumption, 35-0-0, p. Joshua & Naoma Nichols, b. LC, farmer, c/o: Samuel A. Brown, sc: Samuel A. Brown, husband, MT Dist., BVS:1871:5

BROWN, Mary L., B, F, d. 6 Feb 1887, LC, whooping cough, 0-7-0, p. Newman & Jane Brown, b. LC, laborer, unm, sc: Newman Brown, father, 3rd Dist., BVS:1887:6

BROWN, Mercey E., W, F, d. 12 Sep 1872, nr Hillsboro, consumption, 57-8-12, p. Joseph Wells ?, b. LC, c/o: John Brown, sc: John Brown, husband, JF Dist., BVS:1872:1

BROWN, Michel, B, M, d. Oct 1873, Leesburg, insanity, 75-0-0, b. Leesburg, laborer, c/o: Alice Brown, sc: Richard Cross, friend, LE Dist., BVS:1873:2

BROWN, Morris Lee, W, M, d. 1 Jul 1889, LC, unk, 1-3-6, p. Luther A. Brown, b. LC, none, unm, sc: L.A.

Brown, head of family, 2nd Dist., BVS:1889:3

BROWN, Newman, B, M, d. 1 Feb 1887, LC, whooping cough, 11-0-0, p. Newman & Jane Brown, b. LC, laborer, unm, sc: Newman Brown, father, 3rd Dist., BVS:1887:6

[BROWN], no name, W, , d. 26 Dec 1871, Green Alden, 0-0-1, p. T. & J.F. Brown, MC Dist., BVS:1871:2

BROWN, no name,W, M, d. 10 Jun 1876, nr Bloomfield, milk crush, 0-7-0, p. Jas. W. & Eliza A. Brown, b. LC, sc: James W. Brown, father, MC Dist., BVS:1876:4

BROWN, no name, W, M, d. 1 Mar 1884, Philomont, pneumonia, 0-1-0, p. Lot T. & Bettie Brown, b. Virginia, unm, sc: Lot T. Brown, father, 3rd Dist., BVS:1884:6

BROWN, no name, B, F, d. 5 Mar 1888, nr Unison, still born, unk, p. Wm. & Mary E. Brown, b. Unison, sc: Wm. Brown, father, 1st Dist., BVS:1888:3

BROWN, no name, B, F, d. 21 Jul 1888, Unison, unk, unk, p. Wm. & Harriet Brown, b. Unison, sc: Wm. Brown, father, 1st Dist., BVS:1888:3

BROWN, no name, W, M, d. 9 Aug 1892, Mountville, unk, 0-10-0, p. Wm. & Annie Brown, b. Mountville, sc: Wm. Brown, father, 1st Dist., BVS:1892:1

BROWN, Richard, B, M, d. 5 Aug 1888, Poor House, pneumonia, 65-0-0, p. unk, b. LC, sc: F.E. Robey, superintendent of poor, 1st Dist., BVS:1888:3

BROWN, Rosa, B, F, d. 25 May 1875, Leesburg, 26-0-15, p. Daniel & Annett Elgin, c/o: Horace Brown, sc: Annett Elgin, mother, LE Dist., BVS:1875:1

BROWN, Sallie F., B, F, d. 19 Jun 1888, LC, consumption, 28-0-0, p. David & Francis Douglas, b. LC, none, c/o: John Brown, sc: William Douglas, father, 3rd Dist., BVS:1888:1

BROWN, Samuel, W, M, d. 27 May 1890, Farmwell, consumption, 74-0-0, p. John & Margaret Brown, b. LC, laborer, c/o: Pamelia A. Brown, sc: Pamelia A. Brown, wife, 1st Dist., BVS:1890:1

BROWN, Samuel B., W, M, d. 20 Dec 1890, Washington, DC, typhoid fever, 27-0-0, p. Isaac & C. Brown, b. LC, merchant, unm, sc: Isaac Brown, father, 3rd Dist., BVS:1890:6

BROWN, Samuel L., W, M, d. 15 Jan 1856, res of parents, bronchitis, 25-0-0, p. Craven & Maria Brown, b. Leesburg T. Pike, teacher, sc: Craven Brown, father, BVS:1856:6, LC:23

BROWN, Sarah, W, F, d. 4 Sep 1856, LC, old age, 94-5-0, p. Joseph & Sarah Cox, b. New Jersey, c/o: Richard Brown, sc: Richard Brown, son, BVS:1856:1, LC:20

BROWN, Sarah, B, F, d. 8 Apr 1873, Evergreen Mills, old age, 81-0-0, p. unk, b. Maryland, married, sc: John H. Brown, son, MC Dist., BVS:1873:5

BROWN, Sarah, W, F, d. 16 Apr 1877, LC, typhoid fever, 78-0-0, p. Wm. & Mary Piggott, b. LC, unm, sc: Jonathan Brown, brother, JF Dist., BVS:1877:3

BROWN, Sarah E., W, F, d. 17 Mar 1873, nr The Grove, consumption, 30-1-15, p. Richard & Rebecca White, b. nr The Grove, c/o: Benjamin Brown, sc: husband, MT Dist., BVS:1873:3

BROWN, Susan, W, F, d. 9 Jun 1877, LC, paralyzed, 80-0-0, p. unk, b. unk, sc: Eli Harris, friend, JF Dist., BVS:1877:3

BROWN, Susan, B, F, d. 19 Dec 1891, Middleburg, la grippe, 28-0-0, p. Jos. & Sarah Brown, b. LC, farmer, unm, sc: Jos Brown, head of family, 1st Dist., BVS:1891:1

BROWN, Susie M., W, F, d. 17 Mar 1891, Upperville, unk, unk, p. W. T. & Annie B. Brown, b. LC, miller, sc: W.T. Brown, father, 1st Dist., BVS:1891:2

BROWN, Walter, B, M, d. 20 Apr 1893, Hillsboro, blood poison, 1-6-0, p. Newman & Jane Brown, b. LC, miller, husband, JF Dist., BVS:1893:3

BROWN, William, W, M, d. 17 Feb 1876, Lime Kiln, tumor in the side, 68-0-0, b. LC, farmer, c/o: Mary Brown, sc: Geo. G. Utterback, son-in-law, MC Dist., BVS:1876:4

BRUIN, Melinda, W, F, d. 27 Mar 1892, Aldie, pneumonia, 43-0-0, p. Wm & Martha Bruin, b. Paris, unm, sc: D. Bruin, brother, 1st Dist., BVS:1892:1

BRUIN, Robt. H., W, M, d. 23 Jun 1884, LC, cholera, 0-1-21, p. Delancy & Martha Bruin, 1st Dist., BVS:1884:1

BRYANS, Minnie, B, F, d. 4 Feb 1879, Snickersville, congestion of brain, 0-4-0, p. Richd & Mary Bryans, b. Snickersville, laborer, sc: Rich'd Bryan, father, 3rd Dist., BVS:1879:3

BRYANT, Allice, B, F, d. 25 Dec 1891, Hughesville, dropsy, unk, p. unk, b. LC, wife, sc: Lee Bryant, MT Dist., BVS:1891:6

BRYANT, Annie, W, F, d. 16 Mar 1891, Paxson, old age, 70-0-0, p. Samuel Thornton, b. LC, consort, sc: Samuel Bryant, MT Dist., BVS:1891:6

BRYANT, Belle, B, F, d. 8 Feb 1884, Leesburg, consumption, 25-0-0, p. unknown, b. LC, laborer, unm, sc: Geo H. Russ, friend, 2nd Dist., BVS:1884:4

BRYANT, Bettie V., B, F, d. 8 Jun 1880, nr Leesburg, consumption, 13-11-20, p. George & Lucy Bryant, b. LC, sc: Lucy Bryant, mother, 2nd Dist., BVS:1880:6

BRYANT, Gabriel, B, M, d. 2 Aug 1872, LC, burnt to death, 11-0-0, p. Geo. & Lucy Bryant, b. LC, sc: Lucy Bryant, mother, LE Dist., BVS:1872:3

BRYANT, George, B, M, d. 12 Feb 1894, Oatlands, brain fever, 77-0-0, p. unk, b. unk, farmer, consort, sc: Wm. Mason, LE Dist., BVS:1894:3

BRYANT, Hester, B, F, d. 27 Jul 1883, nr Leesburg, consumption, 40-0-0, p. Bushrod & --- Buckman, b. LC, laborer, c/o: Bassil Bryant, sc: Bushrod Bryant, son, 2nd Dist., BVS:1883:3

BRYANT, Jane, B, F, d. [1869], LC, 3-0-0, p. Gregg & Patsy Bryant, b. LC, unm, sc: Gregg Bryant, father, BVS:1869:1

BRYANT, Lucy, B, F, d. 20 Dec 1890, LC, unk, 52-0-0, p. Margaret Johnson, b. LC, none, c/o: Geo Bryant, sc: Geo Bryant, husband, 2nd Dist., BVS:1890:5

BRYANT, Lucy, B, F, d. 10 Dec 1891, Oatlands, consumption, 52-0-0, p. unk, b. unk, consort, sc: daughter, LE Dist., BVS:1891:4

BRYANT, Nelley, B, F, d. Aug 1874, LC, old age, 104-0-0, widow, sc: Lucey Bryant, grandmother, LE Dist., BVS:1874:5

BRYANT, Nora, B, F, d. 26 Nov 1883, Leesburg, pneumonia, 2-9-9, p. Moses & Lucy Bryant, b. LC, sc: Moses Bryant, father, 2nd Dist., BVS:1883:6

BRYANT, Richard, B, M, d. 8 Jun 1883, Leesburg, consumption, 17-0-0, p. Bassil & Hester Bryant, b. LC, laborer, sc: Belle Bryant, sister, 2nd Dist., BVS:1883:6

BRYANT, Thomas, B, M, d. 23 Feb 1884, Leesburg, scrofula, 4-0-0, p. Belle Bryant (unm), b. LC, sc: Geo H. Russ, friend, 2nd Dist., BVS:1884:4

BUBB, Martha J., W, F, d. 20 Apr 1878, nr Guilford Station, consumption, 27-0-0, p. Frederic & Sarah Bubb, b. Pennsylvania, unm, sc: Frederick Bubb, father, BR Dist., BVS:1878:4

BUCHANAN, Robert, B, M, d. 21 Mar 1885, nr Leesburg, consumption, 66-0-0, p. Andrew & Fannie Buchanan, laborer, c/o: Mahala Buchanan, sc: Mahala Buchanan, wife, 2nd Dist., BVS:1885:1

BUCHANNAN, Elizabeth, B, F, d. 6 Jan 1890, nr Aldie, diphtheria, 9-0-0, p. Thornton & Nacy Buchanan, b. nr Aldie, unm, sc: Thornton Buchannan, father, 1st Dist., BVS:1890:1

BUCHANNAN, Fannie, B, F, d. Jan 1890, nr Aldie, diphtheria, 11-0-0, p. Thornton & Nancy Buchannan, b. nr Aldie, unm, sc: Thornton Buchannan, father, 1st Dist., BVS:1890:1

BUCHANNAN, Hellen, B, F, d. 10 Nov 1890, nr Aldie, consumption, 18-0-0, p. Ellen Buchannan (unm), b. nr Aldie, unm, sc: Robt Windsor, brother-in-law, 1st Dist., BVS:1890:1

BUCHANNAN, Mehala, B, F, d. 1 Sep 1888, nr Aldie, dropsy, 7-0-0, p. Fenton & Amy Buchannan, b. LC, sc: Fenton Buchannan, father, 1st Dist., BVS:1888:3

BUCKNER, Joanna, B, F, d. 4 Aug 1887, Middleburg, paralysis, 75-0-0, p. Peter & Peggy Bryant, b. Middleburg, unm, sc: Lee Murray, son-in-law, 1st Dist., BVS:1887:2

BUCKNER, Lucy, W, F, d. 6 Feb 1855, unk, 80-0-0, p. Bernard & Margt. Hooe, b. Prince William Co, sc: S. Ariss Buckner, son, BVS:1855:8, LC:19

BUCKNER, no name, B, M, d. 12 Feb 1890, Middleburg, unk, 0-0-2, p. Joseph & Amanda Buckner, b. Middleburg, sc: Joseph Buchner, father, 1st Dist., BVS:1890:1

BUCKNER, Robert, B, M, d. 15 Apr 1873, Middleburg, consumption, 18-0-0, p. Robt. & Joanna Buckner, b. Middleburg, laborer, unm, sc: Joanna Buckner, mother, MC Dist., BVS:1873:5

BUCKNER, Scipio, B, M, d. 28 May 1854, Poor House, old age, 80-0-0, laborer, sc: Wm. Furr, BVS:1854:11, LC:11

BUGGY, Patrick, W, M, d. 18 May1878, Poor House, paralysis, 72-0-0, b. Ireland, sc: Wm. H. Hibbs, superintendant of poorhouse, MC Dist., BVS:1878:6

BURCH, Chas., W, M, d. 30 Jul 1884, LC, catarrh fever, 0-11-0, p. Thos. F. & Helen Burch, unm, 1st Dist., BVS:1884:1

BURCH, Earnest, W, M, d. Sep 1873, LC, whooping cough, 8-0-0, p. John L. & Margret Burch, b. LC, unm, sc: J.L. Burch, father, LE Dist., BVS:1873:2

BURCH, Maria, W, F, d. 17 Jan 1880, LC, diphtheria, 6-0-0, p. Thomas F. & Helen A. Burch, b. LC, unm, sc: Thomas F. Burch, father, 1st Dist., BVS:1880:1

BURCH, Martena, W, F, d. 1 Mar 1876, nr Mt. Hope Church, pneumonia, 62-0-0, p. unk, b. LC, c/o: L.D. Burch, sc: A.T. Franklin, head of family, BR Dist., BVS:1876:2

[BURCH], no name, W, M, d. 27 Sep 1872, Leesburg, unk, 0-0-1, p. Thos. & Helen Burch, b. Leesburg, sc: Thomas F. Burch, father, LE Dist., BVS:1872:3

BURCH, Thomas, W, M, d. 14 Feb 1884, nr Leesburg, paralysis, 65-0-0, p. unknown, b. LC, farmer, c/o: Lucinda J. Burch, sc: Lucinda J. Burch, wife, 2nd Dist., BVS:1884:4

BURGESS, Lydia J., W, F, d. 12 Feb 1888, nr Farmwell, consumption, 28-0-0, p. Jas W. & Jane Frame, b. Farmwell, c/o: Wm. F. Burgess, sc: Wm. F. Burgess, husband, 1st Dist., BVS:1888:3

BURGESS, Penelope S., W, F, d. 22 Sep 1881, Farmwell, child bed, 23-0-0, b. LC, c/o: Wm F. Burgess, sc: W.F. Burgess, husband, 1st Dist., BVS:1881:1

BURGESS, William, W, M, d. 25 Mar 1880, Leesburg, pneumonia, 64-10-24, p. Wm. & ___ Burgess, b. LC, farmer, c/o: Martha A. Burgess, sc: Martha A. Burgess, wife, 2nd Dist., BVS:1880:6

BURGESS, Wm. F., W, M, d. 20 Jan 1894, Ryan, consumption, 39-11-0, p. Louiza Burgess, b. LC, laborer, c/o: Rachael Burgess, sc: Rachael Burgess, wife, 1st Dist., BVS:1894:1

BURGESS, Wm. L., W, M, d. 3 Feb 1874, Broad Run Dist., whooping cough, 0-11-7, p. Chas. & Mary E. Burgess, b. LC, sc: Chas. Burgess, father, BR Dist., BVS:1874:3

BURKE, Amanda, B, F, d. 1 Oct 1880, Leesburg, consumption, 11-9-0, p. Charles & Hester Burke, b. LC, sc: Lucy Brooks, sister, 2nd Dist., BVS:1880:6

BURKE, James, W, M, d. 18 Jun 1857, Phebe Ewers', pulmonary, 72-2-3, b. Maryland, shoemaker, c/o: Sarah Burke, sc: Phebe Ewers, BVS:1857:3, LC:26

BURKE, Martha F., (f), F, d. 28 Aug 1855, Wm. Wilkinson's, gastric fever, 0-7-0, p. Jno. & Eliz. Burke, b. Wm. Wilkinson's, sc: Eliz. Burke, mother, BVS:1855:5, LC:17

BURKE, Mary M., W, F, d. 20 Jan 1886, acute pneumonia, 43-0-0, p. Absalom & Louise Johnson, c/o: Richard S. Burke, sc: Richd. S. Burke, husband, 2nd Dist., BVS:1886:5

BURKE, [no name], B, F, d. Apr 1875, Forrest Mills, spinal disease, 0-0-21, p. Cornelius & Margaret Burke, b. LC, laborer, unm, sc: Cornelius Burke, father, MT Dist., BVS:1875:8
BURKE, Orra B., W, F, d. 7 Sep 1854, LC, inflammation of brain, 0-10-7, p. Josiah D. & Lucinda Burke, b. LC, sc: Josiah D. Burke, father, BVS:1854:8, LC:7
BURKE, Richard S., W, M, d. 22 Apr 1858, Leesburg, kidney affection, 50-4-2, p. Benjamin & Mildred Burke, b. Fairfax, merchant, c/o: Mary A. Burke, sc: Mary A. Burke, wife, BVS:1858:2, LC:30
BURKETT, John, W, M, d. 14 Nov 1854, Hillsboro, congestion of brain, 56-0-0, b. Frederick nr Winchester, tailor, c/o: Mary Burkett, sc: widow, BVS:1854:12, LC:12
BURR, Jane E., W, F, d. 5 Dec 1888, Sterling, pneumonia, 64-0-0, p. Nicholas & Jane Farr, b. Sterling, c/o: John R. Burr, sc: John R. Burr, husband, 1st Dist., BVS:1888:3
BURR, Mary Ann, W, F, d. 25 Aug 1856, LC, whooping cough, 1-10-0, b. LC, sc: Jane E. Burr, mother, BVS:1856:7, LC:24
BURSON, Beulah, W, F, d. 15 Oct 1881, nr Guilford, diphtheria, 2-6-0, p. Chas N. & Ann C. Burson, b. LC, sc: Dr. Leith, physician, 1st Dist., BVS:1881:1
BUSH, Beni, B, F, d. 12 Oct 1887, LC, heart disease, 27-0-0, p. Henson & M. A. Simpson, none, unm, sc: Henson Simpson, father, 3rd Dist., BVS:1887:7
BUSH, Noah, B, M, d. 20 Oct 1875, Guilford, intermittent fever, 19-0-0, p. Rosanna Bush, b. nr Guilford, laborer, unm, sc: Wm. Bush, head of family, BR Dist., BVS:1875:5
BUSH, Sarah, B, F, d. 10 Apr 1885, nr Guilford, old age, 102-0-0, p. Daniel & Kate Bush, b. nr Guilford, sc: Wm. Bush, son, 1st Dist., BVS:1885:3
BUSH, Stephen, B, M, d. 7 Feb 1876, nr Waterford, cancer, 91-0-0, laborer, widower, sc: Alice Wenner, daughter, LV Dist., BVS:1876:3
BUSHROD, Jas. E., B, M, d. 15 Jul 1892, Dover, diphtheria, 7-3-0, p. Henry Bushrod, b. Dover, sc: Ida Bushrod, mother, 1st Dist., BVS:1892:4
BUSHROD, Lizzie, B, F, d. 5 Sep 1892, Dover, diphtheria, 3-2-0, p. Henry Bushrod, b. Dover, sc: Ida Bushrod, mother, 1st Dist., BVS:1892:4
BUSHROD, Tucker, B, M, d. 10 Mar 1888, Dover, pneumonia, 2-0-0, p. Henry & Ida Bushrod, b. Dover, sc: Henry Bushrod, father, 1st Dist., BVS:1888:3
BUSSARD, Louisa, W, F, d. 7 Oct 1886, LC, consumption, 33-0-0, b. LC, c/o: O.M. Bussard, sc: O.M. Bussard, husband, 3rd Dist., BVS:1886:4
BUTCHER, Mary, W, F, d. 3 Aug 1856, res, tumor, 58-0-0, p. Hezekiah & Sarah Glasscock, b. Fauquier Co., c/o: John H. Butcher, sc: J.H. Butcher, widower, BVS:1856:4, LC:22
BUTLER, Charles, B, M, d. 15 Dec 1886, Middleburg, old age, 83-0-0, p. Lemuel & Fannie Butler, b. Prince William Co, laborer, c/o: Millie Butler, sc: Millie Butler, wife, 1st Dist., BVS:1886:1
BUTLER, Elizabeth, W, F, d. 16 Jan 1873, Maryland, pneumonia, 68-0-0, p. unk, b. Maryland, married, sc: Chas. M. Butler, head of family, BR Dist., BVS:1873:1
BUTLER, Hannah, (f), F, d. 7 Jan 1856, Poor House, suddenly, 80-0-0, b. Leesburg, sc: steward, BVS:1856:4, LC:22
BUTLER, Harrison, B, M, d. 10 May 1874, Wheatland, fever, 60-0-0, p. unk, b. unk, laborer, c/o: Ann Butler, sc: Ann Butler, wife, JF Dist., BVS:1874:2
BUTLER, Julia A., B, F, d. 1 Sep 1887, LC, dropsy, 63-0-0, b. LC, none, c/o: Harrison Butler, sc: Wm. Butler, son, 3rd Dist., BVS:1887:6
BUTLER, Mary F., W, F, d. 7 March 1875, LC, pneumonia, 47-0-0, sc: Jno. S. Cornwell, friend, LE Dist., BVS:1875:1
BUTLER, Sarah, W, F, d. 29 Nov 1853, Upperville, measles, 36-0-0, p. James & Sarah Hamilton, b. Frederick Co., c/o: Jno. Butler, sc: husband, BVS:1854:1, LC:4

BUTTS, Ann Rebecca, W, F, d. Mar 1876, nr Lovettsville, consumption, 22-0-0, b. Washington Co, VA, c/o: Franklin P. Butts, sc: Isaac Butts, father-in-law, LV Dist., BVS:1876:3

BUTTS, John, B, M, d. 6 Sep 1889, Philomont, hemorrhage, 56-0-0, p. unk, b. LC, unk, sc: F.E. Robey, superintendent of poor, 1st Dist., BVS:1889:1

BUTTS, Mary J., W, F, d. 2 Feb 1890, LC, la grippe, 68-8-0, p. Isaac B. & Elizabeth Wells, b. LC, none, c/o: O.S. Butts, sc: O.S. Butts, husband, 2nd Dist., BVS:1890:3

[BUTTS], no name, B, , d. 11 Apr 1877, LC, water on brain, 0-0-3, p. Taylor & Virginia Butts, sc: Taylor Butts, father, LE Dist., BVS:1877:8

BUTTS, Sarah Ann, W, F, d. 20 Feb 1865, nr Hillsboro, typhoid fever, 48-0-0, p. Wm. & Margarett Butts, b. LC, blacksmith, unm, sc: Wm Butts, father, 1st Dist., BVS:1865:2/4

BUTTS, Susan J., W, F, d. 10 Oct 1855, LC, unk, 0-11-16, p. Chas. W. & Mary E. Butts, b. LC, sc: Chas. W. Butts, father, BVS:1855:3, LC:15

BYRD, James, (f), M, d. 5 Sep 1854, LC, unk, 55-0-0, p. unk, b. Richmond City, laborer, c/o: Emily A. Byrd, sc: Loretta Carnes, neighbor, BVS:1854:8, LC:7

BYRNE, Frances, W, F, d. 30 Jul 1853, nr Middleburg, consumption, 30-0-0, p. Ralph & Catharine Murray, b. Fauquier Co., c/o: Chas. Byrne, sc: mother-in-law, BVS:1854:1, LC:4

BYRNE, John F., W, M, d. 30 Jan 1866, Annandale, influenza, 0-7-0, p. A. C. & E. F. Byrne, b. Annandale, sc: father, BVS:1866:2

[BYRON], Asbury H., W, M, d. Jun 1865, nr Aldie, diphtheria, 11-0-0, p. Geo & Jane Byron, b. nr Aldie, sc: father, BVS:1865:1

[BYRON], Catie, W, F, d. Jun 1865, nr Aldie, diphtheria, 6-0-0, p. Geo & Jane Byron, b. nr Aldie, sc: father, BVS:1865:1

[BYRON], Georgia F., W, F, d. Jun 1865, nr Aldie, diphtheria, 8-0-0, p. Geo & Jane Byron, b. nr Aldie, sc: father, BVS:1865:1

BYWATERS, Annie J., W, F, d. 15 Jan 1887, Aldie, dyspepsia, 37-0-0, p. J. P. & D. Bywaters, b. Ohio, unm, sc: Milton McVeigh, step-father, 1st Dist., BVS:1887:2

CALAHAN, David P., W, M, d. 15 Aug 1890, Snickersville, grip, 23-0-0, p. Geo. & Margaret Calahan, b. LC, laborer, unm, sc: Geo Calahan, father, 3rd Dist., BVS:1890:6

CALDWELL, Augusta, W, F, d. 26 Mar 1857, Purcellville, typhoid fever, 17-0-0, p. S.B.T. & Mary Caldwell, b. Mulberry Grove, sc: S.B.T. Caldwell, father, BVS:1857:3, LC:26

CALLAHAN, William E., W, M, d. 24 Feb 1880, Lincoln, unk, 0-4-0, p. Saml. S. & Emma Callahan, b. LC, sc: Saml S. Callahan, father, 3rd Dist., BVS:1880:4

CAMERON, Thos., W, M, d. 25 Jan 1853, Poor House, old age, 75-0-0, p. unk, b. unk, farmer, c/o: Mary Cameron, sc: Wm. Furr, keeper of poor house, BVS:1854:6, LC:6

CAMP, Ada B., W, F, d. 13 Oct 1871, Hillsboro, diphtheria, 1-5-7, p. Thos E. & ___ Camp, b. nr Hillsboro, sc: T.E. Camp, father, JF Dist., BVS:1871:1

CAMP, Mary G., W, F, d. 28 Sep 1871, nr Hillsboro, diphtheria, 3-2-17, p. Thos E. & ___ Camp, b. nr Hillsboro, sc: T.E. Camp, father, JF Dist., BVS:1871:1

CAMP, Sarah, W, F, d. no date, Hillsboro, unk, 77-0-0, sc: T.E. Camp, son, JF Dist., BVS:1871:1

CAMPBELL, Carrie, B, F, d. 26 Dec 1896, nr Unison, consumption, 21-0-0, p. Marshall & Ann Campbell, b. nr Unison, none, unm, sc: Marshall Campbell, father, MC Dist., BVS:1896:1

CAMPBELL, Flavius, W, M, d. 15 Aug 1853, LC, dysentery, 2-0-0, p. Robt & Martha Campbell, b. LC, sc: Robt Campbell, father, BVS:1854:3, LC:1

CAMPBELL, Hatty, W, F, d. 15 Jul 1853, LC, unk, 0-1-15, p. Joseph & Ruth Campbell, b. Fauquier Co., sc: Joseph Campbell, father, BVS:1854:3, LC:1

CAMPBELL, Henry, W, M, d. 8 Nov 1855, LC, dissipation, 42-0-0, p. Jos. & Margt. Campbell, b. LC, shoemaker, c/o: Amelia A.

Loudoun County, Virginia, Death Register, 1853-1896　　61

Campbell, sc: Amelia A. Campbell, wife, BVS:1855:3, LC:15

CAMPBELL, Maria J., B, F, d. 8 Aug 1893, Leesburg, diphtheria, 7-0-0, p. Joseph & Lavinia, b. Leesburg, unm, sc: father, LE Dist., BVS:1893:7

CAMPBELL, Mary E., W, F, d. 14 Mar 1858, LC, typhoid fever, 4-6-0, p. Henry & Amelia A. Campbell, b. LC, sc: Amelia A. Campbell, mother, BVS:1858:1, LC:29

CAMPBELL, Ruth, W, F, d. 1 Jul 1853, LC, unk, 27-0-0, p. Elkanah & Sally Thompson, b. Fairfax, c/o: Joseph Campbell, sc: Joseph Campbell, husband, BVS:1854:3, LC:1

CAMPBELL, Sarah, W, F, d. 25 Nov 1893, Lucketts, consumption, 33-0-0, p. unk, b. Lucketts, consort, sc: B.F. Campbell, LE Dist., BVS:1893:6

CAMPBELL, Viola M., W, F, d. 17 Jul 1884, nr Leesburg, unk, 0-2-9, p. Benj. F. & Sarah P. Campbell, b. LC, sc: Benj. F. Campbell, father, 2nd Dist., BVS:1884:4

CANADA, Milly, B, F, d. 28 Jun 1880, LC, dropsy of heart, 80-0-0, p. unk, b. LC, c/o: Clem Canada, sc: Clem Canada, husband, 1st Dist., BVS:1880:1

CARLISLE, Emily, W, F, d. 10 Mar 1882, LC, hernia, 57-0-0, p. unk, b. LC, c/o: James Carlisle, sc: James Carlisle, husband, 3rd Dist., BVS:1882:3

CARLISLE, Ethel, W, F, d. 11 Dec 1890, Paxson, strangled, 0-0-1, p. James & Susan Carlisle, b. LC, unm, sc: James Carlisle, father, 3rd Dist., BVS:1890:6

CARLISLE, John H., W, M, d. 6 Aug 1889, LC, cholera infantum, 9-0-2, p. Thos. M. & Mary C. Carlisle, b. LC, none, unm, sc: John M. Carlisle, head of family, 2nd Dist., BVS:1889:3

CARLL, Cornelia C., W, F, d. 14 Sep 1864, Langolen, dysentery, 1-2-0, p. Jno & Cornelia Carll, b. Clarke Co., VA, sc: John Carll, father, BVS:1864:1, LC:38

CARNES, Daniel, W, M, d. 13 Mar 1896, Lovettsville, pneumonia, 79-0-0, p. unk, b. unk, farmer, c/o: Elizabeth Carnes, sc: Elizabeth Carnes, consort, LV Dist., BVS:1896:7

CARNES, Jacob, W, M, d. 20 May 1854, Poor House, dropsy, 82-0-0, b. Maryland, Frederick, chair maker, widower, sc: Wm. Furr, BVS:1854:11, LC:11

CARNES, Marrietta, W, F, d. 1 Sep 1865, Taylorstown, child birth, 24-0-0, p. Henry & Cathn Spring, b. nr Taylorstown, carpenter, c/o: A.E. Carnes, sc: A.E. Carnes, husband, BVS:1865:3/5

CARNES, Silas C., W, M, d. 17 Nov 1866, E side of Ketoctin Mountain, rheumatism, 12-0-0, p. Samuel L. & Sarah M. Carnes, b. LC, laborer, sc: Saml. Carnes, father, BVS:1866:1

CARNES, Susan E., W, F, d. 27 Aug 1878, LC, dropsy, 28-0-0, p. Peter & Sarah Carnes, b. LC, unm, sc: Sarah Carnes, mother, LE Dist., BVS:1878:8

CARPENTER, Etta M., W, F, d. 3 Sep 1892, Hillsboro, diabetes, 21-0-0, p. Geo. W. & Delight Smith, b. New York, wife, sc: C.L. Carpenter, JF Dist., BVS:1892:7

CARPENTER, John, W, M, d. 19 Feb 1854, nr Union, chronic affection, 60-0-0, p. Wm. Carpenter, farmer, c/o: Mary Carpenter, sc: John Keen, nephew, BVS:1854:11, LC:11

CARR, Isaac, W, M, d. 27 Jun 1883, nr Leesburg, old age, 80-0-0, b. LC, farmer, unm, sc: Jas M. Kettle, nephew, 2nd Dist., BVS:1883:6

CARR, Martha A., W, F, d. 15 Mar 1893, Leesburg, old age, 78-0-0, p. unk, b. Leesburg, consort, sc: Thos. G. Elgin, LE Dist., BVS:1893:6

CARR, Mollie, W, F, d. 30 Apr 1885, nr Leesburg, cramp colic, 28-0-0, b. Virginia, c/o: John C. Carr, sc: Jno C. Carr, husband, 3rd Dist., BVS:1885:6

CARR, William, W, M, d. 3 Oct 1855, LC, old age, 84-9-0, p. Peter & Rachel Carr, b. LC, unm, sc: David Carr, son, BVS:1855:3, LC:15

CARRINGTON, no name, B, M, d. 6 Dec 1883, nr Leesburg, consumption, 1-7-0, p. Virginia Carrington, b. LC, sc: Hilleary Carington, father, 2nd Dist., BVS:1883:3

CARRINGTON, no name, B, M, d. 20 May 1893, Aldie, still born, p. Jno. &

Martha Carrington, b. Aldie, laborer, sc: Jno Carrington, father, 1st Dist., BVS:1893:2

CARROLL, John, W, M, d. 15 May 1896, nr Upperville, paralysis, 60-0-0, p. unk, b. nr Upperville, farmer, consort, sc: Nimrod Clems, son-in-law, MC Dist., BVS:1896:1

CARRUTHERS, Carrie M., W, F, d. 17 Nov 1882, LC, diphtheria, 7-9-0, p. Thos. & Virga. Carruthers, b. LC, unm, sc: Thos E. Carruthers, parent, 3rd Dist., BVS:1882:3

CARRUTHERS, Gertrude, W, F, d. 26 Nov 1882, LC, diphtheria, 4-1-26, p. Thos. & Virga. Carruthers, b. LC, unm, sc: Thos E. Carruthers, parent, 3rd Dist., BVS:1882:3

CARRUTHERS, John, W, M, d. 20 Aug 1884, Clarkes Gap, consumption, 71-6-12, b. Virginia, farmer, c/o: Malinda Carruthers, sc: Malinda Carruthers, wife, 3rd Dist., BVS:1884:6

CARRUTHERS, John G., W, M, d. 7 Dec 1887, Aldie, whooping cough, 0-1-23, p. Joel & Sarah F. Carruthers, b. Aldie, sc: Joel Carruthers, father, 1st Dist., BVS:1887:2

CARRUTHERS, Virginia L., W, F, d. 5 Nov 1882, LC, diphtheria, 8-9-2, p. Thos. & Virga. Carruthers, b. LC, unm, sc: Thos E. Carruthers, parent, 3rd Dist., BVS:1882:3

CARSON, Jacob, W, M, d. 3 Sep 1896, LC, suicide, 73-0-0, b. Maryland, farmer, husband, sc: wife, LE Dist., BVS:1896:5

CARSON, James H., W, M, d. 13 Jan 1884, Leesburg, kidney affection, 75-11-2, p. Simon & Martha Carson, b. Frederick Co. VA, farmer, c/o: Catharine Carson, sc: Catharine Carson, wife, 2nd Dist., BVS:1884:4

CARSON, Mary R., W, F, d. 3 Jan 1892, Lucketts, pneumonia, 33-0-0, p. Jacob & Eliz. Carson, b. Lucketts, unm, sc: Jacob Carson, LE Dist., BVS:1892:5

[CARSON], no name, W, F, d. 17 Jul 1872, LC, unk, 0-0-20, p. Jacob & Elizabeth Carson, b. LC, sc: Elizabeth Carson, mother, LE Dist., BVS:1872:3

CARTER, Alfred N., W, M, d. 14 Aug 1890, Bloomfield, bright's disease, 70-0-0, p. Richard & Devie Carter, b. LC, farmer, unm, sc: Thos J. Littleton, nephew, 1st Dist., BVS:1890:1

CARTER, Amanda A., W, F, d. Apr 1873, nr Millville, consumption, 40-0-0, p. James A. Carter, b. LC, unm, sc: James Carter, father, MC Dist., BVS:1873:5

CARTER, Amanda A., W, F, d. 10 May 1872, nr Herald's Ship, consumption, 35-0-0, p. James G. & Jemiah Carter, MC Dist., BVS:1872:7

CARTER, Annie, B, F, d. 27 Oct 1878, LC, cholera infantum, 1-6-0, p. Sallie Carter, b. LC, unm, sc: Sallie Carter, mother, LE Dist., BVS:1878:8

CARTER, Catharine, W, F, d. 30 Dec 1888, Aldie, old age, 84-0-0, p. Wm. & Cecil Copen, b. LC, c/o: Wm. B. Carter, sc: Wm. B. Carter, husband, 1st Dist., BVS:1888:3

CARTER, Charles, B, M, d. 1 Oct 1891, nr Lovettsville, old age, 80-0-0, p. unk, b. unk, laborer, unm, sc: nephew, LV Dist., BVS:1891:5

CARTER, Cordelia, W, F, d. 15 Feb 1886, Mountville, old age, 73-0-0, p. John & Sarah Abell, b. LC, unk, sc: Joseph Bolen, son-in-law, 1st Dist., BVS:1886:1

CARTER, Courtney Newton, W, F, d. 12 May 1865, Woodland farm, diphtheria, 7-2-18, p. E.L. & M.L. Carter, b. Woodland Farm, unm, sc: E.L. Carter, father, BVS:1865:2

CARTER, Deborah, W, F, d. 11 Sep 1854, res, nr Bloomfield, apoplexy, 70-0-4, p. Wm. & Margaret Newlon, b. Berkley County, c/o: Richard Carter, sc: husband & son, BVS:1854:12, LC:12

CARTER, Dilwin S., W, M, d. 11 Jun 1864, Louisa Co., killed in battle, 21-0-0, p. J.S. & Jemima Carter, b. Millville, soldier, sc: Jas S. Carter, father, BVS:1864:1, LC:38

CARTER, Edward L., W, M, d. 12 Aug 1871, kidney disease, 60-0-0, farmer, married, BR Dist., BVS:1871:3

CARTER, Ema, B, F, d. Sep 1873, Leesburg, consumption, 62-0-0, b.

Loudoun County, Virginia, Death Register, 1853-1896   63

LC, laborer, unm, sc: Matthew Lucket, friend, LE Dist., BVS:1873:2
CARTER, Emma L., W, F, d. 15 May 1865, Woodland farm, diphtheria, 6-0-0, p. E.L. & M.L. Carter, b. Woodland Farm, unm, sc: E.L. Carter, father, BVS:1865:2
CARTER, Fannie, B, F, d. Aug 1873, nr Unison, bite of a dog, 45-0-0, p. unk, b. Rappahannock, c/o: Harrison Carter, sc: Edward Carter, grandson, MC Dist., BVS:1873:5
CARTER, Henry, W, M, d. 3 Mar 1883, nr Lovettsville, paralysis, 73-0-0, p. Richard & Deborah Carter, b. LC, farmer, c/o: Mary Carter, sc: Thos W. Carter, son, 2nd Dist., BVS:1883:3
CARTER, Henry Arthur, W, M, d. 17 May 1857, res of parents, putrid sore throat, 4-0-14, p. B.F. & Rebecca M. Carter, b. place of death, sc: R.M. Carter, mother, BVS:1857:5, LC:27
CARTER, Herbert R., W, M, d. 2 Apr 1857, res of father, putrid sore throat, 3-9-19, p. John R. & Maria E. Carter, b. place of death, sc: J.R. Carter, father, BVS:1857:5, LC:27
CARTER, James, W, M, d. 6 Aug 1882, LC, old age, 88-0-0, p. James & Mary Carter, farmer, widower, sc: Fannie Carter, daughter, 1st Dist., BVS:1882:1
CARTER, Jesse, B, M, d. 13 Dec 1896, nr Unison, unk, 75-0-0, p. unk, b. unk, none, unm, sc: F.E. Robey, head of house, MC Dist., BVS:1896:1
CARTER, John W., W, M, d. Feb 1871, LC, 0-2-15, p. N.T. & Margaret Carter, b. LC, unm, LE Dist., BVS:1871:4
CARTER, Juliet N., W, F, d. 18 May 1865, Woodland farm, diphtheria, 3-0-0, p. E.L. & M.L. Carter, b. Woodland Farm, unm, sc: E.L. Carter, father, BVS:1865:2
CARTER, Landon, W, M, d. 31 Jul 1858, LC, old age, 87-0-0, p. John & Jane Cockerille[sic], b. LC, sc: Edward L. Carter, son, BVS:1858:6, LC:33
CARTER, Landon W, M, d. 1 Jun 1872, 1-6-0, p. Richard W. & Sophia Carter, MC Dist., BVS:1872:7

CARTER, Madie, W, F, d. 15 Dec 1896, Aldie, consumption, 26-0-0, p. M. & S. B. Carter, b. Aldie, none, unm, sc: M. Carter, father, MC Dist., BVS:1896:1
CARTER, Margaret, W, F, d. 5 Dec 1887, LC, consumption, 27-0-0, p. Thomas & Margaret Green, b. LC, none, c/o: Burr Carter, sc: Thomas Green, father, 2nd Dist., BVS:1887:4
CARTER, Martha, (f), F, d. Mar 1857, B.W. Skillman's, typhoid fever, 30-0-0, sc: B.W. Skillman, employer, BVS:1857:5, LC:28
CARTER, Mary E., W, M, d. 23 Apr 1857, putrid sore throat, 5-4-26, p. John R. & Maria E. Carter, b. place of death, sc: J.R. Carter, father, BVS:1857:5, LC:27
[CARTER], Natalie B., W, F, d. 16 Nov 1854, Meadow View, dysentery, 2-6-0, p. Addison B. & Lucy G. Carter, b. Winchester, sc: father & mother, BVS:1854:11, LC:11
CARTER, Nettie M., W, F, d. 1 Dec 1887, LC, consumption, 0-11-0, p. Burr F. & Margaret Carter, b. LC, none, unm, sc: Thomas Green, grandfather, 2nd Dist., BVS:1887:4
[CARTER], no name, (f), F, d. Feb 1854, John Cockerill's, 0-0-1, p. Martha Carter, sc: mother, BVS:1854:12, LC:12
CARTER, no name,W, M, d. 6 Jun 1876, nr Mountville, from a fall, 0-0-1, p. Jno & Emily M. Carter, b. LC, sc: Jno. Carter, father, MC Dist., BVS:1876:4
CARTER, Rebecca, W, F, d. 20 Dec 1896, nr Middleburg, old age, 80-0-0, p. unk, b. unk, housekeeper, consort, sc: B.F. Carter, son, MC Dist., BVS:1896:1
CARTER, Richard, W, M, d. 5 Oct 1866, nr Bloomfield, jaundice, 75-0-0, p. Henry & Sarah Carter, farmer, sc: Alfred N. Carter, son, BVS:1866:2
CARTER, Richard H., W, M, d. 10 Dec 1880, LC, congestion of brain, 0-18-0, p. Jno. A. & Sophia D. Carter, b. LC, unm, sc: Jno. A. Carter, father, 1st Dist., BVS:1880:1
CARTER, Richard W., W, M, d. 20 Dec 1888, Unison, unk, 52-0-0, p. John A. & Rebecca Carter, b. Unison, c/o:

Sarah D. Carter, sc: John A. Carter, brother, 1st Dist., BVS:1888:3

CARTER, Richd. A., W, M, d. 15 Feb 1881, LC, unk, 1-6-0, p. Jno A. & Sophia Carter, b. LC, sc: Jno A. Carter, father, 1st Dist., BVS:1881:1

CARTER, Robert, W, M, d. 5 Apr 1881, LC, brain fever, 0-6-0, p. Thos. J. & Phebe Carter, b. LC, sc: Thos J. Carter, father, 3rd Dist., BVS:1881:4

CARTER, Robert, B, M, d. Apr 1874, LC, apoplexy, 0-3-0, p. Emily Carter, sc: Emily Carter, mother, LE Dist., BVS:1874:5

CARTER, Robt. C., W, M, d. Aug 1873, nr Millville, consumption, 35-0-0, p. James L. Carter, b. LC, farmer, married, sc: James L. Carter, father, MC Dist., BVS:1873:5

CARTER, T. H., W, M, d. 12 Oct 1892, Lenah, bright's disease, 45-0-0, p. unk, b. Mount Gilead, unm, 1st Dist., BVS:1892:1

CARTER, Thomas, B, M, d. 19 May 1876, nr Millville, pneumonia, 58-0-0, b. LC, laborer, c/o: Jane Carter, sc: Luke Howard, neighbor, MC Dist., BVS:1876:4

CARTER, Thos. Arthur, W, M, d. 20 Jun 1873, Hillsboro, unk, 0-2-3, p. Thos. A. & Mary E. Carter, b. LC, sc: Thos. A. Carter, father, JF Dist., BVS:1874:1

CARTER, Wm. M., W, M, d. 14 Aug 1891, nr Unison, unk, 75-0-0, p. Richd. & Debora Carter, b. LC, farmer, c/o: Cassandra Carter, sc: Edwd Carter, son, 1st Dist., BVS:1891:2

CARUTHERS, Edith, W, F, d. 17 Aug 1887, LC, 0-0-1, p. Jas. E. & S. L. Caruthers, b. LC, sheriff, sc: James E. Caruthers, father, 3rd Dist., BVS:1887:6

CARUTHERS, Mary C., W, F, d. 23 Dec 1853, LC, croup, 10-4-0, p. John & Malinda Caruthers, b. LC, sc: John Carruthers, father, BVS:1854:4, LC:2

CARUTHERS, Victoria V., W, F, d. 13 Mar 1888, LC, pneumonia, 49-0-0, p. unk, b. LC, none, c/o: John E. Caruthers, sc: J.E. Caruthers, husband, 3rd Dist., BVS:1888:1

CARUTHERS, William, W, M, d. 13 Dec 1876, nr Woodburn, consumption, 59-2-18, p. Thos. & Martha Caruthers, b. LC, farmer, married, sc: William T. Caruthers, son, MT Dist., BVS:1876:1

CASE, Mabel A., W, F, d. 4 Jul 1890, LC, cholera infantum, 0-11-0, p. Geo. W. & Rosa B. Case, b. LC, none, unm, sc: Geo W. Case, father, 2nd Dist., BVS:1890:3

CASTER, Richard Thomas, W, M, d. 10 Jan 1877, nr Bloomfield, brain fever, 7-0-0, p. Wm. & Casandra Caster, b. LC, sc: Wm. M. Caster, father, MC Dist., BVS:1877:5

CASTLE, Anna B., W, F, d. 20 Jun 1859/60, Leesburg, unk, 6-10-0, p. Eli S. & Rowena E. Castle, b. Leesburg, sc: Eli S. Castle, father, BVS:1859:2, 1860:5, LC:37

CASTLE, Virginia B., W, F, d. 15 Sep 1858, Leesburg, cholera infantum, 1-2-0, p. Eli S. & Roena E. Castle, b. Leesburg, sc: Roena E. Castle, mother, BVS:1858:1, LC:29

CATON, Bertha M, W, F, d. 1 Mar 1884, LC, diphtheria, 0-4-0, p. Erasmus G. & A. Caton, 1st Dist., BVS:1884:1

CATON, Clyde, W, M, d. 8 Mar 1884, LC, diphtheria, 0-2-0, p. Erasmus G. & A. Caton, 1st Dist., BVS:1884:1

CATON, Collie L., W, M, d. 8 Feb 1884, LC, erysipelas, 0-0-20, p. Erasumus G. & A. Caton, b. LC, 1st Dist., BVS:1884:1

CATON, John R., W, M, d. 15 Jun 1866, Old Road, heart disease, 21-0-0, p. Hannah Caton, b. Fauquier Co., farmer, sc: E.G. Caton, son, BVS:1866:3

CAYLOR, Nellie O., W, F, d. 6 Oct 1886, nr Farmwell, brain fever, 3-0-0, p. John A. & Priscilla Caylor, b. LC, sc: John A. Caylor, father, 1st Dist., BVS:1886:1

CEASER, no name, B, M, d. 10 Mar 1883, James Chapel, unk, 0-0-1, p. Julius & Anna Ceasar, b. LC, sc: Julius Ceaser, father, 3rd Dist., BVS:1883:5

CHAMBERLAYNE, Sue, W, F, d. 13 Jun 1888, Middleburg, gastritis, 0-5-13, p. Eugene & Bessie Chamberlayne, b. Middleburg, sc: Eugene Chamberlayne, father, 1st Dist., BVS:1888:3

CHAMBLIN, A. Rush, W, M, d. 23 Dec 1876, nr Bloomfield, consumption, 26-0-0, p. A. G. & E. B. Chamblin, b. LC, school teacher, unm, sc: Brooke Chamblin, brother, MC Dist., BVS:1876:4

CHAMBLIN, Anna, W, F, d. 2 Apr 1883, nr Bloomfield, burnt, 19-0-0, p. Richard C. & Sarah E. Chamblin, b. nr Bloomfield, unm, sc: Richard C. Chamblin, father, 1st Dist., BVS:1883:1

CHAMBLIN, Asenath, W, F, d. 3 Aug 1874, nr Unison, typhoid fever, 68-0-0, b. LC, c/o: Wm. Chamblin, sc: Thos. S. Chamblin, son, MC Dist., BVS:1874:4

CHAMBLIN, Catharine, W, F, d. 14 Dec 1884, LC, dropsy, 31-0-0, p. Gill & Mary A. Furr, c/o: John W. Chamblin, 1st Dist., BVS:1884:1

CHAMBLIN, Charles J., W, M, d. 2 Feb 1859/60, res of parents, consumption, 24-11-0 or 24-1-0, p. Mason & Duanna Chamblin, b. Chamblin's Mill, salesman, sc: Mason Chamblin, father, BVS:1859:5, 1860:2, LC:35

CHAMBLIN, Chas. Isaac, W, M, d. 2 Feb 1859/60, father's res, consumption, 24-4-0 or 24-11-0, p. Mason & Duanna Chamblin, b. Chamblin's Mill, salesman, sc: M. Chamblin, father, BVS:1859:3, 1860:1, LC:34

CHAMBLIN, Chas. T., W, M, d. Dec 1871, Leesburg, consumption, 30-0-0, p. J.H. & Octavia Chamblin, b. LC, merchant, unm, LE Dist., BVS:1871:4

CHAMBLIN, Elsy, W, M, d. 15 May 1892, Mechanicsville, old age, 84-0-0, b. Mechanicsville, farmer, husband, sc: Jacob Allen, head of family, JF Dist., BVS:1892:7

CHAMBLIN, Henry K., W, M, d. 12 Nov 1857, Leesburg, unk, 0-6-4, p. James H. & Octavia Chamblin, b. Leesburg, sc: Jas. H. Chamblin, father, BVS:1857:2, LC:25

CHAMBLIN, Jas. H., W, M, d. 6 Jul 1883, nr Leesburg, old age, 73-0-0, p. Chas. & --- Chamblin, b. LC, merchant, c/o: Octavia Chamblin, sc: A. Dibrill, son-in-law, 2nd Dist., BVS:1883:3

CHAMBLIN, Jno. L., W, M, d. 7 Dec 1892, Philomont, bladder trouble, 81-0-0, p. Jno & Mary Chamblin, b. Philomont, farmer, married, sc: Jno M. Chamblin, son, MT Dist., BVS:1892:8

CHAMBLIN, John, W, M, d. 8 Sep 1890, Hillsboro, cancer on face, 38-0-0, p. Elza & Mary Chamblin, b. LC, farmer, unm, sc: Elza Chamblin, father, 3rd Dist., BVS:1890:6

CHAMBLIN, Mary, W, F, d. 20 Mar 1881, LC, old age, 86-0-0, b. LC, c/o: Burr P. Chamblin, sc: Jno H. Lynch, friend, 3rd Dist., BVS:1881:4

CHAMBLIN, Mary A., W, F, d. 19 Aug 1887, LC, consumption, 73-0-0, b. LC, none, c/o: John L. Chamblin, sc: Jno L. Chamblin, husband, 3rd Dist., BVS:1887:6

CHAMBLIN, Mary E., W, F, d. Aug 1894, Philomont, stomach trouble, 49-0-0, p. Henry & Charlotte McIlhollen, b. Philomont, consort, sc: R L. Chamblin, husband, 3rd Dist., BVS:1894:5

CHAMBLIN, Peyton W., W, M, d. 24 Nov 1859/60, res, dropsy of brain, 33-10-22, p. Mason & Duanna Chamblin, b. LC, miller, c/o: Sarah C. Chamblin, sc: S. E. Chamblin, widow, BVS:1859:3, 1860:1, LC:34

CHAMBLIN, Phebe Jane, W, F, d. 14 Apr 1858, res of parents, measles etc., 14-0-22, p. Leven P. & Julia Chamblin, b. nr Bloomfield, sc: L.P. Chamblin. father, BVS:1858:5, LC:33

CHAMBLIN, Philip, W, M, d. 31 Jul 1881, LC, unk, 2-0-0, p. Henry M. & Mary F. Chamblin, b. LC, sc: M.F. Chamblin, mother, 1st Dist., BVS:1881:1

CHAMBLIN, Rush, W, M, d. 21 Apr 1884, Caroline Co., VA, lock jaw, 0-3-4, p. Brooke & Annie Chamblin, b. LC, 1st Dist., BVS:1884:1

CHAMBLIN, Ruth, W, F, d. 12 May 1857, her res, dropsy & old age, 88-0-0, p. John & ... Jared, b. nr Taylor's Mill, c/o: Charles Chamblin, decd, sc: Jared Chamblin, son, BVS:1857:3, LC:26

CHAMBLIN, Ruth, W, F, d. 6 Mar 1858, res of parents, measles etc., 7-7-5, p. Leven P. & Julia Chamblin,

b. nr Beatty's Mill, sc: L.P. Chamblin. father, BVS:1858:5, LC:33

CHAMBLIN, Sarah, W, F, d. 13 Mar 1880, LC, old age, 70-0-0, p. unk, b. LC, c/o: A.G. Chamblin, sc: A. G. Chamblin, husband, 1st Dist., BVS:1880:1

CHAMP, Annie, B, F, d. 1 Mar 1883, North Fork, unk, 30-0-0, p. Charles Champ, b. LC, c/o: Charles Champ, sc: Chas Champ, husband, 3rd Dist., BVS:1883:5

CHAMP, Catherine, B, F, d. 27 Jan 1890, Hamilton, 78-0-0, b. LC, none, sc: Ham Wood, friend, 3rd Dist., BVS:1890:6

CHAMP, Clarence, B, M, d. 1 Mar 1882, LC, croup, 4-1-0, p. Charles & Sallie Champ, b. LC, unm, sc: Charles Champ, parent, 3rd Dist., BVS:1882:3

CHAMP, Dade, B, M, d. unk, 1872, Mount Gilead Twp., unk, 0-6-0, p. Dade & Lucy Ellen Champ, b. Mount Gilead Town, unm, sc: Lucy Ellen Champ, mother, MT Dist., BVS:1872:2

CHAMP, Jefferson, B, M, d. 18 Sep 1878, Mountville, typhoid fever, 2-6-0, p. Luke & Amy Champ, b. LC, sc: Luke Champ, father, MC Dist., BVS:1878:6

CHAMP, Joseph, B, M, d. 10 Aug 1888, Mountville, sunstroke, 4-0-0, p. Luke & Amy Champ, b. Mountville, sc: Luke Champ, father, 1st Dist., BVS:1888:3

CHAMP, Joseph, B, M, d. 11 Apr 1873, nr Mountville, consumption, 40-0-0, p. Harriet Payne, b. Mountville, unm, sc: Harriet Payne, mother, MC Dist., BVS:1873:5

CHAMP, Luke, B, M, d. 19 Dec 1891, Mountville, heart failure, 68-0-0, p. Jack & Mary Champ, b. LC, laborer, c/o: Anne Champ, sc: Amos Champ, head of family, 1st Dist., BVS:1891:1

[CHAMP], no name, B, M, d. 14 Sep 1884, LC, unk, 0-1-0, p. Jacob & Agness Champ, 1st Dist., BVS:1884:1

CHAMP, Samuel, B, M, d. 10 Jan 1881, LC, scrofula, 60-0-0, p. Newton & Mary Champ, b. LC, laborer, sc: Mary Champ, mother, 1st Dist., BVS:1881:1

CHAMP, Samuel, B, M, d. 20 Dec 1881, LC, dropsy, 55-0-0, p. Hannah Champ, b. LC, laborer, sc: Hannah Champ, mother, 1st Dist., BVS:1881:1

CHANCELLOR, Ann Maria, W, F, d. 12 Nov 1857, Middleburg, whooping cough, 1-10-12, p. Lorman & Margaret Chancellor, b. Middleburg, sc: father, BVS:1857:3, LC:25

CHANCELLOR, Clarence J., W, M, d. 26 Mar 1853, Middleburg, scarlet fever, 3-6-0, p. Lamar & Margaret Chancellor, b. Spottsylvania, sc: father, BVS:1854:1, LC:4

CHANCELLOR, Hugh M., W, M, d. 10 Apr 1853, Spottsylvania, scarlet fever, 2-5-0, p. Lamar & Margaret Chancellor, b. Spottsylvania, sc: father, BVS:1854:1, LC:4

CHANCELLOR, Mary A., B, F, d. 19 May 1877, Leesburg, burns from coal oil, 22-0-0, p. Jno. & Malinda Harris, b. Leesburg, c/o: Charles Chancellor, sc: Charles Chancellor, husband, LE Dist., BVS:1877:8

CHANCELLOR, Mary R., B, F, d. 18 Feb 1876, Leesburg, brain fever, 0-0-8, p. Charles & Mary Chancellor, b. Leesburg, sc: Charles Chancellor, father, LE Dist., BVS:1876:6

CHANCELLOR, Nannie, B, F, d. 16 Aug 1877, Leesburg, cholera infantum, 0-6-0, p. Chas. & Mary Chancellor, b. Leesburg, sc: Charles Chancellor, father, LE Dist., BVS:1877:8

[CHANCELLOR], no name, W, M, d. 13 Sep 1854, Middleburg, malformation, 0-0-2, p. Lorman & Margaret T. Chancellor, b. Middleburg, sc: Lorman Chanceller, BVS:1854:11, LC:10

[CHAPELL], no name, W, F, d. 1 Jul 1853, on Blue Ridge, 0-0-1, p. James & Susan Chapell, b. on Blue Ridge, sc: father, BVS:1854:1, LC:4

CHAPMAN, Carrol, B, M, d. 21 Feb 1886, Mountville, pneumonia, 1-0-0, p. David & Jane Chapman, b. Middleburg, unm, sc: David Chapman, father, 1st Dist., BVS:1886:1

[CHAPMAN], no name, W, , d. 12 May 1871, Coe's Mill, unk, p. Jane Chapman, MC Dist., BVS:1871:2

Loudoun County, Virginia, Death Register, 1853-1896 67

CHAPMAN, Wm. D., B, M, d. 1 Jun 1871, 0-4-0, p. Wm. D. Chapman, unm, sc: Wm. Carter, MC Dist., BVS:1871:2

CHARITY, Nancy, B, F, d. 27 Jul 1878, Middleburg, erysipelas, 47-0-0, b. Charles Co., c/o: Peter Charity, sc: Peter Charity, husband, MC Dist., BVS:1878:6

CHARITY, Wilson, B, M, d. 12 Sep 1881, LC, unk, 0-9-0, p. Mat & Mary Charity, b. LC, sc: Mary Charity, mother, 1st Dist., BVS:1881:1

CHESHER, John M., W, M, d. Nov 1854, nr Circleville, affection of brain, 0-9-0, p. John W. & Mary Chesher, b. nr Circleville, sc: father, BVS:1854:11, LC:11

CHICHESTER, Mary, W, F, d. 31 Jul 1872, LC, dysentery, 65-8-6, p. unk, b. Maryland, lady, c/o: Geo. M. Chichester, sc: A.W. Chichester, son, LE Dist., BVS:1872:3

CHICHESTER, Washington B., W, M, d. 2 Nov 1879, nr Leesburg, fever, 0-9-0, p. Arthur M. & Mary Chichester, b. LC, sc: Arthur M. Chichester, father, 2nd Dist., BVS:1879:1

CHICK, Harriet, W, F, d. 1 Oct 1854, LC, consumption, 4-8-30, p. Geo. W. & Elizabeth Chick, b. LC, sc: Elizabeth Chick, mother, BVS:1854:9, LC:8

CHICK, Sarah C., W, F, d. 23 Sep 1854, LC, whooping cough, 0-0-28, p. Geo. W. & Elizabeth Chick, b. LC, sc: Elizabeth Chick, mother, BVS:1854:9, LC:9

CHINN, Francis A., W, M, d. 9 Feb 1892, Aldie, old age, 95-4-0, p. Hugh & Chloe Chinn, b. Prince William Co, farmer, c/o: Mary A. Chinn, sc: F. Chinn, son, 1st Dist., BVS:1892:1

CHINN, Mary, B, F, d. 10 Jul 1891, Lincoln, typhoid fever, 5-0-0, p. Henry & Mollie Chinn, b. Lincoln, unm, sc: Henry Chinn, MT Dist., BVS:1891:6

CHINN, Mary A., W, F, d. 27 Nov 1871, neuralgia of the heart, 61-0-0, married, BR Dist., BVS:1871:3

CHINN, no name, W, M, d. 11 Jun 1889, Middleburg, unk, 0-0-1, p. John S. & Ida Chinn, b. Middleburg, sc: John S. Chinn, father, 1st Dist., BVS:1889:1

CHINN, no name, W, M, d. 15 Sep 1889, Middleburg, cholera infantum, 0-3-0, p. John S. & Ida Chinn, b. Middleburg, sc: John S. Chinn, father, 1st Dist., BVS:1889:1

CHINN, R. S., W, M, d. 12 May 1888, Middleburg, thrown from wagon, 69-0-0, p. Samuel & Mildred Chinn, b. LC, c/o: Sallie Chinn, sc: Wm. B. Noland, brother-in-law, 1st Dist., BVS:1888:3

CHINN, Samuel, W, M, d. 25 Jan 1854, Middleburg, heart affected, 75-0-0, p. R. Chinn, b. Recovered Hill, farmer, sc: R. L. Chinn, son, BVS:1854:11, LC:11

CHINN, Sarah M., W, F, d. Aug 1872, nr Middleburg, typhoid fever, 19-0-0, p. R. L. & Sarah Chinn, MC Dist., BVS:1872:7

CHINN, Susan Virginia, W, F, d. 1 Nov 1876, Middleburg, consumption, 44-0-0, p. Saml. & Millie Chinn, b. LC, unm, sc: Wm. B. Noland, brother-in-law, MC Dist., BVS:1876:4

CHRISTIAN, Chas. P., W, M, d. 25 Jun 1881, LC, diphtheria, 5-1-19, p. J. B. & M. P. Christian, sc: C.R. Paxton, grandfather, 2nd Dist., BVS:1881:6

CHURCHMAN, Harriet L., B, F, d. 31 Aug 1877, nr Aldie, affection of throat, 0-0-7, p. Julia Churchman, b. LC, sc: Thomas Churchman, grandfather, MC Dist., BVS:1877:5

CHURCHMAN, Mary, W, F, d. 10 Jan 1881, LC, consumption, 30-0-0, b. LC, sc: Fanny Cockrille, friend, 1st Dist., BVS:1881:1

[CISK], no name,W, F, d. 22 Feb 1857, Jos. G. Gray's, unk, 0-11-0, p. Wm. & Sarah T. Cisk, b. Jos. G. Gray's, sc: Sarah J. Cisk, mother, BVS:1857:4, LC:27

[CISK], no name,W, M, d. Feb 1856, Langolon Farm, 0-0-4, p. Wm. & Sarah Jane Cisk, b. Llangolon Farm, sc: Wm. Cisk, father, BVS:1856:4, LC:22

CLAGETT, Angeline, B, F, d. 1 Sep 1885, Waterford, consumption, 40-0-0, p. Marshal & Angeline Clagett, b. LC, c/o: Marshal Clagett, sc: Marshal Clagett, husband, 3rd Dist., BVS:1885:6

CLAGETT, Eva, B, F, d. 9 Jan 1885, Waterford, consumption, 0-2-0, p. Marshal & Angeline Clagett, b. LC, sc: Marshal Clagett, father, 3rd Dist., BVS:1885:6

CLAGETT, Isaac, B, M, d. 10 Aug 1885, Waterford, consumption, 2-0-0, p. Marshal & Angeline Clagett, b. LC, unm, sc: Marshal Clagett, father, 3rd Dist., BVS:1885:6

CLAGETT, Mrs. Lalla, W, F, d. 13 Dec 1888, LC, paralysis, 62-0-0, p. John & Harriet Gray, b. LC, none, c/o: Dr. Clagett, sc: John Gray, nephew, 2nd Dist., BVS:1888:5

CLAGETT, Mary E., B, F, d. 17 Dec 1876, Leesburg, burnt, 3-10-18, p. Beverly & Lucy Clagett, b. LC, sc: Beverly Clagett, father, LE Dist., BVS:1876:6

CLAGETT, Thomas H., W, M, d. May 1881, LC, paralysis, 42-0-0, p. Thos. H. & C. Clagett, merchant, c/o: H.W. Clagett, sc: H.W. Clagett, wife, 2nd Dist., BVS:1881:6

CLAGETT, Virginia, W, F, d. 20 Oct 1892, Leesburg, unk, 50-0-0, p. unk, b. Leesburg, consort, LE Dist., BVS:1892:5

CLAIGETT, Harris, B, M, d. 12 Oct 1888, Poor House, paralysis, 60-0-0, p. unk, b. unk, sc: F.E. Robey, superintendent of poor, 1st Dist., BVS:1888:3

CLAPHAM, Charlotte, B, F, d. 14 May 1879, Waterford, consumption, 39-0-0, b. LC, c/o: French Clapham, sc: French Clapham, husband, 3rd Dist., BVS:1879:3

CLAPHAM, Hannah W., W, F, d. 13 Jun 1880, nr Lovettsville, old age, 83-6-0, p. Robert H. & Hannah W. Hodge, b. Westmoreland, c/o: Josiah Clapham, sc: Elizabeth Clampham, daughter, 2nd Dist., BVS:1880:6

CLARK, Charles, B, M, d. 15 Mar 1890, Hamilton, pneumonia, 15-0-0, p. Richard & Mary Clark, b. LC, none, unm, sc: Richard Clark, father, 3rd Dist., BVS:1890:6

CLARK, Manuel, B, M, d. Sep 1866, Old Road, found dead, unk, laborer, sc: H.R. Brewer, head of family, BVS:1866:3

CLARKE, Addison H., W, M, d. 8 Sep 1854, LC, dysentery, 63-5-10, p. Thomas & Jemima Clarke, b. Westmoreland, farmer, c/o: Mary Clarke, sc: Mary Clarke, wife, BVS:1854:10, LC:10

CLARKE, Henry, B, M, d. 6 Aug 1893, Hamilton, consumption, 27-0-0, p. W. H. & Maria Clarke, b. LC, husband, sc: wife, MT Dist., BVS:1893:4

CLARKE, James W., B, M, d. 22 Apr 1881, LC, consumption, 20-1-22, p. Ellen Clarke, laborer, unm, sc: Ellen Jones, mother, 2nd Dist., BVS:1881:6

CLARKE, Maria, B, F, d. 16 Jun 1883, nr Leesburg, heart disease, 63-0-0, p. Aleck & Belle Johnson, b. Fauquier Co., laborer, c/o: George Clarke, sc: Geo Clarke, husband, 2nd Dist., BVS:1883:6

CLARKE, Mary, W, F, d. 15 Jany 1876, nr Helmswood, congestion of lungs, 72-0-0, p. Jos. & Elizabeth Vandevanter, b. LC, married, sc: Lewis C. Helm, son-in-law, MT Dist., BVS:1876:1

CLARKSON, Caroline, W, F, d. Aug 1871, LC, shot, 16-0-0, p. T. & Caroline Clarkson, b. LC, unm, LE Dist., BVS:1871:4

CLARKSON, Thomas, W, M, d. 3 Mar 1883, nr Leesburg, consumption, 73-0-0, b. LC, farmer, c/o: Caroline Clarkson, sc: Chas Clarkson, son, 2nd Dist., BVS:1883:3

CLAYBORN, no name, B, M, d. 12 Jul 1878, nr Hoysville, consumption, 58-0-0, laborer, married, sc: John E. Washington, friend, LV Dist., BVS:1878:1/5

CLEMENS, Edna, (f), F, d. 2 Aug 1858, LC, unk, 20-0-0, b. LC, sc: H. Clemens, friend, BVS:1858:6, LC:33

CLEMENS, Margaret, B, F, d. 4 Jul 1893, Sterling, consumption, 18-0-0, p. Henry & Flora Lee, b. Sterling, c/o: Charles Clemens, sc: Charles Clemens, husband, 1st Dist., BVS:1893:2

[CLEMENS], [no name], (f), F, d. 7 Aug 1858, LC, 0-3-0, p. Robison & Edna Clemens, b. LC, sc: H. Clemens, friend, BVS:1858:6, LC:33

CLENDENING, Bernard T., W, M, d. 4 Dec 1878, nr Hillsboro, apoplexy, 22-0-7, p. Saml. & Sarah Clendening, b. LC, farmer, unm, sc: Saml Clendening, father, JF Dist., BVS:1878:10

CLENDENING, Jas. H., W, M, d. Jul 1896, Hillsboro, bright's disease, 72-0-0, p. Ruth & Wm. Clending, b. Hillsboro, farmer, unm, JF Dist., BVS:1896:8

CLENDENING, Mary, W, F, d. 17 Jun 1859/60, LC, old age, 83-6-2, p. Saml & Sarah Clendening, b. LC, unm, sc: Saml Clendening, brother, BVS:1859:1, 1860:4, LC:37

CLENDENING, Wm., W, M, d. 4 Apr 1855, LC, apoplexy, 72-0-0, p. unk, b. LC, c/o: Ruth Clendening, sc: Jno. Clendening, son, BVS:1855:2, LC:15

CLENDENNING, Elizabeth, W, F, d. 1 Jan 1886, LC, general debility, 71-11-25, b. LC, c/o: Saml Clendening, sc: Wm. T. Clending, son, 3rd Dist., BVS:1886:4

CLEVELAND, Adelaide, B, F, d. 21 Aug 1892, Welbourne, typhoid fever, 15-0-0, p. Jas & Annie Cleveland, b. Welbourne, laborer, unm, sc: Jas Cleveland, father, 1st Dist., BVS:1892:4

CLEVELAND, Katie, B, F, d. 3 Oct 1892, Welbourne, typhoid fever, 13-0-0, p. Jas & Annie Cleveland, b. Welbourne, laborer, unm, sc: Jas Cleveland, father, 1st Dist., BVS:1892:4

CLEVELAND, Mary C., B, F, d. 15 Dec 1893, nr Watson, consumption, 24-0-0, p. Adam & Susan Cleveland, b. Watson, unm, sc: Adam Cleveland, father, 1st Dist., BVS:1893:2

CLIFF, Maggie J., W, F, d. Feb 1896, Hillsboro, bright's disease, 18-0-0, p. J. B. & Ginnie Cliff, unm, JF Dist., BVS:1896:8

CLINE, Alfred, W, M, d. 7 Sep 1886, paralysis, 74-0-0, p. William & Margaret, merchant, unm, sc: Mary A. Cline, sister, 2nd Dist., BVS:1886:5

CLINE, Margaret A., W, F, d. 6 Dec 1884, Leesburg, inflammation of stomach, 60-0-0, p. S.M. & Elizabeth Boss, b. LC, sc: William Cline, husband, 2nd Dist., BVS:1884:4

CLINE, Margaret A., W, F, d. 3 Nov 1881, LC, consumption, 65-0-0, p. Wm. & Margaret Cline, unm, sc: A. Cline, brother, 2nd Dist., BVS:1881:6

CLINE, Maria V., W, F, d. 29 Jul 1855, Middleburg, consumption, 25-0-0, p. Edwd & Emily Cochran, b. Middleburg, c/o: Jno. T. Cline, sc: Jno. T. Cline, widower, BVS:1855:6, LC:17

CLINE, William, W, M, d. 2 Jul 1889, LC, heart failure, 71-0-0, p. Wm. & Margaret Cline, b. LC, merchant, widower, sc: C.A. Cline, son, 2nd Dist., BVS:1889:3

CLOW, Louisa, W, F, d. Sep 1871, LC, 73-0-0, b. Prince William Co, c/o: Wm. Clow, LE Dist., BVS:1871:4

COATES, Elizabeth, B, F, d. 18 Jun 1878, nr Hillsboro, croup, 0-7-0, p. Ira & Charity Coates, b. LC, sc: Charity Coates, mother, JF Dist., BVS:1878:10

COATES, James Harrison, W, M, d. 25 Apr 1875, Lovettsville Dist, cholera infantum, 0-10-0, p. ? & Mary J. Coates, b. LC, unm, sc: ? Coates, father, LV Dist., BVS:1875:4

COATES, Mary L., B, F, d. 18 Jun 1878, nr Hillsboro, croup, 0-7-0, p. Ira & Charity Coates, b. LC, sc: Charity Coates, mother, JF Dist., BVS:1878:10

COATES, Virginia, B, F, d. 28 May 1875, LC, consumption, 15-0-0, p. Ira & Charity Coates, b. LC, sc: Charity Coates, mother, JF Dist., BVS:1875:3

COATS, Calvin, W, M, d. 10 Aug 1890, Waterford, cancer on face, 78-0-0, b. LC, farmer, c/o: Elizabeth Coates, sc: Elizabeth Coates, wife, 3rd Dist., BVS:1890:6

COATS, Lacy Cordel, B, M, d. 14 Mar 1894, Lincoln, diphtheria, 5-0-0, p. Sandford Coats, b. Lincoln, sc: Sandford Coats, father, 3rd Dist., BVS:1894:5

COATS, Nathan, B, M, d. Nov 1891, Hillsboro, unk, 1-3-0, p. Ony & Charity Coats, b. Hillsboro, laborer, husband, sc: Ony Coates, head of family, JF Dist., BVS:1891:7

COATS, Phebe, B, F, d. 6 Dec 1876, Poor House, old age, 80-0-0, b. LC, laborer, unm, sc: W.H. Hibbs, superintendent of Poor, MC Dist., BVS:1876:4

COATS, Virginia, B, F, d. 1 Mar 1876, LC, pneumonia, 0-9-0, p. Ira & Charity Coats, b. LC, sc: Ira Coats, father, JF Dist., BVS:1876:8

COATS, Walter H., W, M, d. 20 Apr 1874, E of Lovettsville, measles, 0-10-0, p. Andrew & Mary J. Coats, farmer, LV Dist., BVS:1874:6

COATS, Wm, W, M, d. 12 Sep 1873, nr Lovettsville, unk, 0-3-0, p. Andrew & Mary J. Coats, b. nr Lovettsville, farmer, married, sc: Andrew Coats, father, LV Dist., BVS:1873:4

COCHRAN, Frances, W, F, d. 12 Jun 1854, Cochran's Mill, cancerous affection, 52-0-0, p. Jas. & Nancy Cross, b. LC, c/o: Robt. H. Cochran, sc: husband, BVS:1854:12, LC:12

COCKERELL, Absolem, W, M, d. 28 Apr 1888, LC, consumption, 60-0-0, p. Samuel & Elizabeth Copeland [sic], b. LC, farmer, unm, sc: C.C. Gover, friend, 3rd Dist., BVS:1888:1

COCKERELL, Absolem, W, M, d. 25 Apr 1888, LC, consumption, 62-0-0, p. unk, b. LC, farmer, unm, sc: W.L. Jacobs, cousin, 2nd Dist., BVS:1888:5

COCKERELL, Landon, W, M, d. 15 Aug 1853, nr Purcellville, putrid sore throat 10, unk, p. Harley & Harriet Cockerell, b. nr Purcellville, sc: father, BVS:1854:6, LC:5

COCKERELL, Nancy, W, F, d. 1 Mar 1888, LC, consumption, 59-0-0, p. unk, b. LC, none, unm, sc: W.L. Jacobs, cousin, 2nd Dist., BVS:1888:5

COCKERELL, Nancy, W, F, d. 15 Mar 1888, LC, consumption, 31-0-0, p. Sam & Elizabeth Cockerell, b. LC, none, unm, sc: C.C. Gover, friend, 3rd Dist., BVS:1888:1

COCKERELL, Sarah C., W, F, d. 25 Dec 1855, Gulick's Mill, erysipelas, 23-0-0, p. Westly & Mary Jenkins, b. Fairfax, c/o: Jas. D. Cockerell, sc: Westley Jenkins, father, BVS:1855:5, LC:17

COCKERELL, Thomas, W, M, d. 1 Nov 1853, Oatlands, typhoid fever, 10-0-0, p. Wm. & Sarah Cockerell, b. Fauquier Co., sc: Craven Pierson, grandfather, BVS:1854:6, LC:5

[COCKERELLE], no name, W, M, d. 11 May 1855, unk, 0-9-24, p. Jas. A. & M. E. Cockerelle, b. LC, sc: Jas. A. Cockerelle, father, BVS:1855:8, LC:19

COCKERILL, Jane A., W, F, d. 16 Feb 1880, Hillsboro, cancer, 37-0-0, p. Henry & Harriet Cockerill, b. LC, unm, sc: M.M. Virts, friend, 3rd Dist., BVS:1880:4

COCKERILL, John, W, M, d. 26 Apr 1880, North Fork, bright's disease, 79-0-0, p. Jno. & Mary Cockerill, b. LC, farmer, c/o: Keziah Cockerill, sc: J.A. Cockerill, son, 3rd Dist., BVS:1880:4

COCKERILL, Sanford M., W, M, d. 3 Aug 1882, LC, paralysis, 65-0-0, p. S.M. & Jane Cockerille, b. Fairfax, mechanic, c/o: Annie E. Cockerill, sc: Annie E. Cockerille, wife, 1st Dist., BVS:1882:1

COCKERILLE, Anna, W, F, d. 20 Dec 1858, LC, unk, 0-2-15, p. James & Anna E. Cockerille, b. LC, sc: James Cockerille, father, BVS:1858:6, LC:33

COCKERILLE, Edgar, W, M, d. 24 Jun 1871, Waterford, hip disease, unk, p. E. I. & Samantha Cockerille, sc: E.H. Cockerille, father, JF Dist., BVS:1871:1

COCKERILLE, Laura, W, F, d. 20 Dec 1892, Sycolin, cancer, 67-0-0, p. unk, b. Sycolin, consort, LE Dist., BVS:1892:5

COCKERILLE, Leslie R., W, M, d. 10 Sep 1887, Farmwell, brain fever, 4-0-0, p. David B. & Sarah C. Cockerille, b. Farmwell, sc: Daniel B. Cockerille, father, 1st Dist., BVS:1887:2

COCKERILLE, Sarah B., W, F, d. 29 Sep 1858, LC, unk, 4-6-0, p. Bushrod & Eliza F. Cockerille, b. LC, sc: Eliza F. Cockerille, mother, BVS:1858:6, LC:33

COCKERILLE, William L., W, M, d. 24 Feb 1872, nr Cleveland Grove, pneumonia, 76-0-0, p. unk, b. Fairfax Co., farmer, unm, sc: Chas. C. Mankin, friend, BR Dist., BVS:1872:6

Loudoun County, Virginia, Death Register, 1853-1896   71

COCKERILLE, Winifred, W, F, d. 23 Jun 1872, nr Mt. Hope Church, unk, 78-11-0, p. unk, b. Fairfax Co., unm, sc: Andrew Beach, friend, BR Dist., BVS:1872:6

COCKRELL, Ernest, W, M, d. 15 Mar 1872, Mount Gilead Twp., unk, 0-0-16, p. James A. & Adelia Cockrell, b. Mount Gilead Town, unm, sc: James A. Cockrell, father, MT Dist., BVS:1872:2

COCKRILLE, Florida, W, F, d. 6 Jul 1872, Leesburg, consumption, 32-0-0, p. Richard H. & Ann Cockrille, b. Fairfax Co., unm, sc: Mrs. Rolls, sister, LE Dist., BVS:1872:3

COCKRILLE, Isabella, W, F, d. 11 Nov 1866, nr Gum Spring, typhoid fever, 13-11-0, p. Philip & Isabella Cockrille, b. Prince William Co, unm, sc: Lewis H. Freeman, head of family, BVS:1866:3

COCKRILLE, James, W, M, d. 14 Feb 1880, LC, pneumonia, 56-0-0, p. unk, b. LC, farmer, c/o: Annie E. Cockrille, sc: Annie E. Cockrille, wife, 1st Dist., BVS:1880:1

[COCKRILLE], no name, W, M, d. 28 Apr 1881, LC, unk, 0-0-8, p. Jas F. & Sarah Cockrille, b. LC, sc: Sarah Cockrille, mother, 1st Dist., BVS:1881:1

COCKRILLE, Philip W., W, M, d. 8 Jul 1866, nr Gum Spring, typhoid fever, 57-0-0, p. Jeremiah & ... Cockrille, b. Fairfax, farmer, sc: Lewis H. Freeman, head of family, BVS:1866:3

COE, Cornelia, B, F, d. 17 Jan 1884, Leesburg, brain fever, 0-5-0, p. Mintie Coe (unm), b. LC, sc: Mintie Coe, mother, 2nd Dist., BVS:1884:4

COE, Menan, W, M, d. 18 Nov 1855, Williamsburg, diarrhea, 39-4-23, p. Wm. & Cath'n. Coe, b. nr Coe's Mill, sc: Cath'n Coe, mother, BVS:1855:7, LC:18

[COE], no name, B, , d. 20 Oct 1878, LC, unk, 0-0-2, p. Minta Coe, b. LC, unm, sc: Mintie Coe, mother, LE Dist., BVS:1878:8

COE, Norman, W, M, d. 2 Apr 1876, Oak Grove, heart disease, 0-9-0, p. Aurelius & Maria Coe, b. LC, unm, sc: Aurelius Coe, father, BR Dist., BVS:1876:2

COE, Robert, W, M, d. 6 Sep 1856, his res, disease of kidneys, 67-0-0, p. Edward & --- Coe, b. Prince William Co., farmer & miller, c/o: Elizabeth Coe, sc: Duane Coe, son, BVS:1856:6, LC:23

COE, Thos B., W, M, d. 22 Dec 1864, LC, croup, 3-1-0, p. Arelius & Hana Coe, b. LC, sc: Aurelius Coe, father, BVS:1864:2, LC:39

COE, Valeria, B, F, d. 17 May 1884, Leesburg, insanity, 12-0-0, p. Mintie Coe (unm), b. LC, sc: Mintie Coe, mother, 2nd Dist., BVS:1884:4

COE, Walter R., B, M, d. 2 Mar 1887, LC, consumption, 19-0-0, p. Mintie Coe, b. LC, laborer, unm, sc: Mintie Coe, mother, 2nd Dist., BVS:1887:4

COGLE, Lydia C., W, F, d. 11 Aug 1893, Neersville, cancer, 59-0-0, p. unk, b. unk, consort, sc: Frederick Cogle, LV Dist., BVS:1893:5

COGLIN, Kate, W, F, d. Aug 1874, Leesburg, dysentery, 0-6-0, p. Micheal & Catherine Coglin, sc: Catherine Coglin, mother, LE Dist., BVS:1874:5

COLBERT, Agness, B, F, d. 15 Sep 1884, LC, consumption, 24-0-0, p. Samuel & Hannah Champ, c/o: Jacob Colbert, 1st Dist., BVS:1884:1

COLBERT, Annie M., B, F, d. 30 Apr 1887, Bloomfield, consumption, 0-6-0, p. Jacob & Mollie Colbert, b. Bloomfield, sc: Jacob Colbert, father, 1st Dist., BVS:1887:2

COLBERT, Minnie, B, F, d. 10 Aug 1869, LC, unk, 0-0-1, p. Louisa Colbert, b. LC, sc: James W. Moore, employer of mother, BVS:1869:1

COLBERT, Samuel, B, M, d. 15 Sep 1884, LC, consumption, 2-0-0, p. Jacob & Agnes Colbert, 1st Dist., BVS:1884:1

COLE, Andrew, W, M, d. 29 Feb 1888, Sterling, congestion of lungs, 18-0-0, p. Wm. & Harriet Cole, b. Sterling, sc: Wm. Cole, father, 1st Dist., BVS:1888:3

COLE, Ann, B, F, d. 28 Nov 1892, Aldie, old age, 84-0-0, p. Nancy Heater, b. LC, laborer, sc: Jas Cole, son, 1st Dist., BVS:1892:4

COLE, Elijah, B, M, d. 16 Apr 1893, Sterling, pneumonia, 0-5-0, p. Elijah

& Janie Cole, b. Sterling, sc: Elijah Cole, father, 1st Dist., BVS:1893:2

COLE, Frank W., W, M, d. 11 Aug 1889, Middleburg, blood poison, 56-0-0, p. Bizzell & Rebecca Cole, b. Prince William Co, farmer, c/o: Mary M. Cole, sc: Mary M. Cole, wife, 1st Dist., BVS:1889:1

COLEMAN, Ada, B, F, d. 1 May 1888, LC, catarrh fever, 11-0-0, p. Robert & Sarah Coleman, b. LC, none, unm, sc: Rob Coleman, father, 3rd Dist., BVS:1888:1

COLEMAN, Amanda, B, F, d. 12 Nov 1884, nr Leesburg, unk, 0-8-6, p. Jos. F. & Jane Coleman, b. LC, sc: Joseph F. Coleman, father, 2nd Dist., BVS:1884:4

COLEMAN, Chas. Thos., W, M, d. 25 Aug 1855, Fairfax, bilious inter. fever, 26-0-0, p. Rich. J. & Martha Coleman, b. Fairfax, farmer, c/o: Mary A. Coleman, sc: Mary A. Coleman, widow, BVS:1855:7, LC:18

COLEMAN, David H., B, M, d. 15 Sep 1884, nr Leesburg, unk, 2-8-0, p. Jos. F. & Jane Coleman, b. LC, sc: Joseph F. Coleman, father, 2nd Dist., BVS:1884:4

COLEMAN, Francis E., W, M, d. 8 Sep 1882, LC, heart disease, 40-0-0, p. Francis & Jennie Coleman, farmer, unm, sc: Francis Coleman, father, 1st Dist., BVS:1882:1

COLEMAN, Henry, B, M, d. 30 Dec 1883, nr Middleburg, consumption, 1-4-0, p. David & Fanny Coleman, b. nr Middleburg, unm, sc: David Coleman, father, 1st Dist., BVS:1883:1

COLEMAN, John C., W, F, d. 7 Oct 1882, LC, measles, 0-7-0, p. J. C. & Florence Coleman, unm, sc: Florence Coleman, mother, 1st Dist., BVS:1882:1

COLEMAN, Joseph, B, M, d. 1 May 1881, LC, pneumonia, 50-0-0, p. Margaret Coleman, laborer, c/o: Margaret Coleman, sc: Ginnie Day, friend, 2nd Dist., BVS:1881:6

COLEMAN, Livina, B, F, d. 30 Jun 1871, Trappe, unk, p. Jane Coleman, unm, MC Dist., BVS:1871:2

COLEMAN, Margaret, B, F, d. 10 Jun 1866, Between the Hills, dysentery, 0-9-0, p. David & Margt. Coleman, b. LC, sc: David Coleman, father, BVS:1866:1

COLEMAN, Rose, B, F, d. 30 Nov 1886, pneumonia, 1-2-0, p. Joseph F. & Jane, sc: Jas. F. Coleman, father, 2nd Dist., BVS:1886:5

COLEMAN, Thomas, W, , d. 13 Apr 1869, LC, 23-0-0, p. A. Coleman, b. LC, farmer, unm, sc: Mary Coleman, mother, BVS:1869:1

COLISS, Thomas, W, M, d. 22 Apr 1859/60, Alex. Owen's nr Upperville, dropsy, 75-0-0, p. Thomas & Lydia Coliss, b. MD nr Port Tobacco, farmer, c/o: Lydia Coliss, sc: Mary Owens, daughter, BVS:1859:3, 1860:1, LC:34

COLLIER, Della M., W, F, d. 30 Jan 1878, nr Trappe, inflammation of brain, 0-9-0, p. Charles & Susan A. Collier, b. LC, sc: Chas Collier, father, MC Dist., BVS:1878:6

COLLIER, Herbert, W, M, d. 8 May 1891, nr Upperville, pneumonia, 7-0-0, p. Chas. & Ada Carter: [sic], b. LC, laborer, sc: Chas Collier, father, 1st Dist., BVS:1891:2

COLLIER, John R., W, M, d. 14 Sep 1882, LC, malarial fever, 7-0-0, p. Chas. & Adelaide Collier, sc: Charles Collier, father, 1st Dist., BVS:1882:1

COLLINS, Helen, B, F, d. 11 Jul 1893, Hamilton, unk, 73-0-0, b. LC, wife, JF Dist., BVS:1893:3

COLLINS, Margaret, W, F, d. 1 Oct 1888, LC, old age, 76-0-0, p. unk, b. LC, none, unm, sc: Adam Cooper, son-in-law, 2nd Dist., BVS:1888:5

COLSTON, Hannah, B, F, d. 10 Oct 1877, Leesburg, old age, 87-6-2, b. Leesburg, sc: Mary Williams, friend, LE Dist., BVS:1877:8

COMPHER, Chas C., W, M, d. 10 Jul 1865, Taylorstown, dysentery, 1-0-0, p. Jno H. & M.A. Compher, b. Tankerville, carpenter, unm, sc: Jno H. Compher, father, BVS:1865:3

COMPHER, Chas C., W, M, d. 10 Jul 1865, Taylorstown, dysentery, 1-0-0, p. Jno H. & M.A. Compher, b. Tankerville, carpenter, unm, sc:

John H. Compher, father, 1st Dist., BVS:1865:4
COMPHER, Cora B., W, F, d. Sep 1874, LC, child complaint, 0-15-0, p. Wm. F Compher, sc: Wm. F. Compher, father, LE Dist., BVS:1874:5
COMPHER, David N., W, M, d. 22 Nov 1875, LC, teething, 0-10-0, p. Frank & Anna Compher, sc: Frank Compher, father, LE Dist., BVS:1875:1
COMPHER, E. Almira, W, F, d. 20 Jun 1865, nr Short Hill, typhoid fever, 16-0-0, p. Jos & Susan Compher, b. nr Short Hill, farmer, unm, sc: Joseph Compher, father, 1st Dist., BVS:1865:3/4
COMPHER, Elizabeth, W, F, d. 2 Jan 1890, LC, la grippe, unk, p. John & Margaret Compher, b. LC, none, unm, sc: W.F. Compher, brother, 2nd Dist., BVS:1890:3
COMPHER, Hannah, W, F, d. 1 Sep 1866, nr Taylorstown, typhoid fever, 48-0-0, p. Israel & Mary Williams, b. LC, c/o: Saml. Compher, sc: Saml. Compher, husband, BVS:1866:1
COMPHER, Henry B, W, M, d. 23 May 1880, nr Lovettsville, inflammation of bowels, 0-3-15, p. John W. & Isabella Compher, b. LC, unm, sc: John W. Compher, father, 2nd Dist., BVS:1880:6
COMPHER, Mary, W, F, d. 29 Oct 1854, LC, dysentery, 44-0-0, p. John & Elizth. Compher, b. LC, unm, sc: Wm. Fawley, bro-in-law, BVS:1854:9, LC:9
COMPHER, Mary D., W, F, d. 18 March 1869, LC, child birth, 43-0-0, p. Howson & Eliza J. Hooe, b. LC, sc: Peter Compher, husband, BVS:1869:1
COMPHER, Mary M., W, F, d. 5 Sep 1853, Hillsboro, diarrhea, 0-5-0, p. Peter & Mary Compher, b. nr Hillsboro, sc: father, BVS:1854:1, LC:3
COMPHER, Peter, W, M, d. 5 Nov 1858, LC, old age, 82-2-12, p. John & Maria C. Compher, b. LC, farmer, c/o: Catharine Compher, sc: John Compher, son, BVS:1858:1, LC:30
COMPHER, Samuel, W, M, d. 26 Mar 1883, nr Lovettsville, pneumonia,

70-0-0, p. Jno. & Elizth. Compher, b. LC, farmer, c/o: Hannah & Mary E. Compher, sc: Chas L. Compher, son, 2nd Dist., BVS:1883:3
COMPHER, Sarah E., W, F, d. 23 Sep 1864, LC, diphtheria, 21-0-0, p. Peter & Mary Compher, b. LC, sc: Peter Compher, father, BVS:1864:1, LC:38
COMPHER, Susanna, W, F, d. 23 Oct 1879, nr Taylorstown, colic, 69-0-0, p. Henry & Elizabeth Fawley, b. LC, c/o: John Compher, sc: George W. Compher, son, 2nd Dist., BVS:1879:1
COMPHER, Susannah, W, F, d. 7 Nov 1891, nr Lovettsville, dropsy, 73-0-0, p. unk, b. unk, farmer, c/o: Joseph Compher, sc: husband, LV Dist., BVS:1891:5
CONARD, Barbary, W, F, d. 3 Feb 1855, LC, old age, 85-11-18, p. unk, b. unk, c/o: John Conard, sc: Abner Conard, son, BVS:1855:2, LC:15
CONARD, E. J., W, M, d. 30 Mar 1889, LC, apoplexy, 61-0-0, p. Jonathan & R. Conard, b. LC, farmer, c/o: Rachel Conard, sc: Rachel Conard, wife, 3rd Dist., BVS:1889:5
CONARD, Eliza Ann, W, F, d. 14 Dec 1876, nr Harpers Ferry, cancer, 65-0-0, p. ....Crooks, c/o: Joseph Conard, sc: Joseph Conard, husband, LV Dist., BVS:1876:3
CONARD, James A., W, M, d. 5 Nov 1890, LC, diphtheria, 5-0-0, p. Abner & Belle Conard, b. LC, none, unm, sc: Abner Conard, father, 2nd Dist., BVS:1890:3
CONARD, John, W, M, d. 4 May 1854, Jackson Co., Miss., cholera, 60-0-0, p. John & Barbary Conard, b. LC, farmer, c/o: Mary C. Conard, sc: Jos. M. Conard, son, BVS:1854:8, LC:7
CONARD, John Wm., W, M, d. 21 Oct 1882, LC, heart disease, 56-11-0, p. unk, b. LC, farmer, c/o: Mary A. Conard, sc: Mary A. Conard, wife, 3rd Dist., BVS:1882:3
CONARD, Joseph M., W, M, d. 13 Sep 1886, dropsy, 62-9-17, p. John & Mary, farmer, c/o: Mary J. Conard, sc: Chas. E. Conard, son, 2nd Dist., BVS:1886:5
CONARD, Louisa A., W, F, d. 26 May 1857, LC, pneumonia, 17-6-13, p.

Abner & Mary C. Conard, b. LC, unm, sc: Abner Conard, father, BVS:1857:1, LC:25

CONARD, Mary, W, F, d. 13 Aug 1856, LC, dysentery, 48-4-23, p. Ebenezer & Mary E. Grubb, b. LC, c/o: Joseph Conard, sc: Joseph Conard, husband, BVS:1856:3, LC:21

CONARD, Mary, W, F, d. 22 Feb 1859/60, LC, typhoid fever, 54-4-0, p. John & Barbary Conard, b. LC, unm, sc: Abner Conard, brother, BVS:1859:1, 1860:4, LC:37

CONARD, Mary E. Arabella, W, F, d. May 1876, nr Neersville, 0-4-0, p. Abner W. & Laura Bell Conard, b. nr Neersville, sc: Abner W. Conard, father, LV Dist., BVS:1876:3

CONARD, Mary Mercilva, W, F, d. Jul 1876, nr Harpers Ferry, consumption, 32-0-0, p. Joseph & Mary Conard, b. LC, unm, sc: Joseph Conard, father, LV Dist., BVS:1876:3

[CONARD], no name, W, F, d. 20 Oct 1875, Lovettsville Dist, 0-3-0, p. Joseph M. & Mary Conard, b. LC, unm, sc: Joseph Conard, father, LV Dist., BVS:1875:4

CONNER, Elizabeth, W, F, d. 4 May 1881, LC, consumption, 60-0-0, b. LC, c/o: David Conner, sc: David Conner, husband, 3rd Dist., BVS:1881:4

CONNER, Elizabeth C., W, F, d. 16 Apr 1889, Bloomfield, spasms, 0-0-6, p. Robt. A. & Annie P. Conner, b. Bloomfield, sc: Robt A. Conner, father, 1st Dist., BVS:1889:1

CONNER, Maurice D., W, M, d. 24 Aug 1887, Unison, dysentery, 1-2-0, p. Robt. A. & Annie Conner, b. Unison, sc: Roberrt A. Conner, father, 1st Dist., BVS:1887:2

CONNER, William, W, M, d. 25 May 1888, LC, chronic dyspepsia, 75-0-0, p. unk, b. LC, tanner, unm, sc: Peter Virts, friend, 3rd Dist., BVS:1888:1

CONNER, William W., W, M, d. 25 Jun 1876, LC, pneumonia, 0-9-0, p. Robert & Mary E. Conner, b. LC, sc: Robert T. Conner, father, LE Dist., BVS:1876:6

CONNER, Wm. H., W, M, d. 10 Jul 1877, Woodburn Farm, remittent fever, 6-0-0, p. J. W. & Louisa A. Conner, b. nr Leesburg, sc: J.W. Conner, father, BR Dist., BVS:1877:1

CONNOR, James W, W, M, d. 22 Oct 1875, North Fork, consumption, 33-0-0, p. John & Susan Connor, b. North Fork, blacksmith, unm, sc: Susy Connor, wife, MT Dist., BVS:1875:8

CONRAD, Abner, W, M, d. 7 Nov 1888, LC, old age, 77-0-0, p. John & Barbara Conrad, b. LC, farmer, c/o: Mary Conard, sc: Mary Conard, widow, 2nd Dist., BVS:1888:5

CONRAD, America, W, F, d. 14 Dec 1886, membranous croup, 1-11-14, p. David & Annie B., sc: David Conrad, father, 2nd Dist., BVS:1886:5

CONSTABLE, Eli, W, M, d. 28 Feb 1875, nr Mt. Hope Church, affection of kidneys, 75-2-0, p. unk, b. England, laborer, married, sc: Saml Shryock, friend, BR Dist., BVS:1875:5

COOK, Annie, B, F, d. Jul 1874, Leesburg, 0-6-0, p. Wm & Margret Cook, sc: Margaret Cook, mother, LE Dist., BVS:1874:5

COOK, Charles, B, M, d. 10 Jan 1887, Middleburg, pneumonia, 1-7-0, p. Carr & Joanna Cook, b. Middleburg, sc: Carr Cook, father, 1st Dist., BVS:1887:2

COOK, Jacob, B, M, d. 1 Jun 1876, nr Bloomfield, consumption, 17-0-0, p. Henry & Emily Cook, b. LC, unm, sc: Richard Tebbs, brother-in-law, MC Dist., BVS:1876:4

COOK, Sarah F., B, F, d. 1 Sep 1891, Lincoln, cancer, 57-0-0, b. Lincoln, wife, sc: Marshall Cook, MT Dist., BVS:1891:6

COOKSEY, Caroline L., W, F, d. 1 Jun 1880, nr Lovettsville, typhoid fever, 19-0-15, p. William & Mary C. Cooksey, b. LC, unm, sc: Mary C. Cooksey, mother, 2nd Dist., BVS:1880:6

COOKSEY, Darcas, W, F, d. 26 Jan 1894, Leesburg, fever, 27-0-0, p. unk, b. Leesburg, seamstress, unm, sc: Susan Cooksey, LE Dist., BVS:1894:3

COOKSEY, Elizabeth, W, F, d. 7 Aug 1855, nr Leesburg, child bed, 28-2-1, p. Robt. & Mary Curry, b. nr Francis' Mill, c/o: Jno. Cooksey, sc: Robt. Curry, father, BVS:1855:5, LC:17

COOKSEY, Eliz., W, F, d. 18 Aug 1855, LC, child bed, 27-0-0, p. Robert & Mary Curry, b. LC, c/o: Jno. Cooksey, sc: Geo. W. Campbell, bro.-in-law, BVS:1855:3, LC:15

COOKSEY, John, W, M, d. 27 Sep 1893, Woodburn, old age, 76-0-0, p. unk, b. Woodburn, farmer, consort, sc: Susan Cooksey, LE Dist., BVS:1893:6

COOKSEY, Rosa, W, F, d. 20 Aug 1884, Leesburg, cholera infantum, 0-3-19, p. Obed & Rosa Cooksey, b. LC, sc: Obed Cooksey, father, 2nd Dist., BVS:1884:4

COOPER, Adam, W, M, d. 26 Jun 1890, Hillsboro, paralyzed, 78-8-3, b. LC, farmer, c/o: Mary E. Cooper, sc: Mary E. Cooper, wife, 3rd Dist., BVS:1890:6

COOPER, Alvira A., W, F, d. 3 May 1883, nr Lovettsville, affection of brain, 1-10-0, p. Columbus P. & Cornelia Cooper, b. LC, sc: Camelia Cooper, mother, 2nd Dist., BVS:1883:6

COOPER, Ann E., W, F, d. 15 Sep 1858, LC, dysentery, 1-2-3, p. Peter & Mary E. Cooper, b. LC, sc: Mary E. Cooper, mother, BVS:1858:2, LC:30

COOPER, Ann E., W, F, d. 2 Sep 1872, nr Lovettsville, cramp colic, 29-5-2, p. J. W. & Sophia Goodhart, b. Lovettsville, mechanic, married, sc: J.W. Goodhart, father, LV Dist., BVS:1872:5

COOPER, Cato, B, M, d. 15 Nov 1874, Hamilton, gout, 38-0-0, p. Jno. & Sallie Cooper, b. LC, laborer, c/o: Mollie Cooper, sc: Mollie Cooper, wife, JF Dist., BVS:1874:2

COOPER, Clary E., W, F, d. 5 Sep 1855, LC, water on brain, 0-11-23, p. Geo. & Mary C. Cooper, b. LC, sc: Geo. Cooper, father, BVS:1855:1, LC:14

COOPER, Daniel, W, M, d. 12 Sep 1854, LC, unk, 69-3-11, p. Fredk &

Cathn Cooper, b. LC, miller, c/o: Elizabeth Cooper, sc: Mary A. Cooper, daughter, BVS:1854:9, LC:8

COOPER, David A., W, M, d. 17 Oct 1879, Leesburg, summer complaint, 0-5-0, p. John W. & Sarah A. Cooper, b. LC, sc: John W. Cooper, father, 2nd Dist., BVS:1879:1

COOPER, Emeline, W, F, d. 1 Jun 1881, LC, paralysis, 63-0-0, p. --- Titus, c/o: Solomon Cooper, sc: R.H. Cooper, son-in-law, 2nd Dist., BVS:1881:6

COOPER, Ervie, W, M, d. 8 Jan 1890, LC, unk, 3-0-0, p. Jno. W. & Sarah Cooper, b. LC, none, unm, sc: Jno W. Cooper, father, 2nd Dist., BVS:1890:3

COOPER, Geo., W, M, d. 20 Aug 1889, LC, old age, 73-4-25, p. Philip & Eliz. Cooper, b. LC, farmer, unm, sc: Susan Fulton, friend, 2nd Dist., BVS:1889:3

COOPER, George, W, M, d. 3 Apr 1888, LC, old age, 87-0-0, p. Geo. & Mary Cooper, b. LC, farmer, c/o: Sarah Cooper, sc: Tilghman Cooper, son, 2nd Dist., BVS:1888:5

COOPER, George, W, M, d. 16 Dec 1892, Lovettsville, paralysis, 72-0-0, p. unk, b. unk, farmer, consort, sc: Wm. Cooper, LV Dist., BVS:1892:6

COOPER, Gilbert, B, M, d. 10 Jan 1880, LC, consumption, 21-0-0, p. Hamill & Susan Cooper, b. LC, farmer, unm, sc: Hamill Cooper, father, 1st Dist., BVS:1880:1

COOPER, Harry Linden, W, M, d. 10 Nov 1876, Leesburg, diphtheria, 6-1-0, p. J. A. J. & Mary E. Cooper, b. Leesburg, sc: J.A.J. Cooper, father, LE Dist., BVS:1876:6

COOPER, Hattie Eugene, W, F, d. 13 Nov 1876, Leesburg, diphtheria, 8-3-0, p. J. A. J. & Mary E. Cooper, b. Leesburg, sc: J.A.J. Cooper, father, LE Dist., BVS:1876:6

COOPER, Henry C., W, M, d. 1 Dec 1888, LC, heart disease, 50-0-0, p. Geo. & Amanda Cooper, b. LC, laborer, unm, sc: Geo F. Cooper, brother, 2nd Dist., BVS:1888:5

COOPER, Isaac C., W, M, d. 29 Oct 1876, nr Lovettsville, swallowing ?, 2-0-0, p. John W. & Sarah A.

Cooper, b. LC, sc: John W. Cooper, father, LV Dist., BVS:1876:3

COOPER, John, B, M, d. 30 Jan 1888, Bloomfield, unk, 0-9-0, p. Lillie Cooper, b. Bloomfield, sc: Lillie Cooper, mother, 1st Dist., BVS:1888:3

COOPER, Joshua, W, M, d. 1 Sep 1855, LC, dysentery, 36-0-0, p. Danl. & Eliz Cooper, b. LC, boating, unm, sc: Mary A. Cooper, sister, BVS:1855:1, LC:14

COOPER, Liddia E., W, F, d. 1 Mar 1890, LC, unk, 26-0-0, p. Elias & Rosanna Crim, b. LC, none, c/o: Peter Cooper, sc: Peter Cooper, husband, 2nd Dist., BVS:1890:3

COOPER, Louisa, B, F, d. May 1872, Blue Ridge, 16-0-0, p. Daniel & Mariah Cooper, MC Dist., BVS:1872:7

COOPER, Margaret, W, F, d. 18 Feb 1896, Morrisonville, paralysis, 94-0-0, p. unk, b. unk, c/o: Benj. Cooper, sc: Benj. Cooper, consort, LV Dist., BVS:1896:7

COOPER, Mary E., W, F, d. 10 Jan 1891, Mechanicsville, pneumonia, 58-0-0, p. Margaret Collins, sc: Wm. H. Fillers, JF Dist., BVS:1891:7

COOPER, Michael, W, M, d. 18 May 1884, nr Lovettsville, rheumatism, 85-6-0, p. Geo. & Mary Cooper, b. LC, farmer, c/o: Mary A. Cooper, sc: Mary A. Cooper, wife, 2nd Dist., BVS:1884:4

COOPER, Milly, B, F, d. 15 Aug 1874, Trappe, affection of lungs, 20-0-0, p. Daniel & Maria Cooper, b. LC, unm, sc: Daniel Cooper, father, MC Dist., BVS:1874:4

[COOPER], no name, (f), F, d. 15 Dec 1853, LC, unk, 0-0-3, p. Sarah Cooper FN, b. LC, sc: Sarah Cooper, mother, BVS:1854:4, LC:2

COOPER, no name, B, F, d. 1Jan 1873, nr Millville, unk, 0-0-10, p. Juinie Cooper, b. Millville, sc: Janie Cooper, mother, MC Dist., BVS:1873:5

[COOPER], no name, W, , d. 14 Feb 1876, Leesburg, unk, 0-0-10, p. J. A. J. & Marry E. Cooper, b. Leesburg, sc: J.A.J. Cooper, father, LE Dist., BVS:1876:6

COOPER, no name, W, M, d. 9 Dec 1877, nr Lovettsville, 0-0-21, p. Thomas J. & Catherine Cooper, b. LC, sc: Thomas J. Cooper, father, LV Dist., BVS:1878:1/5

COOPER, Peter, W, M, d. [1879], Goresville, old age, 75-0-0, p. unk, b. LC, laborer, sc: J.R. Barnhouse, friend, 2nd Dist., BVS:1879:1

COOPER, Rachel A. E., W, F, d. Aug 1853, nr Hamilton, water on brain, 0-9-0, p. Peter & Elizabeth Cooper, b. nr Purcell's Store, sc: Mary Sutton, aunt, BVS:1854:6, LC:5

COOPER, Solomon, W, M, d. 2 Aug 1855, LC, suicide, 52-3-2, p. Geo. & Mary Cooper, b. LC, farmer, c/o: Emeline Cooper, sc: Emeline Cooper, wife, BVS:1855:1, LC:14

COPELAND, Andrew, W, M, d. 2 Jan 1854, LC, inflammation of glands, 63-7-0, p. Andrew & Nancy Copeland, b. LC, farmer, c/o: Jane Copeland, sc: Harmon Copeland, son, BVS:1854:9, LC:8

COPELAND, Craven A., W, M, d. 9 Jul 1885, Hillsboro, natural decay, 87-0-0, b. Virginia, farmer, c/o: Maria Copeland, sc: Luther Copeland, son, 3rd Dist., BVS:1885:6

COPELAND, Eliza J., W, F, d. 13 Nov 1859/60, LC, typhoid fever, 30-0-0, p. Danl T. & Margt Crawford, b. Jefferson, c/o: James C. Copeland, sc: James C. Copeland, husband, BVS:1859:1, 1860:3, LC:36

COPELAND, Elizabeth, W, F, d. 25 Feb 1858, her res, paralysis, 84-0-0, p. Richard & ... Roach, b. nr Short Hill, c/o: Richard Copeland, sc: Lindsey Copeland, son, BVS:1858:5, LC:33

COPELAND, Jane, W, F, d. 25 Mar 1888, LC, old age, 95-2-7, p. Andrew & Sarah Copeland, b. LC, none, c/o: Andrew Copeland, sc: Zillah E. Copeland, daughter, 3rd Dist., BVS:1888:1

COPELAND, John, W, M, d. 29 Nov 1859/60, LC, drowned, 44-0-0, p. David & Mary Copeland, b. LC, c/o: Delila Copeland, sc: Delila Copeland, wife, BVS:1859:1, 1860:4, LC:37

COPELAND, Nancy, W, F, d. 18 Jul 1856, LC, suicide, 72-11-0, p.

Andrew & Nancy Copeland, b. LC, unm, sc: Jane Copeland, sister-in-law, BVS:1856:2, LC:20

COPELAND, Nancy, W, F, d. 7 Jul 1865, Round Hill, consumption, unk, p. Jas & Sarah Copeland, b. Hillsboro, unm, sc: Jas. Copeland, father, BVS:1865:1

COPELAND, Richard, W, M, d. 15 Feb 1859/60, his res, old age, 96-3-0 or 90/3/0, p. David & Deborah Copeland, b. Ireland, cabinet maker, c/o: Elizabeth Copeland, dec'd, sc: Lindsey Copeland, son, BVS:1859:5, 1860:2, LC:35

CORBETT, Matthew Zaviour, W, M, d. 25 Aug 1877, LC, pneumonia, 1-3-25, p. James & Mary A. Corbett, b. LC, sc: James Corbett, father, LV Dist., BVS:1877:4/7

CORBIN, Jane, B, F, d. 10 May 1890, Willisville, dropsy, 79-0-0, p. Joseph & Bettie Roy, b. Fauquier Co., c/o: James Corbin, sc: William H. Gaskins, son-in-law, 1st Dist., BVS:1890:1

CORBIN, Mary J., W, F, d. 6 Dec 1881, LC, croup, 3-19-0, p. D. G. & Bettie Corbin, b. LC, sc: D.G. Corbin, father, 3rd Dist., BVS:1881:4

CORBIN, Miriom, W, F, d. Sep 1896, Waterford, bright's disease, 61-0-0, consort, JF Dist., BVS:1896:8

CORDELL, Amanda E., W, F, d. 19 Dec 1890, LC, child birth, 22-0-0, p. John L. Stout, b. LC, none, c/o: J.W. Cordell, sc: J.W. Cordell, husband, 2nd Dist., BVS:1890:3

CORDELL, Esther, W, F, d. 17 Oct 1873, nr Hoysville, unk, 0-0-17, p. Wm & Mary A. Cordell, b. nr Hoysville, shoemaker, married, sc: Wm. M. Cordell, father, LV Dist., BVS:1873:4

CORDELL, Martha, W, F, d. 21 Sep 1859/60, Lovettsville, unk, 75-8-22, p. unk, b. LC, sc: Susan Snoots, daughter, BVS:1859:1, 1860:4, LC:37

CORDELL, no name, W, M, d. 19 Dec 1890, LC, unk, 0-0-1, p. Jos. W. & Amanda Cordell, b. LC, none, unm, sc: J.W. Cordell, father, 2nd Dist., BVS:1890:3

CORDELL, Roger, W, M, d. 22 Jul 1896, Point of Rocks, cholera infantile, 0-8-0, p. Jos. & Hattie, b. Point of Rocks, unm, sc: Jos. Cordell, LV Dist., BVS:1896:7

CORDELL, Susan, W, F, d. 17 Jun 1853, LC, unk, 45-0-0, p. Jacob & Cathn. Slater, b. LC, c/o: Adam Cordel, sc: Jacob Cordell, bro-in-law, BVS:1854:3, LC:1

CORNELL, Clinton, B, M, d. 24 Apr 1886, LC, brain fever, 2-0-0, p. Richard & Laura Cornell, b. LC, none, unm, sc: Richd Cornell, father, 3rd Dist., BVS:1886:4

CORNELL, Dallas W., W, F, d. 14 Jul 1894, Sycolin, dysentery, 3-11-3, p. Dallas & Rosy, b. Sycolin, unm, sc: Dallas W. Cornell, LE Dist., BVS:1894:3

CORNELL, Robt S., W, M, d. 24 Nov 1855, Union, unk, 0-0-18, p. Stephen & Amanda Cornell, b. Union, sc: Stephen Cornell, father, BVS:1855:4, LC:16

CORNELL, Wildman, W, M, d. 3 Sep 1889, Philomont, consumption, 75-0-0, p. unk, b. LC, laborer, unk, sc: F.E. Robey, superintendent of poor, 1st Dist., BVS:1889:1

CORNELL, Wm. H., W, M, d. 4 Dec 1894, nr Lenah, consumption, 19-0-0, p. C. E. & Virginia Cornell, b. LC, laborer, unm, sc: C.E. Cornell, father, 1st Dist., BVS:1894:1

CORNWELL, Clinton, W, M, d. 24 Apr 1885, North Fork, brain fever, 2-0-0, p. Richd. & Cornelia Cornwell, b. Virginia, unm, sc: Richd Cornwell, father, 3rd Dist., BVS:1885:6

CORNWELL, Margaret F., W, F, d. 14 Feb 1893, Point of Rocks, consumption, 45-0-0, p. unk, b. Point of Rocks, consort, sc: R.A. Cornwell, LE Dist., BVS:1893:6

[CORNWELL], no name, W, M, d. 10 Apr 1892, Leesburg, unk, 0-0-8, p. Dallas & Emma Cornwell, b. Leesburg, unm, sc: Dallis Cornwell, LE Dist., BVS:1892:5

CORNWELL, Nora, W, F, d. 17 Nov 1893, Sycolin, pneumonia, 0-6-0, p. Dallis & Nora, b. Sycolin, unm, sc: Dallis Cornwell, LE Dist., BVS:1893:6

CORNWELL, Sarah E., W, F, d. 29 Mar 1889, LC, consumption, 28-0-0, p. A. B. & May Corder, b. LC, none, c/o: Thomas F. Cornwell, sc: Thos F. Cornwell, husband, 3rd Dist., BVS:1889:5

CORUM, Ann, B, F, d. 10 Dec 1881, LC, diphtheria, 7-0-0, p. Morant & Lucinda Corum, b. LC, sc: Alfred White, friend, 1st Dist., BVS:1881:1

CORUM, Ginnie, B, F, d. 14 Sep 1885, nr Aldie, indigestion, 25-0-0, p. Henry & Sarah Thomas, b. nr Aldie, c/o: Marshall Corum, sc: Marshall Corum, husband, 1st Dist., BVS:1885:3

CORUM, Henry, B, M, d. 10 May 1890, nr Aldie, consumption, 73-0-0, p. unk, b. LC, laborer, c/o: Betsey Corum, sc: Ambrose Corum, son, 1st Dist., BVS:1890:1

CORUM, Mary, B, F, d. 15 Apr 1885, nr Aldie, consumption, 6-0-0, p. Marshall & Ginnie Corum, b. nr Aldie, sc: Marshall Corum, father, 1st Dist., BVS:1885:3

CORUM, Mima, B, F, d. 24 Jan 1890, nr Aldie, unk, 70-0-0, p. unk, b. LC, c/o: Cyrus Corum, sc: George Corum, nephew, 1st Dist., BVS:1890:1

CORUM, Sally, B, F, d. 15 Mar 1883, nr Aldie, pneumonia, 18-0-0, p. Waven & Isabella Corum, b. nr Aldie, c/o: Sewell Ramey, sc: Waven Corum, father, 1st Dist., BVS:1883:1

CORUM, Waven, B, M, d. 10 Dec 1893, nr Aldie, heart failure, 82-0-0, p. unk, b. Prince William Co, laborer, c/o: Maria Corum, sc: Maria Corum, wife, 1st Dist., BVS:1893:2

CORUM, William, B, M, d. 20 Oct 1885, nr Aldie, consumption, 17-0-0, p. Ambrose & Ann M. Corum, b. nr Aldie, laborer, sc: Ann Corum, mother, 1st Dist., BVS:1885:3

[COSBERRY], no name, B, F, d. 10 Aug 1875, Leesburg, cholera infantum, 0-6-4, p. Patience Cosberry, b. Leesburg, sc: Mary Davis, friend, LE Dist., BVS:1875:2

[COSBERRY], no name, B, F, d. 15 Aug 1875, Leesburg, thrush, 0-1-9, p. Fannie Cosberry, b. Leesburg, sc: Hannah Hunter, friend, LE Dist., BVS:1875:2

COSBERRY, Willis, B, M, d. 28 Oct 1878, LC, pneumonia, 2-0-0, p. Patience Cosberry, b. LC, unm, sc:

Patience Cosberry, mother, LE Dist., BVS:1878:8

COST, Martha A., W, F, d. 2 Aug 1877, LC, paralysis, 75-6-25, b. LC, widow, sc: Thomas Cost, son, LV Dist., BVS:1877:4/7

[COST], no name, W, F, d. 29 Jul 1865, Lovettsville, strangulation, 0-0-28, p. Thoms J. & Jane A. Cost, b. Waterford, unsettled, unm, sc: Thoms T. Cost, father, 1st Dist., BVS:1865:3/4

COSTELLO, James, W, M, d. 20 Mar 1891, nr Bloomfield, old age, 108-0-0, p. Robt. Costello, b. Warren Co., farmer, c/o: Mary Costello, sc: Jas W. Costello, son, 1st Dist., BVS:1891:2

COSTELLOE, John B., W, M, d. Aug 1854, Bellfield, unk, 0-2-0, p. Robt. & Mary Ann Costelloe, b. Bell Field, sc: father, BVS:1854:12, LC:11

COSTELLOW, Henry T., W, M, d. 31 Mar 1878, Bellfield, pneumonia, 4-4-0, p. Thomas H. & Dinah A. Costellow, b. LC, sc: Thos H. Costellow, father, MC Dist., BVS:1878:6

COSTELLOW, Mary E., W, F, d. 1 Nov 1882, LC, measles, 4-0-0, p. Robert & Arah Costellow, sc: Robert Costellow, father, 1st Dist., BVS:1882:1

[COUGHMAN], no name,W, F, d. 27 Aug 1873, Snickersville, heart disease, 1-6-0, p. Joel & Matilda Coughman, b. Snickersville, sc: parents, MT Dist., BVS:1873:3

COWDEN, Mary, W, F, d. 5 Sep 1864, Pleasant Valley, dysentery, 64-0-0, p. Jas E. & E. Adrain, b. LC, housekeeper, c/o: Henry Cowden, sc: Henry Cowden, husband, BVS:1864:2, LC:39

COX, George L., W, M, d. 3 Oct 1865, nr Middleburg, dysentery, 3-1-1, p. Jas W. & A.C. Cox, b. nr Middleburg, sc: Philo Relerani, BVS:1865:1

COX, Hannah, W, F, d. 23 Mar 1873, nr Ketoctin Mountain, asthma, 82-5-5, p. Maurice Davis, b. LC, widow, sc: Sarah A. Hough, daughter, LV Dist., BVS:1873:4

COX, Lydia A., W, F, d. 21 Oct 1885, Hamilton, general debility, 77-0-0, b.

Loudoun County, Virginia, Death Register, 1853-1896

LC, c/o: James Cox, sc: Jas Cox, son, 3rd Dist., BVS:1885:6

COX, Patty, (f), F, d. 12 Feb 1858, Poor House, paralysis, 75-0-0, sc: W. Furr, steward, BVS:1858:3, LC:31

COX, Roulda, W, M, d. 6 Nov 1872, LC, croup, 0-6-4, p. Malina Cox, b. LC, sc: Malina Cox, mother, LE Dist., BVS:1872:3

CRAIG, Elizabeth, W, F, d. 7 Apr 1892, Mountville, nervous prostration, 60-0-0, p. Geo. & Sarah Gulick, b. Mountville, c/o: Jas Craig, sc: Jas Craig, husband, 1st Dist., BVS:1892:1

CRAIG, James M., W, M, d. 5 Jun 1858, res of parents, consumption, 10-10-0, p. James & Louisa Craig, b. nr Franklin's Mill, sc: James Craig, father, BVS:1858:4, LC:32

CRAIG, Llewellyn, B, M, d. 20 Mar 1876, Leesburg, rheumatism, 38-0-0, p. Ignatius & Elizabeth Craig, b. LC, laborer, sc: Catherine Thomas, friend, LE Dist., BVS:1876:6

[CRAIG], no name, W, M, d. 2 Oct 1876, nr Philomont, 0-0-1, p. John F. & Louisa Craig, b. LC, unm, sc: John F. Craig, father, MT Dist., BVS:1876:1

CRAIN, Catharine J., W, F, d. 8 Dec 1884, LC, typhoid dysentery, 70-0-0, p. Peter & Ann Jett , b. Fairfax Co., VA, c/o: Philo B. Crain, 1st Dist., BVS:1884:1

CRAMPTON, Thary, W, F, d. 7 Sep 1856, Poor House, dropsy, 70-0-0, b. LC, sc: steward, BVS:1856:4, LC:22

CRAVEN, Abigail, W, F, d. 1 Sep 1853, on Goose Creek, bilious fever, 54-0-0, p. Wm. & Abigail Holmes, b. LC, c/o: Jas Craven, sc: Jas Craven, husband, BVS:1854:5, LC:5

CRAVEN, Alice, B, F, d. Oct 1864, Augurne Farm, pneumonia, 4-0-0, p. Chas & Susan Crain, b. LC, sc: S.A. Brickner, head of family, BVS:1864:2, LC:39

CRAVEN, Chas., B, M, d. 15 May 1896, LC, 0-2-0, p. J. B. Craven, b. LC, sc: Jno Craven, father, LE Dist., BVS:1896:5

CRAVEN, Elizabeth A., B, F, d. 14 Aug 1885, nr Leesburg, unk, 0-0-7, p. Julian & Ida Craven, sc: Allison Craven grandfather, 2nd Dist., BVS:1885:1

CRAVEN, Hannah, W, F, d. 29 Jul 1894, Lincoln, heart trouble, 59-0-0, p. Timothy & Harriett Taylor, b. Lincoln, consort, sc: G.G. Craven, husband, 3rd Dist., BVS:1894:5

CRAVEN, Helen W., W, F, d. 8 Sep 1892, Lincoln, cholera infantum, 0-2-0, p. Ross C. & Gracie Craven, b. Lincoln, farmer, married, sc: Ross C. Craven, father, MT Dist., BVS:1892:8

CRAVEN, James F., W, M, d. 8 Apr 1866, Goose Creek, neuralgia, 77-3-10, p. Jas & ...Craven, b. Diggs Valley, farmer, sc: Wm Craven, son, BVS:1866:3

CRAVEN, Mary A., W, F, d. 4 Mar 1885, nr Arcola, rupture, 47-0-0, p. James & Agnes Craven, b. Arcola, sc: Chas E. Maffett, nephew, 1st Dist., BVS:1885:3

CRAVEN, no name, B, M, d. 1 Oct 1892, Arcola, unk, 0-0-6, p. Chas. & Maria Craven, b. Arcola, sc: Chas Craven, father, 1st Dist., BVS:1892:4

CRAVEN, Susan, B, F, d. 15 Jul 1872, nr Broad Run, unk, 32-0-0, p. unk, b. LC, c/o: Charles Craven, sc: Charles Craven, BR Dist., BVS:1872:6

CRAVEN, Thomas, W, M, d. 21 Jan 1894, Lincoln, lung trouble, 80-0-0, p. Joel & Alvira Craven, b. Lincoln, unm, sc: Mary Craven, sister, 3rd Dist., BVS:1894:5

CRAVEN, Wm. H., W, M, d. 11 Sep 1889, Arcola, bronchitis, 67-0-0, p. James S. & Abbie Craven, b. LC, unk, sc: C.J.C. Maffett, nephew, 1st Dist., BVS:1889:1

[CREEL], no name, W, F, d. 12 Aug 1880, LC, unk, 0-0-2, p. M.M. & Georgie Creel, b. LC, unm, sc: M.M. Creel, father, 1st Dist., BVS:1880:1

[CREEL], no name, W, M, d. 12 Aug 1880, LC, unk, 0-0-2, p. M.M. & Georgie Creel, b. LC, unm, sc: M.M. Creel, father, 1st Dist., BVS:1880:1

CRIDLER, John, W, M, d. 16 Nov 1854, Leesburg, consumption, 64-3-20, p. unk, b. Pennsylvania, butcher, c/o: Rebecca Cridler, sc: John W. Cridler, son, BVS:1854:10, LC:10

CRIDLER, John, W, M, d. 16 Nov 1854, Leesburg, consumption, 65-9-30, p. unk, b. Maryland, butcher, c/o: Rebecca Cridler, sc: Rebecca Cridler, wife, BVS:1854:8, LC:7

CRIDLER, John R., W, M, d. 1 Jun 1856, LC, unk, 0-3-0, p. Richard M. & Margaret Cridler, b. LC, sc: Margaret Cridler, mother, BVS:1856:1, LC:20

CRIDLER, Richard M., W, M, d. 1 Mar 1857, LC, consumption, 34-0-0, p. John & Elizth Cridler, b. Leesburg, laborer, c/o: Lydia M. Cridler, sc: Lydia M. Cridler, wife, BVS:1857:1, LC:24

CRIM, Ann S., W, F, d. 28 Aug 1890, LC, unk, 54-5-11, p. John & Catherine Shumaker, b. LC, none, c/o: Arnstead Crim, sc: Catharine Shumaker, mother, 2nd Dist., BVS:1890:4

CRIM, Annie, W, F, d. 13 Oct 1893, Maryland, consumption, 27-0-0, p. Mary & James Carey, b. Maryland, wife, sc: father, JF Dist., BVS:1893:3

CRIM, B. Frank, W, M, d. 9 Nov 1888, LC, r r accident, 23-0-0, p. C. F. & Louisa Crim, b. LC, none, unm, sc: C.F. Crim, father, 2nd Dist., BVS:1888:5

CRIM, Benj. F.L., W, M, d. 29 Jan 1865, Short Hill, croup, 0-2-14, p. C.F. & L.C. Crim, b. Between the Hills, blacksmith, unm, sc: C.F. Crim, father, 1st Dist., BVS:1865:3/4

CRIM, Conard, W, M, d. 1 Mar 1888, LC, old age, 81-0-0, p. Abram & Rosanna Crim, b. LC, none, unm, sc: Elias Crim, brother, 2nd Dist., BVS:1888:5

CRIM, Mary C., W, F, d. 6 Sep 1893, Maryland, unk, 0-3-0, p. Joseph A. & Annie Crim, b. LC, sc: husband, JF Dist., BVS:1893:3

CRIM, Peter, W, M, d. 9 or19 May 1865, Short Hill, consumption, 54-0-0, blacksmith, c/o: Susan Crim, sc: Susan Crim, wife, 1st Dist., BVS:1865:3/4

CRIM, Rosana, W, F, d. 10 Oct 1865, nr Short Hill, old age, 85-0-0, b. LC, farmer, c/o: A. Crim, sc: Conard Crim, son, 1st Dist., BVS:1865:2/4

CRIM, Susan, W, F, d. 24 Dec 1883, nr Lovettsville, old age, 84-0-0, p. Dyer & Catherine Waters, b. LC, c/o: Peter Crim, sc: Ann R. Riley, daughter, 2nd Dist., BVS:1883:3

CRIM, Wm. Asbury, W, M, d. Nov 1876, on Beaverdam Creek, chronic croup, 6-0-0, p. Christian & Louisa Crim, b. On Beaverdam Creek, sc: Christian Crim, father, LV Dist., BVS:1876:3

CRIMM, G.B., W, M, d. 20 Nov 1886, croup, 5-0-0, p. John J. & S. G., sc: John J. Crim, father, 2nd Dist., BVS:1886:5

CRIMM, William, B, M, d. 10 Aug 1888, Poor House, drowned, 40-0-0, p. unk, b. unk, unm, sc: F.E. Robey, superintendent of poor, 1st Dist., BVS:1888:3

CROSBERY, Maria, B, F, d. Oct 1874, Leesburg, old age, 74-0-0, p. Spencer Crosbery, sc: Spencer Crosbery, father, LE Dist., BVS:1874:5

CROSEN, Bettie, W, F, d. 16 Jul 1878, nr Bloomfield, dysentery, 6-0-0, p. Saml & Eliza B. Crosen, b. LC, sc: Saml Crosen, father, MC Dist., BVS:1878:6

CROSEN, Elizabeth, W, F, d. 4 Jan 1878, nr Millville, cancer in stomach, 83-0-0, b. LC, c/o: John Crosen, sc: C.W. Barton, nephew, MC Dist., BVS:1878:6

CROSEN, Mary E., W, F, d. 15 Jul 1896, nr Arcola, heart failure, 47-0-0, p. unk, b. nr Sterling, wife, c/o: Saml Crosen, sc: Saml Crosen, husband, BR Dist., BVS:1896:3

CROSEN, Simpson, W, M, d. Nov 1866, Sterling Branch, paralyzed, 70-0-0, p. unk, b. Fairfax, farmer, sc: S.H. Crosen, grandson, BVS:1866:3

CROSEN, Thomas S., W, M, d. Oct 1866, nr LKT Pike, unk, 40-0-0, p. Simpson & ... Crosen, b. Fairfax, farmer, sc: S.H. Crosen, nephew, BVS:1866:3

CROSS, [no name], W, M, d. 13 Jan 1879, Goresville, unk, 0-0-12, p. George L. & Lucy Cross, b. LC, sc: Fielder Cross, grandfather, 2nd Dist., BVS:1879:1

CROSS, Algernon, W, M, d. 25 May 1858, LC, killed, 19-0-0, p. Harrison & Kitty Cross, b. LC, sc: Harrison Cross, father, BVS:1858:6, LC:33

Loudoun County, Virginia, Death Register, 1853-1896   81

CROSS, James, (f), M, d. 15 Jun 1857, H. Piggott's, consumption, 15-6-0, p. Wesley & Caroline Cross, sc: mother, BVS:1857:3, LC:26

CROSS, John T., B, M, d. 1 Feb 1873, Mountain Gap, consumption, 11-2-0, p. Thomas & Elizabeth Cross, b. Mountain Gap, sc: parents, MT Dist., BVS:1873:3

CROSS, John Thomas, W, M, d. Aug 1875, Black Oak Ridge, brain fever, 0-9-0, p. James & Susan S. Cross, b. Black Oak Ridge, farmer, unm, sc: Samuel Cross, father, MT Dist., BVS:1875:8

CROSS, Mary, (f), F, d. 18 Jan 1856, LC, scrofula, 63-0-0, p. unk, unk, sc: Elizabeth Brooken, daughter, BVS:1856:1, LC:19

CROSS, Molly, (f), F, d. 12 Aug 1858, Leesburg, measles, 2-2-11, p. Jenny Cross, b. Leesburg, sc: Jenny Cross, mother, BVS:1858:1, LC:29

CROSS, Nancy, (f), F, d. 10 Nov 1859/60, LC, unk, 32-0-0, p. Joseph & Polly Cross, b. Leesburg, washer, unm, sc: James Winters, cousin, BVS:1859:2, 1860:5, LC:38

CROSS, no name, B, M, d. 3 May 1883, nr Leesburg, unk, 0-1-0, p. Alice Cross, b. LC, sc: Alice Cross, mother, 2nd Dist., BVS:1883:3

CROSS, Octavia, W, F, d. Jan 1856, LC, unk, 32-0-0, p. Wm. Rollins, b. Prince William Co., sc: Catharine Cross, mother-in-law, BVS:1856:7, LC:23

CROSS, Thomas, (f), M, d. Oct 1857, Joseph L. Hawling's, typhoid pneumonia, 3-0-0, p. Townsend & Elizabeth Cross, b. J.L. Hawling's Farm, sc: Joseph L. Hawlings, master, BVS:1857:4, LC:26

CROSS, William, W, M, d. 9 May 1875, Leesburg, spasms of the heart, 70-3-15, physician, c/o: Mary Cross, sc: Mary Cross, wife, LE Dist., BVS:1875:1

CROUCH, Ernest, W, M, d. 11 Jul 1896, nr Middleburg, diphtheria, 12-1-0, p. Thos. & M. Crouch, b. nr Middleburg, none, unm, sc: Thos Crouch, father, MC Dist., BVS:1896:1

CROUCHE, Ida V., W, F, d. 18 Nov 1882, LC, diphtheria, 7-0-0, p. Jno. W. & Eliz. Crouche, unm, sc: Jno W. Crouche, father, 1st Dist., BVS:1882:1

CROWSEN, Harrison, W, M, d. 24 Oct 1859/60, LC, consumption, 40-0-0, p. Simpson & Sarah Crowsen, b. LC, sc: Alfred Daymoode, brother-in-law, BVS:1859:6, 1860:3, LC:36

CROWSEN, Mary R., W, F, d. Oct 1856, LC, burned, 30-0-0, p. unk, b. LC, c/o: Thomas S. Crowson, sc: T.S. Crowson, head of family, BVS:1856:7, LC:24

CROWTHER, Elizabeth, W, F, d. 29 Feb 1884, Leesburg, old age, 82-0-0, p. --- Wilhelm, b. Baltimore Co. MD, c/o: John Crowther, sc: J.J. Stansbury, relation, 2nd Dist., BVS:1884:4

CROZEN, Sarah, W, F, d. 22 Oct 1879, nr Bolington, old age, 73-0-0, p. Jacob & Mary Ruse, b. LC, farmer, c/o: Jacob Crozen, sc: William T. Crozen, son, 2nd Dist., BVS:1879:1

CULLEN, Armistead, W, M, d. 31 Dec 1856, G.B. McCarty's, pulmonary, 0-5-0, p. John A. & Winifreed H. Cullen, b. Middleburg, sc: J.A. Cullen, father, BVS:1856:5, LC:23

CUMMINS, Edwd H., W, M, d. 25 Nov 1865, Frankville, diphtheria, 1-0-14, p. Jno T. & S.V. Cummins, b. LC, farmer, unm, sc: Jno T. Cummins, father, BVS:1865:1

CUMMINS, Frank, W, M, d. 10 Sep 1881, LC, dysentery, 0-3-0, p. Thos & Mary Cummins, b. LC, sc: Thos. Cummins, father, 3rd Dist., BVS:1881:4

CUMMINS, Hannah E., W, F, d. 6 Apr 1877, LC, pneumonia, 42-0-0, p. Edward & Mary Haines, b. LC, c/o: Jno. T. Cummins, sc: Jno. T. Cummins, husband, JF Dist., BVS:1877:3

CUMMINS, Martha A., W, F, d. 11 Oct 1866, Bellmont, diphtheria, 1-6-0, p. J. T. Cummins, b. Fairfax Co., sc: father, BVS:1866:2

CUMMINS, no name, W, M, d. 10 Jun 1884, Bunker Hill, VA, unk, 0-4-25, p. Thomas & Mollie Cummins, b. Bunker Hill, unm, sc: Thomas Cummins, father, 3rd Dist., BVS:1884:6

CUMMINS, no name, W, M, d. 22 Aug 1888, LC, cholera infantum, 0-0-12, p. Thomas & Molly Cummins, b. LC, none, unm, sc: Thos Cummins, father, 3rd Dist., BVS:1888:1

CUNNING, Ada V., W, F, d. 19 Apr 1888, LC, brain fever, 4-0-0, p. James L. & Ada Cunning, b. LC, none, unm, sc: Ada Cunning, mother, 2nd Dist., BVS:1888:5

CUNNING, John F., W, M, d. 12 Mar 1886, old age, 74-0-0, laborer, c/o: Mary Cunning, sc: Thos. J. Cunning, son, 2nd Dist., BVS:1886:5

CUNNING, Mary, W, F, d. 1 Apr 1885, nr Lovettsville, old age, 73-0-0, p. unk, c/o: John F. Cunning, sc: Jas T. Cunning, son, 2nd Dist., BVS:1885:1

CUNNING, no name, W, F, d. 14 Jul 1885, nr Lovettsville, unk, 0-0-7, p. Jas. T. & Ada V. Cunning, sc: Jas T. Cunning, father, 2nd Dist., BVS:1885:1

CUNNING, no name, W, F, d. 6 Jun 1888, LC, unk, 0-0-4, p. James L. & Ada Cunning, b. LC, none, unm, sc: Ada Cunning, mother, 2nd Dist., BVS:1888:5

CUNNINGHAM, John H., W, M, d. 5 Aug 1857, Middleburg, cholera infantum, 0-9-0, p. John W. & Mary C. Cunningham, b. Middleburg, sc: J.W. Cunningham, father, BVS:1857:4, LC:27

[CUNNINGHAM], no name, W, F, d. Oct 1854, dysentery, 0-3-0, p. Robt. & Ann E. Cunningham, b. LC, sc: R. Cunningham, father, BVS:1854:13, LC:13

[CUNNINGHAM], no name, W, F, d. 21 Oct 1873, nr Gum Spring, unk, 0-0-1, p. Benj. F. & Almira Cunningman, b. LC, sc: Benj. F. Cunningham, head of family, BR Dist., BVS:1873:1

CUNNINGHAM, Robt., Sr., W, M, d. 15 Oct 1874, Broad Run Dist., paralysis, 78-6-3, p. unk, b. LC, farmer, married, sc: Robt. Cunningham Jr., son, BR Dist., BVS:1874:3

CUNNINGHAM, Wilmuth, W, M, d. 15 Apr 1881, nr Pleasant Valley, cancer, 82-0-0, b. LC, sc: Huldah Mershon, friend, 1st Dist., BVS:1881:1

CURNS, Michael, B, M, d. 26 Dec 1880, LC, hernia, 81-0-0, p. unk, b. LC, unm, sc: Benj. F. Hibbs, friend, 1st Dist., BVS:1880:1

CURRELL, John J., W, M, d. 19 Aug 1886, nr Aldie, consumption, 57-0-0, p. John & Pamelia Currell, b. LC, farmer, c/o: Mary A.M. Currell, sc: Mary A.M. Currell, wife, 1st Dist., BVS:1886:1

CURREY, Mary, W, F, d. 23 Jan 1878, LC, pneumonia, 70-0-0, p. unk, b. LC, c/o: Robert Currey, sc: Chas. E. Currey, son, LE Dist., BVS:1878:8

CURRY, Anna, W, F, d. 15 Feb 1875, Leesburg, scarlet fever, 1-3-0, p. Jno R. & Anna Curry, sc: Jno. R. Curry, father, LE Dist., BVS:1875:1

CURRY, Elizabeth, W, F, d. 15 Mar 1884, nr Lovettsville, cold, 79-0-0, p. Andrew & Mary Graham, b. LC, farmer, c/o: John Curry, sc: John Curry, husband, 2nd Dist., BVS:1884:4

CURRY, Harry R., W, M, d. 15 Jun 1888, LC, measles, 1-2-0, p. Chas. E. & Rebecca Curry, b. LC, none, unm, sc: Chas E. Curry, father, 2nd Dist., BVS:1888:5

CURRY, John, W, M, d. 19 Jul 1887, LC, old age, 86-0-0, p. unk, b. LC, farmer, c/o: Margaret Curry, sc: Mary F. Curry, daughter, 2nd Dist., BVS:1887:4

CURRY, John R., W, M, d. 16 Feb 1889/90, LC, pneumonia, 53-0-0, p. unk, b. LC, plasterer, c/o: Ann C. Curry, sc: Ann C. Curry, widow, 2nd Dist., BVS:1889:3, 1890:3

CURRY, R. O. Agnes, W, F, d. 11 Jun 1879, Leesburg, unk, 0-0-14, p. Charles E. & Rebecca Curry, b. LC, sc: Charles E. Curry, father, 2nd Dist., BVS:1879:1

CURSEN, Nathaniel M., W, M, d. 13 Dec 1866, nr Rehoboth, consumption, 23-0-0, p. Jacob & Sarah Cursen, b. LC, unm, sc: Jacob Cursen, father, BVS:1866:1

CURTIS, L. D., B, M, d. 14 Oct 1890, Waterford, croup, 2-9-0, p. L. H. & Cate Curtis, b. LC, unm, sc: L.H. Curtis, father, 3rd Dist., BVS:1890:6

CURTIS, Mariah, B, F, d. 31 Aug 1877, LC, tumor on the bowels, 51-0-0, b. LC, c/o: Edward Curtis, sc: Edward

Loudoun County, Virginia, Death Register, 1853-1896   83

Curtis, husband, LV Dist., BVS:1877:4/7

[DADE], Evaline, (f), F, d. May 1855, Fauquier Co, scarlet fever, 3-0-0, p. Jas & Jane Dade, b. Fauquier Co., sc: James Dade, father, BVS:1855:6, LC:18

[DADE], James Edwards, (f), M, d. May 1855, Fauquier Co, scarlet fever, 4-0-0, p. Jas & Jane Dade, b. Fauquier Co., sc: James Dade, father, BVS:1855:6, LC:18

DADE, Mary R., W, F, d. Mar 1896, Waterford, liver complaint, 20-0-0, b. Waterford, unm, JF Dist., BVS:1896:8

DADE, Sarah E., W, F, d. 25 Sep 1883, nr Leesburg, whooping cough, 0-3-13, p. Lee M. & Medora Dade, b. LC, sc: Lee M. Dade, father, 2nd Dist., BVS:1883:6

DAILEY, Frances A., W, F, d. 23 Feb 1859/60, LC, consumption, 19-3-1, p. Aaron & Hannah Dailey, b. LC, unm, sc: Hannah Dailey, mother, BVS:1859:2, 1860:4, LC:37

DAILEY, William A., W, M, d. 2 Jul 1885, Leesburg, rheumatism of heart, 15-3-27, p. J. Thomas & Melinda Dailey, sc: J.T. Dailey, father, 2nd Dist., BVS:1885:1

DANA, Mary S., W, F, d. 16 Jun 1885, nr Farmwell, heart disease, 70-0-0, p. John & Mary Hamer, b. Pennsylvania, sc: Sarah A.D. Klein, friend, 1st Dist., BVS:1885:3

DANIEL, Elizabeth J., W, F, d. 7 Oct 1873, nr Mountville, stillborn, p. Jas W. & Elizabeth Daniel, b. nr Mountville, sc: James Daniel, father, MC Dist., BVS:1873:5

DANIEL, Forest, W, M, d. 1 Jun 1890, LC, cholera infantum, 0-6-0, p. Lemuel J. D. & Annie Daniel, b. LC, farmer, unm, sc: L.J.D. Daniel, father, 2nd Dist., BVS:1890:3

DANIEL, Goufalls, W, M, d. 22 Feb 1889, LC, unk, 35-0-0, p.__ & T. A. Daniel, b. LC, farmer, unm, sc: F.A. Daniel, head of family, 2nd Dist., BVS:1889:3

DANIEL, John Morrison, W, M, d. 12 Aug 1866, nr Mount Gilead, dysentery, 8-0-0, p. John & Cornelia Morrison, b. nr Mount Gilead, sc: father, BVS:1866:2

DANIEL, John T., W, M, d. 18 Sep 1883, nr Arcola, measles, 52-0-0, p. unk, b. LC, farmer, c/o: Sarah Daniel, sc: Sarah Daniel, wife, 1st Dist., BVS:1883:1

DANIELS, Harriet, B, F, d. 26 May 1887, LC, general debility, 75-0-0, p. unk, b. LC, none, unm, sc: W.G. Burson, friend, 3rd Dist., BVS:1887:6

DAREY, Eli, W, M, d. 4 Feb 1889, Philomont, pneumonia, 65-0-0, p. unk, b. LC, laborer, unk, sc: F.E. Robey, superintendent of poor, 1st Dist., BVS:1889:1

DARKUS, Annie C., B, F, d. 25 Dec 1893, Leesburg, unk, 54-0-0, p. unk, b. Leesburg, consort, sc: husband, LE Dist., BVS:1893:7

DARNE, Chas. W., W, M, d. 20 Jun 1876, nr Belmont, scrofula, 32-0-0, p. Thos. & Fannie Darne, b. LC, farmer, unm, sc: Janie Darne, mother, BR Dist., BVS:1876:2

DARNE, Penelope M., W, F, d. 6 Apr 1896, Ashburn, old age & paralysis, 73-0-0, b. LC, c/o: John A. Darne, sc: Al Saunders, son, BR Dist., BVS:1896:3

DARNE, Thomas, W, M, d. 15 Apr 1871, pneumonia, 78-0-0, farmer, married, BR Dist., BVS:1871:3

DARR, Blanche, W, F, d. 8 Aug 1881, LC, dysentery, 0-4-0, p. Chas. & Rosa Darr, b. LC, sc: C.E. Darr, father, 3rd Dist., BVS:1881:4

DARR, Jonnie, W, M, d. 1 Oct 1887, LC, consumption, 0-11-0, p. Chas. & Rosa Darr, b. LC, none, unm, sc: Charles Darr, father, 3rd Dist., BVS:1887:6

DARR, Margaret, W, F, d. 27 May 1854, LC, unk, 40-2-7, p. unk, b. LC, c/o: Samuel Darr, sc: Priscilla Shoars, neighbor, BVS:1854:9, LC:8

DARR, Mary E., W, F, d. 14 Feb 1881, LC, quinsy, 14-3-0, p. E. W. & M. A. Darr, sc: E.W. Darr, father, 2nd Dist., BVS:1881:6

DARR, Rosie E., W, F, d. 13 Jun 1887, LC, consumption, 30-0-0, p. Jno. & Lizzie Virts, b. LC, none, c/o: Charles Darr, sc: Charles Darr, husband, 3rd Dist., BVS:1887:6

DAVIS, Annie E., W, F, d. 17 Sep 1890, Unison, membranous croup, 1-2-0, p. Chas. E. & Callie Davis, b. Unison, sc: Chas E. Davis, father, 1st Dist., BVS:1890:1

DAVIS, Bertie, W, F, d. 19 Oct 1869, LC, unk, p. Betsy Ann & Benj E. Davis, b. LC, sc: Benjamin Davis, father, BVS:1869:1

DAVIS, Betsy, B, F, d. 26 Jan 1877, nr Bloomfield, consumption, 21-11-0, p. Wesley & Isabella Davis, b. LC, unm, sc: Wesley Davis, father, MC Dist., BVS:1877:5

DAVIS, Bettie, B, F, d. 9 Feb 1883, Leesburg, typhoid pneumonia, 40-0-0, p. unk, b. LC, laborer, c/o: Chas. Davis, sc: Chas Davis, husband, 2nd Dist., BVS:1883:3

DAVIS, Catharine, W, F, d. 17 Apr 1877, Unison, abscess of the stomach, 76-0-0, b. LC, c/o: Jerry Davis, sc: Frank Taylor, friend, MC Dist., BVS:1877:5

DAVIS, Catharine M., W, F, d. 15 Apr 1883, Charles Co., MD, tumor, 60-0-0, p. Geo. & Ellen Goode, b. LC, c/o: Edwin P. Davis, sc: Edwin P. Davis, husband, 1st Dist., BVS:1883:1

DAVIS, Charlotte J., B, F, d. 15 Jan 1878, LC, scrofula, 14-0-0, p. John & Eliza Davis, b. LC, unm, sc: Eliza Davis, mother, LE Dist., BVS:1878:8

DAVIS, Clara, W, F, d. 30 Sep 1882, LC, old age, 85-0-0, p. John & Mary Davis, c/o: Edward K. Davis, sc: Edward K. Davis, husband, 1st Dist., BVS:1882:1

DAVIS, Eliz., (f), , d. Jul 1855, unk, 13-0-0, p. Norvell & E. Davis, b. LC, sc: Eliz. Davis, mother, BVS:1855:8, LC:19

DAVIS, Eliza, W, F, d. Sep 1855, unk, 45-0-0, p. unk, sc: F.F. Luckett, friend, BVS:1855:9, LC:19

DAVIS, Emma, B, F, d. 30 Sep 1873, nr Broad Run, consumption, 18-0-0, p. Lorinda Prim, b. Leesburg, unm, sc: Geo. Binns, head of family, BR Dist., BVS:1873:1

DAVIS, Evaline, B, F, d. 17 Nov 1887, LC, blood poison, unk, p. unk, b. LC, none, c/o: Jamy Davis, sc: Jamy Davis, husband, 3rd Dist., BVS:1887:6

DAVIS, Fanny, B, F, d. 15 Jun 1876, nr Bloomfield, unk, 6-11-15, p. Wesley & Isabella Davis, b. LC, sc: Wesley Davis, father, MC Dist., BVS:1876:4

DAVIS, Frank, B, M, d. 3 Aug 1893, Round Hill, paralysis, 82-0-0, p. Jno. Anderson, b. Carroll Co., Va., miller, husband, JF Dist., BVS:1893:3

DAVIS, Frezina, B, F, d. 9 Jun 1896, North Fork, child birth, 26-0-0, p. Burr & Millen Jones, b. North Fork, sc: Burr Jones, father, MT Dist., BVS:1896:9

DAVIS, Isaac L., W, M, d. 13 May 1864, Mount Gilead, 0-1-21, p. Benj R.J. Davis, b. LC, sc: Benj. Davis, father, BVS:1864:2, LC:39

DAVIS, Jerry, W, M, d. 28 Jun 1853, Poor House, paralysis, 55-0-0, p. unk, b. unk, sc: Wm. Furr, keeper of the poor house, BVS:1854:7, LC:6

DAVIS, Jerry, B, M, d. 10 Apr 1877, Leesburg, pneumonia, 35-0-0, sc: Jos. Valentine, friend, LE Dist., BVS:1877:8

DAVIS, John M., W, M, d. 2 Mar 1894, Taylorstown, dropsy, 85-0-0, p. unk, b. unk, unk, consort, sc: John Davis, LV Dist., BVS:1894:4

DAVIS, Lillian A., W, F, d. 28 Apr 1892, Woodburn, spinal meningitis, 6-11-0, p. Benjamin & Sallie Davis, b. Woodburn, farmer, married, sc: Benjamin Davis, father, MT Dist., BVS:1892:8

DAVIS, Lilly H., W, F, d. 23 Apr 1872, LC, unk, 0-2-0, p. Mary E. Davis, b. Washington DC, sc: F.A. Lutz, grandfather, LE Dist., BVS:1872:3

DAVIS, Margaret, W, F, d. 25 Apr 1892, Purcellville, pneumonia, 36-0-0, b. Purcell's, farmer, married, sc: Margaret Davis, wife, MT Dist., BVS:1892:8

DAVIS, Mary Elizabeth, W, F, d. 13 Feb 1875, Hamilton, pneumonia, unk, p. Albert C. & Susan E. Davis, b. Hamilton, unm, sc: Albert Davis, father, MT Dist., BVS:1875:8

DAVIS, Mollie, B, F, d. Oct 1876, E side of Short Hill, heart disease, 25-0-0, b. Frederick, MD, unm, sc: Margaret Timbers, friend, LV Dist., BVS:1876:3

DAVIS, Nancy, W, F, d. 2 Feb 1857, LC, dropsy, 61-0-0, p. unk, b. LC, unm, sc: John Jones, friend, BVS:1857:1, LC:24

[DAVIS], no name, W, M, d. Oct 1854, Green Garden, 0-11-0, p. Richard G. & Susan Davis, b. Prince William Co, sc: Alexander Pierson, BVS:1854:12, LC:11

[DAVIS], no name, W, , d. Jul 1855, unk, 0-8-0, p. I. F. & Louisa Davis, b. LC, sc: Delilah Piles, neighbor, BVS:1855:8, LC:19

[DAVIS], no name, W, M, d. 25 Jul 1855, Snickersville, 0-0-1, p. E.P. & Eliz. Davis, b. Snickersville, sc: E.P. Davis, father, BVS:1855:7, LC:18

[DAVIS], [no name], W, M, d. Apr 1857, unk, 0-0-15, p. J.F. & Louisa Davis, b. LC, sc: J.F. Davis, father, BVS:1857:7, LC:28

[DAVIS], no name, W, F, d. Feb 1865, Diamondhill farm, unk, 0-1-0, p. I.F. & Louisa Davis, b. Diamond Hill, unm, sc: Isaac F. Davis, father, BVS:1865:2

[DAVIS], no name, B, F, d. 2 Jan 1866, nr Moss's Mill, unk, unk, p. Anderson Davis, b. Moss Mill, sc: Wm. Moss, BVS:1866:2

DAVIS, Rebecca J., W, F, d. 24 May 1864, Mount Gilead, child birth, 40-4-17, p. Isaac & Martina Eaton, b. LC, sc: Benj. Davis, husband, BVS:1864:2, LC:39

DAVIS, Rich. T., W, M, d. 22 Aug 1877, Leesburg, cholera infantum, 0-13-0, p. Rich. T. & L. T. Davis, b. Leesburg, sc: Rich. T. Davis, father, LE Dist., BVS:1877:8

DAVIS, Robt. L., W, M, d. 19 Jun 1889, Farmwell, consumption, 37-0-0, p. Wm. B. & Velinda W. Davis, b. LC, farmer, c/o: Jane A. Davis, sc: Jane A. Davis, wife, 1st Dist., BVS:1889:1

DAVIS, Samuel, W, M, d. 12 Sep 1880, LC, diphtheria, 6-0-0, p. Edward R. & Lucinda Davis, b. LC, unm, sc: Edward K. Davis, father, 1st Dist., BVS:1880:1

DAVIS, Sarah, W, F, d. 12 Aug 1856, res, paralysis, 46-0-13, p. Wm. & Nancy White, b. LC, sc: B. Davis, widower, BVS:1856:5, LC:22

DAVIS, Sarah L., W, F, d. 15 Apr 1876, nr Mount Gilead, pneumonia, unk, p. Benj. & Sarah Davis, b. LC, unm, sc:

Benj. Davis, father, MT Dist., BVS:1876:1

DAVIS, Thomas L., W, M, d. 16 Dec 1856, nr Silcott Springs, typhoid fever, 44-0-0, p. John C. & ---, b. Fauquier Co., blacksmith, c/o: Margaret A. Davis, sc: Joseph Gochnauer, brother-in-law, BVS:1856:4, LC:22

DAVIS, Tobias, B, M, d. 3 Oct 1876, LC, consumption, 23-0-0, p. Jerry & Emiline Davis, b. LC, laborer, unm, sc: Jerry Davis, father, JF Dist., BVS:1876:8

DAVIS, Westly, B, M, d. 4 Dec 1888, Bloomfield, consumption, 58-0-0, p. Philip & Betsey Davis, b. Bloomfield, unm, sc: Philip Davis, brother, 1st Dist., BVS:1888:3

DAVIS, Wm. E., W, M, d. 6 Nov 1854, Boscum, bilious dysentery, 50-0-0, p. Benson & Ann Davis, b. Prince William Co., farmer, c/o: Verlinda Davis, sc: Mrs. Verlinda Davis, BVS:1854:11, LC:10

DAVISON, Agnes, W, F, d. 7 Feb 1856, Hillsboro, inflammation stomach, 18-0-23, p. Fredk. A. & Elizth. Davison, b. Hillsboro, unm, sc: F.A. Davison, father, BVS:1856:1, LC:20

DAWSON, Dickie, B, F, d. 3 Feb 1896, Middleburg, unk, 1-8-24, p. R. P. & Laura Dawson, b. Middleburg, none, unm, sc: R.P. Dawson, father, MC Dist., BVS:1896:1

DAWSON, Ester C., B, F, d. 21 Jun 1884, LC, dropsy, 3-4-0, p. Richard & Lawvina Dawsen, 1st Dist., BVS:1884:1

DAWSON, Jennith, W, F, d. 20 Mar 1866, Ellendale, croup, 3-0-0, p. Benj F. & Jane Dawson, b. Fauquier Co., farmer, sc: father, BVS:1866:3

DAWSON, Laura, W, F, d. 31 Jul 1886, nr Unison, unk, 0-4-10, p. Charles & Henrietta Dawson, b. nr Unison, sc: Charles W. Dawson, father, 1st Dist., BVS:1886:1

DAWSON, Mary A., W, F, d. 18 Mar 1884, LC, scarlet fever, 6-5-0, p. John H. & Sarah Dawson, b. LC, 1st Dist., BVS:1884:1

DAWSON, Robert L., W, M, d. 1 Nov 1890, LC, consumption, 22-0-0, p. Wm. M. Dawson, b. LC, carpenter, unm, sc: Wm. Dawson, father, 2nd Dist., BVS:1890:3

DAY, Andrew, B, M, d. 1 May 1881, LC, bronchitis, 1-3-0, p. Thomas & Harriet Day, sc: Harriet Day, mother, 2nd Dist., BVS:1881:6

DAY, Emanuel, B, M, d. 10 Mar 1883, nr Leesburg, consumption, 55-0-0, p. Julius & Jane Day, b. LC, laborer, c/o: Jennie Day, sc: Jennie Day, wife, 2nd Dist., BVS:1883:3

DAY, Fannie, B, F, d. 3 May 1883, nr Leesburg, pneumonia, 19-0-0, p. Washington & Helen Day, b. LC, laborer, sc: Washington Day, father, 2nd Dist., BVS:1883:6

DAY, Gabriel, B, M, d. 17 Sep 1875, LC, thrush, 0-1-8, p. Bagrield & Dianna Day, sc: Dianna Day, mother, LE Dist., BVS:1875:1

DAY, George W., B, M, d. 10 May 1878, LC, pneumonia, 1-3-0, p. Thomas & Harriett Day, b. LC, unm, sc: Harriett Day, mother, LE Dist., BVS:1878:8

DAY, Harry, B, M, d. 1 Jul 1885, nr Leesburg, unk, 0-2-0, p. Robert & Catherine Day, sc: Robert Day, father, 2nd Dist., BVS:1885:1

DAY, Jane, B, F, d. 18 Mar 1883, nr Leesburg, pneumonia, 20-0-0, p. Washington & Helen Day, b. LC, laborer, sc: Washington Day, father, 2nd Dist., BVS:1883:6

DAY, Julius, B, M, d. 15 May 1881, LC, old age, 80-0-0, p. --- Day, laborer, unk, sc: Ginnie Day, daughter-in-law, 2nd Dist., BVS:1881:6

DAY, Lucinda, B, F, d. 7 Aug 1879, nr Oatlands, consumption, 0-6-17, p. Thomas & Harriet Day, b. LC, sc: Thomas Day, father, 2nd Dist., BVS:1879:1

DAY, no name, B, F, d. 5 May 1884, nr Leesburg, unk, 1-0-0, p. Robert & Catharine Day, b. LC, sc: Robert Day, father, 2nd Dist., BVS:1884:4

DAY, Sarah, B, F, d. 10 Dec 1883, nr Leesburg, consumption, 15-0-0, p. Gabriel & Dinah Day, b. LC, laborer, sc: Dinah Day, mother, 2nd Dist., BVS:1883:6

DAY, Washington, B, M, d. 12 Nov 1891, Sycolin, consumption, unk, p. unk, b. unk, consort, LE Dist., BVS:1891:4

DAYMOODE, Louis, W, M, d. 8 Oct 1853, LC, typhoid fever, 17-0-0, p. John & E. Daymoode, b. LC, sc: Jacob Fox, friend, BVS:1854:2, LC:6

DAYMUDE, Bessie L., W, F, d. 22 Jul 1894, nr Arcola, typhoid fever, 16-0-0, p. A. G. & Julia E. Daymude, b. LC, laborer, unm, sc: Julia E. Daymude, mother, 1st Dist., BVS:1894:1

DAYMUDE, Geo. F., W, M, d. 19 Jul 1894, nr Arcola, typhoid fever, 31-0-0, p. A. G. & Julia E. Daymude, b. LC, laborer, unm, sc: Julia E. Daymude, mother, 1st Dist., BVS:1894:1

DAYMUDE, John, W, M, d. 11 Jul 1865, Skinners Mill, old age, 78-4-29, p. Jacob Daymude, b. Maryland, farmer, consort, sc: A.G. Daymude, son, BVS:1865:2

DAYMUDE, Susan B., W, F, d. 23 Apr 1876, nr Guilford, unk, 0-0-6 hrs, p. Alfred G. & Julia Daymude, b. Broad Run Dist., unm, sc: Alfred Daymude, father, BR Dist., BVS:1876:2

DAYMUDE, Susie B., W, F, d. 15 Apr 1894, nr Arcola, typhoid fever, 18-0-0, p. A. G. & Julia E. Daymude, b. LC, laborer, unm, sc: Julia E. Daymude, mother, 1st Dist., BVS:1894:1

DEAN, George, B, M, d. 20 Mar 1889, Sterling, pneumonia, 28-0-0, p. Jesse & Lorinda Dean, b. LC, laborer, c/o: Frances Dean, sc: Frances Dean, wife, 1st Dist., BVS:1889:1

DEAN, J. William, W, M, d. 14 Jul 1883, Hamilton, paralysis, 39-0-0, b. LC, merchant, c/o: Mary R. Dean, sc: Mary R. Dean, wife, 3rd Dist., BVS:1883:5

DEAN, James H., B, M, d. 25 Nov 1874, Broad Run Dist., typhoid fever, 20-4-0, p. Reuben & Martha Dean, b. LC, sc: Reuben Dean, head of family, BR Dist., BVS:1874:3

DEAN, Martha, B, F, d. 29 Apr 1883, nr Pleasant Valley, malaria fever, 65-0-0, p. unk, b. LC, c/o: Reuben Dean, sc: Reuben Dean, husband, 1st Dist., BVS:1883:1

DEBUTTS, Taylor M., W, M, d. 18 Nov 1886, nr Farmwell, unk, 38-0-0, p.

Loudoun County, Virginia, Death Register, 1853-1896 87

Swanington & Jane Debutts, b. West Virginia, farmer, c/o: Margaret V. Debutts, sc: Margaret V. Debutts, wife, 1st Dist., BVS:1886:1

DEER, James, (f), M, d. 20 Jan 1858, Poor House, old age, 80-0-0, b. Prince William Co., supposed, sc: W. Furr, steward, BVS:1858:3, LC:31

DEMERY, Enos, W, M, d. 18 Dec 1857, LC, unk, 58-0-0, p. Peter & Mary Demery, b. LC, farmer, unm, sc: Mahlon Demery, brother, BVS:1857:1, LC:25

DEMERY, Jane C., W, F, d. 27 Dec 1857, LC, unk, 26-6-0, p. Mahlon & Elizth Demery, b. LC, unm, sc: Mahlon Demery, father, BVS:1857:1, LC:25

[DEMERY], no name, W, F, d. 20 Mar 1853, LC, unk, 0-0-1, p. Mahlon & Sophia Demery, b. LC, sc: Mahlon Demery, father, BVS:1854:4, LC:2

[DEMERY], no name, W, F, d. 24 Dec 1857, LC, unk, 0-0-5, p. Jane C. Demery, b. LC, unm, sc: Mahlon Demery, grandfather, BVS:1857:1, LC:25

DEMORY, Margaret E., W, F, d. 10 Jul 1874, teething, 0-13-0, p. John & Jane Demory, LV Dist., BVS:1874:6

DENEAL, William H., B, M, d. 3 Jul 1890, nr Aldie, consumption, 1-0-0, p. Enoch & Frances DeNeal, b. nr Aldie, sc: Enoch DeNeal, father, 1st Dist., BVS:1890:1

DENNIS, Selina, W, F, d. 5 Jan 1875, LC, inflammation bowels, 68-0-0, c/o: John Dennis, sc: L.D. Thompson, friend, JF Dist., BVS:1875:3

DENNISON, Garland, W, M, d. Dec 1855, unk, 80-0-0, p. unk, b. LC, sc: Eliz. French, head of family, BVS:1855:8, LC:19

DENNY, Mary, B, F, d. 22 Apr 1876, nr Gum Spring, dropsy, 31-0-0, p. unk, b. Fairfax Co., unm, sc: John Denny, brother, BR Dist., BVS:1876:2

DENSMORE, John H., W, M, d. 9 Dec 1890, Round Hill, brain fever, 1-8-0, p. A. E. & A. B. Densmore, b. LC, none, unm, sc: W.E. Densmore, father, 3rd Dist., BVS:1890:6

DENSMORE, Wm. L/S. W.P., W, M, d. 24 Sep 1859/60, LC/Maryland, typhoid fever, 16-5-0, p. Wm. & Sarah Densmore, b. Maine, sc: Wm. Densmore, father, BVS:1859:1, 1860:3, LC:36

DENY, Frances, W, F, d. 15 Nov 1866, Between the Hills, 16-0-0, p. Eli & Elizth. Deny, b. LC, sc: Eli Deny, father, BVS:1866:1

DENY, Sophia, W, F, d. 6 Jul 1866, Between the Hills, cancer, 54-0-0, p. Jacob & Elizth. Hough, b. LC, c/o: Solomon Deny, sc: Soloman Deny, husband, BVS:1866:1

DERRY, Christian, W, M, d. 27 May 1858, LC, dropsy, 62-5-2, p. Philip & Barbary Derry, b. LC, farmer, c/o: Susan Derry, sc: John P. Derry, son, BVS:1858:2, LC:30

DERRY, David, W, M, d. 31 Oct 1854, LC, unk, 49-0-0, p. unk, b. LC, cooper, c/o: Nancy W. Derry, sc: Ann Wolford, neighbor, BVS:1854:8, LC:7

DERRY, Joseph P., W, M, d. 4 Nov 1890, Hillsboro, typhoid fever, 27-0-18, p. Lewis W. & Virginia Derry, b. LC, farmer, unm, sc: Virginia Derry, mother, 3rd Dist., BVS:1890:6

DERRY, Lewis W., W, M, d. 17 Jun 1882, LC, bright's disease, 62-7-0, p. unk, b. LC, farmer, c/o: Virginia Derry, sc: Virginia Derry, wife, 3rd Dist., BVS:1882:3

DERRY, Mary L. A., W, F, d. 15 Nov 1853, LC, dysentery, 1-2-5, p. Absalom P. & Polly Derry, b. LC, sc: John P. Derry, cousin, BVS:1854:4, LC:2

[DERRY], no name, W, F, d. 5 Jul 1856, LC, whooping cough, 0-3-2, p. Philip & Mary E. Derry, b. LC, sc: Philip Derry, father, BVS:1856:2, LC:20

DERRY, no name, W, M, d. 3 May 1874, nr Hillsboro, still born, unk, p. Phillip & Mary Derry, b. LC, sc: Phillip Derry, father, JF Dist., BVS:1874:2

DERRY, no name, W, F, d. Mar 1876, nr Bolivar, Jefferson W Va, 0-0-10, p. Philip V. & Mary E. Derry, b. Jefferson Co., W Va., sc: John P. Derry, cousin, LV Dist., BVS:1876:3

DERRY, no name, W, F, d. Apr 1876, nr Bolivar, Jefferson W Va, 0-1-0, p. Philip V. & Mary E. Derry, b.

Jefferson Co., W Va., sc: John P. Derry, cousin, LV Dist., BVS:1876:3

DERRY, Philip, W, M, d. 20 Sep 1890, LC, heart disease, 70-0-0, p. Philip & Barbara Derry, b. LC, farmer, c/o: Mary E. Derry, sc: Mary E. Derry, widow, 2nd Dist., BVS:1890:3

DERRY, Philip, W, M, d. Apr 1876, nr Bolivar, Jefferson W Va, jaundice, 47-0-0, p. Peter & Eliza Ann Derry, b. LC, farmer, c/o: Mary E. Derry, sc: John P. Derry, cousin, LV Dist., BVS:1876:3

DERRY, William A., W, M, d. 1 Apr 1889, LC, kicked by a horse, 20-0-0, p. Jane & John Derry, b. LC, none, unm, sc: J.P. Derry, head of family, 2nd Dist., BVS:1889:3

DEVENGER, John W., B, M, d. 18 Mar 1885, S. Spring's, whooping cough, 1-2-0, p. Julius & Elizabeth Devenger, b. LC, unm, sc: Julius Devenger, father, 3rd Dist., BVS:1885:6

DIBRELL, Anthony, W, M, d. 3 Apr 1893, Leesburg, heart failure, 46-0-0, p. unk, b. Leesburg, cashier, consort, sc: Agnes Dibrell, LE Dist., BVS:1893:6

DICKEY, Eliza A., W, F, d. 23 Oct 1891, Round Hill, unk, 56-0-0, p. Harrison & Angie Cummins, b. Round Hill, wife, sc: J.K. Reynolds, JF Dist., BVS:1891:7

DIEDERICK, Clara V., W, F, d. 22 Mar 1883, nr Farmwell, scarlet fever, 2-6-0, p. Geo. & Anna Diederick, b. nr Farmwell, unm, sc: Geo Diederick, father, 1st Dist., BVS:1883:1

DIEDRICK, Daniel, W, M, d. 25 Jan 1878, nr Belmont, infirmity, 90-0-0, p. unk, b. Germany, farmer, unk, sc: Geo. W. Diedrick, son, BR Dist., BVS:1878:4

DILLARD, Cora, B, F, d. 1 May 1887, LC, inflammation of brain, 0-8-0, p. Coon & Linda Dillard, b. LC, none, unm, sc: Charles Darr, father, 3rd Dist., BVS:1887:6

DILLON, Anna L., W, F, d. 30 Dec 1857, res of parents, 0-0-1, p. James J. & Mary E. Dillon, b. nr Purcellville, sc: J.J. Dillon, father, BVS:1857:4, LC:26

DILLON, Isaac, W, M, d. 18 Sep 1853, Purcellville, typhoid fever, 37-2-19, p. Abdon & Ann Dillon, b. Purcels Store, farmer, c/o: Lydia Dillon, sc: Jno J. Dillon, brother, BVS:1854:6, LC:5

DILLON, Josiah, W, M, d. 15 Jul 1853, Purcellville, dysentery, 90-0-0, p. unk, b. unk, farmer, sc: Jno T. Smith, neighbor, BVS:1854:6, LC:5

DILLON, Lena, W, F, d. 27 Aug 1876, nr Purcellville, cholera infantum, 0-3-0, p. Joseph A. & Fannie Dillon, b. LC, unm, sc: Joseph A. Dillon, father, MT Dist., BVS:1876:1

DILLON, Lydia, W, F, d. 2 Dec 1853, Purcellville, typhoid fever, 42-7-2, p. Abdon & Ann Dillon, b. nr Purcell's Store, unm, sc: Jno Dillon, brother, BVS:1854:6, LC:5

DINKLE, Daniel, W, F, d. 1 Jan 1875, Snickersville, born dead, p. Daniel & Catharine Dinkle, b. Snickersville, mechanic, sc: D.J. Dinkle, father, MT Dist., BVS:1875:8

DINSMORE, A. E., W, F, d. 20 Aug 1896, LC, fever, 0-6-0, p. A. E. Dinsmore, b. LC, sc: father, LE Dist., BVS:1896:5

DISHMAN, Joseph L., W, M, d. 15 Oct 1880, LC, typhoid fever, 30-0-0, p. unk, b. LC, mechanic, c/o: C.E. Dishman, sc: C.E. Dishman, wife, 1st Dist., BVS:1880:1

DISHMAN, M. F., W, M, d. 6 Nov 1891, nr Unison, diabetes, 43-0-0, p. Marcus & Mary Dishman, b. LC, farmer, c/o: Rosalie Dishman, sc: M.F. Dishman, brother, 1st Dist., BVS:1891:2

DISHMAN, Thos. A., W, M, d. 12 Feb 1881, LC, diabetes, 32-0-0, b. LC, farmer, sc: C.E. Dishman, brother, 1st Dist., BVS:1881:1

DIVINE, Ann N., W, F, d. 22 Apr 1890, Waterford, heart disease, 64-0-0, p. Niland & Nancy Herdle, b. LC, none, c/o: Charles W. Divine, sc: Chas W. Divine, husband, 3rd Dist., BVS:1890:6

DIVINE, Bonham, W, M, d. 15 May 1855, Waterford, old age, 90-0-0, p. Wm. & Rachel Divine, b. LC, stone mason, unm, sc: Jacob Divine, brother, BVS:1855:1, LC:14

DIVINE, Emily, W, F, d. 30 Jul 1890, LC, gen. debility, 62-0-0, p. Abner & Sarah Edwards, b. LC, none, c/o: R.

Divine, sc: J.W. Hammerly, friend, 2nd Dist., BVS:1890:4
DIVINE, Frances, W, F, d. Mar 1896, Waterford, old age, 82-0-0, consort, JF Dist., BVS:1896:8
DIVINE, Maria, W, F, d. 26 Oct 1856, Hillsboro, paralysis, 63-0-0, p. John & Judith Bogue, b. England, c/o: Wm. Divine, sc: W. Divine, widower, BVS:1856:5, LC:22
DIVINE, Minor S., W, M, d. 18 Sep 1889, LC, dysentery, 6-0-0, p. Joseph T. & S. A. Divine, b. LC, none, unm, sc: Jos L. Divine, father, 3rd Dist., BVS:1889:5
DIVINE, Robert, W, M, d. 25 Feb 1888, LC, apoplexy, 62-0-0, p. Jacob Divine (mother unk), b. LC, merchant, c/o: Emily Divine, sc: F. Alonzo Divine, son, 2nd Dist., BVS:1888:5
DIVINE, Robert L., W, M, d. 11 Apr 1873, nr Hillsboro, typhoid fever, 9-3-10, p. Robt & Susan Divine, b. LC, sc: Robert Devine, father, JF Dist., BVS:1874:1
DIVINE, William, W, M, d. 21 Mar 1884, LC, old age, 92-0-0, p. unknown, carpenter, unm, 1st Dist., BVS:1884:1
DIXON, Bell, B, M, d. 1 Mar 1887, LC, consumption, unk, p. Benj. & H. Dixon, b. LC, none, unm, sc: Alexander Smith, friend, 3rd Dist., BVS:1887:6
DIXON, Frank, W, M, d. 14 Oct 1881, LC, dropsy, 5-8-0, p. Catherine Dixon, sc: Elizth Fry, aunt, 2nd Dist., BVS:1881:6
DIXON, Rosa, W, F, d. 15 Jun 1881, LC, unk, 0-7-11, p. Catharine Dixon, b. LC, sc: Elizabeth Fry, aunt, 2nd Dist., BVS:1881:6
DIXON, Thomas, B, M, d. 10 Jan 1875, LC, dysentery, 0-4-0, p. Thos. & May, b. LC, sc: May Dixon, mother, JF Dist., BVS:1875:3
DIXSON, Mary Elizabeth, W, F, d. 20 Jul 1878, nr Potomac, unk, p. Julius S. & A Dixson, b. LC, sc: Julius Dixson, father, LV Dist., BVS:1878:1/5
DIXSON, William Richardson, W, M, d. 25 Jul 1878, nr Potomac, unk, p. Julius S. & A Dixson, b. LC, sc:
Julius Dixson, father, LV Dist., BVS:1878:1/5
DODD, Charles, W, M, d. 3 May 1875, LC, catarrh fever, 0-1-3, p. Chas. H. & Margt E. Dodd, sc: Chas. H. Dodd, father, LE Dist., BVS:1875:1
DODD, Frances E., W, F, d. 30 Jul 1884, LC, dropsy, 62-0-0, p. Geo. W. & Rose Dodd, unm, 1st Dist., BVS:1884:1
DODD, Geo Wm, W, M, d. 8 May 1878, nr Goose Creek Bridge, scrofula, 0-3-0, p. Geo Y. & M. Olivia Dodd, b. LC, sc: Geo Y. Dodd, father, MC Dist., BVS:1878:6
DODD, Jessie, W, F, d. 1 Aug 1884, Waterford, cholera infantum, 1-8-0, p. Joel F. & Mary Dodd, b. Waterford, unm, sc: Joel F. Dodd, father, 3rd Dist., BVS:1884:6
DODD, Margaret E., W, F, d. 6 Aug 1886, nr Mount Gilead, child birth, 39-0-0, p. Robert & Mary Costelloe, b. Upperville, c/o: Charles Dodd, sc: Charles Dodd, husband, 1st Dist., BVS:1886:1
DODD, Rosa, W, F, d. 3 Feb 1872, Middleburg, 82-0-0, MC Dist., BVS:1872:7
DONALDSON, Aaron T., W, M, d. 1 Sep 1853, Waterford, dysentery, 1-6-1, p. Geo. & Patience Donaldson, b. Waterford, sc: Geo R. Donaldson, father, BVS:1854:4, LC:3
DONALDSON, Manley, W, M, d. 8 May 1883, nr Waterford, pneumonia, 20-0-0, p. Geo. R. & Patience Donaldson, b. LC, laborer, sc: Geo R. Donaldson, father, 3rd Dist., BVS:1883:5
[DONALDSON], no name, B, F, d. 10 Nov 1885, nr Unison, unk, 0-0-21, p. John & Caroline Donaldson, b. nr Unison, sc: John Donaldson, father, 1st Dist., BVS:1885:3
DONALDSON, Ruth, W, F, d. 10 Feb 1882, LC, consumption, 20-0-0, p. Saml & Jane Donaldson, b. LC, unm, sc: Samuel Donaldson, father, 1st Dist., BVS:1882:1
DONALDSON, Walter S., W, M, d. 23 Nov 1884, nr Lovettsville, consumption, 52-0-0, p. Thomas & Elizabeth Donaldson, b. LC, mechanic, c/o: Mary C. Donaldson,

sc: Mary C. Donaldson, wife, 2nd Dist., BVS:1884:4

DONALSON, Alfred, B, M, d. 25 Sep 1876, nr Mountville, pneumonia, 1-6-0, p. Jno & Fanny Donalson, b. LC, sc: Jno. Donalson, father, MC Dist., BVS:1876:4

DONALSON, no name., B, F, d. 8 Jul 1877, nr Mountville, spasms, 0-0-7, p. Jno. & Fanny Donalson, b. LC, sc: Fanny Donalson, mother, MC Dist., BVS:1877:5

DONALSON, Wm. Peyton, B, M, d. 21 Aug 1877, nr Pot House, bleeding of the chord, 0-0-7, p. Joseph & Elizabeth Donalson, b. LC, sc: Joseph Donalson, father, MC Dist., BVS:1877:5

DONNELLY, Andrew F., W, M, d. 9 Jul 1866, nr Potomac, dysentery, 3-0-0, p. Robt. & Marcelena Donnelly, b. LC, sc: Robt. Donnelly, father, BVS:1866:1

DONOHOE, Delilah, W, F, d. 18 Aug 1892, Evergreen Mills, old age, 81-0-0, p. unk, b. Evergreen Mills, unm, LE Dist., BVS:1892:5

DONOHOE, Fannie, W, F, d. 8 Apr 1881, LC, consumption, 22-0-0, p. Wm. F. & Ann E. Donohoe, unm, sc: Ann E. Donohoe, mother, 2nd Dist., BVS:1881:6

[DONOHOE], no name, W, M, d. 23 Apr 1889, LC, unk, 0-0-1, p. Samuel E. & M. Donahoe, b. LC, farmer, unm, sc: S.S. Donahoe, head of family, 2nd Dist., BVS:1889:3

DONOHOE, no name, W, M, d. 2 Jul 1890, LC, unk, 0-0-1, p. R. L. & Florence Donahoe, b. LC, farmer, unm, sc: R.L. Donohoe, father, 2nd Dist., BVS:1890:3

DONOHOE, Rebecca, W, F, d. 18 Mar 1883, Leesburg, old age, 89-6-0, p. Samuel & Margaret Donohoe, b. LC, unm, sc: Elizth Norris, neice, 2nd Dist., BVS:1883:3

DONOHOE, Sarah, W, F, d. Feb 1853, nr Gilead, erysipelas, 77-0-0, p. Stephen & Sarah Roszel, b. LC, farmer, c/o: John Donohoe, sc: Ann Donohoe, daughter, BVS:1854:6, LC:5

DORCUS, Milton, B, M, d. 20 Jul 1887, LC, consumption, 22-0-0, p. Fannie Dorcus, b. LC, laborer, unm, sc: Fannie Dorcus, mother, 2nd Dist., BVS:1887:4

DORRELL, Archibald P., W, M, d. 17 Feb 1865, Chester Station, effect of a baler, 23-3-20, p. Thos S. & Mary Dorrell, b. Leesburg, soldier, unm, sc: G.W. Dorrell, uncle, BVS:1865:2

DORRELL, George W., W, M, d. 18 Dec 1885, nr Guilford, cancer, 76-0-0, p. Thomas & Mary Dorrell, b. LC, farmer, c/o: Mary Dorell, sc: Richard Palmer, friend, 1st Dist., BVS:1885:3

DORRELL, James H., W, M, d. 1875, Lovettsville Dist, pneumonia, 84-0-0, b. LC, farmer, LV Dist., BVS:1875:4

DORRELL, Mary A., W, F, d. 21 Nov 1891, nr Daysville, heart failure, 75-0-0, b. LC, unk, c/o: Geo Dorrell, sc: R.H. Palmer, son-in-law, 1st Dist., BVS:1891:2

DORRELL, Olevia, W, F, d. 20 Nov 1880, Woodgrove, dropsy, 0-7-4, p. Jas. A. & Sarah Dorrell, b. LC, sc: Jas. A. Dorrell, father, 3rd Dist., BVS:1880:4

DORSEY, Charlotte, B, F, d. 5 Oct 1876, nr Franklin Mills, child birth, 26-0-0, b. Fauquier Co., laborer, c/o: Wm. Dorsey, sc: H.H. Tolbert, brother-in-law, MC Dist., BVS:1876:4

DORSEY, John R., B, M, d. 10 Jul 1884, LC, dropsy, 10-0-0, p. Marshal & Lucy Dorsey, unm, 1st Dist., BVS:1884:1

DORSEY, Letitia, B, F, d. 19 Sep 1885, nr Bloomfield, paralysis, 72-0-0, p. unk, b. LC, c/o: Marshall Dorsey, sc: Marshall Dorsey, son, 1st Dist., BVS:1885:3

DORSEY, Mary, B, F, d. 1 Dec 1865, nr Potomac, dropsy, 17-0-0, sc: John Bradfield, head of family, BVS:1865:2

DORSEY, Portia, W, F, d. 8 Jun 1882, LC, strangulation, 0-0-2, p. John & Portia R. Dorsey, sc: John Dorsey, father, 1st Dist., BVS:1882:1

DORSEY, Portia R., W, F, d. 11 Dec 1889, Aldie, pneumonia, 56-0-0, p. ___ Castleman, b. Clarke, c/o: Caleb Dorsey, sc: Caleb Dorsey, husband, 1st Dist., BVS:1889:1

DOUGLAS, Amelia A., B, F, d. Jan 1879, Leesburg, cold, 0-9-0, p. Robert & Emily Douglas, b. LC, sc:

Robert Douglas, father, 2nd Dist., BVS:1879:1
DOUGLAS, Catherine, B, F, d. 10 Sep 1891, North Fork, consumption, 27-0-0, p. Wm. Douglas, b. North Fork, wife, sc: Wm. Douglas, MT Dist., BVS:1891:6
DOUGLAS, Charles, W, M, d. 22 Mar 1872, Leesburg, heart disease, 78-0-0, p. Hugh & Catharine Douglas, b. Albemarle Co., gentleman, c/o: Ann Douglas, sc: A.R. Mott, Doctor, LE Dist., BVS:1872:3
DOUGLASS, David, B, M, d. 5 May 1888, LC, old age, 79-0-0, b. LC, laborer, sc: L. Douglas, friend, 3rd Dist., BVS:1888:1
DOUGLAS, Henrietta, B, F, d. 10 May 1885, Leesburg, unk, 25-0-0, p. Shirley & Mary Watson, laborer, c/o: Henry Douglas, sc: Henry Douglas, husband, 2nd Dist., BVS:1885:1
DOUGLAS, Jno M., W, M, d. 24 Jul 1878, nr Sulphur Springs, West Va., consumption, 23-10-19, b. LC, unm, sc: Alex B. Moore, uncle, MC Dist., BVS:1878:6
DOUGLAS, Margaret F., W, F, d. Sep 1873, Aldie, consumption, 17-0-0, p. LE Douglas, b. Aldie, sc: Alexander B. Moore, uncle, MC Dist., BVS:1873:5
DOUGLAS, Marion, W, F, d. 30 Mar 1893, Aldie, pneumonia, 35-0-0, p. unk, b. Rectortown, housekeeper, c/o: J.E. Douglas, sc: J.E. Douglas, husband, 1st Dist., BVS:1893:1
[DOUGLAS], no name, B, F, d. Jun 1865, Fairfax line, convulsions, 0-0-10, p. David & Fannie Douglas, b. LC, unm, sc: Chas W. Whaley, head of family, BVS:1865:2
DOUGLAS, no name, B, M, d. 18 Aug 1885, nr Leesburg, unk, 0-0-9, p. Emanuel & Lettie Douglas, sc: Emanuel Douglas, father, 2nd Dist., BVS:1885:1
DOUGLAS, S. Jane, B, F, d. 28 Nov 1876, Leesburg, consumption, 52-0-0, p. unk, b. LC, c/o: Henry Douglas, sc: Robert Douglas, son, LE Dist., BVS:1876:6
DOUGLASS, Henry, B, M, d. Aug 1871, Leesburg, 40-0-0, b. LC, laborer, unm, LE Dist., BVS:1871:4

DOUGLASS, Jack, B, M, d. 25 Aug 1869, LC, typhoid fever, 10-0-0, p. unk, b. Maryland, sc: Mandly Hammerley, neighbor, BVS:1869:1
DOVE, Elizabeth, W, M, d. 25 Jul 1885, nr Farmwell, spinal affection, 71-0-0, p. James & Mary Whaley, b. Virginia, sc: John Dove, son, 1st Dist., BVS:1885:3
DOVE, George Wm., W, M, d. 7 Jul 1871, whooping cough, 2-0-0, p. John & Elizabeth Dove, BR Dist., BVS:1871:3
DOVE, Grace, W, F, d. 5 Mar 1885, nr Leesburg, croup, 0-10-0, p. Thomas & Annie Dove, sc: Thomas Dove, father, 2nd Dist., BVS:1885:1
DOVE, Robert L., W, M, d. 2 Apr 1884, nr Leesburg, remittent fever, 14-10-0, p. Thomas & Annie Dove, b. LC, sc: Harrison Mills, guardian, 2nd Dist., BVS:1884:4
DOVE, William, W, M, d. 25 Aug 1871, congestion of the brain, 61-0-0, farmer, married, BR Dist., BVS:1871:3
DOWDELL, Thomas, W, M, d. 25 Dec 1871, Mount Gilead, consumption, 62-0-0, p. not living, b. LC, farmer, c/o: Sarah Dowdell, sc: Charles F. Dowdell, son, MT Dist., BVS:1871:5
DOWE, Fannie, B, F, d. 24 Oct 1896, nr Unison, unk, 20-0-0, p. unk, b. unk, none, unm, sc: F.E. Robey, head of family, MC Dist., BVS:1896:1
DOWELL, Conrad R., W, M, d. 18 Feb 1857, nr Hamilton, consumption, 53-1-27, p. Elisha & Ann Dowell, b. nr Hamilton, farmer, c/o: Malinda Dowell, sc: John Dowell, son, BVS:1857:5, LC:28
DOWELL, Emaline, W, F, d. 25 Nov 1856, res of parents, 0-1-0, p. C. F. & Emaline M. Dowell, b. place of death, sc: C.F. Dowell, father, BVS:1856:6, LC:23
DOWELL, Emma E., W, F, d. 15 Apr 1879, LC, cancer, 35-0-0, p. Jesse & Mary Dowell, b. LC, c/o: Thaddeus Dowell, sc: Thaddeus Dowell, husbanc, 3rd Dist., BVS:1879:3
DOWNEY, Leila B., W, F, d. 7 Jan 1865, Loudoun Mills, consumption, 16-0-0, p. James M. & Ann E. Downey, b. Wash. Co., MD, miller,

unm, sc: James M. Downy, father, 1st Dist., BVS:1865:4

DOWNEY, Lula B., W, F, d. 2 Jan 1865, Loudoun Mills, consumption, 16-0-0, p. Jas M. & Ann E. Downey, b. Wash. Co., MD, miller, unm, sc: Jas M. Downey, father, BVS:1865:3

DOWNEY, W. S., W, M, d. 8 Feb 1878, nr Taylorstown, kicked by a horse, 26-0-0, p. James M. Downey, b. LC, farmer & miller, c/o: Laura J. Downey, sc: Laura J. Downey, wife, LV Dist., BVS:1878:1/5

DOWNS, Elizabeth, W, F, d. 26 Aug 1858, LC, old age, 78-0-0, p. unk, b. LC, sc: James W. Downs, son, BVS:1858:6, LC:33

DOWNS, Ella M., W, F, d. 11 Aug 1873, nr Hamilton, cholera infantum, 0-6-27, p. Cueso & Martha E. Downs, b. nr Hamilton, sc: parents, MT Dist., BVS:1873:3

DOWNS, Frankie Ellen, W, F, d. 24 Jul 1892, Leesburg, dysentery, 2-0-0, p. John Downs, b. Leesburg, unm, sc: John Downs, LE Dist., BVS:1892:5

DOWNS, Martha E., W, F, d. 19 Feb 1891, Mount Gilead, pneumonia, 46-0-0, p. Cicero Downs, b. Mount Gilead, wife, sc: Cicero Downs, MT Dist., BVS:1891:6

[DOWNS], no name, W, F, d. May 1856, LC, unk, 0-0-1, p. Noah & Mary J. Downs, b. LC, sc: Noah Downs, father, BVS:1856:7, LC:24

DOWNS, Noah, W, M, d. 20 Dec 1896, nr Daysville, killed by runaway horse, 15-0-9, p. Wm. H. & Linnie Downs, b. nr Ashburn, laborer, unm, sc: W.H. Downs, father, BR Dist., BVS:1896:3

DOWNS, William H., W, M, d. 21 Dec 1883, nr Leesburg, whooping cough, 1-11-21, p. Chas. F. & Annie R. Downs, b. LC, sc: Chas F. Downs, father, 2nd Dist., BVS:1883:6

DRAKE, Annie, W, F, d. Jun 1893, Paxson, unk, 0-0-1, p. G.T. & R. H. Drake, b. LC, sc: father, JF Dist., BVS:1893:3

DRAKE, Harold, W, M, d. 1 Sep 1890, LC, scarlet fever, 4-0-0, p. H. S. & Maria Drake, b. LC, vet-surgeon, unm, sc: H.S. Drake, father, 2nd Dist., BVS:1890:3

DRISCOLL, Mary, W, F, d. 1 Jan 1864, Jos Taylor's, consumption, 63-0-0, b. Prince William Co., sc: Jos Taylor, neighbor, BVS:1864:1, LC:38

DRISCOLL, Richd, W, M, d. 19 Jul 1864, Point Lookout, typhoid fever, 33-0-0, p. Mary Driscoll, b. Prince William Co., soldier, sc: Jos Taylor, neighbor, BVS:1864:1, LC:38

DRISH, John H., W, M, d. 19 Jul 1881, LC, general debility, 59-6-1, p. Wm. D. & Harriet Drish, laborer, c/o: Phoebe J. Drish, sc: Phoebe J. Drish, wife, 2nd Dist., BVS:1881:6

DUDLEY, Fanny B., W, F, d. 5 Oct 1865, Middleburg, 26-0-0, p. Wm. B. & Fanny Cochran, b. nr Middleburg, sc: Wm. B. Cochran, father, BVS:1865:1

DULANEY, H. Grafton, W, M, d. 8 Nov 1890, Welbourne, pleurisy, 36-0-0, p. Richd. H. & Rebecca A. Dulaney, b. LC, farmer, unm, sc: Richd H. Dulaney, father, 1st Dist., BVS:1890:1

DULANEY, Rebecca A., W, F, d. 1 Sep 1858, Welbourne, nervous dysentery, 30-0-0, p. Henry Rosia & Fanny A. Dulany, b. Cedar Hill, Fairfax, c/o: R.H. Dulaney, sc: R.H. Dulaney, widower, BVS:1858:4, LC:31

DULANY, Richard H., W, M, d. 15 Sep 1854, Middleburg, unk, 1-3-0, p. D. F. & Margaret A. Dulany, b. Middleburg, sc: Capt. D.F. Dulany U.S.N., BVS:1854:11, LC:10

DULIN, Ann B., W, F, d. 13 Sep 1853, nr Leesburg, water on brain, 6-4-0, p. Alfred & Margaret Dulin, b. Goose Creek, sc: father, BVS:1854:5, LC:5

DULIN, Chas. E., W, M, d. 6 Aug 1853, nr Leesburg, dysentery, 4-5-0, p. Alfred & Margaret Dulin, b. nr Goose Creek, sc: father, BVS:1854:5, LC:5

DULIN, Harry T./Henry, W, M, d. 28 Jul 1853, Leesburg, dysentery, 8-11-0, p. Alfred & Margaret Dulin, b. Goose Creek Bridge, sc: father, BVS:1854:5, LC:4

DULIN, Jas. W., W, M, d. 2 Aug 1853, nr Leesburg, dysentery, 3-0-0, p. Alfred & Margaret Dulin, b. nr Leesburg, sc: father, BVS:1854:5, LC:4

DUNBAR, Grace T., W, F, d. 29 Jul 1884, Hamilton, cholera infantum, 0-7-0, p. Edward & Clyde Dunbar, b. Iowa, unm, sc: Edward Dunbar, father, 3rd Dist., BVS:1884:6

DUNBAR, Herod H., W, M, d. 8 Sep 1891, nr Upperville, inflammation of bowels, 72-0-0, p. John & Lydia Dunbar, b. Fauquier Co., farmer, c/o: Ann E. Dunbar, sc: Ann E. Dunbar, wife, 1st Dist., BVS:1891:2

DUNCAN, George, W, M, d. 5 Oct 1855, congestive chills, 66-0-0, p. Chas. & Susan Duncan, b. LC, sc: M. Orrison, friend, BVS:1855:8, LC:19

DUNHAM, Sarah E., W, F, d. 3 Aug 1858, LC, consumption, 32-0-0, p. Amos & Mary E. Dunham, b. LC, unm, sc: Mary J. Cassady, sister, BVS:1858:1, LC:30

DUNLOP, Rebecca, W, F, d. 15 Jan 1855, Poor House, old age, 100-0-0, sc: steward, BVS:1855:5, LC:17

DUNN, James, W, M, d. 17 May 1884, LC, bright's disease, 62-0-0, p. Wm. & --- Dunn, b. England, 1st Dist., BVS:1884:1

DUTTON, Emma J., W, F, d. 18 Oct 1889, LC, old age, 83-0-0, p. unk, b. LC, none, c/o: John B. Dutton, sc: John B. Dutton, husband, 3rd Dist., BVS:1889:5

DUVAL, Harriet, W, F, d. 21 Nov 1875, Leesburg, cancer, 73-0-0, sc: Louisiana Whitmore, daughter, LE Dist., BVS:1875:1

DUVAL, Laura, B, F, d. 1 Sep 1880, Leesburg, heart disease, 23-0-0, p. unk, b. LC, laborer, unm, sc: Thomas King, friend, 2nd Dist., BVS:1880:6

DYER, Martha, B, F, d. 1 Jul 1869, LC, bilious fever, 0-5-0, p. Samuel & Mary Jane Dyer, b. LC, sc: Sam Dyer, father, BVS:1869:1

DYKE, Margaret H., W, F, d. 21 Dec 1882, LC, consumption, 40-0-0, p. unk, c/o: Nathan Dyke, sc: Nathan Dyke, husband, 1st Dist., BVS:1882:1

EACHES, Delilah, W, F, d. 29 Dec 1888, Unison, old age, 86-0-0, p. Jacob & Jeane Silcott, b. Unison, c/o: Thomas Eaches, sc: Fannie Carter, granddaughter, 1st Dist., BVS:1888:3

EACHES, Thomas, W, M, d. 11 Oct 1865, Union, heart disease, 68-11-25, p. Danl & Mary Eaches, b. nr Union, farmer, sc: Delilah Eaches, wife, BVS:1865:1

EAMICH, Hatie Loudella, W, F, d. 11 Jul 1878, Lovettsville, cholera infantum, 0-7-5, p. George F. & Mary V. Eamich, b. LC, sc: George F. Eamich, father, LV Dist., BVS:1878:1/5

[EAMICH], no name, W, M, d. 6 Nov 1873, Lovettsville, unk, 0-0-2, p. Jno W. & Sarah Eamich, b. Lovettsville, huckster, married, sc: Jno W. Eamich, father, LV Dist., BVS:1873:4

EASTERDAY, Julian, W, M, d. 16 Sep 1876, Leesburg, diphtheria, 3-9-0, p. William & Mary Easterday, b. LC, sc: William D. Easterday, father, LE Dist., BVS:1876:6

EATON, Mary C., W, F, d. 17 Mar 1891, Snickersville, consumption, 34-0-0, p. Jackson & Elizabeth Eaton, b. Clarke Co., WV, wife, sc: John Eaton, head of family, JF Dist., BVS:1891:7

EATON, Melinda, W, F, d. 6 Jun 1873, Mountville, disease of heart, 63-0-0, p. --- Craig, b. LC, c/o: Isaac Eaton, sc: David H.C. Eaton, son, MC Dist., BVS:1873:5

EBERT, Margaret, W, F, d. 9 Dec 1887, LC, old age, 84-0-0, p. unk, b. Frederick Co. MD, none, unm, sc: Annie Riley, neice, 2nd Dist., BVS:1887:4

EDMONDS, Alice, B, F, d. 7 May 1885, Leesburg, unk, 16-9-9, p. Jas. & Mary Edmonds, sc: Mary Edmonds, mother, 2nd Dist., BVS:1885:1

EDMONDS, Littleton, B, M, d. 5 Jun 1885, nr Leesburg, disease of kidneys, 75-0-0, p. --- Edmonds, laborer, c/o: Cynthia & Martha, sc: Mary Edmonds, daughter, 2nd Dist., BVS:1885:1

EDMONDS, Wm., W, M, d. 15 Jul 1874, Washington, DC, cholera infantum, 0-10-0, p. Jno. R. & Annie Edmonds, b. Washington DC, sc: Jno. R. Edmonds, father, MC Dist., BVS:1874:4

EDMUNS, Lee, B, M, d. 18 Apr 1893, Middleburg, unk, 65-0-0, p. unk, b. unk, laborer, unm, sc: Henry Jones, son-in-law, 1st Dist., BVS:1893:2

EDWARDS, Barbara, W, F, d. 1 Jun 1881, LC, heart disease, 70-0-0, p. John & C. Cline, c/o: Mahlon Edwards, sc: B.W. Roby, son-in-law, 2nd Dist., BVS:1881:6

EDWARDS, Edith P., B, F, d. 15 Aug 1888, Poor House, pneumonia, 1-0-0, p. Marie Edwards, b. LC, sc: F.E. Robey, superintendent of poor, 1st Dist., BVS:1888:3

EDWARDS, Howard B., W, M, d. 15 Jan 1890, LC, kidney disease, 6-0-0, p. unk, b. LC, none, unm, sc: S.R. Edwards, grandfather, 2nd Dist., BVS:1890:3

EDWARDS, John, W, M, d. 8 Sep 1886, flux, 8-0-0, p. Samuel R. & Ann V., sc: Wm. T. Edwards, brother, 2nd Dist., BVS:1886:5

EDWARDS, Jonathan, W, M, d. 21 Mar 1873, nr Hoysville, consumption, 27-0-0, p. Mahlon & Barbara Edwards, b. LC, huckster, unm, sc: T. or L.R. Edwards, brother, LV Dist., BVS:1873:4

EDWARDS, Jonathan, W, M, d. 16 Nov 1855, LC, pneumonia, 28-0-20, p. Jos & Eliz. Edwards, b. LC, c/o: Julia A. Edwards, sc: Jos. Edwards, father, BVS:1855:2, LC:15

EDWARDS, Joseph, W, M, d. 1 Nov 1858, LC, bilious colic, 38-0-0, p. Jos. & Lydia D. Edwards, b. LC, sc: J.E. Edwards, brother, BVS:1858:6, LC:33

EDWARDS, Joseph, W, M, d. 4 Oct 1859/60, LC, cancer, 65-3-0, p. Hugh & Eve Edwards, b. LC, farmer, c/o: Elizabeth Edwards, sc: Elizth Edwards, wife, BVS:1859:1, 1860:4, LC:37

EDWARDS, Mahlon, W, M, d. 13 Nov 1880, nr Lovettsville, paralysis, 80-0-0, p. ___ Edwards, b. LC, farmer, c/o: Barbara Edwards, sc: Mahlon Edwards, son, 2nd Dist., BVS:1880:6

EDWARDS, Mortimore, W, M, d. 7 Mar 1887, LC, consumption, 56-0-15, p. Mahlon & Barbara Edwards, b. LC, farmer, c/o: Sarah Edwards, sc: Sarah Edwards, wife, 2nd Dist., BVS:1887:4

EDWARDS, Ned, B, M, d. 1 Dec 1890, Poor House, paralysis, 70-0-0, p. unk, b. LC, laborer, unm, sc: F.E. Robey, superintendent of poor, 1st Dist., BVS:1890:1

EDWARDS, Sarah, B, F, d. 11 May 1889, LC, cramp colic, 30-0-0, p. Edward & Mary Edward, b. LC, none, unm, sc: Edward Edwards, father, 3rd Dist., BVS:1889:5

EDWARDS, William H., W, M, d. 16 May 1856, LC, inflammation brain, 26-0-0, p. Mahlon & Barbary Edwards, b. LC, unm, sc: Mahlon Edwards, father, BVS:1856:2, LC:21

EIDSON, Joseph, W, M, d. 19 Jun 1865, Union, old age, 86-0-0, p. Jos & Rebecca Eidson, b. Northumberlund Co., farmer, sc: wife, BVS:1865:1

ELBERT, Adam, W, M, d. 21 Dec 1876, nr Neersville, consumption, 50-0-0, b. Frederick, MD, farmer, c/o: Harriet Elbert, sc: Margaret Elbert, sister, LV Dist., BVS:1876:3

ELGIN, Annie, W, F, d. 1 Jan 1875, Utopia, scarlet fever, 2-0-0, p. John F. & Annie Elgin, b. Utopia, farmer, unm, sc: John F. Elgin, father, MT Dist., BVS:1875:8

ELGIN, Catharine Rebecca, W, F, d. 25 Sep 1856, res of parents, scarlet sore throat, 6-3-0, p. Ignatius & Mary A. Elgin, b. nr Ball's Mill, sc: Ignatius Elgin, father, BVS:1856:5, LC:23

ELGIN, Daniel, B, M, d. 30 Oct 1875, LC, heart disease, 41-2-0, c/o: Annett Elgin, sc: Annett Elgin, wife, LE Dist., BVS:1875:1

ELGIN, Elizabeth, W, F, d. 12 Aug 1887, LC, paralysis, 81-0-0, p. Manly & Jane Cross, b. LC, none, widow, sc: Chas Elgin, son, 2nd Dist., BVS:1887:4

[ELGIN], Florence, W, F, d. Mar 1858, Mary Elgin's, consumption, 1-0-0, p. Chas. H. & Edmonia Elgin, b. Aldie, sc: Mary Elgin, G-mother, BVS:1858:4, LC:31

ELGIN, Ignatius, W, M, d. 4 Oct 1896, LC, paralysis, 66-0-0, p. Robt. & Elizth. Elgin, b. LC, farmer, husband, sc: son-in-law, LE Dist., BVS:1896:5

ELGIN, Ignatius Sr., W, M, d. 16 Mar 1858, his res, heart affection, 59-5-16, p. Walter & Diadama Elgin, b. 4

miles s of Leesburg, farmer, c/o: Mary A. Elgin, sc: M.A. Elgin, widow, BVS:1858:4, LC:32

ELGIN, John, W, M, d. 15 Sep 1853, nr Sycolin, dysentery, 60-0-0, p. Walter & Damy Elgin, b. LC, farmer, unm, sc: Sarah Elgin, sister, BVS:1854:5, LC:5

ELGIN, John F., W, M, d. 12 Mar 1883, nr Leesburg, cancer on liver, 46-0-0, p. Ignatius & Mary A. Elgin, b. LC, farmer, c/o: Annie Elgin, sc: Annie Elgin, wife, 2nd Dist., BVS:1883:6

ELGIN, Margaret E., W, F, d. 3 Jun 1875, LC, consumption, 49-2-0, c/o: Robert Elgin, sc: Roberta E. Carr, daughter, LE Dist., BVS:1875:1

ELGIN, Mary A., W, F, d. 21 Jul 1879, nr Leesburg, congestion of lungs, 68-0-0, p. Joshua & Theodocia Lee, b. LC, c/o: Ignatious Elgin, sc: John F. Elgin, son, 2nd Dist., BVS:1879:1

ELGIN, Mary J., W, F, d. 19 Mar 1891, Leesburg, unk, 37-0-0, p. Thomas & Mary Elgin, b. nr Leesburg, farmer, unm, sc: brother, LE Dist., BVS:1891:4

ELGIN, Mary S., W, F, d. 27 Sep 1876, LC, liver disease, 43-0-0, p. unk, b. unk, c/o: Ignatius Elgin, sc: Ignatius Elgin, husband, LE Dist., BVS:1876:6

ELGIN, Mary S., W, F, d. 12 Dec 1889, LC, old age, 83-6-0, p. Thos. & Eliz. Elgin, b. LC, none, widow, sc: T.G. Elgin, son, 2nd Dist., BVS:1889:3

ELGIN, Nettie, B, F, d. 16 Feb 1881, LC, pneumonia, unk-0-0, p. Wm. & Rose Smith, laborer, c/o: Daniel Elgin, sc: Helen Elgin, daughter, 2nd Dist., BVS:1881:6

[ELGIN], [no name], W, M, d. Sep 1871, LC, unk, p. Thos G. & Mary Elgin, b. LC, unm, LE Dist., BVS:1871:4

[ELGIN], no name, W, M, d. 3 Sep 1872, LC, unk, 0-1-1, p. Thos.G. & Mary E. Elgin, b. LC, sc: Mary E. Elgin, mother, LE Dist., BVS:1872:3

[ELGIN], no name, W, , d. 9 Mar 1878, LC, unk, 0-0-9, p. Chas. H. & Alice Elgin, b. LC, unm, sc: Alice Elgin, mother, LE Dist., BVS:1878:8

ELGIN, [no name], W, M, d. 9 Mar 1879, nr Leesburg, lockjaw, 0-0-8, p. Chas. H. & Susan A. Elgin, b. LC,

sc: Chas. H. Elgin, father, 2nd Dist., BVS:1879:1

ELGIN, Robert, W, M, d. 17 Oct 1864, Peach Run, consumption, 45-0-0, b. LC, sc: Margt Elgin, widow, BVS:1864:2, LC:39

ELGIN, Thomas, W, M, d. 28 Jul 1876, LC, cholera infantum, 0-6-22, p. Thomas & Mary E. Elgin, b. LC, sc: Thomas G. Elgin, father, LE Dist., BVS:1876:6

ELLIOTT, Daniel, B, M, d. 10 Sep 1873, nr Peugh's Mill, typhoid fever, 33-0-0, p. Enos & Mary Elliott, c/o: Nancy Elliott, sc: Nancy Elliott, wife, JF Dist., BVS:1874:1

ELLIOTT, Elizabeth A., W, F, d. 12 Apr 1885, nr Farmwell, spinal affection, 17-0-0, p. Thos. H. & Elizabeth Elliott, b. Fairfax, sc: Thomas H. Elliott, father, 1st Dist., BVS:1885:3

ELLIOTT, Joseph T., W, M, d. 19 May 1885, nr Farmwell, congestive chills, 4-0-0, p. Thos. H. & Elizabeth Elliott, b. Fairfax, sc: Thomas H. Elliott, father, 1st Dist., BVS:1885:3

ELLIS, Catharine, W, F, d. 4 Mar 1883, nr Leesburg, typhoid fever, 70-0-0, p. Geo. & Nancy Smoot, b. Fairfax, unk, sc: Mary E. Matheis, daughter, 2nd Dist., BVS:1883:6

ELLIS, Evelyn, B, F, d. 10 Oct 1894, Sterling, colic, 2-0-0, p. Wm. & Mary Ellis, b. Sterling, sc: Wm. Ellis, father, 1st Dist., BVS:1894:2

ELLIS, George W., W, M, d. 5 Oct 1883, nr Mount Gilead, unk, 0-0-5, p. Lewis W. & Georgia Ellis, b. LC, sc: Lewis W. Ellis, father, 3rd Dist., BVS:1883:5

ELLIS, Thomas, W, M, d. Mar 1854, old age, 85-0-0, p. James & Rebecca Ellis, b. Maryland, wheelwright, sc: Jos. Piles, friend, BVS:1854:13, LC:13

ELLMORE, A. Eliz., W, F, d. 1 Jul 1864, Farmwell Farm, consumption, 34-0-0, p. Wm. & Mary Mills, b. LC, c/o: Jno W. Elmore, sc: Mary Mills, mother, BVS:1864:2, LC:39

ELLMORE, Ann E., W, F, d. 26 May 1864, nr Farmwell, consumption, 49-0-0, p. Jno & Cathrn Ellmore, b. LC, sc: John Ellmore, father, BVS:1864:2, LC:39

ELLMORE, Charles W., W, M, d. 14 Oct 1857, falling of a tree, 40-0-0, p. John & Catharine Ellmore, b. LC, farmer, sc: John Ellmore, father, BVS:1857:7, LC:28

ELLMORE, John, W, M, d. 1865, nr Farmville, dysentery, 2-0-0, p. J.R. & M.W. Ellmore, b. LC, unm, sc: J. Arundell, grandfather, BVS:1865:2

ELLMORE, John, W, M, d. 1 Apr 1871, pneumonia, 82-0-0, farmer, married, BR Dist., BVS:1871:3

ELLMORE, John F., W, M, d. 30 Jul 1854, LC, dysentery, 1-4-0, p. Edward & Elizabeth Ellmore, b. LC, sc: Elizabeth Ellmore, mother, BVS:1854:14, LC:13

ELLMORE, John J., W, M, d. 7 May 1892, Leesburg, measles, 0-17-0, p. Chas. & Sarah Ellmore, b. Leesburg, unm, sc: Chas Ellmore, LE Dist., BVS:1892:5

ELLMORE, John W., W, M, d. 15 Jun 1864, Farmwell Farm, consumption, 8-1-15, p. J.W. & A.E. Ellmore, b. LC, sc: Mary Mills, grandmother, BVS:1864:2, LC:39

ELLMORE, Margaret L., W, F, d. 18 Jul 1872, nr Guilford, water on the brain, 1-7-0, p. Edward L. & Lucinda Ellmore, b. LC, sc: Edward L. Ellmore, BR Dist., BVS:1872:6

ELLMORE, Mary C., W, F, d. 1 Jun 1864, Farmwell Farm, consumption, 10-7-5, p. J.W. & A.E. Ellmore, b. LC, sc: Mary Mills, grandmother, BVS:1864:2, LC:39

ELLMORE, Mollie, W, F, d. 10 Oct 1873, nr Farmwell Church, unk, 0-6-18, p. Samuel F. & Mary E. Ellmore, b. nr Farmwell Station, sc: Saml F. Ellmore, head of family, BR Dist., BVS:1873:1

[ELLMORE], no name, W, F, d. Oct 1865, nr Farmville, unk, 0-0-1, p. J.R. & M.W. Ellmore, b. LC, unm, sc: J. Arundell, grandfather, BVS:1865:2

ELLMORE, Odie E., W, M, d. 15 Dec 1887, Farmwell, pneumonia, 3-0-0, p. John W. & Mary P. Ellmore, b. Farmwell, sc: John W. Ellmore, father, 1st Dist., BVS:1887:2

ELLMORE, Philip H., W, M, d. 15 Sep 1890, nr Ryan, consumption, 15-0-0, p. John W. & Malinda P. Ellmore, b. nr Ryan, sc: John W. Ellmore, father, 1st Dist., BVS:1890:1

ELLSEY, Rudolph, B, M, d. Jun 1873, Mountville, unk, 0-8-0, p. Wm. & Phrony Ellsey, b. Mountville, sc: Phrony Ellsey, mother, MC Dist., BVS:1873:5

ELLZEY, Helen, W, F, d. 27 Jun 1876, nr Goose Creek, paralysis, 63-0-0, p. George & Betsey Mason, b. Fairfax Co., c/o: T. Ellzey, sc: E. Chancellor, friend, BR Dist., BVS:1876:2

ELLZEY, Mary E., B, F, d. 30 Sep 1875, LC, cholera infantum, 0-9-0, sc: Elizabeth Manly, mother, LE Dist., BVS:1875:1

ELLZEY, Thos. L., W, M, d. 3 Jan 1874, Broad Run Dist., affection of the kidney, 64-0-0, p. Col. Wm. Ellzey & wife, b. LC, farmer, married, sc: Wm. Ellzey, son, BR Dist., BVS:1874:3

ELMORE, John R., W, M, d. 6 Oct 1865, nr Goresville, hemorrhage, 23-0-0, p. Chas. W. & Mary Elmore, b. LC, farmer, unm, sc: George W. Elmore, brother, 1st Dist., BVS:1865:3/4

ELMORE, William, W, M, d. 14 Mar 1880, Woodgrove, inflammatory rheumatism, 72-0-0, p. unk, b. LC, laborer, c/o: Maria Elmore, sc: Jno. Ellmore, friend, 3rd Dist., BVS:1880:4

ELSEA, Winnie Davis, W, F, d. Dec 1894, Snickersville, unk, 0-6-0, p. Thomas & Annie Elsea, b. Snickersville, sc: Annie Elsea, mother, 3rd Dist., BVS:1894:5

EMERICK, Rodney T., W, M, d. 1 Aug 1887, LC, disorder of the blood, 3-0-0, p. John & Carrie Emerick, b. LC, none, unm, sc: John Emerick, father, 3rd Dist., BVS:1887:6

EMERSON, Judson, W, M, d. 5 Sep 1873, LC, unk, 85-0-0, p. unk, b. Leesburg, butcher, sc: G. L. Lightfoot, head of family, BR Dist., BVS:1873:1

ENGLISH, Archibald N., W, M, d. 17 Dec 1865, Hoysville, spasms, 0-2-28, p. Wm. F. & Ellen O. English, laborer, sc: Wm. F. English, father, 1st Dist., BVS:1865:3/4

ENGLISH, Catherine, W, F, d. 15 Dec 1890, LC, consumption, 38-0-0, p.

Loudoun County, Virginia, Death Register, 1853-1896 97

unk, b. LC, none, c/o: C.A. English, sc: C.A. English, father, 2nd Dist., BVS:1890:3

ENGLISH, Chester A., W, M, d. 9 Dec 1881, LC, neuralgia of bowels, 10-0-0, p. Wm. & E. O. English, sc: Wm. English, father, 2nd Dist., BVS:1881:6

ENGLISH, Lucy, W, F, d. 1 Jun 1890, LC, unk, 0-3-0, p. W.T. & Ophilia English, b. LC, farmer, unm, sc: W.T. English, father, 2nd Dist., BVS:1890:3

ENGLISH, Mary W., W, F, d. 1865, Middleburg, dropsy, 36-0-0, p. Pickett & Emily Withers, b. Culpepper Co., farmer, married, sc: Ca? English, husband, BVS:1865:1

ENGLISH, Wilmer, W, M, d. 25 Aug 1878, nr Short Hill, 1-4-0, p. Wm. & Ellen Ophelia English, b. LC, sc: Wm. English, father, LV Dist., BVS:1878:1/5

ETCHER, Annie, W, F, d. 6 Nov 1880, Leesburg, old age, 82-4-18, p. unk, b. LC, c/o: Peter Etcher, sc: Charles L. Etcher, step-son, 2nd Dist., BVS:1880:6

ETCHER, James C., W, M, d. 7 Nov 1892, Leesburg, unk, 57-0-0, p. unk, b. Leesburg, consort, LE Dist., BVS:1892:5

ETCHER, Peter, W, M, d. 8 Jul 1884, nr Leesburg, old age, 87-0-0, p. Peter & --- Etcher, b. LC, farmer, c/o: Annie Etcher, sc: Jas C. Etcher, son, 2nd Dist., BVS:1884:4

EVANS, Jane A., W, F, d. 13 May 1894, Hamilton, heart trouble, 76-0-0, p. Evan & Hannah Evans, b. Hamilton, wife, sc: Annie Evans, daughter, 3rd Dist., BVS:1894:5

EVANS, Jos., B, M, d. 20 Nov 1894, Welbourne, paralysis, 4-0-0, p. Rich. & Jane Evans, b. nr Welbourne, sc: Jane Evans, mother, 1st Dist., BVS:1894:2

EVANS, Julia, B, F, d. 7 May 1896, Willisville, heart disease, 76-0-0, p. unk, b. unk, none, consort, sc: Geo Evans, husband, MC Dist., BVS:1896:1

EVANS, Sarah W., W, F, d. 5 Aug 1885, Wheatland, dropsy, 71-0-0, p. Evan & Hannah Evans, b. LC, unm, sc: Presly Evans, brother, 3rd Dist., BVS:1885:6

EVANS, Thomas F., W, M, d. 17 Jul 1856, LC, unk, 0-2-29, p. Jonathan & Louisa E. Evans, b. LC, sc: Hannah Evans, grandmother, BVS:1856:2, LC:21

EVARD, M. E., W, F, d. 16 Jul 1880, Leesburg, dropsy, 57-1-1, p. J. & Mary A. Wright, b. LC, c/o: Chas. E. Evard, sc: Chas E. Evard, husband, 2nd Dist., BVS:1880:6

EVERETT, no name, W, F, d. 29 Apr 1889, LC, unk, 0-0-1, p. Payten & Venia Everett, b. LC, none, unm, sc: Payten Everett, father, 3rd Dist., BVS:1889:5

EVERHART, Arabella Ann, W, F, d. 5 Aug 1866, nr Hamilton, typhoid fever, 22-5-12, p. Wm. N. & Cath. Everhart, b. LC, unm, sc: father, BVS:1866:2

EVERHART, Augustus S., W, M, d. 10 Aug 1877, LC, consumption, 45-0-0, p. Delilah Everhart, b. LC, unm, sc: Mollie J. Waldron, sister, LV Dist., BVS:1877:4/7

EVERHART, David, W, M, d. 31 Jan 1856, LC, unk, 57-0-0, p. Philip & Charlotte E. Everhart, b. LC, c/o: Elizabeth Everhart, sc: Elizabeth Everhart, wife, BVS:1856:2, LC:21

EVERHART, Elizabeth, W, F, d. 26 Nov 1888, LC, old age, 84-0-0, p. John Long (mother unk), b. LC, none, c/o: Nelson Everhart, sc: F.?, son-in-law, 2nd Dist., BVS:1888:5

EVERHART, Elizabeth, W, F, d. 1 Dec 1887, LC, cancer, 83-0-0, p. unk, b. LC, none, c/o: Joshua Everhart, sc: Joshua Everhart, 2nd Dist., BVS:1887:4

EVERHART, Franklin C., W, M, d. 8 Aug 1875, Lovettsville Dist, 0-0-7, p. ? Everhart, b. LC, sc: ? Everhart, father, LV Dist., BVS:1875:4

EVERHART, Gertrude M., W, F, d. 1 Sep 1880, nr Lovettsville, diphtheria, 2-2-0, p. M. G. & Harriet S. Everhart, b. LC, unm, sc: Maxbury G. Everhart, father, 2nd Dist., BVS:1880:6

EVERHART, John, W, M, d. 28 Jul 1887, LC, cancer, 57-1-28, p. David & Elizabeth Everhart, b. LC, c/o: Delilah Everhart, sc: Delilah

Everhart, sister, 2nd Dist., BVS:1887:4

EVERHART, John, W, M, d. 3 Dec 1879, nr Leesburg, enlargement of liver, 68-9-2, p. Philip & Charlotte Everhart, b. LC, farmer, c/o: Matilda A. Everhart, sc: Matilda A. Everhart, wife, 2nd Dist., BVS:1879:1

EVERHART, John C., W, M, d. 12 Nov 1890, LC, diphtheria, 9-0-0, p. Mabury G. & Catherine Everhart, b. LC, none, unm, sc: M.G. Everhart, father, 2nd Dist., BVS:1890:3

EVERHART, Joseph, W, M, d. 18 Oct 1883, nr Lovettsville, gravel, 81-0-18, p. Michael & Christine Everhart, b. LC, farmer, c/o: Ann E. Everhart, sc: Ann E. Everhart, wife, 2nd Dist., BVS:1883:6

EVERHART, Joshua, W, M, d. 28 Aug 1888, LC, constipation, 81-0-0, p. unk, b. LC, farmer, widower, sc: M.C. Everhart, son, 2nd Dist., BVS:1888:5

EVERHART, Lena Bell, W, F, d. 11 Oct 1894, Round Hill, typhoid fever, 13-0-0, p. Thomas & Ida Everhart, b. Round Hill, unm, sc: Thomas Everhart, father, 3rd Dist., BVS:1894:5

EVERHART, Margaret O., W, F, d. 21 Dec 1890, LC, typhoid fever, 22-0-0, p. John B. & Susan Everhart, b. LC, none, unm, sc: J.B. Everhart, father, 2nd Dist., BVS:1890:3

EVERHART, Mary, W, F, d. 15 Oct 1859/60, LC, consumption, 89-0-0, p. unk, b. Maryland, unm, sc: Tabitha Everhart, daughter, BVS:1859:1, 1860:4, LC:37

EVERHART, Maud M., W, F, d. 25 Jul 1888, LC, brain fever, 0-5-0, p. Geo. O. & Fannie Everhart, b. LC, none, unm, sc: Geo O. Everhart, father, 2nd Dist., BVS:1888:5

EVERHART, no name, W, M, d. 15 Dec 1878, nr Lovettsville, 0-0-9, p. Michael & Fanny Everhart, b. LC, sc: Tilghman Everhart, uncle, LV Dist., BVS:1878:1/5

EVERHART, Susan V., W, F, d. 16 Aug 1854, LC, dysentery, 0-11-14, p. John & Christina A. Everhart, b. LC, sc: John Everhart, father, BVS:1854:8, LC:8

EVERHART, Susanna M., W, F, d. 18 Oct 1855, Hamilton, heart disease, 12-4-14, p. Nathl W. & Darius Everhart, b. LC, sc: N.W. Everhart, father, BVS:1855:6, LC:17

EVERHART, Thos. J., W, M, d. 15 Jan 1866, Between the Hills, 4-0-0, p. Jos. & Elizth. Everhart, b. LC, sc: Jos. Everhart, father, BVS:1866:1

EVERHART, William H., W, M, d. 16 Nov 1888, LC, unk, 0-0-10, p. John G. & Kate Everhart, b. LC, none, unm, sc: John G. Everhart, father, 2nd Dist., BVS:1888:5

EVERHART, Wm. P., W, M, d. 11 Jan 1896, LC, fever, 41-0-0, p. Jno. & Matilda, b. LC, farmer, unm, sc: mother, LE Dist., BVS:1896:5

EVERITT, Amy, W, F, d. 8 Sep 1875, Hamilton, typhoid fever, 6-0-0, p. John & Harriet Everitt, b. Hamilton, unm, sc: John Everitt, father, MT Dist., BVS:1875:8

EWERS, Eliz., W, F, d. 16 Mar 1855, Bacon Fort, inflam. rheumah., 19-11-25, p. Wm. & Ruth Ewers, b. nr Bacon Fort, sc: Franklin Ewers, half-brother, BVS:1855:7, LC:18

FADELEY, Chas. Fenton, W, M, d. 28 May 1872, Leesburg, typhoid fever, 54-8-22, p. Jacob & Mary Fadley, b. LC, livery man, c/o: Orra M. Fadeley, sc: Orra M. Fadeley, consort, LE Dist., BVS:1872:3

FADELEY, Milton W., W, M, d. 15 Jul 1873, Leesburg, whooping cough, 0-0-13, p. Milton M. & Annie M. Fadeley, b. Leesburg, sc: Milton M. Fadeley, head of family, BR Dist., BVS:1873:1

FADELY, Roland Acre, W, M, d. 6 Nov 1885, Waterford, blood poison, 5-8-0, p. Charles W. & Orra Fadely, b. LC, unm, sc: Chas W. Fadely, father, 3rd Dist., BVS:1885:6

[FARR], no name, W, F, d. 15 Aug 1882, LC, unk, 0-3-0, p. Edward L. & A. E. Farr, sc: Edward L. Farr, father, 1st Dist., BVS:1882:1

[FAULKNER], no name, B, F, d. 7 Jan 1876, LC, fever, 0-5-0, p. Jas. & Nettie Faulkner, b. LC, sc: Jas. Faulkner, father, JF Dist., BVS:1876:8

FAUNTLEROY, Chas. W., W, M, d. 28 Jul 1889, LC, paralysis, 67-0-0, p. Thos L. & Ann Fauntleroy, b. LC, none, widower, sc: Janet K. Harrison, daughter, 2nd Dist., BVS:1889:3

FAWLEY, Edith, W, F, d. 6 Jul 1885, nr Goresville, old age, 86-0-0, p. --- Titus, c/o: John H. Fawley, sc: Jeremiah Fawley, son, 2nd Dist., BVS:1885:1

FAWLEY, Henry M., W, M, d. 4 Jun 1887, LC, diphtheria, 5-0-0, p. John H. & Sarah J. Fawley, b. LC, unm, sc: John H. Fawley, father, 2nd Dist., BVS:1887:4

FAWLEY, Lynn, W, F, d. 3 Mar 1873, nr Ketoctin Mountain, consumption, 22-0-0, p. Wm & Eliz Fawley, b. Ketoctin Mountain, unm, sc: Wm Fawley, father, LV Dist., BVS:1873:4

FAWLEY, no name, W, F, d. 29 Apr 1881, LC, unk, 0-0-4, p. Geo. W. & J. V. Fawley, sc: Geo. W. Fawley, father, 2nd Dist., BVS:1881:6

FAWLEY, no name, W, F, d. 26 Apr 1883, nr Lovettsville, unk, 0-0-4, p. George W. & Ida V. Fawley, b. LC, sc: Geo W. Fawley, father, 2nd Dist., BVS:1883:6

FAWLEY, Sally L/S. G., W, F, d. 23 Dec 1858/60, LC, unk, 3-0-23, p. Wm. & Elizth Fawley, b. LC, sc: Wm. Fawley, father, BVS:1859:1, 1860:3, LC:36

FAWLEY, William, W, M, d. 9 Jul 1884, nr Lovettsville, consumption, 72-0-0, p. Henry & Christina Fawley, b. LC, farmer, c/o: Elizabeth Fawley, sc: William B. Fawley, son, 2nd Dist., BVS:1884:4

FEAGAN, Hannah, W, F, d. Nov 1853, nr Mountville, consumption, 61-0-0, p. Sylvester & Frances Welsh, b. Fauquier Co., c/o: Enoch Feagan, sc: husband, BVS:1854:2, LC:4

FEAGANS, Julius R., W, M, d. 10 Sep 1865, Fauquier Co, diphtheria, 9-2-0, p. Wm. F. & Nancy D. Feagans, sc: Wm. F. Feagans, father, BVS:1865:1

FEAGANS, Uriah, W, M, d. 1 Aug 1878, nr Ebenezer M.H., typhoid pneumonia, 53-2-3, b. Prince William Co., farmer, c/o: Margaret Feagans, sc: Margaret Feagans, wife, MC Dist., BVS:1878:6

FEAGANS, William L., W, M, d. 16 Oct 1853, nr Wheatland, consumption, 37-6-0, p. Isaac & Ann Feagans, b. LC, farmer, c/o: Ann Feagans, sc: wife, BVS:1854:1, LC:4

FEASTER, George L., W, M, d. 10 May 1876, LC, bronchitis, 0-5-0, p. Henry A. & Susan A. Feaster, b. Leesburg, sc: Henry A. Feaster, father, LE Dist., BVS:1876:6

FELTNER, John D., W, M, d. 1 Dec 1896, Evergreen Mills, pneumonia, 0-0-21, p. Geo. W. & Sarah B. Feltner, b. Evergreen Mills, sc: Geo W. Feltner, father, BR Dist., BVS:1896:3

FENTON, Thomas N., W, M, d. 23 Dec 1869, LC, measles, 20-0-0, p. Enoch & Ruth E. Fenton, b. LC, farmer, unm, sc: Enoch Fenton, father, BVS:1869:1

[FERGURSON], no name, W, F, d. 16 Aug 1855, unk, unk, p. Jno. H. & V. Fergurson, b. LC, sc: Jno. H. Fergurson, father, BVS:1855:8, LC:19

FERGUSON, Genevieve, B, F, d. 3 Nov 1893, nr Sterling, typhoid fever, 6-0-0, p. Chas. & Rachel Ferguson, b. nr Sterling, laborer, sc: Rachel Ferguson, mother, 1st Dist., BVS:1893:2

FERGUSON, Mary C., W, F, d. 9 Jan 1878, nr Little River Church, general debility, 21-7-0, p. Romulus & Cathe. Ferguson, b. nr Little River Church, unm, sc: Romulus Ferguson, father, BR Dist., BVS:1878:4

FERGUSON, no name, W, M, d. 1 Aug 1882, LC, teething, 0-10-0, p. John & Lucy Ferguson, b. LC, sc: John Ferguson, parent, 3rd Dist., BVS:1882:3

FERGUSON, no name, W, M, d. 30 Jul 1886, LC, unk, 0-0-21, p. John M. & Lucy Ferguson, b. LC, unm, sc: Jno M. Ferguson, father, 3rd Dist., BVS:1886:4

FERGUSON, Walter, B, M, d. 5 Nov 1893, nr Sterling, typhoid fever, 7-10-0, p. Chas. & Rachel Ferguson, b. nr Sterling, laborer, sc: Rachel

Ferguson, mother, 1st Dist., BVS:1893:2

FERGUSON, Walter R., W, M, d. 24 Sep 1874, Broad Run Dist., typhoid fever, 9-4-20, p. Romulus & Catharine Ferguson, b. LC, sc: Romulus Ferguson, father, BR Dist., BVS:1874:3

FERRELL, Amanda, B, F, d. 10 Jul 1891, Hillsboro, consumption, 32-0-0, p. Allen & July Ferrell, b. Hillsboro, sc: Allen Ferrell, head of family, JF Dist., BVS:1891:7

FERRELL, J. Arthur, B, M, d. 28 Mar 1892, Hillsboro, scrofula, 10-0-0, p. James Ferrell, b. Hillsboro, laborer, sc: James Ferrell, father, JF Dist., BVS:1892:7

FERRILL, Amanda, B, F, d. 14 Jul 1896, Elvan, inflammation of bowels, 0-4-0, p. Silas & Sarah, b. Elvan, sc: Silas Ferrill, LV Dist., BVS:1896:7

FIELDS, Albert, W, M, d. 23 Aug 1888, LC, dysentery, 8-0-0, p. James & S. Fields, b. LC, none, unm, sc: S. Fields, mother, 2nd Dist., BVS:1888:5

FIELDS, Blanche C., W, F, d. 26 May 1888, LC, unk, 0-3-0, p. Wm. & Charlotte Fields, b. LC, none, unm, sc: Amanda Conard, grandmother, 2nd Dist., BVS:1888:5

FIELDS, Charlotte, W, F, d. 4 May 1888, LC, consumption, 21-0-0, p. Joseph & Amanda Conard, b. LC, none, c/o: William Fields, sc: Amanda Conard, mother, 2nd Dist., BVS:1888:5

FIELDS, Mary, W, F, d. 8 Oct 1853, nr Mountville, heart disease, 65-0-0, p. A. & Mary Orrison, b. LC, c/o: Jno. Fields Sr., sc: Jas. Fields, grandson, BVS:1854:2, LC:4

[FIELDS], no name, B, F, d. 19 Aug 1872, nr Belmont, unk, 0-0-4, p. Aaron & Melvina Fields, b. LC, sc: Aaron Fields, BR Dist., BVS:1872:6

FIELDS, S., W, F, d. 9 Oct 1889, LC, cancer of womb, 40-0-0, p. Enoch & S. Figgins, b. LC, none, c/o: James Fields, sc: James Fields, husband, 3rd Dist., BVS:1889:5

FIELDS, Susan, B, F, d. 2 Nov 1876, nr Snickersville, asthma, unk, p. Hannah & Peter Thomas, b. LC, c/o: Jas Fields, sc: Jas. Fields, husband, MT Dist., BVS:1876:1

FIGGINS, Enoch, W, M, d. 2 Jun 1859/60, LC, paralyzed, 80-0-0, p. unk, b. LC, miller, sc: Wm. Low, friend, BVS:1859:6, 1860:3, LC:36

FIGGINS, Wilford, W, M, d. 20 Apr 1858, John Sheezer's, consumption, 53-0-0, b. LC, sc: John Shugers, BVS:1858:5, LC:32

FILLER, Geo. W., W, M, d. 17 Nov 1854, LC, unk, 0-2-1, p. Jacob & Mary A. Filler, b. LC, sc: Jacob Filler, father, BVS:1854:8, LC:7

FILLER, Geo. W., W, M, d. 13 Dec 1855, LC, pneumonia, 25-11-13, p. Michl. & Margt Filler, b. LC, unm, sc: Margt. Filler, mother, BVS:1855:2, LC:15

FILLER, James H., W, M, d. 24 May 1880, nr Leesburg, pneumonia, 44-0-0, p. Michael & Margaret Filler, b. LC, c/o: Margaret F. Filler, sc: Margaret F. Filler, wife, 2nd Dist., BVS:1880:6

FILLER, Thomas W., W, M, d. 25 Aug 1859/60, LC, accidental, 19-0-0, p. Michael & Margaret Filler, b. LC, farmer, unm, sc: James Filler, brother, BVS:1859:1, 1860:3, LC:36

FILLINGAME, Ida C., W, F, d. 7 Jul 1877, LC, cholera infantum, 0-6-0, p. Wm. F. & Christina Fillingame, b. LC, sc: Wm. F. Fillingame, father, JF Dist., BVS:1877:3

FILLINGAME, John E., W, M, d. 6 Nov 1888, LC, unk, 0-0-2, p. Wm. F. & Christina Fillingame, b. LC, none, unm, sc: W.F. Fillingame, father, 2nd Dist., BVS:1888:5

FINCH, James, W, M, d. 10 Aug 1866, Fairfax, dysentery, 63-4-21, p. John & Margt Finch, b. Fauquier Co., farmer, sc: Jane Finch, wife, BVS:1866:3

FISHER, Benjamin, B, M, d. 18 Apr 1896, Middleburg, unk, 7-0-0, p. Douglass & M. Fisher, b. Middleburg, none, unm, sc: M. Fisher, mother, MC Dist., BVS:1896:1

FISHER, Bienca, B, F, d. Dec 1873, Middleburg, whooping cough, 3-0-0, p. J.M. & Fannie Fisher, b. Middleburg, sc: John W. Fisher, father, MC Dist., BVS:1873:5

Loudoun County, Virginia, Death Register, 1853-1896   101

FISHER, Hattie, W, F, d. 10 Oct 1889, LC, scarlet fever, 10-6-27, p. Thos. & Julia Fisher, b. LC, none, unm, sc: Thomas Fisher, father, 2nd Dist., BVS:1889:3

FISHER, James F., B, M, d. 30 Mar 1884, LC, unk, 0-1-6, p. Peter & Hester Fisher, b. LC, 1st Dist., BVS:1884:1

FISHER, Jane, B, F, d. 16 Sep 1887, Middleburg, rheumatism of heart, 18-0-0, p. John M. & Francis Fisher, b. Middleburg, unm, sc: John M. Fisher, father, 1st Dist., BVS:1887:2

FISHER, Lizzie T., B, F, d. 28 Dec 1882, LC, scrofula, 8-0-0, p. Jno. M. & Frances Fisher, sc: Jno M. Fisher, father, 1st Dist., BVS:1882:1

FISHER, Minnie B., W, F, d. 17 Aug 1872, Leesburg, cholera infantum, 0-6-4, p. Thos. & Julia A. Fisher, b. LC, sc: Thos. Fisher, father, LE Dist., BVS:1872:3

FISHER, Nelson, W, M, d. 26 Apr 1883, nr Leesburg, old age, 83-0-22, p. --- Fisher, b. LC, laborer, c/o: Hulda Fisher, sc: Thomas N. Fisher, son, 2nd Dist., BVS:1883:6

[FISHER], no name, B, F, d. 15 Mar 1885, nr Middleburg, croup, 0-0-6, p. John M. & Frances Fisher, b. nr Middleburg, sc: John M. Fisher, father, 1st Dist., BVS:1885:3

FISHER, no name, W, F, d. 16 Jul 1886, unk, 0-0-1, p. Thomas N. & Julia, sc: Thos. N. Fisher, father, 2nd Dist., BVS:1886:5

FISHER, no name, B, F, d. 12 Jan 1887, Middleburg, unk, 0-0-3, p. Peter & Hester Fisher, b. Middleburg, unm, sc: Peter Fisher, father, 1st Dist., BVS:1887:2

FITZHUGH, Aquilla, B, M, d. 15 Apr 1879, LC, croup, 0-1-3, p. Tazwell & Mary Fitzhugh, b. LC, sc: Tazwell Fitzhugh, father, 3rd Dist., BVS:1879:3

FITZHUGH, Chester, B, M, d. 31 Dec 1888, LC, consumption, 0-7-11, p. Taz & Mary A. Fitzhugh, b. LC, none, sc: Mary Fitzhugh, mother, 3rd Dist., BVS:1888:1

FITZHUGH, Minnie, B, F, d. 15 Mar 1887, LC, consumption, 1-3-0, p. Tazwell & C. Fitzhugh, b. LC, none, unm, sc: Tazwell Fitzhugh, father, 3rd Dist., BVS:1887:6

FLAHERTY, Ginnie, W, F, d. 10 Feb 1885, nr Farmwell, unk, 20-0-0, p. Robt. W. & Margaret A. Power, b. nr Farmwell, c/o: James G. Flaherty, sc: James G. Flaherty, husband, 1st Dist., BVS:1885:3

FLEMING, Asa G., W, M, d. 20 Sep 1881, LC, diphtheria, 1-10-0, p. Jas F. & Lucinda Fleming, b. LC, sc: J.F. Fleming, father, 1st Dist., BVS:1881:1

FLEMING, Jesse, W, M, d. 6 Feb 1853, foot of Blue Ridge, paralysis, 79-11-20, p. Arch & Sarah Fleming, b. Pennsylvania, farmer, unm, sc: Wm. Fleming, BVS:1854:1, LC:4

FLEMING, Kendall, W, M, d. 30 Sep 1894, nr Paris, cholera infantum, 0-5-6, p. Chas. T. & Lizzie Fleming, b. nr Paris, sc: C.T. Fleming, father, 1st Dist., BVS:1894:1

FLEMING, Theodora, W, F, d. 31 Oct 1869, LC, accidental, 1-9-0, p. Joseph F. & ? Fleming, b. LC, unm, sc: Joseph Fleming, father, BVS:1869:1

FLETCHER, Eddie W., W, M, d. 15 Sep 1887, Mountville, dysentery, 0-10-0, p. Townsend & Martha Fletcher, b. Mountville, sc: Townsend Fletcher, father, 1st Dist., BVS:1887:2

FLETCHER, Gibson, W, M, d. 16 Aug 1866, nr Upperville, dysentery, 6-0-0, p. Joshua & Eliz. A. Fletcher, b. nr Upperville, sc: mother, BVS:1866:2

FLETCHER, Lias T., W, M, d. 14 Oct 1858, LC, dropsy, 9-0-0, p. Mathias & Mary A. Fletcher, b. Prince William Co., sc: Mathias Fletcher, father, BVS:1858:2, LC:30

FLETCHER, Martha A., W, F, d. 22 Jan 1887, Mountville, dysentery, 48-0-0, p. Martin & Betsey Putnam, b. Fauquier Co., c/o: Townsend Fletcher, sc: Townsend Fletcher, father, 1st Dist., BVS:1887:2

FLETCHER, Mary E., W, F, d. 25 Dec 1889, LC, pneumonia, 49-0-0, p. Alfred & S. Cattleman, b. LC, none, c/o: Isaac Fletcher, sc: I. Fletcher, husband, 2nd Dist., BVS:1889:3

[FLETCHER], no name, (f), F, d. 1 Jun 1856, Green Garden Mill, 0-1-0, p.

Lucy Fletcher, b. Green Garden Mills, sc: Lucy Fletcher, mother, BVS:1856:4, LC:22

FLETCHER, Sally, W, F, d. 23 Jul 1878, nr Upperville, child birth, 30-0-0, b. LC, c/o: Robert Fletcher, sc: Thomas Glascock, father, MC Dist., BVS:1878:6

FLETCHER, Susan A., W, F, d. 22 Aug 1873, Middleburg, cancer of liver, 55-0-0, p. George Dodd, b. Fauquier Co., married, sc: Elizabeth Dodd, sister, MC Dist., BVS:1873:5

FLETCHER, Walter T., W, M, d. 10 Jun 1894, nr Waxpool, brain fever, 3-0-0, p. Chas. R. & Mary Fletcher, b. LC, sc: Chas R. Fletcher, father, 1st Dist., BVS:1894:1

FLING, Ellen V., W, F, d. 6 Sep 1888, LC, consumption, 34-0-0, p. Chas. & Delia Henderson, b. LC, none, c/o: W.F. Fling, sc: W.F. Fling, husband, 2nd Dist., BVS:1888:5

FLING, George, W, M, d. 31 Jul 1888, LC, consumption, 0-3-0, p. Wm. F. & Ellen V. Fling, b. LC, none, unm, sc: W.F. Fling, father, 2nd Dist., BVS:1888:5

FLING, Harvey, W, M, d. 10 Aug 1883, nr Leesburg, cholera infantum, 0-3-10, p. Wm. F. & Ella Fling, b. LC, sc: Wm. F. Fling, father, 2nd Dist., BVS:1883:6

FLING, James T., W, M, d. 19 Jan 1886, nr Farmwell, dropsy, 57-0-0, p. Sanford & Elizabeth Fling, b. LC, farmer, c/o: Adaline V. Fling, sc: Adaline V. Fling, wife, 1st Dist., BVS:1886:1

FLING, Mary J., W, F, d. 19 Oct 1865, Horsepen Run, intermitting fever, 3-9-10, p. G.W. & S. Fling, b. Horsepen, unm, sc: G.W. Fling, father, BVS:1865:2

[FLING], no name, W, M, d. 20 Apr 1875, LC, unk, 0-0-2, p. Wm. H. & Louisa Fling, sc: Wm. H. Fling, father, LE Dist., BVS:1875:1

FLING, Norah, W, F, d. 23 Apr 1892, Farmwell, measles, 15-0-0, p. Chas. E. & Alice Fling, b. Farmwell, unm, sc: Alice Fling, mother, 1st Dist., BVS:1892:1

FLING, Rebecca J., W, F, d. 18 Apr 1892, Ryan, measles & la grippe, 43-0-0, p. Wesley & Betsy Bladen, b. Vienna, VA, c/o: B.H. Fling, sc: B.H. Fling, husband, 1st Dist., BVS:1892:1

FLING, Sanford, W, M, d. 1 Sep 1865, Fairfax line, congestive chills, 71-1-0, p. unk, b. Fairfax, farmer, consort, sc: Sallie E. Fling, wife, BVS:1865:2

FLING, Sarah E., W, F, d. 25 Mar 1856, LC, unk, 26-0-0, p. Alexander & Jane Lyon, b. LC, sc: James T. Fling, husband, BVS:1856:7, LC:24

[FLORENCE], no name, B, , d. 8 Aug 1877, LC, 0-3-11, p. John & Nettie Florence, b. Leesburg, sc: John Florence, father, LE Dist., BVS:1877:8

FLOUCK, Lydia A., W, F, d. 8 Jul 1891, Wheatland, old age, 60-0-0, b. Maryland, wife, sc: Wm. Mock, JF Dist., BVS:1891:7

FLYNN, Sallie, W, F, d. 10 mar 1888, Middleburg, pneumonia, 80-0-0, p. John & Sarah Ball, b. Middleburg, unk, sc: John Flynn, son, 1st Dist., BVS:1888:3

FOLEY, Bailiss, W, M, d. 29 May 1871, dyspepsia, 74-0-0, farmer, married, BR Dist., BVS:1871:3

FOLEY, Job. F., W, M, d. 8 Aug 1853, LC, dysentery, 5-7-0, p. Wm. & Abigail Foley, b. LC, sc: Wm. Foley, father, BVS:1854:2, LC:6

FOLEY, Patrick, W, M, d. 16 Sep 1858, Poor House, consumption, 27-0-0, b. Ireland, sc: W. Furr, steward, BVS:1858:3, LC:31

FORD, Amanda L., B, F, d. 22 Oct 1885, nr Trappe, consumption, 24-0-0, p. Robt. S. & Elizabeth Taylor, b. nr Trappe, c/o: Edward Ford, sc: Robt C. Taylor, father, 1st Dist., BVS:1885:3

FORD, Catherine, B, F, d. 5 May 1885, nr Trappe, croup, 0-2-0, p. Edward & Amanda Ford, b. nr Trappe, sc: Robt C. Taylor, grandfather, 1st Dist., BVS:1885:3

FORSYTH, George R., W, F, d. 18 Feb 1886, pneumonia, 0-3-0, p. Geo. R. & Theresa A., sc: George R. Forsythe, father, 2nd Dist., BVS:1886:5

FORSYTHE, Louisa E., W, F, d. 24 Feb 1890, LC, general debility, 64-0-0, p. unk, b. LC, none, c/o: W.J.

Forsythe, sc: W.J. Forsythe, husband, 2nd Dist., BVS:1890:3

FOUCHE, Amos, W, M, d. 11 Dec 1859/60, LC, consumption, 75-0-0, p. Thomas & Sarah Fouche, b. LC, sc: Amos Fouche, son, BVS:1859:6, 1860:3, LC:36

FOUCHE, Elenor, W, F, d. 16 Jun 1878, nr Mt. Hope Church, general debility, 69-0-0, p. Henry Stevens & wife, b. nr Goose Creek, c/o: Amos Fouche, sc: Geo. Fouche, son, BR Dist., BVS:1878:4

FOUCHE, Rebecca, W, F, d. 27 Dec 1859/60, LC, cancer in stomach, 50-5-0, p. John & Amy Torrison, b. Prince William Co, c/o: Temple Fouche, sc: Lewis Torrison, brother, BVS:1859:1, 1860:4, LC:37

FOUCHE, Sydney C., W, M, d. 7 Jul 1892, Waxpool, dysentery, 3-0-0, p. Geo. W. & Mary M. Fouche, b. Waxpool, unm, sc: Geo H. Fouche, 1st Dist., BVS:1892:1

FOWLER, James, B, M, d. 1 Feb 1872, nr Guilford, bilious fever, 38-0-0, p. Charlotte Woodson, b. Alexandria Co., laborer, unm, sc: Charlotte Woodson, BR Dist., BVS:1872:6

FOWLER, Mary E., W, F, d. 19 Dec 1858, LC, consumption, 31-0-0, p. G.A. & Rebecca Geaslin, b. LC, sc: George A. Geaslin, father, BVS:1858:6, LC:33

FOX, Geo. K., W, M, d. 14 Dec 1872, Leesburg, typhoid pneumonia, 40-3-10, p. Geo. K. & Fanny Fox, b. Leesburg, Clerk of Court, c/o: Anna Fox, sc: Edgar Littleton, brother-in-law, LE Dist., BVS:1872:3

FOX, Manzilla V., W, F, d. 16 Nov 1878, LC, puerperal fever, 22-6-0, p. Jonas Snoots, b. LC, c/o: Chas E. Fox, sc: Chas. E. Fox, husband, LE Dist., BVS:1878:9

FOX, Mary D., W, F, d. 29 Jul 1854, LC, consumption, 56-8-3, p. Wm. & Chloe Timms, b. Port Tobacco, MD, c/o: Wm. Fox, sc: Wm. Fox, husband, BVS:1854:9, LC:8

FOX, Maurice F., W, M, d. 3 Jun 1882, LC, whooping cough, 0-5-0, p. N. T. & M. E. Fox, sc: Newton T. Fox, father, 1st Dist., BVS:1882:1

[FOX], no name, W, F, d. 31 Oct 1872, nr Gum Spring, unk, 0-0-1/2, p. Newton T. & Margaret Fox, b. LC, sc: Newton T. Fox, head of family, BR Dist., BVS:1872:6

[FOX], no name, W, F, d. 10 Jul 1874, Broad Run Dist., unk, 0-7-1, p. Newton T. & Margt. E. Fox, b. LC, sc: N.T. Fox, head of family, BR Dist., BVS:1874:3

[FOX], no name, W, , d. 14 Nov 1878, LC, premature, 0-0-2, p. Charles E. & M. V. Fox, b. LC, unm, sc: M.V. Fox, mother, LE Dist., BVS:1878:9

FOX, Sarah R., W, F, d. 11 Jun 1855, LC, consumption, 24-0-0, p. Wm. & Mary Fox, b. LC, unm, sc: Wm. Fox, father, BVS:1855:2, LC:15

FOX, William, B, M, d. 10 May 1881, LC, bright's disease, 76-0-0, p. unk, b. LC, farmer, c/o: Hannah Fox, sc: Hannah Fox, wife, 3rd Dist., BVS:1881:4

FRAME, Martha, W, F, d. 14 Jan 1886, nr Arcola, tetanus, 0-0-14, p. Wm. H. & Virginia B. Frame, b. Arcola, sc: Wm. H. Frame, father, 1st Dist., BVS:1886:1

FRAME, Susan, W, F, d. 5 Jun 1892, Purcellville, la grippe, 29-0-0, p. Charles & Susan Frame, b. Purcellville, farmer, married, sc: Charles Frame, husband, MT Dist., BVS:1892:8

FRANCIS, Hannah Ann, W, F, d. 19 May 1858, A.G. Chamblin's, pneumonia, 24-4-19, p. John & Alferna Francis, b. Mountville, sc: John Francis, father, BVS:1858:3, LC:30

FRANCIS, Henry Jefferson, W, M, d. Jan 1876, nr Waterford, affection of kidneys, 24-0-0, p. Joseph & Mary Francis, b. Buckland, Prince Wm, Va., farmer, unm, sc: John W. Francis, brother, LV Dist., BVS:1876:3

FRANCIS, Ida V., W, F, d. 10 Mar 1878, nr Mountville, whooping cough, 0-1-0, p. Jno E. & Emily G. Francis, b. LC, sc: Jno E. Francis, father, MC Dist., BVS:1878:6

FRANCIS, Isaac, B, M, d. 12 Jun 1871, unk, p. Becca Francis, MC Dist., BVS:1871:2

FRANCIS, Mary, W, F, d. 25 Mar 1856, Middleburg, typhoid fever, 44-0-0, p. Andrew & Elizth. Francis, b.

Fauquier Co., sc: Elizabeth Francis, sister, BVS:1856:4, LC:21

FRANCIS, Sidnor B., W, M, d. 12 Jan 1887, Mountville, consumption, 39-0-0, p. Thomas & Sallie Francis, b. Mountville, c/o: Ella Francis, sc: Edgar McCray, father, 1st Dist., BVS:1887:2

FRANCIS, Willard H., W, M, d. 24 Jan 1892, Willard, scarlet fever, 8-4-14, p. A. B. & Laura P. Francis, b. Pleasant Valley, laborer, unm, sc: H. Frances, father, 1st Dist., BVS:1892:1

FRANKLIN, Dora, W, F, d. 12 Mar 1884, Hamilton, diphtheria, 3-11-0, p. Webster & Lucy Franklin, b. Hamilton, unm, sc: T. Webster Franklin, father, 3rd Dist., BVS:1884:6

FRANKLIN, James R, W, M, d. 25 Nov 1876, Leesburg, diphtheria, 3-0-0, p. James F. & Catharine Franklin, b. Leesburg, sc: James F. Franklin, father, LE Dist., BVS:1876:6

FRANKLIN, Kate, W, F, d. 20 Nov 1876, Leesburg, diphtheria, 5-0-0, p. James F. & Catharine Franklin, b. Leesburg, sc: James F. Franklin, father, LE Dist., BVS:1876:6

FRANKLIN, Susan, (f), F, d. Sep 1855, Michael Plaster's, unk, 0-1-0, p. Sarah Perry, b. Michael Plaster's, sc: Mrs. Michael Plaster, BVS:1855:5, LC:17

FRANKS, Henry, W, M, d. 6 Nov 1890, Poor House, dropsy, 94-0-0, p. unk, b. LC, laborer, c/o: Martha Franks, sc: F.E. Robey, superintendent of poor, 1st Dist., BVS:1890:1

FRANKS, Julia, W, F, d. 10 May 1876, LC, old age, 76-0-0, p. unk, b. unk, c/o: Henry Franks, sc: William Franks, son, LE Dist., BVS:1876:6

FRANKS, Wm. H., W, M, d. 8 Dec 1877, LC, fever, 49-0-0, c/o: Mary F. Franks, sc: Mary F. Franks, wife, LE Dist., BVS:1877:8

FRASIER, Catharine, W, F, d. 1 Jul 1896, nr Upperville, old age, 92-0-0, p. unk, b. unk, none, consort, sc: Geo Frasier, son, MC Dist., BVS:1896:1

FRASIER, Richard, W, M, d. 10 Sep 1889, Trappe, pneumonia, 0-6-0, p. Henry & Lizzie Frasier, b. Trappe, sc: Henry Frasier, father, 1st Dist., BVS:1889:1

FRASIER, Sarah E., W, F, d. 29 Sep 1885, nr Trappe, heart disease, 63-0-0, p. John R. & Hannah Littleton, b. Trappe, c/o: Townsend Frasier, sc: Townsend Frasier, husband, 1st Dist., BVS:1885:3

FRASIER, Willie C., W, M, d. 10 Jul 1891, nr Bloomfield, cholera infantum, 0-7-0, p. Henry & Eliz. Frasier, b. LC, farmer, sc: Townsend Frasier, grandfather, 1st Dist., BVS:1891:2

FRAZIER, John, W, M, d. 29 Aug 1854, LC, consumption, 80-0-0, p. James & Sarah Frazier, b. unk, farmer, sc: Mary Frazier, dau in law, BVS:1854:8, LC:7

[FRAZIER], no name, W, M, d. 26 Oct 1866, Tankerville, 0-0-1, p. Saml H. & Sarah A. Frazier, b. LC, farmer, married, sc: Saml. H. Frazier, father, BVS:1866:1

FRAZIER, Patsey, B, F, d. 6 Feb 1876, Leesburg, old age, 71-0-0, p. unk, b. unk, c/o: Simon Frazier, sc: Elias Rivers, friend, LE Dist., BVS:1876:6

FRAZIER, Samuel H., W, M, d. 8 Dec 1856, LC, paralysis, 53-3-0, p. unk, b. Maryland, c/o: Mary A. Frazier, sc: Mary A. Frazier, wife, BVS:1856:2, LC:21

FRAZIER, Samuel H., W, M, d. 23 Dec 1883, nr Lovettsville, typhoid fever, 48-2-6, p. Saml. H. & Mary A. Frazier, b. LC, farmer, c/o: Sarah A. Frazier, sc: Wm. H. Frazier, son, 2nd Dist., BVS:1883:3

FRED, Frank L., W, M, d. 11 Jul 1894, Middleburg, diphtheria, 2-0-0, p. S. R. & Kate Fred, b. LC, sc: S.R. Fred, father, 1st Dist., BVS:1894:1

FREDERICK, Leonard, W, M, d. 2 Jun 1855, LC, pneumonia, 62-6-0, p. unk, b. Germany, c/o: Sabina Frederick, sc: Sabina Frederick, wife, BVS:1855:2, LC:15

FREE, John L., W, M, d. 1 Jun 1887, LC, dysentery, 1-0-10, p. Jno. L. & M. Free, b. LC, unm, sc: Jno Free, father, 3rd Dist., BVS:1887:6

FREEMAN, Annie L., W, F, d. 7 Oct 1882, LC, diphtheria, 0-18-0, p. L. H. & Annie E. Freeman, sc: L.H.

Loudoun County, Virginia, Death Register, 1853-1896   105

Freeman, father, 1st Dist., BVS:1882:1
FREEMAN, John M., W, M, d. 11 Oct 1882, LC, diphtheria, 4-0-0, p. L. H. & Annie E. Freeman, sc: L.H. Freeman, father, 1st Dist., BVS:1882:1
FREEMAN, Mary J., W, F, d. 16 Dec 1884, LC, premature, 0-0-3, p. Lewis H. & Hattie Freeman, b. LC, 1st Dist., BVS:1884:1
FREER, Arthur Clayton, W, M, d. 6 Mar 1892, Hillsboro, unk, 2-0-0, p. Jacob & Eni E. Freer, b. Hillsboro, mechanic, husband, sc: Jacob Freer, head of family, JF Dist., BVS:1892:7
FRITTS, Elizabeth, W, F, d. 9 Sep 1886, paralysis, 71-0-0, p. George & --- Fritts, c/o: Samuel Fritts, sc: Robert Booth, friend, 2nd Dist., BVS:1886:5
FRY, Anna C., W, F, d. 1 Oct 1889, LC, whooping cough, 18-0-0, p. Martin H. & Sarah Fry, b. LC, none, unm, sc: Martin L. Fry, father, 2nd Dist., BVS:1889:3
FRY, Annie E., W, F, d. 31 Jul 1894, Lucketts, typhoid, 26-0-0, p. Peter & Mary, b. Lucketts, unm, sc: Peter Fry, LE Dist., BVS:1894:3
FRY, Annie J., W, F, d. 15 Oct 1891, nr Lovettsville, pneumonia, 29-0-0, p. Thomas & Sarah Harrison, b. nr Lovettsville, farmer, c/o: John Fry, sc: husband, LV Dist., BVS:1891:5
FRY, Annie V., W, F, d. 4 Nov 1880, nr Leesburg, heart disease, 22-1-0, p. Jacob & Elizabeth Fry, b. LC, unm, sc: Elizabeth Fry, mother, 2nd Dist., BVS:1880:6
FRY, Cary Lorina, W, F, d. 5 Aug 1877, LC, 0-4-19, p. Charles & Catherine Fry, b. LC, sc: Charles W. Fry, father, LV Dist., BVS:1877:4/7
FRY, Catherine, W, F, d. 4 Oct 1888, LC, remittent fever, 40-0-0, p. ___Hefner, b. LC, none, c/o: Julius Fry, sc: Julius Fry, husband, 2nd Dist., BVS:1888:5
FRY, Chas. E., W, M, d. 19 Sep 1892, Lucketts, consumption, 16-0-0, p. Martin & Sarah Fry, b. Lucketts, unm, sc: Martin Fry, LE Dist., BVS:1892:5

FRY, Christina, W, F, d. Jul 1877, LC, dropsy, 73-0-0, p. David & Eve Axline, b. LC, c/o: Late Daniel Fry, sc: David E. Fry, son, LV Dist., BVS:1877:4/7
FRY, Cora D., W, F, d. 10 Sep 1886, congestion of brain, 14-8-17, p. Peter W. & Mary E., sc: Peter W. Fry, father, 2nd Dist., BVS:1886:5
FRY, Daniel N., W, M, d. 1 Mar 1885, nr Lovettsville, unk, 55-0-0, p. John & Elizabeth Fry, farmer, c/o: Adalaide S. Fry, sc: Emma B. Fry, daughter, 2nd Dist., BVS:1885:1
FRY, Edward F., W, M, d. 20 Oct 1881, Ohio, malarial fever, 33-0-0, p. Isaac & C. Fry, mechanic, c/o: Laura Fry, sc: J. W. Fry, brother, 2nd Dist., BVS:1881:6
FRY, Elizabeth, W, F, d. 11 Nov 1890, LC, la grippe, 59-0-0, p. Joseph & Sarah Dixon, b. LC, none, c/o: John M. Fry, sc: J.M. Fry, husband, 2nd Dist., BVS:1890:3
FRY, Elizabeth, W, F, d. 13 Oct 1887, LC, old age, 87-0-0, p. David & Eve Axline, b. LC, c/o: John Fry, sc: John D. Fry, son, 2nd Dist., BVS:1887:4
FRY, Elizabeth, W, F, d. 15 Mar 1888, LC, old age, 80-0-0, p. unk, b. LC, none, unm, sc: A.E. Carner, brother-in-law, 2nd Dist., BVS:1888:5
FRY, Gertrude E., W, F, d. 18 Mar 1885, nr Goresville, spinal affection, 9-4-11, p. Isaac M. & Margaret E. Fry, sc: Margaret E. Fry, mother, 2nd Dist., BVS:1885:1
FRY, Hugh W.W., W, M, d. 22 Nov 1880, nr Lovettsville, diphtheria, 2-10-21, p. Chas. W. & Annie Fry, b. LC, unm, sc: Charles H. Fry, father, 2nd Dist., BVS:1880:6
FRY, Jas. M., W, M, d. 23 Aug 1877, LC, cholera infantum, 0-11-4, p. Jos. F. & Mary C. Fry, sc: Jos. F. Fry, father, LE Dist., BVS:1877:8
FRY, John, W, M, d. 17 Jul 1877, LC, dropsy, 85-0-0, p. Philip & ? Fry, b. LC, farmer, c/o: Elizabeth Fry, sc: Elizabeth Fry, wife, LV Dist., BVS:1877:4/7
FRY, John P., W, M, d. 1 Oct 1888, LC, brain fever, 56-0-0, p. Peter & Sarah Fry, b. LC, laborer, c/o: Amanda Fry, sc: Amanda Fry, widow, 2nd Dist., BVS:1888:5

FRY, John W., W, M, d. 9 Dec 1891, Lucketts, typhoid fever, 20-0-0, p. John & Mary Fry, b. Lucketts, laborer, unm, sc: father, LE Dist., BVS:1891:4

FRY, John W., W, M, d. 6 Mar 1883, nr Leesburg, typhoid fever, 10-5-19, p. Wm. C. & Annie J. Fry, b. LC, laborer, sc: Annie J. Fry, mother, 2nd Dist., BVS:1883:3

FRY, Joseph, W, M, d. 1 Sep 1875, LC, bilious dysentery, 67-11-0, farmer, c/o: Margaret M. Fry, sc: Geo. M. Fry, son, LE Dist., BVS:1875:1

FRY, Joseph W., W, M, d. 14 Aug 1857, LC, unk, 0-5-10, p. Noah & Susanna Fry, b. LC, sc: Susanna Fry, mother, BVS:1857:1, LC:24

FRY, Leonard C., W, M, d. 25 Feb 1853, LC, water on brain, 2-4-8, p. Martin & Susanna Fry, b. LC, sc: Susanna Fry, mother, BVS:1854:2, LC:1

FRY, Lillie B., W, F, d. 4 Sep 1879, nr Goresville, whooping cough, 3-3-21, p. Geo. H. & Rosa B. Fry, b. LC, sc: George H. Fry, father, 2nd Dist., BVS:1879:1

FRY, Margaret, W, F, d. 25 Aug 1853, LC, dysentery, 55-7-11, p. Nichs. & Margaret Fry, b. LC, unk, sc: Saml Shipman, son-in-law, BVS:1854:4, LC:3

FRY, Margaret A., W, F, d. 19 Aug 1854, LC, dysentery, 51-2-11, p. John & Margaret A. Fawley, b. LC, c/o: Joseph Fry, sc: Joseph Fry, husband, BVS:1854:9, LC:9

FRY, Mary F., W, F, d. 26 Apr 1866, E side of Ketoctin Mountain, pneumonia, 26-0-0, p. Wm. & Sarah A. Hough, b. LC, carpenter, c/o: David Fry, sc: Mrs. Cox, grandmother, BVS:1866:1

FRY, Millard A., W, M, d. 16 Jul 1880, nr Leesburg, summer complaint, 1-6-0, p. Isaac W. & Margaret E. Fry, b. LC, unm, sc: Isaac Fry, father, 2nd Dist., BVS:1880:6

FRY, Nancy C., W, F, d. 10 Jun 1877, LC, spasms, 21-3-0, sc: Rich. M. Fry, husband, LE Dist., BVS:1877:8

FRY, Nicholas, W, M, d. 25 Jun 1890, LC, old age, 78-0-0, p. J. Nicholas & Margaret Fry, b. LC, none, unm, sc: D.W. Fry, son, 2nd Dist., BVS:1890:3

FRY, no name, W, M, d. 2 May 1883, nr Leesburg, unk, 0-0-2, p. Martin L. & Sarah M. Fry, b. LC, sc: Sarah M. Fry, mother, 2nd Dist., BVS:1883:6

FRY, no name, W, F, d. 14 Jun 1885, nr Goresville, unk, 0-0-7, p. Martin L. & Sarah M. Fry, sc: Martin L. Fry, father, 2nd Dist., BVS:1885:1

FRY, no name, W, F, d. 11 Jun 1886, unk, 0-0-1, p. Martin L. & Sarah M., sc: Sarah M. Fry, mother, 2nd Dist., BVS:1886:5

FRY, no name, W, F, d. 12 Jun 1886, unk, 0-0-2, p. Martin L. & Sarah M., sc: Sarah M. Fry, mother, 2nd Dist., BVS:1886:5

FRY, no name, W, M, d. 24 Sep 1888, LC, unk, 0-0-14, p. Theadore & Annie Fry, b. LC, none, unm, sc: Theadore Fry, father, 2nd Dist., BVS:1888:5

FRY, no name, W, M, d. 15 Aug 1890, LC, unk, 0-0-1, p. Thoeodore & Annie Fry, b. LC, none, unm, sc: Theadore Fry, father, 2nd Dist., BVS:1890:3

FRY, Nora C., W, F, d. 18 Nov 1896, LC, fever, 21-0-0, p. J. W. & A. S. Fry, b. LC, unm, sc: father, LE Dist., BVS:1896:5

FRY, Samuel, W, M, d. 6 Nov 1866, nr Lovettsville, heart disease, 57-8-11, b. LC, farmer, married, sc: Chas. W. Frye, son, BVS:1866:1

FRY, Sarah, W, F, d. 3 Dec 1866, E side of Short Hill, unk, c/o: Peter Fry, sc: Peter Fry, BVS:1866:1

FRY, Stephen A., W, M, d. 20 Jul 1877, LC, cholera infantum, 0-1-10, p. Rich W. & Nancy C. Fry, sc: Richard W. Fry, father, LE Dist., BVS:1877:8

FRY, Susan, W, F, d. Feb 1871, LC, 62-0-0, b. LC, c/o: Lenard Fry, LE Dist., BVS:1871:4

FRY, Susan H., W, F, d. 21 Mar 1878, LC, brain fever, 3-10-0, p. David W. & Nancy C. Fry, b. LC, unm, sc: Nancy C. Fry, mother, LE Dist., BVS:1878:8

FRY, William, W, M, d. 11 May 1879, nr Lovettsville, heart disease, 72-0-0, p. Peter & ___ Fry, b. LC, farmer,

Loudoun County, Virginia, Death Register, 1853-1896   107

c/o: Elizabeth Fry, sc: Elizabeth Fry, wife, 2nd Dist., BVS:1879:1

FRYE, Elizabeth, W, F, d. 19 Apr 1891, nr Aldie, dropsy, 36-0-20, p. John & Frances Moss, b. LC, farmer, c/o: Saml Frye, sc: Saml Frye, husband, 1st Dist., BVS:1891:2

FRYE, Mary E., W, F, d. 12 Jul 1865, nr Boling Farm, affection lungs, 0-8-12, p. Jos H. & Sarah E. Frye, b. nr Bolington, farmer, unm, sc: Jos H. Frye, father, BVS:1865:3

FRYE, Mary Elizabeth, W, F, d. 12 Jul 1865, nr Bolington, affection lungs, 0-8-12, p. Joseph H. & Sarah E. Frye, b. nr Bolington, farmer, married, sc: Joseph H. Frye, father, 1st Dist., BVS:1865:4

FULTON, James, W, M, d. 14 Aug 1872, nr Valley Church, cramp & cold, 78-0-0, p. Hugh & Susanna Fulton, b. unk, farmer, c/o: Sarah Fulton, sc: Sarah Fulton, consort, LE Dist., BVS:1872:3

FULTON, John Edward, W, M, d. 23 Sep 1873, nr Purcellville, skin disease, 55-10-20, p. Edward & Rebecca Fulton, b. Pennsylvania, farmer, c/o: Maria Fulton, sc: Edward C. Fulton, son, JF Dist., BVS:1874:1

FULTON, Martha, W, F, d. 2 Oct 1857, LC, dropsy, 11-1-1, p. James & Sarah Fulton, b. LC, sc: James Fulton, father, BVS:1857:1, LC:24

FULTON, William, W, M, d. 13 Aug 1885, nr Leesburg, consumption, 33-0-0, p. Wm. & Martha A. Fulton, physician, unm, sc: Arthur H. Fulton, brother, 2nd Dist., BVS:1885:1

FURGERSON, Amos, W, M, d. 1 Apr 1857, old age, 76-0-0, p. unk, b. LC, blacksmith, sc: Romulus Furgerson, son, BVS:1857:7, LC:28

FURR, Arbelin, W, F, d. 14 Nov 1877, on Blue Ridge Mountain, consumption, 40-0-0, b. LC, c/o: Kemp B. Furr, sc: Kemp B. Furr, husband, MC Dist., BVS:1877:5

FURR, Douglass, B, M, d. 24 Mar 1869, LC, typhoid fever, 0-8-0, p. Perry & Ann Furr, b. LC, unm, sc: Jerry Furr, father, BVS:1869:1

FURR, Ebin H., W, M, d. 3 Apr 1881, LC, congestive chill, 3-0-0, p. Jos. P. & Mary Furr, b. LC, sc: J.P. Furr, father, 3rd Dist., BVS:1881:4

FURR, Emsey, W, F, d. 20 Jun 1873, nr Aldie, disease of heart, 61-0-0, p. John & Mary Gillham, b. LC, c/o: Wm. Furr, sc: Dallas Furr, son, MC Dist., BVS:1873:5

FURR, Enoch, W, M, d. 2 Sep 1874, Poor House, old age, 84-0-0, b. Fauquier Co., sc: Wm. H. Hibbs, superintendant, MC Dist., BVS:1874:4

FURR, Francis, B, F, d. 4 Jul 1891, Hillsboro, abscess of stomach, 62-0-0, p. Forrest & Griffey Furr, b. Wheatland, sc: Forrest Furr, head of family, JF Dist., BVS:1891:7

FURR, Kemp G., W, M, d. 12 Nov 1878, nr Trappe, dysentery, 2-9-0, p. Kemp B. & Arbelia Furr, b. LC, sc: Kemp B. Furr, father, MC Dist., BVS:1878:6

FURR, Martha A., W, F, d. 24 Jun 1882, LC, pneumonia, 50-0-0, p. John & Martha Davis, c/o: Dewit C. Furr, sc: Dewitt C. Furr, husband, 1st Dist., BVS:1882:1

FURR, Moses, W, M, d. 5 Jan 1866, Blue Ridge, 71-0-0, farmer, married, sc: Kemp B. Furr, son, BVS:1866:2

[FURR], no name, W, F, d. Jul 1854, foot of Blue Ridge, 0-0-14, p. Kemp B. & Mary Ann Furr, b. foot of Blue Ridge, sc: father, BVS:1854:11, LC:11

[FURR], no name, W, M, d. 7 May 1855, E of Blue Ridge, 0-0-1, p. Dewit C. & Martha A. Furr, b. E of Blue Ridge, sc: B.F. Furr, uncle, BVS:1855:6, LC:18

[FURR], no name, W, M, d. 8 Sep 1855, parents' res, thrush, 0-1-0, p. Fenton & Sarah Furr, b. nr Ebenezer Church, sc: Fenton Furr, BVS:1855:5, LC:17

FURR, Phebe, W, F, d. 22 Oct 1856, res, heart affection, 70-7-0, p. Eli & Sarah Anderson, b. LC, c/o: Minor Furr, sc: Minor Furr, widower, BVS:1856:5, LC:22

FURR, Richard E., W, M, d. 27 Feb 1883, nr Farmwell, pneumonia, 64-0-0, p. unk, b. LC, farmer, c/o: Sally Furr, sc: Sally Furr, wife, 1st Dist., BVS:1883:1

FURR, Susan E., W, F, d. 13 Jun 1876, Bloomfield, consumption, 57-0-0, b. LC, c/o: Fenton Furr, sc: Fenton Furr, husband, MC Dist., BVS:1876:4

FURR, Thompson M., W, M, d. 19 Apr 1864, Lunatic Asylum, Wash, imprisonment, 19-0-0, p. E. & Emily Furr, b. Bloomfield, soldier, sc: B.R. Barton, neighbor, BVS:1864:1, LC:38

FURR, W. G., W, M, d. 18 Sep 1894, nr Bloomfield, old age, 88-0-0, p. unk, b. unk, farmer, c/o: Mary A. Furr, sc: Mary A. Furr, wife, 1st Dist., BVS:1894:1

FURR, William, W, M, d. 11 Jan 1873, nr Aldie, disease of heart, 67-0-0, p. unk, b. LC, farmer, married, sc: Dallas Furr, son, MC Dist., BVS:1873:5

FURR, Wilmer, B, M, d. 21 Nov 1884, Philomont, diphtheria, 1-3-10, p. Gregg & Mary Furr, b. Philomont, unm, sc: Gregg Furr, father, 3rd Dist., BVS:1884:6

GAINES, Agnes Leslie, W, F, d. 18 Nov 1876, nr Bloomfield, affection of the lungs, 0-8-0, p. Jno D. & Flora Gaines, b. LC, sc: Jno. D. Gaines, father, MC Dist., BVS:1876:4

GAINES, Cora Lilian, W, F, d. 19 Nov 1876, nr Bloomfield, scald, 3-9-0, p. Jno D. & Flora Gaines, b. LC, sc: Jno. D. Gaines, father, MC Dist., BVS:1876:4

GAINES, Euphamia, W, F, d. 7 Jan 1881, LC, dysentery, 78-0-0, b. LC, c/o: John Gaines, sc: Frank Robey, friend, 3rd Dist., BVS:1881:4

GAINES, Lucy L., W, F, d. 17 Jul 1889, Farmwell, consumption, 44-0-0, p. Thos. A. & Priscilla A. Jones, b. LC, c/o: David Gaines, sc: David Gaines, husband, 1st Dist., BVS:1889:1

[GAINES], no name, (f), F, d. 26 Feb 1858, LC, unk, 0-0-11, p. Jane Gaines, b. LC, sc: Kitty Gaines, grandmother, BVS:1858:2, LC:30

GAINES, Wm. F., W, M, d. 1865, nr Snickersville, croup, 3-0-21, p. Wm. A. & Masey S. Gaines, b. LC, merchant, BVS:1865:1

GALLEHER, Beatrice, W, F, d. 15 Apr 1876, nr Unison, unk, 1-0-0, p. T. H. & Jane D. Galleher, b. LC, sc: Turner H. Galleher, father, MC Dist., BVS:1876:4

GALLEHER, James W., W, M, d. 7 Dec 1856, LC, typhoid fever, 35-0-0, p. Thomas & Patsy Galleher, b. Fauquier Co., c/o: Elizabeth V. Galleher, sc: Elizabeth V. Galleher, wife, BVS:1856:3, LC:21

GALLEHER, Jno. W., W, M, d. 4 Dec 1883, Washington, DC, consumption, 56-0-0, p. Thos. & Martha Galleher, b. LC, merchant, c/o: Virginia Galleher, sc: Wm. R. Galleher, son, 2nd Dist., BVS:1883:3

GALLEHER, Maria C., W, F, d. 19 Apr 1859/60, her res, consumption, 23-3-6, p. R.B. & Susan B. Jacobs, b. nr Union, c/o: Turner H. Galleher, sc: T. H. Galleher, husband, BVS:1859:3, 1860:1. LC:34

GALLEHER, Marjary, W, F, d. 31 Jan 1857, nr Bloomfield, old age, 80-0-0, p. George & ... Johnston, b. nr Pothouse, c/o: William Galleher, sc: William Galleher, widower, BVS:1857:4, LC:27

GALLEHER, Patsy Violet, W, F, d. 15 Apr 1877, Stoney Point, consumption, 0-4-0, p. Turner H. & Jane D. Galleher, b. LC, sc: Turner H. Galleher, father, MC Dist., BVS:1877:5

GALLEHER, Turner H., W, M, d. 16 Jan 1881, LC, consumption, 51-0-0, p. Thos H. & Patsy V. Galleher, b. LC, farmer, c/o: Jane D. Galleher, sc: J.D. Galleher, wife, 1st Dist., BVS:1881:1

GALLEHER, Willis B., W, M, d. 30 Dec 1859/60, Leesburg, scalded, 4-8-21, p. John W. & Virgina A. Galleher, b. Leesburg, sc: John W. Gallaher, father, BVS:1859:2, 1860:4, LC:37

GALLIGHER, Frank, B, M, d. 9 Aug 1883, Leesburg, cholera infantum, 0-4-0, p. Frank & Rachal Galligher, b. LC, sc: Rachael Galligher, mother, 2nd Dist., BVS:1883:3

GANT, Elizabeth, B, F, d. 20 Aug 1877, LC, pneumonia, 2-4-0, p. Isabella Gant, sc: Isabella Gant, mother, LE Dist., BVS:1877:8

GANT, Ella J., W, F, d. 23 Feb 1875, Leesburg, diphtheria, 5-1-21, p. Jno.

F. & Ann E. Gant, sc: Ann E. Gant, mother, LE Dist., BVS:1875:1

GANT, Johnnie, B, M, d. 8 Jan 1887, Aldie, consumption, 8-0-0, p. Ed & Sarah Gant, b. Aldie, sc: Ed Gant, father, 1st Dist., BVS:1887:2

GANT, Laura J., W, F, d. 26 Dec 1878, LC, consumption, 25-7-0, p. John T. & Annie E. Gant, b. LC, unm, sc: Annie E. Gant, mother, LE Dist., BVS:1878:8

GANT, Margaret, W, F, d. 20 Apr 1878, Aldie, dropsy, 52-0-0, b. LC, c/o: Richard H. Gant, sc: Richard H. Gant, husband, MC Dist., BVS:1878:6

GANT, Margt A., W, F, d. 3 Nov 1864, nr Beaver Dam, dysentery, 5-0-18, p. Jno & Eliz Gant, b. LC, sc: John Gant, father, BVS:1864:2, LC:39

GANT, no name, W, F, d. 2 Oct 1881, LC, unk, 0-0-1, p. Danl. J. & J. E. Gant, sc: Daniel E. Gant, father, 2nd Dist., BVS:1881:6

GANT, Thomas, B, M, d. 2 Oct 1876, LC, diphtheria, 8-0-0, p. Alice Budd, b. LC, sc: Mana Budd, friend, LE Dist., BVS:1876:6

GARDINER, Chas. L., W, M, d. 31 Dec 1889, Arcola, old age, 87-0-0, p. Charles L. & Ann Gardiner, b. LC, Miller, unk, sc: Catharine E. Gardiner, daughter, 1st Dist., BVS:1889:1

GARDINER, Elizabeth, W, F, d. 10 Feb 1881, LC, nervous ?, 74-0-0, b. LC, c/o: Charles Gardiner, sc: C. Gardiner, daughter, 1st Dist., BVS:1881:1

GARDINER, Thomas J., W, M, d. 7 Jun 1886, nr Farmwell, consumption, 20-0-0, p. James L. & Susan Gardiner, b. LC, laborer, sc: James L. Gardiner, father, 1st Dist., BVS:1886:1

GARDINER, Wm., W, M, d. 29 May 1892, Ryan, inflammation of bowels, 76-0-0, p. Chas. L. & Ann Gardiner, b. LC, potter, unm, sc: J.L. Gardiner, nephew, 1st Dist., BVS:1892:1

GARDNER, Mary J., W, F, d. 3 Mar 1884, nr Lovettsville, heart disease, 52-0-0, p. Robert & Malinda Johnson, b. LC, farmer, c/o: William W. Gardner, sc: W.W. Gardner, husband, 2nd Dist., BVS:1884:4

GARNER, Annie L., W, F, d. Apr 1873, Leesburg, consumption, 8-0-0, p. H. & A. Garner, b. Leesburg, unm, sc: Amanda Garner, mother, LE Dist., BVS:1873:2

GARNER, Arthur, W, M, d. 5 Sep 1853, LC, old age, 80-0-0, p. Samuel Garner, b. LC, toll gatherer, sc: Elizabeth Garner, wife, BVS:1854:2, LC:7

GARNER, John, B, M, d. 15 Nov 1896, Middleburg, cancer, 27-0-0, p. Fannie Garner, b. Middleburg, none, unm, sc: Wm. Austin, stepfather, MC Dist., BVS:1896:1

GARNER, Nathan, B, M, d. 12 Jun 1880, LC, unk, 0-6-0, p. Samuel & Sarah Garner, b. LC, unm, sc: Sarah Garner, mother, 1st Dist., BVS:1880:1

GARNER, Sarah J., W, F, d. 27 Apr 1856, Leesburg, pneumonia, 14-9-20, p. Arthur & Elizth. Garner, b. LC, unm, sc: Peter R. Shaffner, half brother-in-law, BVS:1856:1, LC:20

GARNET, Aletis, B, F, d. 25 Nov 1887, Arcola, old age, 93-0-0, p. Henry & Charity Barnett, b. Prince William Co., unk, sc: Aaron Johnson, grandson, 1st Dist., BVS:1887:2

GARRETT, A. L., W, F, d. 1 Apr 1889, LC, consumption, 50-0-0, p. S. & G. Garrett, b. LC, none, unm, sc: Burr Garrett, brother, 3rd Dist., BVS:1889:5

GARRETT, Anna, W, F, d. Spring, 1864, Thos M. Triplett's, consumption, 21-0-0, p. S. & M. Garrett, b. Fauquier Co., sc: Thos M. Triplett, cousin, BVS:1864:1, LC:38

GARRETT, Archibald, W, M, d. 22 Nov 1859/60, LC, consumption, 55-0-0, p. unk, b. unk, farmer, c/o: Susan Garrett, sc: Sydnor Bennett, friend, BVS:1859:1, 1860:3, LC:36

GARRETT, Enoch F., W, M, d. 9 Apr 1864, nr Philomont, scrofula, 0-9-0, p. Jos. & Ester Garrett, b. LC, sc: Jos Garrett, father, BVS:1864:2, LC:39

GARRETT, Hannah, W, F, d. 1 Aug 1858, her res, dropsy, 52-2-9, p. John & Elizth Batson, b. LC, c/o: Enoch Garrett, sc: E. Garrett, husband, BVS:1858:5, LC:33

GARRETT, Josephine, W, F, d. 8 Jan 1873, nr Aldie, cholera infantum, 0-7-0, p. Burr W. & Lucinda Garrett, b. nr Aldie, sc: Burr W. Garrett, head of family, BR Dist., BVS:1873:1

GARRETT, Stephen, W, M, d. Apr 1857, old age, 86-0-0, p. Joseph & Sally Garrett, b. LC, farmer, sc: George W. Garrett, son, BVS:1857:7, LC:28

GARRISON, Elizabeth, W, F, d. 4 Feb 1854, Leesburg, dropsy, 58-2-3, p. unk, b. Accomac Co., c/o: James Garrison, sc: James Garrison, husband, BVS:1854:8, LC:7

GARRISON, James, W, M, d. 10 May 1872, Leesburg, typhoid pneumonia, 80-1-2, p. Jas. & Sarah Garrison, b. Norfolk, merchant, c/o: Mary Garrison, sc: Mary Garrison, consort, LE Dist., BVS:1872:3

GARRISON, Sarah W., W, F, d. 8 Jun 1859/60, Fauquier Co, unk, 0-8-0, p. Washington & M. Garrison, b. Fauquier Co., sc: W. Garrison, father, BVS:1859:6, 1860:3, LC:36

GASKINS, Annie, B, F, d. Jul 1873, nr Aldie, whooping cough, 1-4-0, p. Rose Gaskins, b. nr Aldie, sc: Wm. Gaskins, brother, MC Dist., BVS:1873:5

GASKINS, Charles, B, M, d. 12 Apr 1887, Aldie, consumption, 25-0-0, p. Viola Gaskins (unm), b. Aldie, unm, sc: Edward Moton, cousin, 1st Dist., BVS:1887:2

GASKINS, Geneva, B, F, d. 23 Dec 1890, Bloomfield, consumption, 12-0-0, p. Nathan & Leva Gaskins, b. Bloomfield, unm, sc: Nathan Gaskins, father, 1st Dist., BVS:1890:1

GASKINS, George, B, M, d. 9 Jul 1880, LC, cholera infantum, 0-12-0, p. George & Alice Gaskins, b. LC, unm, sc: Alice Gaskins, mother, 1st Dist., BVS:1880:1

GASKINS, Georgie, B, F, d. 21 Aug 1885, nr Farmwell, consumption, 20-0-0, p. Joseph & Georgie Gaskins, b. nr Farmwell, unm, sc: Joseph Gaskins, father, 1st Dist., BVS:1885:3

GASKINS, Gustave, B, M, d. 20 Nov 1880, LC, unk, 2-0-0, p. John & Rose Gaskins, b. LC, unm, sc: Rose Gaskins, mother, 1st Dist., BVS:1880:1

GASKINS, Henry, B, M, d. 11 Dec 1886, nr Aldie, consumption, 26-0-0, p. Henry & Lucy Gaskins, b. LC, laborer, unm, sc: Edward Moton, cousin, 1st Dist., BVS:1886:1

GASKINS, Henry, B, M, d. 12 Jan 1887, Aldie, consumption, 23-0-0, p. Lashey Gaskins (unm), b. Aldie, unm, sc: Edward Moton, cousin, 1st Dist., BVS:1887:2

GASKINS, Henry Cal, B, M, d. Oct 1878, Guinea, croup, 0-3-0, p. Peter & Frances Gaskins, b. Guinea, sc: P. Gaskins, parent, MT Dist., BVS:1878:2/3

GASKINS, Joseph, B, M, d. 3 Dec 1894, nr Farmwell, consumption, 36-0-0, p. Rebecca Gaskins, b. LC, c/o: Francis Jackson, sc: Geo Jackson, father-in-law, 1st Dist., BVS:1894:2

GASKINS, Mary C., B, F, d. 15 Dec 1884, LC, brain fever, 2-0-0, p. Joseph & Francis Gaskins, b. LC, 1st Dist., BVS:1884:1

GASKINS, Matilda, B, F, d. 20 Oct 1890, nr Aldie, old age, 94-0-0, p. unk, b. LC, unm, sc: Edward Moton, nephew, 1st Dist., BVS:1890:1

[GASKINS], no name, B, F, d. 24 Oct 1875, LC, unk, unk, p. Jas H. & Hannah Gaskins, sc: Hannah Gaskins, mother, LE Dist., BVS:1875:1

[GASKINS], no name, B, M, d. 9 Aug 1880, LC, unk, 0-0-8, p. Wm. & Mary C. Gaskins, b. LC, unm, sc: Mary C. Gaskins, mother, 1st Dist., BVS:1880:1

[GASKINS], no name, B, M, d. 20 Sep 1880, LC, unk, 0-1-5, p. Nathan & Olivia Gaskins, b. LC, unm, sc: Olivia Gaskins, mother, 1st Dist., BVS:1880:1

GASKINS, Robert, B, M, d. 1 Sep 1888, LC, unk, 11-0-0, p. James H. & Hannah Gaskins, b. LC, none, unm, sc: Mahala Buckhanon, grandmother, 2nd Dist., BVS:1888:5

GASKINS, Rosa, B, F, d. 20 Mar 1887, Aldie, consumption, 20-0-0, p. Eliza Gaskins (unm), b. Aldie, sc: Edward Moton, father, 1st Dist., BVS:1887:2

GASKINS, Sallie, B, F, d. 12 Aug 1887, Aldie, consumption, 38-0-0, p.

Matilda Gaskins (unm), b. Aldie, unm, sc: Edward Moton, cousin, 1st Dist., BVS:1887:2

GASKINS, Serena, B, F, d. 21 Aug 1887, Aldie, dropsy, 25-0-0, p. Matilda Gaskins (unm), b. Aldie, unm, sc: Edward Moton, cousin, 1st Dist., BVS:1887:2

GASKINS, William, B, M, d. 10 Sep 1890, Willisville, consumption, 15-0-0, p. Wm. & Rose Gaskins, b. LC, laborer, sc: William Gaskins, father, 1st Dist., BVS:1890:1

GAULT, Elizabeth, W, F, d. 28 Jun 1876, nr Short Hill, dropsy, 77-0-0, p. .....Jackson, c/o: John Gault, sc: Blanco Branhall, son-in-law, LV Dist., BVS:1876:3

GAUNT, Ferdinand, W, M, d. 4 Oct 1859/60, Charlottesville O & A RR, typhoid fever, 25-0-0, p. Charles & Margaret Gaunt, b. Purcellville, conductor R.R., sc: C. Gaunt, father, BVS:1859:3, 1860:1, LC:34

GAUNT, Franklin, W, M, d. 1 Oct 1859/60, father's res, sore throat, 9-0-0, p. Charles & Margaret Gaunt, b. Purcellville, sc: C. Gaunt, father, BVS:1859:3, 1860:1, LC:34

GAUNT, Margaret, W, F, d. Aug 1858, nr Purcellville, unk, BVS:1858:5, LC:32

GAYNER, Ann E., W, F, d. 3 Jul 1890, Hillsboro, consumption, 53-0-0, p. Reuben & Ellen Jenkins, b. LC, none, c/o: Patrick Gaynor, sc: Robert McArter, son, 3rd Dist., BVS:1890:6

GAYNOR, Alice, W, F, d. Nov 1859/60, res of parents, 0-0-25, p. James & Mary Jane Gaynor, b. foot of Short Hill, sc: Mary Jane Gaynor, mother, BVS:1859:4, 1860:2, LC:35

GAYNOR, Margaret, W, F, d. 5 Aug 1866, Short Hill, unk, 2-0-0, p. James Gaynor, b. Short Hill, sc: father, BVS:1866:2

GEASLIN, Samuel S., W, M, d. 20 Jun 1886, Farmwell, consumption, 45-0-0, p. Anderson & Mary Geaslin, b. LC, Miller, c/o: Susan A. Geaslin, sc: Susan A. Geaslin, wife, 1st Dist., BVS:1886:1

GEATER, C. F., B, M, d. 20 Jul 1880, LC, unk, 0-0-14, p. Mary Geater, b. LC, unm, sc: Mary Geater, mother, 1st Dist., BVS:1880:1

GENUS, Leroy, B, M, d. 9 Feb 1885, nr Farmwell, brain fever, 1-0-0, p. Chas. & Josephine Genus, b. nr Farmwell, sc: Chas Genus, father, 1st Dist., BVS:1885:3

GENUS, Mary M., B, F, d. 15 Apr 1890, Farmwell, croup, 0-10-0, p. Charles & Josephine Genus, b. Farmwell, sc: Charles Genns, father, 1st Dist., BVS:1890:1

GEORGE, Edith, W, F, d. 10 Sep 1881, LC, scalded, 3-0-0, p. A. C. & E. C. George, sc: A.C. George, father, 2nd Dist., BVS:1881:6

GEORGE, Jno. S., W, M, d. 29 Oct 1872, nr Short Hill, unk, 0-8-2, p. Saml. & Virginia George, b. nr Short Hill, farmer, married, sc: Saml W. George Jr., father, LV Dist., BVS:1872:5

GEORGE, Mary, W, F, d. 8 May 1890, LC, rheumatism, 75-0-0, p. Frederick & Elizabeth Dinges, b. LC, none, c/o: Solomon George, sc: G.W. George, son, 2nd Dist., BVS:1890:3

[GEORGE], no name, W, F, d. 28 Sep 1856, LC, unk, 0-0-6, p. Samuel W. & Eliza C. George, b. LC, sc: Samuel W. George, father, BVS:1856:2, LC:21

GEORGE, no name, W, M, d. 15 Jun 1877, LC, 0-3-15, p. Robert & Florence George, b. LC, sc: Robert L. George, father, LV Dist., BVS:1877:4/7

GEORGE, no name, W, M, d. 30 Jul 1884, nr Lovettsville, unk, 0-5-0, p. Robert & Florence George, b. LC, sc: Robt L. George, father, 2nd Dist., BVS:1884:4

GEORGE, Phebe, W, F, d. 22 Apr 1854, res of Francis Carter, dropsy, 75-1-28, p. Richard & Agness Carter, c/o: Wm. George, decd, sc: Francis Carter, nephew, BVS:1854:13, LC:13

GEORGE, Samuel W., W, M, d. 18 Aug 1889, LC, cancer, 69-0-0, p. John & Eliz. George, b. LC, farmer, c/o: Elizabeth George, sc: E. George, widow, 2nd Dist., BVS:1889:3

GHEEN, Robert N., W, M, d. 25 Mar 1879, nr Leesburg, remitting fever, 2-6-0, p. George H. & Rose V. Gheen, b. LC, sc: George H. Gheen, father, 2nd Dist., BVS:1879:1

GHEEN, Thomas M., W, M, d. 12 Jan 1876, LC, consumption, 26-0-0, p. unk, b. LC, laborer, c/o: Elizabeth Gheen, sc: John W. Sinclair, father-in-law, LE Dist., BVS:1876:7

GIBSON, Aaron, W, M, d. 9 Nov 1857, Addison Stillion's, 78-5-26, p. Moses & Lydia Gibson, b. nr Clifton, carpenter, c/o: Elizabeth Gibson, decd, sc: Susan Shillions, daughter, BVS:1857:3, LC:26

GIBSON, Allen, W, M, d. 10 Apr 1855, Greengarden, typhoid fever, 30-0-0, p. Aaron & Eliz. Gibson, b. on Blue Ridge, Farmhand, c/o: Huldah Gibson, sc: Addison Williams & wife, brother & sister-in-law, BVS:1855:4, LC:16

GIBSON, Elenora, W, F, d. 5 Dec 1855, Fernue, typhoid, 61-0-0, p. Alexr. & Martha Bruce, b. Stafford, c/o: Mahlon Gibson, decd, sc: Bruce Gibson, son, BVS:1855:6, LC:18

GIBSON, Florence, 8 w, F, d. 8 Oct 1894, nr Upperville, cancer, 47-0-6, p. unk, b. nr Upperville, c/o: Jos A. Gibson, sc: Jos A. Gibson, husband, 1st Dist., BVS:1894:1

GIBSON, George, W, M, d. 23 Oct 1855, Joseph Gibson's, typhoid fever, 47-10-2, p. John & Cidney Gibson, b. nr Upperville, farmer, sc: Mrs. Wm. Wilkinson, sister, BVS:1855:4, LC:16

GIBSON, James D., W, M, d. 23 Aug 1890, Unison, typhoid fever, 24-0-0, p. Owen H. & Mary Gibson, b. Unison, unm, sc: Owen H. Gibson, father, 1st Dist., BVS:1890:1

GIBSON, Jesse H., W, M, d. 18 Feb 1853, on Blue Ridge, burnt to death, 1-4-0, p. Alexr. & Huldah Gibson, b. on Blue Ridge, sc: mother, BVS:1854:1, LC:4

GIBSON, Juliet A., W, F, d. 30 Oct 1856, Leesburg, consumption, 41-0-0, p. Levi & Mary Gibson, b. LC, unm, sc: Mary P. Turner, friend, BVS:1856:1, LC:19

GIBSON, Maria, W, F, d. 5 Oct 1882, LC, congestive chill, 74-0-0, p. John & Mary Jones, c/o: Gilbert B. Gibson, sc: G.B. Gibson, husband, 1st Dist., BVS:1882:1

GIBSON, Martha L., W, F, d. 4 Dec 1855, Fernue, typhoid fever, 28-0-0, p. Mahlon & Elenora Gibson, b. nr Green Gardens, sc: Bruce Gibson, brother, BVS:1855:6, LC:17

GIBSON, Nancy, B, F, d. 12 Feb 1877, nr Frankville, pneumonia, 6-0-0, p. Samuel & Louisa Gibson, b. unk, unm, sc: Samuel Gibson, father, BR Dist., BVS:1877:1

GIBSON, Ruth, B, F, d. 6 Jun 1891, Sterling, heart failure, 84-6-0, p. unk, b. Fauquier Co., laborer, c/o: Charles Gibson, decd, sc: Nelson Gaskins, head of family, 1st Dist., BVS:1891:1

GIBSON, Solomon, W, M, d. 14 Feb 1864, Bloomfield, old age, 102-9-0, p. Jas & Ruth Gibson, b. Pennsylvania, farmer, sc: Ruth Arnett, daughter, BVS:1864:1, LC:38

GILBERT, Francis, B, M, d. 1 Apr 1880, nr Leesburg, consumption, 0-9-0, p. Zack & Harriet Gilbert, b. LC, unm, sc: Zack Gilbert, father, 2nd Dist., BVS:1880:6

GILBERT, George V., W, M, d. 4 Aug 1857, Middleburg, inflammation of bowels, 8-10-0, p. Melvina Gilbert, b. Joshua Pancoast's Farm, sc: David E. Adams, employer, BVS:1857:4, LC:26

GILBERT, Margaret, B, F, d. 5 Jun 1875, LC, unk, unk, p. Zachariah & Mary Gilbert, sc: Wm. Ball, friend, LE Dist., BVS:1875:1

GILBERT, Zachariah, B, M, d. 20 Feb 1894, Silcott Springs, milk scales, 0-4-0, p. Zach & Almira Gilbert, b. Silcott Springs, sc: Zacheriah Gilbert, father, 3rd Dist., BVS:1894:5

GILL, John L., W, M, d. 8 Mar 1877, Bloomfield, pneumonia, 84-0-0, b. Prince William Co., farmer, c/o: Hannah Gill, sc: Wm. H. Gill, son, MC Dist., BVS:1877:5

GILL, William H., W, M, d. 8 Jul 1887, Bloomfield, cancer, 67-0-0, p. John L. & Hannah Hunt, b. Bloomfield, c/o: Sarah J. Gill, sc: Sarah J. Gill, wife, 1st Dist., BVS:1887:2

GILMORE, Anna, W, F, d. 30 Apr 1857, Leesburg, unk, 79-4-14, p.

Loudoun County, Virginia, Death Register, 1853-1896   113

Pierce & Mary Bayly, b. unk, c/o: William Gilmore, sc: William Gilmore, husband, BVS:1857:2, LC:25

GILMORE, Bettie, B, F, d. 26 Dec 1880, nr Leesburg, child birth, 51-0-0, p. William & Lucinda Luckett, b. LC, laborer, c/o: James Gilmore, sc: James Gilmore, husband, 2nd Dist., BVS:1880:6

[GILMORE], no name, B, , d. 11 Feb 1877, LC, strangulation, 0-0-1, p. James & Bettie Gilmore, sc: James Gilmore, father, LE Dist., BVS:1877:8

GILSON, Amanda, W, F, d. 23 Aug 1853, nr Sycolin, dysentery, 21-0-0, p. Murphey & Diadama Shumate, b. on Sycolin, c/o: R.G. Gilson, sc: M. Shumate, father, BVS:1854:5, LC:5

GIST, Elizabeth, W, F, d. 10 Oct 1880, LC, cancer, 50-0-0, p. unk, b. LC, unm, sc: John Hutchison, cousin, 1st Dist., BVS:1880:1

GLADSTONE, James, W, M, d. 15 Jan 1896, nr Unison, consumption, 66-0-0, p. unk, b. Rappahannock Co., carpenter, consort, sc: Henry Tavenner, son-in-law, MC Dist., BVS:1896:1

GLASCOCK, B.H., W, M, d. 20 May 1853, nr Philomont, epilepsy, 41-0-0, p. Uriel & Mary Glascock, b. LC, farmer, unm, sc: father, BVS:1854:1, LC:4

GLEAD, Ginnie, B, F, d. 15 Aug 1881, LC, consumption, 39-9-0, p. Robt. & M. Buchannan, laborer, c/o: John Glead, sc: Robert Buchannan, father, 2nd Dist., BVS:1881:6

GLEAD, Lucinda, B, F, d. April 1874, LC, consumption, 40-0-0, c/o: Jack Glead, sc: Jack Glead, father, LE Dist., BVS:1874:5

GLEAD, Mary, B, F, d. 1 Feb 1881, LC, consumption, 1-3-0, p. Jno. & Ginnie Glead, sc: Grace Pierson, aunt, 2nd Dist., BVS:1881:6

GLEAD, Sarah, B, F, d. Dec 1873, LC, whooping cough, 0-15-0, p. John & Hanah Glead, b. LC, unm, sc: J. Glead, father, LE Dist., BVS:1873:2

GLEAD, Wm., B, M, d. 15 Apr 1878, LC, pneumonia, 0-11-0, p. Jacob & Ginny Glead, b. LC, unm, sc: Ginnie Glead, mother, LE Dist., BVS:1878:8

GLEAD, Wm., B, M, d. 20 May 1877, LC, bronchitis, 1-11-4, p. Jack & Ginnie Glead, sc: Jack Glead, father, LE Dist., BVS:1877:8

GOCHNAUER, David, W, M, d. 2 Jul 1859/60, his res, heart affection, 47-9-18, p. Isaac & Nancy Gochnauer, b. nr Middleburg, farmer, c/o: Elizabeth Gochnauer, sc: E. Gochnauer, sister, BVS:1859:4, 1860:2, LC:35

GOCHNAUER, Delia V., W, F, d. 11 Feb 1858, res of mother, tumor on brain, 23-0-0, p. Jacob & Elizabeth Gochnauer, b. nr New Lisbon, sc: Catharine A. Hibbs, sister, BVS:1858:3, LC:31

GOCHNAUER, Elizabeth, W, F, d. 19 Nov 1858, nr Ebenezer Church, epilepsy, 40-0-0, p. Wm. & Letticia Blakely, b. Blakeley's Tan Yards, c/o: David Gochnauer, sc: Elizabeth Gochnauer, sister-in-law, BVS:1858:3, LC:31

GOCHNAUER, Elizabeth L., W, F, d. 19 Mar 1875, LC, consumption, 74-0-0, c/o: Jacob Gochnauer, sc: Frances Daniel, daughter, LE Dist., BVS:1875:1

GOCHNAUER, Mary Adelia, W, F, d. 28 Jan 1858, nr Ebenezer Church, putrid sore throat, 13-10-25, p. David & Elizth Gochnauer, b. Blakeley's Tan Yards, sc: Elizabeth Gochnauer, aunt, BVS:1858:3, LC:31

[GOCHNAUER], no name, W, M, d. 12 Jul 1853, Union, 0-0-1, p. David & Elizabeth Gochnauer, b. Union, sc: father, BVS:1854:1, LC:4

[GOCHNAUER], no name, W, M, d. May 1855, res of parents, unk, p. David & Eliz. Gochnauer, b. nr Ebenezer Church, sc: father, BVS:1855:5, LC:17

GOCHNAUER, Spencer J., W, M, d. 3 Mar 1858, res of parents, whooping cough, 0-4-26, p. Wm. L. & Sallie M. Gochnauer, b. nr New Lisbon, sc: W.L. Gochnauer, father, BVS:1858:3, LC:30

GODFREY, Elizabeth, B, F, d. 15 Dec 1880, LC, unk, 0-7-0, p. Mary A. Godfrey, b. LC, unm, sc: Mary A. Godfrey, mother, 1st Dist., BVS:1880:1

GODFREY, Lizzie F., B, F, d. 10 Jan 1881, LC, consumption, 17-0-0, p. Wm. S. & E. Godfrey, b. LC, sc: W.S. Godfrey, father, 1st Dist., BVS:1881:1

GODFREY, Mary, B, F, d. 29 Oct 1883, nr Aldie, consumption, 25-0-0, p. William & Mary Godfrey, b. nr Aldie, unm, sc: William Godfrey, father, 1st Dist., BVS:1883:1

GODFREY, Wm., B, M, d. 31 Jun 1888, Aldie, consumption, 56-0-0, p. unk, b. Alexandria, c/o: Elizabeth Godfrey, sc: Elizabeth Godfrey, wife, 1st Dist., BVS:1888:3

GOINGS, Matilda, B, F, d. 15 Jun 1880, LC, bronchitis, 40-0-0, p. Benj. & Emily Goings, b. LC, unm, sc: Emily Goings, mother, 1st Dist., BVS:1880:1

GOLDEN, Elizabeth M., W, F, d. 1 Aug 1883, nr Arcola, paralysis, 59-0-0, p. Alias & Margaret Utterback, b. Fauquier Co., c/o: John W. Golden, sc: John W. Golden, husband, 1st Dist., BVS:1883:1

GOOD, no name, W, F, d. 6 Oct 1889, LC, lock jaw, 0-0-6, p. Samuel & Maggie Good, b. LC, none, unm, sc: Samuel Good, father, 3rd Dist., BVS:1889:5

GOOD, Saml. P., W, M, d. 5 Jul 1892, Purcell's, typhoid fever, 42-0-0, p. Perry & Ellen Good, b. Purcell's, farmer, married, sc: Ellen Good, wife, MT Dist., BVS:1892:8

GOODHART, A. L., W, M, d. 3 Jun 1890, LC, r. r. accident, 19-0-0, p. Chas. W. & Mary C. Goodhart, b. LC, none, unm, sc: G.W. Goodhart, father, 2nd Dist., BVS:1890:3

GOODHART, John, W, M, d. 28 Feb 1875, Lovettsville Dist, paralysis, 63-0-0, b. LC, LV Dist., BVS:1875:4

GOODHART, Mary, W, F, d. 4 Sep 1853, LC, paralysis, 65-10-14, p. John & Eve Fawley, b. LC, farmer, c/o: Jacob Goodhart, sc: Mary E. Goodhart, dau-in-law, BVS:1854:3, LC:1

GOODIN, John, W, M, d. 19 Oct 1887, LC, bright's disease, 79-0-0, p. David & Ann Goodin, b. LC, unm, sc: Jonathan Goodin, brother, 3rd Dist., BVS:1887:6

GOODIN, Mortimor F., W, M, d. 6 Jun 1858, R. F. Gorden's, dropsy of brain, 4-6-0, p. R.F. & Letitia A. Goodin, b. place of death, sc: R.F. Goodin, father, BVS:1858:4, LC:32

GOODING, Anna, W, F, d. 14 Oct 1875, LC, unk, 0-0-5, p. Jno.J. & Levia J. Gooding, sc: Jno. J. Gooding, father, LE Dist., BVS:1875:1

GOODING, Wm. D., W, M, d. 12 Jan 1864, Hillsboro, effect of fall, 22-0-0, p. Wm. D. & N.W. Gooding, b. Fairfax, soldier, sc: Jno J. Gooding, father, BVS:1864:2, LC:39

GOOSEBERRY, Abigail, B, F, d. Oct 1873, nr Mountville, dropsy, 30-0-0, p. unk, b. Fauquier Co., farmer, unm, sc: Richard ?, friend, MC Dist., BVS:1873:5

GORAM, John, (f), M, d. 10 May 1858, LC, consumption, 25-0-0, b. LC, sc: George Clarke, friend, BVS:1858:1, LC:29

GORAM, no name, B, M, d. 23 Aug 1883, Leesburg, unk, 0-0-3, p. Geo. W. & Lucy Goram, b. LC, sc: Geo W. Goram, father, 2nd Dist., BVS:1883:3

GORAM, Tincianna, (f), F, d. 14 May 1853, LC, unk, 3-4-1, p. Margaret Goram, b. LC, sc: Richard M. Cridler, head of family, BVS:1854:3, LC:1

GORDON, Hester Ann, B, F, d. 8 Oct 1877, Lincoln, burned, 6-0-0, p. Oscar & Anna B. Gordon, b. LC, sc: Oscar Gordon, father, MT Dist., BVS:1877:2

GORE, Catherine, W, F, d. 16 Mar 1873, Broad Run, unk, 83-0-0, p. Michael & Catharine Whitacre, b. LC, widow, sc: Wm Beatty, son, LV Dist., BVS:1873:4

GORE, Phebe Ann, W, F, d. Sep 1858, Thomas Gore's, child bed, 24-0-0, p. Joshua & Naomi Nichols, b. nr Goose Creek Meeting House, c/o: Jonathan Gore, sc: Wm. Nichols, uncle, BVS:1858:5, LC:32

GORE, Roena, W, F, d. 25 Aug 1855, LC, disease of kidneys, 59-3-10, p. John & Eleanor Drish, b. Leesburg, c/o: Tilghman Gore, sc: Tilghman Gore, husband, BVS:1855:2, LC:15

GORE, Shadrack, B, M, d. 9 Jul 1877, Poor House, old age, 85-0-0, b. LC, unm, sc: Wm. H. Hibbs, superintendent of poor, MC Dist., BVS:1877:5

GORE, William, W, M, d. 5 Aug 1857, res of parents, consumption, 25-0-0, p. Thomas & Mary Gore, b. nr Hughesville, farmer, sc: father, BVS:1857:3, LC:26

GORE, Wm., W, M, d. 3 Aug 1894, Mechanicsville, paralysis, 71-0-0, p. Marcus Gore, b. Mechanicsville, sc: Susan Gore, wife, 3rd Dist., BVS:1894:5

GOVER, Henry, W, M, d. 5 Sep 1888, LC, apoplexy, 68-6-19, b. Frederick Co. MD, manufacturer, c/o: Hannah Gover, sc: Chester C. Gover, son, 3rd Dist., BVS:1888:1

GOVER, John W., W, M, d. Mar 19 1857, LC, intemperance, 33-0-0, p. Samuel & Susanna Gover, b. Fauquier Co., farmer, c/o: Sarah J. Gover, sc: Sarah J. Gover, wife, BVS:1857:2, LC:25

GOVER, Margaret Anne, W, F, d. 16 Dec 1865, nr Waterford, consumption, 35-0-0, b. Baltimore, MD, merchant, married, sc: Saml A. Gover, husband, 1st Dist.BVS:1865:3/4

GOVER, Samuel, W, M, d. 26 Jun 1875, Leesburg, dropsy of chest, 80-1-0, minister, c/o: Susannah Gover, sc: Sarah J. Gover, daughter-in-law, LE Dist., BVS:1875:1

GOVER, Sarah J., W, F, d. Mar 1883, nr Lovettsville, dropsy of chest, 80-0-0, p. --- Simpson, b. LC, c/o: John Gover, sc: John McCabe, friend, 2nd Dist., BVS:1883:6

GOVER, Susanna, W, F, d. 5 Apr 1854, Leesburg, consumption, 59-3-17, p. Spencer & Susanna Anderson, b. Prince William Co, c/o: Samuel Gover, sc: Samuel Gover, husband, BVS:1854:8, LC:7

GOVER, Virginia, W, F, d. 5 Mar 1872, Leesburg, consumption, 19-1-5, p. John & Jane Gover, b. Leesburg, unm, sc: Jane Gover, mother, LE Dist., BVS:1872:3

GRADY, Sarah, W, F, d. 18 Aug 1873, Levenworth, old age, 92-3-0, p. Manly & Sarah Taylor, b. nr Upperville, c/o: Edward B. Grady, sc: Maria Powell, daughter, MT Dist., BVS:1873:3

GRAHAM, Mary C., W, F, d. 1 Oct 1858, LC, dysentery, 0-11-21, p. John & Mary C. Graham, b. LC, sc: John Graham, father, BVS:1858:2, LC:30

GRAHAM, William, W, M, d. Nov 1857, Wheatland, 0-0-14, p. Wm. & Elizth R. Graham, b. Wheatland, sc: father, BVS:1857:3, LC:26

GRANT, Edwd M, W, M, d. 20 Oct 1893, Middleburg, brain trouble, 0-6-0, p. H.G.F. & H.F. Grant, b. Middleburg, sc: H.F. Grant, mother, 1st Dist., BVS:1893:1

GRASON, Mary F., (f), F, d. 6 May 1856, LC, consumption, 23-5-0, p. Matthew & Kitty Grason, b. Stafford, unm, sc: Julian Howard, sister, BVS:1856:2, LC:20

GRAY, Alice W., W, F, d. 17 Jun 1855, LC, consumption, 9-10-0, p. Wm. S. & Sarah Gray, b. LC, sc: Wm. S. Gray, father, BVS:1855:1, LC:14

GRAY, Carrie, B, F, d. 6 Jul 1888, Middleburg, consumption, 30-0-0, p. unk, b. Clarke Co., Va., c/o: Albert Gray, sc: Albert Gray, husband, 1st Dist., BVS:1888:3

GRAY, Cora, B, F, d. 12 Mar 1880, nr Leesburg, teething, 1-6-0, p. John & Belle Gray, b. LC, unm, sc: Mary Neuman, aunt, 2nd Dist., BVS:1880:6

GRAY, Edward, B, M, d. 15 Oct 1865, Saml C. Luckett's, typhoid f, 6-0-0, p. Dolly Gray, b. S.C. Luckett's, unm, sc: Saml C. Luckett, former owner, 1st Dist., BVS:1865:3/4

GRAY, Henry, (f), M, d. 20 Nov 1859/60, Poor House, paralysis, 55-0-0, sc: steward, BVS:1859:4, 1860:2, LC:35

GRAY, Jane, W, F, d. 5 Aug 1887, Middleburg, dropsy, 56-0-0, p. James & Elizabeth Gray, b. Fauquier Co., c/o: James Gray, sc: James Gray, husband, 1st Dist., BVS:1887:2

GRAY, Jenetta, W, F, d. 28 Sep 1885, nr Unison, thrush, 0-5-0, p. Jerome B. & Martha J. Gray, b. Unison, sc: Jerome B. Gray, father, 1st Dist., BVS:1885:3

GRAY, Jennie, W, F, d. Mar 1873, LC, consumption, 24-0-0, p. Sarah Gray, b. LC, unm, sc: Samuel Gray, brother, LE Dist., BVS:1873:2

GRAY, John, W, M, d. 12 Sep 1884, Leesburg, consumption, 44-0-0, p. Joseph & --- Gray, b. LC, merchant, c/o: Rebecca Gray, sc: J.B. Beverley, brother-in-law, 2nd Dist., BVS:1884:4

GRAY, Lillie, W, F, d. 29 Jul 1885, Leesburg, consumption, 32-0-0, p. Joseph & Jane A. Pancoast, c/o: R. Benteley Gray, sc: Jane A. Pancoast, mother, 2nd Dist., BVS:1885:1

GRAY, Lucy E., W, F, d. 9 May 1878, LC, heart disease, 42-0-0, p. Joseph & Mary E. Gray, b. LC, unm, sc: A.M. Chichester, friend, LE Dist., BVS:1878:8

GRAY, Mary E., W, F, d. 2 Jul 1853, Llangolon, confinement, 40-0-0, p. Wm. & Frances Elzey, b. LC, c/o: Dr. Joseph Gray, sc: Dr. Joseph Gray, husband, BVS:1854:1, LC:4

GRAY, Mary E., W, F, d. 2 Feb 1885, Leesburg, pneumonia, 66-0-0, p. Robert & Kitty Benteley, c/o: Robert W. Gray, sc: Rebecca Gray, daughter, 2nd Dist., BVS:1885:1

GRAY, Minnie, W, F, d. 6 May 1887, Unison, unk, 0-9-0, p. Jerome B. & Martha J. Gray, b. Unison, sc: Jerome B. Gray, father, 1st Dist., BVS:1887:2

GRAY, no name, B, M, d. 17 Jul 1888, Middleburg, consumption, 0-6-0, p. Albert & Cary Gray, b. Middleburg, sc: Albert Gray, father, 1st Dist., BVS:1888:3

GRAY, Robert W., W, M, d. 3 Nov 1879, nr Hoysville, consumption, 21-0-0, p. Wm. S. & Sarah A. Gray, b. LC, farmer, sc: Edward B. Gray, brother, 2nd Dist., BVS:1879:1

GRAY, Samuel I., W, M, d. 20 Apr 1875, Lovettsville Dist, consumption, 33-0-0, b. LC, farmer, unm, LV Dist., BVS:1875:4

GRAYSON, Annie B., B, F, d. 3 Aug 1888, LC, teething, 0-7-5, p. Web & Nancy Grayson, b. LC, none, unm, sc: Mary Grayson, mother, 3rd Dist., BVS:1888:1

GRAYSON, George W., W, M, d. 1 Aug 1874, nr Millville, consumption, 60-0-0, p. unk, b. Kentucky, farmer, sc: Henry W. Chamblin, son-in-law, MC Dist., BVS:1874:4

GRAYSON, James Herbert, B, M, d. 1875, nr Snickersville, unk, p. Julia Jackson, b. nr Snickersville, sc: Henry Jackson, MT Dist., BVS:1875:8

GRAYSON, Rebecca, B, F, d. 28 Aug 1892, Mountville, typhoid fever, 8-0-0, p. Thos. & Sylvia Grayson, b. Mountville, sc: Thos Grayson, father, 1st Dist., BVS:1892:4

GRAYSON, Saml., B, M, d. 31 Jul 1896, Woodburn, accident, 77-0-0, b. Woodburn, laborer, MT Dist., BVS:1896:9

GRAYSON, Saml. B., B, M, d. 6 Nov 1879, Waterford, consumption, 31-0-0, p. Saml. & Harriet Grayson, b. LC, laborer, sc: Saml Grayson, father, 3rd Dist., BVS:1879:3

GREEN, Alberta, W, F, d. 14 Aug 1857, Aldie, purple fever, 33-0-0, p. Richard & ... Osburn, b. nr Woodgrove, c/o: J.P. Green, sc: T.N. Green, bro-in-law, BVS:1857:4, LC:26

GREEN, Calvin, B, M, d. 10 Apr 1881, LC, pneumonia, 80-0-0, b. LC, unm, sc: Elzey Furr, friend, 3rd Dist., BVS:1881:4

GREEN, John E., W, M, d. 20 Mar 1889, LC, old age, 89-0-0, p. unk, b. LC, none, widower, sc: R.H. Green, son, 2nd Dist., BVS:1889:3

GREEN, Lizzie M., W, F, d. 17 Jun 1877, Unison, fever, 0-8-0, p. Chas. P. & Mary E. Green, b. LC, sc: Chas. P. Green, father, MC Dist., BVS:1877:5

GREEN, Mary J., W, F, d. 3 Aug 1880, Leesburg, paralysis, 66-0-0, p. William & Sarah E. Woody, b. LC, c/o: John Green, sc: John Green, husband, 2nd Dist., BVS:1880:6

GREEN, Mason Mack, W, M, d. 15 Mar 1875, Snickersville, cold, 0-0-15, p. Albert & Mary G. Green, b. Snickersville, laborer, unm, sc: Albert Green, father, MT Dist., BVS:1875:8

[GREEN], no name, B, , d. 28 Feb 1876, LC, unk, unk, p. Washington &

Loudoun County, Virginia, Death Register, 1853-1896 117

Charlotte Green, b. LC, sc: Charlotte Green, mother, LE Dist., BVS:1876:6

[GREEN], no name, B, , d. 29 Sep 1876, LC, unk, unk, p. Washington & Charlotte Green, b. LC, sc: Charlotte Green, mother, LE Dist., BVS:1876:6

GREEN, no name, B, M, d. 30 Oct 1877, Middletown, cra colic, 0-0-7, p. Edward & Sina Green, b. LC, sc: Sina Green, mother, MC Dist., BVS:1877:5

GREEN, no name, B, M, d. 29 May 1884, nr Leesburg, unk, 0-0-4, p. Samuel & Elizabeth Green, b. LC, sc: Elizabeth Green, mother, 2nd Dist., BVS:1884:4

GREEN, Richard H., B, M, d. 30 Jan 1884, LC, measles, 0-2-0, p. Richard & Flora Green, b. LC, 1st Dist., BVS:1884:1

GREEN, Sallie, B, F, d. 22 Dec 1890, nr Pilomont, paralysis, 50-0-0, p. unk, b. LC, unm, sc: F.E. Robey, superintendent of poor, 1st Dist., BVS:1890:1

GREEN, Samuel W., W, M, d. 4 Jul 1853, nr Hamilton, pneumonia, 0-6-0, p. T. W. & Elizabeth Green, b. nr Hamilton, sc: father, BVS:1854:7, LC:6

GREEN, Theodotia, W, F, d. 6 Sep 1882, LC, apoplexy, 73-0-0, p. Wm. & Ann Davis, b. LC, c/o: Henry Green, sc: Henry Green, husband, 1st Dist., BVS:1882:1

GREEN, Thomas, W, M, d. 11 Jan 1886, Daysville, old age, 93-0-0, p. Thomas Green, b. LC, farmer, unk, sc: John Z. Daily, son-in-law, 1st Dist., BVS:1886:1

GREEN, Walter, B, M, d. 1 Dec 1864, LC, 1-6-0, p. Francis Green, b. LC, sc: Harmon Lodge, BVS:1864:1, LC:38

GREEN, William D., W, M, d. 5 Jul 1873, nr Potomac, whooping cough, 0-2-0, p. Wm. F. & Sarah Green, b. LC, unm, sc: Wm. F. Green, head of family, BR Dist., BVS:1873:1

GREEN, Winfield S., W, M, d. 7 Nov 1853, LC, water on brain, 2-7-0, p. Curtis & Rachel A. Grubb, b. LC, sc: Curtis Grubb, father, BVS:1854:4, LC:2

GREENLEASE, Lena E., W, F, d. 7 Dec 1886, affection of brain, 0-5-22, p. Wm. H. & Annie E., sc: Wm H. Greenlease, father, 2nd Dist., BVS:1886:5

GREENLEASE, Mary A., W, F, d. 4 Mar 1880, nr Leesburg, pneumonia, 69-0-0, p. Isaac & Sally Hughes, b. LC, c/o: William Grealease, sc: Isaac J. Greenlease, son, 2nd Dist., BVS:1880:6

GREENLEASE, Wm. S., W, M, d. 9 Apr 1878, LC, paralysis, 69-0-0, p. unk, b. LC, unm, sc: Wm. J. Greenlease, son, LE Dist., BVS:1878:8

GREENWALT, Abraham, W, M, d. 25 Oct 1894, Harpers Ferry, unk, 54-0-0, p. unk, b. unk, unk, consort, LV Dist., BVS:1894:4

GREENWELL, Mary Ellen, W, F, d. Jun 1858, nr Silcott Springs, summer complaint 11, 11-6-0, p. Francis R. & Sarah E. Greenwell, b. Washington DC, sc: F.R. Greenwell, father, BVS:1858:4, LC:32

GREGG, Alfred, B, M, d. 23 Dec 1888, LC, consumption, 25-0-0, p. Benja. & Margaret Gregg, b. LC, none, unm, sc: Benj Gregg, father, 2nd Dist., BVS:1888:5

GREGG, Assenith, W, M, d. 19 Dec 1885, Silcott Springs, old age, 84-0-0, p. Joseph & Mary Gregg, b. LC, unm, sc: J.H. Thatcher, friend, 3rd Dist., BVS:1885:6

GREGG, Benjamin, B, M, d. 20 Oct 1880, Leesburg, croup, 7-8-0, p. Benj. & Margaret Gregg, b. LC, unm, sc: Margaret Gregg, mother, 2nd Dist., BVS:1880:6

GREGG, Charles, B, M, d. 3 Aug 1885, nr Leesburg, cholera infantum, 0-3-0, p. Frank & Kate Gregg, sc: Frank Gregg, father, 2nd Dist., BVS:1885:1

GREGG, Elizabeth, W, F, d. 24 Jun 1896, Hamilton, tumor, 78-0-0, p. Wm. & Elizabeth Gregg, b. Hamilton, MT Dist., BVS:1896:9

GREGG, Emily J., W, F, d. 4 May 1855, LC, typhoid fever, 17-1-28, p. Peter & Emily J. Gregg, b. LC, sc: Emily J. Gregg, mother, BVS:1855:3, LC:16

GREGG, Florence, W, F, d. May 1896, Purcellville, unk, 0-0-7, p. Daniel &

Laura Gregg, b. Purcellville, sc: Daniel Gregg, father, MT Dist., BVS:1896:9

GREGG, Geo., W, M, d. 9 Aug 1855, LC, old age, 80-1-7, p. Wm. & Rebecca Gregg, b. LC, c/o: Ann Gregg, sc: Ann Gregg, wife, BVS:1855:2, LC:15

GREGG, Hannah, W, F, d. 14 Apr 1855, Phebe Gregg's, dropsy, 74-0-0, p. Jno. & Martha Gregg, b. Middleburg, sc: Wm. Gregg, nephew, BVS:1855:7, LC:18

GREGG, James, B, M, d. 20 Jun 1881, LC, unk, 19-1-0, p. Benj. & M. Gregg, unm, sc: Reuben Gregg, brother, 2nd Dist., BVS:1881:6

GREGG, John, W, M, d. 30 Aug 1896, Lincoln, bright's disease, 77-0-0, p. John & Phebe Gregg, b. Lincoln, sc: John Gregg, father, MT Dist., BVS:1896:9

GREGG, John C., W, M, d. 3 Oct 1875, Round Hill, cancer, 68-0-0, b. LC, married, sc: Lucinda McPherson, housekeeper, MT Dist., BVS:1875:8

GREGG, John F., W, M, d. 17 Apr 1855, LC, typhoid fever, 22-1-8, p. Peter & Emily J. Gregg, b. LC, school teacher, sc: Emily J. Gregg, mother, BVS:1855:3, LC:16

GREGG, Kate, B, F, d. 15 Aug 1880, Leesburg, unk, 0-2-0, p. Frank & Kate Gregg, b. LC, unm, sc: Kate Gregg, mother, 2nd Dist., BVS:1880:6

GREGG, Lula, B, F, d. 6 Oct 1884, LC, consumption, 8-0-0, p. Anderson & Louisa Gregg, b. LC, 1st Dist., BVS:1884:1

GREGG, Mary C., W, F, d. 3 Sep 1858, LC, typhoid fever, 33-0-0, p. John & Catharine Johnson, b. LC, c/o: Wilson Gregg, sc: Wilson Gregg, husband, BVS:1858:1, LC:29

GREGG, Nathan, W, M, d. 2 Jun 1869, LC, paralyzed, 68-0-0, p. Thomas Gregg, b. LC, farmer, sc: William Beans, neighbor, BVS:1869:1

GREGG, Peter, W, M, d. 27 Apr 1855, LC, typhoid fever, 54-11-24, p. Josiah & Margt A. Gregg, b. LC, farmer, c/o: Emily J. Gregg, sc: Emily J. Gregg, widow, BVS:1855:3, LC:16

GREGG, Robert, B, M, d. 19 Jun 1881, LC, unk, 0-7-0, p. Benj. & M. Gregg, sc: Reuben Gregg, brother, 2nd Dist., BVS:1881:6

GREGG, Sallie Ann, W, F, d. 29 Apr 1857, res of father, pulmonary, 27-0-0, p. Nathan & Susan R. Gregg, b. place of death, sc: Nathan Gregg, father, BVS:1857:4, LC:27

GREGG, Sampson, B, M, d. 10 Nov 1882, LC, smothered, 0-4-0, p. Anderson & Sarah Gregg, sc: Anderson Gregg, father, 1st Dist., BVS:1882:1

GREGG, Sarah, W, F, d. 17 Jun 1856, res of brother, 61-0-0, p. Thomas & Ann Gregg, b. nr Short Hill, sc: Smith Gregg, brother, BVS:1856:6, LC:23

GREGG, Smith, W, M, d. 2 Sep 1879, LC, general debility, 81-0-0, p. Thomas & Ann Gregg, b. LC, farmer, unm, sc: Susan Gregg, sister, 3rd Dist., BVS:1879:3

GREGG, Thomas, W, M, d. 15 Aug 1858, R. F. Gorden's, old age, 87-0-0, p. Thomas & ... Gregg, sc: R.F. Goodin, BVS:1858:4, LC:32

GREGG, Thomas, W, M, d. 12 Dec 1873, nr Purcellville, consumption, 61-1-19, p. Thos & Alma Gregg, b. LC, farmer, c/o: Laura Gregg, sc: Smith Gregg, brother, JF Dist., BVS:1874:1

GREGG, Thomas L., W, M, d. 3 Mar 1878, LC, strangulation, 0-0-1, p. Elijah & Catharine Gregg, b. LC, unm, sc: Catherine Gregg, mother, LE Dist., BVS:1878:8

GREGG, William, W, M, d. 20 Sep 1888, LC, enlargement of intestines, 65-0-0, p. John & Phebe Gregg, b. LC, farmer, c/o: Elizabeth Gregg, sc: Elizabeth Gregg, wife, 3rd Dist., BVS:1888:1

GREGG, William, B, M, d. 27 Jul 1893, Sycolin, consumption, 22-0-0, p. unk, b. Sycolin, unm, sc: father, LE Dist., BVS:1893:7

GREY, Thomas G., W, M, d. 19 Jul 1853, Middleburg, scarlet fever, 3-10-0, p. Caleb & Mary Grey, b. nr Middleburg, sc: mother, BVS:1854:5, LC:4

GRIFFITH, Chas., B, M, d. 10 Mar 1892, Conklin, la grippe, 9-0-0, p.

Fred & Martha Griffith, b. Conklin, laborer, unm, sc: Fred Griffith, father, 1st Dist., BVS:1892:4

GRIFFITH, John, B, M, d. 10 Oct 1890, Arcola, measles, 10-0-0, p. Frederick & Martha Griffith, b. Arcola, sc: Frederick Griffith, father, 1st Dist., BVS:1890:1

GRIFFITH, Juliet A., W, F, d. 7 Jul 1878, nr Haymarket, Prince Wm Co., unk, 0-6-27, p. Robt P & Martha Griffith, b. Prince William Co., sc: Robt P. Griffith, father, MC Dist., BVS:1878:6

GRIFFITH, Lorenda M., W, F, d. Nov 1856, nr Scotland, inflammation bowels, 7-0-0, p. Thos. & Sarah Griffith, b. LC, sc: Thomas Griffith, father, BVS:1856:6, LC:23

GRIFFITH, Martha, B, F, d. 16 Apr 1890, Arcola, lagrippe, 22-0-0, p. Wm. & Martha Stewart, b. LC, laborer, c/o: Frederick Griffith, sc: Frederick Griffith, husband, 1st Dist., BVS:1890:1

GRIFFITH, no name, W, M, d. 27 Mar 1878, nr Mountain Gap, unk, 0-0-1, p. Edward & Mary L. Griffith, b. LC, sc: Edward Griffith, father, MC Dist., BVS:1878:6

GRIFFITH, Susie, B, F, d. 10 Nov 1890, Arcola, measles, 5-0-0, p. Frederick & Martha Griffith, b. Arcola, sc: Frederick Griffith, father, 1st Dist., BVS:1890:1

GRIFFITH, Sylva, B, F, d. 15 May 1890, Arcola, measles, 2-0-0, p. Frederick & Martha Griffith, b. Arcola, sc: Frederick Griffith, father, 1st Dist., BVS:1890:1

GRIGSBY, George, B, M, d. 19 Oct 1876, LC, heart disease, 70-0-0, p. unk, b. unk, laborer, sc: Jas. W. Russell, friend, JF Dist., BVS:1876:8

GRIMES, Annie, W, F, d. 12 Nov 1891, Leesburg, old age, 83-0-0, p. unk, b. unk, c/o: John Grimes, sc: Son, LE Dist., BVS:1891:4

GRIMES, Beverley, W, M, d. 26 Oct 1881, LC, spasms, 1-0-21, p. Wm. & Miranda Grimes, sc: Wm. Grimes, father, 2nd Dist., BVS:1881:6

GRIMES, Edwin C.Z., W, M, d. 31 Dec 1858, G.L. Bitzer's Farm, scarlet fever, 0-11-22, p. Greenbury & Elizabeth Grimes, b. G.L. Bitzer's Farm, sc: Elizabeth Grimes, mother, BVS:1858:4, LC:31

GRIMES, Eliza, W, F, d. 20 Jul 1889, Upperville, Fauquier Co., old age, 83-0-0, p. Samuel & Mollie Henderson, b. LC, unk, sc: Samuel Grimes, son, 1st Dist., BVS:1889:1

GRIMES, John T., W, M, d. 26 Dec 1880, Leesburg, catarrh, 39-5-0, p. Henry & Nancy Grimes, b. LC, farmer, c/o: Mary J. Grimes, sc: George W. Grimes, brother, 2nd Dist., BVS:1880:6

GRIMES, Lizzie, W, F, d. [1880], Leesburg, unk, 0-0-14, p. William & Miranda Grimes, b. LC, unm, sc: William Grimes, father, 2nd Dist., BVS:1880:6

GRIMES, Martha R., W, F, d. 3 Jun 1853, nr Union, inflammation of brain, 0-2-20, p. Frank & Naomi Grimes, b. nr Union, sc: grandmother, BVS:1854:7, LC:6

[GRIMES], no name, W, M, d. Sep 1853, nr Aldie, inflammation brain, 0-2-0, p. Greenbury & Betsy Grimes, b. nr Aldie, sc: J. Lynn, neighbor, BVS:1854:6, LC:6

[GRIMES], no name, W, M, d. 3 Apr 1872, nr Hillsboro, unk, 0-0-3, p. George & Sarah Grimes, b. nr Hillboro, sc: George Grimes, father, JF Dist., BVS:1872:1

GRIMES, no name, W, F, d. 15 Jan 1874, nr Hillsboro, fever, 0-0-14, p. G. W. & Sarah Grimes, b. LC, farmer, sc: G.W. Grimes, father, JF Dist., BVS:1874:2

[GRIMES], no name, W, M, d. 20 Feb 1875, LC, still born, unk, p. George & Sarah, b. LC, sc: George Grimes, father, JF Dist., BVS:1875:3

[GRIMES], no name, W, , d. 14 Jul 1876, Leesburg, spasms, 0-0-5, p. William & Miranda Grimes, b. Leesburg, sc: William Grimes, father, LE Dist., BVS:1876:6

GRIMES, no name, W, M, d. 10 Oct 1878, nr Hillsboro, cholera infantum, 0-1-7, p. Geo. W. & Sarah E. Grimes, b. LC, sc: Geo. W. Grimes, father, JF Dist., BVS:1878:10

GROOMS, Cecelia, B, F, d. 10 Mar 1880, LC, unk, 16-0-0, p. Saiteford & Mary Grooms, b. LC, unm, sc: Mary

Grooms, mother, 1st Dist., BVS:1880:1

GROOMS, Emma, B, F, d. 29 Mar 1885, nr Mountville, whooping cough, 1-0-0, p. Sanford & Sallie Grooms, b. Mountville, sc: Sanford Grooms, father, 1st Dist., BVS:1885:3

GROOMS, Jane, B, F, d. 25 Sep 1896, nr Middleburg, old age, 94-0-0, p. unk, b. unk, none, consort, sc: Jno H. Jackson, head of family, MC Dist., BVS:1896:1

GROSS, Patience, W, F, d. 21 Apr 1856, LC, mumps, 39-3-10, p. John & Betsy Ramsey, b. LC, c/o: John Gross, sc: Elizabeth S. Gross, daughter, BVS:1856:2, LC:21

GROSZ, Charles ., W, M, d. 14 Dec 1883, nr Lovettsville, whooping cough, 1-10-14, p. Geo. & Mary Grosz, b. LC, sc: Mary Grosz, mother, 2nd Dist., BVS:1883:3

GRUBB, Catharine, W, F, d. 31 Oct 1878, Lovettsville, heart disease, 61-0-0, p. Peter & Susannah Wire, b. LC, c/o: Wm. D. Grubb, sc: Luther H. Potterfield, nephew, LV Dist., BVS:1878:1/5

GRUBB, Curtis, W, M, d. 7 Feb 1883, nr Lovettsville, paralysis, 86-0-0, p. Ebeneezer & Esther Grubb, b. LC, farmer, c/o: Harriet Hough, sc: Marrietta Grubb, daughter, 2nd Dist., BVS:1883:6

GRUBB, Elizabeth J., W, F, d. 14 Aug 1890, LC, paralysis, 72-0-0, p. Susanah Shriver, b. LC, none, c/o: John Grubb, sc: John Grubb, husband, 2nd Dist., BVS:1890:3

GRUBB, John E., W, M, d. 21 Aug 1855, LC, unk, 0-7-3, p. Ebenezer L. & Cecelia Grubb, b. LC, sc: E. L. Grubb, father, BVS:1855:1, LC:14

GRUBB, Lina Grace, W, F, d. 25 Jun 1887, LC, typhoid fever, 9-0-0, p. W. H. & Matilda Grubb, b. LC, unm, sc: W.H. Grubb, father, 3rd Dist., BVS:1887:6

GRUBB, Margaret, W, F, d. 15 Jan 1892, Lovettsville, consumption, 54-0-0, p. unk, b. unk, consort, sc: Benj. Grubb, LV Dist., BVS:1892:6

GRUBB, Mary D., W, F, d. 2 Sep 1889, LC, dropsy, 80-0-0, b. LC, none, c/o: Joseph Grubb, sc: Hannah Grubb, daughter, 3rd Dist., BVS:1889:5

GRUBB, Maud W., W, F, d. 20 Sep 1879, nr Hoysville, croup, 2-3-19, p. Benj. J. & Margaret A. Grubb, b. LC, sc: Margaret A. Grubb, mother, 2nd Dist., BVS:1879:1

GRUBB, Rachel S., W, F, d. 29 Mar 1853, LC, disease of kidneys, 3-3-7, p. Sarah A. Riney, b. LC, unm, sc: Benj. Grubb, head of family, BVS:1854:3, LC:1

GRUBB, Richard C., W, M, d. 28 Dec 1893, Lovettsville, gun shot wound, 23-0-0, p. Saml. & Elizabeth, b. Lovettsville, laborer, unm, sc: Samuel Grubb, LV Dist., BVS:1893:5

GRUBB, Virginia E., W, F, d. 15 Jul 1854, LC, unk, 0-0-11, p. Benjn. H. & Jane E. Grubb, b. LC, sc: Benj. H. Grubb, father, BVS:1854:8, LC:8

GRUBB, Wm. D., W, M, d. 3 Nov 1855, LC, dropsy, 39-11-3, p. Adam & Eliz. Grubb, b. LC, farmer, c/o: Mary C. Grubb, sc: Mary C. Grubb, wife, BVS:1855:1, LC:14

GULATT, Elenor, W, F, d. 6 Nov 1890, LC, old age, 89-0-0, p. George Sinclair, b. LC, none, c/o: ___ Gulatt, sc: David Conard, son-in-law, 2nd Dist., BVS:1890:3

GULICK, Ann V., W, F, d. 21 Dec 1882, LC, unk, 66-0-0, p. unk, widow, sc: James H. Gulick, husband, 1st Dist., BVS:1882:1

GULICK, Arthur H., W, M, d. Apr 1864, Sanford Gulick's, heart disease, 8-8-0, p. S. & W.B. Gulick, b. LC, sc: Sanford Gulick, father, BVS:1864:1, LC:38

GULICK, Edna Jane, W, F, d. May 1858, res of parents, whooping cough, 8-1-15, p. Francis & Nancy Gulick, b. Ketoctin Mountain, sc: F. Gulick, father, BVS:1858:4, LC:31

GULICK, Geo Milton, W, M, d. 29 Oct 1864, nr Upperville, killed in battle, 19-0-0, p. Francis & Nancy Gulick, b. Ketoctin Mountain, soldier, sc: Jas W. Gulick, brother, BVS:1864:1, LC:38

GULICK, George, W, M, d. 21 Apr 1856, his res, quinsy, 80-0-15, p. John & --- Gulick, b. New Jersey, farmer, c/o: Sarah Gulick, sc:

Sanford Gulick, son, BVS:1856:5, LC:23
GULICK, Henry H., W, M, d. 21 Nov 1873, nr Aldie, typhoid fever, 17-14-0, p. James H. & Ann V. Gulick, b. nr Aldie, farmer, unm, sc: brother, MT Dist., BVS:1873:3
GULICK, Jas H., W, M, d. 27 Mar 1864, Age Institute, heart disease, 49-5-16, p. Wm. & Mary Gulick, b. LC, farmer, c/o: Ann V. Gulick, sc: Ann V. Gulick, widow, BVS:1864:1, LC:38
GULICK, Mary, W, F, d. 18 Mar 1864, Sanford Gulick's, pneumonia, 71-3-18, p. Jas & Isabella Hixon, b. Leesburg, c/o: Wm. Gulick decd, sc: Ann V. Gulick, daughter-in-law, BVS:1864:1, LC:38
GULICK, Sanford, W, M, d. 15 Nov 1878, Aldie, disease of lungs, 65-0-5, b. LC, farmer, c/o: Nancy R. Gulick, sc: Nancy R. Gulick, wife, MC Dist., BVS:1878:6
GULICK, William, W, M, d. 12 Mar 1859/60, his res, paralysis, 68-0-0, p. Moses & ___ Gulick, b. Aldie, farmer, c/o: Mary Gulick, sc: H. B. Gulick, son, BVS:1859:5, 1860:2, LC:35
GULICK, Wm., W, M, d. Jul 1858, Sanford Gulick's, suddenly, 38-5-0, p. George & Sarah Gulick, b. place of death, sc: F. Gulick, brother, BVS:1858:4, LC:32
GUMLEY, Jack, (f), M, d. 7 Feb 1856, Poor House, old age, 80-0-0, b. Gum Spring, sc: steward, BVS:1856:4, LC:22

HAGAN, Amanda M., W, F, d. 13 Oct 1969, LC, scalded, 3-10-0, p. Benjamin & Hanah Hagan, b. LC, sc: Benjamin F. Hagan, father, BVS:1869:1
HAINES, Addison, W, M, d. 11 Mar 1879, Hughesville, general debility, 58-0-0, b. LC, mechanic, unm, sc: May Haines, friend, 3rd Dist., BVS:1879:3
HAINES, Francis Ann, W, F, d. Feb 1865, Frankville, consumption, 35-0-0, p. Ed & Sarah Haines, b. Frankville, unm, sc: Edwd Haines, father, BVS:1865:2

HAINES, Mary, W, F, d. Jan 1896, Hamilton, heart disease, 77-0-0, consort, JF Dist., BVS:1896:8
HALEY, Fannie, W, F, d. 27 Nov 1881, LC, typhoid fever, 24-0-0, p. John & Emily Haley, b. LC, unm, sc: Ella Haley, sister, 3rd Dist., BVS:1881:4
HALEY, Jno., W, M, d. 30 Jul 1853, nr Bloomfield, thurston on bowels, 0-3-0, p. Jno. & Emily Haley, b. nr Bloomfield, sc: mother, BVS:1854:7, LC:6
HALEY, Mary, W, F, d. 13 Dec 1881, LC, typhoid fever, 39-0-0, p. John & Emily Haley, b. LC, unm, sc: Ella Haley, sister, 3rd Dist., BVS:1881:4
[HALEY], no name, W, F, d. Sep 1858, croup, 0-5-0, p. John & Emily J. Haley, b. Welbourne, sc: E.J. Haley, mother, BVS:1858:3, LC:31
HALL, Ann B., W, F, d. Dec 1871, LC, croup, 2-0-0, p. G.M. & Martha Hall, b. LC, unm, LE Dist., BVS:1871:4
HALL, Anna V., W, F, d. 18 Aug 1872, LC, cholera infantum, 1-8-18, p. Jas. M. & Martha H. Hall, b. LC, sc: Jas. M. Hall, father, LE Dist., BVS:1872:3
HALL, Beckie, B, F, d. 10 Aug 1887, Aldie, croup, 0-3-0, p. Louis & Mary E. Hall, b. Aldie, sc: Louis Hall, father, 1st Dist., BVS:1887:1
HALL, Eva, B, F, d. 3 May 1892, Middleburg, whooping cough, 8-0-0, p. Nathan & Cornelia Hall, b. Middleburg, laborer, sc: Nathan Hall, father, 1st Dist., BVS:1892:4
HALL, James, B, M, d. 16 Mar 1884, LC, premature, 0-0-1, p. Louis & Mary E. Hall, b. LC, 1st Dist., BVS:1884:1
HALL, John, W, M, d. 10 Jul 1896, Mountain Gap, cholera infantum, 0-4-4, p. Jno. K. & Mary Hall, b. Mountain Gap, none, unm, sc: Mary Hall, mother, MC Dist., BVS:1896:1
HALL, Martha, W, F, d. 2 Sep 1880, nr Leesburg, diphtheria, 8-7-0, p. James M. & Martha A. Hall, b. LC, unm, sc: James M. Hall, father, 2nd Dist., BVS:1880:6
HALL, Mary, W, F, d. 4 May 1853, LC, old age, 83-10-3, p. Thos. & Mary Carr, b. LC, c/o: Wm. Hall, sc: William Hall, son, BVS:1854:5, LC:3
HALL, Mary E., B, F, d. 1 Dec 1887, Aldie, consumption, 26-0-0, p. Alfred

& Eliza Roberson, b. LC, c/o: Louis Hall, sc: Alfred Roberson, father, 1st Dist., BVS:1887:1

HALL, Susie, W, F, d. 19 Aug 1896, Mountain Gap, cholera infantum, 1-6-0, p. Jno. K. & Mary Hall, b. Mountain Gap, none, unm, sc: Mary Hall, mother, MC Dist., BVS:1896:1

HALL, Thomas, B, M, d. 29 Apr 1892, Middleburg, whooping cough, 3-0-0, p. Nathan & Cornelia Hall, b. Middleburg, laborer, sc: Nathan Hall, father, 1st Dist., BVS:1892:4

HALL, Willie, W, M, d. 28 May 1894, Upperville, cholera infantum, 0-7-0, p. John & Mary, b. Leesburg, unm, sc: John Hall, LE Dist., BVS:1894:3

HALLEY, Catharine J., W, F, d. 19 May 1885, nr Leesburg, paralysis, 64-0-0, p. Gustavus & Elizabeth Elgin, c/o: Edgar Halley, sc: Edgar Halley, husband, 2nd Dist., BVS:1885:1

HALLEY, Martha, W, F, d. 2 Oct 1871, whooping cough, 0-1-0, p. R. N. & V. Halley, BR Dist., BVS:1871:3

HALLEY, Mary, W, F, d. 14 Jun 1887, LC, consumption, 29-0-0, p. Jno. & Mary Hall, b. LC, c/o: A.C. Halley, sc: A.C. Halley, husband, 3rd Dist., BVS:1887:6

[HALLEY], no name, W, F, d. 15 Jan 1873, nr Cub Run, unk, 0-0-24, p. Richd N. & Virginia Halley, b. LC, sc: Richd N. Halley, head of family, BR Dist., BVS:1873:1

HAMILTON, Caroline A., W, F, d. 4 May 1853, LC, consumption, 29-5-10, p. Gideon & Julia A. Householder, b. LC, c/o: Jas. W. Hamilton, sc: Jas W. Hamilton, husband, BVS:1854:4, LC:2

HAMILTON, Edward J., W, M, d. 2 Apr 1875, Lovettsville Dist, consumption, 42-0-0, b. LC, LV Dist., BVS:1875:4

HAMILTON, George, W, M, d. 8 Apr 1855, consumption, 36-0-0, p. unk, b. New York, sc: S.L. Hodgson, friend, BVS:1855:9, LC:19

HAMILTON, John, W, M, d. 16 Dec 1856, LC, cancer, 58-11-20, p. James & Elizabeth Hamilton, b. LC, farmer, c/o: Permelia Hamilton, sc: Edward F. Hamilton, son, BVS:1856:2, LC:21

HAMILTON, Mary, W, F, d. 10 May 1855, John Tavenner's, chronic, 56-6-12, p. Swithen & Rebecca Nichols, b. nr Goose Creek Meeting House, c/o: Jno. Hamilton, decd, sc: Jno. Tavenner, brother-in-law, BVS:1855:6, LC:18

[HAMILTON], no name, W, M, d. May 1858, Wheatland, 0-1-14, p. Oliver & Lorenza C. Hamilton, b. Wheatland, sc: Owen Hamilton, father, BVS:1858:5, LC:32

HAMILTON, no name, W, , d. 19 Apr 1893, Waterford, 0-0-3, p. Jos. A. Hamilton, b. Waterford, sc: father, JF Dist., BVS:1893:3

HAMILTON, no name, W, F, d. 18 Apr 1894, Wheatland, hemorrhage, 0-0-3, p. James & Mary Hamilton, b. Wheatland, sc: James Hamilton, father, 3rd Dist., BVS:1894:5

HAMILTON, S.N., W, M, d. 29 Mar 1857, consumption, 33-0-0, p. John & Mary Hamilton, b. LC, physician, sc: Ellen V. Hamilton, wife, BVS:1857:7, LC:28

HAMILTON, Sarah, W, F, d. 28 Sep 1881, LC, dropsy, 77-0-0, b. LC, c/o: Jas. Hamilton, sc: JW. Hamilton, son, 3rd Dist., BVS:1881:4

HAMILTON, Thomas J., W, M, d. 12 Oct 1859/60, LC, consumption, 28-0-0, p. John & Maria Hamilton, b. LC, miller, unm, sc: Sarah E. Hamilton, sister, BVS:1859:1, 1860:4, LC:37

HAMMERLEY, Ella Virginia, W, F, d. May 1869, LC, measles, 3-0-0, p. Mandly & Eliza A. Hammerley, b. LC, sc: Mandly Hammerley, neighbor, BVS:1869:1

HAMMERLEY, Ruth, W, F, d. Feb 1896, Round Hill, pneumonia, 62-0-0, p. Joe Worthington, b. Woodgrove, consort, JF Dist., BVS:1896:8

HAMMERLEY, Cath. A., W, F, d. 9 Oct 1877, LC, nervous prostration, 57-11-0, c/o: John Hammerly, sc: John Hammerly, husband, LE Dist., BVS:1877:8

HAMMERLY, Charles L., W, M, d. 6 Jul 1887, LC, cholera infantum, 0-6-12, p. Jno. & Mary Hammerly, b. LC, sc: John Hammerly, father, 3rd Dist., BVS:1887:6

HAMMERLY, Ella Virginia, W, F, d. 16 May 1892, Hillsboro, catarrh fever,

Loudoun County, Virginia, Death Register, 1853-1896

4-0-0, p. J. W. & M. V. Hammerly, b. Hillsboro, JF Dist., BVS:1892:7

HAMMERLY, John, W, M, d. 23 Nov 1881, LC, heart disease, 61-5-13, p. Wm. Hammerly, butcher, c/o: Catharine A. Hammerly, sc: J.A. Hammerly, son, 2nd Dist., BVS:1881:6

HAMMERLY, Wm., W, M, d. 15 Oct 1855, Leesburg, cholera morbus, 63-0-0, p. unk, b. Berkley Co., laborer, c/o: Eliz. Hammerly, sc: Eliz. Hammerly, wife, BVS:1855:3, LC:15

HAMMOND, Herbert S., W, M, d. 3 Aug 1886, cholera infantum, 0-3-7, p. Chas M. & Catherine A., sc: Chas M. Hammond, father, 2nd Dist., BVS:1886:5

HAMPTON, Caroline, B, F, d. 10 Jul 1891, Bloomfield, consumption, 72-0-0, p. Gilbert & Chancy Green, b. Page Co., laborer, c/o: Mark Hampton, sc: Mark Hampton, head of family, 1st Dist., BVS:1891:1

HAMPTON, Charles, B, M, d. 14 Jan 1884, nr Leesburg, pneumonia, 3-0-0, p. F. Thomas & Laura Hampton, b. LC, sc: F. Thomas Hampton, father, 2nd Dist., BVS:1884:4

HAMPTON, Charles, W, M, d. 5 Feb 1871, Silcott Springs, consumption, 20-2-0, p. Fenton & Sarah Hampton, b. LC, farmer, unm, sc: Fenton Hampton, father, MT Dist., BVS:1871:5

HAMPTON, James, W, M, d. 4 Dec 1857, his res, pneumonia, 67-0-0, p. Jeremiah & ... Hampton, b. LC, farmer, c/o: Eleanor Hampton, sc: Wm. F. Hampton, son, BVS:1857:4, LC:27

HAMPTON, Mary Ethel, W, F, d. 10 Apr 1891, Dry Mill, drowned, 8-8-0, p. George & Ella Hampton, b. Dry Mill, c/o: child, sc: George Hampton, MT Dist., BVS:1891:6

[HAMPTON], no name, W, M, d. Jun 1856, nr North Fork Church, erysipelas, 0-3-0, p. Manley & E. J. Hampton, b. North Fork, sc: M. Hampton, father, BVS:1856:4, LC:22

HAMPTON, Wade, W, M, d. 27 Apr 1890, nr Bloomfield, lock jaw, 5-6-0, p. John A. & Jennie Hampton, b. nr Bloomfield, sc: John A. Hampton, father, 1st Dist., BVS:1890:1

HAMPTON, William A., W, M, d. 12 Jul 1880, Purcellville, dysentery, 0-4-0, p. J. N. & Manerva Hampton, b. LC, sc: J.N. Hampton, father, 3rd Dist., BVS:1880:4

HANCOCK, Ann Jane, W, F, d. 20 Mar 1874, Broad Run Dist., consumption, 76-11-0, p. Jas. & Elizabeth Lewis, b. LC, c/o: Saml Hancock, sc: Martha V. Holtzclaw, daughter, BR Dist., BVS:1874:3

HANCOCK, James W., W, M, d. 10 Dec 1885, nr Arcola, peritonitis, 47-0-0, p. Samuel G. & Jane T. Hancock, b. Arcola, farmer, unm, sc: Martha V. Holtzclaw, sister, 1st Dist., BVS:1885:3

HANCOCK, Susan, W, F, d. 19 Mar 1865, Thistlewood farm, old age, 89-10-2, p. Lebberton & L. Raidan, b. Fairfax, housekeeper, consort, sc: C.F. Hancock, son, BVS:1865:2

HANDY, Jno. C., W, M, d. 22 Oct 1855, Albert Harding's, unk, 55-0-0, p. Jno. & Germina Handy, b. nr Handy's Mill, physician, sc: Jos. A. Hanes, nephew, BVS:1855:6, LC:17

HANFORD, Lizzie, W, F, d. 18 Jun 1875, Guilford, brain fever, 0-3-15, p. John M. & Julia Hanford, b. LC, sc: Julia Hanford, mother, BR Dist., BVS:1875:5

HANGARTER, Ansel, W, M, d. 3 Sep 1872, LC, heart disease, 24-0-0, p. Jos. & Ginser Hangarter, b. Germany, brewer, unm, sc: Jos. Hangarter, father, LE Dist., BVS:1872:3

HANLEY, Mary B., W, F, d. 20 Aug 1878, nr Hamilton, pneumonia, 0-10-29, p. Bayless & Martha Hanley, b. LC, sc: Baylen Hanley, father, JF Dist., BVS:1878:10

HANSBURY, Lizzie, B, F, d. 4 Apr 1882, LC, unk, 9-0-0, p. John & Betsy Hansbury, unm, sc: Jno Hansbury, father, 1st Dist., BVS:1882:1

HANSEY, Elizabeth, W, F, d. 1878, Waterford, pneumonia, 64-0-0, p. unk, b. Frederick Co. Va., c/o: John Hansey, decd, sc: James Hansey, son, JF Dist., BVS:1878:10

HARDING, Bessie, W, F, d. 10 Apr 1892, Waxpool, measles & typhoid pneumonia, 7-0-0, p. Chas. W. &

Arabell Harding, b. Waxpool, unm, sc: C.W. Harding, father, 1st Dist., BVS:1892:1

HARDING, Daisy, W, F, d. 17 Apr 1892, Waxpool, convulsions, 4-0-0, p. Chas. W. & Arabell Harding, b. Waxpool, unm, sc: C.W. Harding, father, 1st Dist., BVS:1892:1

HARDING, Edward, W, M, d. 9 Nov 1873, nr Hillsboro, old age, 86-1-0, p. Job & Nancy Harding, b. LC, farmer, unm, sc: Samuel F. Harding, son, JF Dist., BVS:1874:1

HARDING, Herbert, W, M, d. 1 Mar 1875, Farmwell Church, measles, 2-0-0, p. H. Clay & Nettie B. Harding, b. LC, unm, sc: H.C. Harding, father, BR Dist., BVS:1875:5

HARDING, Mabyl, W, F, d. 1 Mar 1876, nr Farmwell Church, water on the brain, 0-6-0, p. H. Clay & Nellie Harding, b. LC, sc: H.C. Harding, father, BR Dist., BVS:1876:2

HARDING, Nettie B., W, F, d. 23 Mar 1884, LC, hemorrhage, 34-0-0, p. Fenton & Susan Myers, b. LC, c/o: Henry Harding, sc: Henry Harding, husband, 1st Dist., BVS:1884:1

HARDING, Rachael, W, F, d. 15 Sep 1894, Waxpool, bronchitis, 77-0-0, p. unk, b. unk, c/o: Jos Harding, sc: C.W. Harding, son, 1st Dist., BVS:1894:1

HARDING, Wm. H., W, M, d. 12 Jul 1864, Petersburg, VA, killed in battle, 25-0-20, p. Albert & E.E. Harding, b. LC, farmer, sc: Ellen E. Harding, mother, BVS:1864:2, LC:39

HARDY, Anne M., W, F, d. 30 March 1878, LC, consumption, 63-7-0, b. LC, c/o: Henry M. Hardy, sc: Henry M. Hardy, husband, LE Dist., BVS:1878:8

HARDY, Harrison K., W, M, d. 23 Jul 1883, Leesburg, concussion of brain, 9-2-12, p. Howard S. & Mary M. Hardy, b. LC, sc: Howard S. Hardy, father, 2nd Dist., BVS:1883:6

HARDY, Hattie A., W, F, d. 29 May 1883, Leesburg, pneumonia, 3-9-22, p. Howard S. & Mary M. Hardy, b. LC, sc: Howard S. Hardy, father, 2nd Dist., BVS:1883:6

HARLOW, Edward H., W, M, d. 11 Mar 1896, nr Trappe, rheumatism, 70-0-0, p. unk, b. unk, minister, consort, sc: Mary Harlow, wife, MC Dist., BVS:1896:1

HARMAN, Laura E., W, F, d. 20 Dec 1875, Hamilton, consumption, 27-0-0, p. R. & Malinda Dowell, b. LC, physician, married, sc: J.D. Harmon, husband, MT Dist., BVS:1875:8

HARMON, Harriet Emeline, W, F, d. 14 Feb 1876, nr Hamilton, consumption, unk, p. J.D. & Laura E. Harmon, b. LC, unm, sc: J.D. Harmon, father, MT Dist., BVS:1876:1

HARNY, Sarah A., W, F, d. 2 Jul 1894, Taylorstown, rheumatism, 63-0-0, p. unk, b. unk, unk, consort, LV Dist., BVS:1894:4

HARPER, Catherine, W, F, d. 13 Apr 1854, LC, affection of the kidneys, 58-0-0, p. unk, b. LC, sc: Julius Harper, son, BVS:1854:8, LC:8

HARPER, Catherine, W, F, d. 3 Feb 1872, LC, unk, 45-0-0, p. Jas. & Catherine Harper, b. unk, unm, sc: James Harper, friend, cousin, LE Dist., BVS:1872:3

HARPER, Daniel H., W, M, d. 30 Aug 1885, nr Goresville, typhoid fever, 22-3-22, p. Chas. F. & Elizabeth Harper, c/o: Eliza Harper, sc: Chas F. Harper, father, 2nd Dist., BVS:1885:1

HARPER, Elizabeth A., W, F, d. 28 Feb 1892, Goresville, la grippe, 62-0-0, p. unk, b. Goresville, consort, LE Dist., BVS:1892:5

HARPER, George W., W, M, d. 15 Mar 1877, LC, brain fever, 4-6-0, p. W. H.H. & Susan Harper, sc: W.H.H. Harper, father, LE Dist., BVS:1877:8

HARPER, Georgianna, W, F, d. 28 Apr 1881, LC, labor, 31-8-19, p. Wm. & Nancy Harper, c/o: J.C. Harper, sc: Nancy Harper, mother, 2nd Dist., BVS:1881:6

HARPER, Henry C., W, M, d. 5 Oct 1872, LC, dysentery, 10-3-4, p. Harrison & Susan Harper, b. LC, sc: Susan Harper, mother, LE Dist., BVS:1872:3

HARPER, Julius, W, M, d. 15 Apr 1884, nr Leesburg, pneumonia, 61-0-0, p. John & Catharine Harper, b. LC, farmer, c/o: Virginia Harper, sc: Virginia Harper, wife, 2nd Dist., BVS:1884:4

HARPER, Mahala A., W, F, d. 5 Aug 1854, LC, dysentery, 15-0-0, p. Catherine Harper, b. LC, unm, sc: Eliza W. Harper, sister, BVS:1854:8, LC:8

[HARPER], no name, W, M, d. 31 Jan 1877, LC, strangulation, 0-3-0, p. Jabez & G. L. Harper, sc: Jabez Harper, father, LE Dist., BVS:1877:8

[HARPER], no name, W, , d. 28 Mar 1878, LC, unk, unk, p. Jabez & Georgina Harper, b. LC, sc: Georgianna Harper, mother, LE Dist., BVS:1878:8

HARPER, no name, W, M, d. 10 Apr 1880, Leesburg, unk, 0-2-18, p. Ida Harper, b. LC, unm, sc: James W. Harper, grandfather, 2nd Dist., BVS:1880:6

HARPER, Robert, W, M, d. 11 Jan 1882, LC, unk, 0-2-0, p. Nancy Harper, unm, sc: Nancy Harper, mother, 1st Dist., BVS:1882:2

HARPER, Stephen H., W, M, d. 8 Nov 1853, LC, unk, 8-3-5, p. Jonathan & Mary J. Harper, b. LC, sc: Mary J. Harper, mother, BVS:1854:3, LC:1

HARPER, Wm. H., W, M, d. 29 Apr 1854, LC, pneumonia, 51-5-2, p. John & Eusatia Harper, b. LC, carpenter, c/o: Nancy Harper, sc: Rachel A. Harper, dau., BVS:1854:8, LC:8

[HARRINGTON], [no name], W, M, d. 4 Oct 1857, unk, 0-0-1, p. George & Sarah A. Harrington, b. LC, sc: George Harrington, father, BVS:1857:7, LC:28

HARRIS, Caroline, B, F, d. 2 Mar 1885, Leesburg, rheumatism, 87-0-0, p. --- Booth, c/o: John Harris, sc: Joseph Waters. friend, 2nd Dist., BVS:1885:1

HARRIS, Charles W., B, M, d. 16 Feb 1875, Leesburg, pneumonia, 1-4-0, p. Flavius & Mary A. Harris, b. Leesburg, sc: Wm. Robey, grandfather, LE Dist., BVS:1875:1

HARRIS, Daphney, B, F, d. 12 Apr 1876, Leesburg, heart disease, 42-9-0, p. unk, b. unk, c/o: James Harris, sc: James Harris, husband, LE Dist., BVS:1876:6

HARRIS, Ed, B, M, d. 14 Jan 1886, nr Guilford, rheumatism, 60-0-0, p. Wm. & Mary Harris, b. LC, c/o: Nancy Harris, sc: Presley Jones, son-in-law, 1st Dist., BVS:1886:1

HARRIS, Jas. G., W, M, d. 5 Jun 1875, Leesburg, consumption, 20-5-5, p. Wm. J. & Ruth Harris, b. Clarke, laborer, sc: Saml N. Harris, brother, LE Dist., BVS:1875:1

HARRIS, Jas. W., B, M, d. 6 Feb 1875, Leesburg, measles, 1-3-0, p. Jas & Dafney Harris, b. Leesburg, sc: Jas. Harris, father, LE Dist., BVS:1875:1

HARRIS, John H., B, M, d. 24 Jun 1879, nr Leesburg, typhoid fever, 12-6-6, p. Philip & Maria Harris, b. LC, sc: Philip Harris, father, 2nd Dist., BVS:1879:1

HARRIS, Kate, B, F, d. 1 Sep 1881, LC, labor, unk-0-0, p. Jno. & L. Philips, c/o: William Harris, sc: Isabell Philips, step-mother, 2nd Dist., BVS:1881:6

HARRIS, Lee, W, M, d. 19 Nov 1869, Clarke Co., VA, pneumonia, 6-11-21, p. William & Ruth Harris, b. Clark Co. VA, sc: Wm. Harris, father, BVS:1869:1

HARRIS, Lutie, W, F, d. 20 Mar 1896, nr Arcola, consumption, 18-0-0, p. Sam Harris, b. LC, laborer, unm, sc: A.C. Gant, friend, BR Dist., BVS:1896:3

HARRIS, Mabel V., W, F, d. 17 Dec 1894, Lovettsville, membranes comp., 6-0-0, p. Geo. & Lucy Harris, b. Lovettsville, unm, sc: Geo. W. Harris, LV Dist., BVS:1894:4

HARRIS, Marietta, B, F, d. 18 Jun 1874, Poor House, typhoid fever, 16-0-0, p. Marlow & Sarah Harris, b. LC, laborer, sc: Marlow Harris, father, MC Dist., BVS:1874:4

HARRIS, Nancy, B, F, d. 5 Jun 1886, nr Guilford, dropsy, 55-0-0, p. Thomas & Fannie Jones, b. LC, laborer, c/o: Ed Harris, sc: Presley Jones, son-in-law, 1st Dist., BVS:1886:1

HARRIS, Nancy, B, F, d. 7 Dec 1894, nr Sterling, consumption, 29-0-0, p. unk, b. nr Sterling, c/o: Henry Harris, sc: Henry Harris, husband, 1st Dist., BVS:1894:2

[HARRIS], no name, B, F, d. May 1877, Snickersville, unk, p. Benj. & Sallie Harris, b. LC, sc: B. Harris, father, MT Dist., BVS:1877:2

HARRIS, Rich. A., B, , d. 18 Oct 1877, LC, jaundice, 3-11-0, p. Philip & Maria Harris, sc: Philip Harris, father, LE Dist., BVS:1877:8

HARRIS, Sallie, B, F, d. 9 Oct 1894, nr Ryan, heart failure, 50-0-0, p. unk, b. LC, c/o: Chas Harris, sc: Chas Harris, husband, 1st Dist., BVS:1894:2

HARRIS, Sarah V., W, F, d. 12 Mar 1883, nr Lovettsville, typhoid pneumonia, 1-8-12, p. Richard & Sallie M. Harris, b. LC, sc: Sallie M. Harris, mother, 2nd Dist., BVS:1883:3

HARRIS, Sissy, B, F, d. 10 Dec 1875, Blue Ridge nr Snickersville, unk, p. Benj. & Sarah Jane Harris, b. nr Snickersville, laborer, sc: Benj. Harris, father, MT Dist., BVS:1875:8

HARRIS, Susie, B, F, d. 10 Oct 1884, LC, burned to death, 7-0-0, p. Wilson & Mary Harris, b. LC, 1st Dist., BVS:1884:1

HARRIS, William P., W, M, d. 15 Aug 1888, LC, old age, 87-0-0, p. Isaac & Sallie Harris, b. LC, none, unm, sc: James Harris, brother, 2nd Dist., BVS:1888:6

HARRIS, Wm. T., W, M, d. 23 Feb 1875, Leesburg, consumption, 50-11-27, laborer, c/o: Ruth Harris, sc: Geo. W. Harris, son, LE Dist., BVS:1875:1

HARRISON, Burr W., W, M, d. 9 Aug 1873, Culpeper Co., cholera infantum, 0-13-0, p. Powell & Jennett Harrison, b. LC, lawyer, unm, sc: P. Harrison, father, LE Dist., BVS:1873:2

HARRISON, Cecelia, W, F, d. 10 Mar 1859/60, Thomas Hensey's, dropsy, 84-0-0, c/o: James Harrison, sc: Thomas Hensey, son-in-law, BVS:1859:5, 1860:2, LC:35

HARRISON, Frances L., W, F, d. 10 Nov 1855, LC, unk, 0-0-1, p. Francis & Mary M. Harrison, b. LC, sc: Francis Harrison, father, BVS:1855:1, LC:14

HARRISON, Henry T., W, M, d. 19 Jun 1881, LC, old age, 84-0-0, p. ___ Harrison, merchant, c/o: M.E. Harrison, sc: Walter J. Harrison, son, 2nd Dist., BVS:1881:6

HARRISON, John F., W, M, d. 27 Aug 1873, Hamilton, whooping cough, 1-0-0, p. John D. & Louisa Harrison, b. Hamilton, sc: parents, MT Dist., BVS:1873:3

HARRISON, Laura, W, F, d. Jul 1856, Aldie, scarlet fever, 7-0-0, p. J. P. H. & Alverda Green, b. Aldie, sc: J.P.H. Green, father, BVS:1856:4, LC:22

HARRISON, Matthew, W, M, d. 18 Jan 1875, Leesburg, consumption, 52-0-0, p. Burr W. & Sally Harrison, lawyer, c/o: H.T. Harrison, sc: Powell Harrison, brother, LE Dist., BVS:1875:1

HARRISON, Nellie, W, F, d. 20 Jul 1893, Lovettsville, unk, 0-2-0, p. Geo. & Alberta, b. Lovettsville, farmer, unm, sc: Geor. H. Harrison, LV Dist., BVS:1893:5

[HARRISON], no name, W, F, d. 16 Oct 1856, LC, unk, 0-0-2, p. Francis & Mary M. Harrison, b. LC, sc: Mary M. Harrison, mother, BVS:1856:1, LC:20

HARRISON, no name, W, F, d. 7 Apr 1890, LC, unk, unk, p. Geo. & Alberta Harrison, b. LC, none, unm, sc: Geo Harrison, father, 2nd Dist., BVS:1890:3

HARRISON, Susan E., W, F, d. 4 Mar 1876, Windsor, pneumonia, 65-0-0, c/o: Jno. W. Harrison, sc: Douglas Iden, son-in-law, MC Dist., BVS:1876:4

HARRISON, Thomas, W, M, d. 15 Feb 1890, LC, unk, 23-0-0, p. Thomas Harrison, b. LC, none, unm, sc: T. Harrison, father, 2nd Dist., BVS:1890:3

HARRISON, Virginia, W, F, d. 24 Apr 1887, LC, consumption, 18-0-0, p. Thomas & Sarah Harrison, b. LC, unm, sc: Thomas Harrison, father, 2nd Dist., BVS:1887:4

HART, Elizabeth S., W, F, d. 14 Sep 1872, nr Wheatland, unk, 0-1-2, p. Joseph & Rachel Hart, b. Wheatland, sc: Joseph S. Hart, father, JF Dist., BVS:1872:1

HART, Emily J., W, F, d. 31 Jun[sic] 1858, LC, unk, 0-9-0, p. Joseph S. & Rachel A. Hart, b. LC, sc: Rachel A. Hart, mother, BVS:1858:2, LC:30

HARTMAN, Ery M., W, F, d. 4 Nov 1886, consumption, 61-10-21, p. Jacob & --- Stoutsenberger, c/o: Thomas J. Hartman, sc: Thos. J.

Hartman, husband, 2nd Dist., BVS:1886:5

HARVEY, Samuel L., W, M, d. 24 Oct 1885, nr Wheatland, typhoid fever, 22-7-0, p. Jonas A. & Sarah Harvey, unm, sc: John C. Harvey, brother, 2nd Dist., BVS:1885:1

HATCHER, J. Thomas, W, M, d. 24 Jan 1884, Lincoln, consumption, 40-0-0, p. Joshua & Sallie Hatcher, b. LC, farmer, c/o: Sallie J. Hatcher, sc: Sallie J. Hatcher, wife, 3rd Dist., BVS:1884:6

HATCHER, Rodney G., W, M, d. 8 Dec 1872, Hamilton, consumption, 39-5-22, p. Thos. & Nancy Hatcher, b. Hamilton, farmer, c/o: Mary T. Hatcher, sc: Mary T. Hatcher, wife, JF Dist., BVS:1872:1

HATCHER, T. Elwood, W, M, d. 1 Dec 1883, Purcellville, paralysis, 79-0-0, b. LC, farmer, unm, sc: Susan Hatcher, daughter, 3rd Dist., BVS:1883:5

HATTEN, Harry D., W, M, d. 10 Dec 1888, LC, pneumonia, 25-0-0, p. Harry & Sarah Hatten, b. Washington DC, laborer, unm, sc: W.D. Vincel, brother-in-law, 2nd Dist., BVS:1888:6

HAUR, Minnie J., W, F, d. 12 Nov 1882, LC, croup, 2-4-0, p. Wm. & Mary Haur, b. LC, unm, sc: Wm. Haur, parent, 3rd Dist., BVS:1882:3

HAVENER, Ada J., W, F, d. 7 Nov 1874, Broad Run Dist., brain fever, 0-2-11, p. E. B. & Anna E. Havener, laborer, sc: Edgar B. Havener, father, BR Dist., BVS:1874:3

HAVENER, Catherine P., W, F, d. 14 Jan 1884, Leesburg, consumption, 20-0-0, p. Jas. B. & Hortentia Havener, b. LC, unm, sc: Hortentia E. Havener, mother, 2nd Dist., BVS:1884:4

HAVENER, Dora L., W, F, d. 9 Mar 1883, nr Belmont, spasmodic asthma, 9-0-0, p. Edgar B. & Anna E. Havener, b. nr Belmont, unm, sc: Edgar B. Havener, father, 1st Dist., BVS:1883:1

HAVENER, Henry M., W, M, d. Aug 1854, LC, unk, 0-8-0, p. Philip F. & L. Havener, b. LC, sc: P. F. Havener, father, BVS:1854:14, LC:13

HAVENER, Jesse W., W, M, d. 1 Sep 1884, LC, unk, 0-0-21, p. Benja. L.& Lucretia Havener, b. LC, sc: Benja Havener, father, 1st Dist., BVS:1884:1

HAVENER, John A., W, M, d. 24 Jan 1854, consumption, 25-11-14, b. LC, wheelwright, sc: John Lee, father-in-law, BVS:1854:13, LC:13

HAVENER, Julia E., W, F, d. 20 Sep 1883, nr Farmwell, deformed, 0-1-3, p. Benja. L. Havener, b. nr Farmwell, unm, sc: Benja L. Havener, father, 1st Dist., BVS:1883:1

HAVENER, L. H., W, M, d. 7 Apr 1892, Ryan, typhoid fever, 36-0-0, p. Wm. H. & Julia Havener, b. Bloomfield, carpenter, c/o: Alice Havener, sc: Alice Havener, wife, 1st Dist., BVS:1892:1

HAVENER, Mary C., W, F, d. 8 Feb 1885, nr Farmwell, blood poison, 48-0-0, p. Catharine B. Moran, c/o: Thomas A. Havener, sc: T.H. Havener, husband, 2nd Dist., BVS:1885:1

HAVENER, Wm. E., W, M, d. 23 Jun 1871, consumption, 69-0-0, married, BR Dist., BVS:1871:3

HAVENER, Wm. W., W, M, d. 30 Sep 1859/60, LC, unk, 1-2-0, p. Wm. H. & Julia E. Havener, b. LC, sc: Wm. Havener, father, BVS:1859:6, 1860:3, LC:36

HAVENNER, Bazell, W, M, d. 12 Jul 1855, pleurisy, 54-0-0, p. unk, sc: Rachael Havenner, wife, BVS:1855:9, LC:19

HAVENNER, John, W, M, d. Jul 1865, Hamilton, dropsy, 37-0-0, p. Jeremiah & M. Havener, b. LC, farmer, sc: father, BVS:1865:1

HAWK, Susan, W, F, d. 4 Jul 1854, LC, dysentery, 0-4-1, p. Elijah & Eliza Hawk, b. LC, sc: Eliza Hawk, mother, BVS:1854:9, LC:8

HAWKINS, Joseph N., W, M, d. 25 Jun 1871, Washington, DC, hemorrhage, 18-11-5, p. John W. & Mary Hawkins, b. nr Pughs Mill, sc: Mary Hawkins, mother, JF Dist., BVS:1871:1

HAWLEY, Wm., B, , d. 25 May 1877, LC, pneumonia, 2-3-0, p. Geo. & Winnie Hawley, sc: Winnie Hawley, mother, LE Dist., BVS:1877:9

HAWLING, Charlie, W, M, d. 29 May 1891, nr Oatlands, membranous croup, 0-8-0, p. C. T. & Jennie Hawling, b. LC, farmer, sc: C.T. Hawling, father, 1st Dist., BVS:1891:2

HAWLING, Frances, W, F, d. 12 Jun 1880, Leesburg, dropsy, 86-9-0, p. James & Martha Best, b. LC, c/o: Isaac Hawling, sc: Jemima Hawling, daughter, 2nd Dist., BVS:1880:6

HAWLING, Isaac W., W, M, d. 24 Sep 1854, White Hall, bilious dysentery, 68-0-0, p. John & Jemina Hawling, b. Rivers farm, farmer, c/o: Frances Hawling, sc: Jemima Hawling, dau, BVS:1854:12, LC:11

HAWLING, Jemima, W, F, d. 2 Apr 1883, nr Leesburg, apoplexy, 39-0-0, p. Isaac & Frances Hawling, b. LC, unm, sc: E.A. Trundle, sister, 2nd Dist., BVS:1883:3

HAWLING, Jno. Wm., W, M, d. 10 Nov 1878, LC, congestion of lungs, 40-0-0, p. Isaac & Frances Hawling, b. LC, unm, sc: Jemima Hawling, sister, LE Dist., BVS:1878:8

HAWLING, Joseph L., W, M, d. 5 Jan 1884, nr Leesburg, heart disease, 68-0-0, p. --- Hawling, b. LC, farmer, c/o: Martha D. Hawling, sc: Martha D. Hawling, wife, 2nd Dist., BVS:1884:4

HAWS, Bertha C., W, F, d. 25 Aug 1882, LC, diphtheria, 0-2-0, p. Isaac & Sarah Haws, unm, sc: Isaac Haws, father, 1st Dist., BVS:1882:1

HAWS, Nettie, W, F, d. 11 Sep 1890, nr Mountville, consumption, 57-0-0, p. Asa & Betty Haws, b. nr Mountville, unm, sc: Thomas Haws, brother, 1st Dist., BVS:1890:1

HAWS, no name, W, M, d. 21 Mar 1891, Mountville, premature, 0-0-1, p. J. W. & Sarah Haws, b. LC, laborer, sc: J.W. Haws, father, 1st Dist., BVS:1891:2

HAWS, W. E., W, M, d. Dec 1871, LC, 46-0-0, b. LC, farmer, c/o: Elizabeth Haws, LE Dist., BVS:1871:4

HAY, no name, W, F, d. 26 Dec 1887, Farmwell, unk, 0-0-18, p. Geo. & Elizabeth Hay, b. Farmwell, sc: George Hay, father, 1st Dist., BVS:1887:1

HAYES, William, W, M, d. 12 May 1885, nr Lovettsville, paralysis, 53-5-9, p. John & Elizabeth Hayes, farmer, c/o: Lydia J. Hayes, sc: Lydia J. Hayes, wife, 2nd Dist., BVS:1885:1

HEAD, Arabella F., W, F, d. 10 May 1885, Leesburg, consumption, 41-0-0, p. Jesse & --- McIntosh, c/o: Benjamin F. Head, sc: B.F. Head, husband, 2nd Dist., BVS:1885:1

HEAD, Clarence, W, M, d. 20 mar 1889, LC, typhoid fever, 37-0-0, p. Col. & Emily Head, b. LC, printer, c/o: Maggie Head, sc: Maggie Head, widow, 2nd Dist., BVS:1889:3

HEAD, Columbus, W, M, d. 10 Nov 1855, Leesburg, unk, 0-4-12, p. C. C. & Emily J. Head, b. Leesburg, sc: C. C. Head, father, BVS:1855:1, LC:14

HEAD, Eley H., W, M, d. 9 Nov 1854, Leesburg, unk, 0-0-26, p. Geo. R. & Sarah V. Head, b. Leesburg, sc: Geo. R. Head, father, BVS:1854:8, LC:7

HEAD, Geo. R. Jr., W, M, d. 10 Aug 1881, LC, consumption, 40-11-10, p. Columbus & E. J. Head, mechanic, c/o: Mary L. Head, sc: Mary L. Head, wife, 2nd Dist., BVS:1881:6

HEAD, Maggie, W, F, d. 31 Mar 1885, nr Leesburg, congestion of brain, 6-6-0, p. Clarence G. & Maggie Head, sc: C.G. Head, father, 2nd Dist., BVS:1885:1

HEAD, Margaret N. G., W, F, d. 7 May 1883, Leesburg, heart disease, 70-0-0, p. Richard & Margaret Morton, b. LC, c/o: Nelson Head, sc: Nelson Head, husband, 2nd Dist., BVS:1883:6

HEAD, Martha E., W, F, d. 23 Dec 1878, LC, gastric fever, 43-0-0, p. Wm H. & Mary Saunders, b. LC, c/o: Benj. F. Head, sc: Benj. F. Head, husband, LE Dist., BVS:1878:8

HEAD, Mary, W, F, d. 5 Aug 1885, Leesburg, cholera infantum, 0-4-0, p. Benj. F. & Arabella F. Head, sc: B.F. Head, father, 2nd Dist., BVS:1885:1

[HEAD], no name, W, M, d. 22 Apr 1858, Leesburg, unk, 0-0-2, p. George R. & Sarah V. Head, b.

Leesburg, sc: George R. Head, father, BVS:1858:1, LC:29
[HEAD], no name, W, M, d. 28 Apr 1859/60, Leesburg, unk, 0-0-10, p. Geo. R. & Sarah V. Head, b. Leesburg, sc: George R. Head, father, BVS:1859:2, 1860:4, LC:37
HEAD, Walter, W, M, d. 15 Aug 1884, Leesburg, cholera infantum, 1-3-0, p. Benj. F. & Arabella Head, b. LC, sc: Benj. F. Head, father, 2nd Dist., BVS:1884:4
HEADLEY, Archie, B, M, d. 31 Jul 1879, Leesburg, summer complaint, 0-6-14, p. Michael & Marie Headley, b. LC, sc: Mary Headley, mother, 2nd Dist., BVS:1879:1
HEADLEY, Michael, B, M, d. 25 Sep 1881, LC, dysentery, 40-0-0, p. Arthur & Sarah Headley, laborer, c/o: Mary Headley, sc: Chas. Headley, brother, 2nd Dist., BVS:1881:6
HEADLEY, no name, B, M, d. 25 Nov 1886, unk, 0-0-7, p. Charles & Fannie, sc: Chas. Headley, father, 2nd Dist., BVS:1886:5
HEARNS, no name, B, F, d. 18 Jul 1893, nr Arcola, unk, 0-2-0, p. Richd & Mary Hearns, b. nr Arcola, laborer, sc: Richd Hearns, grandfather, 1st Dist., BVS:1893:2
HEATER, Alice A., W, F, d. 15 Sep 1896, Lovettsville, unk, 43-0-0, p. Samuel & Sarah, b. Lovettsville, c/o: William C. Heater, sc: William C. Heater, consort, LV Dist., BVS:1896:7
HEATER, Cornelia A., W, F, d. 8 Oct 1893, Lovettsville, dyspepsia, 78-0-0, p. unk, b. Lovettsville, consort, sc: Eli Heater, LV Dist., BVS:1893:5
HEATER, Philip Henry, W, M, d. 1 Jun 1872, Leesburg, stabbed in an affray, 25-8-6, p. Jno. & Margaret Heater, b. LC, farmer, unm, sc: Margaret Heater, mother, LE Dist., BVS:1872:3
HEATH, Diadema, W, F, d. 15 Apr 1866, Rosedale, mental derangement, 67-0-0, b. LC, sc: F.M. Paxson, son-in-law, BVS:1866:1
HEATON, Henry, W, M, d. 17 May 1890, Leesburg, apoplexy, 57-0-0, p. J. & P. Heaton, b. LC, attorney at law, unm, sc: N.R. Heaton, brother, 3rd Dist., BVS:1890:6
HEATON, J.T.W., W, M, d. 18 Jan 1865, nr Woodgrove, falling from a horse, 56-0-0, p. Jonathan Heaton, b. nr Purcellville, farmer, unm, sc: James Heaton, nephew, BVS:1865:1
HEATON, James, W, M, d. 27 Dec 1883, Woodgrove, heart disease, 65-7-15, b. LC, farmer, unm, sc: N.R. Heaton, brother, 3rd Dist., BVS:1883:5
HEATON, James D., W, M, d. 15 Feb 1859/60, his res, Exedra, consumption, 42-9-20, p. Jos & Lydia Heaton, b. place of death, physician, c/o: Cecelia M. Heaton, sc: C.M. Heaton, widow, BVS:1859:4, 1860:2, LC:35
HEATON, Patience, W, F, d. 24 Mar 1855, Woodgrove, inflammation lung, 58-5-21, p. Abner & Patience Osburn, b. nr Woodgrove, c/o: Jonathan Heaton, decd, sc: Eliz. Heaton, daughter, BVS:1855:7, LC:18
[HEDLEY], no name, B, , d. 17 Apr 1876, Leesburg, spasms, 0-0-14, p. Michael & Mary Hedley, b. LC, sc: Mary Hedley, mother, LE Dist., BVS:1876:6
HEFLIN, Jane, W, F, d. Jan 1873, Leesburg, dyspepsia, 75-0-0, b. Leesburg, sc: J.A. Anderson, friend, LE Dist., BVS:1873:2
HEFLIN, John H., W, M, d. 25 Oct 1886, Fauquier Co, unk, 0-5-2, p. John C. & Mattie B. Heflin, b. Fauquier Co., sc: John C. Heflin, father, 1st Dist., BVS:1886:1
HELM, Joseph, W, M, d. 25 Jul 1890, LC, dysentery, 84-0-0, p. unk, b. LC, minister, unm, sc: L.M. Shumate, son-in-law, 2nd Dist., BVS:1890:4
HEMPSTON, Cephas, W, M, d. Mar 1874, LC, infection of bowels, 69-0-0, widower, sc: G. Giddings, son-in-law, LE Dist., BVS:1874:5
HENDERSON, Andrew, B, M, d. 1 Apr 1891, nr Aldie, consumption, 13-0-0, p. Andrew Henderson, b. LC, laborer, unm, sc: Andrew Henderson, head of family, 1st Dist., BVS:1891:1

HENDERSON, Emma, B, F, d. 2 Jun 1891, nr Aldie, consumption, 37-0-0, p. unk, b. LC, laborer, c/o: Andrew Henderson, sc: Andrew Henderson, head of family, 1st Dist., BVS:1891:1

HENDERSON, Francis P., W, F, d. Oct 1894, Guinea Mills, diphtheria, 23-0-0, p. J.K.P. & Francis A. Henderson, b. Guinea Mills, sc: J.K.P. Henderson, father, 3rd Dist., BVS:1894:5

HENDERSON, Louisa, B, F, d. 13 Aug 1873, nr Gum Spring, hemorrhage, 60-0-0, p. unk, b. nr Gum Spring, married, sc: Geo. Henderson, head of family, BR Dist., BVS:1873:1

HENDERSON, Maria E., W, F, d. 26 Mar 1857, Leesburg, dropsy, 26-3-0, p. George T. & Ann Thomas, b. Rappahannock Co., c/o: Fenton M. Henderson, sc: F.M. Henderson, husband, BVS:1857:2, LC:25

HENDERSON, Maria Lee, W, F, d. 23 Oct 1857, Leesburg, premature birth, 0-7-0, p. F.M. & Maria E. Henderson, b. Leesburg, sc: F.M. Henderson, father, BVS:1857:2, LC:25

HENDERSON, Mary A.V., W, F, d. 21 Aug 1857, res of parents, cholera infantum, 1-5-0, p. George & Lucinda Henderson, b. place of death, sc: father, BVS:1857:3, LC:25

HENDERSON, no name, B, M, d. 3 Jun 1891, nr Aldie, premature, 0-0-1, p. Andrew Henderson, b. LC, laborer, sc: Andrew Henderson, head of family, 1st Dist., BVS:1891:1

HENDERSON, Rebecca, W, F, d. Mar 1873, LC, consumption, 22-0-0, p. E. W. & Delsa Henderson, b. LC, unm, sc: Chas. W. Henderson, father, LE Dist., BVS:1873:2

HENDERSON, William E., W, M, d. 29 Jul 1880, nr Leesburg, unk, 0-4-25, p. R. H. & M. E. Henderson, b. LC, unm, sc: R.H. Henderson, father, 2nd Dist., BVS:1880:6

HENRY, Henry, B, M, d. 10 Jun 1887, LC, dysentery, 1-6-0, p. Jno. & Lydia Henry, b. LC, unm, sc: John Henry, father, 3rd Dist., BVS:1887:6

HENRY, Katie, B, F, d. 1 Feb 1888, LC, bronchitis, 1-6-0, p. John & Lydia A. Henry, b. LC, none, unm, sc: John Henry, father, 3rd Dist., BVS:1888:1

HENRY, Sarah A., B, F, d. 31 Mar 1887, LC, consumption, 18-0-0, p. Jno. & Lydia Henry, b. LC, unm, sc: John Henry, father, 3rd Dist., BVS:1887:6

HENSEY, George, W, M, d. 7 Dec 1854, nr North Fork, typhoid fever, 18-0-0, p. Rhoda Hensey & Nancy, b. Prince William Co, bricklayer, sc: J. Hensey, brother, BVS:1854:11, LC:11

HENSIA, Cornelia, W, F, d. 20 Mar 1885, nr Guilford, scarlet fever, 14-0-0, p. Wm. & Julia Hensia, b. New Jersey, sc: Cyrus B. Rees, friend, 1st Dist., BVS:1885:4

HERN, John, W, M, d. 6 Dec 1890, Round Hill, thrown from horse, 41-0-0, p. Thomas & Jabel Hern, b. LC, laborer, c/o: E. Hern, sc: E. Hern, wife, 3rd Dist., BVS:1890:6

HERNDON, Bessie V., W, F, d. 7 Apr 1885, nr Leesburg, unk, 0-2-25, p. Jno. W. & Mattie Herndon, sc: Jno W. Herndon, father, 2nd Dist., BVS:1885:1

HERNDON, no name, W, M, d. 14 Aug 1883, nr Leesburg, unk, 0-1-10, p. Geo. & Martha Herndon, b. LC, sc: Geo W. Herndon, father, 2nd Dist., BVS:1883:6

HESKETT, Sarah E., W, F, d. 19 Jul 1888, LC, heart disease, 50-0-0, p. Peter & Emily Cole, b. LC, none, c/o: William Heskett, sc: Wm. Heskett, husband, 3rd Dist., BVS:1888:1

HESS, Charles B., W, M, d. 1 Nov 1887, LC, diphtheria, 3-6-0, p. Chas. B. & Fannie A. Hess, b. LC, unm, sc: Chas B. Hess, father, 2nd Dist., BVS:1887:4

HESS, Chas. B., W, M, d. 15 Oct 1889, LC, heart failure, 33-0-0, p. Abram & Catherine Hess, b. LC, merchant, c/o: Fannie A. Hess, sc: Fannie A. Hess, widow, 2nd Dist., BVS:1889:3

HESS, Clarence R., W, M, d. 10 Feb 1877, nr Bloomfield, unk, 0-2-2, p. Jno. A. & Mollie Hess, b. LC, sc: Jno. A. Hess, father, MC Dist., BVS:1877:5

HESS, Ethell Boyd, W, F, d. 1 Nov 1887, LC, diphtheria, 5-0-0, p. Chas. B. & Fannie A. Hess, b. LC, unm, sc:

Chas B. Hess, father, 2nd Dist., BVS:1887:4
HESS, Mary M., W, F, d. 10 Dec 1882, LC, general debility, 69-0-0, p. David & Annie Hess, b. Jefferson Co., WV, unm, sc: L.D. Hoge, brother, 3rd Dist., BVS:1882:3
HESSER, Alcinda, W, F, d. 13 Dec 1881, LC, heart disease, 78-0-0, b. LC, c/o: Thomas Hesser, sc: A.T. Hesser, son, 3rd Dist., BVS:1881:4
HESSER, Sallie M., W, F, d. 19 Oct 1875, LC, cancer, unk, p. Alcinda & David Hesser, b. LC, unm, sc: David Hesser, father, MT Dist., BVS:1875:8
HEWES, John W., B, M, d. 1 Dec 1890, Clarkes Gap, unk, 1-0-0, p. Geo. & May A. Hewes, b. LC, laborer, unm, sc: Geo Hughes, father, 3rd Dist., BVS:1890:6
HEWITT, Unity, W, F, d. 3 Aug 1855, Leesburg, unk, 0-1-11, p. Abrahm & Isabella Hewitt, b. Leesburg, sc: Abraham Hewitt, father, BVS:1855:1, LC:14
HIBBS, Elizabeth, W, F, d. Jan 1858, Wm Roby's, dropsy, 61-0-0, p. Amos & Mary Hibbs, b. nr Union, sc: Wm. Robey, nephew-in-law, BVS:1858:3, LC:30
HIBBS, George W., W, M, d. 26 Oct 1876, nr Aldie, affection of the brain, 2-3-0, p. Jos. L. & Alvorna D. Hibbs, b. LC, sc: Jos. L. Hibbs, father, MC Dist., BVS:1876:4
HIBBS, John R., W, M, d. 10 Sep 1855, Hibbs Mill, typhoid fever, 42-9-15, p. Mary Hibbs, b. LC, boot & shoemaker, c/o: Catherine Ann Hibbs, sc: Stephen Hibbs, stepfather, BVS:1855:7, LC:18
HIBBS, Mariah P., W, F, d. 24 Dec 1853, Nichols Mill, dropsy of brain, 1-7-0, p. Wm. & Mary P. Hibbs, b. Nichols Mill, sc: father, BVS:1854:7, LC:6
[HIBBS], no name, W, F, d. Nov 1855, Goose Creek Bridge, 0-7-0, p. Wm. & Mary Jane Hibbs, b. Goose Creek Bridge, sc: Wm. Hibbs, father, BVS:1855:7, LC:18
[HIBBS], no names, W, M, d. March 1859/60, nr North Fork Meeting House, dropsy on brain, 0-6-0, p. Wm. & Mary J. Hibbs, b. nr North Fork Meeting House, sc: W. Hibbs, father, BVS:1859:3, 1860:1, LC:34
HIBBS, Rebecca, W, F, d. 14 Jul 1981, Aldie, catarrh cons, 67-0-0, p. unk, b. LC, unk, c/o: Benj Hibbs, sc: Benj Hibbs, husband, 1st Dist., BVS:1891:2
HIBBS, William, W, M, d. 10 Dec 1887, Philomont, chronic diarrhea, 69-11-12, p. Joseph & Nancy Hibbs, b. Rappahannock, c/o: Mary J. Hibbs, sc: Mary E. Pierson, daughter, 1st Dist., BVS:1887:2
HIBLER, Henry, W, M, d. 16 Aug 1877, LC, teething, 0-9-0, p. H. B. & Louisa Hibler, sc: H.B. Hibler, father, LE Dist., BVS:1877:8
HICKMAN, Bessie M., W, F, d. 23 Nov 1881, LC, croup, 2-1-22, p. Geo. L. K. & R. M. Hickman, b. LC, sc: Geo L.K. Hickman, father, 2nd Dist., BVS:1881:6
HICKMAN, Carolina R., W, F, d. 15 Aug 1866, nr Lovettsville, typhoid fever, 22-0-0, p. Geo. & Eleanora Hickman, b. LC, unm, sc: Eleanora Hickman, mother, BVS:1866:1
HICKMAN, Catharine A., W, F, d. 21 Apr 1856, LC, typhoid fever, 8-3-0, p. Peter & Mary E. Hickman, b. LC, sc: Peter Hickman, father, BVS:1856:1, LC:20
HICKMAN, Catharine E., W, F, d. 16 Aug 1878, nr Lovettsville, 0-1-10, p. L. W. & Annie M. Hickman, b. LC, sc: L.W. Hickman, father, LV Dist., BVS:1878:1/5
HICKMAN, Ellen B., W, F, d. 20 Jun 1883, nr Lovettsville, whooping cough, 0-3-0, p. Luther W. & Annie Hickman, b. LC, sc: L.W. Hickman, father, 2nd Dist., BVS:1883:3
HICKMAN, George, W, M, d. 27 Aug 1866, nr Lovettsville, typhoid fever, 50-0-0, p. Peter & Mary Hickman, b. LC, farmer, married, sc: Eleanora Hickman, wife, BVS:1866:1
HICKMAN, Jerry, B, M, d. 25 Nov 1884, Hillsboro, burned, 4-1-0, p. Lewis & Harriet Hickman, b. Hillsboro, unm, sc: Lewis Hickman, father, 3rd Dist., BVS:1884:6
HICKMAN, Lewis, B, M, d. 1 Dec 1888, LC, consumption, 51-0-0, p. unk, b. West Virginia, laborer, unm, sc:

Newman Brown, friend, 3rd Dist., BVS:1888:1

HICKMAN, Nellie J., W, F, d. 1 Oct 1879, nr Lovettsville, drowned, 2-7-0, p. Luther W. & Annie M. Hickman, b. LC, sc: Luther W. Hickman, father, 2nd Dist., BVS:1879:1

[HICKMAN], no name, W, M, d. 23 Jun 1857, LC, unk, 0-0-3, p. George & Eleanor M. Hickman, b. LC, sc: Eleanor M. Hickman, mother, BVS:1857:1, LC:24

HICKMAN, Thomas W., W, M, d. 1 Oct 1890, LC, unk, 0-0-1, p. M. E. Hickman, b. LC, none, unm, sc: T.W. Hickman, father, 2nd Dist., BVS:1890:3

HICKS, Jane, B, F, d. 25 Apr 1886, LC, dropsy, 75-0-0, b. LC, c/o: Richd Hicks, sc: Jas R. Hicks, son, 3rd Dist., BVS:1886:4

HIGGINS, Katie, W, F, d. 18 Sep 1878, nr Farmwell Station, typhoid pneumonia, 15-9-2, p. Hugh & Harriet Higgins, b. nr Farmwell Station, unm, sc: Harriet Higgins, mother, BR Dist., BVS:1878:4

HIGHT, Ida B, F, d. 12 Jan 1887, LC, mal. fever, 1-5-0, p. Jordan & Susan Hight, b. LC, unm, sc: Jordan Hight, father, 3rd Dist., BVS:1887:6

HILL, Chas., B, M, d. 28 Oct 1894, nr Sterling, tumor, 9-0-0, p. Marshal & Emma Hill, b. nr Sterling, sc: Marshall Hill, father, 1st Dist., BVS:1894:2

HILL, Elizabeth, W, F, d. 14 Jun 1871, Round Hill, old age, 89-0-0, p. not living, b. LC, c/o: James W. Hill, decd, sc: Priscilla Palmer, no relation, MT Dist., BVS:1871:5

HILL, Henry, B, M, d. 4 Mar 1874, Poor House, consumption, 60-0-0, p. unk, b. Fauquier Co., sc: Wm. H. Hibbs, superintendant, MC Dist., BVS:1874:4

HILL, Mary J., B, F, d. 1 Mar 1874, Hamilton, fever, 27-0-0, p. Lewis & Dusey Hill, b. LC, unm, sc: George Hill, brother, JF Dist., BVS:1874:2

HILL, Matilda, B, F, d. 3 Sep 1873, nr Unison, old age, 83-0-0, p. unk, b. unk, married, sc: Wm. H. Hibbs, superintendent of Poor, MC Dist., BVS:1873:5

HILLARY, Rosa, W, F, d. 14 Apr 1856, Lovettsville, pneumonia, 0-1-27, p. Wm. P. & Anna Hillary, b. Lovettsville, sc: Wm. P. Hillery, father, BVS:1856:1, LC:20

HILLEARY, Fannie, W, F, d. 10 Jul 1891, Lovettsville, consumption, 24-0-0, p. Henry & Sophia Hilleary, boarding house, unm, sc: mother, LV Dist., BVS:1891:5

HILLERY, Henry, W, M, d. 1874, Williamsburg, insanity, 35-0-0, LV Dist., BVS:1874:6

HINDMAN, Franklin P., W, M, d. 2 Jun 1853, LC, croup, 2-0-0, p. Saml. & Barbary Hindman, b. LC, sc: Saml Hindman, father, BVS:1854:4, LC:2

HINDMAN, Harriet E., W, F, d. 31 Aug 1853, LC, consumption, 3-0-0, p. Saml. & Barbary Hindman, b. LC, sc: Saml Hindman, father, BVS:1854:4, LC:2

HINDMAN, Hattie, W, F, d. 8 Apr 1876, nr Round Hill, unk, p. Mathew J. & Elizabeth F. Hindman, b. LC, unm, sc: Mathew J. Hindman, father, MT Dist., BVS:1876:1

HINDMAN, Mathew J., W, M, d. 10 Sep 1878, Round Hill, consumption, unk, p. Matthew & Sarah Hindman, carpenter, c/o: Elizabeth E. Hindman, sc: E.E. Hindman, wife, MT Dist., BVS:1878:2/3

HIRST, Elizabeth J., W, F, d. 10 Jan 1859/60, Leesburg, asthma, 24-3-6, p. Saml M. & Elizth F. Boss, b. Leesburg, c/o: Samuel N. Hirst, sc: Saml. N. Hirst, husband, BVS:1859:2, 1860:4, LC:37

HIRST, Mary, W, F, d. 6 Nov 1864, Hestin Hirst's, old age, 88-9-0, b. Frederick Co. MD, sc: Heston Hirst, son, BVS:1864:2, LC:39

HIRST, Samuel S., W, M, d. 22 Oct 1884, Lincoln, blood poison, 51-5-10, p. Heston & Ellen Hirst, b. Lincoln, farmer, c/o: Mary F. Hirst, sc: John T. Hirst, brother, 3rd Dist., BVS:1884:6

HISKETT, Susannah, W, F, d. 17 Jul 1875, nr Hillsboro, dropsy, 52-0-0, p. unk, b. Ohio, sc: Saml Clendening, friend, JF Dist., BVS:1875:3

HITAFFER, Elizabeth, W, F, d. 16 Nov 1877, nr Farmwell Station, dropsy etc., 58-0-0, p. Peyton & Pamela

Loudoun County, Virginia, Death Register, 1853-1896   133

Powell, b. LC, c/o: Wm. Hitaffer, sc: Wm. Hitaffer, husband, BR Dist., BVS:1877:1
HITAFFER, Sarah, W, F, d. 25 Sep 1831, LC, old age, 90-0-0, p. ___ Detrol, b. Pennsylvania, c/o: John Hitaffer, sc: Jas. A. Rollins, son-in-law, 2nd Dist., BVS:1881:6
HITT, Mary A., W, F, d. 4 Nov 1881, LC, dropsy, 79-0-0, b. LC, sc: W.L. Hitt, son, 1st Dist., BVS:1881:1
HIXON, John W., W, M, d. 29 Oct 1883, nr Dover, unk, 0-0-8, p. William N. & Mary E. Hixon, b. nr Dover, sc: William A. Hixon, father, 1st Dist., BVS:1883:1
HIXON, Maria J., W, F, d. 6 Aug 1887, Dover, consumption, 71-0-0, p. Joseph & Sarah Lynn, b. Louis Williams', LC, c/o: John H. Hixon, sc: John H. Hixon, husband, 1st Dist., BVS:1887:1
[HIXON], no name, W, M, d. 31 May 1884, LC, unk, 0-0-1, p. Wm. & Martha Hixon, b. LC, sc: William N. Hixon, father, 1st Dist., BVS:1884:1
HIXSON, Benjamin, W, M, d. 25 Mar 1857, res of John H. Hixson, paralysis, 68-0-0, p. James & Isabella Hixson, b. LC, miller, c/o: Tacy Hixson, sc: John D. Hixson, son, BVS:1857:4, LC:26
HIXSON, David, W, M, d. Jun 1865, Aldie, shot, 24-6-0, p. Al & Harriet Hixson, b. LC, soldier, unm, sc: Eliz Hutchison, cousin, BVS:1865:2
HIXSON, Tacy, W, F, d. 15 Sep 1854, son John's res, dropsy, 67-0-0, p. Abner & Mary Humphrey, b. nr Bloomfield, c/o: Benjamin Hixson, sc: John Hixson, son, BVS:1854:12, LC:11
HOCKLEY, Rosy, W, M, d. 11 Sep 1889, LC, unk, 0-1-0, p. A. J. & Eliza Hockley, b. LC, none, unm, sc: A.J. Hockley, father, 2nd Dist., BVS:1889:3
HODGE, Susan A., W, F, d. 11 Aug 1876, Lovettsville, paralysis, 67-0-0, p. Robert & Hannah Hodge, b. LC, unm, sc: Hannah M. Clapham, sister, LV Dist., BVS:1876:3
HOFFMAN, Eliza, W, F, d. 3 Mar 1857, LC, old age, 78-0-0, p. Peter & Mary D. Hoffman, b. Frederick City, MD,

unm, sc: Sophia Hoffman, niece, BVS:1857:1, LC:25
HOFFMAN, John, W, M, d. 10 Jun 1854, Snickersville, consumption, 70-0-0, p. Henry & Nancy Hoffman, b. Fairfax Co., farmer, c/o: Phebe Hoffman, sc: Phebe Hoffman, BVS:1854:11, LC:11
HOFFMAN, John, W, M, d. 31 Oct 1876, LC, kidney disease, 72-0-0, p. unk, b. unk, sc: Peter C. Hoffman, brother, LE Dist., BVS:1876:6
HOFFMAN, Otterbine, W, M, d. Oct 1883, nr Leesburg, unk, 70-0-0, p. Jacob & Elizth. Hoffman, b. Alexandria, farmer, unm, sc: Emily Hoffman, sister, 2nd Dist., BVS:1883:6
HOFFMAN, Peter E., W, M, d. Feb 1880, Leesburg, old age, 80-0-0, p. Jacob & Elizth. Hoffman, b. Alexandria, Va., farmer, unm, sc: Otterbein Hoffman, brother, 2nd Dist., BVS:1880:6
HOFFMAN, Selman A., W, M, d. 16 Mar 1893, Middleburg, pneumonia, 16-0-0, p. W. H. & Mary H. Hoffman, b. Middleburg, laborer, sc: W.H. Hoffman, father, 1st Dist., BVS:1893:1
HOFFMAN, Sophia, W, F, d. 21 Oct 1876, LC, old age, 70-0-0, p. unk, b. unk, sc: Peter C. Hoffman, brother, LE Dist., BVS:1876:6
HOGAN, Eugene, W, M, d. 6 Apr 1886, unk, 0-7-5, p. Jesse E. & Sarah C., sc: Jesse Hogans, father, 2nd Dist., BVS:1886:5
HOGAN, Fredie, B, M, d. 4 Oct 1891, nr Morrisonville, unk, 0-4-0, p. Wesley & Annie Hogan, b. Lovettsville, laborer, unm, sc: father, LV Dist., BVS:1891:5
HOGAN, Mary, W, F, d. 9 Dec 1884, LC, broken hip, 70-0-0, p. James & Bridget Mulhen, b. Ireland, c/o: Nicholas Hogan, sc: Nicholas Hogan, husband, 1st Dist., BVS:1884:1
HOGAN, Nicholas, W, M, d. 28 Feb 1888, Oatlands, old age, 72-0-0, p. unk, b. Ireland, sc: James W. Hogan, son, 1st Dist., BVS:1888:3
HOGAN, Patrick, W, M, d. 6 Jun 1891, Aldie, old age, 78-0-0, p. Michael & Mary Hogan, b. Ireland, laborer, c/o:

Bettie Hogan, sc: Jas W. Hogan, nephew, 1st Dist., BVS:1891:2

HOGAN, Zella, B, F, d. 10 Jul 1894, nr Arcola, consumption, 15-0-0, p. Fenton & Cath. Hogan, b. nr Sterling, sc: Cath. Hogan, mother, 1st Dist., BVS:1894:2

HOGE, Annie E., W, F, d. 9 May 1891, Unison, consumption, 21-0-0, p. G.D. & Lucy Hoge, b. Virginia & Ohio [sic], physician, unm, sc: G.D. Hoge, father, 1st Dist., BVS:1891:2

HOGE, Edward A., W, M, d. 1865, nr Hughesville, diphtheria, 11-0-0, p. Wm. & Rachell E. Hoge, b. nr Hughesville, farmer, sc: father, BVS:1865:1

HOGE, Emma, W, F, d. 31 Dec 1876, nr Philomont, diphtheria, unk, p. Geo. W. & Susan M. Hoge, b. LC, unm, sc: Geo. W. Hoge, father, MT Dist., BVS:1876:1

HOGE, Henrietta, W, F, d. 6 Nov 1871, Hughesville, consumption, 18-0-0, p. Jesse & Mary Ellen Hoge, b. LC, merchant, unm, sc: Jesse Hoge, father, MT Dist., BVS:1871:5

HOGE, Isaac F., W, M, d. 1 Jan 1884, Hamilton, internal injuries, 5-5-15, p. Isaac C. & Freddie Hoge, b. LC, unm, sc: Isaac Hoge, father, 3rd Dist., BVS:1884:6

HOGE, James, W, M, d. 28 Apr 1885, Hughesville, rheumatism etc., 72-0-0, b. LC, farmer, c/o: Phila Hoge, sc: Phila Hoge, wife, 3rd Dist., BVS:1885:6

HOGE, James R., W, M, d. Aug 1857, res of parents, bilious dysentery, 9-1-18, p. Thomas & Mary A. Hoge, b. res of parents, sc: Thomas Hoge, BVS:1857:3, LC:26

HOGE, Mary E., W, F, d. 17 Aug 1857, LC, dysentery, 27-0-0, p. Henry S. & Hannah J. Taylor, b. LC, c/o: Jesse Hoge, sc: Jesse Hoge, husband, BVS:1857:1, LC:25

HOGELAND, Jane T., W, F, d. 16 Feb 1889, LC, old age, 71-0-0, p. Samuel & Mary Ayers, b. LC, none, c/o: J.J. Hogeland, sc: J.J. Hogeland, husband, 2nd Dist., BVS:1889:3

HOGELAND, John, W, M, d. 12 Jun 1858, Hogeland's Factory, heart disease, 74-6-16, p. John & Frances Hogeland, b. Huntington Co., NJ, carder & fuller, c/o: Massie Hogeland, sc: Massie Hogeland, widow, BVS:1858:3, LC:30

HOLIDAY, Caldwell, W, M, d. 1 Jun 1874, nr Middleburg, pneumonia, 45-0-0, b. Fauquier Co., farmer, c/o: Mary J. Holiday, sc: Mary J. Holiday, wife, MC Dist., BVS:1874:4

[HOLIDAY], no name, B, M, d. 18 Oct 1865, nr Farmville, unk, 0-0-16, p. Stella Holiday, b. LC, unm, sc: Jas H. Palmer, head of family, BVS:1865:2

HOLLIDAY, Charles C., W, M, d. 10 Oct 1882, LC, diphtheria, 11-0-0, p. Henry & Mary Holliday, unm, sc: Henry Holliday, father, 1st Dist., BVS:1882:1

HOLLINGSWORTH, Abby, W, F, d. 9 Sep 1856, Waterford, whooping cough, 2-8-12, p. Robt. J. & Rachel J. Hollingsworth, b. LC, sc: Robert I. Hollingsworth, father, BVS:1856:1, LC:20

HOLLINGSWORTH, Lydia J, W, F, d. 20 Oct 1879, Waterford, cancer, 53-0-0, p. Lewis & Abigail Hollingsworth, b. LC, unm, sc: S.P. Sythe, friend, 3rd Dist., BVS:1879:3

HOLLINGSWORTH, Rob. P., W, M, d. 14 Oct 1888, LC, dyspepsia, 26-0-0, p. Chs. L. & Nancy C. Hollingsworth, b. LC, laborer, unm, sc: Chas L. Hollingsworth, father, 3rd Dist., BVS:1888:1

HOLLINGSWORTH, Robert J., W, M, d. Sep 1871, Waterford, unk, 57-0-0, b. Frederick Co. VA, sc: C. L. Hollingsworth, brother, JF Dist., BVS:1871:1

HOLLINGSWORTH, Sally A., W, F, d. 25 Oct 1853, LC, quinsy, 5-3-2, p. Rachel J. & Robt J. Hollingsworth, b. LC, sc: Robert Hollingsworth, father, BVS:1854:3, LC:2

HOLMES, Blanche, W, F, d. 15 Jul 1883, Hamilton, cholera infantum, 0-4-0, p. George W. & Rebecca Holmes, b. LC, sc: Geo W. Holmes, father, 3rd Dist., BVS:1883:5

HOLMES, Elisha, W, M, d. 28 Apr 1873, nr Mount Gilead, pneumonia, 63-6-6, p. William & Abigal Holmes, b. Green Hill, farmer, c/o: Hester J.

Holmes, sc: wife, MT Dist., BVS:1873:3

HOLMES, Elizabeth R., W, F, d. 5 Nov 1873, nr Hamilton, consumption, 72-1-5, p. Hamilton & Dinah Rogers, b. nr Hamilton, c/o: Elijah Holmes, sc: George T. Holmes, MT Dist., BVS:1873:3

HOLMES, Emily, W, F, d. 2 Mar 1882, LC, dyspepsia, 55-0-0, p. Elijah & Mary Holmes, b. LC, unm, sc: Hugh R. Holmes, brother, 3rd Dist., BVS:1882:3

HOLMES, Emily, W, F, d. 2 Mar 1881, LC, dyspepsia, 55-0-0, p. Elijah & Elizabeth Holmes, b. LC, unm, sc: Hugh R. Holmes, brother, 3rd Dist., BVS:1881:4

HOLMES, Mary Ann, B, F, d. 15 Aug 1892, Mountain Gap, child birth, 20-0-0, p. John & Sarah Utterback, b. Mountain Gap, consort, LE Dist., BVS:1892:5

HOLMES, no name, B, M, d. 15 Nov 1892, Mountain Gap, unk, 0-2-0, p. Robt. & Mary Holmes, b. Mountain Gap, unm, sc: Robert Holmes, LE Dist., BVS:1892:5

HOLMES, Warner, W, M, d. 14 Apr 1886, nr Mountville, old age, 80-0-0, p. unk, b. LC, wheelwright, unk, sc: Geo. McCarty, friend, 1st Dist., BVS:1886:1

HOLSTEN, Harmon, W, M, d. Dec 1857, unk, 32-0-0, p. unk, b. Germany, carpenter, sc: B.F. Saffer, friend, BVS:1857:7, LC:28

HOLTZCLAW, Jas. M., W, M, d. 3 Dec 1871, disease of the kidney, 40-0-0, farmer, married, BR Dist., BVS:1871:3

HOOE, Chas., B, M, d. 24 Dec 1896, nr Unison, consumption, 17-3-0, p. Clifford F. Hooe, b. nr Unison, none, unm, sc: Clifford Hooe, father, MC Dist., BVS:1896:1

HOOE, Nancy, W, F, d. 4 Oct 1881, LC, bright's disease, 73-0-0, b. LC, c/o: Harmon Hooe, sc: Harmon Hooe Jr., son, 3rd Dist., BVS:1881:4

HOOE, Sallie, W, M, d. 27 Dec 1857, res of parents, croup, 3-8-11, p. Jas. B. & Eliza J. Throckmorton, b. foot of Blue Ridge, sc: James B. Throckmorton, father, BVS:1857:5, LC:27

HOPE, Alice R., W, F, d. 4 Dec 1876, LC, inflammation bowels, 0-3-3, p. Chas. W. & Anna Hope, b. LC, sc: Chas. W. Hope, father, JF Dist., BVS:1876:8

HOPE, Lydia, W, F, d. 12 Oct 1883, nr Leesburg, consumption, 26-11-10, p. Jno. A. & Lydia Hope, b. LC, unm, sc: Lydia Hope, mother, 2nd Dist., BVS:1883:3

HOPE, Lydia, W, F, d. 20 Jul 1884, LC, heart disease, 68-0-0, p. James & Charlotte Reed, b. LC, c/o: John A. Hope, sc: John A. Hope, husband, 1st Dist., BVS:1884:1

HOPE, Mary E., W, F, d. 25 May 1855, LC, consumption, 16-3-7, p. John A. & Lydia Hope, b. LC, unm, sc: John A. Hope, father, BVS:1855:2, LC:15

HOPE, Robert F., W, M, d. 13 Dec 1883, nr Leesburg, affliction of spine, 0-2-15, p. Chas. W. & Annie C. Hope, b. LC, sc: Chas W. Hope, father, 2nd Dist., BVS:1883:3

HOPKINS, Betsy, B, F, d. 10 May 1880, Waterford, old age, 94-0-0, p. unk, b. unk, c/o: Harry Hopkins, sc: Alfred Craven, friend, 3rd Dist., BVS:1880:4

HORELL, Emma Ann, W, F, d. 20 Mar 1864, Girisley Reeder's, small pox, 18-9-0, p. Geo & Emssy Horell, b. LC, sc: Wm. A. Reeder, BVS:1864:1, LC:38

HORNSLEY, Elizabeth, W, F, d. 27 May 1854, Mavins Mill, pneumonia, 66-0-0, p. Robt. & Mary Mavin, b. Northumberland, England, c/o: George Hornsley, sc: Robt. & Wm. Mavin, brothers, BVS:1854:12, LC:11

HORSEMAN, Mary S., W, F, d. 23 Jan 1887, Farmwell, whooping cough, 2-0-0, p. James H. & Susan Horseman, b. Farmwell, sc: James H. Horseman, father, 1st Dist., BVS:1887:1

HORSEMAN, Sarah, W, F, d. 9 Nov 1886, nr Farmwell, pneumonia, 82-0-0, p. Stephen & Mary Horseman, b. LC, unm, sc: Wm. H. Horseman, brother, 1st Dist., BVS:1886:1

[HORSMAN], no name, W, F, d. 20 Mar 1873, nr Broad Run, unk, 0-0-15, p. William & Susan Horsman, b. nr Broad Run, sc: Wm. Horsman, head of family, BR Dist., BVS:1873:1

HORSMAN, Saml E., W, M, d. 28 Jan 1865, Bull Run, general debility, 31-6-0, p. Steven & S. Horsman, b. LC, soldier, unm, sc: Sallie Horsman, mother, BVS:1865:2

HOSKINSON, Ann A., W, F, d. 20 Jul 1853, LC, dysentery, 1-8-16, p. Robt. L. & Elizth. A. Hoskinson, b. LC, sc: Elizth A. Hoskinson, mother, BVS:1854:4, LC:3

HOSKINSON, Ellen, W, F, d. 18 Mar 1854, old age, 85-0-0, b. LC, c/o: Andrew Hoskinson, sc: Wm. A. Lanham, friend, BVS:1854:13, LC:13

HOSKINSON, Francis E., W, M, d. 25 Aug 1858, LC, measles, 0-9-0, p. Robt I. & Elizth A. Hoskinson, b. LC, sc: Robt J. Hoskinson, father, BVS:1858:1, LC:29

HOSKINSON, Ida V., W, F, d. 24 Sep 1865, nr Goresville, typhoid fever, unk, p. Thoms H. & Ann V. Hoskinson, b. LC, S. teacher, married, sc: Thoms H. Hoskinson, father, 1st Dist., BVS:1865:3/4

HOSKINSON, James A., W, M, d. 30 Dec 1894, Bolington, pneumonia, 0-2-0, p. Robt. & Laura, b. Bolington, unm, sc: R. H. Hoskinson, LV Dist., BVS:1894:4

HOSKINSON, James F., W, M, d. 13 Dec 1889, LC, cholera, 1-0-0, p. R. H. & Laura Hoskinson, b. LC, none, unm, sc: R.H. Hoskinson, father, 2nd Dist., BVS:1889:3

HOSKINSON, Jesse R., W, M, d. 11 Dec 1888, LC, choked, 1-10-27, p. R. H. & Laura Hoskinson, b. LC, none, unm, sc: R.H. Hoskinson, father, 2nd Dist., BVS:1888:6

HOSKINSON, Laura B., W, F, d. 2 Jul 1853, LC, dysentery, 0-0-11, p. Thos. W. & Virginia Hoskinson, b. LC, sc: Thomas W. Hoskinson, father, BVS:1854:4, LC:3

HOSKINSON, Thomas, W, M, d. 15 Nov 1880, Mt. Hope, Md., complication of diseases, 69-0-0, p. --- Hoskinson, b. LC, teacher, c/o: Virginia Hoskinson, sc: Clinton Hoskinson, son, 2nd Dist., BVS:1880:6

HOSKINSON, Thos. L, W, M, d. 27 Nov 1875, Hamilton, pneumonia, 74-0-0, p. Nathan & Elizabeth, b. Maryland, carpenter, unm, sc: Robert Hoskinson, son, MT Dist., BVS:1875:8

[HOSPITTLE], Rebecca Jane, W, F, d. 14 Jan 1854, Millville, scarlet fever, 4-4-14, p. Lucellus & Catherine Hospittle, b. Millville, sc: Lucellus Hospittle, BVS:1854:11, LC:10

HOUGH, Abner E., W, M, d. 8 Jul 1884, Waterford, brain fever, 6-10-0, p. Beverly R. & Mary C.Hough, b. LC, unm, sc: B.R. Hough, father, 3rd Dist., BVS:1884:6

HOUGH, Charles S., W, M, d. 5 Sep 1858, Leesburg, unk, unk, p. L.W.S. & Sarah Hough, b. Leesburg, sc: L.W.S. Hough, father, BVS:1858:1, LC:29

HOUGH, Cora O., W, F, d. 27 Aug 1856, Lovettsville, unk, 0-2-0, p. Derizo C. & Mattie A. Hough, b. Lovettsville, sc: Derizo C. Hough, father, BVS:1856:1, LC:20

HOUGH, Eliza N., W, F, d. 15 Apr 1881, LC, tumor, 78-0-0, b. LC, c/o: Wm. Hough, sc: David Hough, son, 3rd Dist., BVS:1881:4

HOUGH, Faith, W, F, d. 2 Aug 1872, Stumptown, cholera infantum, 0-9-4, p. Wm. & Duana Hough, b. LC, sc: Duanna Hough, mother, LE Dist., BVS:1872:3

HOUGH, Fannie A., W, F, d. 10 Mar 1887, LC, dropsy, 51-0-0, p. Thos. & Ann Rinker, b. LC, c/o: Louis N. Hough, sc: Louis N. Hough, husband, 3rd Dist., BVS:1887:6

HOUGH, Hattie, W, F, d. 15 Aug 1871, Alexandria, 0-0-16, p. Sarah P. & Duane Coe, MC Dist., BVS:1871:2

HOUGH, I. ? A., W, F, d. 29 Nov 1890, Waterford, heart disease, 37-0-0, p. John P. & Annie Robb, b. LC, none, c/o: Robt. W. Hough, sc: Robt. W. Hough, husband, 3rd Dist., BVS:1890:6

HOUGH, Ida, W, F, d. 18 Jul 1875, Waterford, consumption, 18-0-0, p. Samuel & Polly Hough, b. LC, sc: Samuel Hough, father, JF Dist., BVS:1875:3

HOUGH, Isaac S., W, M, d. 28 Sep 1866, Milltown, mental

derangement, 57-0-0, p. Wm. H. & Phebe Hough, b. LC, manufacturer, married, sc: Isaac S. Hough, son, BVS:1866:1

HOUGH, James A., W, M, d. 30 Jun 1891, nr Upperville, dropsy, 64-0-0, p. J. I. & Nancy Hough, b. LC, farmer, unm, sc: Chas Hough, brother, 1st Dist., BVS:1891:2

HOUGH, John, W, M, d. 5 Jan 1854, LC, unk, 0-0-1, p. Wm. & Sarah A. Hough, b. LC, sc: Wm. Hough, father, BVS:1854:8, LC:8

HOUGH, John J., W, M, d. 8 Aug 1890, Hamilton, typhoid fever, 30-0-0, b. LC, laborer, unm, sc: W. Hough, father, 3rd Dist., BVS:1890:6

HOUGH, John R., W, M, d. 14 Aug 1885, Waterford, spasms, 1-0-9, p. Robt. W. & Ida Hough, b. LC, sc: R.W. Hough, father, 3rd Dist., BVS:1885:6

HOUGH, Leven W. S., W, M, d. Aug 1890, LC, paralysis, 70-0-0, p. unk, b. LC, none, c/o: Mary L. Hough, sc: M.L. Hough, widow, 2nd Dist., BVS:1890:4

HOUGH, Mahala F., W, F, d. 12 Dec 1893, Purcellville, paralysis, 65-0-0, p. unk, b. Fauquier Co., wife, sc: husband, JF Dist., BVS:1893:3

HOUGH, Mahala F., W, F, d. Dec 1892, Purcellville, paralysis, 65-0-0, p. Nelson & Ellen Garrison, b. Fauquier Co., farmer, wife, sc: Saml Hough, JF Dist., BVS:1892:7

HOUGH, Mary A., W, F, d. 28 Sep 1854, LC, consumption, 31-0-0, p. Nancy Bramhall, b. LC, c/o: John Hough, sc: Ann S. Hough, step-dau, BVS:1854:8, LC:7

HOUGH, Mary C., W, F, d. 29 Sep 1855, LC, croup, 2-9-0, p. Jno. & Mary A. Hough, b. LC, sc: John Grubb, friend, BVS:1855:1, LC:14

HOUGH, Mary C., W, F, d. 12 Jun 1884, Waterford, consumption, 33-0-0, p. David & Mary Orrison, b. LC, c/o: Beverly R. Hough, sc: B.R. Hough, husband, 3rd Dist., BVS:1884:6

HOUGH, Mary T., W, F, d. 6 Dec 1853, LC, cancer, 63-0-0, p. Thomas & Mary A. Hough, b. LC, unm, sc: Wm. Hough, brother, BVS:1854:4, LC:2

HOUGH, Nelson B., W, M, d. 29 Apr 1888, LC, unk, 0-0-13, p. B. R. & S. A. Hough, b. LC, none, unm, sc: B.R. Hough, father, 3rd Dist., BVS:1888:1

HOUGH, Oscar B., W, M, d. 12 May 1856, Waterford, croup, 2-6-0, p. Geo. W. & Margaret J. Hough, b. Waterford, sc: George W. Hough, father, BVS:1856:1, LC:19

HOUGH, Rosa A., W, F, d. 18 Jan 1892, Waterford, lagrippe, 29-3-20, p. William & Hannah, b. LC, unm, sc: Irwin Hough, LV Dist., BVS:1892:6

HOUGH, Sarah M., W, F, d. 18 Apr 1890, Hillsboro, grip, 72-0-11, p. Samuel & Rebecca Love, b. LC, c/o: W.N. Hough, sc: W.N. Hough, husband, 3rd Dist., BVS:1890:6

HOUGH, Sarah V., W, F, d. 15 Nov 1854, LC, water on brain, 4-1-5, p. Denzo C. & Eleanor Hough, b. LC, sc: Wm. H. Hough, uncle, BVS:1854:8, LC:7

HOUGH, Silas F., W, M, d. 2 Aug 1881, LC, consumption, 37-0-0, p. Saml. & Polly Hough, b. LC, painter, unm, sc: Saml Hough, father, 3rd Dist., BVS:1881:4

HOUGH, Stanley, W, M, d. 20 Oct 1884, Waterford, diphtheria, 3-10-0, p. Ida & E.P. Hough, b. Waterford, unm, sc: Ida Hough, mother, 3rd Dist., BVS:1884:6

HOUGH, Thaddeus, W, M, d. 6 Oct 1878, nr Farmwell Station, typhoid fever, 19-9-12, p. Calhoun & Ann Hough, b. nr Lovettsville, farmer, unm, sc: C.C. Hough, father, BR Dist., BVS:1878:4

HOUGH, Virginia, W, F, d. 15 Sep 1856, LC, typhoid fever, 5-0-3, p. Isaac S. & Mary J. Hough, b. LC, sc: Isaac S. Hough, father, BVS:1856:2, LC:20

HOUGH, William, W, M, d. 25 Nov 1886, LC, apoplexy, 71-1-0, b. LC, merchant, c/o: Louisa Hough, sc: Thos E. Hough, son, 3rd Dist., BVS:1886:4

HOUGH, William, W, M, d. 15 May 1877, LC, rupture of tumor, 75-0-0, p. Garrett & Elizabeth Hough, b. Leesburg, carpenter, c/o: Sarah A.

Hough, sc: Sarah A. Hough, wife, LV Dist., BVS:1877:4/7

HOUGH, William H., W, M, d. 19 Feb 1892, Waterford, lagrippe, 74-2-19, p. unk, b. LC, farmer, consort, sc: Irwin Hough, LV Dist., BVS:1892:6

HOUGH, Wilson S., W, M, d. 14 Apr 1878, LC, pneumonia, 0-3-6, p. L. W. & Mary Lou Hough, b. LC, unm, sc: L.W.S. Hough, father, LE Dist., BVS:1878:8

HOUGH, Wm. N., W, F[sic, d. 7 Sep 1891, Hillsboro, canker, 78-0-0, p. Wm. & Jane Hough, b. Hillsboro, husband, sc: Saml W. Hough, JF Dist., BVS:1891:7

HOUGHTON, Hannah J., W, F, d. 10 Mar 1885, nr Guilford, scarlet fever, 22-0-0, p. John & Mary Houghton, b. Pennsylvania, sc: Cyrus Baker, friend, 1st Dist., BVS:1885:3

HOURIHANE, Johanna, W, F, d. 23 Feb 1888, LC, spinal meningitis, 48-0-0, p. unk, b. Ireland, none, c/o: Michael Hourihane, sc: Michael Hourihane, husband, 2nd Dist., BVS:1888:6

HOUSE, Sarah Ann, W, F, d. 23 Oct 1854, res, spinal affection, 32-0-0, p. Eli & Hannah Pierpoint, b. father's res, c/o: E. C. H. House, sc: husband, BVS:1854:13, LC:12

HOUSEHOLDER, Catharine, W, F, d. 15 Aug 1859/60, LC, apoplexy, 42-0-0, p. Peter & Catherine Compher, b. LC, c/o: Jacob Householder, sc: Jacob Householder, husband, BVS:1859:1, 1860:4, LC:37

HOUSEHOLDER, Daniel, W, M, d. 17 Nov 1865, nr Lovettsville, old age, 91-6-2, p. Daniel Householder, b. Berks Co., Penn, c/o: Priscilla Householder, sc: Adam Householder, son, 1st Dist., BVS:1865:4

HOUSEHOLDER, Gideon, W, M, d. 1 Feb 1896, Lovettsville, gen. debility, 76-0-0, p. unk, b. unk, farmer, consort, sc: Eugene Householder, LV Dist., BVS:1896:7

HOUSEHOLDER, Jacob, W, M, d. 2 Nov 1866, nr Stone Church, typhoid fever, 54-0-0, p. Danl. & Cathrn. Housholder, b. LC, married, sc: Oscar Householder, son, BVS:1866:1

HOUSEHOLDER, Sarah C., W, F, d. 23 Nov 1866, nr Stone Church, typhoid fever, 29-0-0, p. Thos. & Fanney A. Johnson, b. LC, c/o: Jacob Householder, sc: T. Johnson, father, BVS:1866:1

HOUSEHOLDER, Silas A., W, M, d. 10 Mar 1888, LC, consumption, 61-0-0, p. Daniel & Priscilla Householder, b. LC, farmer, c/o: Roxanne Householder, sc: R. Housholder, widow, 2nd Dist., BVS:1888:5

HOUSEHOLDER, Veleina G., W, F, d. 4 Nov 1866, nr Stone Church, typhoid fever, 10-0-0, p. Jacob & Cath. Householder, b. LC, sc: Oscar Householder, brother, BVS:1866:1

HOUSEHOLDER, Virginia C., W, F, d. 28 Nov 1866, nr Stone Church, typhoid fever, 23-0-0, p. Jacob & Cath. Householder, b. LC, unm, sc: Oscar Householder, brother, BVS:1866:1

HOUSER, Mary F., W, F, d. 1 Aug 1887, LC, consumption, 39-0-0, b. LC, c/o: Charles Howser, sc: Chas Howser, husband, 3rd Dist., BVS:1887:6

HOUSER, Philip, W, M, d. 15 Oct 1876, nr Farmwell Station, chronic rheumatism, 61-1-0, p. Philip & Deliverance Houser, b. LC, merchant, married, sc: B.A. Houser, son, BR Dist., BVS:1876:2

HOUSER, Sarah E., W, F, d. 12 May 1890, Farmwell, pneumonia, 36-0-0, p. Hugh & Harriet Higgins, b. Farmwell, c/o: Philip A. Howser, sc: Philip A. Houser, husband, 1st Dist., BVS:1890:1

HOUSER, Ziephie A., W, F, d. 12 Oct 1865, Mount Middleton farm, typhoid fever, 23-0-12, p. Richd & M.W. Houser, b. Farmwell, unm, sc: Richd Houser, father, BVS:1865:2

HOUSHOLDER, Adam, W, M, d. 14 Sep 1883, nr Lovettsville, diabetes, 74-0-0, p. David & --- Housholder, b. LC, farmer, unm, sc: Silas Housholder, brother, 2nd Dist., BVS:1883:7

HOUSHOLDER, Danl, W, M, d. 17 Nov 1865, nr Lovettsville, old age, 91-6-2, p. Adam Housholder, b. Bucks Co., PA, c/o: Priscella Householder,

Loudoun County, Virginia, Death Register, 1853-1896

sc: Adam Housholder, son, BVS:1865:3

HOWARD, Aleck, B, M, d. 11 Dec 1883, nr Leesburg, typhoid fever, 30-0-0, p. ---Howard, b. LC, laborer, c/o: Martha Howard, sc: Jno M. Orr, friend, 2nd Dist., BVS:1883:3

HOWARD, Almarian, W, M, d. 27 Dec 1875, nr Guilford, croup, 4-4-0, p. Chas. O. & Harriet B. Howard, b. nr Guilford, unm, sc: C.O.. Howard, head of family, BR Dist., BVS:1875:5

HOWARD, Burrell, B, M, d. 25 Jun 1887, Unison, consumption, 1-0-0, p. Chas. & Adelaide Howard, b. Unison, sc: Charles Howard, father, 1st Dist., BVS:1887:2

HOWARD, Charles, W, M, d. 8 Dec 1881, LC, unk, 1-0-0, p. Chas O. & H.O. Howard, b. LC, sc: C.O. Howard, father, 1st Dist., BVS:1881:1

HOWARD, Harriet A., W, F, d. 11 Dec 1875, nr Guilford, croup, 3-3-11, p. Chas. O. & Harriet B. Howard, b. nr Guilford, unm, sc: C.O.. Howard, head of family, BR Dist., BVS:1875:5

HOWARD, Jno., B, M, d. 11 Oct 1893, nr Unison, typhoid fever, 17-2-0, p. Chas. & Ada Howard, b. nr Unison, laborer, sc: Chas Howard, father, 1st Dist., BVS:1893:2

HOWARD, Joseph, B, M, d. 20 Jun 1880, LC, consumption, 0-10-0, p. Charles & Adelaide Howard, b. LC, unm, sc: Adelaide Howard, mother, 1st Dist., BVS:1880:1

HOWARD, Joseph, B, M, d. 20 Sep 1881, LC, pneumonia, 1-0-0, p. Jos & Adalaid Howard, b. LC, sc: A. Howard, mother, 1st Dist., BVS:1881:1

HOWARD, Mary, B, F, d. 20 Apr 1894, nr Bloomfield, typhoid fever, 17-0-0, p. Jacob & Sophia Howard, b. nr Bloomfiled, sc: Jacob Howard, father, 1st Dist., BVS:1894:2

HOWARD, Nancy, B, F, d. 29 Dec 1882, LC, strangulation, 0-0-28, p. Charles & Nancy Howard, b. LC, unm, sc: Charles Howard, father, 1st Dist., BVS:1882:1

HOWARD, no name, B, M, d. 15 Dec 1877, St. Louis, unk, 0-0-2, p. Burson & Sarah Howard, b. LC, sc: Burson Howard, father, MC Dist., BVS:1877:5

HOWARD, Roy, B, M, d. 10 Dec 1890, nr Bloomfield, croup, 0-10-0, p. Chas & Alice Howard, b. nr Bloomfield, sc: Burr Stiles, brother-in-law, 1st Dist., BVS:1890:1

HOWARD, Sarah A., B, F, d. 1 Sep 1872, William Seaton's, 50-0-0, sc: William Seaten, MC Dist., BVS:1872:7

HOWARD, Tad, B, M, d. 15 Sep 1881, LC, consumption, 27-0-0, p. Burns & Ann Howard, b. LC, sc: Burns Howard, father, 1st Dist., BVS:1881:1

HOWELL, David, W, M, d. 19 Sep 1871, Bunker Hill, fever, 69-0-0, p. not living, b. LC, mechanic, c/o: Hannah Howell, sc: Joseph W. Howell, son, MT Dist., BVS:1871:5

HOWELL, Geans, W, F, d. 8 Oct 1873, nr Bunkers Hill, information brain(twin), 0-1-22, p. Joseph & Amanda A. Howell, b. nr Bunkers Hill, sc: parents, MT Dist., BVS:1873:3

HOWELL, Harmon C., W, M, d. 15 Aug 1857, Missouri, lightning, 27-0-0, p. David & Mahala Howell, b. LC, cabinet maker, c/o: Rachel Howell, sc: David J. Howell, father, BVS:1857:4, LC:27

HOWELL, Jeanetta, W, F, d. 8 Oct 1873, nr Bunkers Hill, information brain(twin), 0-1-22, p. Joseph & Amanda A. Howell, b. nr Bunkers Hill, sc: parents, MT Dist., BVS:1873:3

HOWELL, Jesse, W, M, d. 1 Feb 1854, son Craven's, old age, 83-11-22, p. Wm. & Martha Howell, b. Pennsylvania, likely, farmer, c/o: Hannah Howell, decd, sc: Craven Howell, son, BVS:1854:12, LC:12

HOWELL, Mary, W, F, d. 24 Aug 1877, LC, old age, 93-0-0, p. Jno. & Sarah Smith, b. LC, c/o: Israel Howell, sc: Sarah B?, daughter, JF Dist., BVS:1877:3

HOWELL, Mary B., W, F, d. 23 Apr 1876, nr Lincoln, 0-0-4, p. John M. & Fanniel L. Howell, b. LC, unm, sc: John M. Howell, father, MT Dist., BVS:1876:1

HOWELL, no name, W, M, d. 30 Aug 1885, Mount Gilead, unk, 0-0-15, p. Jos. M. & Rose Howell, b. LC, sc: Jos M. Howell, father, 3rd Dist., BVS:1885:6

HOWELL, Thompson J., W, M, d. 11 Oct 1857, Missouri, dysentery, 22-2-0, p. Craven & Anna Howell, b. on Blue Ridge, sc: Craven Howell, father, BVS:1857:5, LC:27

HOWSER, Catherine, W, F, d. Oct 1894, Woodburn, old age, 74-0-0, p. Charles Howser, b. Woodburn, wife, sc: Charles Howser, son, 3rd Dist., BVS:1894:5

HOWSER, Mary Ann, W, F, d. 25 Nov 1876, LC, heart disease, 65-0-0, p. unk, b. unk, c/o: Richard Howser, sc: James R. Howser, son, LE Dist., BVS:1876:6

[HOWSER], no name, W, M, d. 2 Oct 1876, LC, spasms, 0-1-0, p. William & Linna C. Howser, b. LC, sc: W.C. Howser, father, LE Dist., BVS:1876:6

HOWSER, Rebecca, W, F, d. 10 Jun 1856, LC, bilious fever, 56-0-0, p. unk, b. Maryland, c/o: Samuel H. Howser, sc: Samuel H. Howser, husband, BVS:1856:2, LC:21

HOWSER, Richard, W, M, d. 19 Nov 1883, nr Leesburg, gravel, 75-0-0, p. Wm. Howser, b. LC, c/o: Mary A. Howser, sc: James R. Howser, son, 2nd Dist., BVS:1883:6

HUGHES, Ada Lee, W, F, d. 25 Mar 1866, Missouri, diphtheria, 14-0-0, p. Jno H. & Martha Hughes, b. Hughesville, sc: father, BVS:1866:2

HUGHES, Amos, W, M, d. 27 Jan 1890, Hughesville, pneumonia, 67-0-0, p. Thomas & Martha Hughes, b. LC, farmer, c/o: Cornelia Hughes, sc: Cornelia Hughes, wife, 3rd Dist., BVS:1890:6

HUGHES, Betsey, B, F, d. 16 Mar 1882, LC, unk, 35-0-0, p. unk, c/o: Wormley Hughes, sc: Wormley Hughes, husband, 1st Dist., BVS:1882:1

HUGHES, Elias, W, M, d. 6 Sep 1890, Hughesville, unk, 65-0-0, p. Thomas & Martha Hughes, b. LC, farmer, c/o: Virginia Hughes, sc: Virginia Hughes, wife, 3rd Dist., BVS:1890:6

HUGHES, Wallis, B, M, d. 5 Oct 1882, LC, general debility, 80-0-0, p. unk, b. LC, laborer, c/o: Priscilla Hughes, sc: Priscilla Hughes, wife, 3rd Dist., BVS:1882:3

HULFISH, Arthur, W, M, d. 20 Aug 1887, LC, dysentery, 9-0-0, p. Garrett & Sorona Hulfish, b. LC, unm, sc: Garrett Hulfish, father, 3rd Dist., BVS:1887:6

HULFISH, Herbert, W, M, d. 13 Nov 1888, LC, consumption, 18-0-0, p. G. D. & S. M. Hulfish, b. LC, none, unm, sc: G.L. Hulfish, father, 3rd Dist., BVS:1888:1

HUMES, Sylvester, B, M, d. 10 Aug 1887, Mountville, consumption, 7-0-0, p. Julius & Gertie Humes, b. Mountville, sc: Edward Moton, cousin, 1st Dist., BVS:1887:2

HUMMER, Alice M., W, F, d. 4 Jun 1865, Guilford Station, diphtheria, 0-10-0, p. B.E. & L.S. Hummer, b. LC, unm, sc: B.E. Hummer, father, BVS:1865:1

HUMMER, Erasmus K., W, M, d. 4 Apr 1858, LC, unk, 18-0-0, p. Wash. & Martena Hummer, b. LC, sc: W. Hummer, father, BVS:1858:6, LC:33

HUMMER, Laura T., W, F, d. 21 Oct 1874, Broad Run Dist., scarlet fever, 33-8-9, p. Jas. & Amelia M. Whaley, b. LC, c/o: Braden E. Hummer, sc: Braden E. Hummer, husband, BR Dist., BVS:1874:3

HUMMER, Leah J., W, F, d. 18 Apr 1866, nr Guilford Station, consumption, 34-1-32, p. John & Leah H. Tippett, b. Guilford Station, sc: G.W. Hummer, husband, BVS:1866:3

HUMMER, Martha B., W, M[sic], d. 8 Nov 1882, LC, old age, 86-0-0, p. W. G. F. & Mary Hummer, widower, sc: G.W. Hummer, brother, 1st Dist., BVS:1882:1

HUMMER, Martha V., W, F, d. 1 Sep 1883, nr Guilford, consumption, 30-0-0, p. unk, b. LC, c/o: Alpheus Hummer, sc: Alpheus Hummer, husband, 1st Dist., BVS:1883:1

HUMMER, Virginia, W, F, d. 2 Oct 1892, Philomont, diphtheria, 6-0-0, p. Maurice & Kate Hummer, b. Philomont, farmer, sc: Maurice

Loudoun County, Virginia, Death Register, 1853-1896 141

Hummer, father, MT Dist., BVS:1892:8

HUMMER, W. Roy, W, F, d. 12 Oct 1892, Philomont, diphtheria, 0-9-0, p. Maurice & Kate Hummer, b. Philomont, sc: Maurice Hummer, father, MT Dist., BVS:1892:8

HUMMER, Washg, W, M, d. 8 Jul 1865, Guilford Station, gravel, 68-4-15, p. Wm. & Rachel Hummer, b. LC, farmer, consort, sc: G.W.F. Hummer, son, BVS:1865:1

HUMPHREY, Jane, B, F, d. 1 Aug 1884, Hamilton, asthma, 52-0-0, b. Hamilton, c/o: Wm. Humphrey, sc: Wm. Humphrey, husband, 3rd Dist., BVS:1884:6

HUMPHREY, Jane, W, F, d. 5 Aug 1881, LC, dyspepsia, 55-0-0, b. LC, c/o: Thos C. Humphry, sc: T.C. Humphry, husband, 1st Dist., BVS:1881:1

HUMPHREY, Jas. R., W, M, d. 24 Jul 1853, nr Poor House, dysentery, 3-9-16, p. Wm. & Jane Humphrey, b. nr Poor House, sc: mother, BVS:1854:7, LC:6

HUMPHREY, Joseph G., W, M, d. 27 Sep 1856, res of parents, 0-0-14, p. Abner G. & Mary C. Humphrey, b. Bunker Hill, sc: A.G. Humphrey, father, BVS:1856:4, LC:22

HUMPHREY, Luther, W, M, d. 5 Jun 1866, nr Bunkers Hill, inflammation bowel, 16-0-0, p. Thos L. & Dorcas Humphrey, b. Bunker Hill, sc: father, BVS:1866:2

HUMPHREY, Mary A., W, F, d. 15 Aug 1881, LC, consumption, 46-0-0, b. LC, sc: A.G. Chamblin, friend, 1st Dist., BVS:1881:1

HUMPHREY, Thomas G., W, M, d. 16 Aug 1856, res, poison, 56-4-10, p. Abner & Mary Humphrey, b. place of death, farmer, c/o: Phebe Humphrey, sc: Margaret A. Humphrey, daughter, BVS:1856:5, LC:22

HUMPHREY, Thomas M., W, M, d. 18 Oct 1869, LC, paralysis, 65-0-0, b. LC, farmer, married, sc: Lydia Humphrey, wife, BVS:1869:1

HUMPHREY, Wm., B, M, d. 1 Jul 1891, Irene, old age, 80-0-0, b. Ireland, laborer, husband, sc: Mary

Humphrey, head of family, JF Dist., BVS:1891:7

HUMPHREYS, Thos. H., W, M, d. 10 Jun 1884, LC, snake bite, 37-0-0, p. Thos. & Mary Humphreys, b. England, farmer, c/o: Tacey Humphreys, sc: Tacy Humphreys, wife, 1st Dist., BVS:1884:1

HUMPHRIES, Richard T., W, M, d. 21 Sep 1878, Bellfield, unk, 0-0-3, p. Thomas & Gertrude Humphries, b. LC, sc: Thomas Humphries, father, MC Dist., BVS:1878:6

HUNT, Mary, W, F, d. Sep 1874, Leesburg, summer complaint, unk, c/o: Lewis Hunt, sc: Lewis Hunt, husband, LE Dist., BVS:1874:5

HUNT, Taylor, W, M, d. 10 Jan 1889, LC, bright's disease, 38-0-0, b. LC, merchant, unm, sc: Anzy Hunt, father, 3rd Dist., BVS:1889:5

HUNT, William, W, M, d. 6 Aug 1857, LC, consumption, 65-0-0, p. unk, b. LC, blacksmith, c/o: Elizth Hunt, sc: Elizth Hunt, wife, BVS:1857:1, LC:25

HUNT, William, W, M, d. 4 Aug 1869, LC, drunkenness, 51-3-0, p. Lewis & Mary Hunt, b. LC, shoemaker, married, sc: Mary Jane Hunt, wife, BVS:1869:1

HUNTER, A., B, M, d. 28 Aug 1896, nr Unison, old age, 80-0-0, p. unk, b. unk, none, unm, sc: F.E. Robey, head of family, MC Dist., BVS:1896:1

HUNTER, Ann, W, F, d. 28 Apr 1859/60, LC, old age, 88-6-5, p. unk, b. LC, unm, sc: Mary A. Titus, daughter, BVS:1859:1, 1860:3, LC:36

HUNTER, Ednor Leola, W, F, d. Sep 1896, Snickersville, cholera phantum, 0-7-0, p. W. & Lillian Hunter, b. Snickersville, laborer, sc: W. Hunter, father, MT Dist., BVS:1896:9

HUNTER, Florence, W, F, d. 20 Aug 1889, LC, unk, 0-0-1, p. W. H. & Margaret Hunter, b. LC, none, unm, sc: W.H. Hunter, father, 2nd Dist., BVS:1889:3

HUNTER, Harriet, B, F, d. 5 Oct 1888, LC, old age, 72-0-0, p. unk, b. LC, none, unm, sc: Henry Cully, brother-in-law, 2nd Dist., BVS:1888:5

HUNTER, Ida S., W, F, d. 25 Feb 1866, E side of Short Hill, unk, p. M. L. & Mary Hunter, b. LC, sc: Michl. Hunter, father, BVS:1866:1

HUNTER, Ida V., W, F, d. 12 Aug 1865, nr Short Hill, diphtheria, 2-1-17, p. Geo & Amanda Hunter, b. LC, farmer, sc: George P. Hunter, father, 1st Dist., BVS:1865:3/4

HUNTER, Joshua, B, M, d. 11 Apr 1885, nr Leesburg, old age 75, unk, p. unk, c/o: Rosetta Hunter, sc: Rosetta L. Hunter, daughter, 2nd Dist., BVS:1885:1

HUNTER, Margaret, W, F, d. 17 Sep 1865, nr Short Hill, typhoid fever, 27-0-0, p. Michael & Sarah Virts, b. LC, farmer, c/o: M. Hunter, sc: Michael Hunter, husband, 1st Dist., BVS:1865:3/4

HUNTER, Mary A., W, F, d. Oct 1856, LC, unk, 0-10-10, p. John & Mary Hunter, b. LC, sc: John Hunter, father, BVS:1856:7, LC:24

HUNTER, Michael, W, M, d. 3 Jun 1876, nr Short Hill, killed by lightning, 42-0-0, p. Wm & Elizabeth Hunter, b. LC, farmer, c/o: Ruth H. Hunter, sc: Ruth H. Hunter, wife, LV Dist., BVS:1876:3

HUNTER, Walter, W, M, d. 5 Oct 1873, nr Short Hill, unk, 0-3-16, p. Richd L. & Ruth H. Hunter, b. nr Short Hill, farmer, married, sc: ___ Hunter, father, LV Dist., BVS:1873:4

HURLEY, Reuben, (f), M, d. 1 Nov 1858, LC, murdered, 55-0-0, b. LC, sc: A.W. Johnson, friend, BVS:1858:6, LC:33

HURST, Bettie R., W, F, d. 27 Sep 1886, Bloomfield, unk, 0-0-12, p. Edwards S. & Ann V. Hurst, b. Bloomfield, sc: Edward S. Hurst, father, 1st Dist., BVS:1886:1

HURST, Heaton, W, M, d. 27 Jul 1873, nr Lincoln, pressure of the brain, 73-11-11, p. John & Mary Hurst, b. nr Lincoln, farmer, c/o: Leah Hurst, sc: Samuel S. Hurst, MT Dist., BVS:1873:3

HURST, Hope, W, F, d. 22 Mar 1886, Trappe, unk, 0-0-6, p. Samuel G. & Lucy Hurst, b. Trappe, sc: Samuel G. Hurst, father, 1st Dist., BVS:1886:1

HURST, Mamie L., W, F, d. 3 Sep 1890, Lincoln, inflammation stomach, 18-0-0, p. Smith & May F. Hurst, b. LC, farmer, unm, sc: May F. Hurst, mother, 3rd Dist., BVS:1890:6

HURST, Robert C., W, M, d. 8 Apr 1880, LC, teething, 1-3-0, p. R. S. & Mary Hurst, b. LC, unm, sc: Mary Hurst, mother, 1st Dist., BVS:1880:1

HUTCHISON, Andrew J., W, M, d. 19 Apr 1854, unk, 32-8-0, p. Richard & Eliz. Hutchison, b. LC, sc: Pickering Hutchison, brother-in-law, BVS:1854:13, LC:13

HUTCHISON, Annie, W, F, d. 23 Sep 1881, LC, consumption, 29-0-0, p. Jos. Hutchison, b. LC, sc: S.J. Clark, friend, 1st Dist., BVS:1881:1

HUTCHISON, Charles J., W, M, d. 19 Sep 1854, dysentery, 16-3-0, p. Sampson & R. Hutchison, b. LC, sc: Catherine Hutchison, aunt, BVS:1854:13, LC:13

HUTCHISON, Ethel G., W, F, d. 2 Nov 1891, Leesburg, membranous croup, 3-0-0, p. Thos. & Mary Hutchison, b. Leesburg, farmer, unm, sc: father, LE Dist., BVS:1891:4

HUTCHISON, Hanson, W, M, d. 8 Jun 1896, nr Lenah, consumption, 22-0-0, p. H. B. & S. E. Hutchison, b. nr Lenah, laborer, unm, sc: S.E. Hutchison, mother, BR Dist., BVS:1896:3

HUTCHISON, Harry, W, M, d. 31 Dec 1891, Farmwell, meningitis, 5-0-0, p. R. W. & Margaret Hutchison, b. LC, laborer, sc: R.W. Hutchison, father, 1st Dist., BVS:1891:2

[HUTCHISON], J. W., W, M, d. 13 Feb 1859/60, res of parents, spasms, 0-0-1, p. Jos A. & Sarah E. Hutchison, b. res of parents, sc: Jos. A. Hutchison, father, BVS:1859:3, 1860:1, LC:34

HUTCHISON, Julia F., W, F, d. 1 Apr 1892, Arcola, la grippe, 83-0-0, p. Wm. & Susan Ambler, b. LC, c/o: Llewellyn Hutchison, sc: Jas A. Orrison, nephew, 1st Dist., BVS:1892:1

HUTCHISON, Lewellon T., W, M, d. 28 Aug 1858, LC, typhoid fever, 23-0-0, p. Andrew & Maria Hutchison, b. LC,

Loudoun County, Virginia, Death Register, 1853-1896 143

sc: Andrew Hutchison, father, BVS:1858:6, LC:33
HUTCHISON, Lucinda, W, F, d. 31 Mar 1877, nr Gum Spring, chronic affection, 71-0-0, p. Richd. & Ann Presgraves, b. nr Gum Spring, c/o: M.B. Hutchison, sc: M.B. Hutchison, husband, BR Dist., BVS:1877:1
HUTCHISON, Lucy, W, F, d. 21 May 1881, LC, diphtheria, 6-0-0, p. Geo C. & Maria Hutchison, b. LC, sc: G.C. Hutchison, father, 1st Dist., BVS:1881:1
HUTCHISON, M. B., W, M, d. 9 Mar 1893, Arcola, heart failure, 83-11-0, p. Geo. Hutchison, b. Arcola, farmer, sc: C.L. Hutchison, son, 1st Dist., BVS:1893:1
HUTCHISON, Maria, W, F, d. 5 Feb 1878, nr Pleasant Valley, infirmity, 84-0-0, p. Geo. & Susan Hutchison, b. LC, c/o: Andrew Hutchison, sc: A.M. Hutchison, son, BR Dist., BVS:1878:4
HUTCHISON, Martha, W, F, d. 25 Apr 1871, disease of the heart, 50-0-0, farmer, married, BR Dist., BVS:1871:3
HUTCHISON, Mary C., W, F, d. 6 Jan 1873, nr Gum Spring, consumption, 38-0-0, p. Elias & Nancy Matthews, b. LC, c/o: John Hutchison, sc: Edgar E. Matthews, brother, BR Dist., BVS:1873:1
HUTCHISON, Mary E., W, F, d. 3 Jan 1873, nr Gum Spring, inflammatory rheumatism, 58-0-0, p. Rector Gist & wife, b. LC, c/o: Thos Hutchison, sc: Thos Hutchison, head of family, BR Dist., BVS:1873:1
HUTCHISON, Mary V., W, F, d. 17 Jul 1876, nr Pleasant Valley, consumption, 33-0-0, p. Andrew & Maria Hutchison, b. LC, unm, sc: A.M. Hutchison, brother, BR Dist., BVS:1876:2
[HUTCHISON], no name, W, M, d. Dec 1854, unk, 0-0-1, p. Jas. S. & F. Hutchison, b. LC, sc: James S. Hutchison, father, BVS:1854:13, LC:13
HUTCHISON, no name, W, F, d. 26 Apr 1890, nr Arcola, unk, 0-0-3, p. Wilmer G. & Clara Hutchison, b. nr Arcola, sc: Wilmer G. Hutchison, father, 1st Dist., BVS:1890:1

HUTCHISON, Pickering, W, M, d. 1 Nov 1896, Arcola, cancer, 84-0-0, b. LC, farmer, c/o: Sarah E. Hutchison, sc: L.D. Hutchison, son, BR Dist., BVS:1896:3
HUTCHISON, Richard H., W, M, d. 6 Sep 1854, dysentery, 11-6-0, p. Sampson & R. Hutchison, b. LC, sc: Catherine Hutchison, aunt, BVS:1854:13, LC:13
HUTCHISON, Sallie B., W, F, d. 6 Sep 1857, Middleburg, putrid sore throat, 2-1-0, p. George H. & Susan Hutchison, b. Middleburg, sc: G.H. Hutchison, father, BVS:1857:6, LC:28
HUTCHISON, Sampson, W, M, d. 8 Oct 1855, old age, 79-10-3, p. Joseph Hutchison, b. LC, sc: Eliz. Hutchison, wife, BVS:1855:8, LC:19
HUTCHISON, Sarah A, W, F, d. 17 Jul 1893, nr Arcola, heart trouble, 79-0-0, p. Richd. Hutchison, b. LC, housekeeper, c/o: Pickering Hutchison, sc: A.B. Hutchison, son, 1st Dist., BVS:1893:1
HUTCHISON, Sina, W, F, d. 15 Apr 1884, LC, scarlet fever, 40-0-0, p. Thos. & Mary E. Hutchison, b. LC, sc: Robt Hutchison, brother, 1st Dist., BVS:1884:1
HUTCHISON, Thos., W, M, d. 15 Aug 1875, nr Sudley Mill, chronic rheumatism, 78-1-0, p. unk, b. LC, farmer, widower, sc: Webster Hutchison, son, BR Dist., BVS:1875:5
HUTCHISON, W.B., W, M, d. Feb 1857, unk, 4-0-0, p. G.W. & C.A. Hutchison, b. LC, sc: C.B. Wrenn, friend, BVS:1857:7, LC:28
HUTCHISON, Wm., W, M, d. 11 Apr 1865, Fairfax line, old age, 79-0-0, p. Lewis & Keiziah Hutchison, b. LC, farmer, consort, sc: Pickering Hutchison, cousin, BVS:1865:2

IDEN, Carl, W, M, d. 19 Mar 1892, Bloomfield, unk, 0-1-0, p. T. C. & L. T. Iden, b. Bloomfield, sc: Thos C. Iden, father, 1st Dist., BVS:1892:1
IDEN, Edwin, W, M, d. 20 Dec 1853, Middleburg, found dead, 0-8-0, p. Lott & Lucy Iden, b. Middleburg, sc: father, BVS:1854:1, LC:4

IDEN, Edwin, W, M, d. Jan 1854, Middleburg, unk, 0-8-0, p. Lot W. & Lucy Ann Iden, b. Middleburg, sc: Lot W. Iden, BVS:1854:11, LC:10

IDEN, Francis, W, M, d. Jul or Aug 1856, res of parents, 0-8-0, p. Lot W. & Lucy A. Iden, b. Middleburg, sc: L.W. Iden, father, BVS:1856:6, LC:23

IDEN, Jno. T., W, M, d. 4 Dec 1875, LC, apoplexy, 52-6-5, b. Leesburg, farmer, c/o: Virginia Iden, sc: Virginia Iden, wife, LE Dist., BVS:1875:1

IDEN, Mary A., W, F, d. Mar 1853, Middleburg, typhus fever, 2-0-0, p. Lott & Lucy Iden, b. Middleburg, sc: father, BVS:1854:1, LC:4

IRISH, William S., W, M, d. 27 Jul 1882, LC, typhoid fever, 39-0-0, b. LC, mechanic, c/o: Mary Irish, sc: Rachel ?, friend, 3rd Dist., BVS:1882:3

[ISH], no name, W, F, d. 18 Sep 1886, nr Aldie, unk, 0-0-2, p. Frank & Alice Ish, b. nr Aldie, sc: Frank Ish, father, 1st Dist., BVS:1886:1

JACKSON, Alice, B, F, d. 2 Aug 1887, LC, consumption, 25-0-0, b. LC, c/o: Frank Jackson, sc: Frank Jackson, husband, 3rd Dist., BVS:1887:6

JACKSON, Alpheus, B, M, d. 1 Oct 1876, LC, diphtheria, 6-0-0, p. Clarence & Ellen Jackson, b. LC, sc: Ellen Jackson, mother, JF Dist., BVS:1876:8

JACKSON, Amanda Catharine, B, F, d. Aug 1875, nr Snickersville, unk, p. Wm. & Virginia Jackson, b. nr Snickersville, laborer, sc: Wm. Jackson, father, MT Dist., BVS:1875:8

JACKSON, Arthur, B, M, d. 2 Sep 1881, LC, brain fever, 0-10-0, p. Thos. & Eliza Jackson, b. LC, sc: Eliza Jackson, mother, 3rd Dist., BVS:1881:4

JACKSON, Benj., B, M, d. 9 Jan 1892, Sterling, pneumonia, 60-0-0, p. unk, b. Sterling, laborer, c/o: Jane Jackson, sc: Jas F. Jackson, son-in-law, 1st Dist., BVS:1892:4

JACKSON, Bertha, B, F, d. 5 Jul 1882, LC, cholera infantum, 0-9-0, p. Henry & Mary Jackson, unm, sc: Henry Jackson, father, 1st Dist., BVS:1882:1

JACKSON, Betsy, B, F, d. 20 Oct 1883, Snickersville, dyspepsia, 65-0-0, b. LC, farmer, c/o: Henry Jackson, sc: Henry Jackson, husband, 3rd Dist., BVS:1883:5

JACKSON, Charles, B, M, d. 11 Mar 1881, LC, consumption, 25-0-0, b. LC, laborer, c/o: Alice Jackson, sc: Alice Jackson, wife, 1st Dist., BVS:1881:1

JACKSON, Chas. B., B, M, d. 22 Sep 1874, Broad Run Dist., lung fever, 0-5-0, p. James B. & Frances Jackson, b. LC, sc: Jas. B. Jackson, father, BR Dist., BVS:1874:3

JACKSON, Clara, W, F, d. 14 Jul 1872, LC, brain fever, 0-6-4, p. Thos. H. & Lucinda Jackson, b. LC, sc: Lucinda Jackson, mother, LE Dist., BVS:1872:3

JACKSON, Clinton, B, M, d. 26 Jul 1887, LC, consumption, 4-0-0, p. Frank & Alice Jackson, b. LC, unm, sc: Frank Jackson, father, 3rd Dist., BVS:1887:6

JACKSON, Delia, B, F, d. 3 Dec 1877, Bellfield, consumption, 26-0-0, p. Henry & Fanny Jackson, b. LC, unm, sc: ? Green, neighbor, MC Dist., BVS:1877:5

JACKSON, Delia, B, F, d. 6 Apr 1876, nr Unison, consumption, 28-0-0, p. Mary Jackson, b. LC, unm, sc: Henry Jackson, grandfather, MC Dist., BVS:1876:4

JACKSON, Edith, B, F, d. 5 Oct 1894, nr Leithtown, unk, 52-0-0, p. unk, b. unk, c/o: Lewis Jackson, sc: Lewis Jackson, husband, 1st Dist., BVS:1894:2

JACKSON, Elen, B, F, d. 16 Jul 1873, nr Philomont, whooping cough, 0-6-1, p. Obediah & Maria Jackson, b. nr Philomont, sc: parents, MT Dist., BVS:1873:3

JACKSON, Eliza, B, F, d. 29 Aug 1894, Purcell's Factory, typhoid fever, 13-0-0, p. Scott & Hattie Jackson, b. LC, sc: Scott Jackson, father, 3rd Dist., BVS:1894:5

JACKSON, Elizabeth, B, F, d. 1 Nov 1880, Leesburg, unk, 0-5-25, p. Albert & Mary J. Jackson, b. LC,

Loudoun County, Virginia, Death Register, 1853-1896   145

unm, sc: Albert Jackson, father, 2nd Dist., BVS:1880:6

JACKSON, Fanny, B, F, d. 15 May 1871, nr Dodd's Mill, 0-5-0, p. Virginia & R.R.S. Hough, MC Dist., BVS:1871:2

JACKSON, Fanny, B, F, d. 15 May 1872, 20-0-0, p. Lee & Louise Jackson, MC Dist., BVS:1872:7

JACKSON, Floyd R., B, M, d. 4 Aug 1889, LC, thrown from vehicle, 0-0-11, p. Isaac & Sarah Jackson, b. LC, none, unm, sc: Isaac Jackson, husband, 3rd Dist., BVS:1889:5

JACKSON, Geo. R., W, M, d. 26 Dec 1855, Leesburg, typhoid fever, 30-0-0, p. Asa & Susan Jackson, b. LC, merchant, c/o: Anna Jackson, sc: L. W. S. Hough, head of family, BVS:1855:3, LC:15

JACKSON, Gertie, B, F, d. 18 Mar 1893, Evergreen Mills, heart failure, 40-0-0, p. unk, b. LC, laborer, c/o: Joshua Jackson, sc: Joshua Jackson, husband, 1st Dist., BVS:1893:2

JACKSON, Giles, W, M, d. 7 Jul 1893, Philomont, heart trouble, 76-0-0, b. LC, farmer, husband, MT Dist., BVS:1893:4

JACKSON, Gorton, B, M, d. 20 Jul 1887, LC, whooping cough, 2-0-0, p. Frank & Alice Jackson, b. LC, unm, sc: Frank Jackson, father, 3rd Dist., BVS:1887:6

JACKSON, Hammond, B, M, d. 28 Aug 1888, LC, unk, 2-0-0, p. Leven & Emma Jackson, b. LC, laborer, unm, sc: Leven Jackson, father, 2nd Dist., BVS:1888:6

JACKSON, Hannah, B, F, d. 20 Nov 1878, LC, old age, 100-2-0, b. LC, unm, sc: Robert Buckhannon, son-in-law, LE Dist., BVS:1878:8

JACKSON, Harriet, B, F, d. 10 Jul 1880, LC, old age, 70-0-0, p. unk, unm, sc: Benj. F. Hibbs, friend, 1st Dist., BVS:1880:2

JACKSON, Harry G., B, M, d. Sep 1866, nr Hillsboro, unk, 0-3-0, p. Lucretia Jackson, b. nr Hillsboro, sc: Edward D. Potts, BVS:1866:2

JACKSON, Hattie, B, F, d. 7 Nov 1876, nr Philomont, unk, 0-2-9, p. Obediah & Maria Jackson, b. LC, unm, sc: Obadiah Jackson, father, MT Dist., BVS:1876:1

JACKSON, Henry, B, M, d. 9 Jun 1875, LC, consumption, 20-0-0, sc: Eliza Bank?, friend, LE Dist., BVS:1875:1

JACKSON, Henry, B, M, d. 17 Mar 1887, LC, heart disease, 65-0-0, b. LC, farmer, c/o: Lettie Jackson, sc: Uriah Jackson, son, 3rd Dist., BVS:1887:7

JACKSON, Henry, B, M, d. 10 Jul 1892, Unison, whooping cough, 2-0-0, p. Chas. & Lucy Jackson, b. Unison, laborer, sc: Chas Jackson, father, 1st Dist., BVS:1892:4

JACKSON, Herbert, B, M, d. 14 May 1892, Unison, pneumonia, 1-9-0, p. Henry & Nellie Jackson, b. Unison, laborer, unm, sc: Henry Jackson, father, 1st Dist., BVS:1892:4

JACKSON, Jemima, B, F, d. Jun 1865, old age, 84-0-0, sc: Sarah Wilson, BVS:1865:1

JACKSON, Jennie, B, F, d. 28 Apr 1885, Leesburg, unk, 2-5-0, p. Albert & Mary J. Jackson, sc: Albert Jackson, father, 2nd Dist., BVS:1885:1

JACKSON, John W., W, M, d. 30 Oct 1854, LC, dropsy, 43-2-17, p. unk, b. unk, shoemaker, sc: Frances J. Dailey, friend, BVS:1854:9, LC:9

JACKSON, Julia, W, F, d. Jul 1874, Leesburg, 10-0-0, c/o: Wm. Jackson, sc: Wm. Jackson, husband, LE Dist., BVS:1874:5

JACKSON, Landon, B, M, d. 18 Jan 1879, LC, pneumonia, 0-1-10, p. John & Margaret Jackson, b. LC, sc: John Jackson, father, 3rd Dist., BVS:1879:3

JACKSON, Lee, B, M, d. 10 Jul 1880, LC, old age, 80-0-0, p. unk, unm, sc: John Hutchison, friend, 1st Dist., BVS:1880:2

JACKSON, Lettie, B, F, d. 17 Feb 1887, LC, heart disease, 60-0-0, b. LC, none, c/o: Henry Jackson, sc: Uriah Jackson, son, 3rd Dist., BVS:1887:7

JACKSON, Lizzie, B, F, d. 3 May 1878, Snickersville, unk, p. Henry & Bettie Jackson, b. Snickersville, sc: H. Jackson, father, MT Dist., BVS:1878:2/3

JACKSON, Louisa, B, F, d. 29 Oct 1892, Welbourne, typhoid fever, 12-0-0, p. Alfred & Patsy Jackson, b. Welbourne, laborer, unm, sc: Alfred Jackson, father, 1st Dist., BVS:1892:4

JACKSON, Louisa, B, F, d. 15 Apr 1873, nr Gum Spring, typhoid fever, 32-0-0, p. unk, b. Georgetown, unm, sc: Benj. Bias, head of family, BR Dist., BVS:1873:1

JACKSON, Lydia, B, F, d. 1 Mar 1887, LC, catarrh fever, 10-0-0, p. Frank & Alice Jackson, b. LC, unm, sc: Frank Jackson, father, 3rd Dist., BVS:1887:6

JACKSON, Malinda, (f), F, d. 29 Jan 1854, nr Nichols Mill, consumption, 32-0-0, p. Wm. & Elizabeth Goorelin, b. Welbourne, c/o: John Jackson, sc: mother, BVS:1854:12, LC:12

JACKSON, Margaret Ann, B, F, d. 18 Jul 1869, LC, thrush, 0-0-10, p. William & Virginia Jackson, b. LC, sc: Virginia Jackson, mother, BVS:1869:1

JACKSON, Mary, B, F, d. Jul 1894, Hillsboro, consumption, 49-0-0, p. Wm. & Harriett Saunders, b. Hillsboro, wife, sc: Wm. Saunders, son, 3rd Dist., BVS:1894:5

JACKSON, Mary, W, F, d. 4 Jul 1854, LC, old age, 73-0-0, p. Giles & Honor Tillett, b. LC, c/o: John Jackson, sc: Julia A. Jackson, dau-in-law, BVS:1854:10, LC:9

JACKSON, Mary, B, F, d. 25 Nov 1884, Hillsboro, 3-5-0, p. Frank & Alice Jackson, b. Hillsboro, unm, sc: Frank Jackson, father, 3rd Dist., BVS:1884:6

JACKSON, Mary E., B, F, d. 14 Oct 1884, LC, thresh, 1-4-0, p. Chas. & Lucy Jackson, b. LC, unm, sc: Chas Jackson, father, 1st Dist., BVS:1884:2

[JACKSON], Mary Elizabeth, W, F, d. 28 Jul 1856, Leesburg, congestion brain, 1-0-0, p. Giles & Sephionia Jackson, b. nr Shreve's Mill, sc: S.E. Jackson, mother, BVS:1856:4, LC:21

JACKSON, Matilda, W, F, d. Oct 1871, LC, 65-0-0, b. LC, c/o: George Jackson, LE Dist., BVS:1871:4

JACKSON, Melville, B, M, d. 25 Nov 1896, Middleburg, diphtheria, 2-0-0, p. Arch & M. Jackson, b. Middleburg, none, unm, sc: Arch. Jackson, father, MC Dist., BVS:1896:1

JACKSON, Mollie, B, F, d. Sep 1896, Hillsboro, heart disease, 52-0-0, consort, sc: daughter, JF Dist., BVS:1896:10

JACKSON, Nancy, B, F, d. Jul 1896, Lincoln, 23-0-0, p. Henry & Francis Jackson, b. Lincoln, sc: Henry Jackson, father, MT Dist., BVS:1896:9

JACKSON, Nancy, B, F, d. 14 May 1878, nr Bloomfield, old age, 84-0-0, b. Fauquier Co., c/o: Garrett Jackson, sc: Wm. H. Jackson, friend, MC Dist., BVS:1878:6

JACKSON, Nancy, B, F, d. 2 Jul 1879, nr Leesburg, burned, 13-0-0, p. Denis & Matilda Johnson [sic], b. LC, sc: T.S. Titus, friend, 2nd Dist., BVS:1879:1

JACKSON, Nellie, B, F, d. 10 Mar 1887, Sterling, unk, 2-0-0, p. Robt. & Jane Jackson, b. Fairfax Co., sc: Webster Bradford, friend, 1st Dist., BVS:1887:1

JACKSON, Nelly, (f), F, d. 7 Dec 1855, Poor House, paralysis, 70-0-0, sc: steward, BVS:1855:5, LC:17

[JACKSON], no name, (f), M, d. 16 Jan 1854, nr Nichols Mill, 0-0-1/4, p. Malinda Jackson, b. Nichols Mill, sc: grandmother, BVS:1854:12, LC:12

[JACKSON], no name, (f), F, d. Jun 1855, unk, 0-3-0, p. Geo. & Mahala Jackson, b. LC, sc: George Jackson, father, BVS:1855:8, LC:19

[JACKSON], no name, (f), F, d. Feb 1856, LC, unk, 0-0-21, p. George & Mahala Jackson, b. LC, sc: George Jackson, father, BVS:1856:7, LC:24

[JACKSON], no name, B, F, d. Jul 1865, Guilford Station, whooping cough, 1-2-0, p. Kizzie Jackson, b. LC, sc: Jon Lewis, head of family, BVS:1865:1

[JACKSON], no name, B, M, d. 17 Jul 1869, LC, inflammation of lungs, 0-8-0, p. William & Virginia Jackson, b. Clarke Co. VA, sc: Virginia Jackson, mother, BVS:1869:1

[JACKSON], no name, B, M, d. 11 Apr 1873, nr Hamilton, unk, 0-0-1, p. Clarence & Elen Jackson, b. nr Hamilton, sc: parents, MT Dist., BVS:1873:3

JACKSON, no name, B, F, d. 10 May 1880, Round Hill, unk, 0-3-0, p. Rice & Maria Jackson, b. LC, sc: Maria Jackson, mother, 3rd Dist., BVS:1880:4

[JACKSON], no name, B, F, d. 15 May 1882, LC, unk, 0-0-5, p. Jane Jackson, b. LC, sc: Jane Jackson, mother, 1st Dist., BVS:1882:1

JACKSON, no name, B, F, d. 20 Jul 1884, Leesburg, cold, 0-0-5, p. Sallie Jackson (unm), b. LC, sc: Sallie Jackson, mother, 2nd Dist., BVS:1884:4

JACKSON, no name, B, M, d. 25 Nov 1884, Hillsboro, burned, 0-9-0, p. Frank & Alice Jackson, b. Hillsboro, unm, sc: Frank Jackson, father, 3rd Dist., BVS:1884:6

JACKSON, no name, B, F, d. 18 Dec 1891, Evergreen Mills, unk, 0-0-9, p. Josh & Gertie Jackson, b. LC, unm, sc: Josh. Jackson, head of family, 1st Dist., BVS:1891:1

JACKSON, no name, B, F, d. 16 May 1892, Unison, whooping cough, 0-1-0, p. Chas. & Lucy Jackson, b. Unison, laborer, sc: Chas Jackson, father, 1st Dist., BVS:1892:4

JACKSON, Oscar, B, M, d. 11 Apr 1894, Hillsboro, consumption, 0-1-0, p. ___ Jackson, b. Hillsboro, unm, sc: W. Jackson, father, 3rd Dist., BVS:1894:5

JACKSON, Patsy, B, F, d. 7 Apr 1891, Welbourne, unk, 25-0-0, p. unk, b. Fauquier Co., laborer, c/o: Robert Jackson, sc: Alfred Jackson, head of family, 1st Dist., BVS:1891:1

JACKSON, Rachael, W, F, d. 10 Oct 1878, LC, pneumonia, 1-9-0, p. Albert & Mary Jackson, b. LC, unm, sc: Mary Jackson, mother, LE Dist., BVS:1878:8

JACKSON, Rebecca, (f), F, d. 30 Jan 1857, Poor House, old age, unk, b. Alexandria, sc: steward of poorhouse, BVS:1857:3, LC:26

JACKSON, Richard, B, M, d. Jun 1879, nr Leesburg, unk, 0-5-0, p. Albert & Mary Jackson, b. LC, sc: Mary J. Jackson, mother, 2nd Dist., BVS:1879:1

JACKSON, Robert, B, M, d. 5 Aug 1876, nr Unison, scrofula, 5-0-0, p. Mary Jackson, b. LC, sc: Henry Jackson, grandfather, MC Dist., BVS:1876:4

JACKSON, Rosa B., B, , d. 25 Dec 1877, LC, pleurisy, 1-2-0, p. Henry & Sallie Jackson, sc: Henry Jackson, father, LE Dist., BVS:1877:8

JACKSON, Sarah F., B, F, d. 1 Sep 1880, Philomont, croup, 1-7-0, p. Albert & America Jackson, b. LC, sc: America Jackson, mother, 3rd Dist., BVS:1880:4

JACKSON, Sarah F., B, F, d. 8 Feb 1886, nr Arcola, diphtheria, 7-0-0, p. Joshua & Gertrude Jackson, b. nr Arcola, unm, sc: Joshua Jackson, father, 1st Dist., BVS:1886:1

JACKSON, Sidney V., B, M, d. 1 Jun 1888, LC, whooping cough, 1-8-0, p. Albert & Mary Jackson, b. LC, laborer, unm, sc: Albert Jackson, father, 2nd Dist., BVS:1888:6

JACKSON, Susan, (f), F, d. 30 Sep 1856, LC, unk, 14-0-0, p. Sally Johnson, b. LC, sc: Sally Johnson, mother, BVS:1856:2, LC:21

JACKSON, Susannah, B, F, d. 10 Jul 1878, nr Bloomfield, scrofula, unk, p. Wm. H. & Martha Jackson, b. Fauquier Co., sc: Wm. H. Jackson, father, MC Dist., BVS:1878:6

JACKSON, Topsey, B, F, d. 3 Oct 1883, Leesburg, smothered, 0-3-0, p. Ellen Jackson, b. LC, sc: Henry Stringfellow, friend, 2nd Dist., BVS:1883:3

JACKSON, Walker, B, M, d. 5 Oct 1887, Philomont, unk, 70-0-0, p. unk, b. LC, sc: F.E. Robey, superintendent of poor, 1st Dist., BVS:1887:1

JACKSON, Walter, B, M, d. 25 Nov 1884, Hillsboro, burned, 2-1-0, p. Frank & Alice Jackson, b. Hillsboro, unm, sc: Frank Jackson, father, 3rd Dist., BVS:1884:6

JACKSON, Welby, B, M, d. 15 Aug 1892, Welbourne, unk, 21-0-0, p. Alfred & Patsy Jackson, b. Welbourne, laborer, unm, sc: Alfred Jackson, father, 1st Dist., BVS:1892:4

JACKSON, William B., W, M, d. 29 Jan 1881, LC, unk, 72-5-18, p. __ Jackson, b. LC, farmer, c/o: Rebecca Jackson, sc: Geo W. Jackson, son, 2nd Dist., BVS:1881:6

JACKSON, William D., B, M, d. 1 Jun 1883, nr Unison, crippled, 10-0-0, p. Joseph & Laura Jackson, b. nr Unison, laborer, sc: Joseph Jackson, father, 1st Dist., BVS:1883:1

JACKSON, Willie, B, M, d. 20 Dec 1879, LC, croup, 0-6-0, p. Frank & Alice Jackson, b. LC, sc: Frank Jackson, father, 3rd Dist., BVS:1879:3

JACOBS, Ann, W, F, d. 7 Oct 1877, Poor House, congestive chill, 60-0-0, b. LC, c/o: Rozzell P. Jacobs, sc: Jos. Howell, step-grandson-in-law, MC Dist., BVS:1877:5

JACOBS, Annie A., W, F, d. 9 Nov 1889, LC, birth of child, 38-0-0, p. Henry & Mary Adams, b. LC, none, c/o: Leven T. Jacobs, sc: Leven T. Jacobs, husband, 3rd Dist., BVS:1889:5

JACOBS, Bertha, W, F, d. 4 Aug 1876, Leesburg, water on the brain, 1-4-0, p. George & Kate Jacobs, b. Leesburg, sc: Kate Jacobs, mother, LE Dist., BVS:1876:6

JACOBS, Catharine, W, F, d. 10 Jun 1858, LC, pneumonia, 37-0-0, p. John & Sarah Wolf, b. LC, c/o: Rynard Jacobs, sc: Rynard Jacobs, husband, BVS:1858:1, LC:29

JACOBS, Chester A., W, M, d. 26 Aug 1892, Britain, cholera infantum, 0-8-0, p. John & Mary, b. LC, unm, sc: John Jacobs, LV Dist., BVS:1892:6

JACOBS, George, W, M, d. 15 Feb 1857, LC, dropsy, 76-0-0, p. unk, b. LC, c/o: Elizabeth Jacobs, sc: Elizth Jacobs, wife, BVS:1857:1, LC:24

JACOBS, Harry, W, M, d. 4 Apr 1876, Leesburg, water on the brain, 0-0-4, p. George & Kate Jacobs, b. Leesburg, sc: Kate Jacobs, mother, LE Dist., BVS:1876:6

JACOBS, Jacob T., W, M, d. 3 Jan 1853, Leesburg, pneumonia, 30-9-4, p. Elizabeth Hipkins, b. LC, shoemaker, unk, sc: Elizabeth Hipkins, mother, BVS:1854:5, LC:3

JACOBS, John H., B, M, d. 24 Dec 1880, Hillsboro, dysentery, 2-0-0, p. Henry & Fannie Jackson[sic], b. LC, sc: Fanny Jacobs, mother, 3rd Dist., BVS:1880:4

JACOBS, Margaret A., W, F, d. 6 May 1858, res of parents, inflammation of bowels, 0-2-1, p. Roszel P. & Ann C. Jacobs, b. place of death, sc: Ann C. Jacobs, mother, BVS:1858:3, LC:31

JACOBS, Mary L., W, F, d. 8 Jun 1890, Bloomfield, unk, 0-7-0, p. Len & Annie Jacobs, b. Bloomfield, sc: Henry H. Taylor, uncle, 1st Dist., BVS:1890:2

JACOBS, Michael T., W, M, d. 27 Aug 1864, Richmond Hospital, tumor on the brain, 30-0-0, p. Rosel P. & S. Jacobs, b. LC, soldier, c/o: Susan Jacobs, sc: R.P. Jacobs, father, BVS:1864:1, LC:38

JACOBS, Nellie A., W, F, d. 20 Aug 1892, Britain, cholera infantum, 8-0-0, p. John & Mary, b. LC, unm, sc: John Jacobs, LV Dist., BVS:1892:6

JACOBS, Raymon K., W, M, d. 17 Jul 1886, putrid sore throat, 4-4-0, p. George & Catharine, sc: Geo. Jacobs, father, 2nd Dist., BVS:1886:5

JACOBS, Robert C., W, M, d. 25 Mar 1881, LC, croup, 0-9-0, p. Jas. W. & C. A. Jacobs, b. LC, sc: Jas W. Jacobs, father, 2nd Dist., BVS:1881:6

JACOBS, Rynard, W, M, d. 25 Apr 1889, LC, old age, 92-0-0, p. unk, b. LC, farmer, unm, sc: J.W. Jacobs, son, 2nd Dist., BVS:1889:3

JACOBS, Sarah, W, F, d. 17 Apr 1881, LC, bronchitis, 65-0-0, p. Geo. & __ Fritts, b. LC, c/o: Rynard Jacobs, sc: Rynard Jacobs, husband, 2nd Dist., BVS:1881:7

JACOBS, Susan R., W, F, d. 1 May 1855, nr Poor House, stomach thrush, 38-7-6, p. Michael & Jane Plaster, b. nr Union, c/o: Roszel P. Jacobs, sc: Jane Plaster, mother, BVS:1855:5, LC:17

JACOBS, Theadore, W, M, d. 28 Mar 1858, res of parents, spasms, 0-0-23, p. Roszel P. & Ann C. Jacobs, b. place of death, sc: Ann C. Jacobs, mother, BVS:1858:3, LC:31

JACOBS, Venn E., W, M, d. 21 Dec 1878, nr Rectors X Roads, unk, 0-4-21, p. Chas J.B. & Ida A. Jacobs, b.

Loudoun County, Virginia, Death Register, 1853-1896   149

LC, sc: Chas J.B. Jacobs, father, MC Dist., BVS:1878:6
JACOBS, Willie, W, M, d. 19 May 1887, Trappe, cold, 0-0-3, p. Franklin & Frances Jacobs, b. Trappe, sc: Franklin P. Jacobs, father, 1st Dist., BVS:1887:1
JACOBS, Wm. H., W, M, d. 7 Sep 1859/60, LC, typhoid fever, 62-0-0, p. Edwd & Mary Jacobs, b. Alexandria, tailor, c/o: Catharine Jacobs, sc: John S. Jacobs, son, BVS:1859:1, 1860:4, LC:37
JACOBS, Wm. R., W, M, d. 25 Jun 1874, W of Lovettsville, teething, 0-5-0, p. James W. & Catharine Jacobs, LV Dist., BVS:1874:6
JAMES, Catharine, W, F, d. 25 Jun 1859/60, LC, unk, 0-0-3, p. Richd & Sarah A. James, b. LC, sc: Richard James, father, BVS:1859:1, 1860:4, LC:37
JAMES, Elijah, W, M, d. 7 Aug 1880, Waterford, old age, 90-4-20, p. --- James, b. LC, c/o: Sarah James, sc: Chas. E. James, son, 2nd Dist., BVS:1880:6
JAMES, Eliza P., W, F, d. 20 Mar 1883, Bunker Hill, consumption, 37-0-0, p. Wm. & Emily Bleakley, b. LC, c/o: T. Benton James, sc: T. Benton James, husband, 3rd Dist., BVS:1883:5
JAMES, Estelle G., W, F, d. 12 May 1884, Hamilton, measles, 5-1-3, p. A. C. & Sarah F. James, b. Virginia, unm, sc: A. Caldwell James, father, 3rd Dist., BVS:1884:6
JAMES, Ida C., W, F, d. 30 Jun 1893, Waterford, consumption, 34-0-0, p. James W. & Sarah Tennyson, b. Waterford, wife, sc: husband, JF Dist., BVS:1893:3
JAMES, Lester, W, M, d. 24 Sep 1887, LC, dysentery, 0-7-0, p. Oscar & Susan F. James, b. LC, unm, sc: Oscar James, father, 3rd Dist., BVS:1887:6
JAMES, Lucy E., B, F, d. 21 May 1892, Middleburg, whooping cough, 2-6-0, p. Otho & Lucy James, b. Middleburg, sc: Otho James, father, 1st Dist., BVS:1892:4
JAMES, Mahlon, W, M, d. 6 Aug 1890, LC, la grippe, 74-0-0, p. Elisha & Sallie James, b. LC, none, sc: T.S.

Yakey, son-in-law, 2nd Dist., BVS:1890:4
JAMES, Mary E., W, F, d. Oct 1896, Waterford, pneumonia, 71-0-0, consort, JF Dist., BVS:1896:8
JAMES, Matson, W, M, d. 21 Oct 1853, nr Scotland, drinking, 40-10-0, p. Thomas & Mary James, b. foot of Blue Ridge, farmer, c/o: Hannah James, sc: Jonah Thomas, brother in law, BVS:1854:1, LC:4
JAMES, Matson, W, M, d. 20 Nov 1877, Round Hill, consumption, unk, p. Mason & Patience James, sc: M. Jones, father, MT Dist., BVS:1877:2
JAMES, Nellie, W, F, d. 30 Jun 1889, LC, unk, 0-11-5, p. unk, b. LC, none, unm, sc: J.James, father, 2nd Dist., BVS:1889:3
[JAMES], no name, W, M, d. Dec 1857, res of parents, 0-1-14, p. Levi & Martha E. James, b. nr Peugh's Mill, sc: father, BVS:1857:3, LC:26
JAMES, Robert, W, M, d. 8 Nov 1869, LC, cancer of stomach, 53-0-0, p. Thomas & Mary James, b. LC, farmer, married, sc: Winifred James, wife, BVS:1869:1
JAMES, Roger, W, M, d. 1 Oct 1892, Waterford, meningitis, 0-7-0, p. P. C. & Jane C. James, JF Dist., BVS:1892:7
[JAMES], Rosaline Gertrude, W, F, d. Jul 1856, res of parents, 5-0-0, p. Mason & Patience James, b. res of parents, sc: M. James, father, BVS:1856:5, LC:22
JAMES, Sallie, W, F, d. 14 Dec 1865, nr Mt. Zion, general debility, 79-0-0, p. Jno & Mary Crain, b. Fauquier Co., housekeeper, consort, sc: Eliz Hutchison, sister, BVS:1865:2
JAMES, Sarah, W, F, d. 19 Nov 1893, Waterford, unk, 65-0-0, p. Israel & Miranda, b. Waterford, consort, sc: Chas. James, LV Dist., BVS:1893:5
JAMES, Winifred, W, F, d. 4 Sep 1885, Lincoln, dropsy, 72-0-0, p. John & Nancy Simpson, b. LC, c/o: Robert James, sc: Octavius Osburn, son-in-law, 3rd Dist., BVS:1885:6
JANNEY, Albert, W, M, d. 10 Jul 1853, nr Circleville, killed by a horse, 30-0-0, p. Daniel & Elizabeth Janney, b. Janney's Mill, farmer, c/o: Lydia

Janney, sc: Thos. Nichols, father-in-law, BVS:1854:6, LC:5

JANNEY, Bettie, W, F, d. Sep 1876, nr Hamilton, cancer, 33-0-0, p. John & Elizabeth Janney, b. LC, unm, sc: Jane Janney, MT Dist., BVS:1876:1

JANNEY, Bula M., W, F, d. 23 Nov 1859/60, Waterford, pneumonia, 75-2-3, p. Isaac & Hannah Thomas, b. Pennsylvania, c/o: Moses Janney, sc: Hannah M. Worley, daughter, BVS:1859:1, 1860:3, LC:36

JANNEY, Daniel, W, M, d. 17 Oct 1859/60, Fairfax, unk, 72-0-0, p. Israel & Anna Janney, b. LC, physician, c/o: Elizth Janney decd, sc: Daniel Janney, son, BVS:1859:4, 1860:2, LC:35

JANNEY, Frank H., W, M, d. 25 Jun 1883, Lincoln, dyspepsia, 52-0-0, b. LC, farmer, c/o: Emily C. Janney, sc: Emily C. Janney, wife, 3rd Dist., BVS:1883:5

JANNEY, Horace H., W, M, d. Aug 1864, Purcellville, dysentery, 11-0-0, p. Asa & Mary Janney, b. LC, sc: Asa Janney, father, BVS:1864:2, LC:39

JANNEY, James C., W, M, d. 25 Feb 1877, LC, general infirmity, 74-0-0, p. Elisha & Mary Janney, b. Alexandria, miller, c/o: Rebecca Janney, sc: M.P. Janney, son, JF Dist., BVS:1877:3

JANNEY, John, W, M, d. 5 Jan 1872, Leesburg, old age, 74-0-0, p. Elisha & Mary Janney, b. Alexandria Co., lawyer, c/o: Alice S. Janney, sc: Chas P. Janney, nephew, LE Dist., BVS:1872:3

JANNEY, John Jr., W, M, d. 8 Mar 1858, res of father, consumption, 31-1-21, p. Samuel & Elizth Janney, b. Alexandria, merchant, c/o: Eliza F. Janney, sc: S.M. Janney, father, BVS:1858:4, LC:32

JANNEY, Joseph, W, M, d. 25 Mar 1866, Lincoln, 66-0-0, p. John & Eliz. Janney, b. Alexandria, miller, unm, sc: Saml M. Janney, brother, BVS:1866:2

JANNEY, Nathan H., W, M, d. 30 Nov 1857, Hamilton, accident, 39-0-0, p. Daniel & Elizth Janney, b. Janney's Mill, physician, c/o: Lydia J. Janney,

sc: E.R. Purcell, brother-in-law, BVS:1857:3, LC:26

JANNEY, Phillips Lee, W, M, d. 26 Apr 1885, Leesburg, typhoid fever, 2-8-3, p. Chas. P. & Nannie L. Janney, sc: Chas P. Janney, father, 2nd Dist., BVS:1885:1

JANNEY, Phineas A., W, M, d. 29 Aug 1857, nr Thos Nichols', dysentery, 5-3-20, p. Albert H. & Lydia A. Janney, b. nr Thomas Nichols, sc: Lydia A. Janney, mother, BVS:1857:5, LC:28

JANNEY, Pleasant, W, F, d. 28 Sep 1881, LC, dropsy, 84-0-0, b. LC, c/o: Jonas Janney, sc: Amos Hughes, friend, 3rd Dist., BVS:1881:4

JANNEY, Rebecca, W, F, d. 23 Nov 1875, LC, diphtheria, 4-0-0, p. Chas. P. & Nannie L. Janney, b. Leesburg, sc: Chas. P. Janney, father, LE Dist., BVS:1875:1

JANNEY, Thamsin, W, F, d. 17 Dec 1890, Lincoln, pneumonia, 52-0-0, p. Asa M. & Lydia Janney, b. LC, physician, unm, sc: Lydia N. Janny, sister, 3rd Dist., BVS:1890:6

JARVIS, Edgar Jarnett, W, M, d. 8 Feb 1872, Leesburg, consumption, 48-0-0, p. Geo. W. & Louisa Jarvis, b. Leesburg, stage contractor, c/o: Elizabeth Jarvis, sc: Mary Evard, aunt, LE Dist., BVS:1872:3

JARVIS, Louisa A., W, F, d. 24 Mar 1859/60, Leesburg, paralysis, 58-0-0, p. Jonathan & Mary A. Wright, b. Frederick Co., c/o: Washington Jarvis, sc: Edgar Jarvis, son, BVS:1859:2, 1860:4, LC:37

JEFFRIES, Stacy Humphrey, W, , d. 5 Feb 1854, Mill Port, child bed, 34-10-20, p. Jos. & Tacy Daniel, b. Retirement nr Dover, c/o: Braxton B. Jeffries, sc: B.B. Jeffries, BVS:1854:11, LC:10

JENKINS, Bessie, W, F, d. 23 Jun 1892, Philomont, cholera measles, 20-0-0, p. H. H. & Clarissa Jenkins, b. Hillsboro, unm, sc: father, JF Dist., BVS:1892:7

JENKINS, Betsy, W, F, d. 2 Apr 1858, Poor House, paralysis, 80-0-0, b. nr Waterford, sc: W. Furr, steward, BVS:1858:3, LC:31

JENKINS, Carruthers, W, M, d. 2 Aug 1881, LC, dysentery, 2-4-2, p. Henry & Bettie Jenkins, b. LC, sc: Henry

Jenkins, father, 3rd Dist., BVS:1881:4

JENKINS, Charles, W, M, d. 14 Nov 1887, Fairfax line, heart disease, 85-0-0, p. Elijah & Delilah Jenkins, b. LC, sc: Webster Bradford, son-in-law, 1st Dist., BVS:1887:1

JENKINS, Charlotte, W, F, d. 16 Sep 1859/60, LC, unk, 1-6-0, p. Saml L. & Nancy Jenkins, b. LC, sc: Saml Jenkins, father, BVS:1859:6, 1860:3. LC:36

JENKINS, Elizabeth, W, F, d. 20 Aug 1873, Georgetown, chronic diarrhea, 0-6-0, p. James G. & Margaret Jenkins, b. Georgetown, unm, sc: Jas. G. Jenkins, head of family, BR Dist., BVS:1873:1

JENKINS, Elizabeth, W, F, d. 10 Oct 1882, LC, dropsy, 66-0-0, p. Wm. & Henry Furr, c/o: Wm. Jenkins, sc: Wm. Jenkins, husband, 1st Dist., BVS:1882:1

JENKINS, Elizabeth A., W, F, d. 28 Feb 1882, LC, consumption, 44-0-0, p. John & Mary Jackson, c/o: Chas T. Jenkins, sc: Chas T. Jenkins, husband, 1st Dist., BVS:1882:1

JENKINS, Hannah, W, F, d. 19 Nov 1894, Hillsboro, pneumonia, 47-0-0, p. Joseph & Sallie Worthington, b. Hillsboro, wife, sc: ___ Jenkins, son, 3rd Dist., BVS:1894:5

JENKINS, Jas L., W, M, d. 4 Dec 1865, on Potomac, pneumonia, 67-10-3, p. Sylvester & E. Jenkins, b. Fairfax, farmer, consort, sc: Nancy Jenkins, wife, BVS:1865:2

JENKINS, Joseph H., W, M, d. 17 Nov 1857, Gulick's Mill, spine disease, 39-6-17, p. Wesley & Nancy Jenkins, b. New Valley Mill, farmer, sc: Wesley Jenkins, father, BVS:1857:4, LC:26

JENKINS, Josiah, W, M, d. 21 Feb 1855, LC, pneumonia, 25-2-3, p. unk, b. Pennsylvania, engineer, unm, sc: Saml. H. Houser, friend, BVS:1855:2, LC:15

[JENKINS], Margaret Ann, W, F, d. 20 Dec 1854, Blue Ridge, 0-0-9, p. Eben & Mary Ann Jenkins, b. Blue Ridge, sc: mother, BVS:1854:11, LC:11

JENKINS, Martha, W, F, d. 5 May 1891, Mount Gilead, typhoid fever, 60-0-0, p. Wm. Smith, b. LC, wife, unm, sc: Jos S. Jenkins, MT Dist., BVS:1891:6

JENKINS, Martha F., W, F, d. 11 Oct 1872, nr Broad Run, unk, 5-1-0, p. Saml. & Mary Jenkins, b. LC, sc: Saml Jenkins, head of family, BR Dist., BVS:1872:6

JENKINS, Mary F., W, F, d. 16 Dec 1880, LC, child birth, 26-0-0, p. unk, c/o: Elijah Jenkins, sc: Elijah Jenkins, husband, 1st Dist., BVS:1880:2

JENKINS, Nellie, W, F, d. 13 Nov 1892, Leesburg, diphtheria, 8-0-0, p. H. L. & Rosa Jenkins, b. Leesburg, unm, sc: H.L. Jenkins, LE Dist., BVS:1892:5

[JENKINS], no name, W, M, d. 20 Mar 1872, LC, unk, 0-0-11, p. Henry & Sarah E. Jenkins, b. LC, sc: Sarah E. Jenkins, mother, LE Dist., BVS:1872:3

JENKINS, no name, W, M, d. 29 Oct 1892, Sterling, hemorrhages, 0-3-0, p. E. V. & Rose L. Jenkins, b. Sterling, sc: E.V. Jenkins, father, 1st Dist., BVS:1892:1

JENKINS, Noral, W, M, d. 6 Dec 1887, LC, dropsy of heart, 50-0-0, p. Novel & Hannah Jenkins, b. LC, c/o: Hannah Jenkins, sc: Hannah Jenkins, wife, 3rd Dist., BVS:1887:6

JENKINS, Pearly M., W, F, d. 10 Apr 1884, LC, bronchitis, 0-9-0, p. Chas. W. & Mary Jenkins, b. LC, sc: Chas W. Jenkins, father, 1st Dist., BVS:1884:2

JENKINS, Porter, W, M, d. 11 Jul 1871, whooping cough, 0-4-18, p. Wash. & Mollie Jenkins, BR Dist., BVS:1871:3

JENKINS, Rosa M., W, F, d. 24 Jan 1890, nr Unison, influenza, 0-11-0, p. James C. & Emma Jenkins, b. nr Unison, sc: James C. Jenkins, father, 1st Dist., BVS:1890:2

JENKINS, Saml. R., W, M, d. 10 Feb 1886, LC, catarrh fever, 0-11-3, p. Robert & Mary Jenkins, b. LC, sc: Robt Jenkins, father, 3rd Dist., BVS:1886:4

JENKINS, Samuel, W, M, d. 8 Sep 1854, LC, diarrhea, 2-0-0, p. Saml. L. & N. Jenkins, b. LC, sc: S. L. Jenkins, father, BVS:1854:14, LC:13

JENKINS, Wesley, W, M, d. 4 Nov 1872, LC, paralysis, 76-0-0, p. unk, b. Fairfax Co., farmer, widower, sc: Chas T. Jenkins, son, LE Dist., BVS:1872:3

JENKINS, Wm. G., W, M, d. 10 Nov 1891, Mount Gilead, typhoid fever, 63-0-0, p. Wm. Jenkins, b. LC, farmer, husband, unm, sc: W.S. Jenkins, MT Dist., BVS:1891:6

JENYES, Alexander, W, M, d. 30 Aug 1854, LC, abscess on liver, 45-1-16, p. unk, b. Pennsylvania, merchant, c/o: Sarah Jeynes, sc: Michael Mullen, friend, BVS:1854:8, LC:8

JET, Eliza, W, F, d. 9 Mar 1888, LC, unk, 67-0-0, p. Benja. & Eliza Jet, b. LC, none, unm, sc: Leven Jackson, friend, 2nd Dist., BVS:1888:6

JEWELL, James L., W, M, d. 5 Sep 1885, nr Pleasant Valley, spasms, 0-0-9, p. John H. & Bettie Jewell, b. Pleasant Valley, sc: John H. Jewell, father, 1^{St} Dist., BVS:1885:4

JEWETT, T. M., W, F, d. 28 Oct 1894, Lincoln, heart trouble, 75-0-0, p. Abijah & Mary A. Janney, b. LC, wife, c/o: Joseph H. Jewett, sc: Joseph H. Jewett, husb., 3rd Dist., BVS:1894:5

JOHNS, Henry V.D., W, M, d. 11 Sep 1878, Middleburg, cholera infantum, 0-4-17, p. Arthur S. & Helen L. Johns, b. Spotsylvania Co., sc: Arthur S. Johns, father, MC Dist., BVS:1878:6

JOHNSON, Andrew, B, M, d. 27 Aug 1883, Leesburg, measles, 1-4-0, p. Jno. & Louisa Johnson, b. LC, sc: Jno Johnson, father, 2nd Dist., BVS:1883:3

JOHNSON, Ann L., W, F, d. 15 Oct 1866, inflammation brain, 1-9-0, p. Jas. W. & Minnie Johnson, b. nr Hillsboro, sc: father, BVS:1866:2

JOHNSON, Arthur, B, M, d. 3 Sep 1881, LC, unk, 2-0-0, p. Jno. & L. Johnson, sc: Jno. Johnson, father, 2nd Dist., BVS:1881:6

JOHNSON, Bernard G., W, M, d. 16 Oct 1881, LC, croup, 3-0-0, p. Chas. W. & J. E. Johnson, b. LC, sc: Chas. W. Johnson, father, 2nd Dist., BVS:1881:7

JOHNSON, Beverley, B, M, d. Sep 1864, Jonah Orrison's, typhoid fever, unk, p. Elizabeth Nelson, farm hand, sc: Nancy Orrison, BVS:1864:1, LC:39

JOHNSON, Catharine, W, F, d. 10 Aug 1878, LC, consumption, 17-0-0, b. LC, unm, sc: Julius Harper, friend, LE Dist., BVS:1878:8

JOHNSON, Celias, B, F, d. 9 Apr 1876, LC, brain fever, 8-0-0, p. Sandy & Lethia Johnson, b. LC, sc: Sandy Johnson, father, LE Dist., BVS:1876:6

JOHNSON, Charles, B, M, d. 1 May 1872, LC, consumption, 15-7-2, p. Gurala & Mary Johnson, b. LC, laborer, sc: Mary Johnson, mother, LE Dist., BVS:1872:3

JOHNSON, Daniel, W, M, d. 15 Oct 1876, nr Gum Spring, chronic diarrhea, 0-5-0, p. G. & Isabella Johnson, b. LC, unm, sc: G. Johnson, father, BR Dist., BVS:1876:2

JOHNSON, Daniel W., W, M, d. 27 Nov 1885, nr Arcola, scrofula, 15-0-0, p. Lawson & Lydia Johnson, b. Arcola, laborer, unm, sc: Lawson Johnson, father, 1^{St} Dist., BVS:1885:4

JOHNSON, David, B, M, d. 28 Mar 1888, Sterling, typhoid pneumonia, 10-0-0, p. Silas & Belle Johnson, b. LC, sc: Silas Johnson, father, 1^{St} Dist., BVS:1888:4

JOHNSON, Dusey, B, F, d. 1 Sep 1881, LC, sun stroke, 22-0-0, b. LC, sc: A. Turner, friend, 1^{St} Dist., BVS:1881:1

JOHNSON, Eliza H., W, F, d. 28 Sep 1880, LC, consumption, 41-0-0, p. John & Mary Johnson, b. LC, unm, sc: Mary Johnson, mother, 1st Dist., BVS:1880:2

JOHNSON, Elizabeth, B, F, d. 28 Aug 1884, Leesburg, consumption, 0-5-9, p. Thornton & Fannie Johnson, b. LC, sc: Fannie Johnson, mother, 2nd Dist., BVS:1884:4

JOHNSON, Ethel M., B, F, d. 16 Dec 1888, Mount Middleton, gastric catarrh, 1-8-0, p. Harvey & Laura Johnson, b. LC, sc: Harvey Johnson, father, 1st Dist., BVS:1888:3

JOHNSON, Flossie W., B, F, d. 29 Dec 1888, Mount Middleton, spasms, 0-

Loudoun County, Virginia, Death Register, 1853-1896 153

4-0, p. Harvey & Laura Johnson, b. LC, sc: Harvey Johnson, father, 1st Dist., BVS:1888:4

JOHNSON, Frances, B, F, d. 19 May 1876, LC, brain fever, 2-9-0, p. Sandy & Lethia Johnson, b. LC, sc: Sandy Johnson, father, LE Dist., BVS:1876:6

JOHNSON, French L., B, M, d. 10 Apr 1873, nr Lovettsville, bronchitis, unk, p. Mandy Johnson, b. nr Lovettsville, unm, sc: Mandy Johnson, mother, LV Dist., BVS:1873:4

JOHNSON, Garfield, B, M, d. 1 Sep 1881, LC, scrofula, 0-6-0, p. Chas. & M. Johnson, b. LC, sc: Chas. Johnson, father, 2nd Dist., BVS:1881:6

JOHNSON, George, B, M, d. 13 Mar 1888, LC, bronchitis, 0-6-0, p. John W. & Ridey Johnson, b. LC, none, sc: John Johnson, father, 3rd Dist., BVS:1888:1

JOHNSON, George, B, M, d. 31 Jan 1884, Waterford, general debility, 75-0-0, p. unk, b. Virginia, laborer, unm, sc: Alfred Craven, friend, 3rd Dist., BVS:1884:6

JOHNSON, Georgiana, B, F, d. 7 Aug 1885, Leesburg, consumption, 36-0-0, p. --- Burrows, b. LC, laborer, c/o: Palmer Johnson, sc: Palmer Johnson, husband, 2nd Dist., BVS:1885:2

JOHNSON, Hannah, B, F, d. 12 Jan 1876, nr Guilford, heart disease, 48-1-0, p. unk, b. LC, sc: Charles Harris, friend, BR Dist., BVS:1876:2

JOHNSON, Hattie N., W, F, d. 28 Mar 1885, Fairfax Ct. House, scarlet fever, 6-0-0, p. Wm. H. & Mary Johnson, b. LC, sc: Wm. H. Johnson, father, 3rd Dist., BVS:1885:6

JOHNSON, Henry, (f), M, d. 14 Apr 1853, Poor House, old age, 80-0-0, b. unk, sc: Wm. Furr, keeper of poor house, BVS:1854:6, LC:6

JOHNSON, Jane, B, F, d. 25 Apr 1893, nr Unison, pneumonia, 30-0-0, p. Armistead & Henrietta Johnson, b. LC, laborer, unm, sc: Armistead Johnson, father, 1st Dist., BVS:1893:2

JOHNSON, Jane, B, F, d. 20 Nov 1880, LC, burned to death, 27-0-0, p. John & Mary Johnson, unm, sc: Joseph Brown, friend, 1st Dist., BVS:1880:2

JOHNSON, John, B, M, d. 10 Nov 1890, Sterling, consumption, 17-0-0, p. Silas & Isabella Johnson, b. Sterling, unm, sc: Silas Johnson, father, 1st Dist., BVS:1890:1

JOHNSON, John A.P., W, M, d. 8 Nov 1857, Leesburg, croup, 5-5-17, p. Alex. W. & Sally Johnson, b. Leesburg, sc: Sally Johnson, mother, BVS:1857:2, LC:25

JOHNSON, John C., W, M, d. 11 Mar 1858, LC, worms, 2-0-5, p. Alexr & Maranda Johnson, b. LC, sc: Alexr Johnson, father, BVS:1858:1, LC:29

JOHNSON, John T., B, M, d. 19 Aug 1884, LC, consumption, 39-0-0, p. Vertney & Emily Johnson, b. LC, laborer, unm, sc: Aaron Johnson, brother, 1st Dist., BVS:1884:2

JOHNSON, Josephine, B, F, d. 10 May 1894, nr Sterling, unk, 0-11-0, p. Jos. & Olivia Johnson, b. nr Sterling, sc: Jos Johnson, father, 1st Dist., BVS:1894:2

JOHNSON, Julia, B, F, d. 1 May 1880, Waterford, consumption, 41-10-0, p. unk, b. unk, unm, sc: William Williams, friend, 3rd Dist., BVS:1880:4

JOHNSON, Kitty, B, F, d. 29 Oct 1891, Aldie, malarial fever, 20-0-0, p. Robt. & Mary Johnson, b. Mississippi, laborer, unm, sc: Robt. Johnson, head of family, 1st Dist., BVS:1891:1

JOHNSON, Lethia, B, F, d. 30 Dec 1876, LC, consumption, 30-0-0, p. unk, b. unk, c/o: Sandy Johnson, sc: Sandy Johnson, husband, LE Dist., BVS:1876:6

JOHNSON, Lucy, B, F, d. 25 Oct 1880, LC, heart disease, 35-0-0, p. unk, unm, sc: Charles Elgin, friend, 1st Dist., BVS:1880:2

JOHNSON, Maggie, B, M, d. 27 Oct 1892, Waterford, typhoid fever, unk, p. Frank Gibson, b. Waterford, JF Dist., BVS:1892:7

JOHNSON, Manuel, B, M, d. 20 Mar 1882, LC, cancer, 52-0-0, p. Richard & Nancy Johnson, unm, sc: Richd Johnson, father, 1st Dist., BVS:1882:1

JOHNSON, Maria, B, F, d. 15 Apr 1866, Leesburg, consumption, 23-0-0, p. Henrietta Johnson, b. LC, unm, sc: Richard H. Edwards, employer, BVS:1866:1

JOHNSON, Marthenia, B, F, d. 7 Jun 1892, Aldie, whooping cough, 0-2-0, p. Robt. & Mary Johnson, b. Aldie, laborer, sc: Mary Johnson, mother, 1st Dist., BVS:1892:4

JOHNSON, Mary, W, F, d. Sep 1854, Middleburg, old age, 84-0-0, b. Baltimore, MD, sc: A. G. Smith, BVS:1854:11, LC:10

JOHNSON, Mary, B, F, d. 25 Feb 1878, LC, pneumonia, 44-0-0, b. LC, c/o: Gara Johnson, sc: Gara Johnson, father, LE Dist., BVS:1878:8

JOHNSON, Mary, B, F, d. 5 Jun 1892, Aldie, whooping cough, 1-0-0, p. Robt. & Mary Johnson, b. Aldie, sc: Mary Johnson, mother, 1st Dist., BVS:1892:4

JOHNSON, Matilda, B, F, d. 10 Oct 1883, Leesburg, dropsy, 41-0-0, p. Peyton & Millie Lucas, b. LC, laborer, c/o: Dennis Johnson, sc: Dennis Johnson, husband, 2nd Dist., BVS:1883:3

JOHNSON, Millie E., W, F, d. 4 Jun 1882, LC, accident, 4-0-0, p. George & Mary E. Johnson, sc: George Johnson, father, 1st Dist., BVS:1882:1

JOHNSON, Miranda, W, F, d. 22 Jul 1891, Mount Gilead, heart affection, 73-0-0, p. James & Abigal Johnson, b. Mount Gilead, wife, unm, sc: B.S. Johnson, MT Dist., BVS:1891:6

JOHNSON, no name, B, F, d. 21 Jun 1878, Middleburg, unk, 0-1-0, p. Margaret Johnson, b. LC, unm, sc: Saml Nickens, friend, MC Dist., BVS:1878:6

JOHNSON, no name, B, F, d. 19 Jun 1892, Aldie, whooping cough, 0-14-0, p. Robt. & Mary Johnson, b. Aldie, sc: Mary Johnson, mother, 1st Dist., BVS:1892:4

[JOHNSON], no name, B, M, d. 28 Jan 1896, LC, unk, 0-0-4, p. Sandy & Carrie Johnson, b. LC, sc: father, LE Dist., BVS:1896:5

JOHN[SON], Peter W., W, M, d. 12 Dec 1884, Leesburg, dropsy, 63-0-0, p. Wm. & Margt. Johnson, b. LC, merchant, c/o: Annie S. Johnson, sc: Annie S. Johnson, wife, 2nd Dist., BVS:1884:4

JOHNSON, Robert, B, M, d. 2 Feb 1881, LC, pleurisy, 3-0-0, p. John & Mary Johnson, b. LC, sc: Jno Johnson, father, 3rd Dist., BVS:1881:4

JOHNSON, Robt., B, M, d. 5 Dec 1881, LC, cold, 1-6-0, p. Robt. & Mary Johnson, b. LC, sc: Robt Johnson, father, 1st Dist., BVS:1881:1

JOHNSON, Rose H., W, F, d. 3 Aug 1885, Leesburg, congestive chills, 26-0-0, p. Geo. R. & Virginia Head, c/o: Wm. H. Johnson, sc: Annie S. Johnson, mother-in-law, 2nd Dist., BVS:1885:1

JOHNSON, Silas, B, M, d. 25 Apr 1896, nr Sterling, consumption, 59-0-0, b. LC, laborer, c/o: Isabella Thompson, sc: Isabella Thompson, wife, BR Dist., BVS:1896:4

JOHNSON, Stephen, B, M, d. 4 Feb 1872, Leesburg, pneumonia, 31-0-5, p. unk, b. Stafford, blacksmith, unm, sc: Flora Green, friend, LE Dist., BVS:1872:3

JOHNSON, Susan E., W, F, d. 18 Jun 1894, Lenah, diarrhea, 73-0-0, p. unk, b. LC, c/o: Amos W. Johnson, sc: Amos Johnson, son, 1st Dist., BVS:1894:1

JOHNSON, Thomas, B, M, d. 1 Sep 1880, LC, suicide, 31-0-0, p. Samuel & Annie Johnson, unm, sc: Annie Fox, witness, 1st Dist., BVS:1880:2

JOHNSON, Troyless T., W, M, d. 9 Sep 1854, dysentery, 1-6-0, p. A. W. & Susan Johnson, b. LC, sc: Amos W. Johnson, father, BVS:1854:13, LC:13

JOHNSON, Vertnay, B, M, d. 28 Apr 1882, LC, unk, 60-0-0, p. Samuel & Louisa Johnson, c/o: Emily Johnson, sc: Emily Johnson, wife, 1st Dist., BVS:1882:1

JOHNSON, W. W., W, M, d. 24 Jul 1894, nr Waxpool, typhoid fever, 26-0-0, p. Wm. A. & N. E. Johnson, b. nr Waxpool, laborer, unm, sc: W.A. Johnson, father, 1st Dist., BVS:1894:1

Loudoun County, Virginia, Death Register, 1853-1896   155

JOHNSTON, Chas. A., W, , d. 12 Nov 1877, LC, nervous prostration, 72-10-0, c/o: Mary R. Johnston, sc: Saml J. Johnston, son, LE Dist., BVS:1877:8

JOHNSTON, Chas. A., W, M, d. 30 Aug 1891, Leesburg, diphtheria, 6-0-0, p. S. J. & Mollie Johnston, b. Leesburg, merchant, unm, sc: father, LE Dist., BVS:1891:4

JOHNSTON, James, W, M, d. 19 Aug 1853, Bloomfield, spinal affection, 74-6-0, p. unk, b. LC, merchant, c/o: Mary Johnston, sc: James W. Johnston, son, BVS:1854:1, LC:4

JONES, , W, F, d. 15 Feb 1890, LC, unk, 49-0-0, b. LC, none, c/o: Samuel Jones, sc: J.H. Jones, son, 2nd Dist., BVS:1890:4

JONES, Addie, B, F, d. 1 Mar 1881, LC, cramp colic, 0-11-0, p. Geo. & Eliza Jones, b. LC, sc: Eliza Jones, mother, 3rd Dist., BVS:1881:4

JONES, Alice, B, F, d. 26 Aug 1880, LC, old age, 60-0-0, p. unk, unm, sc: Benj. F. Hibbs, friend, 1st Dist., BVS:1880:2

JONES, Ann, B, F, d. 6 Jul 1891, nr Arcola, heart failure, 58-0-0, p. Aws. & Maria Jones, b. LC, laborer, unm, sc: Jake Allen, head of family, 1st Dist., BVS:1891:1

JONES, Ann W., W, F, d. 21 Nov 1853, LC, unk, 0-3-0, p. Lewen T. & Lydia C. Jones, b. LC, sc: Lewen T. Jones, father, BVS:1854:2, LC:1

JONES, Auze, B, M, d. 27 Nov 1878, nr Gum Spring, pneumonia, 84-0-0, p. Sina Jones, b. unk, laborer, c/o: Maria Jones, sc: Maria Jones, wife, BR Dist., BVS:1878:4

JONES, Cecilia, B, F, d. 28 Feb 1873, nr Farmwell Church, bronchitis, 40-0-0, p. unk, b. nr Farmwell Church, married, sc: Wilson Allen, head of family, BR Dist., BVS:1873:1

JONES, Charles, B, M, d. 1 Nov 1866, nr Gum Spring, unk, 1-0-0, p. Ann Jones, b. Gum Spring, unm, sc: L.H. Freeman, head of family, BVS:1866:3

JONES, Dinah, (f), F, d. 20 Aug 1853, nr Philomont, old age, 90-0-0, p. unk, b. unk, sc: Philip Jones, son, BVS:1854:1, LC:4

JONES, Franklin, B, M, d. 25 Apr 1885, nr Arcola, pneumonia, 2-0-0, p. Richard & Alice Jones, b. Arcola, sc: Richd Jones, father, 1st Dist., BVS:1885:4

JONES, George, B, M, d. 20 Dec 1891, Leesburg, la grippe, 0-2-0, p. Riley & Mary Jones, b. Leesburg, laborer, unm, sc: father, LE Dist., BVS:1891:4

JONES, George, B, M, d. 10 Sep 1880, LC, typhoid fever, 22-0-0, p. Henry & Virginia Jones, b. LC, laborer, unm, sc: Virginia Jones, mother, 1st Dist., BVS:1880:1

JONES, Hannah, W, F, d. 23 Mar 1887, LC, kidney affection, unk, p. Jos. & Ruth Thomas, b. LC, none, c/o: Joseph Thomas[sic], sc: Humphrey Thomas, friend, 3rd Dist., BVS:1887:6

JONES, Isaiah, B, M, d. 30 Aug 1880, LC, scrofula, 0-6-27, p. Henry & Annie Jones, unm, sc: Annie Jones, mother, 1st Dist., BVS:1880:2

JONES, Jennie, B, F, d. 1 Sep 1880, LC, murder, 25-0-0, p. James & Susan Jones, unm, sc: Susan Jones, mother, 1st Dist., BVS:1880:2

JONES, John, B, M, d. 10 Feb 1884, LC, measles, 36-0-0, p. Chas. & Nancy Jones, b. LC, laborer, sc: Edgar Harris, friend, 1st Dist., BVS:1884:1

JONES, John, W, M, d. 12 Nov 1881, LC, unk, 67-0-0, b. LC, tailor, sc: J.R. Jones, son, 1st Dist., BVS:1881:1

JONES, John E., W, M, d. 13 Sep 1880, Hillsboro, tumor, 31-0-0, p. John & L. H. Jones, b. LC, farmer, unm, sc: Robt. P. Jones, brother, 3rd Dist., BVS:1880:4

JONES, Lenard, W, M, d. 7 Nov 1889, LC, apoplexy, 63-0-0, p. P. E. & Ann C. Jones, b. LC, farmer, c/o: Lydia C. Jones, sc: L.C. Jones, widow, 2nd Dist., BVS:1889:3

JONES, Leven, B, M, d. 27 Feb 1885, nr Aldie, pneumonia, 56-0-0, p. Millie Jones, b. nr Aldie, laborer, c/o: Ginnie Jones, sc: Enoch Neal, son-in-law, 1st Dist., BVS:1885:4

JONES, Lilly, B, F, d. Dec 1872, 14-0-0, sc: Marcus Hampton, MC Dist., BVS:1872:7

JONES, Lucinda, B, F, d. 29 Oct 1881, LC, dyspepsia, 62-0-0, b. LC, c/o: Thos Jones, sc: Geo Young, friend, 3rd Dist., BVS:1881:4

JONES, Maggie, B, F, d. 15 Aug 1885, nr Aldie, croup, 0-5-0, p. Leven & Ginnie Jones, b. nr Aldie, sc: Enoch Neal, uncle, 1st Dist., BVS:1885:4

JONES, Maria, B, F, d. 20 Apr 1874, Broad Run Dist., paralysis, 66-0-0, p. unk, b. LC, married, sc: Ause Jones, husband, BR Dist., BVS:1874:3

JONES, Mary E., B, F, d. 10 Aug 1880, LC, dropsy, 13-0-0, p. Thomas & Lizzie Jones, unm, sc: Lizzie Jones, mother, 1st Dist., BVS:1880:2

JONES, Mary Ellen, B, F, d. 26 Oct 1866, nr Gum Spring, typhoid fever, 11-0-0, p. Ann Jones, b. nr Gum Spring, sc: L.H. Freeman, head of family, BVS:1866:3

JONES, Millie, B, F, d. 28 Feb 1885, nr Aldie, old age, 78-0-0, p. unk, sc: Enoch Neal, grandson, 1st Dist., BVS:1885:4

JONES, Millie, B, F, d. 10 May 1882, LC, cancer, 25-0-0, p. John & Annie Jones, unm, sc: John Jones, father, 1st Dist., BVS:1882:1

[JONES], no name, (f), F, d. Dec 1855, unk, 0-3-0, p. Leven & Mahala Jones, b. LC, sc: Mahala Jones, mother, BVS:1855:8, LC:19

[JONES], no name, (f), M, d. 15 Aug 1856, Leesburg, unk, 0-0-1/2, p. Elizabeth Jones, b. Leesburg, unm, sc: Priscilla Jones, grandmother, BVS:1856:1, LC:19

[JONES], no name, B, F, d. 1 Dec 1866, Fairfax line, unk, 0-0-1, p. Isabella Jones, b. Fairfax line, sc: Wm A. Hutchison, head of family, BVS:1866:3

[JONES], no name, B, , d. Jul 1869, LC, unk, p. Ady & Jane Jones, b. LC, sc: Ady Jones, father, BVS:1869:1

[JONES], no name, B, M, d. Sep 1873, Leesburg, children's complaint, 0-6-0, p. Charles & Mary Jones, b. Leesburg, unm, sc: Mary Jones, mother, LE Dist., BVS:1873:2

JONES, no name, B, F, d. 11 Jan 1884, nr Leesburg, unk, 0-0-1, p. Riley & Lucy Jones, b. LC, sc: Riley Jones, father, 2nd Dist., BVS:1884:4

JONES, no name, B, M, d. 15 Mar 1885, Leesburg, unk, 0-0-8, p. Wm. L. & Mary Jones, sc: Wm. L. Jones, father, 2nd Dist., BVS:1885:1

JONES, Norah, B, F, d. 10 Apr 1880, LC, teething, 2-0-0, p. Henry & Virginia Jones, b. LC, unm, sc: Virginia Jones, mother, 1st Dist., BVS:1880:1

JONES, Rebecca A., B, F, d. 5 Feb 1885, Lincoln, pneumonia, 28-0-0, b. LC, c/o: Peter Jones, sc: Peter Jones, husband, 3rd Dist., BVS:1885:6

JONES, Robert, B, M, d. 14 Feb 1880, LC, whooping cough, 2-0-0, p. Thomas & Lizzie Jones, unm, sc: Lizzie Jones, mother, 1st Dist., BVS:1880:2

JONES, Ruby, B, M, d. 3 Nov 1887, Farmwell, consumption, 11-0-0, p. Richard & Alice Jones, b. Farmwell, sc: Richard Jones, father, 1st Dist., BVS:1887:1

JONES, Sandy, (f), M, d. 18 Feb 1857, nr Mechanicsville, consumption, 19-0-0, p. Milly Jones, b. Fauquier Co., sc: Milly Jones, mother, BVS:1857:5, LC:27

JONES, Sarah, B, F, d. Oct 1873, Leesburg, spine disease, 13-0-0, p. Lewis & Lena Jones, b. Leesburg, laborer, sc: Lina Jones, mother, LE Dist., BVS:1873:2

JONES, Sarah E., W, , d. 15 Aug 1877, LC, dropsy, 40-0-0, c/o: Robert Jones, sc: Geo. W. Taylor, son-in-law, LE Dist., BVS:1877:8

JONES, Sarah J., B, F, d. 19 Aug 1876, nr Mount Gilead, unk, unk, p. Riley & Priscilla Jones, b. LC, unm, sc: Nelson Jones, son, MT Dist., BVS:1876:1

JONES, Susan, B, F, d. 1 Aug 1876, nr Mountville, dropsy, 30-0-0, c/o: Harrison Jones, sc: Moton Harris, father, MC Dist., BVS:1876:4

JORDAN, Martha, B, F, d. 10 Sep 1896, LC, consumption, 27-0-0, wife, sc: Noble Adams, no kin, LE Dist., BVS:1896:5

Loudoun County, Virginia, Death Register, 1853-1896 157

KAIGHN, Henrietta E., W, F, d. 1 Mar 1893, Leesburg, pneumonia, 43-0-0, p. unk, b. Leesburg, unm, sc: S.H. Kaighn, LE Dist., BVS:1893:6

KAIGHN, Mary E., W, F, d. 1 Jul 1883, Leesburg, paralysis, 75-0-0, p. Simon & Ebenzer Triplett, b. Kentucky, c/o: John Kaighn, sc: Isabella Kaighn, daughter, 2nd Dist., BVS:1883:7

KAIN, William, W, M, d. 31 Jan 1857, Poor House, frozen, 28-0-0, b. Ireland, sc: steward of poorhouse, BVS:1857:3, LC:26

KALB, Chas. K., W, M, d. 15 Aug 1874, W of Lovettsville, brain fever, 3-0-0, p. Saml S. & Lydia Kalb, LV Dist., BVS:1874:6

KALB, John G. R., W, M, d. 25 Nov 1886, cancer of stomach, 63-0-0, p. Samuel & Susannah, farmer, c/o: Ellen H. Kalb, sc: Harry P. Kalb, son, 2nd Dist., BVS:1886:5

KALB, Lydia A., W, F, d. 1 May 1885, nr Lovettsville, cancer, 53-8-15, p. Philip & Louisa Vincel, b. LC, c/o: Samuel J. Kalb, sc: Samuel J. Kalb, husband, 2nd Dist., BVS:1885:2

KALB, Saml., W, M, d. 18 April 1855, LC, dropsy, 58-8-3, p. Jno. & Susanna Kalb, b. Maryland, farmer, sc: Susanna Kalb, wife, BVS:1855:1, LC:14

KALB, Willie M., W, M, d. 17 Mar 1859/60, Washington, DC, congestion of brain, 7-1-0, p. John G.R. & Ellen H. Kalb, b. LC, sc: Ellen H. Kalb, mother, BVS:1859:1, 1860:4, LC:37

KARNER, T. S., W, F, d. 23 Dec 1896, Arcola, typhoid fever, 66-0-0, b. LC, c/o: Hylor Karner, sc: Hylor Karner, husband, BR Dist., BVS:1896:3

KARNES, Eliza, W, F, d. 22 Jul 1865, Brook Farm, typhoid dysentery, 41-3-16, p. S. & Mercy Karnes, b. New York, housekeeper, unm, sc: Scilanslet Karnes, father, BVS:1865:2

KARNES, Mercy J., W, F, d. 14 Jul 1865, Brook Farm, typhoid dysentery, 63-3-19, p. Amos & K. Upson, b. Connecticut, housekeeper, consort, sc: Scilanslet Karnes, husband, BVS:1865:2

KEEN, Benjamin, W, M, d. 31 Aug 1885, nr Guilford, cholera infantum, 0-3-0, p. Benjamin B. & Annie Keen, b. Guilford, sc: Benj. B. Keen, father, 1st Dist., BVS:1885:4

KEEN, Clemence, W, F, d. 21 Mar 1886, nr Unison, brain fever, 17-0-0, p. Jonathan & Amanda Keen, b. nr Unison, unm, sc: Jonathan Keen, father, 1st Dist., BVS:1886:1

KEEN, Jonathan, W, M, d. 10 Mar 1890, nr Unison, thrown from horse, 62-0-0, p. Geo. & Nancy Keen, b. LC, farmer, c/o: Amanda S. Keen, sc: Amanda S. Keen, wife, 1st Dist., BVS:1890:2

KEENE, Elizabeth, W, F, d. 24 Dec 1874, Broad Run Dist., paralysis, 68-8-13, p. John & Rebecca Dulin, b. LC, c/o: Newton Keene, sc: Newton Keene, husband, BR Dist., BVS:1874:3

KEENE, Harriet, W, F, d. Mar 1857, unk, 45-0-0, p. unk, b. LC, sc: John J. Coleman, neighbor, BVS:1857:7, LC:28

KEENE, J. J., W, M, d. 12 Dec 1891, Unison, cons of lungs, 6-0-0, p. C. F. & Elizabeth Keene, b. LC, farmer, sc: C.F. Keene, father, 1st Dist., BVS:1891:2

KEENE, Newton, W, M, d. 8 Apr 1880, LC, paralysis of heart, 76-0-0, p. unk, c/o: Elizabeth Keene, sc: Elizabeth Keene, wife, 1st Dist., BVS:1880:2

KEENE, Thompson, W, M, d. May 1857, unk, 50-0-0, p. unk, b. LC, farmer, sc: John J. Coleman, neighbor, BVS:1857:7, LC:28

KEENE, Wm. H., W, M, d. 24 Aug 1865, Coton Farm, inflammation brain, 1-9-0, p. A.D. & C.J. Keene, b. LC, unm, sc: A.D. Keene, father, BVS:1865:2

KEES, Richd. F., W, M, d. Apr 1855, Jesse Piggott's farm, catarrh fever, 2-0-0, p. Wm. & Alcinda Kees, b. Jose Piggott farm, sc: Alcinda Kees, mother, BVS:1855:7, LC:18

KEEYS, James F., W, M, d. 21 Sep 1858, LC, typhoid fever, 35-0-0, p. unk, b. LC, c/o: Louisa A. Keeys, sc: Robt J. Hoskinson, friend, BVS:1858:1, LC:29

KELLY, Caroline, B, F, d. Sep 1880, Leesburg, chills, 33-0-0, p. Robt & Maria Washington, b. LC, laborer, c/o: James Kelly, sc: Arch. Lee, step-father, 2nd Dist., BVS:1880:6

KELLY, Catherine, W, F, d. 4 Jan 1854, LC, croup, 0-7-2, p. Patrick & Ellen Kelly, b. LC, sc: Ellen Kelly, mother, BVS:1854:9, LC:9

KELLY, John, W, M, d. 8 Sep 1866, Carolina Road, cancer, 63-5-10, p. unk, b. Pennsylvania, blacksmith, sc: Wm A. Dennis, son-in-law, BVS:1866:3

KELLY, Lawson, W, M, d. 25 Aug 1891, nr Sterling, brain fever, 3-0-0, p. J. S. & A. V. Kelly, b. LC, farmer, sc: J.S. Kelly, father, 1st Dist., BVS:1891:2

KELLY, Patrick, W, M, d. 24 Nov 1859/60, LC, dropsy, 42-0-0, p. Thos. & Catharine Kelly, b. Ireland, laborer, c/o: Ellen Kelly, sc: Wm. Kelly, brother, BVS:1859:1, 1860:4, LC:37

KELLY, Saml D., W, M, d. 27 May 1881, LC, unk, 1-6-0, p. Robt & S.C. Kelly, sc: Robert Kelly, father, 1st Dist., BVS:1881:1

KELLY, Wm., W, M, d. 17 Oct 1865, nr Lovettsville, typhoid fever, 47-0-0, p. unk, b. Ireland, laborer, married, sc: Mary Kelly, wife, 1st Dist., BVS:1865:3/4

KENDALL, Clabourn, W, M, d. 8 Dec 1883, nr Upperville, Fauquier Co., paralysis, 64-0-0, p. Francis & Mary Kendall, b. LC, farmer, married, sc: John M. Gibson, friend, 1st Dist., BVS:1883:1

KENDALL, Clifton, W, M, d. 24 Sep 1891, Bloomfield, jaundice, 0-0-9, p. A. F. & Martha Kendall, b. LC, farmer, sc: A.F. Kendall, father, 1st Dist., BVS:1891:2

KENDALL, no name, W, F, d. 17 Feb 1888, nr Bloomfield, unk, 0-0-7, p. Amos F. & Martha Kendall, b. LC, sc: Amos F. Kendall, father, 1st Dist., BVS:1888:4

KENT, Arthur C., W, M, d. 28 Dec 1893, Leesburg, diphtheria, 2-0-0, p. Nelson & Annie, b. Leesburg, unm, sc: Nelson H. Kent, LE Dist., BVS:1893:6

KENT, Jessie S., W, F, d. 12 Jan 1894, Leesburg, diphtheria, 3-10-0, p. Nelson & Mamie, b. Leesburg, unm, sc: Nelson H. Kent, LE Dist., BVS:1894:3

KENT, Wm H., W, M, d. 4 Jan 1889, LC, heart disease, 80-0-0, p. Samuel & E. Kent, b. LC, none, c/o: Elizabeth Kent, sc: Elizabeth Kent, wife, 3rd Dist., BVS:1889:5

KERN, Hannah, W, F, d. 1 Oct 1875, Lovettsville Dist, dropsy, 6-0-0, b. LC, c/o: Conway M. Kern, LV Dist., BVS:1875:4

KERN, Mary, W, F, d. 5 Mar 1890, LC, unk, 75-9-2, p. Jacob & Elizabeth Kern, b. LC, unm, sc: N.H. Bartlett, son-in-law, 2nd Dist., BVS:1890:4

KERNAN, Thomas, W, M, d. 23 May 1873, Middleburg, consumption, 14-0-0, p. Thos. & Mary Kernan, b. Middleburg, laborer, sc: John ?, step father, MC Dist., BVS:1873:5

[KERNS], no name, W, M, d. 2 Dec 1874, Broad Run Dist., unk, 0-0-1/2, p. John N. & Martha A. Kerns, sc: John N. Kerns, father, BR Dist., BVS:1874:3

KERRICK, Agnes, W, F, d. 11 Jul 1883, nr Middleburg, pneumonia, 1-1-0, p. Francis M. & Sarah Kerrick, b. nr Middleburg, sc: Francis M. Kerrick, father, 1st Dist., BVS:1883:1

KERRICK, Lucy Ann, W, F, d. 20 Jul 1873, nr Welbourne, brain fever, 0-0-5, p. F. M. & Lucy Kerrick, b. Welbourne, sc: Francis M. Kerrick, father, MC Dist., BVS:1873:5

KERSEY, Maria Louisa, W, F, d. 27 May 1874, Aldie, consumption, 32-0-0, p. Saml & Catharine Simpson, b. LC, c/o: W.W. Kersey, sc: W.W. Kersey, husband, MC Dist., BVS:1874:4

KETTLE, Amanda E., W, F, d. 1 May 1883, nr Leesburg, pneumonia, 48-0-0, p. Jas. & Mary Kettle, b. LC, unm, sc: Jas M. Kettle, brother, 2nd Dist., BVS:1883:3

KETTLE, Mary E., W, F, d. 27 Sep 1872, LC, pneumonia, 30-3-15, p. Jas. & Nancy Kettle, b. LC, unm, sc: Isaac Carr, friend, uncle, LE Dist., BVS:1872:3

KEYES, Janie, W, F, d. 16 Oct 1887, Mountville, pneumonia, 1-2-0, p.

Loudoun County, Virginia, Death Register, 1853-1896   159

James H. & Annie Keys, b. Mountville, unm, sc: James H. Keys, father, 1st Dist., BVS:1887:1

KEYS, Freddie, W, M, d. 22 mar 1885, nr Mountville, unk, 0-3-7, p. Howard & Annie Keys, b. Mountville, sc: Howard Keys, father, 1st Dist., BVS:1885:4

KEYS, Jane E., W, F, d. 17 May 1880, Waterford, heart disease, 65-0-0, p. unk, b. LC, c/o: Wm. Keys, sc: Chas. Ball, friend, 3rd Dist., BVS:1880:4

KEYS, John, W, M, d. 1 May 1880, LC, bronchitis, 3-0-0, p. Jno L. & Martha Keys, unm, sc: Martha Keys, mother, 1st Dist., BVS:1880:2

[KEYS], no name, W, M, d. 10 Sep 1884, LC, cholera infantum, 0-7-0, p. John & Mollie Keys, b. LC, sc: John Keys, father, 1st Dist., BVS:1884:2

KEYS, Samuel, W, M, d. 10 Nov 1880, LC, bronchitis, 3-0-0, p. Jno L. & Martha Keys, unm, sc: Martha Keys, mother, 1st Dist., BVS:1880:2

KEYS, Susan, W, F, d. 15 Aug 1880, Silcott Springs, croup, 2-0-0, p. Jno. W. & Alice Keys, b. LC, sc: Jno. W. Keys, father, 3rd Dist., BVS:1880:4

KIDWELL, Bessie V., W, M, d. Mar 1874, LC, choked to death, 1-0-0, p. Jas & Mary E. Kidwell, sc: Jas. Kidwell, father, LE Dist., BVS:1874:5

KIDWELL, Cecelia A., W, F, d. 5 Dec 1856, LC, unk, 0-1-0, p. Hezekiah & Cecelia A. Kidwell, b. LC, sc: Cecelia A. Kidwell, mother, BVS:1856:2, LC:21

KIDWELL, Chas. F., W, M, d. 26 Feb. 1871, whooping cough, 0-3-0, p. J. H. & L. Kidwell, BR Dist., BVS:1871:3

KIDWELL, Eliza, W, F, d. Oct 1854, L. Luckett's Farm, hemorrhage of stomach, 24-0-0, sc: Michael Moraity, BVS:1854:13, LC:13

KIDWELL, Emaline, W, F, d. 30 Jul 1856, LC, whooping cough, 17-10-10, p. Wm. & Maria Kidwell, b. LC, unm, sc: Maria Kidwell, mother, BVS:1856:3, LC:21

KIDWELL, Fannie, W, F, d. 3 May 1878, LC, paralysis, 75-0-0, b. LC, c/o: Ellzey Kidwell, sc: James E. Kidwell, son, LE Dist., BVS:1878:8

KIDWELL, Franklin, W, M, d. 5 Sep 1885, nr Lovettsville, killed by bomb shell, 18-0-0, p. Thomas E. & Mary E. Kidwell, b. LC, laborer, unm, sc: Thomas E. Kidwell, father, 2nd Dist., BVS:1885:2

KIDWELL, Geo. Rust, W, M, d. 20 Jul 1854, LC, dysentery, 10-2-20, p. Wm. & Maria Kidwell, b. LC, sc: Maria Kidwell, mother, BVS:1854:9, LC:9

KIDWELL, George F., W, M, d. 26 Mar 1874, nr Hillsboro, dyspepsia, 60-0-0, p. unk, b. LC, merchant, sc: R. Goodchilds, friend, JF Dist., BVS:1874:2

KIDWELL, John H., W, M, d. 25 Aug 1880, LC, worms, 2-0-0, p. John H. & Laura Kidwell, unm, sc: Laura F. Kidwell, mother, 1st Dist., BVS:1880:2

KIDWELL, John W., W, M, d. 6 Aug 1866, b. dysentery, 10-0-0, p. John F. & Susan Kidwell, b. Fauquier Co., sc: father, BVS:1866:2

KIDWELL, Mary E., W, M[sic], d. 15 Jun 1883, nr Leesburg, vertigo, 37-0-0, p. Israel & Mary Myers, b. LC, c/o: James E. Kidwell, sc: James E. Kidwell, husband, 2nd Dist., BVS:1883:7

KIDWELL, May, W, F, d. 10 Aug 1875, nr Hillsboro, apoplexy, 65-0-0, b. LC, c/o: Zedekial Kidwell, sc: Zedekial Kidwell, husband, JF Dist., BVS:1875:3

[KIDWELL], no name, W, M, d. 27 May 1896, LC, 0-1-4, p. R. A. & Y. Kidwell, b. LC, farmer, unm, sc: father, LE Dist., BVS:1896:5

KIDWELL, Thomas A., W, M, d. 13 Aug 1889, LC, heart disease, 67-0-0, p. W. & Maria Kidwell, b. LC, laborer, c/o: Mary Kidwell, sc: Mary Kidwell, widow, 2nd Dist., BVS:1889:3

KIDWELL, Thos., W, M, d. 9 Aug 1866, b. dysentery, 0-6-0, p. John F. & Susan Kidwell, b. Fauquier Co., sc: father, BVS:1866:2

KIDWELL, Wm. H. H., W, M, d. 20 Aug 1854`, LC, dysentery, 13-2-6, p. Wm. & Maria Kidwell, b. LC, sc: Maria Kidwell, mother, BVS:1854:9, LC:9

KILE, Sarah, W, F, d. 28 Nov 1858, her res, Kile's Store, dropsy, 65-0-0, p. Abraham & ... Palmer, b. nr

Ebenezer Church, c/o: George Kile, sc: George Kile, widower, BVS:1858:3, LC:31

KILGORE, Mary, W, F, d. May 1864, Hillsboro, 0-1-0, p. Jas M. Kilgore, b. LC, sc: Jas M. Kilgore, father, BVS:1864:1, LC:38

KILGOUR, Charlotte, W, F, d. unk, nr Hillsboro, general debility, 80-0-0, p. James & Margaret Kilgour, b. Maryland, unm, sc: James M. Kilgour, nephew, JF Dist., BVS:1874:1

KILLEN, Richard S., W, M, d. 11 Aug 1853, LC, dysentery, 38-0-0, p. unk, b. England, minister, sc: Jno Hoffman, head of family, BVS:1854:4, LC:2

KING, Edwin, W, M, d. 16 Sep 1889, LC, unk, 0-0-15, p. E. & Sarah King, b. LC, none, unm, sc: E.J. King, father, 3rd Dist., BVS:1889:5

KING, Hannah, B, F, d. 15 Jun 1866, Carolina Road, old age, 71-0-0, b. Carolina Road, sc: John J. Tyler, former master, BVS:1866:3

KING, Harriet, W, F, d. 21 Feb 1872, Mount Gilead Twp., heart disease, 75-0-0, p. unk, b. unk, unm, sc: George F. Alder, physician, MT Dist., BVS:1872:2

KING, Ida, W, F, d. 10 Aug 1893, Pleasant Valley, cholera infantum, 0-5-0, p. Wm. & Rosa King, b. Pleasant Valley, sc: Wm. King, father, 1st Dist., BVS:1893:1

KING, Willie, W, M, d. 23 Jun 1872, Woodgrove, 3-0-0, p. James H. & Fannie King, MC Dist., BVS:1872:7

KINSEY, Nancy, W, F, d. 14 Mar 1887, Fauquier Co, old age, 77-0-0, p. unk, b. Rappahannock, unm, sc: James W. McDonald, nephew, 1st Dist., BVS:1887:1

KIRKPATRICK, Catherine, W, F, d. 19 Mar 1892, Mount Gilead, child birth, 39-0-0, p. Jno. & Jane Gray, b. Mount Gilead, laborer, married, sc: Jno Kirkpatrick, husband, MT Dist., BVS:1892:8

KIRKPATRICK, Mary J., W, F, d. 20 Mar 1891, nr Upperville, consumption, 50-0-0, p. Wesley & Ann Edwards, b. Fauquier Co., farmer, c/o: J.F. Kirkpatrick, sc: J.F.

Kirkpatrick, husband, 1st Dist., BVS:1891:2

KIRKPATRICK, Thomas J., W, M, d. 11 Jul 1857, on F.M. Carter's Farm, putrid sore throat, 6-0-0, p. Hugh & Mary Kirkpatrick, b. Jas. B. Wilson's Farm, sc: H. Kirkpatrick, father, BVS:1857:6, LC:28

KIRKPATRICK, Wm. E., W, M, d. 6 Jan 1854, Francis Mill, bowel complaint, 1-0-13, p. Hugh & Mary E. Kirkpatrick, b. nr Mountville, sc: father, BVS:1854:12, LC:12

KITCHEN, Hannah C., W, F, d. 7 Dec 1853, LC, croup, 4-3-0, p. Wm. & Eliz. Kitchen, b. Fairfax, sc: Wm. Kitchen, father, BVS:1854:3, LC:1

KITZMILLER, Archibald, W, M, d. 9 Sep 1876, Leesburg, diphtheria, 1-5-0, p. Jennings & Mary E. Kitzmiller, b. Washington DC, sc: F.J. Crissey, grandfather, LE Dist., BVS:1876:6

KLINE, Mary A., W, F, d. 3 Jun 1888, LC, congestion of brain, 71-0-0, p. James & Sarah Hurst, b. Jefferson Co. WV, none, c/o: James Kline, sc: John A. Kline, son, 3rd Dist., BVS:1888:1

KNOX, Catharine, W, F, d. 15 Sep 1855, Leesburg, cancer, 57-6-3, p. unk, b. Fauquier Co., c/o: Thos. P. Knox, sc: Thos. P. Knox, husband, BVS:1855:3, LC:15

KOLB, Rose, W, F, d. 23 May 1858, Leesburg, unk, 0-8-0, p. Jacob & Johanna Kolb, b. Leesburg, sc: Jacob Kolb, father, BVS:1858:1, LC:29

KOLB, Virginia, W, F, d. 27 Apr 1858, Leesburg, croup, 2-0-0, p. Jacob & Johanna Kolb, b. Leesburg, sc: Jacob Kolb, father, BVS:1858:1, LC:29

KUTHER, Geo., W, M, d. 22 Jul 1888, nr Arcola, paralysis, 64-0-0, p. unk, b. Europe, sc: John Schneider, friend, 1st Dist., BVS:1888:4

LACEY, Cath B., W, F, d. 24 Sep 1865, Snickersville, unk, b. Clarke Co., married, sc: B.R. Lacey, husband, BVS:1865:1

LACEY, Francis, W, M, d. 12 Jun 1858, Jesse Richards', inflammatory rheumatism, 7-6-10, p. Jos & Mary F. Lacey, b. Jesse Richards', sc:

Jesse Richards, grandfather, BVS:1858:4, LC:31

LACEY, Israel, W, M, d. 22 Aug 1857, LC, dysentery, 65-11-16, p. Samuel & Mary Lacey, b. LC, carpenter, c/o: Ann Lacey, sc: Ann Lacey, wife, BVS:1857:1, LC:25

LACEY, M. H., W, M, d. 16 Oct 1856, LC, unk, 38-2-0, p. Elias & Mary Lacey, b. LC, sc: Mary Lacey, consort, BVS:1856:7, LC:24

[LACEY], no name, W, M, d. 22 Apr 1871, nr Woodgrove, unk, 0-0-5, p. S. E. & Patience Lacey, b. nr Woodgrove, sc: S.E. Lacey, father, JF Dist., BVS:1871:1

LACEY, Richard H., W, M, d. 5 Jan 1857, LC, unk, 0-6-0, p. Mesheck & M.L. Lacy, b. LC, sc: Mary L. Lacy, mother, BVS:1857:7, LC:28

LACK, Mary, W, F, d. 11 May 1881, LC, dropsy, 77-0-0, p. Wm. & Mary Milne, b. Scotland, c/o: William Lack, sc: Wm. Lack, husband, 2nd Dist., BVS:1881:7

LACOCK, Frances A., W, F, d. 25 Dec 1859/60, LC, scarlet fever, 6-9-7, p. James & Mary A. Lacock, b. LC, sc: James Lacock, father, BVS:1859:1, 1860:4, LC:37

LACY, Benj. R., W, M, d. 6 Oct 1883, nr Bloomfield, old age, 82-0-0, p. Ellis & Mary Lacy, b. nr Aldie, physician, married, sc: Joseph B. Lacy, son, 1st Dist., BVS:1883:1

LAKE, Bettie B., W, F, d. 29 Aug 1890, Philomont, typhoid fever, 11-6-0, p. T. W. & F. Lake, b. LC, none, unm, sc: F.O. Lake, mother, 3rd Dist., BVS:1890:6

LAKE, E., W, F, d. 15 Aug 1888, LC, cholera infantum, 0-4-12, p. T. W. & T. O. Lake, b. LC, none, unm, sc: T.W. Lake, father, 3rd Dist., BVS:1888:1

LAMB, Anna C., W, F, d. 20 Aug 1858, Leesburg, whooping cough, 2-4-0, p. Saml & Lucy J. Lamb, b. Leesburg, sc: Samuel Lamb, father, BVS:1858:2, LC:30

LAMBERT, Edward, W, M, d. 30 Jan 1896, Ryan, pneumonia, 0-15-2, p. J. D. & Sarah P. Lambert, b. Ryan, sc: J.D. Lambert, father, BR Dist., BVS:1896:3

LAMBERT, Francis, W, M, d. 22 Sep 1891, Arcola, diarrhea, 74-0-0, p. unk, b. France, unk, c/o: Susan Lambert, sc: J.D. Lambert, son, 1st Dist., BVS:1891:2

LAMBERT, Francis C., W, M, d. 15 Apr 1859/60, LC, unk, 0-2-15, p. Francis & M.L. Lambert, b. LC, sc: Francis Lambert, father, BVS:1859:6, 1860:3, LC:36

LAMBERT, Francis D., W, M, d. 11 Sep 1891, Ryan, brain fever, 1-0-0, p. J. D. & Sarah Lambert, b. LC, merchant, sc: J.D. Lambert, father, 1st Dist., BVS:1891:2

LAMBERT, Lee J., W, M, d. 25 Sep 1875, Gum Spring, dropsy, 12-0-12, p. Francis & Mary L. Lambert, b. LC, unm, sc: Francis Lambert, father, BR Dist., BVS:1875:5

LANDHAM, Sarah Catherine, W, F, d. 30 Jan 1891, Woodgrove, heart disease, 64-0-0, p. Robert & Barbry Ashby, b. Woodgrove, farmer, wife, sc: Minor Landham, JF Dist., BVS:1891:7

LANDSDOWN, Jesse, B, M, d. 5 Sep 1885, Middleburg, pneumonia, 22-0-0, p. Edward & Kizzie Landsdown, b. Middleburg, laborer, unm, sc: Edward Landsdown, father, 1st Dist., BVS:1885:4

LANE, Alice, B, F, d. 1 Aug 1891, nr Aldie, consumption, 16-0-0, p. John & Bettie Lane, b. LC, laborer, unm, sc: John Lane, head of family, 1st Dist., BVS:1891:1

LANE, David D., W, M, d. 9 Jul 1876, nr Pleasant Valley, paralysis, 85-6-0, p. unk, b. LC, farmer, married, sc: John Lane, grandson, BR Dist., BVS:1876:2

LANE, James W., W, M, d. 6 May 1855, P. R. Crane's, typhoid fever, 20-0-21, p. A. F. & Cathrn. Lane, b. Centerville, Fairfax Co., teacher, sc: P. B. Crane, uncle, BVS:1855:3, LC:16

LANE, Jas. L., W, M, d. 26 Oct 1875, Gum Spring, unk, 23-0-0, p. Chas. W. & Mary P. V. Lane, b. LC, laborer, married, sc: Chas. W. Lane, father, BR Dist., BVS:1875:5

LANE, Jos. B., W, M, d. 2 Mar 1874, Broad Run Dist., pneumonia, 22-0-0, p. Chas. W. Lane & wife, b. LC, farmer, sc: Chas. W. Lane, head of family, BR Dist., BVS:1874:3

LANE, Linnic, B, M, d. 19 Mar 1890, nr Aldie, unk, 0-5-0, p. John & Bettie Lane, b. nr Aldie, sc: John Lane, father, 1st Dist., BVS:1890:2

LANG, Elizabeth A., W, F, d. 13 May 1854, nr Union, cancer on throat, 51-0-0, p. Samuel & Elizabeth Richards, b. nr Union, c/o: Claybourn Lang, sc: husband, BVS:1854:11, LC:11

LANG, S. E., W, M, d. Apr 1896, Hillsboro, rheumatism, 57-0-0, laborer, consort, JF Dist., BVS:1896:8

LANG, Sally, W, F, d. 1 Nov 1853, nr Hillsboro, dysentery, 70-0-0, p. unk, b. Stafford Co., c/o: Jno. Lang, sc: Wm. Lang, son, BVS:1854:1, LC:4

LANHAM, Betsey, W, F, d. 10 Sep 1882, Poor House, unk, 80-0-0, p. unk, unm, sc: Jno R. Carter, superintendent, 1st Dist., BVS:1882:2

LANHAM, Minor, W, M, d. May 1896, Round Hill, old age, 76-0-0, farmer, consort, JF Dist., BVS:1896:8

LANHAN, Ellen H., W, F, d. 29 Jul 1882, LC, general debility, 84-11-29, b. LC, c/o: John Lanham, sc: Bethanie McFarland, daughter, 3rd Dist., BVS:1882:3

LATIMER, Sophia, W, F, d. 3 Aug 1853, LC, paralysis, 67-1-0, p. Peter & Mary Hoffman, b. Frederick, MD, c/o: ___ Latimer, sc: Jno Hoffman, nephew, BVS:1854:4, LC:2

LAUCK, Eliz B., W, F, d. 17 Dec 1865, nr J.P. Dulany's, consumption, 24-4-16, p. Isaac H. & Sarah E. Lauck, b. Page Co., unk, sc: father, BVS:1865:1

LAWSON, Mary S., W, , d. 12 Aug 1877, LC, cholera infantum, 0-9-0, p. J. H. & S. E. Lawson, sc: J.H. Lawson, father, LE Dist., BVS:1877:8

LAWSON, Samuel, W, M, d. 18 Jul 1888, LC, unk, 0-3-0, p. James H. & S. Lawson, b. LC, none, unm, sc: J.H. Lawson, father, 2nd Dist., BVS:1888:6

LAWSON, Sarah E., W, F, d. 16 Apr 1888, LC, child birth, 42-0-0, p. R. S. & Sarah Howser, b. LC, none, c/o:

J.H. Lawson, sc: J.H. Lawson, husband, 2nd Dist., BVS:1888:6

LAWSON, Sarah E., W, F, d. 16 Apr 1886, complications of disease, 41-0-0, p. unk, c/o: James H. Lawson,, sc: J. H. Lawson, husband, 2nd Dist., BVS:1886:5

LAY, Francis M., W, M, d. 15 Jul 1873, nr Hillsboro, diphtheria, 0-1-5, p. George H. & Virginia Lay, b. LC, sc: George H. Lay, father, JF Dist., BVS:1874:1

LAY, Franky, W, M, d. 30 Apr 1869, LC, measles, 2-6-0, p. George H. & Virginia Lay, b. LC, sc: Virginia Lay, mother, BVS:1869:1

LAY, George W., W, M, d. 7 Aug 1856, LC, dysentery, 1-10-0, p. Jos. E. & Susan Lay, b. LC, sc: Joseph E. Lay, father, BVS:1856:2, LC:21

LAYCOCK, Elizabeth, B, F, d. Aug 1871, LC, 31-0-0, p. M. & Maria Mathias, b. LC, c/o: C.A. Laycock, LE Dist., BVS:1871:4

LAYCOCK, Emily, W, F, d. 28 Dec 1884, Woodburn, pneumonia, 76-0-0, b. Virginia, c/o: Joseph Laycock, sc: Joseph Laycock, husband, 3rd Dist., BVS:1884:6

LAYCOCK, Joseph, W, M, d. 23 Aug 1891, Woodburn, heart failure, 89-0-0, p. Saml. & Ann Laycock, b. Woodburn, farmer, husband, unm, sc: Saml Laycock, MT Dist., BVS:1891:6

LAYCOCK, Laurence A., W, M, d. 26 Jun 1893, Leesburg, diphtheria, 4-0-0, p. Adin & Maggie, b. Leesburg, unm, sc: A.W. Laycock, LE Dist., BVS:1893:6

LAYCOCK, Lucy E., W, , d. 12 Jul 1877, LC, consumption, 24-1-0, p. Saml. & Matilda Laycock, sc: Robt. Davis, brother-in-law, LE Dist., BVS:1877:8

LAYCOCK, Maggie M., W, F, d. 27 May 1893, Leesburg, child birth, 27-0-0, p. unk, b. Leesburg, consort, sc: A.W. Laycock, LE Dist., BVS:1893:6

LEE, Alfred, B, M, d. 20 Jun 1885, Middleburg, consumption, 4-0-0, p. Alfred & Mildred Lee, b. Middleburg, sc: Alfred Lee, father, 1st Dist., BVS:1885:4

LEE, Alice, W, F, d. 14 Dec 1859/60, LC, consumption, 53-0-0, p. John &

Loudoun County, Virginia, Death Register, 1853-1896

Sarah Jones, b. LC, sc: A.D. Lee, husband, BVS:1859:6, 1860:3, LC:36

LEE, Amanda, B, F, d. 1 Apr 1874, Hamilton, child birth, 17-0-0, p. Geo. & Ellen Lee, b. LC, unm, sc: Ellen Lee, mother, JF Dist., BVS:1874:2

LEE, Amos, B, M, d. 10 Jun 1880, LC, typhoid fever, 21-0-0, p. Lewis A. & Martha Lee, laborer, unm, sc: Martha Lee, mother, 1st Dist., BVS:1880:2

LEE, Braxton, B, M, d. 30 Mar 1894, Middleburg, pneumonia, 21-0-0, p. Alfred & Mildred Lee, b. Middleburg, sc: Alfred Lee, father, 1st Dist., BVS:1894:2

LEE, Carrie, -, -, d. 15 Nov 1885, Aldie, scrofula, 34-0-0, p. Wm. & Mary Toliver, b. nr Aldie, c/o: James Lee, sc: Louis W. Lee, brother-in-law, 1st Dist., BVS:1885:4

LEE, Catharine V., W, F, d. 10 Mar 1874, Broad Run Dist., consumption, 29-0-0, p. Richd. Y. & Emily Moran, b. LC, c/o: John G. Lee, sc: John G. Lee, head of family, BR Dist., BVS:1874:3

LEE, Charles, B, M, d. 23 Dec 1890, Hillsboro, heart disease, 18-0-0, p. John & Caroline Lee, b. LC, laborer, unm, sc: John Lee, father, 3rd Dist., BVS:1890:6

LEE, Ella May, W, F, d. 17 Jul 1864, Leesburg Road, while ?, 8-6-15, p. J.F. & S.E. Lee, b. LC, sc: J.F. Lee, father, BVS:1864:2, LC:39

LEE, Eva, B, F, d. Oct 1874, LC, child complaint, 0-4-0, p. Rachel Lee, sc: Rachel Lee, mother, LE Dist., BVS:1874:5

LEE, George, W, M, d. 9 Feb 1858, Leesburg, inflammation of bladder, 57-0-10, p. Geo & Evelyn B. Lee, b. LC, physician, c/o: Sallie M. Lee, sc: F.M. Henderson, wife's brother, BVS:1858:2, LC:30

LEE, Harriet, B, F, d. 27 May 1866, Francis Shreve's, fall from a tree, 8-0-0, p. Ann Lee, sc: Francis Shreve, BVS:1866:2

LEE, Isabela, B, F, d. 24 Dec 1886, nr Arcola, consumption, 15-0-0, p. Henry & Flora Lee, b. nr Arcola, sc: William Lee, uncle, 1st Dist., BVS:1886:1

LEE, James, B, M, d. 10 Dec 1881, LC, fever, 35-0-0, b. LC, sc: Danl Lee, friend, 1st Dist., BVS:1881:2

LEE, James, B, M, d. 20 Nov 1891, nr Aldie, brain fever, 4-0-0, p. Lewis & Jennie Lee, b. LC, laborer, unm, sc: Jennie Lee, head of family, 1st Dist., BVS:1891:1

LEE, Judith B., W, F, d. 9 Mar 1855, LC, unk, 0-0-14, p. Richd E. & Ann C. Lee, b. LC, sc: Rich. E. Lee, father, BVS:1855:3, LC:15

LEE, Julia May, B, F, d. 28 Aug 1894, Hamilton, pneumonia, 9-0-0, p. Daniel & Julia Lee, b. Hamilton, unm, sc: Daniel Lee, father, 3rd Dist., BVS:1894:5

LEE, Lawson, B, M, d. 31 Jan 1873, nr Lovettsville, consumption, unk, p. Lawson Lee, b. nr Lovettsville, unm, sc: Mary A. Boger, mother, LV Dist., BVS:1873:4

LEE, Leah F., W, F, d. 8 Apr 1872, nr Broad Run, child birth, 23-1-0, p. Daniel T. & Leah Palmer, b. LC, c/o: George W. Lee, sc: Geo. W. Lee, head of family, BR Dist., BVS:1872:6

LEE, Lucilia, B, F, d. 17 Mar 1880, Waterford, unk, 0-0-2, p. Daniel & Julia Lee, b. LC, sc: Julia Lee, mother, 3rd Dist., BVS:1880:4

LEE, Margaret, W, F, d. 10 Nov 1883, nr Gum Spring, consumption, 62-0-0, p. unk, b. Fairfax Co., c/o: Laridy Lee, decd, sc: John F. Ryan, son, 1st Dist., BVS:1883:1

LEE, Martha, B, F, d. 10 Jun 1876, LC, fever, 19-0-0, p. George & Mary Lee, b. LC, sc: Mary Lee, mother, JF Dist., BVS:1876:8

LEE, Mary Ellen, B, F, d. 12 May 1876, LC, fever, 0-4-12, p. Daniel & Julia Lee, b. LC, sc: Julia Lee, mother, JF Dist., BVS:1876:8

[LEE], no name, B, M, d. 1 Feb 1874, Broad Run Dist., unk, 0-0-12, p. Rachel Lee, unm, sc: Rachel Lee, mother, BR Dist., BVS:1874:3

[LEE], no name, W, M, d. 16 Oct 1883, nr Arcola, chronic infantum, 0-0-9, p. Thos. A. & Cornelia Lee, b. nr Arcola, sc: Thos A. Lee, father, 1st Dist., BVS:1883:1

LEE, Thomas, B, M, d. 20 Sep 1880, LC, brain fever, 1-0-0, p. Alfred &

Annie Lee, b. LC, unm, sc: Annie Lee, mother, 1st Dist., BVS:1880:2

LEE, Thomas, B, M, d. 5 Jul 1886, nr Arcola, consumption, 13-0-0, p. Henry & Flora Lee, b. nr Arcola, unm, sc: William Lee, uncle, 1st Dist., BVS:1886:1

LEFEVER, Dewit, W, M, d. 27 Feb 1864, Farmwell, whooping cough, 0-1-6, p. Henry & Sallie Lefever, b. LC, sc: Henry S. Lefever, father, BVS:1864:2, LC:39

LEFEVER, Henry, W, M, d. 29 Jun 1892, Waxpool, dysentery, 69-0-0, p. Wm & Mary Lefever, b. Waxpool, laborer, c/o: Sallie Lafever, sc: Sallie Lefever, wife, 1st Dist., BVS:1892:1

LEFEVER, Herbert, W, M, d. 18 Mar 1886, brain fever, 0-6-0, p. Luther & Mary E., sc: Wm. E. McPherson, grandfather, 2nd Dist., BVS:1886:5

[LEFEVER], no name, W, M, d. 6 Feb 1856, LC, unk, 0-0-1, p. Peter & Frances A. Lefever, b. LC, sc: F.A. Lefever, mother, BVS:1856:7, LC:24

LEGG, Wm., W, M, d. 25 Nov 1896, Rectortown, unk, 0-2-0, p. Luke & Lula Legg, b. nr Rectortown, none, unm, sc: Luke Legg, father, MC Dist., BVS:1896:1

LEITH, Christiana, W, F, d. 27 Dec 1880, LC, apoplexy, 65-0-0, p. John & Mary Beavers, b. LC, c/o: Wm. Leith, sc: Frank Leith, step-son, 1st Dist., BVS:1880:2

LEITH, Mary L., W, F, d. 15 Sep 1887, Mountville, unk, 0-3-0, p. Laurence & Louisa Leith, b. Mountville, sc: Lawrence Leith, father, 1st Dist., BVS:1887:1

[LEITH], no name, W, F, d. 14 Aug 1855, Farmer's Delight, 0-0-7, p. Randh H. & Martha C. Leith, b. nr New Lisbon, sc: Randolph H. Leith, father, BVS:1855:7, LC:18

LEITH, Sarah Francis, W, F, d. 10 Oct 1876, nr Pot House, diphtheria, 7-5-20, p. B. F. & Mary L. Leith, b. LC, sc: B.F. Leith, father, MC Dist., BVS:1876:4

LEITH, T. B., W, M, d. 15 May 1896, nr Middleburg, consumption, 62-10-0, p. Wm. & Fannie Leith, b. nr Middleburg, farmer, consort, sc: Walter Leith, son, MC Dist., BVS:1896:1

LEITH, Thomas W., W, M, d. 21 Feb 1882, LC, diphtheria, 11-0-0, p. B. F. & Peni Leith, sc: B.F. Leith, father, 1st Dist., BVS:1882:1

LEITH, Veturia A., W, F, d. 19 Nov 1887, Unison, meningitis, 67-0-0, p. Henry & Frances Plaster, b. LC, c/o: Richard Leith, sc: Ernest Leith, son, 1st Dist., BVS:1887:1

LEMON, Henry T., W, M, d. 28 Dec 1885, Lincoln, accidentally shot, 16-0-0, p. Wm. T. & Mary J. Lemon, b. LC, sc: Wm. T. Lemon, father, 3rd Dist., BVS:1885:6

LEMON, Jacob, W, M, d. 16 Mar 1887, LC, heart disease, 79-9-0, b. LC, laborer, c/o: Jane Lemon, sc: Henry Lemon, son, 3rd Dist., BVS:1887:7

LENT, Abram, W, M, d. 14 Dec 1880, LC, old age, 97-0-0, p. unk, widower, sc: Samuel E. Lent, son, 1st Dist., BVS:1880:2

LENT, Casper, W, M, d. 9 Nov 1880, LC, accident, 21-0-0, p. Saml. C. & Martha A. Lent, unm, sc: Martha A. Lent, mother, 1st Dist., BVS:1880:2

LENT, Edna M., W, F, d. 16 Jun 1888, Sterling, diphtheria, 9-0-0, p. Franklin P. & Alverta Lent, b. Sterling, sc: Franklin P. Lent, father, 1st Dist., BVS:1888:4

LENT, Henry, W, M, d. 15 Feb 1877, nr Guilford Station, croup, 0-5-0, p. Saml. E. & Alverda Lent, b. nr Guilford, unm, sc: Saml E. Lent, father, BR Dist., BVS:1877:1

LESLIE, Joseph K., W, M, d. 15 Sep 1853, LC, dysentery, 5-1-12, p. Benja. & Johanna E. Leslie, b. LC, sc: Benj Leslie Jr., father, BVS:1854:4, LC:2

LESLIE, Rebecca K., W, F, d. 24 Oct 1853, LC, dysentery, 74-11-2, p. unk, b. unk, sc: Benj Leslie Jr., son, BVS:1854:4, LC:2

LESLIE, Samuel B., W, M, d. 10 Jan 1866, Hillsboro, cancer, 81-0-0, farmer, sc: Saml D. Leslie,?, BVS:1866:2

LEUT, Abram, W, M, d. 9 Jan 1881, LC, old age, 96-0-0, c/o: Ann Leut, sc: S.E. Leut, son, 1st Dist., BVS:1881:1

[LEVENBERG], no name, B, F, d. 6 Aug 1866, nr Round Hill, smothered by accident, unk, p. Winifred

Loudoun County, Virginia, Death Register, 1853-1896 165

Levenberg, b. nr Round Hill, sc: Wm. Chamblin, BVS:1866:1

LEVENBERRY, Elwood, B, M, d. 10 Oct 1879, LC, heart disease, 44-0-0, p. Jacob & Winefred Levenberry, b. LC, laborer, c/o: Louisa Levenberry, sc: Louisa Levenberry, wife, 3rd Dist., BVS:1879:3

LEVENBERRY, Helen, B, F, d. 21 Feb 1890, Hamilton, indigestion, 22-0-0, p. Elwood & Louisa Levenberry, b. LC, none, unm, sc: C.F. Levenberry, son, 3rd Dist., BVS:1890:6

LEVENBERRY, Louisa, B, F, d. 4 Jul 1890, Hamilton, indigestion, 53-0-0, p. Elwood & Louisa Levenberry, b. LC, none, c/o: Elwood Levenberry, sc: C.F. Levenberry, son, 3rd Dist., BVS:1890:6

LEVENBERRY, Martha, B, F, d. 1 Nov 1887, LC, spinal affection, 27-0-0, p. Chas. & M. Levenberry, b. LC, none, unm, sc: Chas Levenberry, father, 3rd Dist., BVS:1887:7

LEVENBERRY, Vier, B, F, d. Sep 1896, Round Hill, dysentery, 3-0-0, p. Bud & Fannie Levenberry, b. Round Hill, sc: brother, JF Dist., BVS:1896:10

LEWIN, Mittee Lee, W, F, d. 25 Jqn 1892, Purcellville, pneumonia, 0-0-14, p. Geo. H. & Fannie Lewin, b. Purcellville, sc: George H. Lewin, father, JF Dist., BVS:1892:7

LEWIS, Anna J., W, F, d. 7 Jan 1884, nr Lovettsville, unk, 24-0-0, p. unk, b. LC, c/o: Jno H. Lewis, sc: Robert S. Lewis, father-in-law, 2nd Dist., BVS:1884:5

LEWIS, Arthur, W, M, d. 18 Aug 1884, LC, consumption, 22-0-0, p. Harry & Mahala Lewis, b. LC, farmer, unm, sc: Harry Lewis, father, 1st Dist., BVS:1884:2

LEWIS, Caroline, B, F, d. 16 Sep 1871, 20-0-0, p. Luise & Lee Jackson, MC Dist., BVS:1871:2

LEWIS, Catherine, W, F, d. 5 Mar 1896, nr Millville, bronchitis, 11-0-0, p. H. R. & C. Lewis, b. nr Winchester, none, unm, sc: H.R. Lewis, father, MC Dist., BVS:1896:1

LEWIS, Elizabeth, W, F, d. 15 May 1878, nr Bolington, neuralgia, 28-0-0, p. Robert S. & Caroline Lewis, sc: Robert S. Lewis, father, LV Dist., BVS:1878:1/5

LEWIS, Estelle, B, F, d. 10 May 1880, Round Hill, consumption, 6-0-0, p. Chester & Louisa Lewis, b. LC, sc: Chester Lewis, father, 3rd Dist., BVS:1880:4

LEWIS, James, W, M, d. 17 Jul 1875, LC, gen. stroke, 58-3-27, p. Edwin & Sydney Lewis, b. Wilmington, Del., farmer, c/o: Ann Lewis, sc: Ann Lewis, wife, LE Dist., BVS:1875:1

LEWIS, Jenkin, W, M, d. 2 Jan 1853, Poor House, old age, 87-0-0, p. unk, b. PA, sc: Wm. Furr, keeper of poor house, BVS:1854:6, LC:6

LEWIS, John, B, M, d. 4 Jul 1896, Purcellville, old age, 95-0-0, p. unk, b. Purcellville, laborer, sc: Alfred Lewis, son, MT Dist., BVS:1896:9

LEWIS, Laura, B, F, d. 13 May 1874, W of Lovettsville, consumption, 18-0-0, p. Priscilla Lewis, LV Dist., BVS:1874:6

LEWIS, Laura F., W, F, d. 16 Jun 1856, LC, whooping cough, 4-6-16, p. Robert S. & Caroline A. Lewis, b. LC, sc: Caroline A. Lewis, mother, BVS:1856:2, LC:21

LEWIS, Lucinda, (f), F, d. 1 May 1855, LC, dropsy, 13-2-17, p. Elizabeth Lewis, b. LC, sc: Charles Adams, uncle, BVS:1855:3, LC:15

LEWIS, Lucy, (f), F, d. 1 Jan 1858, Waterford, old age, 73-0-0, b. LC, sc: Lucinda Lewis, daughter, BVS:1858:1, LC:29

LEWIS, Lucy, B, F, d. 30 Jun 1884, LC, dropsy, 23-0-0, p. Chas. & Maria Berkley, b. LC, c/o: Robt. Lewis, sc: Chas Berkley, father, 1st Dist., BVS:1884:2

LEWIS, Lydia J., (f), F, d. 12 Oct 1856, Lovettsville, scalded, 5-0-0, p. Priscilla Lewis, b. Lovettsville, sc: Priscilla Lewis, mother, BVS:1856:1, LC:20

LEWIS, Mahala J., W, F, d. 17 Dec 1886, nr Aldie, consumption, 52-0-0, p. Thomas & Priscilla Jones, b. nr Aldie, c/o: Harrison Lewis, sc: Harrison Lewis, husband, 1st Dist., BVS:1886:1

LEWIS, Mariah, B, F, d. 20 Feb 1887, LC, bronchitis, 2-9-0, p. Jamy &

Kate Lewis, b. LC, none, sc: Jamy Lewis, father, 3rd Dist., BVS:1887:7

LEWIS, Martha J., W, F, d. 31 May 1873, nr Gum Spring, consumption, 78-1-11, p. Jas. Lewis & wife, b. LC, unm, sc: Mrs. Jane Haneback, sister, BR Dist., BVS:1873:1

LEWIS, no name, B, F, d. 5 Jun 1883, nr Leesburg, unk, 0-1-0, p. Wesley & Louisa Lewis, b. LC, sc: Catharine Thomas, friend, 2nd Dist., BVS:1883:7

LEWIS, Philips, B, M, d. Jun 1873, Unison, dropsy, 60-0-0, p. unk, b. unk, laborer, married, sc: Armistead Turner, son-in-law, MC Dist., BVS:1873:5

LEWIS, Prissilla, B, F, d. 15 Oct 1889, LC, old age, 87-0-0, p. unk, b. LC, none, unm, sc: F.P. Lewis, son, 2nd Dist., BVS:1889:4

LEWIS, Robert, B, M, d. Dec 1893, Purcell's Factory, Richard Lewis, 0-4-0, p. Richard & Hamitt Lewis, b. LC, sc: father, MT Dist., BVS:1893:4

LEWIS, Robt., B, M, d. 31 Mar 1884, LC, consumption, 37-0-0, p. unk, b. LC, laborer, c/o: Lucy Lewis, sc: Chas Berkley, father-in-law, 1st Dist., BVS:1884:2

LEWIS, Thomas B., W, M, d. 26 Sep 1872, nr Gum Spring, consumption, 73-1-0, p. unk, b. LC, farmer, unm, sc: Jane Hancock, aunt, BR Dist., BVS:1872:6

LICKEY, Eugene, W, M, d. 11 Dec 1894, Round Hill, unk, 20-0-0, p. Charles E. & Mary E. Lickey, b. Round Hill, laborer, sc: Charles Licky, father, 3rd Dist., BVS:1894:5

LICKEY, Mary E., W, F, d. 25 Apr 1893, Round Hill, old age, 76-0-0, b. Maryland, wife, sc: son, MT Dist., BVS:1893:4

LIGGETT, Jas. W., W, M, d. 19 Jul 1853, Waterford, dysentery, 4-0-19, p. Saml. W. & Catherine Liggett, sc: Saml. W. Liggitt, father, BVS:1854:5, LC:3

LIGHTFOOD, John T., W, M, d. 15 Jul 1877, nr Mt. Zion Church, pneumonia, 52-0-0, p. Saml. & Catharine Lightfoot, b. unk, farmer, married, sc: John T. Ball, son-in-law, BR Dist., BVS:1877:1

LIGHTFOOT, Elizabeth, W, F, d. 6 Aug 1872, nr Mt. Zion Church, pneumonia, 47-0-0, p. Thos. Emerson & wife, b. Leesburg, c/o: John T. Lightfoot, sc: John T. Lightfoot, BR Dist., BVS:1872:6

LINCOLN, Annie, B, F, d. 2 Mar 1896, nr Upperville, consumption, 43-0-0, p. unk, b. nr Upperville, none, consort, sc: Samuel Lincoln, husband, MC Dist., BVS:1896:1

LINCOLN, Laura, B, F, d. 15 May 1880, Leesburg, consumption, 2-0-0, p. ___ & Clara Lincoln, b. LC, unm, sc: James Butler, friend, 2nd Dist., BVS:1880:6

LINGHAM, Fanny, B, F, d. 25 Jun 1877, LC, consumption, 56-4-0, p. unk, b. unk, c/o: Leander Lingham, sc: Leander Lingham, husband, JF Dist., BVS:1877:3

LINKINS, May, W, F, d. 15 Nov 1880, LC, diphtheria, 1-4-0, p. H. B. & Caroline Linkins, b. LC, unm, sc: Caroline Linkins, mother, 1st Dist., BVS:1880:2

LITTLE, Robt. H., W, M, d. 10 Feb 1892, Arcola, la grippe, 40-0-0, p. Thos. & Mary Little, b. Arcola, laborer, unm, sc: Thos Little, father, 1st Dist., BVS:1892:1

LITTLE, Thos., W, M, d. 18 Dec 1896, Arcola, old age, 87-0-0, b. New York, farmer, c/o: Rachel Little, sc: Rachael Little, wife, BR Dist., BVS:1896:3

LITTLETON, Dorothy R., W, F, d. 27 Jun 1859/60, her res, brain affection, 42-0-0, p. George & Nancy Noble, b. nr Bellfield, c/o: Chas. M. Littleton, sc: C.M. Littleton, husband, BVS:1859:4, 1860:2, LC:35

LITTLETON, Edgar, W, M, d. 20 Feb 1894, Leesburg, pneumonia, 54-0-0, p. unk, b. unk, lawyer, consort, sc: Ada Littleton, LE Dist., BVS:1894:3

LITTLETON, Elizabeth, W, , d. 8 Feb 1877, LC, pneumonia, 73-6-0, c/o: Thomas Littleton, sc: Thos. Littleton, husband, LE Dist., BVS:1877:8

LITTLETON, Fielding, W, M, d. 30 Mar 1857, Middleburg, cancerous affection, 59-0-0, p. Thomas & ... Littleton, b. Clarke Co., sheriff, sc: R.C. Littleton, nephew, BVS:1857:6, LC:28

LITTLETON, Francis A., W, M, d. Oct 1857, res of parents, 0-8-0, p. Chas. G. & Amanda M. Littleton, b. foot of Blue Ridge, sc: Charles G. Littleton, father, BVS:1857:5, LC:27

LITTLETON, John, W, M, d. 28 Feb 1859/60, Leesburg, paralysis, 77-3-0, p. Chas & Casandria Littleton, b. LC, c/o: Cene Littleton, sc: Thomas Littleton, son, BVS:1859:2, 1860:5, LC:38

LITTLETON, Thomas, W, M, d. 2 May 1857, his res, dropsy, 70-0-0, p. Charles & Cassandra Littleton, b. LC, farmer, c/o: Alvina Littleton, decd, sc: Mrs. John K. Littleton, daughter-in-law, BVS:1857:4, LC:27

LITTLETON, Virginia, W, F, d. 13 May 1855, Leven Richards', typhoid fever, 7-0-0, p. Chas. & Mary Littleton, b. Jenkins Mill, sc: Levin Richards, BVS:1855:5, LC:17

LLOYD, Ida, B, F, d. 5 Feb 1881, LC, unk, 20-0-0, p. Bruce & Jennie Lloyd, b. LC, sc: Bruce Lloyd, father, 1st Dist., BVS:1881:2

LLOYD, John F., W, M, d. 15 Aug 1853, nr Purcellville, dysentery, 1-6-0, p. Jas. & Mary Lloyd, b. nr Nichols Store, sc: father, BVS:1854:6, LC:5

LLOYD, Lillie, B, F, d. 25 Feb 1896, nr Unison, pneumonia, 0-1-1, p. H. & Nancy Lloyd, b. nr Unison, none, unm, sc: Henry Lloyd, father, MC Dist., BVS:1896:1

LLOYD, no name, B, F, d. 22 Mar 1877, on Beaverdam, unk, 0-0-3, p. Susan A. Lloyd, b. LC, sc: Eliza Lloyd, grandfather[sic], MC Dist., BVS:1877:5

LLOYD, Willie, B, M, d. 10 Feb 1894, Unison, pneumonia, 0-1-0, p. Henry & Nancy Lloyd, b. nr Unison, sc: Nancy Lloyd, mother, 1st Dist., BVS:1894:2

LODGE, Joseph, W, M, d. 5 Jun 1877, nr Snickersville, natural cause, 83-0-0, p. Wm. & Polly Lodge, unk, sc: F.J.B. Lodge, son, MT Dist., BVS:1877:2

LODGE, Martha A., W, F, d. 26 Nov 1859/60, res, consumption, 28-8-25, p. Jno/Jos. & Mary Lodge, b. nr Snickersville, c/o: Harmon Lodge, sc: H. Lodge, husband, BVS:1859:4, 1860:2, LC:35

LODGE, Mary, W, F, d. 10 Mar 1892, Round Hill, consumption, 69-0-0, p. Saml. & Rebecca Lodge, b. Snickersville, unm, sc: Henrietta Lodge, sister, MT Dist., BVS:1892:8

LODGE, Nathan, W, M, d. 9 Jun 1894, Round Hill, heart trouble, 76-0-0, p. Samuel & Rebeca Lodge, b. Round Hill, farmer, unm, sc: Henrietta Lodge, sister, 3rd Dist., BVS:1894:5

LODGE, Saml., W, M, d. 25 Dec 1859/60, res, dropsy & asthma, 70-2-7, p. Wm. & Christina Lodge, b. nr Short Hill, farmer, c/o: Rebecca Lodge, sc: R. Lodge, consort, BVS:1859:3, 1860:1, LC:34

LOGAN, Jerry, B, M, d. 20 Mar 1866, Middleburg, gravel, 60-0-0, b. Fauquier Co., farmer, unm, BVS:1866:3

LONG, John, W, M, d. 10 Jan 1866, E side of Short Hill, dropsy, 67-0-0, p. Jacob & Eva Long, b. LC, BVS:1866:1

LONG, William, W, M, d. 10 Apr 1876, nr Harpers Ferry, heart disease, 68-0-0, b. LC, laborer, c/o: Ann Long, sc: James C. Long, son, LV Dist., BVS:1876:3

LONGERBEAM, A. C., W, M, d. Aug 1896, Purcellville, cut with ax, 14-0-0, p. G. & S. Longerbeam, unm, JF Dist., BVS:1896:8

LORENTZ, Octavia A., W, F, d. 23 Sep 1858, LC, unk, 29-0-0, p. Adrian L. & Ann Swarts, b. LC, c/o: J.A. Lorentz, sc: J.A. Lorentz, husband, BVS:1858:6, LC:33

LOVE, Alcinda, W, F, d. 1 Aug 1894, Hillsboro, typhoid fever, 57-0-0, p. Lydia A. & James Love, b. Hillsboro, sc: R.R. Love, husband, 3rd Dist., BVS:1894:5

LOVE, Eli A., W, M, d. 30 Jul 1890, Hillsboro, paralyzed, 85-0-0, p. Thomas & Sarah Love, b. LC, farmer, c/o: Sarah Love, sc: M. R. Love, daughter, 3rd Dist., BVS:1890:6

LOVE, Elizabeth, W, F, d. 9 Dec 1893, nr Hamilton, paralysis, 83-0-0, b. LC, wife, sc: son, JF Dist., BVS:1893:3

LOVE, Laura, W, F, d. Dec 1896, Hillsboro, inflammation stomach., 27-0-0, b. Lincoln, consort, JF Dist., BVS:1896:8

LOVE, Mary Ellen, W, F, d. 25 Dec 1869, LC, unk, 27-0-0, p. Mahlon & Mary S. Taylor, b. LC, sc: Samuel Love, husband, BVS:1869:1

LOVE, Nathan E., W, M, d. 14 Aug 1882, LC, consumption, 61-11-0, b. LC, physician, c/o: Armida Love, sc: Armida Love, wife, 3rd Dist., BVS:1882:3

[LOVE], no name, W, M, d. 1 March 1869, LC, unk, 0-1-0, p. Samuel P. & Eliza Love, b. LC, sc: Samuel P. Love, father, BVS:1869:1

[LOVE], no name, W, M, d. 1 Aug 1875, nr Hillsboro, still born, unk, p. Samuel & Laura, sc: Samuel Love, father, JF Dist., BVS:1875:3

LOVE, no name, W, M, d. 10 Aug 1884, Hamilton, cholera infantum, 0-0-15, p. Joseph & America Love, b. Virginia, unm, sc: Joseph Love, father, 3rd Dist., BVS:1884:6

LOVE, no name twins, W, M, d. 25 Aug 1884, Hamilton, unk, 0-1-0, p. Joseph & America Love, b. Virginia, unm, sc: Joseph Love father, 3rd Dist., BVS:1884:6

LOVE, Samuel P., W, M, d. 25 Apr 1890, Hillsboro, fall from horse, 44-0-0, p. Eli A. & Sarah Love, b. LC, farmer, c/o: Laura Love, sc: W. Love, son, 3rd Dist., BVS:1890:6

LOVE, Thomas, W, M, d. 25 April 1869, LC, unk, 0-3-0, p. Samuel P. & Eliza Love, b. LC, sc: Samuel P. Love, father, BVS:1869:1

LOVELESS, Elizabeth, W, F, d. 1 Jan 1880, Woodburn, heart disease, 65-0-0, p. unk, b. LC, c/o: Thomas Loveless, sc: Wm. Weadon, friend, 3rd Dist., BVS:1880:4

LOVELESS, John R., W, M, d. 30 Sep 1881, LC, typhoid fever, 16-5-8, p. Jno. W. & A. E. Loveless, b. LC, laborer, sc: John W. Loveless, father, 2nd Dist., BVS:1881:7

LOVELESS, William T., W, M, d. 31 Oct 1873, nr Day Mill, epilepsy, 16-0-0, p. John W. & Alcinda Loveless, b. nr Day Mill, sc: father, MT Dist., BVS:1873:3

LOW, Alfred T., W, M, d. 4 May 1864, Bunker Hill, heart disease, 9-0-0, p. Jos & Emily Low, b. LC, sc: Jos Low, father, BVS:1864:1, LC:38

LOWE, Annie A., W, F, d. 4 Aug 1893, Hamilton, cancer, 51-0-0, p. Washington & Kate Silcott, b. LC, c/o: ife, sc: Thomas Lowe, husband, MT Dist., BVS:1893:4

LOWE, Arthur, W, M, d. 6 Aug 1884, nr Leesburg, unk, 0-2-10, p. Rector & Mary E. Lowe, b. LC, sc: Rector Lowe, father, 2nd Dist., BVS:1884:4

LOWE, Benjamin F., W, M, d. 12 Jul 1858, LC, unk, 1-1-5, p. Thos & Eliza A. Lowe, b. LC, sc: Thomas Lowe, father, BVS:1858:1, LC:29

LOWE, Jane, W, F, d. 25 Feb 1880, Leesburg, old age, 81-0-0, p. Moses & Lettie Thomas, b. LC, c/o: Rector Lowe, sc: William Lowe, Son, 2nd Dist., BVS:1880:6

LOWE, John H., W, M, d. 2 Aug 1854, LC, dysentery, 1-0-26, p. Chas. J. & Mary E. Lowe, b. LC, sc: Mary E. Lowe, mother, BVS:1854:9, LC:9

LOWE, John T., W, M, d. 6 Aug 1884, nr Leesburg, tumor on liver, 62-10-0, p. Rector & Jane Lowe, b. LC, farmer, c/o: Ann Lowe, sc: Wm. Lowe, brother, 2nd Dist., BVS:1884:4

LOWE, Mary J., W, F, d. 24 Dec 1885, nr Leesburg, jaundice, 5-1-10, p. Rector & Mary Lowe, b. LC, sc: Rector Lowe, father, 2nd Dist., BVS:1885:2

LOWE, Sophroney, W, F, d. 23 Sep 1866, Poor House, consumption, 36-0-0, married, sc: Wm. Lowe, husband, BVS:1866:2

LOWE, Walter, W, M, d. 27 Aug 1884, nr Leesburg, unk, 0-3-0, p. Rector & Mary E. Lowe, b. LC, sc: Rector Lowe, father, 2nd Dist., BVS:1884:4

LOWENBACH, Chas. L., W, M, d. 3 Jul 1890, LC, inflammation of bowel, 0-10-0, p. Chas. R. & J. Lowenbach, b. LC, none, unm, sc: C.R. Lowenbach, father, 2nd Dist., BVS:1890:4

LOY, Adam, W, M, d. Aug 1874, LC, paralysis, 69-0-0, c/o: Catherine Loy, sc: Geo. H. Loy, son, LE Dist., BVS:1874:5

LOY, Margaret A., W, F, d. 1 May 1853, LC, measles, 15-0-0, p. Adam & Sarah Loy, b. LC, sc: Sarah Loy, mother, BVS:1854:3, LC:1

[LOY], no name, W, , d. 3 Nov 1877, LC, strangulation, 0-0-3, p. R. F. &

L. R. Loy, sc: R.F. Loy, father, LE Dist., BVS:1877:8

LOY, no name, W, F, d. 9 Jan 1881, LC, unk, 0-0-2, p. R. F. & L. R. Loy, b. LC, sc: Richd F. Loy, father, 2nd Dist., BVS:1881:7

LOY, Saml. W., W, M, d. 2 May 1853, LC, measles, 7-6-0, p. Adam & Sarah Loy, b. LC, sc: Sarah Loy, mother, BVS:1854:3, LC:1

LUCAS, Aaron W., B, M, d. 17 Aug 1877, nr Pleasant Valley, spinal affection, 1-6-0, p. Fenton & Ann M. Lucas, b. Pleasant Valley, unm, sc: Ann M. Lucas, mother, BR Dist., BVS:1877:1

LUCAS, Arthur, B, M, d. 15 Dec 1886, whooping cough, 2-0-0, p. Thomas & Ellen Lucas, sc: Thomas Lucas, father, 2nd Dist., BVS:1886:5

LUCAS, Eli, B, M, d. 11 Jun 1877, LC, dysentery, 0-0-25, p. Hiram & Mary Lucas, b. LC, sc: Hiram Lucas, father, LV Dist., BVS:1877:4/7

LUCAS, Elijah, B, M, d. 17 Jun 1877, LC, dysentery, 0-1-15, p. Hiram & Mary Lucas, b. LC, sc: Hiram Lucas, father, LV Dist., BVS:1877:4/7

LUCAS, George, B, , d. 27 Aug 1877, LC, hernia, 72-0-0, c/o: Mary Lucas, sc: Sandy Lucas, son, LE Dist., BVS:1877:8

LUCAS, Jordan, B, M, d. 20 May 1879, LC, inflammation bowels, 0-11-25, p. Phillip & Adaline Lucas, b. LC, sc: Phillip Lucas, father, 3rd Dist., BVS:1879:3

LUCAS, Linda, B, F, d. 1 Dec 1876, nr Summer Hill, unk, 0-5-0, p. Geo W. & Malinda Lucas, b. LC, unm, sc: Geo. W. Lucas, father, MT Dist., BVS:1876:1

LUCAS, Martha, B, F, d. 1 Jul 1883, nr Leesburg, intermittent fever, 0-19-0, p. Angeline Lucas, b. LC, laborer, unm, sc: Alex. Lucas, step-father, 2nd Dist., BVS:1883:3

LUCAS, Mary, (f), F, d. 20 May 1857, nr Thos Nichols', typhoid fever, 30-0-0, p. Malinda Thomas, b. Fauquier Co., c/o: John Lucas, sc: J. Lucas, widower, BVS:1857:5, LC:28

LUCAS, Mary C., B, F, d. 3 May 1875, LC, consumption, 15-0-0, p. Geo. & Lucinda Lucas, b. LC, sc: Geo. Lucas, father, LE Dist., BVS:1875:1

LUCAS, Mary Louisa, B, F, d. 25 May 1892, Hillsboro, consumption, 22-0-0, p. Albert & Emma Lucas, b. Hillsboro, sc: Albert Lucas, father, JF Dist., BVS:1892:7

[LUCAS], no name, B, M, d. 4 Mar 1872, LC, hemorrhage, 0-0-4, p. Sandy & Angeline Lucas, b. LC, sc: Angeline Lucas, mother, LE Dist., BVS:1872:3

[LUCAS], no name, B, M, d. 15 Aug 1881, Pleasant Valley, unk, 0-0-5, p. Fenton & Ann Lucas, sc: Ann Lucas, mother, 1st Dist., BVS:1881:1

LUCAS, Robert, B, M, d. 22 Aug 1873, nr Unison, dropsy, 73-0-0, p. unk, b. unk, married, sc: Wm. H. Hibbs, superintendent of poor, MC Dist., BVS:1873:5

LUCAS, Ruth, B, F, d. 2 Apr 1882, LC, typhoid fever, 42-0-0, b. LC, sc: Albert ?, friend, 3rd Dist., BVS:1882:3

LUCAS, Silena, B, F, d. 8 Apr 1875, LC, jaundice, 2-0-2, p. Sandy & Angelina Lucas, b. LC, sc: Sandy Lucas, father, LE Dist., BVS:1875:1

LUCAS, Soloman, B, M, d. 12 Nov 1883, Hamilton, paralyzed, 79-0-0, b. LC, sc: Mary Dodd, friend, 3rd Dist., BVS:1883:5

LUCAS, Wm., B, M, d. 24 Jul 1891, Pleasant Valley, cholera infantum, 2-0-0, p. Fenton & Ann Lucas, b. LC, laborer, unm, sc: Ann Lucas, head of family, 1st Dist., BVS:1891:1

LUCIUS, Mollie, W, F, d. 2 May 1876, nr Upperville, consumption, 17-0-0, p. Chas. & Mary Lucius, b. LC, unm, sc: Robt C. Lucius, brother, MC Dist., BVS:1876:4

LUCIUS, Nora, W, F, d. 30 Dec 1876, nr Upperville, consumption, 21-0-0, p. Chas. & Mary Lucius, b. LC, unm, sc: Robt C. Lucius, brother, MC Dist., BVS:1876:4

LUCK, Jordan B., W, M, d. 23 Aug 1853, on Goose Creek, dysentery, 61-0-0, p. Jno. & Mildred Luck, b. Caroline Co., farmer, c/o: Adaline Luck, sc: son, BVS:1854:6, LC:5

LUCKETT, Charles W., W, M, d. 5 Oct 1856, LC, typhoid fever, 21-2-5, p. Samuel C. & Mary B. Luckett, b. LC, unm, sc: Samuel C. Luckett, father, BVS:1856:1, LC:20

LUCKETT, Janet, B, F, d. 28 Mar 1881, LC, catarrh fever, 0-7-0, p. Matthew & Kate Luckett, b. LC, sc: Kate Luckett, mother, 2nd Dist., BVS:1881:7

LUCKETT, Mary B., W, F, d. 9 Oct 1853, LC, hemorrhage, 45-0-0, p. Jno. & Winifred Hamilton, b. LC, c/o: Samuel C. Luckett, sc: Saml C. Luckett, husband, BVS:1854:3, LC:1

LUCKETT, Robt. T., W, M, d. 14 Feb 1855, Middleburg, accident, 47-7-1, p. Leven & Lititia Luckett, farmer, c/o: Arabela Luckett, sc: Horace Luckett, brother, BVS:1855:3, LC:16

LUCKETT, Wm. C., W, M, d. 7 Dec 1872, Lucketts + Roads, unk, 68-0-0, p. Saml. & Sally Luckett, b. LC, farmer, c/o: Mary Luckett, sc: Mary Luckett, consort, LE Dist., BVS:1872:3

LUCUS, Catherine, B, F, d. May 1874, LC, consumption, 16-0-0, sc: George Lucus, father, LE Dist., BVS:1874:5

LUCUS, Margaret, B, F, d. 1 Dec 1889, LC, dropsy, 25-0-0, p. Hiram & Mary Lucus, b. LC, none, unm, sc: Hiram Lucus, father, 2nd Dist., BVS:1889:3

LUKE, Sarah, W, F, d. Jan 1853, Snickersville, old age, 79-9-0, p. Wm. & Catharine Clayton, b. Pennsylvania, c/o: Jacob Luke, sc: A. M. Moore, friend, BVS:1854:1, LC:4

LUMM, Ruth, W, F, d. 7 Oct 1858, Nancy Lumm's, old age, 83-9-6, p. Samuel & Mary Lumm, b. LC, sc: Martha Carter, niece, BVS:1858:4, LC:32

LUNCEFORD, Eliza, W, F, d. 2 Nov 1869, LC, measles & pneumonia, 41-0-0, p. John & Nancy McDonald, b. Warren Co. VA, married, sc: Wm. Lunceford, husband, BVS:1869:1

LUNSFORD, Harriet E., W, F, d. 6 Nov 1879, Silcott Springs, consumption, 41-0-0, b. LC, c/o: J. Thomas Lunsford, sc: J.T. Lunsford, husband, 3rd Dist., BVS:1879:3

LUNSFORD, Jordan, W, M, d. 1 Apr 1884, Round Hill, unk, 0-3-6, p. Charles & Mollie Lunsford, b. Virginia, unm, sc: Chas Lunsford, father, 3rd Dist., BVS:1884:6

LUTZ, John A., W, M, d. 30 Nov 1878, LC, consumption, 32-10-11, p. F. A. & Mary A. Lutz, b. LC, sc: F.A. Lutz, father, LE Dist., BVS:1878:8

LYNCH, Wm. P., W, M, c. 4 Aug 1854, Leesburg, dysentery, 0-2-0, p. Wm. B. & Laura R. Lynch, b. Leesburg, sc: Wm. B. Lynch, father, BVS:1854:10, LC:9

LYNE, Minerva A., W, F, d. 2 Feb 1883, nr Farmwell, pneumonia, 60-0-0, p. unk, b. LC, c/o: Geo H. Lyne, sc: Geo H. Lyne, husband, 1st Dist., BVS:1883:1

LYNE, Thos. H., W, M, d. 12 Nov 1877, nr Guilford Station, cancer, 63-7-1, p. Wm. & Susan Lyne, b. LC, farmer, c/o: Minerva Lyne, sc: Minerva Lyne, wife, BR Dist., BVS:1877:1

LYNN, Bertha Elgin, W, F, d. 22 Dec 1876, nr Aldie, inflammation of bowels, 1-3-14, p. J. Humphrey & P.P. Lynn, b. LC, sc: J. Humphrey Lynn, father, MC Dist., BVS:1876:4

LYNN, James, W, M, d. 13 Oct 1871, Union, 0-0-3, p. Mary A. & Wm. F. Lynn, MC Dist., BVS:1871:2

LYNN, Jas F., W, M, d. 30 Oct 1864, nr Bloomfield, bronchitis, 58-0-0, p. Fielding & R. Lynn, b. LC, school teacher, c/o: Verlinda A. Lynn, sc: Wm. F. Lynn, son, BVS:1864:1, LC:38

LYNN, John T., W, M, d. 3 Aug 1872, nr Dover, dropsy, 49-0-0, c/o: Nancy D. Lynn, MC Dist., BVS:1872:7

LYNN, Leroy, W, M, d. 2 Oct 1896, nr Sterling, diphtheria, 2-0-8, p. Lucien & Mary Lynn, b. nr Sterling, sc: Lucien Lynn, father, BR Dist., BVS:1896:3

LYNN, Lester, W, M, d. 5 Sep 1886, nr Aldie, spinal affection, 4-11-0, p. John H. & Rill F. Lynn, b. nr Aldie, sc: John H. Lynn, father, 1st Dist., BVS:1886:1

LYNN, Sarah J., W, F, d. 15 May 1855, Mount Prominent, consumption, 16-3-6, p. Jas. R. & Permelia C. Lynn, b. Mount Prominent, sc: John T. Lynn, brother, BVS:1855:6, LC:18

LYON, Eliza J., W, F, d. 15 Jun 1881, LC, cancer, 66-0-0, c/o: James Lyon, sc: Mary E. Lyon, daughter, 1st Dist., BVS:1881:1

LYON, Jane, W, F, d. 1 Nov 1880, LC, old age, 79-0-0, p. unk, unm, sc: M.B. Lyon, nephew, 1st Dist., BVS:1880:2

LYON, Jno. M., W, M, d. 5 Oct 1893, Ryan, lung trouble, 71-10-0, p. Alex. & Virginia Lyon, b. LC, farmer, sc: Reboa Lyon, sister, 1st Dist., BVS:1893:1

LYON, Mary E., W, F, d. 15 Jan 1880, LC, paralysis, 64-0-0, p. unk, unm, sc: Henry Jones, friend, 1st Dist., BVS:1880:2

LYONS, John H., W, M, d. 8 Aug 1865, nr Farmville, suddenly, 11-4-4, p. H.M. & E.J. Lyon, b. LC, unm, sc: Thornton Lyon, brother, BVS:1865:2

LYONS, Nancy R, W, F, d. 13 Oct 1877, Poor House, diphtheria, 6-0-0, p. Jno V. & Lydia A. Lyons, b. LC, sc: Jno. V. Lyons, father, MC Dist., BVS:1877:5

MACATEE, Jane, W, F, d. 15 May 1865, nr Scotland, consumption, 65-0-0, widow, BVS:1865:1

MACOMB, Richard, W, M, d. 14 Nov 1877, Georgetown, D.C., inflammation of bowels, 36-0-0, p. Samuel & Ann Macomb, b. Washington DC, painter, c/o: Margaret Macomb, sc: Margaret Macomb, wife, LV Dist., BVS:1877:4/7

MADDOX, Elizabeth, W, F, d. 9 Jun 1885, nr Arcola, brain fever, 68-0-0, p. John & Lucy Carter, b. nr Arcola, c/o: Wm. Maddox, sc: James W. Maddox, son, 1st Dist., BVS:1885:4

MADDOX, J. W., W, M, d. 20 Oct 1894, nr Aldie, typhoid fever, 46-0-0, p. unk, b. unk, laborer, c/o: Virginia A. Maddox, sc: Virginia A. Maddox, wife, 1st Dist., BVS:1894:1

MADISON, Lizzie, B, , d. 1 May 1877, LC, cholera infantum, 0-11-0, p. Maria Madison, sc: Maria Madison, mother, LE Dist., BVS:1877:8

MAFFETT, Chas. W., W, M, d. 25 Mar 1877, nr Gum Spring, pneumonia heart disease, 49-0-0, p. Henry & Linnie Maffett, b. LC, farmer, c/o: Martha Maffett, sc: Wm. Craven, brother-in-law, BR Dist., BVS:1877:1

MAFFETT, Jas. A., W, M, d. 8 Feb 1893, nr Waxpool, dropsy, 60-0-0, p. Henry & Linnie Maffett, b. LC, farmer, married, sc: Jno J. Maffett, son, 1st Dist., BVS:1893:1

MAFFETT, Leven C., W, M, d. 7 May 1882, LC, pneumonia, 40-0-0, p. James & Mary A. Maffett, b. LC, farmer, unm, sc: James Maffett, father, 1st Dist., BVS:1882:2

MAFFETT, Linny, W, F, d. 1 Sep 1880, LC, cancer, 81-0-0, p. unk, b. LC, c/o: Henry Maffett, sc: Henry Maffett, husband, 1st Dist., BVS:1880:2

MAFFETT, Marth A., W, F, d. 18 Apr 1891, Arcola, pneumonia, 62-0-0, p. William & Mary (decd) Craven, b. LC, farmer, c/o: William Maffett, sc: C.J.C. Maffett, son, 1st Dist., BVS:1891:2

MAFFETT, Peter F., W, M, d. 23 Nov 1893, nr Evergreen Mills, heart failure, 63-11-0, p. Henry & Linnie Maffett, b. LC, farmer, c/o: Ellen V. Maffett, sc: Ellen V. Maffett, wife, 1st Dist., BVS:1893:1

MAGAHA, Armistead, W, M, d. 8 Dec 1879, nr Waterford, congestion of brain, 51-4-0, p. David & Dorcas C. Magaha, b. LC, farmer, c/o: Margaret C. Magaha, sc: H.H. Russell, friend, 2nd Dist., BVS:1879:1

MAGAHA, Catharine, W, F, d. 15 Jan 1853, LC, palsy, 47-3-10, p. unk, b. unk, unk, sc: Wm. Magaha, head of family, BVS:1854:4, LC:2

MAGAHA, George W., W, M, d. 5 Sep 1858, LC, unk, 1-2-0, p. James & Sarah A. Magaha, b. LC, sc: Frederick Roller, neighbor, BVS:1858:1, LC:29

MAGAHA, George W., W, M, d. 29 Jul 1872, nr Short Hill, scarlet fever, 1-4-0, p. George W. & M. Magaha, b. nr Short Hill, laborer, married, sc: George W. Magaha, father, LV Dist., BVS:1872:5

MAGAHA, Mary C. D., W, F, d. 31 Jul 1872, nr Short Hill, scarlet fever, 3-11-4, p. George W. & M. Magaha, b. nr Short Hill, laborer, married, sc: George W. Magaha, father, LV Dist., BVS:1872:5

MAHONEY, Daisy, B, F, d. 18 Sep 1891, Hillsboro, brain fever, 1-6-0, p. Wm. & Martha Mahoney, b. Hillsboro, laborer, sc: Wm. Mahoney, JF Dist., BVS:1891:7

MAHONEY, Martha Ellen, (f), F, d. 10 Mar 1854, LC, pneumonia, 5-3-14, p. John & Elizabeth Mahoney, b. LC, sc: Elizabeth Mahoney, mother, BVS:1854:8, LC:7

MALORY, Carrie, B, F, d. 8 Apr 1884, nr Leesburg, pneumonia, 11-0-0, p. Virginia Malory (unm), b. LC, sc: Mary Malory, grandmother, 2nd Dist., BVS:1884:5

MALORY, Laura, B, F, d. 8 Oct 1888, LC, unk, 3-0-0, p. Ann Malory, b. LC, none, unm, sc: Mary Malory, grandmother, 2nd Dist., BVS:1888:6

MALORY, Virginia, B, F, d. 1 Mar 1888, LC, pneumonia, 4-3-0, p. Jane Malory, b. LC, none, unm, sc: Mary Malory, grandmother, 2nd Dist., BVS:1888:6

MANKIN, Christiana M., W, F, d. Feb 1866, Oatlands Farm, paralyzed, 49-0-0, p. Wm. & Mary Moore, b. New York, sc: Jas W. Mankin, husband, BVS:1866:3

MANKIN, James W., W, M, d. 11 Mar 1872, nr Gum Spring, pneumonia, 65-0-0, p. unk, farmer, married, sc: Geo. F. Mankin, son, BR Dist., BVS:1872:6

MANKIN, Julia E., W, F, d. 28 Dec 1859/60, LC, consumption, 14-10-0, p. Jas W. & Christina Mankin, b. LC, sc: James W Mankin, husband, BVS:1859:6, 1860:3, LC:36

MANKIN, Virginia C., W, F, d. 1865, Fairfax line, dysentery, 1-0-0, p. Geo W. & M.C. Mankin, b. LC, farmer, unm, sc: G.W. Mankin, father, BVS:1865:1

MANLY, Craven, B, M, d. 1864, Wm. Tate's, old age, 75-0-0, sc: William Tate, BVS:1864:2, LC:39

MANLY, Eliza J., B, F, d. 28 Apr 1887, LC, consumption, 48-0-0, p. Caroline Manly, b. LC, none, unm, sc: Caroline Manly, mother, 2nd Dist., BVS:1887:4

MANLY, Ellen, B, F, d. 15 Aug 1872, nr Mt. Hope Church, cancer, 60-0-0, p. unk, b. LC, unm, sc: Thos. Manly, BR Dist., BVS:1872:6

MANLY, James, B, M, d. 28 Nov 1896, LC, consumption, 27-0-0, b. LC, laborer, unm, sc: Roxey Manly, mother, LE Dist., BVS:1896:5

MANLY, James, B, M, d. Aug 1879, nr Leesburg, sun stroke, 29-0-0, p. Mary Manly, b. LC, laborer, sc: Mary Manly, mother, 2nd Dist., BVS:1879:1

MANLY, Louisa, B, F, d. 9 Mar 1883, Leesburg, dropsy, 19-0-0, p. Caroline Manly, b. LC, unm, sc: Laura Manly, sister, 2nd Dist., BVS:1883:7

MANLY, Mollie, B, F, d. 20 Sep 1872, nr Gum Spring, consumption, 22-2-0, p. Caroline Manly, b. LC, unm, sc: Thos. Manly, uncle, BR Dist., BVS:1872:6

MANN, Catherine R. J., W, F, d. 28 May 1890, LC, womb disease, 13-0-0, p. John S. & Mary C. Mann, b. LC, none, unm, sc: J.S. Mann, father, 2nd Dist., BVS:1890:4

MANN, Edward C., W, M, d. 4 Apr 1892, George's Mill, membranous croup, 7-0-0, p. J. H. & Rebecca Mann, b. LC, unm, sc: J. H. Mann, LV Dist., BVS:1892:6

MANN, Geo. B., W, M, d. 29 Jan 1891, nr Point of Rocks, MD, railway accident, 28-0-0, p. Joseph & Mary Mann, b. Morrisonville, laborer, unm, sc: father, LV Dist., BVS:1891:5

MANN, Geo. B. M., W, M, d. 28 Jan 1890, LC, r. r. accident, 28-0-0, p. John S. & Mary C. Mann, b. LC, RR man, unm, sc: J.S. Mann, father, 2nd Dist., BVS:1890:4

MANN, Jacob, W, M, d. 12 May 1884, nr Lovettsville, old age, 89-0-0, p. Jno. & Mary Mann, b. LC, farmer, c/o: Ann Brown[sic], sc: Martin L. Mann, son, 2nd Dist., BVS:1884:5

MANN, Jacob F., W, M, d. 19 Jun 1858, LC, measles, 19-0-0, p. Joseph & Elizth Mann, b. LC, sc: Joseph Mann, father, BVS:1858:2, LC:30

MANN, Louisa, B, F, d. May 1866, Hillsboro, unk, 0-8-0, p. Lafayette & Pamelia Mann, sc: father, BVS:1866:2

MANN, Rosetta M., W, F, d. 2 Mar 1874, W of Lovettsville, teething, 0-10-7, p. John & Mary Mann, LV Dist., BVS:1874:6

MANNING, Harvy D., W, M, d. 11 May 1875, Leesburg, scarlet fever, 1-6-0, p. J. W. & C. E. Manning, b. LC, sc:

Loudoun County, Virginia, Death Register, 1853-1896   173

J.A. Manning, father, LE Dist., BVS:1875:1
MANNING, Maud, W, , d. 10 Sep 1877, LC, dropsy, 1-2-0, p. J. H. & C. E. Manning, sc: J.H. Manning, father, LE Dist., BVS:1877:8
MANSFIELD, David, W, M, d. Oct 1871, Waterford, typhoid fever, 50-0-0, b. Baltimore, MD, sc: C.L. Hollingsworth, admr, JF Dist., BVS:1871:1
MANUEL, Elijah, W, M, d. 10 Oct 1892, Unison, inflammation bowels, 0-14-0, p. Duncan & Ida Manuel, b. Unison, sc: Duncan Manuel, father, 1st Dist., BVS:1892:1
MANUEL, Mary Ellen, W, F, d. 18 Dec 1865, Silcott Springs, consumption, 0-1-24, p. A.A. & Sarah E. Manuel, b. nr Silcott Springs, farmer, sc: father, BVS:1865:1
MANUEL, Turner D., W, M, d. 10 Aug 1894, nr Unison, dysentery, 1-2-0, p. Duncan & Ida Manuel, b. nr Bloomfield, sc: Duncan Manuel, father, 1st Dist., BVS:1894:1
MARCELLUS, Rebecca, B, F, d. 15 Jun 1872, nr Hillsboro, consumption, 37-0-0, p. Henry & Rachel Marcellus, b. nr Hillsboro, sc: Lydia H. Jones, friend, JF Dist., BVS:1872:1
MARCH, Martha E., W, F, d. 20 Oct 1882, LC, heart disease, 26-0-0, p. Samuel & Jane Jackson, c/o: Jesse F. March, sc: Jesse F. March, husband, 1st Dist., BVS:1882:1
MARCH, Sallie Ann, W, F, d. 7 Apr 1874, on Blue Ridge, pneumonia, 30-0-0, p. Hesikiah & Kitty Wiley, b. Clarke, c/o: Jno. March, sc: Albert Thompson neighbor, MC Dist., BVS:1874:4
MARCUS, Sarah, W, F, d. 13 Feb 1874, on Blue Ridge, old age, 80-0-0, p. unk, b. LC, c/o: Levi Marcus, sc: Spencer Marcus, son, MC Dist., BVS:1874:4
MARLOW, Lucinda, B, F, d. 10 Nov 1886, nr Trappe, pneumonia, 1-9-0, p. Buck & Hannah Marlow, b. nr Trappe, unm, sc: Abner Casey, grandfather, 1st Dist., BVS:1886:2
[MARLOW], no name, B, M, d. 12 Jun 1884, LC, measles, 0-0-6, p. Buck & Annie Marlow, b. LC, sc: Annie

Marlow, mother, 1st Dist., BVS:1884:2
MARMADUKE, Cathrn., W, F, d. 17 Jul 1855, LC, consumption, 42-0-0, p. Wm. & Phebe McKendra, b. Jefferson, c/o: Silas Marmaduke, sc: Silas Marmaduke, husband, BVS:1855:2, LC:15
MARQUESS, Sarah Elizabeth, W, F, d. 27 Dec 1869, LC, pneumonia, 13-0-0, p. Spencer & Catharine E. Marquess, b. LC, sc: Spencer Marquess, father, BVS:1869:1
MARSHALL, Jacob, W, M, d. 8 Sep 1859/60, his res, old age, 86-0-0, p. Jacob & Sarah Marshall, b. Prince William Co, farmer, c/o: Mary Marshall, sc: Thomas Marshall, son, BVS:1859:5, 1860:3, LC:36
[MARSHALL], James Curr, W, M, d. 28 Jun 1855, Aldie, himal affect, 3-3-20, p. Wm. B. & Jane C. Marshal, b. Aldie, sc: Wm. B. Marshall, father, BVS:1855:4, LC:16
MARSHALL, James Raymond, W, M, d. 18 Jul 1893, Hillsboro, summer trouble, 0-2-25, p. J.T. & S.J. Marshall, b. Hillsboro, sc: father, JF Dist., BVS:1893:3
MARSHALL, John, B, M, d. 5 Aug 1885, nr Unison, consumption, 18-0-0, p. Lucas & Rosetta Marshall, b. Fauquier Co., laborer, unm, sc: Lias Marshall, father, 1st Dist., BVS:1885:4
[MARSHALL], John Thomas, W, M, d. 11 Aug 1854, Aldie, bilious dysentery, 7-0-0, p. Wm. B. & J. C. Marshall, b. Aldie, sc: Wm. B. Marshall, BVS:1854:10, LC:10
MARSHALL, Mrs. W.B., W, F, d. 23 Feb 1857, Aldie, chronic gastritis, unk, BVS:1857:4, LC:26
MARSHALL, Robt, W, M, d. 4 Mar 1865, Snickersville, pneumonia, 36-9-5, farmer, married, BVS:1865:1
MARSHALL, William G., W, M, d. 1 Sep 1854, Aldie, summer complaint, 0-8-0, p. Wm. B. & J. C. Marshall, b. Aldie, sc: Wm. B. Marshall, BVS:1854:10, LC:10
MARTIN, ? B., B, F, d. 15 Sep 1878, nr Middleburg, unk, 0-4-20, p. Wm F. & Ella J. Martin, b. LC, sc: Wm. F. Martin, father, MC Dist., BVS:1878:6

MARTIN, Theresa, W, F, d. 13 Apr 1877, nr Guilford Station, consumption, 32-0-0, p. John Quin & wife, b. Ireland, c/o: Wm. Martin, sc: Wm. Martin, husband, BR Dist., BVS:1877:1

MARTS, John, W, M, d. 7 Dec 1855, Dover, croup, 2-1-14, p. Jno & Christina Marts, b. Dover, sc: John Marts, father, BVS:1855:5, LC:17

MARTYN, Ida F., W, F, d. 8 Aug 1886, nr Arcola, unk, 11-0-0, p. Wm. H. & Ellen Martyn, b. LC, unm, sc: Wm. H. Martyn, father, 1st Dist., BVS:1886:2

MARTZ, Ann Maria, W, F, d. Nov 25 1875, nr Snickersville, consumption, 47-0-0, p. Edward & Rachel Furr, b. LC, married, sc: Saml T. Martz, husband, MT Dist., BVS:1875:8

MASON, Ann, W, F, d. 1 Sep 1855, Leesburg, typhoid fever, 67-0-0, p. Philip & Mary Noland, b. LC, unm, sc: Catharine B. Gassway, niece, BVS:1855:3, LC:15

MASON, Campbell, W, M, d. 18 Apr 1887, LC, rheumatism, 18-4-6, p. John F. & Caroline Mason, b. Washington, school boy, unm, sc: John F. Mason, father, 2nd Dist., BVS:1887:4

MASON, Constantia, (f), F, d. 6 Sep 1857, LC, unk, 0-5-0, p. Emily Mason, b. LC, sc: Wm. H. Hough, head of family, BVS:1857:1, LC:24

MASON, Jerry, B, M, d. 26 May 1883, nr Leesburg, pneumonia, 45-0-0, p. --- Mason, b. LC, laborer, c/o: Melia Mason, sc: Melia Mason, wife, 2nd Dist., BVS:1883:7

MASON, Mary, B, F, d. 25 Mar 1882, LC, unk, 0-2-7, p. Wm. & Josephine Mason, b. LC, sc: Wm. Mason, parent, 3rd Dist., BVS:1882:3

MASON, Mary, B, F, d. 10 Aug 1887, Middleburg, pneumonia, 75-0-0, p. unk, b. Fairfax Co., sc: John Fauntleroy, son-in-law, 1st Dist., BVS:1887:1

MASON, Richard, B, M, d. 20 Jul 1875, LC, scrofula, 19-0-0, p. Mary Smith, b. LC, sc: Beverly Smith, friend, LE Dist., BVS:1875:1

MASSEY, Henry, B, M, d. 21 Jul 1878, LC, hernia, 54-0-0, b. LC, c/o: Frances Massey, sc: Frances Massey, wife, LE Dist., BVS:1878:8

MATHERS, Joseph, W, M, d. 25 Nov 1881, LC, typhoid fever, 24-10-15, p. Jno. & M. E. Mathers, b. LC, laborer, unm, sc: John Mathers, father, 2nd Dist., BVS:1881:7

MATHERS, Maggie, W, F, d. 15 Dec 1880, nr Leesburg, diphtheria, 7-0-0, p. Jno. & Mary Mathers, b. Fairfax Co., Va., unm, sc: John Mathers, brother, 2nd Dist., BVS:1880:7

MATHERS, Margaret, W, F, d. 25 Nov 1883, nr Leesburg, cancer, 68-0-0, p. --- Brooks, b. LC, c/o: William Mathers, sc: Maria Mathers, daughter-in-law, 2nd Dist., BVS:1883:7

MATHERS, Mary E., W, F, d. 2 Dec 1880, nr Leesburg, diphtheria, 0-10-27, p. Benj. & Margaret Mathers, b. LC, unm, sc: B.F. Mathers, father, 2nd Dist., BVS:1880:7

MATHESS, Sina, W, F, d. 15 Mar 1872, nr Broad Run, disease of the heart, 55-0-0, p. unk, b. LC, c/o: Robert Mathess, sc: Robert Mathess, husband, BR Dist., BVS:1872:6

MATHEWS, Margaret E., W, F, d. 26 Jul 1853, on Sycolin, dysentery, 0-8-2, p. Wm. & Margaret Mathews, b. on Sycolin, sc: father, BVS:1854:5, LC:5

MATHEWS, Marian G., W, F, d. 25 Aug 1853, LC, dysentery, 7-9-9, p. Edward Y. & Sarah Mathews, b. Maryland, sc: Edward Mathews, father, BVS:1854:3, LC:1

MATHEWS, Mary E., W, F, d. 12 Jul 1853, on Sycolin, dysentery, 2-4-8, p. Wm. & Margaret Mathews, b. Sugarland Run, sc: father, BVS:1854:5, LC:5

MATHIAS, L.E., W, M, d. 28 Jun 1871, Sunny Side, dyspepsia, 68-11-0, farmer, MC Dist., BVS:1871:2

MATHIS, Maria, B, F, d. Sep 1871, LC, 0-10-0, p. ... & Sarah Mitchell, b. LC, unm, LE Dist., BVS:1871:4

MATTHEW, Ida Lee, W, F, d. 19 Sep 1883, nr Arcola, typhoid fever, 13-0-0, p. Edgar & Frances Matthew, b. nr Arcola, unm, sc: Edgar Mathew, father, 1st Dist., BVS:1883:1

Loudoun County, Virginia, Death Register, 1853-1896   175

MATTHEW, Jane F., W, F, d. 13 Apr 1875, nr Sudley Mill, paralysis, 64-0-0, p. Elias & Leah Matthew, b. LC, unm, sc: Edgar E. Matthew, friend, BR Dist., BVS:1875:5

MATTHEW, Lizzie A., W, F, d. 11 Dec 1877, LC, consumption, 35-0-0, p. Lewis & Catherine Torreysen, b. LC, c/o: Wm. Matthew, sc: Wm. Matthew, husband, JF Dist., BVS:1877:3

MATTHEW, Martha C., W, F, d. 15 Feb 1887, LC, consumption, 35-0-0, p. unk, b. LC, c/o: William Matthew, sc: William Matthew, husband, 2nd Dist., BVS:1887:4

MATTHEW, Nancy, W, F, d. 1 May 1866, Old Road, consumption, 60-0-0, p. ... Franklin, b. Prince William Co., sc: John W. Hutchison, son-in-law, BVS:1866:3

MATTHEW, William, W, M, d. 13 May 1886, suicide, 47-0-0, p. Jonathan & Rebecca Matthew, lawyer, c/o: Ella C. Matthew, sc: Ella C. Matthew, wife, 2nd Dist., BVS:1886:5

MATTOX, Bessie, W, F, d. 16 Aug 1872, nr Little River Church, unk, 0-3-22, p. Jas. W. & Virginia Mattox, b. LC, sc: Jas. W. Mattox, BR Dist., BVS:1872:6

MATTOX, William, W, M, d. 28 May 1884, LC, paralysis, 75-0-0, p. Joseph & Mary Mattox, b. LC, farmer, c/o: Elizabeth Mattox, sc: Elizabeth Mattox, wife, 1st Dist., BVS:1884:2

MAY, U.S.Grant, W, M, d. 15 Sep 1865, nr Goresville, abscess bowels, 0-14-15, p. James H. & Mary May, b. nr Goresville, shoemaker, married, sc: James H. May, father, 1st Dist., BVS:1865:4

MAY, W.S. Grant, W, M, d. 15 Sep 1865, Goresville, abscess in breast, 1-2-15, p. Jas H. & Mary May, b. nr Goresville, shoemaker, married, sc: Jas H. May, father, BVS:1865:3

MAYHERB, Lydia, W, F, d. 1 Nov 1888, LC, unk, 60-0-0, p. unk, b. LC, none, unm, sc: John Peyton, friend, 2nd Dist., BVS:1888:6

MAYO, Telzy, B, F, d. Feb 1892, Hillsboro, unk, unk, p. Joseph & Malinda Mayo, b. Hillsboro, sc: Joseph Mayo, father, JF Dist., BVS:1892:7

MCABEE, Charles T., W, M, d. 10 Jul 1880, nr Lovettsville, accident, 3-10-0, p. Wm. E. & Annie E. McAbee, b. LC, unm, sc: Wm. McAbee, father, 2nd Dist., BVS:1880:7

MCARTER, Florence, B, F, d. 25 Dec 1882, LC, unk, 25-0-0, p. unk, unm, sc: Jno R. Carter, superintendent, 1st Dist., BVS:1882:2

MCARTER, Samuel, W, M, d. 22 Jul 1889, LC, consumption, 31-0-0, b. LC, laborer, unm, sc: Ann E. Gayner, friend, 3rd Dist., BVS:1889:5

MCARTOR, Annie E., W, F, d. 25 Aug 1888, LC, dysentery, 2-0-0, p. Ths. E. & Ettie C. McArtor, b. LC, none, unm, sc: Ths E. McArtor, father, 3rd Dist., BVS:1888:1

MCATEE, Harrison L., W, M, d. 24 Dec 1857, on Blue Ridge, accident by machine, 76-0-0, p. ... & ... McAtee, b. Prince William Co., farmer, c/o: Jane McAtee, sc: William McAtee, son, BVS:1857:5, LC:27

MCCABE, Aileen, W, F, d. 26 Jul 1883, Leesburg, cholera infantum, 0-10-27, p. J. B. & Ella McCabe, b. LC, sc: J.B. McCabe, father, 2nd Dist., BVS:1883:3

MCCABE, Elizabeth, W, F, d. Nov 1879, nr Leesburg, old age, 78-0-0, p. ___ Simpson, b. LC, c/o: John McCabe, sc: John McCabe, husband, 2nd Dist., BVS:1879:1

MCCABE, Ernest L., W, M, d. 14 Mar 1872, Leesburg, croup, 1-10-0, p. Thos H. & Ann J. McCabe, b. LC, sc: Thos A. McCabe, father, LE Dist., BVS:1872:3

MCCABE, Jane, W, F, d. 17 Jan 1853, Leesburg, old age, 96-0-0, p. unk, b. unk, c/o: Henry McCabe, sc: James E. McCabe, grandson, BVS:1854:5, LC:3

MCCABE, John, W, M, d. 10 Jun 1889, LC, old age, 94-0-0, p. unk, b. LC, none, widower, sc: C.R. McCabe, son, 2nd Dist., BVS:1889:3

MCCABE, Joseph L., W, M, d. 1 Oct 1893, Leesburg, membranous croup, 3-0-0, p. J. B. & L. E. McCabe, b. Leesburg, unm, sc: J.B. McCabe, LE Dist., BVS:1893:6

MCCARTY, Billington J., W, M, d. 25 Oct 1864, LC, dysentery, 7-1-0, p. Dennis & W.E. McCarty, b. LC, sc: Ann E. McCarty, mother, BVS:1864:2, LC:39

MCCARTY, George W., W, M, d. 27 Jun 1856, res on Goose Creek T. Pike, old age, 80-0-0, p. Thadius & Sarah E. McCarty, b. Fairfax Co., farmer, c/o: Winifred H. McCarty, sc: George B. McCarty, son, BVS:1856:4, LC:21

MCCARTY, Maria F., W, F, d. 29 Mar 1864, Geo B.McCarty's, consumption, 59-11-29, p. Wesley & Margaret McCarty, b. LC, sc: Geo B. McCarty, brother, BVS:1864:1, LC:38

MCCARTY, Massanills, W, M, d. 11 Dec 1892, Aldie, apoplexy, 25-0-0, p. Wm. M. & Florence McCarty, b. Venezuela, So. Am., laborer, unm, sc: Wm. M. McCarty, father, 1st Dist., BVS:1892:1

MCCARTY, Rachel, (f), F, d. 1 Jun 1857, LC, unk, 0-1-7, p. Daniel & Rachel McCarty, b. Leesburg, sc: Rachel McCarty, mother, BVS:1857:2, LC:25

MCCARTY, Sarah A., W, F, d. 26 Jun 1854, Leesburg, unk, 2-9-11, p. Daniel & Rachel McCarty, b. LC, sc: Rachel McCarty, mother, BVS:1854:10, LC:9

MCCARTY, Susan F., W, F, d. 18 Nov 1881, LC, diphtheria, 6-0-0, p. B. & Mary McCarty, b. LC, sc: M.J. McCarty, mother, 1st Dist., BVS:1881:2

MCCARTY, Wm. T., W, M, d. no date, Newington, disease of heart, unk, b. LC, farmer, c/o: Hannah McCarty, sc: Hannah McCarty, husband, MC Dist., BVS:1874:4

MCCAULEY, Edward, W, M, d. 1 Mar 1896, nr Upperville, killed, 25-0-0, p. Jno. O. & M. McCauley, b. nr Upperville, none, consort, sc: M.McCauley, mother, MC Dist., BVS:1896:1

MCCORMICK, Katie, W, F, d. 25 Mar 1873, Dover, brain fever, 46-0-0, p. Thos. & Elizabeth Renolds, b. Clarke Co., c/o: Robert McCormack, sc: Robert McCormack, husband, MC Dist., BVS:1872:7

[MCCORMICK], no name, W, , d. 18 May 1854, Paris, Fauquier Co, 0-0-2, p. Robt. R. & Kate A. McCormick, b. Paris Fauquier Co, sc: R. R. McCormick, BVS:1854:11, LC:10

MCCRAY, Byron, W, M, d. 8 Sep 1855, res of parents, croup, 3-11-3, p. Wm. & Eliz. McCray, b. res of parents, sc: Eliz. McCray, mother, BVS:1855:6, LC:18

[MCCRAY], Byron, W, M, d. 27 Aug 1854, res of parents, croup, 3-0-0, p. Wm. & Elizabeth McCray, b. res of parents, sc: father, BVS:1854:13, LC:12

MCCRAY, Elizabeth, W, F, d. 9 Feb 1890, Hamilton, unk, 76-0-0, p. John & Sally Gregg, b. LC, none, c/o: Wm. McCray, sc: Wm. McCray, husband, 3rd Dist., BVS:1890:6

MCCULLOW, Archibald, W, M, d. 3 Aug 1871, unk, p. Christy & Jno D. McCullow, MC Dist., BVS:1871:2

MCDANIEL, James H., W, M, d. 9 Dec 1892, Purcellville, pneumonia, 61-0-0, p. Archibald McDaniel, b. Purcellville, farmer, husband, sc: son, father, JF Dist., BVS:1892:7

MCDANIEL, Mary A. M., W, F, d. 25 May 1858, LC, unk, 15-7-13, p. Augustus & Elizth McDaniel, b. LC, sc: Augustus McDaniel, father, BVS:1858:2, LC:30

[MCDANIEL], [no name], B, , d. May 1878, Round Hill, unk, p. Henry & Levinia McDaniel, b. Round Hill, sc: H. McDaniel, father, MT Dist., BVS:1878:2/3

MCDANIEL, Priscella, W, F, d. 2 Dec 1865, nr Wheatland, consumption, 65-0-0, widow, sc: Jas W. McDaniel, son, BVS:1865:1

MCDANIEL, Thomas, W, M, d. 11 Apr 1853, Poor House, dropsy, 25-0-0, p. unk, b. Ireland, ditcher, sc: Wm. Furr, keeper of poor house, BVS:1854:6, LC:6

MCDONALD, Herbert B., W, M, d. 7 Nov 1893, Front Royal, unk, 0-3-0, p. S. R. & Roberta McDonald, b. Upperville, sc: S.P. McDaniel, father, 1st Dist., BVS:1893:1

MCDONOUGH, Florence, W, F, d. 25 Jun 1896, Leesburg, child birth, 22-0-0, p. M. & A. McFarland, b. LC, housewife, wife, sc: husband, LE Dist., BVS:1896:5

MCFARLAND, Annie, W, F, d. 24 Oct 1882, LC, consumption, 32-0-0, p. James & Kate Saunders, c/o: Maurice McFarland, sc: Maurice McFarland, husband, 1st Dist., BVS:1882:1

MCFARLAND, Elizabeth L., W, F, d. 21 Jan 1858, LC, unk, 0-9-20, p. Alex. & Bethana McFarland, b. LC, sc: Alexr McFarland, father, BVS:1858:6, LC:33

MCFARLAND, James A., W, M, d. 18 Nov 1857, consumption, 45-0-0, p. James & Hannah McFarland, b. LC, farmer, sc: Margaret A. Ryan, sister, BVS:1857:7, LC:28

MCFARLAND, Joseph, W, M, d. 6 Aug 1874, Broad Run Dist., shot by John W. Golden, 50-6-0, p. Jas. McFarland & wife, merchant, married, sc: John F. Ryan, nephew, BR Dist., BVS:1874:3

MCFARLAND, Landen, W, M, d. 31 Mar 1883, nr Leesburg, pneumonia, 68-0-0, p. --- McFarland, b. LC, farmer, c/o: Mary A. McFarland, sc: Mary A. McFarland, wife, 2nd Dist., BVS:1883:7

MCFARLAND, Mary E., W, F, d. 6 Feb 1896, Arcola, consumption, 66-0-0, b. nr Sterling, c/o: Jos McFarland, sc: Edgar McFarland, son, BR Dist., BVS:1896:3

MCFARLAND, Oscar M., W, M, d. 7 Dec 1855, LC, typhoid fever, 6-4-3, p. Landon & M. A. McFarland, b. LC, sc: Mary A. McFarland, mother, BVS:1855:3, LC:15

MCFARLAND, Virginia P., W, F, d. 7 Jul 1872, Leesburg, consumption, 17-8-4, p. Landon & Mary A. McFarland, b. LC, unm, sc: Mary A. McFarland, mother, LE Dist., BVS:1872:3

MCGAHA, Julia A., W, F, d. 22 May 1881, LC, irritation bowels, 50-0-0, p. Wm. & Catharine McGaha, b. LC, laborer, unm, sc: George W. McGaha, brother, 2nd Dist., BVS:1881:7

MCGAHA, Mary E., W, F, d. 19 Aug 1896, LC, consumption, 52-0-0, p. Thos. Bales, b. LC, wife, sc: husband, LE Dist., BVS:1896:5

MCGINN, Charles R., W, M, d. Jul 1858, Middleburg, cholera infantum, 0-6-0, p. J.H. & Charlotte M. McGinn, b. Middleburg, sc: J.H. McGinn, father, BVS:1858:5, LC:33

MCGRAW, John, W, M, d. Mar 1857, Poor House, 30-0-0, p. Margaret McGraw, b. Leesburg, sc: steward of poorhouse, BVS:1857:3, LC:26

MCILHANEY, Sarah A., W, F, d. 17 Jan 1853, Hillsboro, excess of brain, 19-10-0, p. James & Margaret McIlhaney, b. nr Hillsboro, unm, sc: step-mother, BVS:1854:1, LC:3

MCILHANY, May, W, F, d. 10 Oct 1855, Jas. M. Kilgour's, pulmonary, 20-11-5, p. Jas. & Margt. McIlhany, b. Mount Calm, sc: Jas. McIlhaney, father, BVS:1855:6, LC:18

MCINTOSH, Ann W., W, F, d. 9 Mar 1864, LC, consumption, 63-0-0, p. Wm. B. & Susan Thompson, b. Middleburg, sc: Loudonia McIntosh, daughter, BVS:1864:2, LC:39

MCINTOSH, Catharine, W, F, d. Aug 1853, on Sycolin, dysentery, 9-0-0, p. Isaac & Ann McIntosh, b. Ball's Mill, sc: father, BVS:1854:5, LC:5

[MCINTOSH], Edward H., W, M, d. 22 Nov 1854, Between the Hills, caused by strangling with a grain of corn, 1-0-21, p. Robt. & Jane McIntosh, b. Between the Hills, sc: Ann McIntosh, aunt, BVS:1854:12, LC:12

MCINTOSH, Laura V., W, F, d. 12 Aug 1856, LC, consumption, 1-6-0, p. Job P. & Angelina McIntosh, b. Washington City, sc: Alex. Newton, step grand-father, BVS:1856:3, LC:21

MCKENZIE, Sallie, B, F, d. 10 Aug 1883, Leesburg, unk, 32-0-0, p. Eli & Millie Ward, b. LC, laborer, c/o: Henson McKenzie, sc: Charles Lucas, brother, 2nd Dist., BVS:1883:7

MCKIMMEY, S. Alice, W, F, d. 26 Jun 1883, nr Lovettsville, child birth, 28-0-0, p. John & Sarah McGavack, b. LC, c/o: A. G. McKimmey, sc: A.G. McKimmey, husband, 2nd Dist., BVS:1883:7

MCKINNEY, Annie B., W, F, d. 12 Jun 1889, LC, consumption, 33-0-0, p. John & May Hough, b. LC, laborer, c/o: J.W. McKinney, sc: J.W. McKinny, husband, 3rd Dist., BVS:1889:5

MCKINNEY, Arthur, W, M, d. 16 Apr 1859/60, Waterford, unk, 0-1-3, p. Jas W. & Cornelia I. McKinney, b. Waterford, sc: Jas. W. McKinney, father, BVS:1859:1, 1860:3, LC:36

MCKINNEY, Lovetta, W, F, d. 6 Dec 1886, diphtheria, 5-0-24, p. C. Francis & Sarah, sc: C. F. McKinney, father, 2nd Dist., BVS:1886:5

MCKINNEY, no name, W, M, d. 30 Nov 1888, LC, unk, 0-0-1, p. John W. & Annie B. McKinney, b. LC, none, unm, sc: John W. McKinney, father, 3rd Dist., BVS:1888:1

MCLAUGHLIN, Fannie, W, F, d. 9 Sep 1880, LC, diphtheria, 3-0-0, p. Thomas B. & Fannie McLaughlin, LC, unm, sc: Fannie McLaughlin, mother, 1st Dist., BVS:1880:2

MCLAUGHLIN, John, W, M, d. 9 Sep 1880, LC, diphtheria, 10-0-0, p. Thomas B. & Fannie McLaughlin, b. LC, unm, sc: Fannie McLaughlin, mother, 1st Dist., BVS:1880:2

MCLENARD, Sarah A., W, F, d. 20 Sep 1890, Lincoln, paralysis of brain, 60-0-0, p. Jonas & Pleasant Janney, b. LC, none, c/o: W.B. McLenard, sc: W.B. McLenard, husband, 3rd Dist., BVS:1890:6

MCLOUGHLIN, Thomas B., W, M, d. 14 Apr 1890, Washington, DC, killed by cars, 32-0-0, p. unk, b. Ireland, c/o: Mary McLoughlin, sc: Mary McLoughlin, wife, 1st Dist., BVS:1890:2

MCNEALEA, Elton, W, M, d. 3 Jul 1896, Ashburn, cholera infantum, 0-3-21, p. Americus & Martha McNealea, b. Ashburn, sc: Americus McNealea, father, BR Dist., BVS:1896:3

MCNEALEA, Jno. R., W, M, d. 27 Apr 1892, Farmwell, typhoid pneumonia, 58-1-28, p. Sanford & Sallie McNealea, b. Farmwell, stone mason, c/o: Martha McNealea, sc: Martha S. McNealea, wife, 1st Dist., BVS:1892:1

MCNEALEA, Robert, W, M, d. 20 Dec 1875, Lovettsville Dist, pneumonia, 35-6-0, p. Jacob & Mary McNealea, b. LC, married, LV Dist., BVS:1875:4

MCNEALEA, Sarah, W, F, d. 4 Oct 1878, nr Mt. Hope Church, consumption, 76-0-0, p. unk, b. LC, c/o: Sanford McNealea, sc: Chas. Wiley, son-in-law, BR Dist., BVS:1878:4

MCNEALEA, W. H., W, M, d. 18 Jul 1893, Farmwell, typhoid fever, 26-0-0, p. W. H. & Susan McNealea, b. Farmwell, laborer, unm, sc: W.H. McNealea, father, 1st Dist., BVS:1893:1

MCNEALEA, Wm. H., W, M, d. 21 Mar 1894, nr Ryan, congestive chill, 56-0-0, p. Sanford & Sallie McNealea, b. LC, stone mason, c/o: Susan McNealea, sc: Susan McNealea, wife, 1st Dist., BVS:1894:1

MCNEALY, Mary E., W, F, d. 15 Nov 1890, LC, paralysis, 80-0-0, p. unk, b. LC, none, unm, sc: M.J. McNealy, daughter, 2nd Dist., BVS:1890:4

MCNULTY, Hugh, W, M, d. 5 Nov 1854, LC, pneumonia, 60-0-0, p. Thos. & Mary McNulty, b. Ireland, tailor, c/o: Mary E. McNulty, sc: Mary E. McNulty, wife, BVS:1854:10, LC:9

MCPHERSON, Charlotte, B, F, d. 5 Oct 1878, LC, pneumonia, 17-0-0, p. Robert & Eliza McPherson, b. LC, unm, sc: Robert McPherson, father, LE Dist., BVS:1878:8

MCPHERSON, Daisy, B, F, d. 26 Sep 1875, Leesburg, cholera infantum, 1-4-27, p. Jas. & Susan McPherson, b. LC, sc: Jas. McPherson, father, LE Dist., BVS:1875:1

MCPHERSON, Harvey Lee, W, M, d. 1 Aug 1875, LC, cholera infantum, 0-4-2, p. Wm. E. & Mary A. McPherson, b. LC, sc: Mary A. McPherson, mother, LE Dist., BVS:1875:1

MCPHERSON, Lucinda, W, F, d. 23 Mar 1889, Philomont, pneumonia, 70-0-0, p. unk, b. LC, unk, sc: F.E. Robey, superintendent of poor, 1st Dist., BVS:1889:1

MCPHERSON, Samuel M., B, M, d. 27 May 1876, LC, shot in a fight, 24-0-0, p. Robert & Eliza McPherson, b. LC, laborer, sc: Joseph McPherson, brother, LE Dist., BVS:1876:6

MCQUAY, Fannie, B, F, d. 25 Dec 1894, Liethtown, burned to death, 6-0-0, p. Jas. & Fannie McQuay, b. Liethtown, sc: Jas McQuay, father, 1st Dist., BVS:1894:2

MCQUAY, George, B, M, d. 16 Jun 1885, nr Unison, croup, 1-4-0, p. Benja & Josephine McQuay, b. nr Unison, sc: Benja McQuay, father, 1st Dist., BVS:1885:4

MCQUAY, John A., B, M, d. 16 Feb 1883, nr Pot House, pneumonia, 1-3-0, p. Benja. & Josephine McQuay, b. nr Pot House, sc: Benja McQuay, father, 1st Dist., BVS:1883:1

MCQUAY, Mary, B, F, d. 10 Mar 1885, nr Unison, croup, 3-0-0, p. James & Fannie McQuay, b. nr Unison, sc: James McQuay, father, 1st Dist., BVS:1885:4

MCVEIGH, Fannie E., W, F, d. 5 Aug 1887, Middleburg, consumption, 64-0-0, p. Jesse & Elizabeth McVeigh, b. Middleburg, unm, sc: Richard L. Rogers, brother-in-law, 1st Dist., BVS:1887:1

MCVEIGH, Jesse, W, M, d. 4 Sep 1856, nr Middleburg, old age, 86-0-5, p. Jonathan & Elizth. McVeigh, b. Pennsylvania, farmer, c/o: Elizabeth McVeigh, sc: Milton McVeigh, son, BVS:1856:4, LC:21

MEAD, Mrs. Mary A., W, F, d. 17 Apr 1896, LC, old age, 85-0-0, b. LC, widow, sc: sister, LE Dist., BVS:1896:5

MEDLEY, Margaret, W, F, d. 3 Jul 1853, LC, paralyzed, 75-0-0, p. Henry & Sarah Russeau, b. LC, c/o: Robert Medley, sc: John Rasseau, brother, BVS:1854:2, LC:7

MEGEATH, Alfred, W, M, d. 11 Jul 1876, nr Mt. Zion, dyspepsia, 69-0-0, p. unk, b. LC, married, sc: physician, friend, BR Dist., BVS:1876:2

MEGEATH, Joseph P., W, M, d. 31 Jul 1858, Philomont, kidney affection, 55-0-0, p. Gabriel & Martha Megeath, b. nr Philomont, merchant, c/o: Elizabeth Megeath, sc: B.H. Richards, son-in-law, BVS:1858:4, LC:31

MELLONTREE, Jesse, B, M, d. 30 Nov 1876, nr Bloomfield, affection of the lungs, 35-0-0, laborer, c/o: Patty Mellontree, sc: Cyrus Young, father-in-law, MC Dist., BVS:1876:4

MENNEFEE, Daniel, B, M, d. 15 May 1896, Middleburg, old age, 90-0-0, p. unk, b. LC, laborer, consort, sc: ___ Mennefee, wife, MC Dist., BVS:1896:2

MERCHANT, Isaac O., W, M, d. 10 Aug 1876, LC, bronchitis, 2-3-0, p. Jas & Sarah Merchant, b. LC, sc: Sarah Merchant, mother, JF Dist., BVS:1876:8

MERCHANT, Mary, W, F, d. 27 Jun 1855, LC, paralyzed, 68-0-0, p. Arch. & Jane Morrison, b. LC, c/o: James Merchant, sc: James Merchant, husband, BVS:1855:2, LC:15

[MERCHANT], no name, W, M, d. Feb 1873, Leesburg, children's complaint, 0-8-0, p. Sarah C. Merchant, b. Leesburg, sc: Sarah C. Merchant, mother, LE Dist., BVS:1873:2

MERCHANT, W. E., W, M, d. 1 Jul 1890, Wheatland, cholera infantum, 0-5-28, p. J. H. & Annie Merchant, b. LC, none, unm, sc: J.H. Merchant, father, 3rd Dist., BVS:1890:7

MERSHON, Henry, W, M, d. 30 Apr 1857, unk, 57-0-0, p. Thomas B. & Betsy Mershon, b. LC, farmer, sc: Benjn Mershon, brother, BVS:1857:7, LC:28

MICKENS, Eliza, B, F, d. Sep 1871, LC, 40-0-0, b. LC, married, LE Dist., BVS:1871:4

MICKENS, Jane, B, F, d. 18 Dec 1883, Leesburg, unk, 65-0-0, p. Kate Mickens, b. LC, laborer, unm, sc: Mark Smith, son-in-law, 2nd Dist., BVS:1883:3

MIDDLETON, Frances P., W, F, d. 13 Sep 1883, nr Gum Spring, inflammation bowels, 35-0-0, p. Lovel & Susan Middleton, b. nr Gum Spring, unm, sc: Susan Middleton, mother, 1st Dist., BVS:1883:1

MIDDLETON, Lovell H., W, M, d. 13 Dec 1872, nr Gum Spring, paralysis, 69-0-0, p. unk, b. Fauquier Co., farmer, c/o: Susan Middleton, sc: Susan Middleton, wife, BR Dist., BVS:1872:6

MILBOURN, A. Jefferson, W, M, d. 31 May 1882, LC, kidney disease, 65-

11-20, b. LC, farmer, c/o: Mary Milbourn, sc: C.S. Milbourn, son, 3rd Dist., BVS:1882:3

MILBOURN, Ann E., W, F, d. 1 Nov 1853, Middleburg, inflammation of blood, 0-8-20, p. Zenas & Adeline Milbourn, b. Middleburg, sc: father, BVS:1854:1, LC:4

MILBOURN, Jonathan, W, M, d. 18 Sep 1854, B. R. M. res of father, cholera, 34-10-0, p. John & Mary Milbourn, b. Blue Ridge Mountain, Engineer R. R., c/o: Massie Milbourn, sc: father, BVS:1854:13, LC:12

MILBURN, Cecelia A., W, F, d. 12 Sep 1859/60, Leesburg, water on brain, 6-10-4, p. John F. & Joanna Milburn, b. LC, sc: John F. Milburn, father, BVS:1859:2, 1860:5, LC:37

MILBURN, J. Fletcher, W, M, d. 9 Oct 1878, LC, heart disease, 64-0-0, b. LC, c/o: Virginia Milburn, sc: Virginia Milburn, wife, LE Dist., BVS:1878:8

MILBURN, Jena F., W, M, d. 18 Nov 1894, Leesburg, cancer, 73-0-0, p. unk, b. unk, unk, consort, sc: Ann Milburn, LE Dist., BVS:1894:3

MILBURN, John, W, M, d. 18 Jan 1873, nr Purcellville, paralysis, 79-0-0, p. Johnathan & Elizabeth Milburn, b. nr Purcellville, farmer, c/o: Mary Milburn, sc: Franklin Milburn, son, MT Dist., BVS:1873:3

MILBURN, Sarah A., W, , d. 24 Nov 1877, LC, drowning, 27-10-0, sc: J.F. Milburn, father, LE Dist., BVS:1877:8

MILES, Sarah, W, F, d. 15 Feb 1893, Lovettsville, indigestion, 65-0-0, p. unk, b. Lovettsville, unm, sc: B. F. Miles, LV Dist., BVS:1893:5

MILEY, Catharine, W, F, d. 7 Nov 1886, Bloomfield, old age, 80-0-0, p. unk, b. LC, unm, sc: Marshall Carpenter, friend, 1st Dist., BVS:1886:2

MILEY, Christopher, W, M, d. Sep 1854, foot of Blue Ridge, old age, 83-0-0, p. Jacob Miley, b. on Potomac River, farmer, unm, sc: Favius G. Miley, nephew, BVS:1854:11, LC:11

MILEY, Hannah, W, F, d. 17 Mar 1858, John Marts', old age, 76-0-0, p. John & ... Boley, b. Frederick Co., c/o:

John Miley decd, sc: Christina Miley, daughter, BVS:1858:4, LC:31

MILEY, James U., W, M, d. 3 Jan 1866, pneumonia, 0-8-0, p. C. G. & Charlotte Miley, b. Trappe, sc: Caldwell G. Miley, father, BVS:1866:2

MILLER, Annie C., W, F, d. 29 Jul 1886, bright's disease, 40-0-0, p. Enoch G. & Eliza B. Rex, c/o: P. H. Miller, sc: P. H. Miller, husband, 2nd Dist., BVS:1886:5

MILLER, Armistead M., W, M, d. 25 Aug 1881, LC, cancer, 66-0-0, p. Geo. & Mary Miller, b. LC, farmer, c/o: Mary Miller, sc: Joseph Connard, daughter[sic], 2nd Dist., BVS:1881:7

MILLER, Elizabeth, W, F, d. 8 Oct 1888, LC, old age, 75-0-0, p. unk, b. LC, none, c/o: Frederick Miller, sc: L.H. Potterfield, adm., 2nd Dist., BVS:1888:6

MILLER, Frederick, W, M, d. 16 Aug 1876, Lovettsville, dropsy of the heart, 75-0-0, b. LC, farmer, c/o: Elizabeth Miller, sc: Elizabeth Miller, wife, LV Dist., BVS:1876:3

MILLER, Frederick, W, M, d. 11 Dec 1856, LC, unk, 33-0-0, p. George & Eliz. Miller, b. LC, sc: ....Miller, wife, BVS:1856:7, LC:24

MILLER, Geo. R., W, M, d. May 1871, LC, 26-0-0, p. Dr. T. & Virginia J. Miller, b. Washington, physician, unm, LE Dist., BVS:1871:4

MILLER, Lydia A, W, F, d. 5 Jul 1880, nr Leesburg, cancer, 42-0-0, p. Jas. & --- Zellers, b. Maryland, c/o: Samuel H. Miller, sc: Saml H. Miller, husband, 2nd Dist., BVS:1880:7

MILLER, no name, W, M, d. 28 Jan 1884, nr Lovettsville, unk, 0-0-2, p. P.H. & Annie C. Miller, b. LC, sc: P.H. Miller, father, 2nd Dist., BVS:1884:5

MILLER, Rosa, W, F, d. Dec 1859/60, 0-3-0, p. Michael & Rosanna Mills, b. nr Janney's Mill, sc: M. Miller, father, BVS:1859:4, 1860:2, LC:35

MILLER, Susan E., W, F, d. 12 Sep 1865, nr Waterford, typhoid f, 20-0-0, p. Wm. & Susan Miller, b. nr Waterford, farmer, unm, sc: Wm. H. Miller, father, 1st Dist., BVS:1865:3/4

Loudoun County, Virginia, Death Register, 1853-1896 181

MILLS, Anna E., W, F, d. 20 Dec 1876, nr Mt. Hope Church, diphtheria, 9-0-0, p. Robt & Sarah E.W. Mills, b. LC, sc: Robert Mills, father, BR Dist., BVS:1876:2

MILLS, Elizabeth, W, F, d. 2 Feb 1873, nr Mt. Hope Church, consumption, 68-0-0, p. Joseph Havener & wife, b. LC, c/o: Wm. Mills, decd, sc: Jas. C. Mills, son, BR Dist., BVS:1873:1

MILLS, Ellen, W, F, d. 8 Feb 1875, Mt. Hope Church, consumption, 75-1-0, p. unk, b. LC, unm, sc: a friend, BR Dist., BVS:1875:5

MILLS, Mary A., W, F, d. 21 Jun 1892, Conklin, consumption, 60-0-0, p. Cornelius & Eliza Williams, b. Fairfax, c/o: Jno H. Mills, sc: Jno H. Mills, husband, 1st Dist., BVS:1892:1

MILLS, Rebecca F., W, F, d. 1 Mar 1883, nr Leesburg, tumor, 55-0-0, p. --- & Frances Muse, b. LC, c/o: Harrison Mills, sc: Jno. W. Lawson, son-in-law, 2nd Dist., BVS:1883:7

MILLS, Sarah E., W, F, d. 2 Oct 1881, LC, croup, 2-0-0, p. Wm M. & Sarah Mills, b. LC, sc: S. Mills, mother, 1st Dist., BVS:1881:2

MILLS, Lucy, (f), F, d. Mar 1854, Charles Byrne's, 1-0-0, p. Sally Mills, b. Ch. Byrnes', sc: Charles Byrne, BVS:1854:11, LC:10

MILLS, Wm., W, M, d. 12 Aug 1855, unk, 60-0-0, p. Jno. & Mary Mills, b. Maryland, farmer, sc: Mary Mills, wife, BVS:1855:8, LC:19

MILSTEAD, Bertie, W, F, d. 9 Jan 1892, Sterling, la grippe & pneumonia, 40-0-0, p. Townsend & Cath. Milstead, b. Sterling, unm, sc: J.E. Milstead, brother, 1st Dist., BVS:1892:1

MILSTEAD, Catharine E., W, F, d. 8 Jan 1892, Sterling, la grippe & pneumonia, 58-0-0, p. Wm. & Sallie Havener, b. Sterling, c/o: Townsend Milstead, sc: J.E. Milstead, son, 1st Dist., BVS:1892:1

MILSTEAD, Townsend, W, M, d. 5 Nov 1858, LC, unk, 29-0-0, p. Noah & Kitty Milstead, b. LC, sc: Noah Milstead, father, BVS:1858:6, LC:33

MILTON, Alexander R., W, M, d. 15 Aug 1857, LC, interception intestines, 16-0-0, p. Alex. R. & Cecelia Milton, b. LC, sc: Joshua White, second cousin, BVS:1857:1, LC:25

MINNIGERODE, Roberta R., W, F, d. 8 Sep 1884, nr Leesburg, cholera infantum, 0-9-2, p. Chas. & Virginia Minnigerode, b. New Orleans, LA, sc: George Carter, uncle, 2nd Dist., BVS:1884:5

MINOR, Benjamin, W, M, d. 15 May 1875, LC, spinal affection, 3-0-0, p. Benj S. & Mary E. Minor, b. LC, sc: Daniel Shreve, grandfather, LE Dist., BVS:1875:1

MINOR, Benjamin S., W, M, d. 14 Apr 1878, LC, consumption, 35-9-0, p. J. M. & Ann E. Minor, b. LC, c/o: Mary E. Minor, sc: Mary E. Minor, wife, LE Dist., BVS:1878:8

MINOR, Colville, W, M, d. 30 Sep 1854, LC, dysentery, 2-3-0, p. John W. & Louise F. Minor, b. LC, sc: John W. Minor, father, BVS:1854:10, LC:10

MINOR, Colville, W, M, d. 25 Sep 1855, LC, dysentery, 3-0-0, p. Jno. W. & L. F. Minor, b. LC, sc: John W. Minor, father, BVS:1855:3, LC:16

MINOR, Flora, B, F, d. 3 May 1878, LC, paralysis, 60-0-0, b. LC, sc: Laura Page, friend, LE Dist., BVS:1878:8

MINOR, Jackson M., W, M, d. 25 Apr 1893, Taylorstown, unk, 66-0-0, p. unk, b. Taylorstown, farmer, consort, sc: Mary C. Minor, LV Dist., BVS:1893:5

MINOR, John W., W, M, d. 24 Dec 1876, LC, gravel, 72-0-0, p. unk, b. LC, farmer, c/o: Louisa Minor, sc: F. C. Minor, son, LE Dist., BVS:1876:6

MINOR, Jos., B, M, d. 10 Mar 1891, Mountville, brain fever, 14-0-0, p. Henry & Jane Minor, b. Culpeper Co., laborer, unm, sc: Henry Minor, head of family, 1st Dist., BVS:1891:1

MINOR, Mary E., W, F, d. 18 Nov 1894, Taylorstown, dropsy, 67-0-0, p. unk, b. unk, unm, sc: Jas. Williams, LV Dist., BVS:1894:4

MINOR, Thos. B., W, M, d. 17 Sep 1855, LC, typhoid fever, 20-2-18, p. Spence & Mary Minor, b. LC, farmer, unm, sc: Spence Minor, father, BVS:1855:1, LC:14

MISKELL, Unali, W, F, d. 18 Feb 1889, LC, unk, 0-2-4, p. J. H. & Lillian

Miskell, b. LC, none, unm, sc: J.H. Miskell, father, 2nd Dist., BVS:1889:3

MISKELL, Uriah, W, F, d. 14 Feb 1890, LC, unk, 0-3-28, p. John H. & Lillia Miskell, b. LC, none, unm, sc: J.H. Miskell, father, 2nd Dist., BVS:1890:4

MISKELL, Willard H., W, M, d. 14 Jan 1892, Lucketts, pneumonia, 0-6-0, p. John & Sallie Miskell, b. Lucketts, unm, sc: John Miskell, LE Dist., BVS:1892:5

MISKELL, Wm., W, M, d. 18 Jan 1865, on Potomac, pneumonia, 76-0-0, b. Richmond, carpenter, consort, sc: F.J. Miskell, son, BVS:1865:2

MITCHEL, Ann L., W, F, d. Feb 1871, LC, 4-0-0, b. LC, unm, LE Dist., BVS:1871:4

MITCHELL, Mary A., B, F, d. 15 Jan 1884, Hamilton, unk, 1-2-0, p. Wm. & Sarah Mitchell, b. Virginia, unm, sc: Wm. Mitchell, father, 3rd Dist., BVS:1884:6

MITCHELL, no name, B, F, d. 18 Jul 1889, Philomont, unk, 0-5-0, p. Ida Mitchell, b. Philomont, sc: F.E. Robey, superintendent of poor, 1st Dist., BVS:1889:1

MITCHELL, Sallie, W, F, d. 25 Jul 1891, Evergreen Mills, heart failure, 64-0-0, p. John & Lucy Mitchell, b. Madison Co., farmer, unm, sc: W.R. Mitchell, brother, 1st Dist., BVS:1891:2

MOBBERLY, Charles F., W, M, d. 25 Jul 1854, LC, dysentery, 1-9-21, p. Jesse W. & Catherine Mobberly, b. LC, sc: Catherine Mobberly, mother, BVS:1854:9, LC:9

MOBERLY, John, W, M, d. 5 Apr 1865, nr Short Hill, gun shot, 20-0-0, p. ___ & Mary Moberly, b. Between the Hills, unm, sc: Mary Moberly, mother, 1st Dist., BVS:1865:3/4

MOBERLY, Maria, W, F, d. 26 Jan 1889, LC, old age, 80-3-7, p. unk, b. LC, none, widow, sc: E.H. Waters, daughter, 2nd Dist., BVS:1889:4

MOBERLY, Thoms J., W, M, d. 9 Jan 1865, Between the Hills, shot in the thigh, 16-0-0, p. John & Maria Moberly, b. Between the Hills, gun smith, married, sc: John Moberly, father, 1st Dist., BVS:1865:3/4

MOCK, Armistead M., W, M, d. 9 Mar 1858, LC, pneumonia, 33-11-5, p. Henry & Barbary Mock, b. LC, unm, sc: Thomas Mock, brother, BVS:1858:1, LC:29

MOCK, Barbary, W, F, d. 15 Jul 1858, LC, paralyzed, 73-5-12, p. unk, b. LC, widow, sc: Thomas Mock, son, BVS:1858:1, LC:29

MOCK, Elizabeth V., W, F, d. 11 Sep 1857, nr Harmony, typhoid dysentery, 13-0-0, p. Jos. C. & Mary Mock, b. nr Peugh's Mill, sc: Joseph C. Mock, father, BVS:1857:3, LC:26

MOCK, Gary C., W, M, d. 22 Nov 1884, nr Lovettsville, gastric fever, 1-6-28, p. Albert & Elizabeth A. Mock, b. LC, sc: Albert Mock, father, 2nd Dist., BVS:1884:5

MOCK, Geo. C. C., W, M, d. 26 Jul 1855, LC, diabetes, 0-3-28, p. Ths. & Rebecca Mock, b. LC, sc: Rebecca Mock, mother, BVS:1855:2, LC:15

MOCK, Grace V., W, F, d. 5 Jul 1881, LC, unk, 2-11-0, p. Albert E. A. Mock, b. LC, sc: Albert Mock, father, 2nd Dist., BVS:1881:7

MOCK, James R., W, M, d. 2 Aug 1872, nr Short Hill, scarlet fever, 1-11-13, p. Jno. C. & Rosana Mock, b. nr Short Hill, laborer, married, sc: Jno C. Mock, father, LV Dist., BVS:1872:5

MOCK, John, W, M, d. 9 Aug 1865, Sarah Heaters, typhoid fever, 55-0-0, p. Henry & Barbary Mock, b. LC, farmer, unm, sc: John Virts, friend, 1st Dist., BVS:1865:3/4

MOCK, Mary Susan, W, F, d. 1 May 1865, nr Waterford, croup, 3-3-0, p. John C. & Marg Mock, b. nr Waterford, laborer, married, sc: John C. Mock, father, 1st Dist., BVS:1865:3/4

MOCK, Rosana, W, F, d. 15 Jul 1872, nr Short Hill, scarlet fever, 8-9-24, p. Jno. C. & Rosana Mock, b. nr Short Hill, laborer, married, sc: Jno C. Mock, father, LV Dist., BVS:1872:5

MOCK, Sarah E., W, F, d. 15 Oct 1855, Cobb Co., IL, intermittent fever, 2-6-14, p. Isaac & Lydia A. Mock, b. Muskingum, Ohio, sc: Isaac L. Mock, father, BVS:1855:1, LC:14

MOFFETT, Drusilla T., W, F, d. 26 Jul 1883, nr Leesburg, heart disease,

56-0-0, p. Benj. & Elizth Prichard, b. Maryland, c/o: Benj. Moffett, sc: Benj Moffett, husband, 2nd Dist., BVS:1883:7

MOFFETT, Elizth. Ann, W, F, d. 15 Jan 1856, res of parents, consumption, 22-0-0, p. Thomas J. & Eliza Moffett, b. G.H. Henderson's, sc: Thomas J. Moffett, father, BVS:1856:5, LC:23

MOFFETT, James E., W, M, d. 22 Apr 1884, LC, spasms, 0-2-20, p. Marcellus & E. Moffett, b. LC, sc: Marcellus Moffet, father, 1st Dist., BVS:1884:2

MOFFETT, Mary, W, F, d. Sep 1853, nr Waterford, consumption, 22-0-0, p. Thos. & Eliza Moffett, b. on Goose Creek, unm, sc: father, BVS:1854:6, LC:5

MOFFETT, Sarah, W, F, d. 12 Jan 1853, nr Waterford, contraction of brain, 12-0-0, p. Thos. & Eliza Moffett, b. Ohio, sc: father, BVS:1854:6, LC:5

MOFFETT, Thos. D., W, M, d. 16 Dec 1896, LC, paralysis, 53-0-0, p. Thos. & Eliza Moffett, b. LC, farmer, husband, sc: wife, LE Dist., BVS:1896:5

MOFFETT, Virginia, W, F, d. Jul 1853, nr Waterford, dysentery, 3-0-0, p. Thos. & Eliza Moffett, b. Waterford, sc: father, BVS:1854:6, LC:5

[MONDAY], Robert Henry, W, M, d. Apr 1854, Jas. Whitacre's farm, influenza, 0-3-9, p. John L. & Sarah Monday, b. Jas. Whitacres farm, sc: father, BVS:1854:12, LC:12

MONDAY, Rosannah, W, F, d. 20 Aug 1873, nr Morristown, dropsy, 74-0-0, p. Nicholas & M. Fry, b. LC, widow, sc: Margaret A. Snoots, daughter, LV Dist., BVS:1873:4

MONEY, Nancy, W, F, d. 20 Nov 1872, Chestnut Hill, pneumonia, 80-0-0, p. Francis & Betsey Hutchins, b. LC, c/o: Nicholas Money, sc: Mary Simmons, daughter, LE Dist., BVS:1872:4

MONEY, Nicholas, W, M, d. 4 May 1855, LC, consumption, 73-0-0, p. unk, b. unk, farmer, c/o: Nancy Money, sc: Ephraim Money, son, BVS:1855:1, LC:14

MONEY, Sarah C., W, F, d. 29 Aug 1883, nr Leesburg, bilious dysentery, 40-4-14, p. Wm. & Mary A. Compher, b. LC, c/o: Samuel Money, sc: Samuel Money, husband, 2nd Dist., BVS:1883:3

MONROE, Alferna, W, F, d. 25 Jan 1888, Unison, measles, 1-10-0, p. Madison & Susan Monroe, b. Unison, sc: Madison Monroe, father, 1st Dist., BVS:1888:4

MONROE, Caroline F., W, F, d. 12 Feb 1871, unk, p. Susan & Wm. M. Monroe, farmer, MC Dist., BVS:1871:2

MONROE, Eaton, W, M, d. 18 Oct 1881, LC, cholera infantum, 0-6-0, p. Mast & Susan Monroe, b. LC, sc: S. Monroe, mother, 1st Dist., BVS:1881:2

MONROE, George, B, M, d. 20 May 1887, Farmwell, sore throat, 6-0-0, p. George & Harriet Monroe, b. Farmwell, sc: George Monroe, father, 1st Dist., BVS:1887:1

MONROE, Michael H.P., W, M, d. 25 Jun 1878, nr Unison, brain fever, 0-5-0, p. Wm M. & Susan V. Monroe, b. LC, sc: Wm M. Monroe, father, MC Dist., BVS:1878:7

MONROE, Mollie A., W, F, d. 17 Apr 1878, nr Unison, consumption, 30-0-0, c/o: Chas A. Monroe, sc: Chas A. Monroe, husband, MC Dist., BVS:1878:7

MONROE, Mrs. M. F., W, F, d. 13 Jul 1896, LC, old age, 71-0-0, p. S.M. & N. Edwards, b. LC, widow, sc: Thos M. Wood, LE Dist., BVS:1896:5

MONROE, no name, B, M, d. 16 Apr 1887, Unison, unk, 0-0-1, p. John & Henrietta Monroe, b. Unison, sc: John Monroe, father, 1st Dist., BVS:1887:1

MONROE, Susan E., W, F, d. 8 Jan 1888, Unison, croup, 2-5-0, p. Alfred C. & Mollie Monroe, b. Unison, sc: Alfred C. Monroe, father, 1st Dist., BVS:1888:4

MONROE, Thos., W, M, d. 14 Aug 1877, nr Philomont, neuralgia of bowels, 49-0-0, p. Wm. & Euphany Monroe, b. LC, farmer, c/o: Julia Ann Monroe, sc: J.A. Monroe, wife, MT Dist., BVS:1877:2

MONROE, William H., W, M, d. 3 Sep 1853, Bloomfield, croup, 0-11-0, p. Thomas & Julia Monroe, b.

Bloomfield, sc: father, BVS:1854:1, LC:4

MOORE, Ann A., W, F, d. 2 Jan 1894, Wheatland, old age, 75-0-0, p. Henry & Matilda Russell, b. Wheatland, wife, sc: Samuel L. Moore, son, 3rd Dist., BVS:1894:5

MOORE, Awrena, B, F, d. 12 Feb 1873, Aldie, unk, 0-0-6, p. Henry & Esther Moore, b. nr Aldie, sc: ? Moore, father, MC Dist., BVS:1873:5

MOORE, Charley, W, M, d. 6 Dec 1859/60, LC, unk, 0-4-0, p. Geo. L. & Ann A. Moore, b. LC, sc: George L. Moore, father, BVS:1859:2, 1860:4, LC:37

MOORE, Charlotte, W, F, d. 16 Mar 1875, Purcellville, fever, 44-0-0, b. LC, c/o: Presley Moore, sc: Presley Moore, husband, JF Dist., BVS:1875:3

MOORE, Chas. P., W, M, d. 9 Aug 1855, Moore's Mill, hemorrhage lungs, 22-0-0, p. Peyton & Araminda Moore, b. Moore's Mill, Miller, sc: Peyton Moor, father, BVS:1855:5, LC:17

MOORE, Edward, W, M, d. 27 Dec 1858, res of parents, croup, 6-11-22, p. James W. & Matilda Moore, b. nr Union, sc: James W. Moore, father, BVS:1858:3, LC:31

MOORE, Elizabeth, B, F, d. 16 Apr 1880, LC, consumption, 24-0-0, p. unk, b. LC, c/o: John H. Moore, sc: John H. Moore, husband, 1st Dist., BVS:1880:2

MOORE, Ella, B, F, d. 10 Jul 1877, St. Louis, consumption, 12-0-0, p. Thomas & Milly Moore, b. LC, sc: Jno. Moore, father, MC Dist., BVS:1877:5

MOORE, Emanuel, B, M, d. 1 Sep 1883, nr Lovettsville, tetanus, 11-0-0, p. Jerry & --- Moore, b. LC, sc: Leven T. Jones, friend, 2nd Dist., BVS:1883:7

MOORE, Emily, W, F, d. 7 May 1896, nr Unison, cancer, 85-0-0, p. unk, b. unk, none, unm, sc: H.L. Keen, head of family, MC Dist., BVS:1896:1

MOORE, Emily Jane, W, F, d. Dec 1865, Purcellville, dropsy, 32-0-0, unm, sc: Oscar Nesmith, brother-in-law, BVS:1865:1

MOORE, F. F., W, M, d. 10 Sep 1896, LC, unk, 0-2-0, p. G.W. S. & E. M. Moore, b. LC, unm, sc: father, LE Dist., BVS:1896:5

MOORE, Hannah, W, F, d. 27 Dec 1866, nr Unison, unk, unk, sc: Edw B. Moore, husband, BVS:1866:2

MOORE, Henry, B, M, d. 25 Apr 1880, LC, consumption, 18-0-0, p. Thos. L. & Annie Moore, b. LC, unm, sc: Annie Moore, mother, 1st Dist., BVS:1880:2

MOORE, Isaac, W, M, d. 21 Apr 1882, Poor House, unk, 78-0-0, p. unk, widower, sc: Jno R. Carter, superintendent, 1st Dist., BVS:1882:2

MOORE, James W., W, M, d. 10 Nov 1878, nr Short Hill Church, consumption, 58-10-2, p. Wm. & Tamar Moore, b. nr Middleburg, farmer, unk, sc: Wm. Moore, son, BR Dist., BVS:1878:4

MOORE, Jeremiah, W, M, d. 11 Feb 1859/60, Poor House, rheumatism, 85-0-0, b. LC, sc: steward, BVS:1859:4, 1860:2, LC:35

MOORE, Jerry, B, M, d. 10 May 1876, Leesburg, kidney disease, 30-0-0, p. unk, b. unk, laborer, sc: Maria Simmons, friend, LE Dist., BVS:1876:6

MOORE, John, W, M, d. 12 Nov 1878, Aldie, old age, 77-9-12, b. Culpepper Co., miller, c/o: Matilda Moore, sc: Alex W. Moore, son, MC Dist., BVS:1878:7

MOORE, Laura, B, F, d. 5 Sep 1883, nr Unison, consumption, 30-0-0, p. Wm. & Mary Thorndley, b. LC, c/o: Geo Moore, sc: Geo Moore, husband, 1st Dist., BVS:1883:1

MOORE, M. L., W, M, d. 3 May 1877, Aldie, heart disease, 72-7-0, b. LC, c/o: Jno. Moore, sc: A.B. Moore, son, MC Dist., BVS:1877:5

MOORE, Mary E., B, F, d. 10 Feb 1877, St. Louis, consumption, 9-0-0, p. Thomas & Milly Moore, b. LC, sc: Jno. Moore, father, MC Dist., BVS:1877:5

MOORE, Matilda, W, F, d. 22 Oct 1859/60, M.M. Plaster's, typhoid fever, 35-8-8, p. Edward & Mary Dulin, b. nr Goresville, c/o: Jas. W.

Moore, sc: Jas. W. Moore, husband, BVS:1859:3, 1860:1, LC:34

MOORE, Mordecai, W, M, d. 1 Jan 1892, Unison, la grippe, 65-0-0, p. Peyton & Arminda Moore, b. Unison, Miller, unm, sc: sister, 1st Dist., BVS:1892:1

MOORE, Nancy, W, F, d. 25 Aug 1866, Unison, 37-0-0, p. Wm. & Margt. Wright, married, sc: Jas W. Moore, husband, BVS:1866:2

[MOORE], no name, B, , d. 24 Aug 1871, 0-0-4, p. Alice & Jno Moore, c/o: James Mount, MC Dist., BVS:1871:2

MOORE, Virginia, W, F, d. 1 Oct 1876, LC, consumption, 26-0-0, p. Jas. & Matilda Moore, b. LC, sc: Jas. Moore, father, JF Dist., BVS:1876:8

MOORE, Walter S., W, M, d. 22 Nov 1880, Hillsboro, membrane croup, 10-3-0, p. Lee L. & Mary C. Moore, b. LC, sc: Lee L. Moore, father, 3rd Dist., BVS:1880:4

MOORE, William B., W, M, d. 18 May 1888, nr Aldie, whooping cough, 0-3-12, p. Alex B. & Lucy B. Moore, b. Aldie, sc: Alex B. Moore, father, 1st Dist., BVS:1888:4

MOORE, William H., W, M, d. 14 Feb 1865, Bond's Mill, croup, 0-8-4, p. Johnathan & Mary Moore, b. Bonds Mill, miller, married, sc: Johnathan Moore, father, 1st Dist., BVS:1865:3/4

MOORELAND, Wm. T., W, M, d. 9 Feb 1875, LC, brain fever, unk, p. Wm H. & Rachel Moreland, b. LC, sc: Wm. H. Moreland, father, LE Dist., BVS:1875:1

MORAN, Albert, W, M, d. 30 Jun 1888, nr Farmwell, consumption, 25-0-0, p. Wm. & Polly Moran, b. Farmwell, c/o: Mary L. Moran, sc: Mary L. Moran, wife, 1st Dist., BVS:1888:4

MORAN, Catharine, W, F, d. 22 Feb 1872, nr Belmont, paralysis, 75-0-0, p. Mivart Moran & wife, b. LC, unm, sc: Thos. A. Havener, son-in-law, BR Dist., BVS:1872:6

MORAN, Chas. E., W, M, d. 3 Aug 1878, nr Mt. Hope Church, brain fever, 0-5-0, p. John & Margaret Moran, b. nr Mt. Hope Church, unm, sc: John W. Moran, father, BR Dist., BVS:1878:4

MORAN, Claudius C., W, M, d. 12 Nov 1886, Farmwell, lung disease, 6-11-0, p. James T. & Maggie E. Moran, b. Farmwell, sc: James T. Moran, father, 1st Dist., BVS:1886:1

MORAN, Edward F., W, F, d. 27 Nov 1881, LC, consumption, 32-0-0, b. LC, c/o: H.T. Moran, sc: H.T. Moran, husband, 1st Dist., BVS:1881:2

MORAN, Elizabeth, W, F, d. 21 Jan 1866, Peyton Hill, pneumonia, 62-0-0, p. Mivert & Mary Moran, b. Broad Run, unm, sc: John W. Moran, nephew, BVS:1866:3

MORAN, Emily, W, F, d. 16 Aug 1887, Farmwell, heart disease, 74-0-0, p. George & Polly Shryock, b. Farmwell, c/o: Richard Moran, sc: William H. Harris, son-in-law, 1st Dist., BVS:1887:1

MORAN, Helen N., W, F, d. 2 Nov 1890, Hamilton, brain disease, 2-6-0, p. W. H. Moran, b. LC, none, unm, sc: W.H. Moran, father, 3rd Dist., BVS:1890:6

MORAN, Jno. M., W, M, d. 16 Mar 1892, Farmwell, typhoid fever, 31-0-0, p. Alexa. & Vilinda Moran, b. Farmwell, laborer, unm, sc: J.T. Moran, brother, 1st Dist., BVS:1892:1

MORAN, Jno. M. Sr., W, M, d. 21 Jun 1891, Ryan, gangrene, 84-0-0, p. John & Mary Moran, b. LC, farmer, c/o: Drusilla Moran, decd, sc: Jno M. Lyon, nephew, 1st Dist., BVS:1891:2

MORAN, Jno. T., W, M, d. 35 Nov 1892, Ryan, pneumonia, 24-0-0, p. Jno. W. & Margaret Moran, b. Ryan, laborer, unm, sc: Jno W. Moran, father, 1st Dist., BVS:1892:1

MORAN, Joshua G., W, M, d. 24 Apr 1896, Ryan, yellow jaundice & wound, 58-0-6, b. nr Ryan, farmer, c/o: Mary J. Moran, sc: Jos R. Moran, son, BR Dist., BVS:1896:3

MORAN, Lizzie J., W, F, d. 20 Dec 1886, Farmwell, consumption, 16-0-0, p. Joshua G. & Mary J. Moran, b. Farmwell, unm, sc: Joshua G. Moran, father, 1st Dist., BVS:1886:2

MORAN, Lydia, W, F, d. 27 Mar 1871, unk, 85-0-0, married, BR Dist., BVS:1871:3

MORAN, Maggie E., W, F, d. 3 Jul 1983, Ryan, child birth, 18-0-0, p.

Pierson & Laurie Crosen, b. Fairfax, c/o: Geo W. Moran, sc: Geo W. Moran, husband, 1st Dist., BVS:1893:1

MORAN, Mary L., W, F, d. 13 Apr 1896, Ryan, consumption, 48-0-0, b. nr Leesburg, c/o: Frank Moran, sc: R.E. Moran, son, BR Dist., BVS:1896:3

[MORAN], no name, W, F, d. 12 Apr 1873, nr Goose Creek, unk, 0-0-2, p. Joshua G. & Mary J. Moran, b. LC, unm, sc: Joshua G. Moran, head of family, BR Dist., BVS:1873:1

MORAN, Nora, W, F, d. 19 Feb 1883, Farmwell, consumption, 16-0-0, p. Joshua G. & Mary J. Moran, b. nr Farmwell, unm, sc: Joshua G. Moran, father, 1st Dist., BVS:1883:1

MORAN, Thos J., W, M, d. 14 Jul 1864, Point Lookout, diarrhea, 23-10-9, p. R.Y. & M.E. Moran, b. LC, farmer, sc: R.Y. Moran, father, BVS:1864:2, LC:39

MORAN, Wm. M., W, M, d. 3 Apr 1892, Sterling, paralysis, 68-0-0, p. Gustave & Lydia Moran, b. LC, farmer, c/o: M.E. Moran, sc: C.L. Moran, son, 1st Dist., BVS:1892:1

MORELAND, Elizabet, W, F, d. 3 Aug 1891, Silcott Springs, old age, 86-0-0, p. George & Catherine Moreland, b. LC, wife, unm, sc: Charles F. Otley, MT Dist., BVS:1891:6

MORELAND, Geo. W., W, M, d. 11 Jul 1853, Waterford, dysentery, 10-8-5, p. Thos. & Sarah Moreland, b. LC, sc: Sarah Moreland, mother, BVS:1854:4, LC:3

MORELAND, John R., W, M, d. 8 Apr 1858, Waterford, scrofula, 20-0-18, p. Thomas & Sarah Moreland, b. Washington City, unm, sc: Sarah Moreland, mother, BVS:1858:1, LC:29

MORELAND, Kate, W, F, d. 10 Jul 1892, Snickersville, heart disease, 32-0-0, p. George Wright, b. LC, wife, sc: Jeremiah Moreland, father-in-law, MT Dist., BVS:1892:8

MORELAND, no name, B, F, d. 15 Feb 1873, nr Bloomfield, still born, unk, p. Wm. & Mary Moreland, b. Bloomfield, sc: Wm. Moreland, father, MC Dist., BVS:1873:5

MORGAN, Henry, B, M, d. 1 May 1887, LC, consumption, 1-1-0, p. Columbus & Amy Morgan, b. LC, unm, sc: Columbus Morgan, father, 2nd Dist., BVS:1887:4

MORGAN, John, W, M, d. 7 Aug 1866, nr Hamilton, dropsy, 72-0-0, p. unk, b. LC, c/o: Sarah Morgan, sc: John W. Morgan, son, BVS:1866:1

MORGAN, Lilly, W, F, d. 16 Feb 1883, Guilford, rheumatism, 9-0-0, p. Benj. F. & Harriet Morgan, b. Guilford, unm, sc: Benja F. Morgan, father, 1st Dist., BVS:1883:1

[MORGAN], no name, W, F, d. 16 Oct 1865, nr Goresville, born dead, unk, p. Benj F. & Hannah G. Morgan, b. nr Goresville, farmer, married, sc: Benj F. Morgan, father, 1st Dist., BVS:1865:3/4

MORGAN, Sarah, W, F, d. 15 May 1866, nr Hamilton, fever, 58-0-0, p. unk, b. LC, c/o: John Morgan, sc: John W. Morgan, son, BVS:1866:1

MORIARITY, Michael, W, M, d. Feb 1874, LC, pneumonia, 54-0-0, c/o: Jane Moriarity, sc: John Moriarity, father, LE Dist., BVS:1874:5

MORIARTY, Jane, W, F, d. 29 May 1883, nr Leesburg, consumption, 59-0-0, p. Henry & --- Kidwell, b. Prince William Co., c/o: Michael Moriarty, sc: John H. Moriarty, son, 2nd Dist., BVS:1883:7

MORIARTY, Jane. F., W, , d. 30 Sep 1853, Fauquier Co, croup, 1-10-0, p. Patrick & Margaret Moriarty, b. Clifton, sc: mother, BVS:1854:7, LC:6

MORIARTY, Sarah A., W, F, d. 7 Aug 1883, nr Leesburg, whooping cough, 0-7-8, p. Jno. H. & Sarah J. Moriarty, b. LC, sc: Jno H. Moriarty, father, 2nd Dist., BVS:1883:7

MORIUS, Nancy, B, F, d. 20 Mar 1882, Poor House, unk, 92-0-0, p. unk, unm, sc: Jno R. Carter, superintendent, 1st Dist., BVS:1882:2

MORRIS, Ann, W, M, d. 17 Feb 1879, Davis Mill, age, 98-3-0, p. Robert Ogden, b. LC, c/o: Mahlon Morris, sc: Leven Ogden, nephew, 3rd Dist., BVS:1879:3

MORRIS, Caroline, B, F, d. 2 Mar 1873, Dover, whooping cough, 3-0-

Loudoun County, Virginia, Death Register, 1853-1896   187

0, p. Robt. & Amanda Morris, b. Middleburg, sc: Lydia Shelton, grandmother, MC Dist., BVS:1873:5

MORRIS, Dora, W, F, d. 5 Jan 1886, nr Unison, whooping cough, 0-6-0, p. John T. & Virginia Morris, b. nr Unison, unm, sc: John T. Morris, father, 1st Dist., BVS:1886:2

MORRIS, Lillie B., B, F, d. 15 Feb 1885, nr Mountville, whooping cough, 0-9-0, p. Robert & Sarah Morris, b. nr Mountville, sc: Robt Morris, father, 1st Dist., BVS:1885:4

MORRIS, Mahlon, W, M, d. 26 Aug 1859/60, his res, old age, 81-8-0, p. John & Sarah Morris, b. nr Hillsboro, farmer, c/o: Ann Roberts, sc: Leven Ogden, uncle, BVS:1859:4, 1860:2, LC:35

MORRIS, no name, B, M, d. 1 Jan 1896, nr Mountville, unk, 0-0-1, p. Robt. & Sarah Morris, b. nr Mountville, none, unm, sc: Robt Morris, father, MC Dist., BVS:1896:1

MORRIS, Robert M., W, M, d. 15 Oct 1866, nr Taylor's Mill, unk, 0-0-6, p. Robt. & Edith A. Morris, sc: father, BVS:1866:2

MORRISON, Edward, W, M, d. 13 Apr 1858, LC, abscess of stomach, 72-10-16, p. Archibald & Jane Morrison, b. LC, farmer, c/o: Frances E. Morrison, sc: Frances E. Morrison, wife, BVS:1858:2, LC:30

MORRISON, Geo. H. C., W, M, d. 16 Sep 1854, LC, dysentery, 1-3-0, p. Arch. & Mary M. Morrison, b. LC, sc: Archd. Morrison, father, BVS:1854:9, LC:9

MORRISON, Sophia E., W, F, d. 14 Sep 1854, LC, dysentery, 11-5-0, p. Archd. & Rachel Morrison, b. LC, sc: Archd. Morrison, father, BVS:1854:9, LC:9

MORRMAN, no name, W, F, d. 16 Jun 1881, LC, unk, 0-5-8, p. A. J. & M. A. Morrman, b. LC, laborer, unm, sc: A.J. Morrman, father, 2nd Dist., BVS:1881:7

MORRMAN, Sarah, W, F, d. 1 Aug 1881, LC, cancer, 52-5-16, p. Jno. & Susan McOldrick, b. Pennsylvania, laborer, c/o: Frank Morrman, sc: Mary Morrman, daughter, 2nd Dist., BVS:1881:7

MORTON, Robert, B, M, d. 25 May 1892, Hillsboro, whooping cough, 5-0-0, p. Philip & Ann Lucilia Morton, b. Hillsboro, blacksmith, sc: Philip Morton, father, JF Dist., BVS:1892:7

MOSES, John, W, M, d. Apr 1854, res of father, 0-10-0, p. unk, sc: father, BVS:1854:11, LC:11

MOSS, Annabell, W, F, d. 6 Sep 1864, Mountain Gap, dysentery, 7-0-0, p. Wm. & Mary J. Moss, b. LC, sc: Wm. Moss, father, BVS:1864:2, LC:39

MOSS, Catharine E., W, F, d. 9 Apr 1894, nr Upperville, unk, 72-0-0, p. unk, b. unk, c/o: Wm. Moss, sc: Wm. Moss, husband, 1st Dist., BVS:1894:1

MOSS, Effa, W, F, d. 19 Apr 1855, nr Ball's Mill, dysentery, 60-0-0, p. Paterson & Nancy Wright, b. nr Waterford, c/o: John Moss, decd, sc: William Moss, son, BVS:1855:5, LC:17

MOSS, Frances J., W, F, d. 6 Feb 1884, Mountain Gap, pneumonia, 57-0-0, p. Wm. & Elizabeth Wildman, b. Virginia, c/o: John C. Moss, sc: Jno C. Moss, husband, 3rd Dist., BVS:1884:6

MOSS, John, W, M, d. 7 Apr 1855, nr Ball's Mill, dropsy, 60-0-0, p. Thos. & ___ Moss, b. nr Balls Mill, farmer, c/o: Effa Moss, sc: Wm. Moss, son, BVS:1855:5, LC:17

MOSS, John W., W, M, d. 18 Jul 1853, on Goose Creek, consumption, 0-3-0, p. Wm. & Mary Moss, b. nr Goose Creek, sc: grandfather, BVS:1854:5, LC:5

MOSS, Nancy, W, F, d. 23 Jul 1871, nr Upperville, cancer, 88-0-0, b. Fauquier Co., VA, c/o: Vincine Moss decd, MC Dist., BVS:1871:2

MOSS, Nancy, W, F, d. 3 Apr 1855, nr Ball's Mill, dysentery, 39-0-0, p. John & Effa Moss, b. nr Balls Mill, sc: William Moss, brother, BVS:1855:5, LC:17

MOSS, Susan Cathn, W, F, d. 25 Aug 1864, Mountain Gap, dysentery, 3-0-0, p. Wm. & Mary J. Moss, b. LC, sc: Wm. Moss, father, BVS:1864:2, LC:39

MOTEN, Matilda, B, F, d. 22 Jan 1896, LC, unk, 54-0-0, p. S. H. Hogans, b.

LC, seamstress, wife, sc: Jesse Moten, husband, LE Dist., BVS:1896:5

MOTT, A. R., W, M, d. 19 Jan 1894, Leesburg, old age, 72-0-0, p. unk, b. unk, physician, consort, sc: Virginia Mott, LE Dist., BVS:1894:3

MOUNT, Fitzhugh, W, M, d. Sep 1857, Mountville, putrid sore throat, 8-0-0, p. John E. & Mary J. Mount, b. Middleburg, sc: Mrs. Mount, grandmother, BVS:1857:3, LC:25

MOUNT, Hannah, W, F, d. 4 Mar 1871, Mountville, 76-0-0, MC Dist., BVS:1871:2

MOUNT, Mary Jackson, W, F, d. 28 Sep 1854, Middleburg, consumption, 26-0-0, p. Wm. & Matilda Fitzhugh, b. Grove res., c/o: Dr. John E. Mount, sc: husband, BVS:1854:12, LC:12

[MOUNT], Mary Jane, W, F, d. 21 Sep 1854, Middleburg, cholera infantum, 0-8-18, p. John E. & Mary Jane Mount, b. Middleburg, sc: father, BVS:1854:12, LC:12

MOZEL, Phillip, B, M, d. 12 Mar 1884, LC, pneumonia, 2-0-0, p. Richard & Kate Mozel, b. LC, sc: Richard Mozel, father, 1st Dist., BVS:1884:2

MULBERRY, Thomas, B, M, d. 1 May 1879, LC, diphtheria, 1-0-0, p. Edward & Lucy Mulberry, b. LC, sc: Edward Mulberry, father, 3rd Dist., BVS:1879:3

MULHOLLAND, Mary J., W, F, d. 13 Jan 1856, Leesburg, consumption, 42-0-0, p. Nicholas & Catharine Martin, b. Ireland, c/o: Thomas Mulholland, sc: James Martin, brother, BVS:1856:1, LC:19

MULLEN, Annie B., W, F, d. 28 Apr 1888, LC, whooping cough, 3-0-0, p. Chas. F. & Mary Mullen, b. LC, none, unm, sc: C.F. Mullen, father, 2nd Dist., BVS:1888:6

MULLEN, Barbary, W, F, d. 1 May 1854, LC, old age, 95-0-0, p. unk, b. LC, c/o: Samuel Mullen, sc: Elizabeth Stoneburner, dau-in-law, BVS:1854:9, LC:8

MULLEN, Charles, W, M, d. 27 Mar 1887, LC, paralysis, 30-0-0, p. Samuel & Lydia Mullen, b. LC, laborer, unm, sc: Samuel Mullen, father, 2nd Dist., BVS:1887:4

MULLEN, Charles, W, M, d. 9 Apr 1881, LC, pneumonia, 0-0-21, p. Chas. F. & M. A. Mullen, b. LC, sc: C.F. Mullen, father, 2nd Dist., BVS:1881:7

MULLEN, Elizabeth, W, F, d. 25 Jul 1853, LC, unk, 0-0-24, p. Saml. & Mary A. Mullen, b. LC, sc: Saml. Mullen, father, BVS:1854:2, LC:1

MULLEN, Jas. H., W, M, d. 7 Nov 1853, LC, water on brain, 0-9-5, p. Saml. & Lydia A. Mullen, b. LC, sc: Saml Mullen, father, BVS:1854:3, LC:1

MULLEN, Lillie, B, F, d. 10 Mar 1880, LC, old age, 90-0-0, p. unk, b. LC, unm, sc: Benj. F. Hibbs, friend, 1st Dist., BVS:1880:2

MULLEN, Mary F., W, F, d. 31 Aug 1855, Leesburg, diarrhea, 1-1-0, p. Saml. & Mary A. Mullen, b. LC, sc: Samuel Mullen Jr., father, BVS:1855:3, LC:15

MULLEN, Mary J., W, F, d. 9 Apr 1881, LC, pneumonia, 2-0-0, p. Chas. F. & M. A. Mullen, b. LC, sc: C.F. Mullen, father, 2nd Dist., BVS:1881:7

MULLEN, Norman L., W, M, d. 3 Aug 1896, LC, unk, 1-1-4, p. R. L. & O. Mullen, b. LC, sc: father, LE Dist., BVS:1896:5

MULLEN, Roger, W, M, d. 26 Feb 1876, LC, congestion of the brain, 4-7-0, p. Samuel H. & Lydia Mullen, b. LC, sc: Samuel H. Mullen, father, LE Dist., BVS:1876:6

MULLEN, Samuel H., W, M, d. 7 Aug 1889, LC, unk, 62-0-0, p. unk, b. LC, none, widower, sc: Arthur Mullen, son, 2nd Dist., BVS:1889:3

MULLEN, Samuel P., W, M, d. 25 Mar 1886, erysipelas, 0-1-11, p. Samuel P. & Mary F., sc: Samuel P. Mullen, father, 2nd Dist., BVS:1886:5

MULLEN, Samuel, W, M, d. 29 Jan 1880, nr Leesburg, consumption, 61-3-0, p. Samuel & Sarah Mullen, b. LC, mechanic, c/o: Mary L. Mullen, sc: Mary L. Mullen, wife, 2nd Dist., BVS:1880:7

MUNDAY, Charles W., W, M, d. 17 May 1876, LC, typhoid fever, 28-0-0, p. unk, b. unk, laborer, sc: W.H.H. Harper, friend, LE Dist., BVS:1876:6

MUNEMAKER, E. L., W, F, d. 13 Nov 1888, LC, tumor, 38-0-0, p. unk, b.

Loudoun County, Virginia, Death Register, 1853-1896   189

LC, none, unm, sc: William Butts, friend, 2nd Dist., BVS:1888:6

MURPHEY, James, W, M, d. 28 Nov 1856, Snickersville, dropsy, 59-0-0, p Eli & Susanna Murphey, b. Frederick or Clarke, shoemaker, c/o: Mary H. Murphey, sc: James F. Murphey, son, BVS:1856:5, LC:22

MURPHY, James W., W, M, d. 21 Nov 1878, Unison, structure of bowels, 21-4-0, p. Hiram & Juddah Murphy, b. Prince William Co., unm, sc: Hiram Murphy, father, MC Dist., BVS:1878:6

MURRAY, Alfred, B, M, d. 15 Nov 1883, nr Aldie, indigestion, 0-7-0, p. Chas. & Fannie Murray, b. nr Aldie, sc: Chas Murray, father, 1st Dist., BVS:1883:1

MURRAY, James F., (f), M, d. 29 Jul 1857, nr Snickersville, inflammatory rheum, 11-9-0, p. Samuel & Elizth Murray, b. Jos Lodge's Farm, sc: E. Murray, mother, BVS:1857:6, LC:28

MURREY, Alfred, B, M, d. 15 Sep 1884, LC, dysentery, 0-7-0, p. Chas. & Fannie Murrey, b. LC, unm, sc: Chas Murrey, father, 1st Dist., BVS:1884:2

MURRY, Lewis, B, M, d. 6 Nov 1873, nr Farmwell Station, unk, 2-0-5, p. James & Adaline Murry, b. nr Farmwell Station, sc: Jas. Murry, head of family, BR Dist., BVS:1873:1

MURRY, Lizzie, B, F, d. 15 Apr 1881, LC, hemorrhage, 1-10-0, p. Jas & Martha Murry, b. LC, sc: Jas Murry, father, 1st Dist., BVS:1881:2

MURRY, Mary, B, F, d. 25 Apr 1892, Lincoln, paralysis, unk, p. Ruben Murry, b. LC, sc: Ruben Murry, father, MT Dist., BVS:1892:8

MURRY, Mary, B, F, d. 17 May 1888, Poor House, consumption, 30-0-0, p. unk, b. unk, sc: F.E. Robey, superintendent of poor, 1st Dist., BVS:1888:4

MURRY, Parker, B, M, d. 15 Sep 1873, nr Hamilton, typhoid fever, 35-0-0, p. Edward & Bettie Murry, b. nr Hamilton, laborer, c/o: Nancy Murry, sc: wife, MT Dist., BVS:1873:3

MURRY, Susie, B, F, d. 15 Jun 1877, nr Pleasant Valley, deformity, 4-0-0, p. James Murry & wife, b. Pleasant Valley, unm, sc: James Murry, father, BR Dist., BVS:1877:1

MUSE, Ann E., W, F, d. 11 Jul 1858, Leesburg, convulsion, 37-3-1, p. Wm. & Sarah Seeders, b. Leesburg, c/o: James H. Muse, sc: James H. Muse, husband, BVS:1858:1, LC:29

MUSE, Blanche E., W, F, d. 15 Sep 1884, LC, burned to death, 0-6-0, p. Thomas S. & Mary F. Muse, b. LC, sc: Thos S. Muse, father, 1st Dist., BVS:1884:2

MUSE, James H., W, M, d. 20 Jul 1882, LC, brain fever, 3-0-0, p. Thomas S. & Mary Muse, sc: Thomas S. Muse, father, 1st Dist., BVS:1882:1

MUSE, Mary, W, F, d. 28 Nov 1857, pneumonia, 64-0-0, p. unk, b. LC, c/o: Thomas H. Muse, sc: John W. Muse, son, BVS:1857:7, LC:28

MUSE, Mary E., W, F, d. 26 Nov 1880, Hamilton, dropsy, 58-0-0, p. unk, b. LC, c/o: James Muse, sc: James Muse, husband, 3rd Dist., BVS:1880:4

MUSE, Owen C., W, M, d. 30 Jul 1858, Leesburg, unk, 0-1-1, p. James H. & Ann E. Muse, b. Leesburg, sc: James H. Muse, father, BVS:1858:1, LC:29

MUSE, Rebecca, W, F, d. 28 May 1853, LC, unk, 63-5-6, p. unk, b. unk, c/o: Jesse Muse, sc: John O. Muse, son, BVS:1854:4, LC:2

MUSE, Thomas W., W, M, d. 14 Apr 1885, Farmwell, consumption, 63-0-0, p. Thomas & Polly Muse, b. Farmwell, farmer, c/o: Nancy Muse, sc: Nancy Muse, wife, 1st Dist., BVS:1885:4

MUSE, Walker J., W, M, d. Dec 1854, LC, unk, 35-0-0, p. Jesse & Rebecca Muse, b. LC, farmer, sc: G. W. Dorrell, friend, BVS:1854:14, LC:13

MUSE, Willie D., W, M, d. 25 Jun 1884, LC, premature, 0-0-5, p. Chas. & Ida J. Muse, b. LC, sc: Chas F. Muse, father, 1st Dist., BVS:1884:2

MYERS, Arthur C., W, M, d. 23 Oct 1891, Leesburg, dropsy, 12-0-0, p. M. H. & Sallie Myers, b. Leesburg, farmer, unm, sc: father, LE Dist., BVS:1891:4

MYERS, Edward T., W, M, d. 2 Feb 1865, Diggs Vally, diphtheria, 4-10-0, p. Wm. & Susan Myers, b. nr Waterford, wheelwright, married, sc: Wm. Myers, father, 1st Dist., BVS:1865:3/4

MYERS, Florence, W, F, d. 22 Oct 1889, LC, child birth, 24-0-0, p. John & Ann Curry, b. LC, none, c/o: E. H. Myers, sc: E.H. Myers, husband, 2nd Dist., BVS:1889:3

MYERS, Henry, W, M, d. 6 Feb 1896, LC, unk, 0-0-3, p. Ish & Annie Myers, b. LC, unm, sc: father, LE Dist., BVS:1896:5

MYERS, Israel, W, M, d. 10 Oct 1874, nr Hamilton, heart disease, 60-0-0, p. Mahala & Mahlon Myers, b. LC, farmer, c/o: Mary Myers, sc: Jonathan Myers, son, JF Dist., BVS:1874:2

MYERS, John C., W, M, d. 24 Aug 1872, LC, dysentery, 77-0-0, p. unk, b. Pennsylvania, farmer, c/o: Mary A. Myers, sc: Mary A. Myers, consort, LE Dist., BVS:1872:4

MYERS, Lester S., W, M, d. 15 Sep 1893, Leesburg, bright's disease, 4-0-0, p. unk, b. Leesburg, unm, sc: Jonathan Myers, LE Dist., BVS:1893:6

MYERS, Margaret, W, F, d. 18 Apr 1896, Ryan, inflammation bowels, 23-0-0, b. LC, c/o: E.P. Myers, sc: E.P. Myers, husband, BR Dist., BVS:1896:3

MYERS, Mary, W, F, d. 8 Jan 1881, LC, asthma, 59-0-0, b. LC, c/o: Mahlon Myers, sc: M.H. Myers, son, 3rd Dist., BVS:1881:4

MYERS, Mary H., W, F, d. 18 May 1890, Hughesville, old age, 70-0-0, p. Thomas & Elizabeth Donaldson, b. LC, none, c/o: W.W. Myers, sc: W.W. Myers, husband, 3rd Dist., BVS:1890:7

MYERS, Mary J., W, F, d. 8 Jan 1885, Clarkes Gap, consumption, 26-0-0, p. Calvin & Jane Coats, b. LC, c/o: Mahlon H. Myers, sc: M.H. Myers, husband, 3rd Dist., BVS:1885:6

MYERS, no name, W, M, d. 6 Jul 1880, nr Leesburg, premature birth, 0-0-3, p. Jas. & Mary M. Myers, b. LC, unm, sc: Jas. W. Myers, father, 2nd Dist., BVS:1880:7

MYERS, Olivia, W, F, d. 1 Apr 1889, LC, consumption, 47-0-0, p. David & Elizabeth Steadman, b. LC, none, c/o: T.J. Myers, sc: F.J. Myers,, 2nd Dist., BVS:1889:4

MYERS, Pearl A., W, F, d. 10 Jun 1890, LC, cholera infantum, 0-2-15, p. Geo. W. & Mary V. Myers, b. LC, none, unm, sc: S.W. Myers, father, 2nd Dist., BVS:1890:4

MYERS, Sarah E., W, F, d. 12 Dec 1865, Frankville, consumption, 25-0-0, p. Ed & Sarah Haines, b. Frankville, housekeeper, consort, sc: Edwd Haines, father, BVS:1865:2

MYERS, Sarah J., W, F, d. 30 Sep 1854, LC, water on the brain, 3-1-2, p. Peter & Catherine Myers, b. LC, sc: Peter Myers, father, BVS:1854:10, LC:9

MYERS, Virginia, W, F, d. 3 Sep 1886, LC, bright's disease, 31-5-1, p. Mary Hawkins, b. LC, c/o: Israel Myers, sc: Israel Myers, husband, 3rd Dist., BVS:1886:4

MYERS, Virginia C., W, F, d. 25 Jul 1854, LC, water on brain, 4-1-2, p. Elijah P. & Margaret C. Myers, b. LC, sc: Elijah P. Myers, father, BVS:1854:10, LC:9

MYERS, William R., W, M, d. 25 Jul 1890, LC, diphtheria, 0-9-0, p. Elijah & Florence Myers, b. LC, none, unm, sc: E.F. Myers, father, 2nd Dist., BVS:1890:4

MYERS, Wm., W, M, d. 5 Dec 1891, Waterford, la grippe, 84-0-0, p. Lambert & Mary Myers, b. Waterford, husband, sc: J. Myers, JF Dist., BVS:1891:7

NALLS, Carr B., W, M, d. 17 Feb 1890, nr Trappe, old age, 84-0-0, p. unk, b. LC, c/o: Eliza Nalls, sc: John T. Nalls, son, 1st Dist., BVS:1890:2

NALLS, Eugene, W, M, d. 20 Dec 1891, nr Paris, abscess of brain, 9-9-0, p. Jno. T. & Adelaide Nalls, b. LC, laborer, sc: Jno T. Nalls, father, 1st Dist., BVS:1891:2

NALLS, Eugene, W, M, d. 8 Mar 1892, nr Paris, Fauq. Co., abscess on brain, 0-3-0, p. Jno T. & Mary Nalls, b. nr Paris, Va., sc: Mary Nalls, mother, 1st Dist., BVS:1892:2

NALLS, Sarah A., W, F, d. 12 Apr 1877, on Blue Ridge, old age, 74-0-0, b. LC, c/o: Carr B. Nalls, sc: C.B. Nalls, husband, MC Dist., BVS:1877:5

NEAL, Caroline, B, F, d. 12 Aug 1882, LC, consumption, 36-11-0, sc: Lewis Neal, parent, 3rd Dist., BVS:1882:3

NEAL, Charlotte, B, F, d. 10 Nov 1872, Leesburg, dropsy of chest, 85-0-0, p. unk, unm, sc: R.H. Edwards, doctor, LE Dist., BVS:1872:4

NEAL, Lucinda, B, F, d. 23 Dec 1885, Aldie, heart disease, 55-0-0, p. James & Lucy Williams, b. Clarke Co., c/o: John Neal, sc: John Neal, husband, 1st Dist., BVS:1885:4

NEAL, Mary, B, F, d. 25 Aug 1875, LC, teething, 1-2-10, p. Elizabeth Neal, b. LC, sc: Elizabeth Neal, mother, LE Dist., BVS:1875:1

NEAL, Thomas, B, M, d. Jul 1871, 22-0-0, p. Lucinda & John Neal, MC Dist., BVS:1871:2

NEAL, W. H., B, M, d. 13 Aug 1896, nr Bloomfield, cholera infantum, 0-4-5, p. Louis & Mary Neal, b. nr Bloomfield, none, unm, sc: Mary Neal, mother, MC Dist., BVS:1896:2

NEER, Eliza, W, F, d. 26 Aug 1884, Hillsboro, pneumonia, 83-0-0, p. Jonas & Patsie Potts, b. Virginia, c/o: Nathan Neer, sc: David C. Neer, son, 3rd Dist., BVS:1884:6

NEILL, Fannie L., W, F, d. 18 Sep 1887, Mountville, dysentery, 0-4-7, p. Dangerfield F. & Mollie Neill, b. Mountville, sc: Dangerfield F. Neill, father, 1st Dist., BVS:1887:1

NELSON, Daniel, B, M, d. 31 Mar 1878, nr Bolington, old age, 80-0-0, laborer, married, sc: Margaret Nelson, daughter-in-law, LV Dist., BVS:1878:1/5

NELSON, Jennie, B, F, d. 10 Mar 1883, nr Leesburg, old age, 80-0-0, p. --- Buchanan, b. LC, c/o: Julius Day, sc: Jennie Day, daughter, 2nd Dist., BVS:1883:4

NELSON, Philip, B, M, d. 30 Apr 1878, nr Bolington, old age, 84-0-0, laborer, unm, sc: Margaret Nelson, niece, LV Dist., BVS:1878:1/5

NELSON, Wesley, W, M, d. 15 Aug 1876, LC, dropsy, 70-0-0, p. unk, b. LC, unk, c/o: Ginnie Nelson, sc: William Haines, friend, LE Dist., BVS:1876:7

NESMITH, Susan, W, F, d. 15 Sep 1865, Purcellville, heart disease, 29-0-0, married, sc: Oscar Nesmith, husband, BVS:1865:1

NETTLE, William, W, M, d. 6 Oct 1856, Waterford, typhoid fever, 77-6-5, b. Pennsylvania, c/o: Sally Nettle, sc: Sally Nettle, wife, BVS:1856:1, LC:19

NEUMAN, George, W, M, d. 4 Mar 1880, Lincoln, dysentery, 0-5-0, p. Caroline Neuman, b. LC, sc: Caroline Neuman, mother, 3rd Dist., BVS:1880:4

NEUMAN, Mary, B, F, d. 27 Apr 1879, LC, typhoid fever, 40-0-0, p. Wm. & Harriet Neuman, b. LC, unm, sc: Wm. Neuman, father, 3rd Dist., BVS:1879:3

NEWLON, Amery, W, F, d. 23 Feb 1894, Pleasant Grove, rheumatism, 78-0-0, p. Hesekiah & Edith Glascock, b. Pleasant Grove, wife, sc: Mason Newlon, husband, 3rd Dist., BVS:1894:5

NEWLON, Mary N., W, F, d. 19 May 1866, nr Unison, consumption, 20-0-0, p. John F. & Sarah A. Newlon, b. nr Unison, unm, sc: John F. Newlon, father, BVS:1866:2

NEWLON, Thomas H., W, M, d. Oct 1869, LC, 2-0-0, p. John F. & Sarah A. Newlon, b. LC, farmer, sc: John F. Newlon, father, BVS:1869:1

NEWMAN, E ?, B, M, d. Aug 1892, Silcott Springs, unk, 1-0-0, p. Isaac Newman, b. LC, sc: Isaac Newman, father, MT Dist., BVS:1892:8

NEWMAN, Elijah, B, M, d. Oct 1873, LC, 0-9-0, p. Elijah & Frances Newman, b. LC, unm, sc: Elijah Newman, friend, LE Dist., BVS:1873:2

NEWMAN, Hannah, (f), F, d. 15 Aug 1857, LC, unk, 10-6-7, p. Benjn & Eliza Newman, b. LC, sc: Eliza Newman, mother, BVS:1857:1, LC:25

NEWMAN, Harriet, B, F, d. 13 May 1866, Lincoln, paralyzed, 35-0-0, p. Wm. & Martha Nichols, b. Lincoln, wife, married, sc: Wm. Newman, husband, BVS:1866:2

NEWMAN, Harry, B, M, d. 5 Sep 1893, nr Willard, old age, 90-0-0, p. unk, b. unk, laborer, c/o: Mary Newman, sc: Mary Newman, wife, 1st Dist., BVS:1893:2

NEWMAN, Nancy, (f), F, d. 28 Aug 1859/60, LC, dropsy, 60-0-0, p. unk, b. LC, sc: Sarah Newman, daughter, BVS:1859:2, 1860:4, LC:37

NEWMAN, no name, B, M, d. 5 Aug 1883, Leesburg, unk, 1-5-0, p. Elijah & May Newman, b. LC, sc: Mary Newman, mother, 2nd Dist., BVS:1883:3

NEWMAN, Tho., (f), M, d. 17 Jul 1855, LC, drowned, 55-0-0, p. unk, b. LC, ferryman, sc: L. L. Beall, friend, BVS:1855:1, LC:14

NEWMAN, Virginia, W, F, d. 10 Jun 1882, LC, dropsy, 6-0-0, p. James F. & Mary Newman, sc: Jos F. Newman, father, 1st Dist., BVS:1882:2

NEWMAN, Wm., B, M, d. 15 Oct 1896, Guinea Mills, internal injuries, 67-0-0, p. Harry & Amy Newman, b. LC, tanner, sc: Lucy N. Newman, wife, MT Dist., BVS:1896:9

NEWTON, Charles, W, M, d. 2 Mar 1872, Leesburg, pneumonia, 64-0-0, p. Robt. & Nancy Newton, b. LC, shoemaker, c/o: Magdelin Newton, sc: Magdelin Newton, consort, LE Dist., BVS:1872:4

NEWTON, Chas. H., W, M, d. 10 Mar 1892, Arcola, paralysis, 51-0-0, p. C. H. & Ann Newton, b. LC, shoemaker, c/o: Mary C. Newton, sc: Mary C. Newton, wife, 1st Dist., BVS:1892:2

NEWTON, Elizabeth, W, F, d. 22 Sep 1875, LC, heart disease, 70-0-0, b. LC, c/o: Alexander Newton, sc: Alexander Newton, husband, LE Dist., BVS:1875:1

NEWTON, Fanny H., W, F, d. 21 Aug 1890, LC, diabetes, 16-0-0, p. C. A. & S. W. Newton, b. LC, unm, sc: C.A. Newton, father, 2nd Dist., BVS:1890:4

NEWTON, Frances, W, F, d. 28 Feb 1853, Leesburg, disease of the heart, 0-0-14, p. Chas. C. & Magdeline Newton, b. Leesburg, sc: Chas. W. Newton, father, BVS:1854:2, LC:1

NEWTON, Sarah, W, F, d. 25 Jul 1854, LC, dysentery, 57-0-0, p. Samuel & Mary Dorsett, b. LC, sc: Sarah Offutt, sister, BVS:1854:14, LC:13

NICHOLS, Annie J., W, F, d. 26 Nov 1882, LC, unk, 0-1-10, p. Saml. & Mollie Nichols, b. LC, sc: Saml E. Nichols, parent, 3rd Dist., BVS:1882:3

NICHOLS, Annie V., W, F, d. 16 May 1888, nr Middleburg, consumption, 29-1-0, p. Levi & Harriet Nichols, b. Middleburg, sc: Levi Nichols, father, 1st Dist., BVS:1888:4

NICHOLS, Chas. H., W, M, d. 14 Mar 1878, LC, pneumonia, 34-4-8, p. Isaac J. & Louisa Nichols, b. LC, unm, sc: L.T. Nichols, brother, LE Dist., BVS:1878:8

NICHOLS, Eli, W, M, d. 26 Jun 1859/60, res, suicide, 48-0-29, p. Samuel & Mary Nichols, b. nr Philomont, farmer, sc: Saml Nichols, brother, BVS:1859:3, 1860:1, LC:34

NICHOLS, Eli, W, M, d. 25 Dec 1881, LC, diphtheria, 7-0-0, p. Eli J. & Lydia Nichols, b. LC, sc: Eli J. Nichols, father, 3rd Dist., BVS:1881:4

NICHOLS, Eli H., W, M, d. 28 Mar 1885, nr Mountville, paralysis, 62-7-0, p. Thos. & Letitia Nichols, b. LC, farmer, c/o: Elizabeth Nichols, sc: Elizabeth Nichols, wife, 1st Dist., BVS:1885:4

NICHOLS, Elizabeth, W, F, d. 15 May 1875, nr L.B.T. Pike, unk, 80-0-14, p. Thos. & Anna Nichols, b. LC, unm, sc: Jas. W. Darne. nephew, BR Dist., BVS:1875:5

NICHOLS, Fanny W, F, d. 23 Jan 1885, Hamilton, paralyzed, 88-0-0, p. Edwd. & Ann McDaniel, b. LC, c/o: Thos Nichols, sc: Lydia Nichols, daughter, 3rd Dist., BVS:1885:6

NICHOLS, Jno. B., W, M, d. 9 Aug 1894, Purcellville, killed in cyclone, 26-0-0, p. Phineas Nichols & wife, b. Philomont, farmer, unm, sc: Phineas Nichols, father, 3rd Dist., BVS:1894:5

NICHOLS, Joshua, W, M, d. 17 Aug 1854, res, nr Goose Creek Meeting House, cholera, 50-0-0, p. Isaac & Mary Nichols, b. nr Bacon Fort, farmer, c/o: Neomi Nichols, sc: widow, BVS:1854:12, LC:12

NICHOLS, Letitia, W, F, d. 8 Mar 1857, her res, dropsy, 67-6-23, p. Stacy & Hannah Janney, c/o: Thomas Nichols, sc: Thomas Nichols, widower, BVS:1857:3, LC:26

NICHOLS, Louisa, W, F, d. 26 Feb 1864, nr Mount Gilead, typhoid fever, 44-7-5, p. Levi & Mary White, b. LC, sc: Thos D. Nichols, son, BVS:1864:2, LC:39

NICHOLS, Lydia Jane, W, F, d. 26 Apr 1856, res of parents, consumption, 18-0-0, p. Thomas J. & Nancy Nichols, b. nr Purcellville, sc: Thomas J. Nichols, father, BVS:1856:6, LC:23

[NICHOLS], Maria Jane, W, F, d. 13 Jul 1854, res of parents, suddenly & unk, 0-8-0, p. Isaac G. & Louisa Nichols, b. res of parents, sc: father, BVS:1854:11, LC:11

NICHOLS, Mariah I., W, F, d. 15 Jul 1853, nr Gilead, convulsions, 0-8-0, p. Isaac & Louisa Nichols, b. LC, sc: father, BVS:1854:6, LC:5

NICHOLS, Martha J., W, F, d. 29 May 1890, nr Unison, consumption, 54-0-0, p. Thomas & Delilah Beavers, b. LC, c/o: Eli Nichols, sc: Charles Nichols, son, 1st Dist., BVS:1890:2

NICHOLS, Mary, W, F, d. 7 Mar 1856, Thomas Brown's, old age, 79-0-0, p. Blexton & Mary Janney, b. Goose Creek Meeting House, c/o: Samuel Nichols, decd, sc: Thomas Brown, son-in-law, BVS:1856:4, LC:22

NICHOLS, Mary Ann, W, F, d. 15 Jul 1892, Lincoln, cong, 82-0-0, p. Daniel & Susan McPherson, b. Lincoln, married, sc: Joseph Nichols, husband, MT Dist., BVS:1892:8

NICHOLS, Mary E., W, F, d. 8 Feb 1885, Purcellville, pneumonia, 37-0-0, b. LC, c/o: Saml E. Nichols, sc: Saml E. Nichols, husband, 3rd Dist., BVS:1885:6

NICHOLS, Sarah, W, F, d. 4 Apr 1879, LC, general debility, 60-0-0, b. LC, c/o: John Nichols, sc: Jno. Nichols, husband, 3rd Dist., BVS:1879:3

NICHOLS, Thomas P., W, M, d. 11 Aug 1869, LC, dysentery, 1-0-24, p. James W. & Hanna E. Nichols, b. LC, sc: James Nichols, father, BVS:1869:1

NICHOLS, Virginia T., W, F, d. 19 May 1866, nr Unison, dysentery, 1-6-0, b. nr Unison, sc: Wm. Nichols, father, BVS:1866:2

NICHOLS, Wilmer, W, M, d. 22 Jul 1894, Philomont, typhoid fever, 21-0-0, p. Eli & Lydia E. Nichols, b. Philomont, farmer, unm, sc: Eli Nichols, father, 3rd Dist., BVS:1894:5

NICHOLSON, A. Jessup, W, M, d. 22 May 1893, Hamilton, bright's disease, 46-0-0, p. A.S. & J.J. Nicholson, b. Hamilton, U.S. officer, sc: father, JF Dist., BVS:1893:3

NICKENS, Amanda, B, F, d. 25 Nov 1874, nr Unison, consumption, 24-0-0, p. Marcus & Carolina Hampton, b. LC, c/o: Clayton Nickens, sc: Caroline Hampton, mother, MC Dist., BVS:1874:4

NICKENS, Eliza, B, F, d. 20 Jan 1880, LC, tumor, 65-0-0, p. unk, b. LC, c/o: Lewis Nickens, sc: Lewis Nickens, husband, 1st Dist., BVS:1880:2

NICKENS, Hampton, B, M, d. 24 May 1874, nr Unison, scrofula on lungs, 0-10-0, p. Clayton & Amanda Nickins, b. LC, sc: Caroline Hampton, grandmother, MC Dist., BVS:1874:4

NICKENS, J. C., B, M, d. Oct 1873, Leesburg, 0-0-6, p. J. C. & Fanny Nickens, b. Leesburg, unm, sc: J.C. Nickens, father, LE Dist., BVS:1873:2

NICKENS, Judy, B, F, d. 1869, LC, 0-6-0, b. LC, sc: father, BVS:1869:1

NICKENS, Lydia, B, F, d. 10 Jun 1888, nr Bloomfield, consumption, 70-0-0, p. Mark & Violet Nickens, b. Bloomfield, sc: Thomas Nickens, son-in-law, 1st Dist., BVS:1888:4

NICKENS, Mary, B, F, d. 22 Jul 1885, nr Mountville, croup, 0-5-0, p. Henry & Martha Nickens, b. nr Mountville, sc: Henry Nickens, father, 1st Dist., BVS:1885:4

NICKENS, Mary, (f), F, d. 14 Nov 1856, his res, 47-0-0, p. Charlotte Lucas, b. Fauquier Co., c/o: Barney Nickens, sc: B. Nickens, widower, BVS:1856:5, LC:23

NICKENS, no name, B, F, d. 14 Nov 1877, Mount Defiance, unk, 0-3-0, p. Samuel & Fannie Nickens, b. LC, sc:

Saml Nickens, father, MC Dist., BVS:1877:5

[NICKENS], no name, B, M, d. 6 May 1883, Middleburg, pneumonia, 1-15-0, p. Levenia Nickens, b. Middleburg, sc: Levinia Nickens, mother, 1st Dist., BVS:1883:1

NICKENS, Willie, B, M, d. 2 Jun 1888, nr Bloomfield, tumor, 9-0-0, p. Clayton & Ellen Nickens, b. Bloomfield, sc: Clayton Nickens, father, 1st Dist., BVS:1888:4

NICKINS, Elizabeth, B, F, d. 10 Jul 1881, LC, consumption, 14-0-0, b. LC, sc: Henly Kid, friend, 1st Dist., BVS:1881:2

NICKINS, Elizabeth, B, F, d. 4 Jul 1881, LC, unk, 16-0-0, b. LC, sc: Saml Nickins, brother, 1st Dist., BVS:1881:2

NISEWARNER, Wilmer, W, M, d. 2 Oct 1891, nr Lovettsville, spasms, 0-0-9, p. Henry & Rosa Nisewarner, b. nr Lovettsville, farmer, unm, sc: father, LV Dist., BVS:1891:5

NIXON, Asbury, W, M, d. 25 Sep 1872, Mount Gilead Twp., apoplexy, 65-0-0, p. Joel & Hannah Nixon, b. LC, farmer, c/o: Hannah Nixon, sc: J.B. Nixon, son, MT Dist., BVS:1872:2

NIXON, Blanch, W, F, d. 1 Oct 1883, nr Leesburg, sore throat, 0-1-0, p. Saml. J. & Blanch Nixon, b. LC, sc: Saml J. Nixon, father, 2nd Dist., BVS:1883:7

NIXON, Geo. L., W, M, d. 30 Jun 1893, Leesburg, membranous croup, 8-0-0, p. Geo. H. & Hattie, b. Leesburg, unm, sc: Geo H. Nixon, LE Dist., BVS:1893:6

NIXON, Hannah, W, F, d. 22 Sep 1891, Clarkes Gap, cancer, 80-0-0, p. Benjamin & Sarah Brown, b. Clark's Gap, wife, unm, sc: J.B. Nixon, MT Dist., BVS:1891:6

NIXON, J. Lewis, W, M, d. 6 Feb 1896, LC, erysipelas, 78-0-0, p. J. & H. Nixon, b. LC, retired, husband, sc: daughter, LE Dist., BVS:1896:5

NIXON, Jessie, W, F, d. 13 Apr 1884, Leesburg, pneumonia, 1-0-4, p. Geo. H.& Hattie Nixon, b. LC, sc: Geo H. Nixon, father, 2nd Dist., BVS:1884:5

NIXON, Jno. E., W, M, d. 25 Mar 1853, LC, pneumonia, 32-2-20, p. Joel &

Hannah Nixon, b. LC, c/o: Rebecca J. Nixon, sc: Rebecca J. Nixon, wife, BVS:1854:3, LC:1

NIXON, Joel W., W, M, d. 4 Jan 1853, LC, croup, 2-1-2, p. Levi W. & Margaret Nixon, b. LC, sc: Levi W. Nixon, father, BVS:1854:4, LC:3

NIXON, John W., W, M, d. 12 Dec 1853, LC, croup, 3-4-23, p. Levi W. & Margaret Nixon, b. LC, sc: Levi W. Nixon, father, BVS:1854:4, LC:3

NIXON, Jonathan W., W, M, d. 3 Nov 1874, Broad Run Dist., paralysis, 66-10-14, p. Joel & Hannah Nixon, b. LC, farmer, married, sc: Mary F. Nixon, wife, BR Dist., BVS:1874:3

NIXON, Mary, W, F, d. 10 Jul 1890, LC, unk, 74-0-0, p. unk, b. LC, none, unm, sc: E. Hawley, nephew, 2nd Dist., BVS:1890:3

NIXON, Walter J., W, M, d. Oct 1865, nr Nixon's Mill, inflammation throat, 0-7-0, p. Jonah & Mary Nixon, b. nr Nixon's Mill, sc: Jonah Nixon, father, BVS:1865:1

NIXON, Westwood B., W, M, d. 28 May 1853, LC, disease of brain, 7-1-15, p. Asbury M. & Hannah Nixon, b. LC, sc: Asbury M. Nixon, father, BVS:1854:4, LC:2

NOGGLE, Sarah C., W, F, d. 30 Sep 1857, LC, convulsions, 0-0-14, p. Ellen Noggle, b. LC, unm, sc: Ellen Noggle, mother, BVS:1857:1, LC:24

NOLAND, Brook P., W, M, d. 1857, Middleburg, suicide, 22-0-0, p. Thomas J. & Sarah C. Noland, b. Middleburg, sc: Wm. B. Noland, brother, BVS:1857:6, LC:28

NOLAND, Burr P., W, M, d. 22 Oct 1889, Middleburg, heart disease, 71-0-0, p. unk, b. LC, lawyer, c/o: Alice Noland, sc: Bolling Halley, son-in-law, 1st Dist., BVS:1889:1

NOLAND, Carrie, W, F, d. 6 Sep 1879, Round Hill, consumption, 18-0-0, p. George & Amanda Noland, b. LC, unm, sc: George W. Noland, father, 3rd Dist., BVS:1879:3

NOLAND, Carrie H., W, F, d. 13 Aug 1876, Middleburg, constipation of the bowels, 37-0-0, p. Burr W. & Sallie Harrison, b. LC, c/o: Burr P. Noland, sc: B.P. Noland, husband, MC Dist., BVS:1876:4

NOLAND, Fanny B., W, F, d. 18 Oct 1864, Middleburg, diphtheria, 2-8-0, p. Wm. B. & Lucy T. Noland, b. Middleburg, sc: Wm. B. Noland, father, BVS:1864:1, LC:38

NOLAND, Maud R., W, F, d. 8 Nov 1864, Middleburg, diphtheria, 5-11-0, p. Wm. B. & Lucy T. Noland, b. Middleburg, sc: Wm. B. Noland, father, BVS:1864:1, LC:38

NOLAND, Susannah C., W, F, d. 17 Mar 1872, Middleburg, unk, Lawyer, c/o: B. A. Noland, sc: B.A. Noland, husband, MC Dist., BVS:1872:7

NOLAND, Thos E., W, M, d. 22 Aug 1864, Locust Valley, dysentery, 3-3-2, p. Geo W. & R.H. Noland, b. LC, sc: Ruth H. Noland, mother, BVS:1864:1, LC:39

NOLAND, Virginia L., W, F, d. 8 Jul 1885, Farmwell, tubercular meningitis, 0-11-0, p. Benjamin F. & R. B. Noland, b. nr Farmwell, sc: Benja F. Noland, father, 1st Dist., BVS:1885:4

NORMAN, Eppa H., W, M, d. 16 Jun 1881, LC, unk, 0-1-2, p. Eppa & R.F. Norman, b. LC, sc: Eppa Norman, father, 1st Dist., BVS:1881:2

NORMAN, Jno F., W, M, d. 23 Jul 1883, nr Leesburg, unk, 0-9-0, p. Andrew & Ida Norman, b. LC, sc: Andrew Norman, father, 2nd Dist., BVS:1883:4

NORRIS, Frank, B, M, d. 18 Jan 1883, nr Leesburg, unk, 20-0-0, p. Amos & Sarah Norris, b. LC, laborer, unm, sc: Amos Norris, father, 2nd Dist., BVS:1883:4

NORRIS, Ida S., W, F, d. 30 Oct 1876, Leesburg, cholera infantum, 0-1-5, p. Thomas B. & Amanda V. Norris, b. Leesburg, sc: Thomas B. Norris, father, LE Dist., BVS:1876:7

NORRIS, John, B, M, d. 7 Feb 1883, nr Leesburg, unk, 12-0-0, p. Amos & Sarah Norris, b. LC, laborer, sc: Amos Norris, father, 2nd Dist., BVS:1883:4

NORRIS, Mary E., B, F, d. 15 Sep 1880, Washington, DC, malarial fever, 12-0-0, p. Amos & Sarah Norris, b. LC, sc: Sarah Norris, mother, 2nd Dist., BVS:1880:7

NOTT, Cecelia, B, F, d. 10 Dec 1880, LC, unk, 18-0-0, p. Samuel & Ann Nott, b. LC, unm, sc: Annie Nott, sister, 1st Dist., BVS:1880:2

NOTT, Samuel, B, M, d. 18 Oct 1880, LC, paralysis, 60-0-0, p. unk, b. LC, widower, sc: Annie Nott, daughter, 1st Dist., BVS:1880:2

NOURSE, Lucy H., W, F, d. 24 Apr 1857, LC, inflammation of brain, 2-6-0, p. Chas. H. & Elizth J. Nourse, b. Montgomery Co., MD, sc: Charles H. Nourse, father, BVS:1857:2, LC:25

NUGENT, Mary E., W, F, d. 20 Jun 1864, Castleman's Ferry, burned by accident, 4-5-0, p. Jas & Eliza Nugent, b. Jefferson Co., VA, sc: Eliza Nugent, mother, BVS:1864:1, LC:38

O'BANNON, L. B., W, M, d. 30 Aug 1896, Pleasant Valley, dysentery, 75-0-0, b. LC, wheelwright, unm, sc: H.J. O'Bannon, brother, BR Dist., BVS:1896:3

OBANNON, Saml., W, M, d. 2 Feb 1853, Poor House, found dead, 70-0-0, p. unk, b. Fauquier Co., carpenter, sc: Wm. Furr, keeperof poor house, BVS:1854:6, LC:6

OBANON, Charles B., W, M, d. 5 Mar 1854, cancer, 65-0-0, b. LC, sc: Henry J. Obanon, son, BVS:1854:13, LC:13

ODEN, Dr. J. Beverley, W, M, d. 2 Jul 1864, Wm. F. Adam's, consumption, 35-4-9, p. W.S. & Huldah Oden, b. LC, physician, c/o: J.C.H. Oden, sc: J.C.H. Oden, widower, BVS:1864:1, LC:38

ODEN, Jane, (f), F, d. 15 Sep 1853, Poor House, old age, 85-0-0, p. unk, b. LC, sc: Wm. Furr, keeper of the poor house, BVS:1854:7, LC:6

ODEN, Nathaniel S., W, M, d. 18 Jul 1854, LC, typhoid, 63-0-0, p. Richard & Mary Oden, b. LC, sc: John B. Oden, son, BVS:1854:13, LC:13

OFFUTT, Charles, W, M, d. 18 May 1854, consumption, 75-0-0, p. Wm. M. & Alice Offutt, b. Maryland, farmer, sc: Sarah Offutt, wife, BVS:1854:13, LC:13

OGDEN, Andrew, W, M, d. 15 Feb 1855, Mahlon Morris', 73-0-0, p. Robt. & Ann Ogden, b. Maryland, farmer & mill right, sc: Mahlon Morris, brother-in-law, BVS:1855:7, LC:18

OGDEN, Benjamin, W, M, d. 29 Nov 1853, Hillsboro, spinal affection, 62-0-0, p. unk, b. LC, farmer, c/o: Sarah Ogden, sc: Levin Ogden, son, BVS:1854:1, LC:3

OGDEN, Thomas, W, M, d. 28 Jun 1892, Daysville, consumption, 25-0-0, p. Jno & Mary Ogden, b. LC, laborer, c/o: Annie Ogden, sc: Annie Ogden, wife, 1st Dist., BVS:1892:2

OLDEN, Mary, B, F, d. 25 May 1876, nr Unison, unk, 0-0-18, p. Willis & Louisa Olden, b. LC, sc: Willis Olden, father, MC Dist., BVS:1876:4

OLDEN, Nancy, B, F, d. 28 Feb 1894, nr Unison, dropsy & heart failure, 44-0-0, p. unk, b. unk, c/o: Samuel Olden, sc: Saml Olden, husband, 1st Dist., BVS:1894:2

OMEARA, Thos. R., Sr., W, M, d. 25 Dec 1874, Broad Run Dist., consumption, 65-3-25, p. Michael & Nancy Omeara, b. Prince William Co., farmer, married, sc: Thos. B. O'Meara Jr., son, BR Dist., BVS:1874:3

OREM, Mary, W, F, d. 31 Nov 1883, nr Lovettsville, consumption, 32-0-0, p. Burr & Mary R. Tarleton, b. LC, c/o: Nathaniel Orem, sc: Nathaniel Orem, husband, 2nd Dist., BVS:1883:7

ORME, Martha, W, F, d. 17 Aug 1858, LC, unk, 4-0-0, p. Robt & Eliza Orme, b. LC, sc: Robert Orme, father, BVS:1858:1, LC:29

ORME, Robert S., W, M, d. 21 Jan 1884, nr Lovettsville, dropsy, 73-0-0, p. Archibald & Etta Orme, b. LC, mechanic, c/o: Ann E. Orme, sc: Jacob H. Stream, friend, 2nd Dist., BVS:1884:5

ORR, Preston, W, M, d. 15 Sep 1878, LC, cholera infantum, 0-3-14, p. Jno. M. & Orra V. Orr, b. LC, unm, sc: Jno. M. Orr, father, LE Dist., BVS:1878:8

ORR, Sally M., W, F, d. 15 Sep 1854, Leesburg, dysentery, 1-9-2, p. John M. & Orra L. Orr, b. Leesburg, sc: John M. Orr, father, BVS:1854:10, LC:9

ORR, Wm. G., W, M, d. 21 Nov 1853, Leesburg, scarlet fever, 3-2-17, p. Jno. M. & Orra M. Orr, b. Leesburg, sc: John M. Orr, father, BVS:1854:5, LC:3

ORRISON, Amelia, W, F, d. 24 Aug 1888, LC, dysentery, 3-4-0, p. Geo. W. & Sarah Orrison, b. LC, none, unm, sc: Geo W. Orrison, father, 2nd Dist., BVS:1888:6

ORRISON, America, W, F, d. 24 May 1854, LC, consumption, 28-2-17, p. Arthur & Elizth. Orrison, b. LC, unm, sc: Elizabeth Orrison, mother, BVS:1854:8, LC:8

ORRISON, Annanias, W, M, d. 1 Apr 1859/60, LC, pneumonia, 60-0-0, p. Andrew & Catharine Orrison, b. LC, farmer, c/o: Catharine Orrison, sc: Cath. Orrison, wife, BVS:1859:1, 1860:3, LC:36

ORRISON, Arthur, W, M, d. 7 Jun 1887, LC, consumption, 73-0-0, p. unk, b. LC, farmer, c/o: Elizabeth Orrison, sc: Stephen Orrison, father, 2nd Dist., BVS:1887:4

ORRISON, Bula A., W, F, d. 11 Sep 1888, LC, brain fever, 1-8-0, p. Isaac A. & Annie Orrison, b. LC, none, unm, sc: Isaac Orrison, father, 3rd Dist., BVS:1888:1

ORRISON, Catherine E., W, F, d. 14 Apr 1875, nr Waterford, consumption, 14-0-0, p. Annanias & Mary Orrison, b. LC, sc: James Orrison, brother, JF Dist., BVS:1875:3

ORRISON, David, W, M, d. 1 Sep 1876, LC, consumption, 50-4-0, p. Annamias & Catherine Orrison, b. LC, farmer, c/o: Mary Orrison, sc: Mary Orrison, wife, JF Dist., BVS:1876:8

ORRISON, Earnest M., W, M, d. 2 Aug 1883, nr Lovettsville, summer complaint, 1-2-0, p. Thos. S. & Mary E. Orrison, b. LC, sc: Thos S. Orrison, father, 2nd Dist., BVS:1883:4

ORRISON, Elizabeth, W, F, d. 7 Apr 1893, Taylorstown, heart failure, 83-0-0, p. unk, b. Taylorstown, consort, sc: Fred A. Orrison, LV Dist., BVS:1893:5

ORRISON, Elizabeth A., W, F, d. 30 Sep 1883, Arcola, paralysis, 80-0-0,

p. Louis & Ann Gardner, b. Arcola, married, sc: Frank Orrison, son, 1st Dist., BVS:1883:1
ORRISON, Esther V., W, F, d. 22 Aug 1888, LC, dysentery, 5-11-0, p. Geo. W. & Sarah Orrison, b. LC, none, unm, sc: Geo W. Orrison, father, 2nd Dist., BVS:1888:6
ORRISON, George F., W, M, d. 28 Aug 1857, LC, pneumonia, 21-1-3, p. Samuel & Margaret Orrison, b. LC, unm, sc: Samuel Orrison, father, BVS:1857:1, LC:24
ORRISON, James H., W, M, d. 1866, nr Hillsboro, kicked by horse, 21-4-0, p. Wm. Orrison, b. LC, unm, sc: Wm. Orrison, father, BVS:1866:1
ORRISON, Jemima S., W, F, d. 4 Oct 1864, nr Wheatland, typhoid fever, 22-2-1, p. Jonah & Mary Orrison, b. LC, sc: Nancy Orrison, mother, BVS:1864:1, LC:38
ORRISON, John, W, M, d. 15 Jan 1856, Scotland, consumption, 46-0-0, b. LC, farmer & Miller, c/o: Sarah Orrison, sc: Townsend Shorb, step son, BVS:1856:6, LC:23
ORRISON, Lillian, W, F, d. 25 Jul 1872, Mount Gilead Twp., cholera infantum, 0-3-20, p. Chas. W. & Sarah E. Orrison, b. Mount Gilead Town, unm, sc: Chas. W. Orrison, father, MT Dist., BVS:1872:2
ORRISON, Lillian M., W, F, d. 23 Jan 1871, unk, 0-2-0, p. F. & Kate B. Orrison, BR Dist., BVS:1871:3
ORRISON, Lillie P., W, F, d. 6 Sep 1886, unk, 0-0-4, p. Jno. P. & Lillie B., sc: Jno. P. Orrison, father, 2nd Dist., BVS:1886:5
ORRISON, Lydia E., W, F, d. 30 Nov 1857, LC, consumption, 25-9-13, p. Thomas & Margaret Hanes, b. LC, c/o: Cumberland G. Orrison, sc: C.G. Orrison, husband, BVS:1857:1, LC:24
ORRISON, Margaret, W, F, d. 21 Apr 1882, LC, general debility, 72-0-27, c/o: Samuel Orrison, sc: John H. Orrison, son, 3rd Dist., BVS:1882:3
ORRISON, Maria E., W, F, d. 24 Aug 1888, LC, dysentery, 2-0-0, p. Geo. W. & Sarah Orrison, b. LC, none, unm, sc: Geo W. Orrison, father, 2nd Dist., BVS:1888:6

ORRISON, Maria E., W, F, d. 10 May 1878, nr Gum Spring, child birth, 38-0-0, p. Llewellyn & Julia Hutchison, b. nr Gum Spring, c/o: Jas W. Orrison, sc: J.W. Orrison, husband, BR Dist., BVS:1878:4
ORRISON, Mary W., W, F, d. 19 May 1855, Rockdale, typhoid fever, 19-2-1, p. Jonah & Nancy Orrison, b. LC, sc: Jonah Orrison, father, BVS:1855:6, LC:17
ORRISON, Mollie, W, F, d. 5 Mar 1884, Waterford, consumption, 27-0-0, p. C.W. & Ann Rinker, b. Waterford, c/o: Daniel Orrison, sc: Danl Orrison, husband, 3rd Dist., BVS:1884:6
ORRISON, Morris H., W, M, d. 17 Jun 1873, nr Hillsboro, unk, 0-0-14, p. Thos. A. & Amanda Orrison, b. LC, sc: T. J. Orrison, father, JF Dist., BVS:1874:1
ORRISON, no name twins, W, F, d. 12 Apr 1874, Hillsboro, unk, 0-0-1, p. F A. & Amanda Orrison, b. LC, sc: F.A. Orrison, father, JF Dist., BVS:1874:2
[ORRISON], no name, W, F, d. 18 Mar 1878, nr Gum Spring, unk, 0-0-9, p. J. W. & Maria E. Orrison, b. nr Gum Spring, unm, sc: J.W. Orrison, father, BR Dist., BVS:1878:4
ORRISON, Permelia A., W, F, d. 12 Dec 1893, Hamilton, old age, 75-0-0, p. James Henry & Pleasant McGarvick, b. LC, wife, sc: daughter, MT Dist., BVS:1893:4
ORRISON, Samuel, W, M, d. 6 Oct 1883, Hamilton, paralysis, 73-0-0, b. LC, farmer, c/o: Margaret Orrison, sc: John H. Orrison, son, 3rd Dist., BVS:1883:5
ORRISON, Sarah, W, F, d. Jan 1864, Bunker Hill, consumption, 60-0-0, p. Jno & Hannah West, b. LC, sc: Townsend Short, BVS:1864:2, LC:39
ORRISON, W. P., W, F, d. 12 Mar 1891, Hamilton, paralysis, 77-0-0, p. Mrs. W. P. Orrison [sic], b. Hamilton, husband, unm, sc: Mrs. W. P. Orrison, MT Dist., BVS:1891:6
OSBURN, Adolphus R., W, M, d. 26 Apr 1855, res of parents, consumption, 14-9-4, p. Addison & Lydia Osburn, b. nr Fred's Store, sc:

Addison Osburn, father, BVS:1855:6, LC:18

OSBURN, Annie, W, F, d. 3 Aug 1873, nr Purcellville, diarrhea, 0-4-0, p. Joseph C. & Elizabeth Osburn, b. LC, sc: Joseph C. Osburn, father, JF Dist., BVS:1874:1

[OSBURN], Archibald, W, M, d. 6 Dec 1854, Snickersville, croup, 0-2-17, p. Joab & Emily J. Osburn, b. Snickersville, sc: father, BVS:1854:11, LC:11

OSBURN, Eliz A., W, F, d. 26 Feb 1864, Snickersville, consumption, unk, b. LC, sc: Pheneas Osburn, husband, BVS:1864:1, LC:38

OSBURN, Emily J., W, F, d. 28 Dec 1881, LC, cancer, 61-4-24, p. Israel & Alice Gibson, b. LC, c/o: Jacob Osburn, sc: Herbert Osburn, son, 2nd Dist., BVS:1881:7

OSBURN, Joel, W, M, d. 8 Jul 1855, E of Blue Ridge, old age, 79-0-0, p. Rich. & Hannah Osburn, b. E of Blue Ridge, farmer, sc: William Osburn, son, BVS:1855:7, LC:18

OSBURN, Oscar, W, M, d. 8 Oct 1856, Patsy Osburn's, congestion fever, 9-0-14, p. Richard & Patsy Osburn, b. place of death, sc: Patsy Osburn, mother, BVS:1856:6, LC:23

OSBURN, Patsey, W, F, d. 4 Jul 1875, nr Purcellville, dropsy, 69-0-0, p. Thos & Martha Shepherd, b. LC, sc: Octavius Osburn, son, JF Dist., BVS:1875:3

OSBURN, Welby, W, M, d. Aug 1875, Snickersville, brain fever, 0-7-0, p. Frank & Elizabeth Osburn, b. Snickersville, farmer, sc: Frank Osburn, father, MT Dist., BVS:1875:8

OTLEY, Easter, W, F, d. 31 Aug 1875, nr Silcott Springs, summer complaint, 0-9-24, p. J. Arthur & Emma R. Otley, b. nr Silcott Springs, teacher, sc: J. Arthur Otley, father, MT Dist., BVS:1875:8

OTLEY, Emma R., W, F, d. 12 Dec 1891, Philomont, chronic bronchitis, 44-0-0, b. LC, wife, unm, sc: J. Arthur Otley, MT Dist., BVS:1891:6

OTLEY, James G., W, M, d. 10 Sep 1891, Philomont, grippe, 71-0-0, b. LC, farmer, husband, unm, sc: J. O. Otley, MT Dist., BVS:1891:6

OTLEY, Joshua T., W, M, d. 20 Aug 1854, Purcellville, dysentery, 4-1-0, p. J. G. & Eliza Otley, b. Philomont, sc: father, BVS:1854:11, LC:11

OTLEY, Louisa H., W, F, d. 14 Sep 1891, Philomont, worn out, 75-0-0, b. LC, husband, unm, sc: J.A. Otley, MT Dist., BVS:1891:6

OTLEY, Orra O., W, F, d. 27 Jul 1877, nr Philomont, typhoid pneumonia, 23-0-0, p. Jas. G. & Louisa Otley, b. LC, sc: J.G. Otley, father, MT Dist., BVS:1877:2

OTTLEY, Francis C., W, M, d. 12 Dec 1866, nr Lincoln, pneumonia, 0-1-12, p. John J. & Maria Ottley, b. nr Lincoln, sc: John J. Ottley, father, BVS:1866:2

OTTLEY, Mary Ann, W, F, d. 19 Jul 1856, her res, dysentery child bed, 37-0-0, c/o: William Ottley, sc: Wm. Ottley, husband, BVS:1856:6, LC:23

OTTLEY, Mary L., W, F, d. 1 Aug 1857, res of parents, dysentery, 2-10-27, p. James G. & Eliza Ottley, b. place of death, sc: James G. Ottley, father, BVS:1857:5, LC:27

OVERALL, Armstead, B, M, d. 15 May 1885, nr Arcola, croup, 0-3-0, p. Richard & Hattie Overall, b. nr Arcola, sc: Richard Overall, father, 1st Dist., BVS:1885:4

OVERALL, Bertha, B, F, d. 9 Aug 1886, nr Arcola, unk, 0-3-0, p. Richd. & Elizabeth Overall, b. nr Arcola, unm, sc: Richard Overall, father, 1st Dist., BVS:1886:2

OVERALL, Fannie, B, F, d. 18 May 1890, nr Watson, heart disease, 75-3-0, p. Samuel & Jane Overall, b. LC, c/o: Richard Overall, sc: Louis Hall, friend, 1st Dist., BVS:1890:2

OVERALL, Ginnie, B, F, d. 28 Dec 1885, nr Arcola, consumption, 4-0-0, p. Richard & Bettie Overall, b. nr Arcola, sc: Richard Overall, father, 1st Dist., BVS:1885:4

OVERALL, James, B, M, d. 20 Aug 1889, Arcola, rupture, 14-0-0, p. Richard & Elizabeth Overall, b. LC, sc: Richard Overall, father, 1st Dist., BVS:1889:1

OVERALL, Nancy C., B, F, d. 10 May 1885, nr Arcola, consumption, 2-0-0, p. Thos. & Margaret Overall, b. nr

Loudoun County, Virginia, Death Register, 1853-1896　　199

Arcola, sc: Thomas Piersall, father, 1st Dist., BVS:1885:4

OVERHALL, Fred, B, M, d. 6 Oct 1888, LC, croup, 3-11-0, p. Thomas & Amanda Overhall, b. LC, none, unm, sc: Amanda Overall, mother, 2nd Dist., BVS:1888:6

OVERHALL, Isaac R., B, M, d. 15 Dec 1877, nr Guilford Station, consumption, 19-0-0, p. Wm. Tippett & Alice Overhall, b. nr Guilford Station, unm, sc: Rachel Overhall, grandmother, BR Dist., BVS:1877:1

OVERHALL, Mary J., B, F, d. 10 Jun 1865, Skinners Mill, dropsy, 25-0-0, p. Hennie Overhall, b. LC, sc: Mary J. Skinner, head of family, BVS:1865:2

OWEN, Samuel, B, M, d. 24 Dec 1877, 7th Toll Gate on Little River Tpike, unk, 65-0-0, p. unk, b. unk, laborer, c/o: Caroline Owen, sc: H.M. Smith, employer, BR Dist., BVS:1877:1

OWENS, Geo, B, M, d. [1869], diphtheria, 3-0-0, p. ? Owens, b. LC, sc: ? Owens, father, BVS:1869:1

OWENS, Jane, B, F, d. 1 May 1888, Evergreen Mills, consumption, 16-0-0, p. Samuel & Caroline Owens, b. Evergreen Mills, sc: Caroline Owens, mother, 1st Dist., BVS:1888:4

PAGE, Horace, W, M, d. 30 Mar 1896, Ryan, cholera infantum, 0-11-0, p. C. C. & Florence Page, b. Ryan, sc: C.C. Page, father, BR Dist., BVS:1896:3

PAGE, Jas., B, M, d. 16 Sep 1894, nr Trappe, unk, 19-0-0, p. John & Mary Page, b. nr Trappe, sc: Nancy Page, mother, 1st Dist., BVS:1894:2

PAGE, Marshal, B, M, d. 15 Jun 1896, nr Conklin, consumption, 31-0-0, p. Nat. & Mary Page, b. nr Arcola, laborer, unm, sc: Nat Page, father, BR Dist., BVS:1896:4

PAGE, Mattie, B, F, d. 5 Dec 1881, LC, whooping cough, 0-3-0, p. Andrew & Laura Page, b. LC, sc: Andrew Page, father, 2nd Dist., BVS:1881:7

PAGE, no name, W, F, d. 7 Sep 1893, Ryan, unk, 0-0-7, p. C. C. & Florence Page, b. Ryan, sc: C.C. Page, father, 1st Dist., BVS:1893:1

PAGE, no name, W, F, d. 18 Oct 1893, nr Sterling, premature, 0-0-3, p. H. C. & Mattie C. Page, b. nr Sterling, sc: H.C. Page, father, 1st Dist., BVS:1893:1

PAGE, Theodore, W, M, d. 15 Aug 1887, Farmwell, cholera infantum, 0-5-12, p. Charles C. & Florence Page, b. Farmwell, sc: Charles C. Page, father, 1st Dist., BVS:1887:1

PAINTER, Mary, W, F, d. 10 Feb 1893, Lovettsville, lagrippe, 64-0-0, p. unk, b. Lovettsville, consort, sc: Jas. W. Painter, LV Dist., BVS:1893:5

PAIRPOINT, Rue A., W, F, d. 17 Feb 1888, LC, paralysis, 78-11-20, p. unk, b. LC, c/o: Joseph Pairpoint, sc: Obed Pairpoint, son, 3rd Dist., BVS:1888:1

PALMER, Aubry L., W, M, d. 30 Aug 1886, Arcola, cholera infantum, 0-4-0, p. Walter L. & Cora F. Palmer, b. Pleasant Valley, sc: Walter L. Palmer, father, 1st Dist., BVS:1886:2

PALMER, Chas J., W, M, d. 10 Jul 1865, Fairfax line, dysentery, 2-4-0, p. S.F. & Wm. W. Palmer, b. LC, unm, sc: Wm. W. Palmer, father, BVS:1865:2

PALMER, Corban F., W, M, d. 27 Jun 1878, nr Gum Spring, cholera infantum, 0-6-0, p. L. F. & Mary F. Palmer, b. Gum Spring, unm, sc: L.F. Palmer, father, BR Dist., BVS:1878:4

PALMER, Edna A., W, F, d. 8 Aug 1882, LC, whooping cough, 3-0-0, p. L. F. & Mary F. Palmer, sc: L.F. Palmer, father, 1st Dist., BVS:1882:2

PALMER, Elizabeth, W, F, d. 23 Apr 1881, LC, heart disease, 55-0-0, b. LC, c/o: J.S. Palmer, sc: J.S. Palmer, husband, 1st Dist., BVS:1881:2

PALMER, James F., W, M, d. 11 Jun 1882, LC, fall from house, 38-0-0, p. J. H. & M. F. Palmer, carpenter, unm, sc: James H. Palmer, father, 1st Dist., BVS:1882:2

PALMER, James Henry, W, M, d. 21 Nov 1858, res of father, fits, 29-9-27, p. Saml & Sarah H. Palmer, b. Round Hill, sc: Samuel Palmer, father, BVS:1858:5, LC:33

PALMER, L. F., W, M, d. 13 Feb 1892, Arcola, la grippe, 63-3-10, p. Phillip

& Prudence Palmer, b. Arcola, merchant, c/o: M.F. Palmer, sc: M.F. Palmer, wife, 1st Dist., BVS:1892:2

PALMER, Martha J., W, F, d. 15 Jul 1865, Fairfax line, dysentery, 5-2-15, p. S.F. & Wm. W. Palmer, b. LC, unm, sc: Wm. W. Palmer, father, BVS:1865:2

PALMER, Mortimer, W, M, d. 11 Jun 1882, LC, fall from house, 32-0-0, p. J. H. & M. F. Palmer, carpenter, unm, sc: James H. Palmer, father, 1st Dist., BVS:1882:2

PALMER, Ralph L., W, M, d. 10 Aug 1892, Arcola, unk, 0-8-0, p. W. L. & Cora Palmer, b. Arcola, sc: W.L. Palmer, father, 1st Dist., BVS:1892:2

PALMER, Saml A, W, M, d. 10 Jul 1865, Maryland, dysentery, 1-0-14, p. Saml & Alice Palmer, sc: Saml E. Palmer, father, BVS:1865:1

PALMER, Sarah E., W, F, d. 10 Aug 1893, Daysville, blood poison, 34-0-0, p. Jno. Winslow, b. Fairfax, housekeeper, c/o: Jno T. Palmer, sc: Jno T. Palmer, husband, 1st Dist., BVS:1893:1

PANCOAST, Lydia, W, F, d. 24 Jan 1857, res of John Pancoast, 76-11-26, p. John & Ruth Pancoast, b. Maryland, sc: John Pancoast, brother, BVS:1857:3, LC:26

PANCOAST, S. Thompson, W, M, d. 3 Aug 1884, nr Lincoln, typhoid fever, 42-0-0, p. J.S. & Emily Pancoast, b. Silcott Springs, farmer, c/o: L.A. Pancoast, sc: L.W. Pancoast, wife, 3rd Dist., BVS:1884:6

PANCOAST, Stephen W., W, M, d. Jul 1865, nr Philomont, consumption, 25-3-21, p. Jno S. & Laura Pancoast, b. nr Philomont, farmer, unm, sc: Jno S. Pancoast, father, BVS:1865:1

PANGLE, C. A., W, M, d. 10 Jun 1896, Arcola, unk, 0-0-7, p. Chas. C. & Alice Pangle, b. Arcola, sc: C.C. Pangle, father, BR Dist., BVS:1896:3

PANGLE, Elizabeth C., W, F, d. 10 Jan 1892, Arcola, la grippe, 63-0-0, p. unk, b. Morgan Co., c/o: Milton H. Pangle, sc: Briscoe Pangle, son, 1st Dist., BVS:1892:2

PANGLE, Geo. W., W, M, d. 29 Jun 1896, Arcola, consumption, 39-0-0,

p. Milton & Sarah Pangle, b. LC, laborer, unm, sc: C.C. Pangle, brother, BR Dist., BVS:1896:3

PANGLE, Robt. I., W, M, d. 31 Mar 1892, Aldie, cholera infantum, 4-0-21, p. Robt. N. & Rebecca Pangle, b. Aldie, sc: Rebecca Pangle, mother, 1st Dist., BVS:1892:2

PARKER, Cassius, B, M, d. 15 Mar 1875, nr Sudley Mill, croup, 0-9-0, p. Cassius & Sylvia Parker, b. LC, sc: Sylvia Parker, mother, BR Dist., BVS:1875:5

PARKER, Isaac, B, M, d. 6 Mar 1889, Sterling, bright's disease, 38-0-0, p. Baltimore & Ruth Parker, b. LC, laborer, unm, sc: Nelson Gaskins, brother-in-law, 1st Dist., BVS:1889:1

PARKER, John W., B, F, d. 15 Sep 1889, LC, unk, 0-0-21, p. J. W. & Lydia Parker, b. LC, none, unm, sc: J.W. Park, father, 2nd Dist., BVS:1889:4

PARKER, Lucy E., W, F, d. 22 Jul 1884, LC, croup, 0-0-24, p. Presley & Mary E. Parker, b. LC, sc: Mary Parker, mother, 1st Dist., BVS:1884:2

PARKER, Robert, B, M, d. 9 Sep 1889, LC, consumption, 30-0-0, p. R. S. & Lucy Parker, b. LC, laborer, unm, sc: Robert Parker, father, 3rd Dist., BVS:1889:5

PARKER, Roberta, B, F, d. 15 May 1878, LC, pneumonia, 1-10-0, p. Emily Parker, b. LC, unm, sc: Emily Parker, mother, LE Dist., BVS:1878:8

PARKERSON, Frank, B, M, d. Mar 1873, Leesburg, fever, 19-0-0, p. Frank Parkerson, b. Leesburg, laborer, unm, sc: Frank Parkerson, father, LE Dist., BVS:1873:2

PARKINSON, Amanda, B, , d. 16 Sep 1877, LC, consumption, 47-3-0, c/o: Frank Parkinson, sc: Frank Parkinson, husband, LE Dist., BVS:1877:8

PARKINSON, Amanda R., B, F, d. 21 May 1880, Leesburg, consumption, 0-9-0, p. Mahala Parkinson, b. LC, unm, sc: ?, aunt, 2nd Dist., BVS:1880:7

PARKINSON, Edward, B, M, d. 25 Mar 1880, Leesburg, consumption, 19-0-0, p. Frank & Amanda Parkinson, b.

Loudoun County, Virginia, Death Register, 1853-1896   201

LC, unm, sc: ?, sister, 2nd Dist., BVS:1880:7

PARKINSON, Edward, B, M, d. 28 Mar 1878, LC, consumption, 18-6-0, p. Frank & Amanda Parkinson, b. LC, unm, sc: Frank Parkinson, father, LE Dist., BVS:1878:8

PARKINSON, Frank, B, M, d. 9 Jun 1880, Leesburg, paralysis, 62-0-0, p. --- Parkinson, b. LC, laborer, c/o: Amanda Parkinson, sc: ?, daughter, 2nd Dist., BVS:1880:7

PARMER, Linda, B, F, d. 28 Jul 1888, LC, tumor of brain, 45-0-0, p. Sam & M. Crosburry, b. LC, c/o: Jessie Parmer, sc: Jessie Parmer, husband, 3rd Dist., BVS:1888:1

PARRIS, Alice, B, F, d. 1 May 1887, LC, consumption, 24-0-0, p. Wm. & Louisa Parris, b. LC, unm, sc: William Parris, father, 2nd Dist., BVS:1887:4

PARRIS, Annie, B, F, d. 1 May 1887, LC, croup, unk, p. Alice Parris, b. LC, unm, sc: William Parris, grandfather, 2nd Dist., BVS:1887:4

PARROTT, Eliza Bell, B, F, d. Aug 1875, Snickersville, pneumonia, 3-0-0, p. John & Georgeanna Parrott, b. LC, laborer, married, sc: John Parrott, father, MT Dist., BVS:1875:8

PATTERSON, James, W, M, d. 11 Feb 1856, Poor House, burn, 70-0-0, p. James and Mary Patterson, b. Millville, blacksmith, sc: steward, BVS:1856:4, LC:22

PATTON, John A. F., W, M, d. 28 Jun 1859/60, res of parents, poison, 3-0-28, p. John W. & Mary A. Patton, b. nr North Fork, sc: John W. Patton, father, BVS:1859:3, 1860:1, LC:34

PATTON, Mary J., W, F, d. 10 Nov 1883, nr Upperville, Fauquier Co., inflammation bowels, 0-2-3, p. Joseph M. & Mary H. Patton, b. Middleburg, sc: Joseph Patton, father, 1st Dist., BVS:1883:1

[PATTON], no name,W, M, d. 17 May 1859/60, res of parents, concussion of brain, 0-1-27, p. John W. & Mary A. Patton, b. nr North Fork, sc: John W. Patton, father, BVS:1859:3, 1860:1, LC:34

PAXON, Henrietta C., W, F, d. 31 Dec 1886, nr Farmwell, paralysis, 70-0-0, p. Wm. & Mary A. Hough, b. LC,

unk, sc: Wm. B. Paxon, son, 1st Dist., BVS:1886:2

PAXSON, Amanda, B, F, d. 3 Feb 1888, Farmwell, consumption, 52-0-0, p. Alex & Virginia Lyon, b. Farmwell, c/o: Samuel G. Paxson, sc: Samuel G. Paxson, husband, 1st Dist., BVS:1888:4

PAXSON, Ann, W, F, d. 10 Nov 1854, Waterford, unk, 27-3-11, p. Wm. H. & Mary Hough, b. LC, c/o: Burr H. Paxson, sc: Burr H. Paxson, husband, BVS:1854:10, LC:9

PAXSON, Burr Rodney, W, M, d. 6 & 7 Aug 1855, LC, unk, 0-2-15, p. G. W. & Duanna Paxson, b. LC, sc: Griffith W. Paxson, father, BVS:1855:1, LC:14

PAXSON, Chas. G., W, M, d. 24 Sep 1894, Falls Church, congestion brain, 25-5-6, p. Samuel B. Paxson, b. Hughesville, Miller, sc: Saml B. Paxson, father, 3rd Dist., BVS:1894:5

PAXSON, Chas. R., W, M, d. 1 Feb 1889, LC, angina pectoris, 62-0-0, p. unk, b. Pennsylvania, farmer, c/o: Rachal Paxson, sc: H. Harrison, friend, 2nd Dist., BVS:1889:4

PAXSON, Clayton C., W, M, d. 8 Sep 1885, Paxson, typhoid fever, 27-0-0, p. John C. Louisa Paxson, b. LC, unm, sc: Jno C. Paxson, father, 3rd Dist., BVS:1885:6

PAXSON, Cornelius W., W, M, d. 21 Nov 1883, nr Leesburg, paralysis, 62-0-0, p. John & Ann Paxson, b. LC, merchant, c/o: Sarah F. Paxson, sc: Sarah F. Paxson, wife, 2nd Dist., BVS:1883:7

PAXSON, Frances, W, F, d. 19 Mar 1892, Ryan, la grippe & pneumonia, 26-0-0, p. Josh G. & Mary J. Moran, b. Ryan, c/o: Walter L. Paxson, sc: Josh G. Moran, father, 1st Dist., BVS:1892:2

PAXSON, Georgia, W, F, d. 9 Sep 1875, nr Waterford, consumption, 20-0-0, p. Griff W. & Duana Paxson, b. LC, sc: G. W. Paxson, father, JF Dist., BVS:1875:3

PAXSON, Jane, W, F, d. 10 Feb 1877, LC, consumption, 52-4-25, p. Jacob & Mahala Paxson, b. LC, unm, sc: G.W. Paxson, uncle, JF Dist., BVS:1877:3

PAXSON, Lewis M., W, M, d. 27 May 1853, Waterford, unk, 0-1-8, p. Burr H. & Ann Paxson, sc: Burr H. Paxson, father, BVS:1854:5, LC:3

PAXSON, Townsend M., W, M, d. 20 Mar 1888, LC, paralysis, 63-0-0, unk, b. LC, farmer, c/o: Sallie J. Paxson, sc: John S. Paxson, son, 2nd Dist., BVS:1888:6

PAXSON, William T., W, M, d. 25 Oct 1876, nr Farmwell Church, croup, 4-4-0, p. Edward & Sarah Paxson, b. in the west, sc: Edward Paxson, father, BR Dist., BVS:1876:2

PAYNE, Amanda, B, F, d. 1 Mar 1892, Bloomfield, spasms, 0-3-0, p. Geneva Payne, b. Bloomfield, laborer, unm, sc: Geneva Payne, mother, 1st Dist., BVS:1892:4

PAYNE, Anthony, B, M, d. 24 Jan 1890, nr Aldie, diphtheria, 16-4-0, p. Landon & Eliza Payne, b. Prince William Co., unm, sc: Landon Payne, father, 1st Dist., BVS:1890:2

PAYNE, Eliza, B, F, d. 13 Mar 1885, nr Aldie, confinement, 25-0-0, p. Waren & Isabella Corum, b. nr Aldie, c/o: Willis Payne, sc: Waren Corum, father, 1st Dist., BVS:1885:4

PAYNE, James, B, M, d. 17 Nov 1893, Paxson, diphtheria, 11-0-0, p. Joseph & Elizabeth Payne, b. LC, sc: father, MT Dist., BVS:1893:4

PAYNE, Kitty, B, F, d. 24 Jun 1890, LC, old age, 85-0-0, p. unk, b. LC, none, unm, sc: N. Diggs, friend, 2nd Dist., BVS:1890:5

PAYNE, Malinda, B, F, d. 1 Mar 1869, LC, consumption, 1-7-0, p. Henrietta Payne, b. LC, sc: Chloe Pinkit, grandmother, BVS:1869:1

PAYNE, Matilda, B, F, d. 26 Jul 1881, LC, consumption, 21-0-0, p. Susan Payne, b. LC, unm, sc: Susan Payne, mother, 3rd Dist., BVS:1881:4

[PAYNE], no name,(f), M, d. Mar 1857, Josephus Carr's Farm, 0-0-1, p. James E. & Susan J. Payne, b. Jos. Carr's Farm, sc: father, BVS:1857:3, LC:26

PAYTON, Warner, B, M, d. 1 Aug 1887, LC, pneumonia, 71-0-0, p. Charles & Emily Payton, b. LC, laborer, unm, sc: Charles Payton, father, 3rd Dist., BVS:1887:7

PEACOCK, Carl W., W, M, d. 6 Jul 1884, Wheatland, cholera infantum, 0-4-14, p. Hector & Josephine Peacock, b. Wheatland, unm, sc: H.B. Peacock, father, 3rd Dist., BVS:1884:7

PEACOCK, Jane E,, W, F, d. 30 Sep 1875, nr Belmont, congestion of brain, 45-2-0, p. Walter & Mary Reeves, b. LC, married, sc: C.W. Peacock, husband, BR Dist., BVS:1875:5

PEACOCK, Lymon S., W, M, d. 10 Aug 1886, nr Leesburg, brain fever, 0-2-0, p. James W. & Mollie Peacock, b. nr Farmwell, sc: James W. Peacock, father, 1st Dist., BVS:1886:2

PEACOCK, Maria, W, F, d. 13 Feb 1892, Morrisonville, typhoid fever, 37-0-0, p. Wm. & Hannah Hough, b. LC, consort, sc: Jas. Peacock, LV Dist., BVS:1892:6

PEACOCK, Mary E., W, F, d. 4 Jan 1888, Waxpool, consumption, 25-0-0, p. Isaiah & Mary Bodine, b. Waxpool, c/o: James W. Peacock, sc: James W. Peacock, husband, 1st Dist., BVS:1888:4

PEACOCK, Minnie C., W, F, d. 5 Oct 1888, LC, burned to death, 6-6-2, p. James & R. Peacock, b. LC, none, unm, sc: James Peacock, father, 2nd Dist., BVS:1888:6

PEACOCK, Nancy C., W, F, d. 25 Jan 1858, res of parents, scarlet fever, 6-6-0, p. Noble B. & Lucinda Peacock, b. place of death, sc: N.B. Peacock, father, BVS:1858:5, LC:32

PEACOCK, no name, W, F, d. 1 Apr 1890, LC, whooping cough, 0-1-0, p. J. H. & Rida Peacock, b. LC, farmer, unm, sc: J.H. Peacock, father, 2nd Dist., BVS:1890:4

[PEACOCK], no name, W, F, d. May 1891, Ketoctin Church, cholera infantum, 0-1-15, p. Hector B. & Josephine Peacock, b. Ketoctin Church, c/o: child, sc: Hector B. Peacock, JF Dist., BVS:1891:7

[PEACOCK], no name, W, F, d. 9 Feb 1892, Morrisonville, unk, 0-0-9, p. Jas. & Maria Peacock, b. LC, unm, sc: Jas. Peacock, LV Dist., BVS:1892:6

[PEACOCK], no name, W, M, d. Jun 1892, Waterford, cholera infantum,

0-1-0, p. H. B. & Josephine Peacock, b. Waterford, married, sc: H.B. Peacock, father, JF Dist., BVS:1892:7

PEACOCK, Winfield Scott, W, M, d. 14 Feb 1858, res of parents, scarlet fever, 10-4-0, p. Noble B. & Lucinda Peacock, b. place of death, sc: N.B. Peacock, father, BVS:1858:5, LC:32

PEARCE, Alcinda, W, F, d. 1 Dec 1887, LC, consumption, 54-0-0, p. Hector & M. Pearce, b. LC, none, unm, sc: Nancy E. Pearce, sister, 3rd Dist., BVS:1887:7

PEARSON, James H., B, M, d. 1 Jun 1876, LC, whooping cough, 2-0-0, p. James & Lena Pearson, b. LC, sc: Jas. Pearson, father, JF Dist., BVS:1876:8

PEARSON, James W., B, M, d. 23 Feb 1877, LC, inflammation of bowels, 1-11-0, p. James H. & Lina Pearson, b. LC, sc: James Pearson, father, JF Dist., BVS:1877:3

PEARSON, Mary E., W, F, d. 1896, LC, cancer, 51-0-0, p. Wm. & Mary Hibbs, b. LC, wife, sc: M.F. Brown, friend, LE Dist., BVS:1896:5

PEARSON, Nancy, B, F, d. 24 Aug 1876, Leesburg, brain fever, 0-0-18, p. Newton & Gracie Pearson, b. LC, sc: Gracie Pearson, mother, LE Dist., BVS:1876:7

[PECK], no name, W, M, d. 29 Oct 1853, Purcellville, unk, 0-0-1/4, p. Clement & Mary Peck, b. nr Purcell's Store, sc: father, BVS:1854:6, LC:5

[PECK], no name, W, M, d. 7 Feb 1854, Beaverdam, brain fever, 0-0-15, p. Julius & Amanda C. Peck, b. Beaverdam, sc: father, BVS:1854:13, LC:13

PENDLETON, Robert, B, M, d. 1 Mar 1877, Upperville, lock jaw, 42-0-0, b. Rappahannock Co., c/o: Mary Pendleton, sc: Mary Pendleton, wife, MC Dist., BVS:1877:5

PENICK, Fannie, B, F, d. 24 Mar 1887, Upperville, unk, 30-0-0, p. unk, b. Upperville, c/o: Lorenza Penick, sc: Lorenza Penick, husband, 1st Dist., BVS:1887:1

PERRY, John T., W, M, d. 9 Aug 1884, Leesburg, dysentery, 65-0-0, p. Jno. T. & --- Perry, b. LC, shoe maker, c/o: Mary Perry, sc: P.P. Perry, son, 2nd Dist., BVS:1884:5

PERRY, Madeline, W, M, d. 12 Nov 1893, Leesburg, diphtheria, 6-0-0, p. Chas. & Mary, b. Leesburg, unm, sc: Chas E. Perry, LE Dist., BVS:1893:6

PERRY, Pendleton, W, M, d. 30 Jun 1881, LC, summer complaint, 0-2-5, p. Pendelton P. & L. M Perry, b. LC, sc: P.P. Perry, father, 2nd Dist., BVS:1881:7

PETERS, Garner, B, M, d. 30 Apr 1893, nr Unison, bladder trouble, 65-0-0, p. unk, b. unk, laborer, c/o: Julia Peters, sc: Julia Peters, wife, 1st Dist., BVS:1893:2

PETERS, John H., B, M, d. 13 Jan 1873, nr Cub Run, pneumonia, 0-5-0, p. John & Susan Peters, b. LC, sc: Susan Peters, mother, BR Dist., BVS:1873:1

PETERSON, Hannah C., B, F, d. 21 Jun 1878, nr Bloomfield, scrofula, 3-0-0, p. Jno Lee & Fanny Peterson, b. LC, sc: Jno Lee Peterson, father, MC Dist., BVS:1878:7

PETERSON, Lee, B, M, d. 10 Aug 1880, LC, unk, 1-0-0, p. Robert & Annie Peterson, b. LC, unm, sc: Annie Peterson, mother, 1st Dist., BVS:1880:2

PETERSON, Mary E., B, F, d. 15 Aug 1883, nr Bloomfield, malaria fever, 0-1-6, p. Robert & Rose Peterson, b. nr Bloomfield, unm, sc: Robert Peterson, father, 1st Dist., BVS:1883:2

PETERSON, Mary E., B, F, d. 12 Jul 1872, nr Bloomfield, unk, p. John L. & Fanny Peterson, MC Dist., BVS:1872:7

PEYTON, Elizabeth C., W, F, d. 1875, Lovettsville Dist, heart disease, 23-0-0, b. LC, LV Dist., BVS:1875:4

PEYTON, James W., W, M, d. 18 Feb 1879, nr Neersville, catarrh fever, 1-8-12, p. Joe E. B. & Ruth E. J. Peyton, b. LC, sc: Ruth E.J. Peyton, mother, 2nd Dist., BVS:1879:1

PEYTON, Lydia, B, F, d. 25 Apr 1873, nr Aldie, pneumonia, 0-8-0, p. James & Lucy Peyton, b. LC, sc: Lucy Peyton, mother, MC Dist., BVS:1873:5

PEYTON, Mary Ann, (f), F, d. 7 Feb 1856, Elizth. Peyton's, consumption,

23-0-0, p. Elizabeth Peyton, b. Millville, sc: E. Peyton, mother, BVS:1856:6, LC:23

PEYTON, Mary E., W, F, d. 1 Nov 1878, Waterford, congestion of lungs, 36-0-0, p. Noble & Mary Braden, b. LC, c/o: Col. Henry E. Payton, sc: Co. H.E. Payton, husband, JF Dist., BVS:1878:10

PHILIPS, Catharine, W, F, d. 28 Feb 1860, cancer, 60-0-0, sc: steward, BVS:1860:2

PHILIPS, Elizabeth M. Etta, W, F, d. 25 Oct 1876, nr Lovettsville, inflammation of lungs, 25-3-16, p. Wm & Caroline M. Smith, b. LC, c/o: .....Phillips, sc: Wm Smith, father, LV Dist., BVS:1876:3

PHILIPS, Jos, W, M, d. 15 Oct 1860, Poor House, consumption, 45-0-0, b. Spain, blacksmith, sc: steward, BVS:1860:2

PHILIPS, Wm. F., W, M, d. 4 Sep 1877, LC, pneumonia, 56-6-0, sc: Thos Williamson, friend, LE Dist., BVS:1877:8

PHILLIPS, Catharine, W, F, d. 28 Feb 1859, cancer, 60-0-0, sc: steward, BVS:1859:4, LC:35

PHILLIPS, Ella, B, F, d. 31 Mar 1890, nr Arcola, consumption, 1-3-0, p. Margaret Phillips (unm), b. nr Arcola, sc: Fenton Lucas, grandfather, 1st Dist., BVS:1890:2

PHILLIPS, George L., W, M, d. 18 Mar 1886, Daysville, pneumonia, 16-0-0, p. Levi C. & Mary A. Phillips, b. nr Daysville, unm, sc: Levi C. Phillips, father, 1st Dist., BVS:1886:2

PHILLIPS, Hugh S., W, M, d. 7 Mar 1853, LC, fever, 1-5-0, p. Thos. & Eliz. J. Philips, b. LC, sc: Thos Philips, father, BVS:1854:3, LC:1

PHILLIPS, Hugh S., W, M, d. 1 Mar 1854, Winchester, pneumonia, 1-3-7, p. Thos. & Elizabeth Phillips, b. LC, sc: Thomas Phillips, father, BVS:1854:10, LC:9

PHILLIPS, Joseph, W, M, d. 15 Oct 1859, Poor House, consumption, 45-0-0, b. Spain, blacksmith, sc: steward, BVS:1859:4, LC:35

PHILLIPS, Levi C., W, M, d. 15 Feb 1881, LC, diphtheria, 2-6-0, p. Levi C. & Mary Phillips, b. LC, sc: L.C. Phillips, father, 1st Dist., BVS:1881:2

PHILLIPS, Louisa, B, F, d. 31 Dec 1887, nr Philomont, old age, 90-0-0, p. unk, b. LC, unm, sc: F.E. Robey, superintendent of poor, 1st Dist., BVS:1887:1

PHILLIPS, Maria, B, F, d. 10 Dec 1866, nr Mount Gilead, paralyzed, 60-0-2, sc: Elizabeth Cox, friend, BVS:1866:2

PHILLIPS, no name, B, F, d. 1 Dec 1888, LC, unk, 0-0-7, p. John & Isabelle Philips, b. LC, none, unm, sc: John Philips, father, 2nd Dist., BVS:1888:6

PHILLIPS, Ray, W, M, d. 13 Aug 1891, Sterling, meningitis, 0-5-0, p. Murray D. & Rosa Phillips, b. LC, blacksmith, sc: M.D. Phillips, father, 1st Dist., BVS:1891:2

PHILLIPS, Samuel T., W, M, d. 8 Aug 1887, Daysville, gastric fever, 21-0-0, p. Levi C. & Mary A. Phillips, b. LC, unm, sc: Levi C. Phillips, father, 1st Dist., BVS:1887:1

PHILLIPS, Thoms, W, M, d. 11 Jun 1865, nr Waterford, typhoid fever, 52-0-0, p. Thoms Phillips, b. nr Waterford, farmer, c/o: Eliz. J. Phillips, sc: Eliz J. Phillips, wife, 1st Dist., BVS:1865:4

PHILLIPS, Thos, W, M, d. 11 Jun 1865, nr Waterford, typhoid fever, 55-0-0, p. Thos P. & ... Phillips, b. nr Waterford, farmer, c/o: E.J. Phillips, sc: Eliz I. Phillips, wife, BVS:1865:3

PHILLIPS, Wilson, W, M, d. 17 Nov 1884, LC, congestion of lungs, 2-6-0, p. Levi C. & Mary Phillips, b. LC, sc: Levi C. Phillips, father, 1st Dist., BVS:1884:2

PIERCE, Andrew J., W, M, d. 6 Dec 1864, Lovettsville, killed in battle, 19-8-0, p. John Pierce, b. LC, farmer, sc: Hannah A. Pierce, sister, BVS:1864:1, LC:38

PIERCE, Estella, W, F, d. Apr 1859/60, Dover, jaundice, 0-0-9, p. Mandeville J. & A.E. Pierce, b. Dover, sc: M.J. Pierce, father, BVS:1859:4, 1860:2, LC:35

PIERCE, Mandaval J., W, M, d. 4 Oct 1876, nr Snickersville, dyspepsia, unk, p. John & Charity Pierce, b. LC, married, sc: Mrs. Ann E. Pierce, wife, MT Dist., BVS:1876:1

PIERCE, Mary C., W, F, d. 4 Apr 1885, nr Arcola, bronchitis, 0-1-0, p. Greer & Minnie J. Pierce, b. nr Arcola, sc: Greer Pierce, father, 1st Dist., BVS:1885:4

PIERPOINT, Eli, W, M, d. 19 Feb 1877, LC, old age, 96-0-0, p. Albert ? & Esther Pierpoint, b. LC, farmer, sc: Eli H?, friend, JF Dist., BVS:1877:3

PIERPOINT, Hannah A., W, F, d. 1865, typhoid fever, 28-0-0, p. Saml & Betsey Pierpoint, b. nr Hamilton, unm, sc: Betsy Pierpoint, mother, BVS:1865:1

PIERPOINT, James, W, M, d. 1 May 1882, LC, diarrhea, 0-1-9, p. Obed & Lizzie Pierpoint, b. LC, sc: Obed Pierpoint, parent, 3rd Dist., BVS:1882:3

PIERPOINT, John, W, M, d. 1 Dec 1880, LC, natural decay, 81-0-0, p. Obed & Esther Pierpoint, b. LC, laborer, unm, sc: Levin Ogden, friend, 3rd Dist., BVS:1880:4

PIERPOINT, Joseph, W, M, d. 22 Mar 1881, LC, old age, 86-0-0, b. LC, farmer, c/o: Rue A. Peirpoint, sc: Obed J. Peirpoint, son, 3rd Dist., BVS:1881:4

PIERPOINT, Nancy L., W, F, d. 27 Apr 1858, Samuel Pierpoint's, cancer of breast, 71-0-0, p. Obed & Esther Pierpoint, b. nr place of death, sc: Samuel Pierpoint, brother, BVS:1858:5, LC:32

PIERSON, Alexr., W, M, d. 20 Oct 1891, nr Paris, gravel, 65-0-0, p. unk, b. LC, farmer, c/o: Anna Pierson, sc: Anna Pierson, wife, 1st Dist., BVS:1891:2

PIERSON, Fannie, B, F, d. 15 Sep 1890, Willisville, consumption, 20-0-0, p. James & Sarah Pierson, b. Willisville, unm, sc: Fletcher Pierson, brother, 1st Dist., BVS:1890:2

PIERSON, Jesse, B, M, d. Nov 1896, Hillsboro, bright's disease, 76-0-0, b. Hillsboro, laborer, unm, sc: brother, JF Dist., BVS:1896:10

[PIERSON], no name, B, F, d. 14 Jun 1880, LC, unk, 0-0-4, p. Rachael Pierson, b. LC, unm, sc: Rachel Pierson, mother, 1st Dist., BVS:1880:2

PIERSON, no name, W, F, d. 7 Apr 1893, Rectors', unk, 0-0-3, p. J. T. & Mary Pierson, b. Rector, sc: J.F. Pierson, father, 1st Dist., BVS:1893:1

PIERSON, Squire, B, M, d. 3 May 1883, Leesburg, consumption, 17-0-0, p. Newton & Grace Pierson, b. LC, laborer, sc: Richard Pierson, brother, 2nd Dist., BVS:1883:4

PIERSON, Susan, W, F, d. 10 Sep 1893, Bloomfield, dropsy, 43-0-0, p. unk, b. Bloomfield, c/o: E.B. Pierson, sc: E.B. Pierson, husband, 1st Dist., BVS:1893:1

PIERSON, Tellie, W, F, d. 15 May 1894, nr Aldie, pneumonia, 3-0-0, p. Jas. H. & Annie E. Pearson, b. nr Aldie, sc: Jas H. Pearson, father, 1st Dist., BVS:1894:1

PIGGOT, Isaac, W, M, d. 7 May 1871, Rosa Wade's, paralysis, 70-0-0, MC Dist., BVS:1871:2

PIGGOT, William J., W, M, d. 16 Aug 1872, 0-4-10, p. Jno. W. & Lydia Piggot, MC Dist., BVS:1872:7

PIGGOTT, Delilah R., W, F, d. 6 Jan 1880, LC, spasms, 2-0-0, p. Thomas H. & H. A. Piggott, b. LC, unm, sc: Hannah A. Piggott, mother, 1st Dist., BVS:1880:2

PIGGOTT, Harriet A., W, F, d. 29 Jul 1890, nr Unison, consumption, 46-0-5, p. Thos. & Delilah Beavers, b. LC, c/o: Thos H. Piggott, sc: Thos H. Piggott, husband, 1st Dist., BVS:1890:2

PIGGOTT, Mary, W, F, d. 22 Mar 1887, nr Philomont, consumption, 48-0-0, p. Isaac & Rebecca Piggott, b. LC, sc: Thomas H. Piggott, brother, 1st Dist., BVS:1887:1

PIGGOTT, Mary, W, F, d. 18 Jun 1855, nr Goose Creek Meeting House, dropsy, 79-0-0, p. Wm. & Sarah Nichols, b. Goose Creek Meeting House, c/o: Wm. Piggott, decd, sc: Mary Piggott, daughter, BVS:1855:7, LC:18

PIGGOTT, Rebecca, W, F, d. 11 Mar 1896, nr Philomont, pneumonia, 0-1-11, p. T. H. & D. C. Piggott, b. nr Philomont, none, unm, sc: T.H. Piggott, father, MC Dist., BVS:1896:2

PIGGOTT, Rebecca, W, F, d. 3 Sep 1874, nr Unison, dropsy of heart, 70-

0-0, p. Saml & Sarah Hatcher, b. LC, c/o: Isaac Piggott dec'd, sc: Thos. W. Piggott, son, MC Dist., BVS:1874:4

PIGGOTT, Samuel F., W, M, d. 2 Mar 1884, LC, dropsy, 1-6-0, p. Thos. & Harriett A. Piggott, b. LC, sc: Thomas Piggott, father, 1st Dist., BVS:1884:2

PINKERT, Emma V., B, F, d. 4 Apr 1872, foot of Blue Ridge, 1-9-8, c/o: Adelade Pinkert, sc: Milton B. Waltman, MC Dist., BVS:1872:7

PINKET, Elias, B, M, d. 8 Aug 1882, Poor House, old age, 102-0-0, p. unk, widower, sc: Jno R. Carter, superintendent, 1st Dist., BVS:1882:2

PINKET, Marshall, B, M, d. 11 Feb 1881, LC, cholera infantum, 0-4-0, p. Jemy & Virginia Pinket, b. LC, sc: Jemy Pinket, father, 1st Dist., BVS:1881:2

PINKET, Mima, B, F, d. Jun 1865, nr Bellfield, consumption, 10-0-0, sc: John Cockerille, BVS:1865:1

PINKET, Sarah T., B, F, d. 24 Feb 1881, LC, unk, 60-0-0, b. LC, c/o: James Pinket, sc: Jemy Pinket, son, 1st Dist., BVS:1881:2

PINCKETT, Claiborne, B, M, d. 1 Feb 1874, nr Middleburg, scrofula, 0-10-0, p. Sarah & Simon Pinkett, b. LC, sc: Simon Pinkett Jr., brother, MC Dist., BVS:1874:4

PINCKETT, Edmond, B, M, d. April 1874, nr Aldie, brain fever, 11-0-0, p. Simon & Martha Pinkett, b. LC, sc: Simon Pinkett, father, MC Dist., BVS:1874:4

PINKETT, Eddie, B, M, d. 25 Aug 1880, LC, old age, 105-0-0, p. unk, b. LC, unm, sc: James Johnson, friend, 1st Dist., BVS:1880:2

PINKETT, George, B, M, d. 16 Apr 1890, nr Aldie, unk, 2-11-0, p. Geo. & Nancy Pinkett, b. nr Aldie, sc: Geo Pinkett, father, 1st Dist., BVS:1890:2

PINKETT, Lucy, B, F, d. Jun 1864, Thos Glasscock's, heart disease, 28-0-0, p. Chas & Lydia Robinson, b. Rappahanock, sc: Mrs. Thos Glasscock, BVS:1864:1, LC:38

PINKETT, Nancy, B, F, d. 21 Jan 1890, nr Aldie, consumption, 35-0-0, p. Simon & Martha Pinkett, b. nr Aldie, c/o: George Pinkett, sc: Geo Pinkett, husband, 1st Dist., BVS:1890:2

[PINKETT], no name, B, F, d. 10 Jul 1894, Aldie, unk, 0-2-0, p. Paul & Josephine Pinkettt, b. Aldie, sc: Paul Pinkett, father, 1st Dist., BVS:1894:2

PINKETT, Robt, B, M, d. 22 Jun 1877, Poor House, old age, 85-0-0, b. LC, sc: Wm. H. Hibbs, superintendent of poor, MC Dist., BVS:1877:5

PINKETT, Simon, B, M, d. 15 May 1883, Aldie, old age, 75-0-0, p. unk, b. Aldie, laborer, c/o: Martha Pinkett, sc: Martha Pinkett, wife, 1st Dist., BVS:1883:1

PINKINS, Adeline, B, F, d. Nov 1873, Leesburg, consumption, 14-0-0, b. LC, unm, sc: David Washington, friend, LE Dist., BVS:1873:2

PINKNEY, Catharine, B, M, d. 20 Aug 1878, LC, consumption, 16-0-0, p. Isaac & Sarah Pinkney, b. LC, unm, sc: Isaac Pinkney, father, LE Dist., BVS:1878:8

[PINCKNEY], no name, B, , d. 22 Oct 1876, LC, hemorrhage, 0-0-3, p. Isaac & Sarah Pinkney, b. LC, sc: Sarah Pinkney, mother, LE Dist., BVS:1876:7

PISTON, John F. B., W, M, d. 1 Aug 1882, LC, malarial fever, 22-0-0, p. S.D. & Mary Piston, sc: Leonard Piston, parent, 3rd Dist., BVS:1882:3

PLASTER, Albert, W, M, d. 15 May 1855, nr Union, consumption, 16-0-0, p. George & Mary Plaster, b. nr Union, sc: Jane Plaster, BVS:1855:5, LC:17

PLASTER, Fannie, W, F, d. 13 Jan 1892, Trappe, old age, 100-2-13, p. Geo. E. & Ann Lloyd, b. Fauquier Co., c/o: Henry Plaster, sc: Jno Ross, son-in-law, 1st Dist., BVS:1892:2

PLASTER, Henry, W, M, d. 10 Feb 1875, Snickersville, croup, 0-10-0, p. Geo. E. & Sallie M. Plaster, b. LC, physician, married, sc: Geo. E. Plaster, father, MT Dist., BVS:1875:8

PLASTER, Jane, W, F, d. 28 Aug 1886, nr Unison, old age, 92-0-0, p. John & Rebecca Copeland, b. LC, c/o: Michael Plaster, sc: Madison

Loudoun County, Virginia, Death Register, 1853-1896   207

Monroe, son-in-law, 1st Dist., BVS:1886:2

PLASTER, Michael, W, M, d. 6 Oct 1869, LC, apoplexy, 83-0-0, p. Henry & Susan Plaster, b. LC, sc: J.R. Jacobs, grandfather, BVS:1869:1

PLATER, Mary Salina, B, F, d. 15 Aug 1873, nr Unison, unk, 0-0-5, p. Edward & Eliza Plater, b. LC, sc: Edward Plater, father, MC Dist., BVS:1873:5

PLATER, Rachel, B, F, d. Jul 1871, unk, p. Mahala Plater, unm, MC Dist., BVS:1871:2

POLAND, Frank, B, M, d. 10 Sep 1880, LC, paralysis, 75-0-0, p. unk, unm, sc: Henry Hibbs, friend, 1st Dist., BVS:1880:3

POLAND, George W., W, M, d. 30 Aug 1873, Snickersville, jaundice, 0-4-4, p. Richard & Eliza Poland, b. Snickersville, sc: parents, MT Dist., BVS:1873:3

[POLAND], no name, W, M, d. 18 Nov 1873, LC, unk, 0-0-1/2, p. Robert & Mrs. Poland, b. Goshen, sc: Robt. Poland, head of family, BR Dist., BVS:1873:1

POLAND, Sharper, B, M, d. 10 Mar 1866, paralyzed, 72-0-0, sc: Wm. G. Leith, BVS:1866:2

POLAND, William A., W, M, d. 4 Apr 1857, Leesburg, water on brain, 1-5-0, p. Alex. & Margaret Poland, b. Leesburg, sc: Alexander Poland, father, BVS:1857:2, LC:25

POLEN, Mary J., W, F, d. 19 Mar 1888, LC, cancer, 50-0-0, p. James & Eliza Wadell, b. LC, none, c/o: G.W. Polen, sc: G.W. Polen, husband, 2nd Dist., BVS:1888:6

POLLARD, Lester, B, M, d. 22 Oct 1886, croup, 1-3-0, p. Gabriel & Nancy, sc: Gabriel Pollard, father, 2nd Dist., BVS:1886:5

POLLARD, Lucy, B, F, d. Dec 1893, North Fork, consumption, 23-0-0, b. LC, MT Dist., BVS:1893:4

POOL, Hugh W., W, M, d. 10 Oct 1864, Lowe's Island, drowned, 18-1-0, p. Jesse & Ann Pool, b. LC, farmer, sc: Jesse Pool, father, BVS:1864:2, LC:39

POOL, Jesse, W, M, d. 9 Apr 1882, LC, old age, 82-0-0, p. Jesse &

Catharine Pool, farmer, c/o: Maggie Pool, sc: James Pool, son, 1st Dist., BVS:1882:2

POOLE, Nancy, W, F, d. 12 Apr 1891, nr Farmwell, old age, 76-0-0, p. Arthur & Jane Ankers, b. LC, farmer, c/o: Jessie Pool, decd, sc: John Dove, son-in-law, 1st Dist., BVS:1891:2

POOLE, no name, W, M, d. 20 Jun 1883, Purcellville, unk, 0-0-1, p. Wm. H. & Louisa Poole, b. LC, sc: Wm. H. Poole, father, 3rd Dist., BVS:1883:5

POPKINS, Elizabeth, W, F, d. 13 Feb 1878, Poor House, unk, 76-0-0, b. LC, unm, sc: Wm. H. Hibbs, superintendent of the poor, MC Dist., BVS:1878:7

POPKINS, Marvin W., W, M, d. 15 Nov 1888, Waxpool, gastric fever, 3-10-0, p. Geo. W. & Laura Popkins, b. Waxpool, sc: Geo W. Popkins, father, 1st Dist., BVS:1888:4

POPKINS, Mason F., W, M, d. 1 Sep 1886, nr Farmwell, gastric fever, 0-5-15, p. Geo. W. & Laura W. Popkins, b. nr Farmwell, sc: Geo W. Popkins, father, 1st Dist., BVS:1886:2

POPKINS, Robert, W, M, d. 3 Sep 1857, nr Mountville, mania-a-potie, 22-0-0, p. ... & Elizabeth Popkins, b. Fauquier Co., stone fencer, sc: William Popkins, uncle, BVS:1857:3, LC:26

POPKINS, Sally, W, F, d. 15 Sep 1876, Poor House, consumption, 35-0-0, unm, sc: W.H. Hibbs, superintendant of poor, MC Dist., BVS:1876:5

POPKINS, Sally, W, F, d. 29 May 1877, Poor House, consumption, 22-0-0, b. LC, unm, sc: Wm. H. Hibbs, superintendent of poor, MC Dist., BVS:1877:5

PORTER, Ann Maria, W, F, d. 21 Sep 1855, Mechanicsville, unk, 2-9-0, p. Wm & Mary E. Porter, b. Fauquier Co., sc: W.A. Porter, father, BVS:1855:6, LC:17

PORTER, Elizabeth J., W, F, d. 7 Nov 1857, res of parents, consumption, 24-0-0, p. Jesse & Mary Porter, b. nr Harper's Ferry, sc: Jesse Porter, father, BVS:1857:4, LC:27

PORTER, George W., W, M, d. 10 Jan 1857, Hamilton Rogers' Farm, cold, 0-1-0, p. Wm. A. & Mary E. Porter, b. Hamilton Roger's Farm, sc: Wm. A. Porter, father, BVS:1857:4, LC:26

PORTER, George W., W, M, d. 11 Jul 1866, Bloomfield, lock jaw, 20-0-0, p. Jesse Porter, farmer, sc: Jesse Porter, father, BVS:1866:2

PORTER, Martha V., W, F, d. 8 Feb 1877, Piedmont, Fauquier Co., whooping cough, 0-2-0, p. Lewis F. & Sarah F. Porter, b. Fauquier Co., sc: Lewis F. Porter, father, MC Dist., BVS:1877:5

PORTER, Sarah F., W, F, d. 23 Dec 1889, LC, pneumonia, 38-0-0, p. W. & S. Kilby, b. LC, laborer, c/o: Lewis F. Porter, sc: Lewis T. Porter, husband, 3rd Dist., BVS:1889:5

POSTON, Flora D., W, F, d. 5 Jan 1876, Welbourne, pneumonia, 0-0-12, p. I. J. & Henrietta E. Poston, b. LC, sc: I.J. Poston, father, MC Dist., BVS:1876:5

POSTON, Susan, W, F, d. 19 Mar 1872, Upperville, paralysis, 55-4-18, c/o: William Poston, sc: William Poston, husband, MC Dist., BVS:1872:7

POTTER, Eliza A., W, F, d. 23 Feb 1884, LC, asthma, 31-0-0, p. Carlisle & Ann Waldron, b. LC, c/o: Nelson Potter, sc: Nelson Potter, husband, 1st Dist., BVS:1884:2

POTTER, George, B, M, d. 24 Jul 1883, nr Leesburg, fracture of skull, 65-0-0, p. --- Potter, b. LC, laborer, unm, sc: Chas T. Birkby, undertaker, 2nd Dist., BVS:1883:4

POTTER, John, W, M, d. 4 Nov 1878, nr Dranesville, unk, 74-0-0, p. unk, b. nr Dranesville, farmer, c/o: Margaret L. Potter, sc: Margaret L. Potter, wife, BR Dist., BVS:1878:4

POTTER, Margaret, B, F, d. 10 Dec 1875, Leesburg, inflammation of bowel, 30-0-0, b. Alexandra, Va., c/o: George Potter, sc: George Potter, husband, LE Dist., BVS:1875:2

POTTER, Martha, W, F, d. 2 Feb 1872, nr Sugarland Run, unk, 0-4-0, p. Nelson & Eliza A. Potter, b. LC, sc: Nelson Potter, BR Dist., BVS:1872:6

POTTERFIELD, Elizabeth, W, F, d. 31 Jul 1859/60, LC, old age, 79-1-10, p. Jacob & Catharine Emery, b. LC, c/o: Jacob Potterfield, sc: Mary Wiard, daughter, BVS:1859:1, 1860:4, LC:37

POTTERFIELD, Septimus, W, M, d. 25 Nov 1888, LC, malarial fever, 45-0-0, p. Samuel & Catherine Potterfield, b. LC, laborer, c/o: Alcinda Potterfield, sc: Alcinda Potterfield, widow, 2nd Dist., BVS:1888:6

POTTS, Edwin H., W, M, d. 22 Dec 1878, nr Hillsboro, tumor, 69-7-7, p. Wm. & Isabella Potts, b. LC, farmer, c/o: Mary Potts, sc: Wm. C. Potts, son, JF Dist., BVS:1878:10

POTTS, Eltore Mary, W, F, d. 7 Sep 1889, LC, unk, 0-1-13, p. Jas. W. & Mollie Potts, b. LC, none, unm, sc: J.W. Potts, father, 2nd Dist., BVS:1889:4

POTTS, F. M., W, M, d. Aug 1896, Hillsboro, dysentery, 70-0-0, farmer, consort, JF Dist., BVS:1896:8

POTTS, Helen V., W, F, d. 30 Oct 1890, Hillsboro, typhoid fever, 17-0-0, p. Jonathan & Mary D. Potts, b. LC, none, unm, sc: Jonathan Potts, father, 3rd Dist., BVS:1890:7

POTTS, John, W, M, d. 2 Feb 1884, nr Hillsboro, dropsy, 79-0-0, b. Virginia, farmer, c/o: Ruth Potts, sc: Jonathan Potts, son, 3rd Dist., BVS:1884:6

POTTS, Joseph L., W, M, d. 20 Dec 1874, Broad Run Dist., consumption, 65-0-0, p. unk, farmer, unm, sc: Miss Lowe, friend, BR Dist., BVS:1874:3

POTTS, Mary, W, F, d. 11 Feb 1885, nr Neersville, burned, 85-0-0, p. Peter & Mary Demory, b. LC, c/o: Jonas Potts, sc: Thomas W. Potts, son, 2nd Dist., BVS:1885:2

POTTS, Mary A., W, F, d. 8 Jan 1853, nr Hillsboro, abscess in side, 46-0-0, p. Jas. & Mary White, b. nr Hillsboro, c/o: Thomas Potts, sc: husband, BVS:1854:1, LC:4

POTTS, Ruth, W, F, d. 20 Feb 1884, nr Hillsboro, erysipelas, 78-0-0, b. Virginia, c/o: John Potts, sc: Jonathan Potts, son, 3rd Dist., BVS:1884:6

POTTS, Ruth C., W, F, d. 7 Sep 1 1853, LC, croup, 5-4-5, p. Edwin H.

& Julia E. Potts, b. LC, sc: Edwin W. Potts, father, BVS:1854:4, LC:2
POTTS, Sallie, W, F, d. 6 Sep 1866, nr Hillsboro, c. infantum, unk, p. Thomas & Ann E. Potts, b. LC, sc: Thompson Potts, father, BVS:1866:1
POTTS, Thomas, W, M, d. 4 Apr 1888, LC, general debility, 80-0-0, p. Joshua & Barbary Potts, b. LC, sc: Joshua O. Potts, son, 3rd Dist., BVS:1888:1
POTTS, Virginia, B, F, d. Aug 1866, White Hall, 27-0-0, sc: P.A.L. Smith, BVS:1866:2
POTTS, Willie, W, M, d. 16 Aug 1879, nr Hillsboro, measles, 0-7-28, p. Thomas W. & Mary A. Potts, b. LC, sc: Thomas W. Potts, father, 2nd Dist., BVS:1879:1
POULTON, Saml R., W, M, d. 1 Jun 1864, North Carolina, diphtheria, 21-0-0, p. Reed & Anzy Poulton, b. LC, farmer, sc: Reed Poulton, father, BVS:1864:2, LC:39
POWELL, Ada V., W, F, d. 6 May 1873, nr Leesburg, consumption, 15-0-0, p. Thomas & Elizabeth Powell, b. nr Leesburg, unm, sc: father, MT Dist., BVS:1873:3
POWELL, America V., W, F, d. 12 Feb 1884, LC, measles, 36-0-0, p. Chas. & Adaline Adams, b. LC, c/o: Thomas L. Powell, sc: Thomas L. Powell, husband, 1st Dist., BVS:1884:2
POWELL, Ann P., W, F, d. 15 Jul 1866, nr Bolington, c. infantum, 0-3-6, p. Israel G. Powell, b. LC, sc: Israel G. Powell, father, BVS:1866:1
POWELL, Cecelia, B, F, d. 15 May 1878, LC, spinal affection, 12-6-0, p. Wm. & Hannah Powell, b. LC, unm, sc: Hannah Powell, mother, LE Dist., BVS:1878:9
[POWELL], Charles B., W, M, d. 21 Aug 1855, Middleburg, cholera infantum, 0-8-0, p. F. W. & Harriet Powell, b. Middleburg, sc: F.W. Powell, father, BVS:1855:7, LC:18
POWELL, Charles E., W, M, d. 10 Jul 1892, Woodburn, cholera, 57-0-0, p. Peyton & Amelia Powell, b. LC, unm, sc: Bettie Powell, wife, MT Dist., BVS:1892:8
POWELL, Chas, W, M, d. 26 Apr 1873, nr Bolington, unk, 0-3-3, p. Israel G. & Lydia C. Powell, b. nr Bolington, farmer, married, sc: Israel G. Powell, LV Dist., BVS:1873:4
POWELL, Elizabeth, W, F, d. 20 Aug 1881, LC, croup, 0-2-20, p. J. Gurley & Lydia Powell, b. LC, sc: J.G. Powell, father, 3rd Dist., BVS:1881:4
POWELL, Esther Ann, W, F, d. 10 Oct 1858, Nancy Lumm's, consumption, 44-8-10, p. John & Nancy Lumm, b. LC, c/o: Thomas Powell, sc: Martha Carter, sister, BVS:1858:4, LC:32
POWELL, Fannie, W, F, d. 20 Oct 1890, Hamilton, typhoid fever, 18-0-0, p. I. G. & Lydie C. Powell, b. LC, none, unm, sc: I.G. Powell, father, 3rd Dist., BVS:1890:7
POWELL, Geo. E, W, M, d. 10 Feb 1884, LC, spasms, 0-1-5, p. Thomas L. & America V. Powell, b. LC, sc: Thos L. Powell, father, 1st Dist., BVS:1884:2
POWELL, James E., W, M, d. 3 Mar 1884, LC, catarrh fever, 0-4-27, p. Geo. & Alma Powell, b. LC, sc: George Powell, father, 1st Dist., BVS:1884:2
POWELL, Llewellen, W, M, d. 11 Jul 1880, Mt. Hope, Md., epilepsy, 21-0-0, p. Edward B. & Cordelial Powell, b. LC, unm, sc: E.B. Powell, father, 2nd Dist., BVS:1880:7
POWELL, Maria Louisa, W, F, d. 25 Jan 1891, Warrenton, Fauquier Co, heart trouble, 81-0-0, p. Dr. Ewell B. & Sarah Grady, b. LC, wife, unm, sc: W.L. Powell, MT Dist., BVS:1891:6
POWELL, Mary C., W, F, d. 15 Jul 1886, unk, 0-10-0, p. Lewis H. & J. L., sc: Louis H. Powell, father, 2nd Dist., BVS:1886:5
POWELL, Mary E., W, F, d. 6 Oct 1858, LC, child bed, 27-0-0, p. unk, b. LC, c/o: Thos L. Powell, sc: Peyton Powell, father-in-law, BVS:1858:1, LC:30
POWELL, Mary J., W, F, d. 27 Jul 1865, Leesburg, typhoid fever, 30-0-0, p. Wm. A. & S.P. Powell, b. Leesburg, cashier of the bank, unm, sc: Wm. A. Powell, father, 1st Dist., BVS:1865:4
POWELL, Mary J., W, F, d. 27 Jul 1865, Leesburg, typhoid fever, 30-0-0, p. Wm. A. & L.P. Powell, b.

Leesburg, cashier bank, unm, sc: Wm. A. Powell, father, BVS:1865:3

POWELL, Mary V., B, F, d. 25 Dec 1887, LC, unk, unk, p. William & Eliza Powell, b. LC, none, unm, sc William Powell, father, 2nd Dist., BVS:1887:5

[POWELL], no name, W, M, d. 1875, Lovettsville Dist, 0-1-0, p. Israel G. & Powell?, b. LC, LV Dist., BVS:1875:4

POWELL, R. L., W, M, d. 1 Sep 1887, LC, typhoid fever, 2-0-0, p. C. E. & Jane Powell, b. LC, farmer, unm, sc: O.M. Bussard, friend, 3rd Dist., BVS:1887:7

POWELL, R. R., W, M, d. 9 Dec 1883, nr Leesburg, aneurysm, 51-0-0, p. Geo. C. & Marietta Powell, b. LC, engineer, c/o: Dianna Powell, sc: Geo Carter, brother-in-law, 2nd Dist., BVS:1883:4

POWELL, Richard W., W, M, d. 16 Apr 1853, Middleburg, croup, 1-8-0, p. Frank & Hannah Powell, b. Middleburg, sc: mother, BVS:1854:1, LC:4

POWELL, Saml. L., W, M, d. 21 Oct 1891, Arcola, consumption, 25-0-0, p. Thos. L. & Mary Powell, b. LC, farmer, unm, sc: Geo O. Powell, brother, 1st Dist., BVS:1891:2

POWELL, Sarah Jane, W, F, d. 17 Oct 1871, nr Leesburg, consumption, 42-0-0, p. Joseph & Emily Lacock, b. LC, farmer, c/o: Thomas L. Powell, sc: Thomas L. Powell, husband, MT Dist., BVS:1871:5

POWELL, William, W, M, d. 10 Nov 1886, nr Sudley, kidney disease, 68-0-0, p. unk, b. nr Daysville, farmer, unk, sc: Geo Powell, son, 1st Dist., BVS:1886:2

POWELL, William, B, M, d. Sep 1873, Leesburg, whooping cough, 1-6-0, p. Ann Powell, b. Leesburg, unm, sc: Anne Powell, mother, LE Dist., BVS:1873:2

POWER, Ada, W, F, d. 30 Apr 1892, Farmwell, consumption, 24-0-0, p. H. H. & Jane Bodine, b. Farmwell, c/o: Rev. A. Power, sc: Rev. A. Power, husband, 1st Dist., BVS:1892:2

POWER, Annie G., W, F, d. 30 Jul 1865, nr Goose Creek, diarrhea, 1-12, p. Robt W. & M.S. Power, b. LC, unm, sc: Robt W. Power, father, BVS:1865:2

POWER, Arminda, W, F, d. 25 Aug 1888, Farmwell, old age, 78-0-0, p. Thos & Nancy Gheen, b. Farmwell, sc: John T. Richard, son-in-law, 1st Dist., BVS:1888:4

POWER, Carrie, W, F, d. 22 Apr 1892, Farmwell, measles, 21-0-0, p. Chas. J. & Sallie Power, b. Farmwell, unm, sc: Jno W. Power, brother, 1st Dist., BVS:1892:2

POWER, Chas., W, M, d. 1 May 1892, Farmwell, measles, 45-0-0, p. Robt. & Arminda Power, b. Farmwell, laborer, c/o: Sallie Power, sc: Jno W. Power, son, 1st Dist., BVS:1892:2

POWER, Jos. T., W, M, d. 25 Apr 1892, Farmwell, measles, 23-0-0, p. Chas. J. & Sallie Power, b. Farmwell, laborer, unm, sc: Jno W. Power, brother, 1st Dist., BVS:1892:2

POWER, Juniette, W, F, d. 25 Aug 1875, nr Goose Creek, drowned, 1-6-6, p. Robt W. & Margaret A. Power, b. LC, sc: R.W. Power, father, BR Dist., BVS:1875:5

POWER, Margaret, W, F, d. 15 Nov 1876, nr Mt. Hope Church, dropsy, 20-0-0, p. Robt & Arminda Power, b. LC, sc: Robert Power, father, BR Dist., BVS:1876:2

POWER, Margaret A., W, F, d. 25 Aug 1875, nr Goose Creek, drowned, 0-0-10, p. Robt W. & Margaret A. Power, b. LC, sc: R.W. Power, father, BR Dist., BVS:1875:5

PRALL, Mary F., W, F, d. 12 Sep 1858, LC, unk, 56-0-0, p. Ariss & Lucy Buckner, b. LC, sc: S. Ariss Buckner, brother, BVS:1858:6, LC:33

PRESGRAVE, Richd H., W, M, d. 20 Jan 1865, Elmira, NY, general debility, 56-1-0, p. Richd & Ann Presgraves, b. LC, farmer, consort, sc: E.A. Presgrave, wife, BVS:1865:2

PRESGRAVES, Albt. C., W, M, d. 18 May 1893, Mountville, diphtheria, 7-0-0, p. S. C. & Presgraves, b. Mountville, sc: S.C. Presgraves, father, 1st Dist., BVS:1893:1

PRESGRAVES, Ann A/K., W, F, d. 20 Dec 1859/60, LC, burned, 2-0-0, p. R.H. & Eliza A. Presgraves, b. LC, sc: R. Presgraves, husband, BVS:1859:6, 1860:3, LC:36

PRESGRAVES, Edith L., W, F, d. 27 Mar 1885, nr Pleasant Valley, scarlet fever, 7-0-0, p. John T. & Sarah E. Presgraves, b. nr Pleasant Valley, sc: John T. Presgrave, father, 1st Dist., BVS:1885:4

PRESGRAVES, Nancy, W, F, d. 7 Sep 1858, LC, old age, 78-0-0, p. unk, b. LC, sc: Susan Ambler, neighbor, BVS:1858:6, LC:33

PRESGRAVES, Wm. R., W, M, d. 20 Apr 1889, Mountville, old age, 85-0-0, p. John & Rebecca Presgraves, b. LC, farmer, c/o: Mary Presgraves, sc: Jas R. Presgraves, son, 1st Dist., BVS:1889:1

PRESTON, Adeline, W, F, d. 29 Feb 1894, Hamilton, pneumonia, 35-0-0, p. Zenith & Sarah Milburn, b. LC, sc: Charles W. Preston, brother, 3rd Dist., BVS:1894:5

PRESTON, Aral G., W, F, d. 18 Mar 1894, Hamilton, pneumonia, 1-0-14, p. Edgar T. & Ada Preston, b. Hamilton, sc: Edgar T. Preston, father, 3rd Dist., BVS:1894:5

PRESTON, John, W, M, d. 25 Dec 1881, LC, cramp colic, 40-0-0, p. Thos. & Jan Preston, b. LC, unm, sc: Thos Preston, father, 3rd Dist., BVS:1881:4

PRESTON, Mary E., W, F, d. 27 Jul 1886, LC, heart disease, 53-0-0, p. Landon & Ann Beatty, b. LC, c/o: Geo W. Preston, sc: Geo W. Preston, husband, 3rd Dist., BVS:1886:4

[PRESTON], no name,W, F, d. 5 Jun 1858, Purcellville, whooping cough, 0-1-1, p. Chas W. & Lydia A. Preston, b. Purcellville, sc: C.W. Preston, father, BVS:1858:4, LC:32

PRICE, Rosella, B, F, d. Oct 1896, Hillsboro, rheumatism, 65-0-0, consort, sc: Philip Moten, JF Dist., BVS:1896:10

PRICE, S. C., W, F, d. 12 Jan 1880, nr Lovettsville, child birth, 33-0-0, p. Jno. & Rebecca A. Cockrell, b. Warren Co. VA, c/o: Russell Price, sc: Russell Price, husband, 2nd Dist., BVS:1880:7

PRIEST, Sallie, B, F, d. 1 Jul 1887, LC, cholera infantum, 0-6-0, p. Lucy Priest, b. LC, none, unm, sc: Lucy Priest, mother, 2nd Dist., BVS:1887:5

PRIM, Sophia, W, F, d. Jul 1857, unk, 70-0-0, p. James & Henrietta Prim, b. LC, sc: Jonathan Lewis, friend, BVS:1857:7, LC:28

PRINCE, Alice, B, F, d. 4 Feb 1883, nr Leesburg, consumption, 25-0-0, p. Millie Ayles, b. LC, laborer, unm, sc: Henry Cully, friend, 2nd Dist., BVS:1883:4

PROCTOR, Edgar F., W, M, d. 20 Jun 1882, LC, unk, 26-0-0, p. Edgar & Cath. Proctor, Laborer, unm, sc: Cath. Proctor, mother, 1st Dist., BVS:1882:2

PROCTOR, Hannah, W, F, d. 9 Mar 1880, LC, old age, 80-0-0, p. unk, b. LC, widow, sc: Harriet Proctor, daughter, 1st Dist., BVS:1880:2

PROSER, Mary, W, F, d. 4 Oct 1875, nr Aldie, consumption, 83-0-0, p. Jacob & Susan Ish, b. LC, married, sc: E. Ish, friend, BR Dist., BVS:1875:5

PURCELL, Harriett N., W, F, d. 24 Aug 1892, Purcellville, paralysis, 60-0-0, p. Jonathan & Patience Healey, b. Woodgrove, married, sc: Rodney Purcell, husband, JF Dist., BVS:1892:7

PURCELL, Samuel, W, M, d. 8 Aug 1855, Woodgrove, old age, 75-0-0, p. Thos. & Lydia Purcell, b. Hillsboro, miller, sc: Lydia V. Chamblin, sister, BVS:1855:7, LC:18

PURSELL, James Heaton, W, M, d. 12 Dec 1869, LC, pneumonia, 0-6-0, b. LC, sc: James H. Pursell, father, BVS:1869:1

PURSELL, Julia, W, F, d. 17 Dec 1869, LC, measles, 2-0-0, p. Franklin & Mary Pursell, b. LC, sc: Franklin Pursell, father, BVS:1869:1

[QUICK], Sarah Jane, W, F, d. 1 Oct 1855, Jas. Best's farm, croup, 4-0-0, p. Armsd. & Margt. Quick, b. Jas. Best's farm, sc: Armst. Quick, father, BVS:1855:7, LC:18

RACE, Sally, W, F, d. 25 Sep 1858, LC, consumption, 60-0-0, p. Job & Elizabeth Race, b. LC, unm, sc: Nancy Race, sister, BVS:1858:6, LC:33

RACE, William, W, M, d. 14 Sep 1857, unk, 54-0-0, p. Job & Elizth Race, b. LC, sc: T.W. Newman, friend, BVS:1857:7, LC:28

RADCLIFFE, Ann M., W, F, d. 11 Jan 1875, Waterford, unk, 77-0-0, p. Henry & Ann Taylor, b. LC, c/o: Thos. Radcliff, sc: Mary Radcliff, daughter, JF Dist., BVS:1875:3

RADLEY, William L., W, M, d. 29 Oct 1881, LC, killed on rail road, 44-0-0, p. Peter & ___ Radley, b. New York, Brakeman, c/o: Esther A. Radley sc: Jno. J. Stephens, brother-in-law, 2nd Dist., BVS:1881:7

RALLS, Jane, W, F, d. Mar 1857, Charles Byrne's, 68-0-0, sc: Charles Byrne, son, BVS:1857:6, LC:28

RAMEY, James M., W, M, d. 27 Jun 1857, res of parents, erysipelas, 1-4-2, p. Wm. & Ellen Ramey, b. place of death, sc: Wm. C. Ramey, father, BVS:1857:4, LC:27

RAMSEY, John, W, M, d. 12 Dec 1857, LC, dropsy, 66-0-0, p. unk, b. Prince George, farmer, c/o: Elizth Ramsey, sc: Samuel C.E. Ramsey, son, BVS:1857:1, LC:24

RAMSEY, no name, W, M, d. 11 Oct 1887, Rectortown, whooping cough, 1-1-0, p. James W. & Martha A. Ramsey, b. Fauquier Co., sc: James W. Ramsey, father, 1st Dist., BVS:1887:1

RANDALL, Annie, B, F, d. 12 Oct 1881, LC, cold, 0-1-0, p. Chas & Annie Randall, b. LC, sc: Chas. Randall, father, 2nd Dist., BVS:1881:7

RANDALL, Eliza, B, F, d. 20 Apr 1894, Sycolin, unk, 0-3-0, p. Chas. & Betsy, b. Sycolin, unm, sc: Chas Randall, LE Dist., BVS:1894:3

RANDALL, Elizabeth, B, F, d. 11 Sep 1880, Leesburg, cold, 0-4-4, p. Charles & Elizth. Randall, b. LC, unm, sc: Charles Randall, father, 2nd Dist., BVS:1880:7

RANDALL, Maria, B, F, d. 19 May 1896, LC, whooping cough, 1-5-0, p. Chas. & Bettie Randall, b. LC, sc: father, LE Dist., BVS:1896:5

RANDALL, Maria, B, F, d. 1 Sep 1875, Leesburg, heart disease, 76-0-0, sc: Matilda Randall, grand-daughter, LE Dist., BVS:1875:2

RANDOLPH, Fenton L., B, M, d. 21 Feb 1884, Leesburg, dropsy, 26-0-0, p. --- & Alcinda Randolph, b. LC, laborer, c/o: Ellen Randolph, sc: Helen Brown, mother-in-law, 2nd Dist., BVS:1884:5

[RANDOLPH], no name,(f), F, d. 7 Jan 1858, Poor House, smothered, 0-1-0, p. Sarah Randolph, b. Poor House, sc: W. Furr, steward, BVS:1858:3, LC:31

RANDOLPH, no name, B, M, d. 12 Jan 1873, Dover, still born, unk, p. Josephine Randolph, b. nr Aldie, sc: Robt E. Russell, employer, MC Dist., BVS:1873:5

RANDOLPH, no name, B, M, d. 6 Feb 1884, Leesburg, unk, 0-0-6, p. Fenton L. & Ellen Randolph, b. LC, sc: Helen Brown, grandmother, 2nd Dist., BVS:1884:5

[RANDOLPH], no name, B, F, d. 23 Jun 1885, Aldie, unk, 0-0-5, p. Alsy Randolph (unm), b. Aldie, sc: Sarah Washington, grandmother, 1st Dist., BVS:1885:4

RANDOLPH, Susan P., W, F, d. 29 Oct 1884, LC, paralysis, 75-0-0, p. Addison B. & Mary Armstead, b. Winchester, unk, sc: Susan Randolph, daughter, 1st Dist., BVS:1884:2

RANSELL, Amanda B., B, F, d. 7 Jan 1886, nr Aldie, consumption, 7-0-0, p. Edward & Rena Ransell, b. nr Aldie, unm, sc: Edward Ransell, father, 1st Dist., BVS:1886:2

RANSELL, Cora L., W, F, d. 12 Feb 1885, Aldie, pneumonia, 0-10-0, p. Edward & Rena Ransell, b. nr Aldie, sc: Edward Ransell, father, 1st Dist., BVS:1885:4

RANSELL, Jno. W., B, M, d. 8 Apr 1892, Aldie, colic, 0-0-5, p. Edwd. & Irene Ransell, b. Aldie, laborer, unm, sc: Irene Ransell, mother, 1st Dist., BVS:1892:4

RANSOM, Geo. H., B, M, d. 10 Oct 1893, nr Aldie, cholera infantum, 0-5-0, p. Edwd. & Irene Ransom, b. nr

Aldie, c/o: Edwd Ransom, sc: Edwd Ransom, father, 1st Dist., BVS:1893:2

RATCLIFFE, Emily, W, F, d. 20 Jun 1891, Philomont, paralysis, 72-0-0, b. Rappahannock Co., farmer, c/o: Wm. Ratcliff, sc: Wm. Ratcliff, husband, 1st Dist., BVS:1891:2

RATCLIFFE, Henrietta, B, F, d. 23 Feb 1884, LC, measles, 0-11-0, p. Richard & Marietta Ratcliffe, b. LC, sc: Richard Ratcliffe, father, 1st Dist., BVS:1884:2

RATCLIFFE, R. H., B, M, d. 4 Jul 1894, nr Arcola, spasms, 0-4-28, p. R. H. & Henrietta Ratcliffe, b. nr Arcola, sc: R.H. Ratcliff, father, 1st Dist., BVS:1894:2

RATCLIFFE, Richd. H., B, M, d. 24 Dec 1891, Arcola, unk, 4-6-0, p. R. H. & Henrietta Ratcliffe, b. LC, farmer, unm, sc: Henrietta Ratcliffe, head of family, 1st Dist., BVS:1891:1

RATHIE, Cora K., B, F, d. 23 Aug 1875, Leesburg, heart disease, 14-11-0, p. Jno Rathie & Ann Bell, b. Leesburg, sc: T.E.A. Russell, friend, LE Dist., BVS:1875:2

RATHIE, Elizabeth, W, F, d. 15 Aug 1873, nr Gum Spring, consumption, 70-0-0, p. unk, b. LC, c/o: John Rathie, sc: John M. Rathie, son, BR Dist., BVS:1873:1

RATHIE, John B., W, M, d. 20 Nov 1893, Leesburg, dropsy, 72-0-0, p. unk, b. Leesburg, painter, consort, sc: Sallie P. Rathie, LE Dist., BVS:1893:6

RATHIE, Joseph L., W, M, d. 3 Jan 1884, Leesburg, paralysis, 73-0-0, p. Jno B. & Elizabeth Rathie, b. LC, painter, c/o: Mary E. Rathie, sc: Geo W. Rupp, friend, 2nd Dist., BVS:1884:5

RATHIE, Mary E., W, F, d. 24 Mar 1876, Leesburg, paralysis, 53-0-0, p. Catharine Garner, b. Leesburg, c/o: Joseph L. Rathie, sc: Catharine Garner, mother, LE Dist., BVS:1876:7

[RATHIE], no name, W, M, d. 11 Sep 1854, LC, unk, 0-0-12, p. Benj. D. & Sarah D. Rathie, b. Leesburg, sc: Benj. D. Rathie, father, BVS:1854:10, LC:9

RAWLINGS, John M., W, M, d. 28 Jul 1884, LC, shot, 28-0-0, p. John M. & Ann V. Rawlings, b. LC, farmer, c/o: Mary Rawlings, sc: John M. Rawlings, father, 1st Dist., BVS:1884:2

RAWLINGS, Lucinda, W, F, d. 5 Dec 1864, Union, dropsy, 67-0-0, p. Reuben & ... Strother, b. Fauquier Co., c/o: Wm. Rawlings, sc: Andrew Robey, nephew, BVS:1864:1, LC:38

REAMER, John H., W, M, d. 29 Sep 1884, LC, cholera infantum, 0-4-0, p. Christian & Emma Reamer, b. LC, sc: Christian Reamer, father, 1st Dist., BVS:1884:2

RECTOR, George H., W, M, d. 15 Aug 1866, Short Hill, fall from a horse, 10-0-0, p. Geo. H. & Eliz. Rector, b. nr Short Hill, sc: George H. Rector, father, BVS:1866:2

RECTOR, Sarah, W, F, d. 19 Mar 1878, nr Hillsboro, cancer, 25-11-26, p. Geo. H. & Elizabeth Rector, b. LC, unm, sc: Geo. H. Rector, father, JF Dist., BVS:1878:10

REDD, Emma A., W, F, d. 18 Nov 1885, Aldie, consumption, 22-0-0, p. Joseph S. & Martha S. Kidd, b. Aldie, unm, sc: Joseph S. Redd, father, 1st Dist., BVS:1885:4

REDD, Joseph, W, M, d. 5 Mar 1887, Aldie, cancer of stomach, 62-0-0, p. John & Sarah Redd, b. Frederick Co. [Va.], merchant, c/o: Martha Redd, sc: Martha Redd, wife, 1st Dist., BVS:1887:1

REDMAN, Alice A., B, F, d. 29 Jul 1878, LC, consumption, 19-8-11, p. Amos & Lenora Redman, b. LC, unm, sc: Serina Redman, mother, LE Dist., BVS:1878:8

REDMAN, Amanda, B, F, d. Nov 1896, Hillsboro, consumption, 71-0-0, b. Hillsboro, consort, sc: son, JF Dist., BVS:1896:10

REDMAN, George W., B, M, d. 22 Mar 1889, LC, typhoid fever, 79-0-0, p. Geo. W. & Mary E. Redman, b. LC, laborer, c/o: Mary E. Redman, sc: Jas F. Redman, son, 3rd Dist., BVS:1889:5

REDMAN, Herbert, W, M, d. 20 Sep 1885, Fauquier Co, unk, 0-1-20, p. Samuel D. & Rose Redman, b.

Middleburg, sc: Samuel D. Redman, father, 1st Dist., BVS:1885:5

REDMAN, Julia, W, F, d. 14 Apr 1880, nr Leesburg, consumption, 16-2-0, p. Saml. & Catharine Redman, b. Fairfax Co., Va., unm, sc: Saml Redman, father, 2nd Dist., BVS:1880:7

REDMAN, Mary E., W, F, d. 22 Aug 1889, LC, consumption, 38-0-0, p. John W. & Sarah E. Hall, b. LC, none, c/o: Douglass Redman, sc: D. Redman, husband, 2nd Dist., BVS:1889:4

REDMON, Sarah, W, F, d. 24 May 1890, nr Sterling, consumption, 24-0-0, p. Daniel & Eliza Blundell, b. LC, c/o: Edward Redman, sc: Daniel Blundell, father, 1st Dist., BVS:1890:2

REED, Bettie R., W, F, d. 18 Sep 1881, LC, tumor, 21-0-0, p. Thos. & Sarah A. Reed, b. LC, sc: F.O. Reed, brother, 1st Dist., BVS:1881:2

REED, Harmon, W, M, d. 30 May 1885, Purcellville, bright's disease, 69-4-0, b. LC, farmer, c/o: Hannah Reed, sc: John Reed, son, 3rd Dist., BVS:1885:6

REED, Henry, W, M, d. 6 Aug 1877, LC, dysentery, 66-0-0, b. Montgomery Co., Md., farmer, c/o: Susan Catharine Reed, sc: Susan C. Reed, wife, LV Dist., BVS:1877:4/7

REED, James S., W, M, d. 2 Sep 1853, LC, dysentery, 2-4-15, p. Harmon & Rosanna Reed, b. LC, sc: Harmon Reed, father, BVS:1854:4, LC:2

REED, John Milton, W, M, d. 28 Jul 1876, Millville, pneumonia, 48-7-24, b. LC, miller, c/o: Sarah A. Reed, sc: James Reed, son, MC Dist., BVS:1876:5

REED, Mary, W, F, d. 6 Jul 1869, LC, cancer, 76-0-0, p. Joseph & Mary Reed, b. LC, married, sc: Jackson Reed, son, BVS:1869:1

REED, no name, W, M, d. 10 Jun 1880, Snickersville, unk, 0-0-10, p. Oscar & Sarah Reed, b. LC, sc: Sarah Reed, mother, 3rd Dist., BVS:1880:4

REED, no name, W, F, d. 9 Jun 1890, nr Unison, unk, 0-0-1, p. Thos. Y. &

Elizabeth Reed, b. LC, sc: Thos J. Reed, father, 1st Dist., BVS:1890:2

REED, Presley, W, M, d. 1 Jui 1887, LC, rheumatism, 55-0-0, p. Joseph & Sallie Reed, b. LC, mechanic, c/o: Sallie Reed, sc: John L. Reed, son, 3rd Dist., BVS:1887:7

REED, Presly C., W, M, d. 14 Jan 1892, Philomont, swallowed a cent, 2-10-0, p. Jos. W. & Margaret A. Reed, b. Philomont, sc: Jos W. Reed, father, 1st Dist., BVS:1892:2

REED, Robert, W, M, d. 10 Aug 1880, LC, pneumonia, 35-0-0, p. unk, unm, sc: Benj. F. Hibbs, friend, 1st Dist., BVS:1880:3

REED, Rosanna H., W, F, d. 24 Jun 1883, Purcellville, unk, 58-0-0, p. Wm. H. & Louisa Poole, b. LC, c/o: Harmon Reed, sc: Harman Reed, husband, 3rd Dist., BVS:1883:5

REED, Sarah, W, F, d. 20 Nov 1853, Hillsboro, unk, 76-0-0, p. Andrew & Elizabeth Reed, b. LC, unm, sc: Joshua Reed, brother, BVS:1854:6, LC:5

REED, Thomas, W, M, d. 17 Dec 1854, LC, hemorrhage of lungs, 53-9-17, p. Wm. & Phebe Reed, b. England, miner, c/o: Isabella Reed, sc: Isabella Reed, wife, BVS:1854:8, LC:8

REED, Virginia, W, F, d. 9 Sep 1881, LC, pneumonia, 48-0-0, b. LC, c/o: Charles Reed, sc: W.S. Green, friend, 1st Dist., BVS:1881:2

REED, Wm., W, M, d. 27 Dec 1853, LC, inflammation brain, 11-2-0, p. Thomas & Isabella Reed, b. England, sc: Isabella Reed, mother, BVS:1854:4, LC:2

REEDER, Gourley, W, M, d. 1875, nr Silver Springs, paralysis, unk, p. Wm. & Mary Reeder, b. LC, farmer, sc: Wm. A. Reeder, son, MT Dist., BVS:1875:8

REEDER, Mary, W, F, d. 5 Mar 1864, Girisley Reeder's, heart disease, 36-0-0, p. Wm. & Ruth Ewers, b. LC, c/o: Wm. A. Reeder, sc: Wm. A. Reeder, husband, BVS:1864:1, LC:38

REESE, Emanuel, W, M, d. 29 Aug 1891, Lovettsville, diabetes, 63-0-0, p. unk, b. nr Lovettsville, mechanic,

Loudoun County, Virginia, Death Register, 1853-1896 215

consort, sc: wife, LV Dist., BVS:1891:5

REEVES, John F., W, M, d. 14 Apr 1888, LC, consumption, 48-0-0, p. Walter & Nancy Reeves, b. LC, merchant, c/o: Lydia C. Reeves, sc: Lydia C. Reeves, widow, 2nd Dist., BVS:1888:6

REEVES, Walter C., W, M, d. 11 Oct 1872, LC, dropsy, 78-0-0, p. unk, b. Prince William Co., farmer, c/o: Nancy A. Reeves, sc: John F. Reeves, son, LE Dist., BVS:1872:4

REMUS, Mary A., B, F, d. 3 Jul 1876, Leesburg, brain fever, 6-3-0, p. Henry & Hannah Remus, b. Leesburg, sc: Hannah Remus, mother, LE Dist., BVS:1876:7

RHODES, Geo. W., W, M, d. 23 Sep 1892, Upperville, typhoid fever, 23-0-0, p. Jno. & Celia Rhodes, b. Leesburg, laborer, c/o: Annie Rhodes, sc: John Rhodes, father, 1st Dist., BVS:1892:2

RHODES, H. A., W, F, d. 5 Jan 1881, LC, consumption, 26-0-0, p. J. K. & Mary A. Rhodes, b. LC, unm, sc: J. R. Rhodes, brother, 2nd Dist., BVS:1881:7

RHODES, Mary A., W, F, d. 19 Dec 1892, Upperville, typhoid fever, 13-0-0, p. Jno. & Celia Rhodes, b. Leesburg, unm, sc: John Rhodes, father, 1st Dist., BVS:1892:2

RHODES, Parmelia, B, F, d. 2 Mar 1879, LC, unk, 0-0-2, p. Burr & Mary Rhodes, b. LC, sc: Burr Rhodes, father, 3rd Dist., BVS:1879:3

RHODES, Randolph, W, M, d. 3 Aug 1857, his res, chronic rheumatism, 87-0-0, p. Tholemiah & Mary Rhodes, b. nr Aldie, c/o: Mary Rhodes, decd, sc: Fanny Leith, daughter, BVS:1857:3, LC:26

RICE, Elizabeth, W, F, d. 7 Aug 1853, LC, intermittent fever, 24-11-13, p. Ezra & Ellen Bolon, b. LC, c/o: David J. Rice, sc: David J. Rice, husband, BVS:1854:5, LC:3

RICHARDS, Barton, W, M, d. 3 Apr 1877, Unison, paralysis, 77-8-3, b. LC, farmer, c/o: Maria Richards, sc: Levin Richards, nephew, MC Dist., BVS:1877:5

[RICHARDS], Delia Elizabeth, B, F, d. 10 Oct 1872, Mount Gilead Twp.,

unk, 5-0-0, p. Silas & Anna Richards, b. Mount Gilead Town, unm, sc: Silas Richards, father, MT Dist., BVS:1872:2

RICHARDS, Evaline, W, F, d. 14 May 1855, nr Bloomfield, typhoid fever, 34-11-0, p. Jno. & Margt. Jenkins, b. nr Bloomfield, c/o: Levin Richards, sc: Levin Richards, widower, BVS:1855:5, LC:17

RICHARDSON, Eliza, B, F, d. 10 May 1890, Woodburn, croup, 0-4-0, p. W. & Alice Richardson, b. LC, none, unm, sc: W. Richardson, father, 3rd Dist., BVS:1890:7

RICHEY, Ann Bell, W, F, d. 8 Aug 1865, nr Taylorstown, dysentery, 4-0-0, p. John & Ann Richey, b. Taylorstown, market man, sc: John W. Richey, father, 1st Dist., BVS:1865:3/4

RICHEY, Mary Ellen, W, F, d. 30 Dec 1865, nr Taylorstown, whooping cough, 2-0-0, p. John & Ann Richey, b. Taylorstown, Market Man, sc: John W. Richey, father, 1st Dist., BVS:1865:3/4

RICHIE, Catherine, W, F, d. 4 Jul 1888, LC, paralysis, 67-0-0, p. unk, b. LC, none, c/o: Geo Richie, sc: Geo Richie, husband, 2nd Dist., BVS:1888:6

RICHIE, John, W, M, d. 15 Sep 1890, LC, consumption, 68-0-0, p. Soloman Richie, b. LC, none, unm, sc: Samuel Smith, nephew, 2nd Dist., BVS:1890:4

RICHIE, Philip, W, M, d. Jun 1896, Morrisonville, old age, 94-0-0, distiller, consort, JF Dist., BVS:1896:8

RIDENBAUGH, John W., W, M, d. 7 Oct 1888, LC, r r accident, 22-0-0, p. Geo. W. & Susan Ridenbaugh, b. LC, laborer, unm, sc: Henry Jones, step-father, 2nd Dist., BVS:1888:6

RIDENBAUGH, no name, W, F, d. 1 Aug 1889, LC, cholera infantum, 0-4-0, p. Geo. & Lizzie Ridenbaugh, b. LC, none, unm, sc: Geo Ridenbaugh, father, 2nd Dist., BVS:1889:4

RIDEOUT, Jefferson, B, M, d. 1865, Edwd D. Potts', consumption, 1-0-0, p. Charity Rideout, b. E.D. Potts', sc: E.D. Potts, BVS:1865:1

RIDGEWAY, George H., W, M, d. 6 Jul 1874, brain fever, 1-0-0, p. Wm F. & Frances Ridgway, LV Dist., BVS:1874:6

RIDGEWAY, James W., W, M, d. 8 Jan 1884, nr Lovettsville, typhoid fever, 22-0-0, p. James W. & Susan Ridgeway, b. LC, laborer, unm, sc: Jas W. Ridgeway, father, 2nd Dist., BVS:1884:5

RIDGEWAY, Nellie C., W, F, d. 12 Mar 1892, Bolington, brain fever, 2-3-0, p. Saml. & Jennie, b. LC, unm, sc: S. R. Ridgeway, LV Dist., BVS:1892:6

[RIDGEWAY], no name, B, M, d. 15 Jun 1854, Union, 0-0-1, p. Rom R. & Elizabeth Ridgway, b. Union, sc: R. R. & E. Ridgeway, BVS:1854:11, LC:10

RIDGEWAY, Sarah E., W, F, d. 1 Jun 1888, LC, paralysis, 68-0-0, p. James & Mary Ridgeway, b. LC, none, unm, sc: James Ridgeway, brother, 2nd Dist., BVS:1888:6

RIDGWAY, James, W, M, d. 10 May 1858, M.N. Union, pneumonia, 77-3-1, p. James & Susan Ridgway, b. Philadelphia, laborer, sc: Benjamin Ridgway. son, BVS:1858:3, LC:31

RILEY, Ann R., W, F, d. 31 Oct 1886, LC, softening of brain, 65-0-0, p. --- & Susan Crim, b. LC, c/o: John Riley, sc: Annie B. Riley, daughter-in-law, 2nd Dist., BVS:1886:6

RILEY, Betsey, (f), F, d. 30 Dec 1855, LC, consumption, 73-0-0, p. unk, b. unk, sc: Jacob Bantz, son-in-law, BVS:1855:2, LC:15

RILEY, George, B, M, d. 8 Dec 1877, nr Guilford Station, croup, 2-0-0, p. Chas. Riley & wife, b. nr Guilford Station, unm, sc: Chas. Riley, father, BR Dist., BVS:1877:1

RILEY, Napoleon B., W, M, d. 12 Aug 1865, nr Hamilton, dysentery, 12-0-0, p. Isaac & Adaline Riley, b. nr Hamilton, laborer, sc: Isaac Riley, father, 1st Dist., BVS:1865:3/4

RILEY, Neal, B, M, d. 10 Aug 1882, LC, unk, 0-7-0, p. Ann Riley, unm, sc: Ann Riley, mother, 1st Dist., BVS:1882:2

RILEY, Richard, W, M, d. 10 May 1855, LC, paralyzed, 70-0-0, p. unk, b. unk, c/o: Elizabeth Riley, sc: Sarah A. Harrison, daughter, BVS:1855:2, LC:15

RILEY, Robert, W, M, d. 2 Jul 1884, Woodburn, unk, 0-1-0, p. Saml. & Susan Riley, b. Mountville, unm, sc: Saml Riley, father, 3rd Dist., BVS:1884:7

RILEY, Robert E., W, M, d. 1 May 1886, Harpers Ferry WV, drowned, 24-0-0, p. John & Ann, b. LC, laborer, unm, sc: Annie B. Riley, sister-in-law, 2nd Dist., BVS:1886:6

RILEY, Rosa Bell, W, F, d. 20 Nov 1865, nr Hamilton, dysentery, 0-18-0, p. Isaac & Adaline Riley, b. nr Hamilton, laborer, sc: Isaac Riley, father, BVS:1865:3

RILEY, Rosa Bell, W, F, d. 20 Mar 1865, nr Hamilton, dysentery, 0-18-0, p. Isaac & Adaline Riley, b. nr Hamilton, laborer, sc: Isaac Riley, father, 1st Dist., BVS:1865:4

RILEY, Virginia, B, F, d. 7 Feb 1884, Leesburg, old age, 97-0-0, p. unknown, b. LC, laborer, c/o: John Riley, sc: Hilleary Carrington, friend, 2nd Dist., BVS:1884:5

RILEY, William, W, M, d. 16 Jul 1877, Bloomfield, old age, 90-9-1, b. Page Co., farmer, c/o: Julia Riley, sc: Julia Riley, wife, MC Dist., BVS:1877:5

RINKER, Ann, W, F, d. 6 Mar 1877, LC, consumption, 65-0-0, p. John & Mary Lumbaugh, b. LC, c/o: Thomas Rinker, sc: Thos. Rinker, husband, JF Dist., BVS:1877:3

RINKER, Asa J., W, M, d. 4 Sep 1876, Leesburg, diphtheria, 3-5-0, p. James F. & Susan J. Rinker, b. Leesburg, sc: James F. Rinker, father, LE Dist., BVS:1876:7

RINKER, Charles, W, M, d. 6 May 1891, Waterford, consumption, 44-0-0, p. Thomas & Annie Rinker, b. Waterford, husband, sc: Annie Rinker, JF Dist., BVS:1891:7

RINKER, Ernest L., W, M, d. 15 Jul 1872, Waterford, cold & croup, 0-11-13, p. George E. & Massa Rinker, b. Waterford, mechanic, sc: George C. Rinker, father, JF Dist., BVS:1872:1

RINKER, Susan, W, F, d. 14 Oct 1890, LC, old age, 76-0-0, p. unk, b. LC, none, c/o: John Rinker, sc: J.A. Rinker, son, 2nd Dist., BVS:1890:4

RITCHIE, Virginia Gray, W, F, d. 4 Jul 1876, nr Taylorstown, sun stroke, 29-0-0, p. Geo M. & Catharine Ritchie, b. LC, unm, sc: Geo M. Ritchie, father, LV Dist., BVS:1876:3

RITICOR, Charles, W, M, d. 29 Jun 1877, Aldie, dropsy of the bladder, 78-11-3, b. LC, farmer, c/o: Susan Riticor, sc: Jno. Riticor, son, MC Dist., BVS:1877:5

RITICOR, Charles Alexander, W, M, d. 14 Feb 1873, nr Aldie, typhoid, 35-0-0, p. John & Eliza Riticor, b. nr Aldie, farmer, unm, sc: John Riticor, father, MC Dist., BVS:1873:5

RITICOR, Chas. F., W, M, d. 7 Feb 1890, LC, measles, 1-6-0, p. Chas. F. & Constance Riticor, b. LC, merchant, unm, sc: C.F. Riticor, father, 2nd Dist., BVS:1890:4

RITICOR, Elizabeth Jane, W, F, d. 3 Jul 1877, nr Aldie, bilious dysentery, 68-0-0, b. LC, c/o: Jno. Riticor, sc: Jno. Riticor, husband, MC Dist., BVS:1877:5

RITICOR, Malinda, W, F, d. 26 Jul 1882, LC, paralysis, 74-0-0, p. Jno. Malinda Riticor, unm, sc: Zylpha Riticor, sister, 1st Dist., BVS:1882:2

RITICOR, Susan, B, F, d. 25 Oct 1885, Aldie, heart disease, 71-0-0, p. --- Moss, b. LC, c/o: Chas Riticor, sc: John T. Riticor, son, 1st Dist., BVS:1885:4

RIVERS, Mary, B, F, d. 1 Sep 1881, LC, dropsy, 70-0-0, p. Danl. & ___ Saunders, b. LC, laborer, c/o: Elias Rivers, sc: Elias Rivers, husband, 2nd Dist., BVS:1881:7

ROACH, James, W, M, d. 10 Jan 1854, LC, dyspepsia, 60-0-24, p. James & Elizabeth Roach, b. LC, farmer, unm, sc: Smith Reed, head of the family, BVS:1854:8, LC:8

ROACH, Phebe E., W, F, d. Aug 1854, bilious dysentery, 8-0-0, p. Daniel & Ann Roach, b. LC, sc: Wesley Roach, uncle, BVS:1854:13, LC:13

ROANE, Maude N., B, F, d. 15 Apr 1896, LC, consumption, 24-0-0, p. Thos. & Roberta Waters, b. LC, wife, sc: Roberta Waters, mother, JF Dist., BVS:1896:6

ROBERSON, James H, B, M, d. 18 Jun 1885, Middleburg, pneumonia, 0-9-0, p. Henry & Margaret Roberson, b. Middleburg, sc: Henry Roberson, father, 1st Dist., BVS:1885:5

ROBERSON, Martha, B, F, d. 20 Mar 1888, Mountville, consumption, 16-0-0, p. Alfred & Elizabeth Roberson, b. Mountville, sc: Sanford Grooms, bro-in-law, 1st Dist., BVS:1888:4

ROBERSON, Nellie, B, F, d. 4 Feb 1885, Mount Gilead, croup, 2-0-0, p. Wm. & Alice Roberson, b. LC, sc: Wm. Roberson, father, 1st Dist., BVS:1885:4

ROBERTS, Landon, W, M, d. 5 Feb 1893, Waterford, kidney trouble, 76-0-0, p. Jonah & Sarah Roberts, b. LC, miller, husband, sc: sister, JF Dist., BVS:1893:3

ROBERTSON, Jane B., W, F, d. 20 Aug 1854, LC, consumption, 65-0-0, p. Robert Beverly, b. Bradfield, Essex Co., unm, sc: John M. Orr, friend, BVS:1854:10, LC:9

ROBERTSON, Seth D., W, M, d. 11 Nov 1853, LC, disease of kidneys, 48-10-19, p. Jno. & Elizabeth Robertson, b. unk, ferryman, c/o: Elizabeth M. Robertson, sc: Elizabeth M. Robertson, daughter, BVS:1854:2, LC:1

ROBEY, Alpheus A., W, M, d. 22 Jul 1877, nr Philomont, dysentery, unk, p. F. E. & Martha Robey, b. LC, sc: F.E. Robey, father, MT Dist., BVS:1877:2

ROBEY, Annie E., W, F, d. 10 Apr 1874, nr Mountville, brain fever, 0-1-0, p. Jno. W. & Emma F. Robey, b. LC, sc: Jno. W. Robey, father, MC Dist., BVS:1874:4

ROBEY, Jane, W, F, d. 11 Nov 1854, Union, paralysis, 70-0-0, p. Thomas Blandon, b. Fairfax, probably, c/o: Michael Roby, decd, sc: Andrew Roby, son, BVS:1854:12, LC:12

ROBEY, Lucinda, W, F, d. Mar 1853, Union, congestion of brain, 0-14-0, p. Andrew & Martha Robey, b. Union, sc: father, BVS:1854:1, LC:4

ROBEY, Mildred, W, F, d. 6 Dec 1884, LC, consumption, 50-0-0, p. Carr B. & Sarah A. Nalls, b. LC, c/o: John F. Robey, sc: Carr B. Nalls, father, 1st Dist., BVS:1884:2

ROBEY, Sarah E., W, F, d. 19 Apr 1893, nr Paris, consumption, 50-0-0,

p. Robt & Mary Leonard, b. Fauquier Co., wife, c/o: W.S. Robey, sc: W.S. Robey, husband, 1st Dist., BVS:1893:1

ROBEY, William O., B, M, d. 21 Sep 1888, LC, dyspepsia, 72-0-0, p. unk, b. LC, minister, unm, sc: Mary Harris, daughter, 2nd Dist., BVS:1888:6

ROBINSON, Harry, B, M, d. 17 Dec 1886, LC, whooping cough, 0-1-15, p. Noble & Alice Robinson, b. LC, sc: Noble Robinson, father, 3rd Dist., BVS:1886:4

ROBINSON, Herbert, B, M, d. 10 Nov 1886, LC, whooping cough, 1-10-0, p. Noble & Alice Robinson, b. LC, sc: Noble Robinson, father, 3rd Dist., BVS:1886:4

ROBINSON, Lizzie, B, F, d. 15 Oct 1881, LC, hemorrhage of lungs, 38-0-0, b. LC, c/o: Albert Robinson, sc: A. Robinson, husband, 1st Dist., BVS:1881:2

ROBINSON, Lucy, B, F, d. 12 Jun 1873, nr Purcell Factory, whooping cough, 2-2-0, p. Alfred & Elizabeth Murry, b. nr Purcell factory, sc: parents, MT Dist., BVS:1873:3

ROBINSON, Nancy, B, F, d. 2 May 1884, Waterford, asthma, 80-0-0, b. Virginia, c/o: Wm. Robinson, sc: Noble Robinson, son, 3rd Dist., BVS:1884:7

ROBINSON, no name, B, M, d. 30 May 1878, nr Newington, pneumonia, 0-2-29, p. Alfred & Lizzie Robinson, b. LC, sc: Alfred Robinson, father, MC Dist., BVS:1878:7

ROBINSON, Rebecca, B, F, d. 10 Jun 1873, nr Purcell Factory, whooping cough, 3-3-0, p. Alfred & Elizabeth Murry, b. nr Purcell factory, sc: parents, MT Dist., BVS:1873:3

ROBINSON, William A., B, M, d. 13 Jun 1873, nr Purcell Factory, whooping cough, 0-11-0, p. Alfred & Elizabeth Murry, b. nr Purcell factory, sc: parents, MT Dist., BVS:1873:3

ROBINSON, Willie, B, M, d. 22 Sep 1880, LC, diphtheria, 0-9-0, p. Henry & Margaret Robinson, b. LC, unm, sc: Margaret Robinson, mother, 1st Dist., BVS:1880:3

ROBISON, Anne B., B, F, d. 25 Dec 1882, LC, consumption, 4-0-0, p. Daniel & Mary Robison, sc: Daniel Robison, father, 1st Dist., BVS:1882:2

ROBISON, Bell, B, F, d. 25 Mar 1885, nr Daysville, scarlet fever, 4-0-0, p. Fayette & Fannie Robison, b. nr Daysville, sc: Fayette Robison, father, 1st Dist., BVS:1885:4

ROBISON, Danl., B, M, d. 17 Jan 1891, Unison, heart failure, 56-0-0, p. unk, b. unk, unk, c/o: Sarah Robison, sc: Sarah Robison, head of family, 1st Dist., BVS:1891:1

ROBISON, Emma, B, F, d. 22 Dec 1883, nr Leesburg, unk, 0-0-6, p. Wm. & Emily Robison, b. LC, sc: Ernest Robison, brother, 2nd Dist., BVS:1883:4

ROBISON, Henry, B, M, d. 5 Dec 1893, nr Sterling, constipation, 70-0-0, p. unk, b. LC, laborer, c/o: Francis Robison, sc: Francis Robison, wife, 1st Dist., BVS:1893:2

ROBISON, John, B, M, d. 15 Oct 1896, Middleburg, whooping cough, 5-0-0, p. Henry & M. Robison, b. Middleburg, none, unm, sc: Henry Robison, father, MC Dist., BVS:1896:2

ROBISON, Lucy, B, F, d. 30 May 1894, nr Leithtown, consumption, 20-0-0, p. Squire & Lucy Robison, b. nr Leithtown, sc: Squire Robison, father, 1st Dist., BVS:1894:2

ROBISON, Nellie, B, F, d. 1 Mar 1889, LC, pneumonia, 1-0-0, p. W. & Alice Robison, b. LC, none, unm, sc: W. Robison, father, 3rd Dist., BVS:1889:5

ROBISON, Sallie, B, F, d. 1 Mar 1889, LC, pneumonia, 0-0-2, p. W. & Alice Robison, b. LC, none, unm, sc: W. Robison, father, 3rd Dist., BVS:1889:5

ROBY, Charles F., (f), M, d. 13 Feb 1857, Leesburg, unk, 0-10-11, p. Wm. & Rachel A. Roby, b. Leesburg, sc: William Robey, father, BVS:1857:2, LC:25

ROBY, Mary Jane, W, F, d. 10 Apr 1855, Greengarden, typhoid fever, 24-0-0, p. Wm Stephin Ross, b. on Blue Ridge, c/o: Alex. Robey, sc:

Loudoun County, Virginia, Death Register, 1853-1896   219

Alex. Robey, widower, BVS:1855:4, LC:17

ROBY, Rachel A., (f), F, d. 24 Aug 1857, Leesburg, consumption, 26-0-12, p. Wm. & Emily Watson, b. LC, c/o: William Roby, sc: William Robey, husband, BVS:1857:2, LC:25

ROBY, William, W, M, d. 1859/60, his res, suicide, 45-0-0, b. nr Union, farmer, c/o: Mary S. Robey, sc: M. S. Roby, widow, BVS:1859:5, 1860:3, LC:36

ROBY, Wm. H., W, M, d. 11 Aug 1858, Union, croup, 3-10-6, p. Andrew J. & Martha C. Robey, b. Union, sc: Martha E. Robey, mother, BVS:1858:3, LC:31

RODERICK, Fannie, W, F, d. 9 May 1886, paralysis of heart, 26-0-0, p. Wm. & Harriet Hough, c/o: Wm. L. Roderick, sc: Wm. L. Roderick, husband, 2nd Dist., BVS:1886:5

RODERICK, Robert L., W, M, d. 21 Sep 1883, nr Lovettsville, spasms, 0-7-1, p. Wm. L. & Mary C. Roderick, b. LC, sc: Jacob R. Roderick, grandfather, 2nd Dist., BVS:1883:4

RODERICK, Robert L., W, M, d. 22 Sep 1883, nr Lovettsville, spasms, 0-7-1, p. William L. & Frances Roderick, b. LC, sc: Jacob R. Roderick, grandfather, 2nd Dist., BVS:1883:7

ROGERS, A. H., W, M, d. 10 Apr 1894, Roanoake, Va., consumption, 32-0-0, p. A. H. & Julia Rogers, b. Woodburn, engineer, sc: A.H. Rogers, father, 3rd Dist., BVS:1894:5

ROGERS, Arthur F., W, M, d. 13 Sep 1871, Middleburg, apoplexy, 35-0-0, married, sc: Charlotte Rogers, MC Dist., BVS:1871:2

ROGERS, Chas. H., W, M, d. 7 Apr 1853, LC, scarlet fever, 11-0-5, p. Thos. & Elmina S. Rogers, b. LC, sc: Elmina S. Rogers, mother, BVS:1854:4, LC:3

ROGERS, Ernest B., W, M, d. Jun 1864, nr Mount Gilead, drowned, 7-0-0, p. S.P. & Susan E. Rogers, b. LC, sc: S.P. Rogers, father, BVS:1864:1, LC:39

ROGERS, George, W, M, d. Jun 1858, nr Mount Gilead, pneumonia, 6-0-0, p. S.P. & Susan E. Rogers, b. place of death, sc: S.P. Rogers, father, BVS:1858:4, LC:31

ROGERS, Hamilton, W, M, d. 20 Aug 1882, LC, heart disease, 82-0-0, p. W. H. & Mary Rogers, b. LC, farmer, c/o: Mary Rogers, sc: Mary Rogers, wife, 1st Dist., BVS:1882:1

ROGERS, Henry, W, M, d. 20 Aug 1887, LC, malaria fever, 23-0-0, p. Hugh & Sallie Rogers, b. LC, farmer, sc: Powell Rogers, brother, 3rd Dist., BVS:1887:7

ROGERS, Lillian, W, F, d. 15 Mar 1877, Aldie, unk, 0-0-1, p. Jesse S. & M. A. Rogers, b. LC, sc: Jesse S. Rogers, father, MC Dist., BVS:1877:5

ROGERS, Margt, W, F, d. 27 Apr 1864, Mount Pleasant, unk, 77-2-0, p. Jas & A. Hixson, b. Prince William Co., c/o: Sanford Rogers, sc: Sanford Rogers, husband, BVS:1864:1, LC:38

ROGERS, Milton M., W, M, d. 30 Oct 1889, Dover, inflammatory rheumatism, 48-0-0, p. Wm. H. & Jane Rogers, b. LC, farmer, c/o: Mollie H. Rogers, sc: Mollie H. Rogers, wife, 1st Dist., BVS:1889:1

ROGERS, Nancy H., W, F, d. 11 Aug 1886, nr Middleburg, heart disease, 70-0-0, p. Jessie & Elizabeth McVeigh, b. LC, c/o: Richard L. Rogers, sc: Richard L. Rogers, husband, 1st Dist., BVS:1886:2

ROGERS, Robert, W, M, d. 11 Sep 1869, LC, erysipelas, 26-0-0, b. LC, farmer, unm, sc: aunt, BVS:1869:1

ROGERS, Ruth, W, F, d. 12 Dec 1874, Dover, heart disease, 48-0-0, b. LC, c/o: Wm. Rogers, sc: Mollie Rogers, daughter, MC Dist., BVS:1874:4

ROGERS, Thomas, W, M, d. 17 Dec 1853, LC, pneumonia, 60-4-0, p. Hamilton & Dinah Rogers, b. LC, farmer, c/o: Elmina S. Rogers, sc: Elmina S. Rogers, wife, BVS:1854:4, LC:3

ROLISON, Bessie A., W, F, d. 1 Sep 1888, LC, unk, 0-9-0, p. Philip & Emma Rollins [sic], b. LC, none, unm, sc: Philip Rollison, father, 2nd Dist., BVS:1888:6

ROLLINS, Ada Gray, W, , d. 1 Sep 1877, Leesburg, cholera infantum,

0-11-3, p. Jas. H & M. A. Rollins, b. LC, sc: Jas. H. Rollins, father, LE Dist., BVS:1877:9

ROLLINS, Ann A., W, F, d. Sep 1873, Leesburg, child birth, 35-0-0, b. Leesburg, c/o: Chas. E. Rollins, sc: C.E. Rollins, husband, LE Dist., BVS:1873:2

ROLLINS, Chas. U., W, M, d. 1 Dec 1866, Leesburg, water on the brain, 2-0-0, p. Chas. & Mary Rollins, b. LC, sc: Chas. Rollins, father, BVS:1866:1

ROLLINS, Clifton M., W, --, d. 12 Mar 1889, LC, consumption, 8-0-0, p. Saml W. & Laura Rollins, b. LC, none, c/o: none, sc: S.W. Rollins, father, 2nd Dist., BVS:1889:4

ROLLINS, Harry M., W, M, d. 23 Dec 1881, LC, cholera infantum, 1-7-0, p. Saml. & Laura Rollins, b. LC, sc: Saml M. Rollins, father, 2nd Dist., BVS:1881:7

ROLLINS, Hattie W., W, F, d. 28 Sep 1875, Leesburg, scrofula, 11-1-0, p. Lewis F. & May J. Rollins, b. Leesburg, sc: Mary J. Rollins, mother, LE Dist., BVS:1875:2

ROLLINS, Lewis, W, M, d. 21 Aug 1857, Charles Shreve's Farm, bilious dysentery, 60-0-0, p. Rhodes & Nancy Rawlings, b. Hagerstown, MD, miller, c/o: Margaret M. Rawlings, sc: widow, BVS:1857:3, LC:25

ROLLISON, John C., W, M, d. 15 Jul 1876, LC, congestion of lungs, 28-0-0, p. William & Henrietta Rollison, b. LC, laborer, sc: William Rollison, father, LE Dist., BVS:1876:7

ROLLISON, Mary, W, F, d. 18 Nov 1896, Lovettsville, pneumonia, 7-0-0, p. Phillip & Emma, b. Lovettsville, unm, sc: Phillip Rollison, LV Dist., BVS:1896:7

ROOF, John, W, M, d. 28 Jun 1881, LC, old age, 88-0-0, p. John & Margaret Roof, b. LC, farmer, c/o: Elizabeth Roof, sc: Amanda Roof, daughter, 2nd Dist., BVS:1881:7

ROPP, Samuel, W, M, d. 26 Aug 1886, heart disease, 73-0-0, p. Nicholas & ___ Ropp, farmer, c/o: Rachel Ropp, sc: Geo. A. Ropp, son, 2nd Dist., BVS:1886:5

ROSE, Alexander W., W, M, d. 14 Apr 1877, nr Frankville, consumption, 24-1-0, p. Geo. W. & Mary F. Rose, b. unk, carpenter, unm, sc: Mary F. Rose, mother, BR Dist., BVS:1877:1

ROSE, Jas. W., W, M, d. 13 Jan 1892, Ryan, consumption, 63-0-0, p. Jno. W. & Kitty Rose, b. Leesburg, laborer, unm, sc: M.F. Nixon, sister, 1st Dist., BVS:1892:2

ROSE, Maria, W, F, d. 12 Jul 1885, nr Arcola, old age, 78-0-0, p. Geo. & Elizabeth Rose, b. Virginia, unm, sc: Jane Rose, sister, 1st Dist., BVS:1885:4

ROSE, Mary, W, F, d. 10 Jun 1892, Waxpool, consumption, 68-0-0, p. unk, b. Fairfax, c/o: Geo Rose, sc: F.E. Rose, son, 1st Dist., BVS:1892:2

ROSE, Ruth W., W, F, d. 18 Feb 1854, LC, consumption, 28-8-0, p. John W. & Kitty S. Rose, b. LC, sc: Kitty S. Rose, mother, BVS:1854:14, LC:13

ROSS, Amanda, W, F, d. 30 Mar 1885, nr Trappe, consumption, 52-0-0, p. Herrod & Mary A. Thomas, b. nr Trappe, c/o: John T. Ross, sc: John T. Ross, husband, 1st Dist., BVS:1885:5

ROSS, Ann, W, F, d. 21 Apr 1857, John Ross', dropsy, 71-0-0, p. John & Agness Ross, b. Frederick Co., sc: John Ross, brother, BVS:1857:4, LC:27

ROSS, John, W, M, d. 21 Feb 1876, foot of Blue Ridge, pneumonia, 87-11-13, b. Clarke Co., farmer, c/o: Susan Ross, sc: Wm. H. Ross, son, MC Dist., BVS:1876:5

ROSS, John W., W, M, d. 9 May 1857, LC, unk, 0-0-21, p. Simon M. & Sarah A. Ross, b. LC, sc: Simon M. Ross, father, BVS:1857:1, LC:25

ROSS, John Wm., W, M, d. 8/28 Mar 1859/60, res of parents, congestion of brain, 0-2-0, p. James & Mary J. Ross, b. nr Union, sc: James F. Ross, father, BVS:1859:5, 1860:3. LC:36

ROSS, Joseph, W, M, d. 15 Aug 1887, Trappe, consumption, 28-0-0, p. John & Amanda Ross, b. Trappe, farmer, unm, sc: John T. Ross, father, 1st Dist., BVS:1887:1

ROSS, Martha A., W, F, d. 11 Mar 1885, Trappe, consumption, 16-0-0, p. John T. & Amanda Ross, b. nr Trappe, unm, sc: John F. Ross, father, 1st Dist., BVS:1885:4

ROSS, Sallie, W, F, d. 29 Jun 1892, Trappe, apoplexy, 83-0-0, p. John & Agnes Ross, b. Old Country, unm, sc: J. T. Ross, brother, 1st Dist., BVS:1892:2

ROSZEL, Lucy B., W, F, d. 29 Mar 1859/60, LC, cold, 0-0-12, p. Saml S. & Julia A.B. Roszel, b. LC, sc: Saml S. Roszel, father, BVS:1859:1, 1860:4, LC:37

ROSZEL, Phebe, W, F, d. 20 Jan 1856, res on Beaverdam, erysipelas, 78-0-0, p. Stephen & Sarah Roszel, b. place of death, sc: Frances Shepherd, BVS:1856:5, LC:22

ROY, no name, B, F, d. 18 Dec 1883, Leesburg, unk, 0-0-1, p. Spencer & Martena Roy, b. LC, sc: Spencer Roy, father, 2nd Dist., BVS:1883:7

[ROYSTEN], no name, B, M, d. Jul 1896, Round Hill, dysentery, 0-4-0, p. W. & N. Roysten, b. Round Hill, sc: father, JF Dist., BVS:1896:10

ROYSTON, Eliza, B, F, d. 16 Apr 1880, Round Hill, consumption, 16-0-0, p. Thornton & Priscilla Royston, b. LC, unm, sc: Priscilla Royston, mother, 3rd Dist., BVS:1880:4

ROYSTON, James C., W, M, d. 20 Dec 1893, Leesburg, diphtheria, 9-0-0, p. Geo. & Annie, b. Leesburg, unm, sc: Geo Royston, LE Dist., BVS:1893:6

ROYSTON, Thornton, B, M, d. 26 Dec 1882, LC, consumption, 46-0-0, c/o: Priscilla Royston, sc: Priscilla Royston, wife, 3rd Dist., BVS:1882:3

RUNNER, William N., B, M, d. 10 Jun 1884, LC, unk, 14-0-0, p. William & Mary F. Runner, b. LC, sc: William Runner, father, 1st Dist., BVS:1884:2

RUSE, Alice M., W, F, d. 11 Jul 1859/60, Lovettsville, unk, 0-4-0, p. Emanuel & Harriet A. Ruse, b. Lovettsville, sc: Emanual Ruse, father, BVS:1859:1, 1860:4, LC:37

RUSE, Laney E., W, F, d. 25 Aug 1858, LC, unk, 0-8-20, p. Emanuel & Hannah Ruse, b. LC, sc: Harriet Ruse, mother, BVS:1858:1, LC:29

RUSE, William, W, M, d. 15 Jul 1856, res, nr Hamilton, constipation of bowel, 32-0-0, p. Solomon & Tabitha Ruse, b. nr Hamilton, farmer, c/o: Louisa Ruse, sc: Solomon Ruse, father, BVS:1856:4, LC:22

RUSK, Anna M., W, F, d. 23 Aug 1889, LC, dysentery, 52-0-0, p. John & Casandra Nixon, b. LC, none, c/o: Manly Rusk, sc: Manly Rusk, husband, 2nd Dist., BVS:1889:4

RUSK, Jno. J., W, M, d. 11 Dec 1877, - - Mill, rupture of the bowels, 51-0-0, b. LC, farmer, c/o: Susan M. Rusk, sc: Jno. T. Rusk, son, MC Dist., BVS:1877:5

RUSK, Mary A. C., W, F, d. 23 Jul 1896, Pleasant Valley, catarrh of stomach, 0-10-0, p. Ham. & Mary Rusk, b. Pleasant Valley, sc: Ham. Rusk, father, BR Dist., BVS:1896:3

RUSK, Molly H., W, --, d. 25 Aug 1889, LC, dysentery, 1-7-0, p. Manly & Maria Rusk, b. LC, none, c/o: none, sc: Manly Rusk, grandfather, 2nd Dist., BVS:1889:4

RUSK, Samuel, W, M, d. 17 Mar 1881, LC, old age, 85-0-0, b. LC, farmer, c/o: Margie Rusk, sc: M. Rusk, wife, 1st Dist., BVS:1881:2

RUSK, Susan C., W, F, d. 19 Dec 1880, LC, consumption, 39-0-0, p. Samuel & Marizee Rusk, b. LC, unm, sc: Marizee Rusk, mother, 1st Dist., BVS:1880:2

RUSK, Susan M., W, F, d. 20 Dec 1882, LC, consumption, 51-0-0, p. John & Sallie Riticor, c/o: Jno. T. Rusk, sc: Jno T. Rusk, husband, 1st Dist., BVS:1882:2

RUSS, George, B, M, d. 11 Jul 1883, Leesburg, unk, 0-7-4, p. Geo. & Frances Russ, b. LC, sc: Geo Russ, father, 2nd Dist., BVS:1883:7

RUSS, Joseph S., B, M, d. 30 Nov 1886, LC, unk, 1-5-0, p. Geo. H. & Frances, b. LC, sc: Geo. H. Russ, father, 2nd Dist., BVS:1886:6

RUSS, Louisa, B, F, d. 4 Aug 1896, Ketoctin Mountain, consumption, 22-0-0, p. Chra. Russ, b. LC, sc: Edmund Parke, uncle, MT Dist., BVS:1896:9

RUSS, Mary V., B, F, d. 6 Feb 1884, Leesburg, heart disease, 0-3-27, p. Geo. H. & Frances Russ, b. LC, sc:

Geo H. Russ, father, 2nd Dist., BVS:1884:5

RUSSELL, Annie, W, F, d. Nov 1883, nr Lovettsville, unk, 0-1-21, p. Jas. G. & Martha Russell, b. LC, sc: Jas G. Russell, father, 2nd Dist., BVS:1883:4

RUSSELL, Etheline, W, , d. 8 May 1877, LC, paralysis, 87-6-0, sc: Saml Shipman, friend, LE Dist., BVS:1877:9

RUSSELL, G. W., W, M, d. 13 Apr 1894, Waterford, heart trouble, 75-0-0, p. Wm. & Caroline Russell, b. Waterford, farmer, husband, sc: Wm. Russell, son, 3rd Dist., BVS:1894:5

RUSSELL, Georgia L., W, F, d. 5 Mar 1883, nr Lovettsville, unk, 14-0-0, p. Geo. B. & Mary A. Russell, b. LC, sc: Geo B. Russell, father, 2nd Dist., BVS:1883:7

RUSSELL, Harriet, W, F, d. 1 Sep 1853, nr Hamilton, dysentery, 4-9-0, p. Caleb & Elizabeth Russell, b. R.B. factory, sc: mother, BVS:1854:6, LC:5

RUSSELL, John, W, M, d. 19 Oct 1853, LC, rheumatism, 40-7-10, p. Robt. & Elizabeth Russell, b. LC, farmer, c/o: Amanda Russell, sc: Amanda Russell, wife, BVS:1854:4, LC:2

RUSSELL, John G., W, M, d. 18 Oct 1881, LC, malarial fever, 2-8-7, p. Geo. R. & Alice A. Russell, b. LC, sc: Geo. R. Russell, father, 2nd Dist., BVS:1881:7

RUSSELL, Lucy E., W, F, d. 29 May 1880, Leesburg, heart disease, 59-0-0, p. Thomas & Ellen Russell, b. LC, unm, sc: Anne J. Beales, sister, 2nd Dist., BVS:1880:7

RUSSELL, Martin L., W, M, d. 17 May 1880, nr Lovettsville, unk, 0-0-1, p. George R. & Alice Russell, b. LC, unm, sc: George R. Russell, father, 2nd Dist., BVS:1880:7

RUSSELL, Robert E., W, M, d. 10 Sep 1891, Dover, dysentery, 57-0-0, p. Thadeus & Catherine Russell, b. LC, farmer, c/o: Mary E. Russell, sc: Brewis Russell, son, 1st Dist., BVS:1891:2

RUSSELL, Susan A, W, F, d. 12 Jun 1866, brain fever, 3-9-0, p. Robt. E. & Ellen Russell, sc: Robt E. Russell, father, BVS:1866:2

RUSSELL, Wm., W, M, d. 17 Jun 1874, nr Dover, chronic diarrhea, 0-3-0, p. Robt E & Ellen Russell, b. LC, sc: Robt. E. Russell, father, MC Dist., BVS:1874:4

RUSSELL, Wm., W, M, d. 3 Sep 1872, nr Waterford, unk, 30-0-0, p. unk, b. nr Waterford, farmer, widower, sc: Wm. H. Russell, son, LV Dist., BVS:1872:5

RUST, Armistead T. M., W, M, d. 17 Jul 1887, LC, unk, 67-0-0, p. George & Maria Rust, b. LC, farmer, c/o: Ida L. Rust, sc: Ida L. Rust, widow, 2nd Dist., BVS:1887:5

RUST, Eliza S., W, F, d. 13 Feb 1858, LC, dropsy, 29-3-7, p. John W. & Mary K. Lawrence, b. LC, c/o: A.T.M. Rust, sc: A.T.M. Rust, husband, BVS:1858:1, LC:30

RUST, George, B, M, d. 1 May 1875, Oatlands, consumption, 21-0-0, p. James & Susan Rust, b. Oatlands, farmer, sc: James Rust, father, MT Dist., BVS:1875:8

RUST, Lizzie, B, F, d. 25 Aug 1875, Oatlands, consumption, 25-0-0, p. James & Susan Rust, b. Oatlands, farmer, sc: James Rust, father, MT Dist., BVS:1875:8

RUST, Margaret, W, F, d. 2 Jun 1887, LC, heart disease, 52-0-0, p. Michael & Elizabeth Sanbower, b. LC, none, c/o: Manly Rust, sc: John J. Roderick, son-in-law, 2nd Dist., BVS:1887:5

RUST, Maria, B, F, d. 8 Feb 1881, LC, consumption, 13-0-0, p. James & Susan Rust, b. LC, sc: James Rust, father, 2nd Dist., BVS:1881:7

RUST, Phebe, B, F, d. 1 May 1879, nr Oatlands, consumption, 22-0-0, p. James & Susan Rust, b. LC, sc: Susan Rust, mother, 2nd Dist., BVS:1879:1

RUST, Samuel, B, M, d. 1 May 1878, LC, spinal affection, 3-0-0, p. James & Susan Rust, b. LC, unm, sc: James Rust, father, LE Dist., BVS:1878:8

RYAN, Alfred, W, M, d. 15 May 1857, Leesburg, measles, 1-2-0, p. Alfred & Catharine T. Ryan, b. Leesburg,

Loudoun County, Virginia, Death Register, 1853-1896   223

sc: Alfred Ryan, father, BVS:1857:2, LC:25

RYAN, Alpheus, W, M, d. 23 Aug 1853, Leesburg, consumption, 1-6-0, p. Alfred & Emaline Ryan, b. Leesburg, sc: Alfred Ryan, father, BVS:1854:5, LC:3

RYAN, Edward, W, M, d. 30 Jan 1879, LC, paralyzed, 80-0-0, p. Christian & Rebecca Ryan, b. LC, farmer, c/o: Jane Ryan, sc: Wilson Barrett, nephew, 3rd Dist., BVS:1879:3

RYAN, Frederic, W, M, d. 16 Jul 1871, congestion of the lungs, 0-2-12, p. J. W. & M. E. Ryan, BR Dist., BVS:1871:3

RYAN, James H., W, M, d. 10 May 1871, congestion of the lungs, 2-0-0, p. J. W. & M. E. Ryan, BR Dist., BVS:1871:3

RYAN, Laura O., W, F, d. May 1860, Jefferson, unk, 1-3-0, p. Thos D. & Laura Ryan, b. LC, sc: M.A. Ryan, aunt, BVS:1860:3

[RYAN], no name, W, M, d. 10 Jul 1872, nr Gum Spring, unk, 0-0-1/2, p. J. Wm. & Mary E. Ryan, b. LC, sc: J. Wm. Ryan, head of family, BR Dist., BVS:1872:6

RYON, Beulah, W, F, d. 10 Aug 1879, Leesburg, cholera infantum, 1-10-10, p. Theodore & Ann F. Ryon, b. LC, sc: Theodore Ryan, father, 2nd Dist., BVS:1879:1

RYON, Jno. H., W, M, d. 26 Dec 1875, Leesburg, paralysis, 55-0-0, restaurant keeper, c/o: Ann Ryon, sc: Ann Ryon, wife, LE Dist., BVS:1875:2

RYON, Laura C., W, F, d. May 1859, Jefferson, unk, 1-3-0, p. Thos D. & Laura Ryon, sc: Margaret Ryan, aunt, BVS:1859:6, LC:36

RYON, Susan A, W, F, d. 6 Jan 1880, Leesburg, consumption, 52-0-0, p. -- Solomon, b. LC, c/o: John Ryon, sc: Jas. E. Ryon, nephew, 2nd Dist., BVS:1880:7

SAFFEL, Sela Jane, W, F, d. Sep 1878, Philomont, summer complaint, 0-9-2, p. Henry W. & Mary F. Saffel, b. Philomont, sc: H. W. Saffel, father, MT Dist., BVS:1878:2/3

SAFFER, Rosa B., W, F, d. 2 Dec 1886, nr Aldie, heart disease, 22-0-0, p. Wm. T. & Emma R. Saffer, b. nr Aldie, unm, sc: Wm. T. Saffer, father, 1st Dist., BVS:1886:2

SAFFER, Susan, W, F, d. 14 Oct 1874, Broad Run Dist., asthma, 79-3-0, p. unk, b. Prince William Co., c/o: Wm. Saffer, sc: Benj. Saffer, son, BR Dist., BVS:1874:3

SAFFER, Viola D., W, F, d. 25 Feb 1886, nr Aldie, pneumonia, 1-10-26, p. Wm. T. & Emma R. Saffer, b. nr Aldie, unm, sc: Wm. T. Saffer, father, 1st Dist., BVS:1886:2

SAFFLE, Mary J., W, F, d. 8 Jul 1855, nr North Fork Church, unk, 23-4-14, p. Fielding & H. Tavenner, b. nr Philomont, c/o: Thos. Saffle, sc: Fielding Tavenner, father, BVS:1855:5, LC:17

SAFFLE, Thos., W, M, d. 8 Aug 1894, Unison, spasms, 0-6-0, p. H. W. & Bettie Saffle, b. Unison, sc: H.W. Saffle, father, 1st Dist., BVS:1894:1

SAGLE, Catherine, W, F, d. 20 Aug 1854, LC, dysentery, 67-2-17, p. Henry & Darcus Sagle, b. LC, unm, sc: Eliza A. Sagle, sister-in-law, BVS:1854:9, LC:8

SAGLE, Charles E., W, M, d. 12 Aug 1854, LC, dysentery, 0-6-7, p. Michl. & Eliza A. Sagle, b. LC, sc: Eliza A. Sagle, mother, BVS:1854:9, LC:8

SAGLE, Michael, W, M, d. 15 Aug 1854, LC, dysentery, 53-7-9, p. Henry & Darcus Sagle, b. LC, farmer, c/o: Eliza A. Sagle, sc: Eliza A. Sagle, wife, BVS:1854:9, LC:8

SANBOWER, Elizabeth, W, F, d. 13 Jul 1885, nr Lovettsville, old age, 84-9-0, p. unk, b. LC, c/o: Simon Sanbower, sc: Simon Sanbower, son, 2nd Dist., BVS:1885:2

SANBOWER, John H., W, M, d. 14 Dec 1887, LC, unk, 0-0-1, p. John H. & Emily Sanbower, b. LC, none, unm, sc: Emily Sanbower, mother, 2nd Dist., BVS:1887:5

SANBOWER, John W., W, M, d. 5 Jul 1884, nr Lovettsville, 61-8-7, p. Adam & Christina Sanbower, b. LC, farmer, c/o: Fannie E. Sanbower, sc: Fannie E. Sanbower, wife, 2nd Dist., BVS:1884:5

SANBOWER, Lucinda, W, F, d. 30 Apr 1875, Lovettsville Dist, dropsy, unk, b. LC, LV Dist., BVS:1875:4

SANBOWER, Mary E., W, F, d. Feb 1877, LC, paralysis, 55-0-0, p. Adam Sanbower, b. LC, unm, sc: George W. Sanbower, brother, LV Dist., BVS:1877:4/7

SANBOWER, Mary E., W, F, d. 5 Dec 1890, LC, unk, 66-1-28, p. Jonathan & M. Cost, b. LC, none, c/o: Simeon Sanbower, sc: Simon Sanbower, husband, 2nd Dist., BVS:1890:4

SANBOWER, Michael, W, M, d. 28 Mar 1884, nr Lovettsville, old age, 86-9-13, p. John & Ann Sanbower, b. LC, farmer, c/o: Elizabeth Sanbower, sc: Elizabeth Sanbower, wife, 2nd Dist., BVS:1884:5

SANBOWER, Odie, W, F, d. 13 May 1887, LC, croup, 2-7-0, p. John H. & Emily Sanbower, b. LC, none, unm, sc: Emily Sanbower, mother, 2nd Dist., BVS:1887:5

SANBOWER, Simon, W, M, d. 26 Jun 1893, Lovettsville, bright's disease, 64-0-0, p. unk, b. Lovettsville, consort, sc: Florence Sanbower, LV Dist., BVS:1893:5

SANBOWER, Thomas, W, M, d. 10 Aug 1890, LC, unk, 66-0-0, p. Geo. Sanbower, b. LC, farmer, c/o: Rachel Sanbower, sc: Rachael Sanbower, widow, 2nd Dist., BVS:1890:4

SANDERS, Beverly, W, M, d. 9 Aug 1879, nr Goresville, consumption, 30-10-10, p. Wilson C. & Sarah Sanders, b. LC, clerk, sc: Wilson C. Sanders, father, 2nd Dist., BVS:1879:1

SANDERS, George, W, M, d. 25 Aug 1873, LC, unk, 88-0-0, p. unk, b. nr Gum Spring, farmer, married, sc: John Sanders, son, BR Dist., BVS:1873:1

SANDERS, Nellie, W, F, d. 26 Nov 1876, Leesburg, diphtheria, 2-6-0, p. Lewis H. & Mollie Sanders, b. Leesburg, sc: John B. Sanders, uncle, LE Dist., BVS:1876:7

SANDERS, Thomas J., B, M, d. 17 Oct 1876, Leesburg, spinal disease, 21-0-0, p. Daniel & Letty Sanders, b. Leesburg, laborer, sc: Kate Luckett, sister, LE Dist., BVS:1876:7

SANDERS, Wilson C., W, M, d. 23 Aug 1885, nr Goresville, bilious colic, 74-1-13, p. Britton & Mary Sanders, b. LC, farmer, c/o: Sarah A. Sanders, sc: Sarah A. Sanders, wife, 2nd Dist., BVS:1885:2

SANDS, Jonah, W, M, d. 10 Aug 1858, his res, old age, 83-0-0, p. ...Sands, b. LC, farmer, c/o: Sarah Sands, sc: Sarah Sands, widow, BVS:1858:5, LC:32

SANFORD, Sarah J., W, F, d. 30 Dec 1885, Aldie, heart disease, 59-0-0, p. unk, b. Louisiana, c/o: Wm. L. Sanford, sc: Wm. L. Sanford, husband, 1st Dist., BVS:1885:5

SANTMYER, Evaline L., W, F, d. 25 Oct 1881, LC, consumption, 2-0-4, p. Isaac & Kessiah Santmyer, b. LC, 3rd Dist., BVS:1881:5

SANTMYER, Kaziah T., W, F, d. 27 Dec 1887, LC, consumption, 40-0-0, p. Wm. & Lucy Arnett , c/o: Isaac Santmyer, sc: Isaac Santmyer, husband, 3rd Dist., BVS:1887:7

SANTMYER, M. E., W, F, d. 11 Jul 1889, LC, unk, 0-0-11, p. J. B. & May Santmyers, b. LC, none, unm, sc: J.B. Santmyers, father, 3rd Dist., BVS:1889:5

SAPPINGTON, Irene, W, F, d. 25 Apr 1887, LC, unk, 0-0-25, p. Wm. D. & Permilia Sappington, none, sc: Wm. D. Sappington, father, 3rd Dist., BVS:1887:7

SAUNDERS, Annie, B, F, d. 1 Aug 1878, LC, consumption, 27-0-0, b. LC, c/o: Geo. H. Saunders, sc: George H. Saunders, husband, LE Dist., BVS:1878:9

SAUNDERS, Annie May, W, F, d. 18 Jul 1891, Woodburn, cholera infantum, 0-4-0, p. Cat. Saunders, b. Woodburn, unm, sc: C.N. Saunders, MT Dist., BVS:1891:6

SAUNDERS, Delia N., W, F, d. 1 Feb 1878, LC, pneumonia, 76-0-0, c/o: Henry Saunders, sc: Mrs. Dowell, friend, LE Dist., BVS:1878:8

SAUNDERS, Henrietta, W, F, d. 5 Jun 1855, LC, dropsy on brain, 1-2-0, p. Henry & Sarah F. Saunders, b. LC, sc: Henry Saunders, father, BVS:1855:2, LC:15

SAUNDERS, James W., W, M, d. 11 Oct 1866, E side of Ketoctin Mountain, jaundice, 44-0-0, b. LC, BVS:1866:1

SAUNDERS, John, W, M, d. 23 Jul 1880, Leesburg, old age, 83-3-0, p. Henry & Patience Saunders, b. LC, merchant, c/o: Mary Saunders, sc: R. Eludin Saunders, son, 2nd Dist., BVS:1880:7

SAUNDERS, Mary, W, F, d. 14 Aug 1855, Leesburg, consumption, 66-4-17, p. John & Mary Saunders, b. LC, c/o: Presley Saunders, sc: Presley Saunders, husband, BVS:1855:1, LC:14

SAUNDERS, Mary, W, F, d. 27 Dec 1866, nr Dry Mill, consumption, 59-0-0, b. LC, married, sc: Benj. Saunders, husband, BVS:1866:1

[SAUNDERS], no name, W, F, d. 2 Jul 1878, nr Pleasant Valley, consumption, 0-0-7, p. John H. & Lucy E. Saunders, b. nr Pleasant Valley, unm, sc: John W. Saunders, father, BR Dist., BVS:1878:4

SAUNDERS, Philip, W, M, d. 7 Dec 1859/1860, LC, paralysis, 59-0-0, p. James & Elizth Saunders, b. LC, farmer, c/o: Amanda C. Saunders, sc: Amanda C. Saunders, wife, BVS:1859:1, 1860:4, LC:37

SAUNDERS, Sarah A., W, F, d. 11 Dec 1891, Goresville, old age, 81-0-0, p. unk, b. unk, unk, c/o: Wilson Saunders, sc: son-in-law, LE Dist., BVS:1891:4

SAUNDERS, William H., W, M, d. 1 Jan 1883, Leesburg, typhoid fever, 71-0-0, p. Geo. & Sarah Saunders, b. Fairfax Co., laborer, c/o: Mary Saunders, sc: Mary V. Saunders, daughter, 2nd Dist., BVS:1883:7

SAUNDERS, Wm. H. H., W, F[sic, d. 8 Sep 1892, Leesburg, whooping cough, 4-6-0, p. Henry & Annie Saunders, b. Leesburg, unm, sc: Henry Saunders, LE Dist., BVS:1892:5

SCATTERDAY, Ann Matilda, W, F, d. 28 Jul 1893, Purcellville, bilious colic, 80-0-0, p. David & Hester Beatty, b. LC, wife, sc: daughter, JF Dist., BVS:1893:3

SCHACKLEFORD, Arthur, W, M, d. Dec 1874, LC, pneumonia, 53-0-0, c/o: Susan Shackleford, sc: Susan Shackleford, wife, LE Dist., BVS:1874:5

SCHLEIF, Bessie, W, F, d. 10 Jul 1883, Leesburg, cholera infantum, 0-7-6, p. Geo. W. & Laura L. Schleif, b. Richmond, sc: John V. Schlerf, grandfather, 2nd Dist., BVS:1883:7

SCHOFIELD, Mahlon, W, M, d. 28 May 1853, LC, old age, 84-7-23, p. Jno. & Ann Scofield, b. Maryland, farmer, sc: Rachel N. Hoge, daughter, BVS:1854:4, LC:2

SCHOOLEY, Catherine, W, F, d. 3 Jun 1886, LC, tumor, 54-0-0, b. Warren Co. VA, c/o: Milton Schooley, sc: Milton Schooley, husband, 3rd Dist., BVS:1886:4

SCHOOLEY, Charles W., W, M, d. 9 May 1891, Waterford, apoplexy, 72-0-0, p. Aaron Schooley, b. Waterford, husband, sc: George W. Schooley, JF Dist., BVS:1891:7

SCHOOLEY, Cora Mildred, W, F, d. Dec 1894, North Fork, pneumonia, 1-0-22, p. C. W. & Emma O. Schooley, b. North Fork, sc: C. W. Schooley, father, 3rd Dist., BVS:1894:5

SCHOOLEY, Eliza Bonet, W, F, d. 9 Apr 1876, nr Hoysville, inflammation of bowels, 29-0-0, p. Jones P. & Sarah A. Schooley, b. LC, unm, sc: Sarah A. Schooley, mother, LV Dist., BVS:1876:3

SCHOOLEY, Jno. H., W, M, d. April 9 1892, Round Hill, la grippe, 75-0-0, b. Round Hill, blacksmith, married, sc: Mollie Schooley, daughter, JF Dist., BVS:1892:7

SCHOOLEY, Jonas B., W, M, d. 3 Aug 1854, LC, inflammation of bowels, 0-3-15, p. Wm. H. & Hannah Schooley, b. LC, sc: Wm. H. Schooley, father, BVS:1854:8, LC:8

SCHOOLEY, Mary, W, F, d. 10 Apr 1885, Waterford, consumption, 64-6-0, b. LC, c/o: Chas W. Schooley, sc: C.W. Schooley, husband, 3rd Dist., BVS:1885:6

SCHOOLEY, R. S., W, F, d. Aug 1896, Waterford, dysentery, 70-0-0, consort, JF Dist., BVS:1896:8

SCHOOLEY, Sarah A., W, F, d. 8 Nov 1894, Lovettsville, old age, 85-0-0, p. unk, b. unk, consort, sc: Dr. A. B. Householder, LV Dist., BVS:1894:4

SCIPPIO, no name, B, --, d. Nov 1893, Snickersville, unk, 0-2-0, p.

Christopher & Rose Scippio, b. LC, sc: father, MT Dist., BVS:1893:4

SCOFIELD, Ann N., B, F, d. 20 Oct 1886, LC, tumor, 70-0-0, b. Frederick Co. Va., sc: Isaac Hoge, friend, 3rd Dist., BVS:1886:4

SCOTT, Belle, B, F, d. 12 Mar 1896, nr Bloomfield, pneumonia, 38-0-0, p. unk, b. nr Bloomfield, none, unm, sc: T. Pearson, head of family, MC Dist., BVS:1896:2

SCOTT, Gilbert, W, M, d. 3 May 1885, nr Lovettsville, bronchial trouble, 85-0-0, p. unk, b. LC, laborer, c/o: Mary A. Scott, sc: Mary A. Scott, wife, 2nd Dist., BVS:1885:2

SCOTT, John Marshall, W, M, d. 31 Jul 1858, res of parents, dysentery, 0-8-0, p. John M. & Mary Scott, b. nr Upperville, BVS:1858:4, LC:31

SCOTT, Lucinda, W, F, d. 15 Aug 1858, res of parents, dysentery, 3-3-0, p. John M. & Mary Scott, b. Upperville, BVS:1858:4, LC:31

SCOTT, Martha J., W, F, d. 17 Dec 1890, LC, unk, 27-0-0, p. Gilbert & Mary Scott, b. LC, none, unm, sc: R.A. Scott, brother, 2nd Dist., BVS:1890:4

SCOTT, Mary, B, F, d. May 1878, Snickersville, phth, unk, p. John & Lizzie Scott, b. Snickersville, sc: J. Scott, parent, MT Dist., BVS:1878:2/3

SCOTT, Mary A., W, F, d. 3 Nov 1892, Lovettsville, pneumonia, 79-0-0, p. Saml. & Ann, b. LC, consort, sc: Robert Scott, LV Dist., BVS:1892:6

[SCOTT], no name, W, , d. 28 Jul 1871, nr Aldie, 0-0-1, p. Susan B. & C. E. Scott, MC Dist., BVS:1871:2

SCOTT, Rebecca, W, F, d. 19 Dec 1880, Waterford, heart disease, 57-0-0, p. unk, b. LC, c/o: Jacob Scott, sc: Jacob Scott, husband, 3rd Dist., BVS:1880:4

SEATON, Adrian, W, M, d. 26 Feb 1881, LC, croup, 0-7-0, p. Wm. & Mary Seaton, b. LC, sc: Wm. Seaton, father, 3rd Dist., BVS:1881:5

SEATON, Alice V., W, F, d. 10 Jan 1890, North Fork, old age, 87-0-0, b. LC, none, c/o: Samuel Seaton, sc: Samuel Seaton, husband, 3rd Dist., BVS:1890:7

SEATON, Amos A., W, M, d. 11 Feb 1888, LC, old age & cons, 83-0-0, p. unk, b. LC, farmer, c/o: Sarah Seaton, sc: Samuel R. Seaton, father, 3rd Dist., BVS:1888:2

SEATON, Arminda, W, F, d. 25 May 1884, LC, brain fever, 0-6-0, p. James & Arminda Seaton, b. LC, sc: James Seaton, father, 1st Dist., BVS:1884:2

SEATON, Charlotte, W, F, d. 22 May 1857, her res, dropsy, 58-0-0, p. John & Edith Florrey, b. Fauquier Co., c/o: William Seaton, sc: William Seaton, widower, BVS:1857:3, LC:26

SEATON, Cornelias E., W, M, d. 19 Oct 1888, LC, typhoid fever, 19-0-0, p. Wm. H. & Annie Seaton, b. LC, laborer, unm, sc: W.H. Seaton, father, 3rd Dist., BVS:1888:2

SEATON, John W., W, M, d. 12 Jun 1865, on Ketoctin Mountain, scrofula, 64-11-28, p. Jas & Eliz Seaton, b. Fauquier Co., married, sc: Nancy Seaton, wife, BVS:1865:1

SEATON, Mary P., W, F, d. 23 Feb 1883, nr Upperville, Fauquier Co., congestion, 53-0-0, p. James J. & Susan Randolph, b. nr Winchester, Frederick Co., c/o: Townsend Seaton, sc: Townsend Seaton, husband, 1st Dist., BVS:1883:2

SEATON, Sarah E., W, F, d. 1 Nov 1858, res of parents, 13-1-20, p. John W. & Nancy Seaton, b. on M. Rawling's Farm, sc: John W. Seaton, father, BVS:1858:3, LC:31

SEATON, Sarah E., W, F, d. 23 Dec 1880, LC, diphtheria, 7-0-0, p. J.H. & Arminda Seaton, unm, sc: Arminda Seaton, mother, 1st Dist., BVS:1880:3

SEATON, Wm. H., W, M, d. 20 Feb 1891, Purcellville, typhoid fever, 59-0-0, p. Amos Seaton, b. Purcellville, husband, sc: Arthur L. Seaton, JF Dist., BVS:1891:7

SEEBRACH, Ida Eliz, W, F, d. 25 Mar 1873, nr Upperville, heart disease, 1-0-0, p. J.P. & Helen Seebrach, b. nr Upperville, sc: Helen Seebrach, mother, MC Dist., BVS:1873:5

SEIBER, Susan, W, F, d. 11 Jul 1879, Leesburg, cancer, 52-11-0, p. John

& Delilah Seiber, b. LC, sc: Rebecca Seiber, sister, 2nd Dist., BVS:1879:1
SEITZ, Amanda, W, F, d. 30 Dec 1883, nr Lovettsville, complication of disease, 67-0-0, p. --- Russell, b. LC, c/o: Andrew Seitz, sc: Chas F. Williams, friend, 2nd Dist., BVS:1883:7
SEITZ, Andrew, W, M, d. 8 Jul 1888, LC, cancer in stomach, 65-0-0, p. unk, b. unk, teacher, unm, sc: C.T. Williams, son-in-law, 2nd Dist., BVS:1888:6
SEITZ, Lottie Bell, W, F, d. 16 Sep 1878, nr Lovettsville, cholera infantum, 1-1-0, p. Winfield S. & Annie B. Seitz, b. LC, sc: W.S. Seitz, father, LV Dist., BVS:1878:1/5
SERWICK, Christian, W, M, d. 18 May 1854, Leesburg, dissipation, 70-0-0, p. unk, b. Germany, butcher, c/o: Elizabeth D. Serwick *, sc: George Serwick, son, BVS:1854:8, LC:7
SETTLE, Naomi, W, F, d. 17 Mar 1856, LC, old age, 78-0-0, b. LC, c/o: Reuben Settle, sc: Thomas Settle, son, BVS:1856:7, LC:24
SETTLE, Nelson, W, M, d. 20 Apr 1890, nr Arcola, old age, 85-0-0, p. Israel & Marian Settle, b. LC, unm, sc: Chas Dean, old servant, 1st Dist., BVS:1890:2
SETTLE, Thomas, W, M, d. 13 Mar 1890, nr Arcola, old age, 89-0-0, p. Israel & Marian Settle, b. LC, unm, sc: Chas Dean, old servant, 1st Dist., BVS:1890:2
SEWELL, Chas. J., W, M, d. 4 Nov 1872, LC, consumption, 11-0-0, p. Thos. S. & Mary Sewell, b. LC, sc: Thos. S. Sewell, father, LE Dist., BVS:1872:4
SEXTON, Florence M., W, F, d. unk [1877], Guilford Station, unk, 1-2-9, p. Thos. F. & Florence Sexton, b. Guilford Station, unm, sc: Thos. F. Sexton, father, BR Dist., BVS:1877:1
SEXTON, John F., W, M, d. 24 Dec 1878, nr Guilford Station, whooping cough, 0-5-20, p. T. F. & Florence Sexton, b. LC, unm, sc: Thomas F. Sexton, father, BR Dist., BVS:1878:4
[SEXTON], no name, W, F, d. 6 Feb 1874, Broad Run Dist., unk, 0-0-1/2,

p. Thos. F. & Florence Sexton, b. LC, sc: Thos. F. Sexton, head of family, BR Dist., BVS:1874:3
SHAFER, Joseph, W, M, d. 29 Jul 1887, LC, pneumonia, 25-0-0, p. Frederick & Susan Shafer, b. LC, physician, unm, sc: Frederick Shafer, father, 2nd Dist., BVS:1887:5
SHAFER, Susan, W, F, d. 20 Apr 1888, LC, heart trouble, 64-0-0, p. Daniel & L. Leazer, b. Frederick, MD, none, c/o: F.W. Shafer, sc: F.W. Shafer, husband, 2nd Dist., BVS:1888:6
SHAFFER, John, W, M, d. 29 Aug 1876, LC, chronic diarrhea, 81-0-0, p. John & Margaret Shaffer, b. unk, Fence builder, c/o: Ellen Shaffer, sc: Danl Shaffer, son, JF Dist., BVS:1876:8
SHAFFER, John W., W, M, d. 16 Apr 1853, LC, inflammation brains, 0-6-2, p. Joseph & Susan Shaffer, b. LC, sc: Joseph H. Shaffer, father, BVS:1854:3, LC:1
SHAFFER, Mary E., W, F, d. 15 May 1854, LC, quinsy, 17-0-0, p. John & Susan Shaffer, b. LC, unm, sc: John Shaffer, brother, BVS:1854:9, LC:8
SHAFFNER, Ann C., W, F, d. 28 Apr 1856, Leesburg, consumption, 25-0-0, p. James & Elizth. Solomon, b. LC, c/o: Peter R. Shaffner, sc: Peter R. Shaffner, husband, BVS:1856:1, LC:20
SHAFFNER, Franklin P., W, M, d. 8 Apr 1856, Leesburg, whooping cough, 3-5-23, p. Peter R. & Ann C. Shaffner, b. Washington City, sc: Peter R. Shaffner, father, BVS:1856:1, LC:20
SHANKS, Thos. P., W, M, d. 12 Sep 1894, nr Sterling, unk, 10-8-0, p. Geo. P. & Dolley E. Shanks, b. LC, sc: Geo P. Shanks, father, 1st Dist., BVS:1894:1
SHAWEN, David, W, M, d. 21 Feb 1858, LC, unk, 0-8-28, p. Wm. & Ann C. Shawen, b. LC, sc: Wm. C. Shawen, father, BVS:1858:1, LC:29
SHEA, Ellen, W, F, d. Aug 1858, LC, unk, 0-3-0, p. James & Mary Shea, b. LC, sc: James Shea, father, BVS:1858:6, LC:33
SHEETZ, B. F., W, M, d. 28 Jun 1896, LC, heart trouble, 66-0-0, b.

Jefferson Co., WV, editor, husband, sc: wife, LE Dist., BVS:1896:5

SHEID, Emma, W, F, d. 8 Jul 1853, LC, whooping cough, 2-6-0, p. Orlando & Amanda Sheid, b. LC, sc: Orlando Sheid, father, BVS:1854:2, LC:7

SHELHORN, Auton, W, M, d. 10 Aug 1881, LC, broke neck in fall, 29-0-0, p. Godfrey & Barbara Shelhorn, b. LC, c/o: Annett Shelhorn, sc: B. Shelhorn, mother, 1st Dist., BVS:1881:2

SHELL, Tamar, W, F, d. 31 May 1866, nr Rehoboth, dropsy, 40-0-0, p. John & Mary Shell, unm, sc: John W. Shell, brother, BVS:1866:1

SHELLHORN, Godfrey, W, M, d. 7 May 1889, Farmwell, consumption, 77-0-0, p. unk, b. Germany, farmer, c/o: Catharine Shellhorne, sc: Catharine Shiner, daughter, 1st Dist., BVS:1889:1

SHELLY, Fannie, B, F, d. 30 Spet 1873, nr Guilford, whooping cough, 0-1-0, p. Turner & Fannie Shelly, b. LC, sc: Turner Shelly, head of family, BR Dist., BVS:1873:1

SHELLY, Nancy, B, F, d. 15 Dec 1871, consumption, 16-0-0, p. T. & F. Shelly, BR Dist., BVS:1871:3

SHELTON, John W., B, M, d. 1 Mar 1873, nr Dover, whooping cough, 1-3-0, p. Nimrod & Lydia Shelton, b. Middleburg, sc: Lydia Shelton, mother, MC Dist., BVS:1873:5

SHEPPARD, Frances, W, F, d. 9 Jan 1880, Leesburg, old age, 74-2-24, p. Chas. & Ellen Sheppard, b. LC, unm, sc: L.W.S. Hough, nephew, 2nd Dist., BVS:1880:7

SHERLY, Rosie, W, F, d. 16 Mar 1874, Gainsville, Prince Wm Co, old age, 81-0-0, b. Prince William Co, c/o: G.W. Sherly, sc: Mrs. E.J.T. Clark, niece, MC Dist., BVS:1874:4

SHERZER, Emsy Ann M., W, F, d. 12 Nov 1859/60, nr Bean's Shop, child bed, 32-0-0, p. Wilford & Elizth Feagans, b. nr Dover, c/o: John Sherzer, sc: Martha Feagans, sister, BVS:1859:4, 1860:2, LC:35

SHINER, Bismark Oswald, W, M, d. 9 Aug 1878, LC, cholera infantum, 0-1-7, p. Albert & Katherine Shiner, b.

LC, sc: Albert Shiner, father, LE Dist., BVS:1878:8

SHINER, Emma, W, F, d. 25 Jun 1876, Leesburg, diphtheria, 0-6-0, p. Albert & Catherine Shiner, b. Leesburg, sc: Albert Shiner, father, LE Dist., BVS:1876:7

SHOEMAKER, Ann, W, F, d. 21 Sep 1890, Wheatland, indigestion, 72-0-0, p. Simon & Betsy Shoemaker, b. LC, none, unm, sc: Thomas Bell, friend, 3rd Dist., BVS:1890:7

SHOEMAKER, Lemuel, W, M, d. 30 Jan 1853, Goose Creek Meeting House, croup, 3-4-0, p. Basil & Caroline Shoemaker, b. nr Goose Creek Meeting House, sc: mother, BVS:1854:6, LC:5

SHOEMAKER, Levi T., W, M, d. 19 Apr 1866, Philomont, consumption, 34-3-1, p. Naylor & Sarah Shoemaker, b. Philomont, farmer, sc: Naylor Shoemaker, father, BVS:1866:2

[SHOEMAKER], no name, W, F, d. Jan 1866, Silcott Springs, unk, 0-0-14, p. Basil & Caroline Shoemaker, b. Silcott Springs, sc: Naylor Shoemaker, father, BVS:1866:2

SHORT, Lettie, B, F, d. 15 Jan 1891, Middleburg, consumption, 29-0-0, p. Thos. & Fannie Smith, b. LC, laborer, c/o: Henry Short, sc: Henry Short, head of family, 1st Dist., BVS:1891:1

SHORT, William Isaac, W, M, d. 1875, Lovettsville Dist, 10-0-0, p. Jacob & Eliza Short, b. LC, laborer, unm, LV Dist., BVS:1875:4

SHORTS, Nancy, B, F, d. 5 Jun 1896, nr Bloomfield, la grippe, 0-5-0, p. Shed & Julia Shorts, b. nr Bloomfield, none, unm, sc: Shed Shorts, father, MC Dist., BVS:1896:2

SHREVE, Daniel, W, M, d. 15 Apr 1884, nr Leesburg, dropsy, 73-0-0, p. Benj. & --- Shreve, b. LC, farmer, c/o: Hannah E. Shreve, sc: Mary E. Minor, daughter, 2nd Dist., BVS:1884:5

SHREVE, Elizth. W., W, F, d. 10 May 1856, res of parents, whooping cough, 1-9-0, p. Francis E. & Minerva A. Shreve, b. res of parents, sc: F.E. Shreve, father, BVS:1856:5, LC:23

Loudoun County, Virginia, Death Register, 1853-1896   229

SHREVE, Eugenia, W, F, d. 1 Jan 1889, Sterling, tuberculosis, 3-2-0, p. Benj. A. & Sallie W. Shreve, b. Sterling, sc: Sallie W. Shreve, mother, 1st Dist., BVS:1889:1

SHREVE, Francis A., W, M, d. 19 May 1878, nr Gum Spring, dropsy, 64-0-0, p. Benj. & Nancy Shreve, b. LC, farmer, c/o: Minerva A. Shreve, sc: B.A. Shreve, son, BR Dist., BVS:1878:4

SHREVE, Henrietta W., W, F, d. 19 May 1856, res of parents, whooping cough, 2-6-0, p. Francis E. & Minerva A. Shreve, b. res of parents, sc: F.E. Shreve, father, BVS:1856:5, LC:23

SHREVE, Matilda, W, F, d. 27 Sep 1881, LC, unk, 0-6-4, p. Benj. & Sallie N. Shreve, b. LC, sc: Benj A. Shreve, father, 1st Dist., BVS:1881:2

SHREVE, Minerva A., W, F, d. 9 Jun 1878, nr Gum Spring, dropsy, 64-0-0, p. J. D. & Matilda Warfield, b. Frederick Co. MD, c/o: Francis E. Shreve, sc: B.A. Shreve, son, BR Dist., BVS:1878:4

SHREVE, no name, W, M, d. 1 Jun 1883, nr Leesburg, unk, 0-0-4, p. A.B. & Annie M. Shreve, b. LC, sc: A.B. Shreve, father, 2nd Dist., BVS:1883:4

SHRIDAL, no name, W, F, d. 15 Mar 1887, nr Philomont, unk, 0-0-5, p. Sarah Shridal (unm), b. nr Philomont, sc: F.E. Robey, superintendent of poor, 1st Dist., BVS:1887:1

SHRIEVE, Benjamin, W, M, d. 1 Feb 1853, nr Sycolin, fall, 82-0-0, p. Benj. & Nancy Shrieve, b. LC, farmer, sc: son, BVS:1854:5, LC:5

SHRIEVE, Jacob, W, M, d. 6 Jul 1876, nr Neersville, worn-out with age, 84-0-0, p. Christopher & Elizabeth Shrieve, b. LC, cooper, widower, sc: Ann E. Shrieve, daughter-in-law, LV Dist., BVS:1876:3

SHRY, Nina B., W, F, d. 2 Oct 1891, nr Taylorstown, heart trouble, 0-1-15, p. Frank & Mary Shry, b. nr Taylorstown, farmer, sc: mother, LV Dist., BVS:1891:5

SHRY, Wallace, W, M, d. 10 Nov 1894, Taylorstown, unk, 0-0-2, p. John & Florence, b. Taylorstown, sc: John Shry, LV Dist., BVS:1894:4

SHRYOCK, Anna, W, F, d. 28 Dec 1872, nr Farmwell Church, child bed, 22-0-0, p. G. & Alice Johnson, b. LC, c/o: John Shryock, Jr., sc: John Shryock, husband, BR Dist., BVS:1872:6

SHRYOCK, Elizabeth, W, F, d. 28 Feb 1892, Waxpool, a fall, 78-0-0, p. Jno. & Elizabeth Moffett, b. LC, c/o: Saml Shryock, sc: Saml Shryock, husband, 1st Dist., BVS:1892:2

SHRYOCK, George W., W, M, d. 5 Jul 1885, Farmwell, bright's disease, 41-0-0, p. John & Mary Shryock, b. Farmwell, farmer, c/o: Lavernia M. Shryock, sc: Lavernia Shryock, wife, 1st Dist., BVS:1885:5

SHRYOCK, Gordon J., W, M, d. 14 Nov 1891, nr Ryan, brain fever, 0-3-0, p. J. F. & Mary Shryock, b. LC, merchant & farmer, sc: J.F. Shryock, father, 1st Dist., BVS:1891:3

SHRYOCK, John, W, M, d. 21 Apr 1890, nr Waxpool, pneumonia, 76-0-0, p. John & Sarah Shryock, b. LC, c/o: Lucy Shryock, sc: John H. Shryock, uncle, 1st Dist., BVS:1890:2

[SHRYOCK], no name, W, M, d. 20 Dec 1865, nr Mount Middleton, unk, 0-0-1, p. G.H. & R.J. Shryock, b. Middleton, housekeeper, unm, sc: R.Jane Shryock, mother, BVS:1865:2

SHUGAR, Joseph, W, M, d. 1 Sep 1881, LC, old age, 90-0-0, b. LC, farmer, c/o: Louisa Shugar, sc: James Shugar, son, 3rd Dist., BVS:1881:5

SHUGAR, Louisa, W, F, d. 2 Jul 1881, LC, general debility, 76-0-0, b. LC, c/o: Joseph Shugar, sc: James Shugar, son, 3rd Dist., BVS:1881:5

SHUGARS, Annie, W, F, d. 3 Oct 1888, LC, typhoid fever, 26-0-0, p. Samuel & Nancy Breckenridge, b. LC, none, c/o: J.A. Shugars, sc: J.A. Shugars, husband, 2nd Dist., BVS:1888:6

SHULLY, Lewis, W, M, d. 20 May 1878, nr Waterford, pneumonia, 76-0-0, b. Maryland, farmer, c/o: Sarah Shully, sc: John T. Shully, son, JF Dist., BVS:1878:10

SHUMAKER, Catharine, W, F, d. 23 Feb 1857, LC, paralysis, 66-5-2, p. Jacob & Catharine Emery, b. LC, c/o: Simon Shumaker, sc: Jonathan Shumaker, son, BVS:1857:1, LC:24

SHUMAKER, Jacob, W, M, d. 16 Dec 1880, nr Lovettsville, old age, 85-0-0, p. George & Mary Shumaker, b. LC, c/o: Sarah Shumaker, sc: Jno. Shumaker, son, 2nd Dist., BVS:1880:7

SHUMAKER, John, W, M, d. 18 Nov 1894, Leesburg, unk, 0-11-0, p. Wm. & Anna, b. Leesburg, unm, sc: Wm. Shumaker, LE Dist., BVS:1894:3

SHUMAKER, John, W, M, d. 14 May 1881, LC, gravel, 84-6-8, p. Geo. & Mary Shumaker, b. LC, farmer, c/o: Catharine Shumaker, sc: Catharine Shumaker, wife, 2nd Dist., BVS:1881:7

SHUMAKER, Josia, W, M, d. 7 Jan 1865, nr Neersville, ulcer, 52-0-0, p. Danl & Manah Shumaker, b. LC, farmer, c/o: A. Shumaker, sc: Amanda Shumaker, wife, BVS:1865:3

SHUMAKER, Josiah, W, M, d. 7 Jan 1865, nr Neersville, ulcer, 52-0-0, p. Danl & Maria Shumaker, b. LC, farmer, c/o: Amanda Shumaker, sc: A. Shumaker, wife, 1st Dist., BVS:1865:4

SHUMAKER, Mary, W, F, d. 1 Jun 1879, LC, heart disease, 68-0-0, p. Simon & Catherine Shumaker, b. LC, unm, sc: Margaret Shumaker, sister, 3rd Dist., BVS:1879:3

SHUMAKER, Mary E., W, F, d. 7 Oct 1855, LC, choked, 2-8-2, p. Geo. & Euphemia Shumaker, b. LC, sc: Geo. Shumaker, father, BVS:1855:2, LC:15

SHUMAKER, Maud E., W, F, d. 24 Aug 1881, LC, unk, 0-1-8, p. Wm. & E. A. Shumaker, b. LC, sc: Saml W. Myers, grandfather, 2nd Dist., BVS:1881:7

[SHUMAKER], no name, W, M, d. 3 Dec 1856, res of parents, 0-0-7, p. Basil & Caroline T. Shumaker, b. nr Goose Creek Meeting House, sc: B. Shoemaker, father, BVS:1856:6, LC:23

SHUMAKER, no name, W, M, d. 30 Dec 1878, nr Morrisonville, croup, 0-1-5, p. Eli & Mary Shumaker, b. LC, sc: Eli Shumaker, father, JF Dist., BVS:1878:10

SHUMAKER, no name, W, M, d. 11 Dec 1885, nr Lovettsville, spasms, 0-0-14, p. Jas. S. & Maggie Shumaker, b. LC, sc: James S. Shumaker, father, 2nd Dist., BVS:1885:2

[SHUMAKER], no name, W, F, d. 16 Apr 1896, Elvan, unk, 0-0-24, p. William & Christian, b. Elvan, unm, sc: William Shumaker, LV Dist., BVS:1896:7

SHUMAKER, Sarah, W, F, d. 18 Dec 1890, LC, old age, 80-0-0, p. Frederick & Catherine Filler, b. LC, none, c/o: Jacob Shumaker, sc: John Shumaker, son, 2nd Dist., BVS:1890:4

SHUMAKER, Simon, W, M, d. 10 Apr 1857, LC, unk, 72-5-7, p. George & Mary Shumaker, b. LC, farmer, c/o: Catharine Shumaker, sc: Jonathan Shumaker, son, BVS:1857:1, LC:24

SHUMAKER, Virginia, W, F, d. 1 Jul 1875, nr Waterford, consumption, 26-0-0, p. Annanias & Mary Orrison, b. LC, c/o: Saml Shumaker, sc: Samuel Shumaker, husband, JF Dist., BVS:1875:3

SHUMAN, Geo. W., W, M, d. 21 Apr 1894, Middleburg, pneumonia, 86-0-0, p. unk, b. unk, post master, c/o: Harriet Shuman, sc: Harriet Shuman, wife, 1st Dist., BVS:1894:1

SHUMAN, Harriet P., W, F, d. 1 Dec 1887, Middleburg, unk, 66-0-0, p. James & Harriet Surghnour, b. Millwood, Clark Co., c/o: Geo W. Shuman, sc: Geo W. Shuman, husband, 1st Dist., BVS:1887:1

[SHUMAN], no name,W, F, d. 10 Aug 1855, Middleburg, congestion of brain, 0-4-8, p. G. W. & Harriet Shuman, b. Middleburg, sc: Geo. W. L. Shuman, father, BVS:1855:4, LC:16

SHUMATE, Diadama, W, F, d. 13 Nov 1886, LC, old age, 83-0-0, p. Walter & --- Elgin, b. LC, c/o: Murphy C. Shumate, sc: L. M. Shumate, son, 2nd Dist., BVS:1886:6

SHUMATE, Lewis M., W, M, d. 4 Feb 1883, nr Leesburg, typhoid fever, 4-9-12, p. L. M. & Mary T. Shumate, b.

Loudoun County, Virginia, Death Register, 1853-1896 231

LC, sc: L.M. Shumate, father, 2nd Dist., BVS:1883:4

SHUMATE, Murphy C., W, M, d. 12 Feb 1883, nr Leesburg, old age, 83-1-17, p. Lewis D. & --- Shumate, b. Fauquier Co., teacher, c/o: Diadama Shumate, sc: L.M. Shumate, son, 2nd Dist., BVS:1883:4

SHUMATE, Sally A., W, F, d. 15 Aug 1853, nr Sycolin, dysentery, 15-0-0, p. Murphey & Dedama Shumate, b. on Sycolin, unm, sc: father, BVS:1854:5, LC:5

SIDEBOTTOM, Mert, W, M, d. 5 Feb 1887, nr Philomont, unk, 60-0-0, p. unk & Betsey Sidebottom, b. Middleburg, unm, sc: F.E. Robey, superintendent of poor, 1st Dist., BVS:1887:3

SIDNEY, James, B, M, d. 1890, LC, dropsy, 12-0-0, p. Wm. Sidney, b. LC, none, unm, sc: W. Signey, father, 2nd Dist., BVS:1890:5

SIEBER, Delilia, W, F, d. 7 Aug 1855, Leesburg, dysentery, 54-0-0, p. unk, b. Baltimore City, MD, c/o: John Sieber, sc: John Sieber, husband, BVS:1855:1, LC:14

SILCOTT, Armstead, W, M, d. 4 Apr 1890, Silcott Springs, pneumonia, 68-0-0, b. LC, laborer, unm, sc: Mrs. Silcott, wife, 3rd Dist., BVS:1890:7

SILCOTT, Chester, W, M, d. 16 Oct 1891, Lincoln, unk, 0-2-0, p. Wm. Howard & Laura A. Silcott, b. Lincoln, unm, sc: W. Howard Silcott, MT Dist., BVS:1891:6

SILCOTT, Elizabeth, W, F, d. 22 Sep 1859/60, nr Wm. Ewers', tumor, 42-0-0, p. Wm. A. & ___Hutchison, b. Prince William Co/nr North Fork, laborer, c/o: Albert Silcott, sc: A. Silcott, husband, BVS:1859:3, 1860:1, LC:34

SILCOTT, James, W, M, d. 13 Nov 1876, LC, consumption, 55-0-0, p. Jessee & Jane Silcott, b. LC, farmer, c/o: Catherine Silcott, sc: Catherine Silcott, wife, JF Dist., BVS:1876:8

SILCOTT, Jane A., W, F, d. 5 Oct 1883, nr Lovettsville, tumor of stomach, 64-0-0, p. Jesse & Sarah Silcott, b. LC, unm, sc: Sydney Bennett, brother-in-law, 2nd Dist., BVS:1883:4

SILCOTT, Jas. Buchanan, W, M, d. 17 Sep 1878, Snickersville, consumption, unk, p. Norval & Margaret Silcott, carpenter, c/o: Emma V. Silcott, sc: F.M. Bradfield, friend, MT Dist., BVS:1878:2/3

SILCOTT, Louisa E., W, F, d. 1864, nr Mount Gilead, 16-0-0, p. Washg & Cath Silcott, b. LC, sc: Washg Silcott, father, BVS:1864:1, LC:39

SILCOTT, Mason, W, M, d. 24 Jul 1853, Goose Creek Meeting House, putrid sore throat, 3-0-0, p. Wm. & Frances Silcott, b. nr Goose Creek Meeting House, sc: mother, BVS:1854:6, LC:5

SILCOTT, no name, W, F, d. 20 Aug 1880, Hamilton, unk, 0-0-14, p. Jas E. & Mary Silcott, b. LC, sc: Jas. E. Silcott, father, 3rd Dist., BVS:1880:4

[SILCOTT], Sarah Rebecca, W, F, d. Aug 1855, Snickersville, unk, 0-5-0, p. Meshack & Emily Silcott, b. Snickersville, sc: M. Silcott, father, BVS:1855:7, LC:18

SIMMONS, Albert, W, M, d. 15 Mar 1888, LC, measles, 1-4-0, p. H. A. & Virginia Simmons, b. LC, unm, sc: H.A. Simmons, father, 3rd Dist., BVS:1888:1

SIMMONS, Benjn. F. P., W, M, d. 16 Oct 1858, Addison Osburn's Farm, scarlet sore throat, 3-0-0, p. Benjn & Catharine Simmons, b. place of death, sc: Effa A. Simmons, sister, BVS:1858:3, LC:31

SIMMONS, Lula A., W, F, d. 25 Dec 1880, Purcellville, pneumonia, 0-0-22, p. Henry & Virgie Simmons, b. LC, sc: Henry Simmons, father, 3rd Dist., BVS:1880:4

[SIMMONS], no name, W, M, d. 25 Dec 1881, LC, unk, 0-0-21, p. A.S. & Virginia Simmons, b. LC, sc: Virg Simmons, mother, 1st Dist., BVS:1881:2

SIMMONS, Virginia, W, F, d. Jul 1896, Round Hill, confinement, 39-0-0, consort, JF Dist., BVS:1896:8

SIMMS, Frances, B, F, d. 10 Aug 1886, nr Daysville, croup, 0-8-0, p. Louis & Frances Simms, b. nr Daysville, sc: Louis Simms, father, 1st Dist., BVS:1886:2

SIMMS, Louis, B, M, d. 10 Aug 1886, nr Daysville, croup, 0-8-0, p. Louis &

Frances Simms, b. nr Daysville, sc: Louis Simms, father, 1st Dist., BVS:1886:2

SIMMS, Malinda, B, F, d. Aug 1875, Leesburg, dropsy, 68-0-0, married, sc: Lewis Simms, MT Dist., BVS:1875:8

SIMMS, Virginia, B, F, d. 29 Jun 1883, nr Lovettsville, deranged, 51-0-0, p. Jane & Tenas Simms, b. LC, laborer, unm, sc: Lee Simms, brother, 2nd Dist., BVS:1883:7

SIMONS, Charlotte, B, F, d. 23 Jan 1866, Carolina Road, old age, 74-0-0, p. S, sc: John J. Tyler, head of family, BVS:1866:3

SIMPSON, Catharine, W, F, d. 8 Jun 1855, Mountain Farm, paralysis, 58-0-0, b. nr Leesburg, widow of Saml Simpson, sc: R.H. Turner, son-in-law, BVS:1855:6, LC:17

SIMPSON, Eben W., W, M, d. 9 Sep 1896, Paxson, typhoid fever, 18-6-0, p. Thomas P. & Eliza Simpson, b. Paxson, LC, mechanic, sc: Thos P. Simpson, father, MT Dist., BVS:1896:9

SIMPSON, Eliza, W, F, d. 15 Oct 1856, Thomas Hoge's, congestive fever, 28-0-0, p. John & Nancy Simpson, b. Ketoctin Mountain, Mount Gilead, sc: Thomas Hoge, brother-in-law, BVS:1856:6, LC:23

SIMPSON, Elizabeth, W, F, d. 5 May 1891, nr Bolington, paralysis, 53-0-0, p. unk, b. LC, farmer, c/o: Burr Simpson, sc: head of family, LV Dist., BVS:1891:5

SIMPSON, Elizabeth, W, F, d. 24 Jun 1876, Leesburg, general prostration, 64-0-0, p. unk, b. unk, sc: J.L. Nixon, friend, LE Dist., BVS:1876:7

SIMPSON, French, W, M, d. 27 May 1855, nr Mount Gilead, paralysis, 59-11-21, p. Jno. & Mary Simpson, b. nr Oatlands, farmer, c/o: Eliz. Simpson, sc: Jas. H. Simpson, son, BVS:1855:5, LC:17

SIMPSON, J. G., W, M, d. 3 Aug 1888, LC, dysentery, 28-0-0, p. Henson & Mary Simpson, b. LC, farmer, unm, sc: Henson Simpson, father, 3rd Dist., BVS:1888:2

SIMPSON, John, W, M, d. 7 Aug 1854, his res, 62-0-0, p. John & Mary Simpson, farmer, c/o: Mary Simpson, decd, sc: Henson Simpson, son, BVS:1854:13, LC:12

SIMPSON, Jonah S., W, M, d. 7 Oct 1864, nr Beaver Dam, 7-1-7, p. Jno H. & E. Simpson, b. LC, sc: Jno H. Simpson, father, BVS:1864:2, LC:39

SIMPSON, Mary A., W, F, d. 10 Nov 1874, LC, inflammation of bowels, 49-0-0, p. Rich. & Rebecca Adams, b. LC, c/o: Jno. W. Simpson, sc: Jno. W. Simpson, husband, JF Dist., BVS:1874:2

SIMPSON, Sally Wily, W, F, d. 14 Jun 1891, Gerrardstown, WV, unk, 20-0-0, p. John & Nannie Wily, b. Gerrardstown, WV, teacher, c/o: John S. Simpson, sc: husband, LE Dist., BVS:1891:4

SIMPSON, Silas, W, M, d. 15 Sep 1876, nr Belmont, heart disease, 40-0-0, p. Frank Simpson & wife, b. LC, farmer, married, sc: Susan Simpson, wife, BR Dist., BVS:1876:2

SINCLAIR, Alcinda, W, F, d. 23 Nov 1857, res of parents, putrid sore throat, 0-8-18, p. Elijah B. & Mary P. Sinclair, b. Bitzers Shop, sc: E.B. Sinclair, father, BVS:1857:4, LC:26

SINCLAIR, John, W, M, d. 13 Feb 1857, old age, 87-0-0, p. James & Mary Sinclair, b. LC, sc: Francis M. Sinclair, son, BVS:1857:7, LC:28

SINGLETON, Jno., B, M, d. 15 Sep 1896, nr Watson, consumption, 16-0-0, p. unk, b. nr Watson, none, unm, sc: J.J. Tyler, neighbor, MC Dist., BVS:1896:2

SINKFIELD, Mary A., B, F, d. 10 Mar 1883, Round Hill, pneumonia, 2-10-0, p. John & Louisa Sinkfield, b. LC, sc: John Sinkfield, father, 3rd Dist., BVS:1883:5

SISK, Carrie A., W, M, d. 2 Apr 1889, Mountville, dropsy, 1-3-0, p. James H. & Nora Sisk, b. Mountville, sc: James H. Sisk, father, 1st Dist., BVS:1889:1

SKILLMAN, Catharine J., W, F, d. 20 Apr 1887, Aldie, unk, 44-0-0, p. Samuel & Caroline Tillett, b. Aldie, c/o: Lemuel Skillman, sc: Lemuel Skillman, husband, 1st Dist., BVS:1887:1

SKILLMAN, Dela, W, F, d. 5 Oct 1856, res, consumption, 65-0-0, p. ---Alexander, b. Ireland, c/o: Abraham

Skillman, sc: A. Skillman, widower, BVS:1856:4, LC:22

SKILLMAN, Ernest, W, M, d. 26 Aug 1890, nr Arcola, typhoid fever, 22-0-0, p. Bush W. & Annie Skillman, b. LC, unm, sc: Chas W. Skillman, brother, 1st Dist., BVS:1890:2

SKILLMAN, Evie, W, F, d. 10 Oct 1893, Aldie, cholera infantum, 0-6-0, p. J. W. & Annie Skillman, b. Aldie, sc: J.W. Skillman, father, 1st Dist., BVS:1893:1

SKILLMAN, Franklin, W, M, d. 4 Jul 1889, Arcola, cholera infantum, 1-6-0, p. Bush W. & Lula Skillman, b. Arcola, sc: Bush W. Skillman, father, 1st Dist., BVS:1889:1

SKILLMAN, Harriet, W, F, d. 25 Dec 1880, LC, paralysis, 46-0-0, p. unk, c/o: John W. Skillman, sc: John W. Skillman, husband, 1st Dist., BVS:1880:3

SKILLMAN, L. F., W, M, d. 2 Jul 1892, Aldie, congestion of lungs, 53-0-0, p. John & Lucinda Skillman, b. Aldie, farmer, c/o: Ella Skillman, sc: Ella Skillman, wife, 1st Dist., BVS:1892:2

SKILLMAN, Mamie V., W, F, d. 12 Jun 1894, Pleasant Valley, unk, 0-5-0, p. W. L. & Cornelia Skillman, b. nr Pleasant Valley, sc: Cornelia Skillman, mother, 1st Dist., BVS:1894:1

SKILLMAN, Maria, W, F, d. 31 Dec 1887, Unison, old age, 80-0-0, p. Samuel & Elizabeth Dishman, b. Unison, c/o: Abraham Skillman, sc: James R. Benton, grandson, 1st Dist., BVS:1887:3

SKINNER, Clinton R., W, M, d. 4 Oct 1857, unk, 7-0-0, p. N.J. & Lucy E. Skinner, b. LC, sc: N.J. Skinner, father, BVS:1857:7, LC:28

SKINNER, Henry W., W, M, d. 15 May 1885, nr Aldie, bright's disease, 56-0-0, p. Gabriel & Elizabeth Skinner, b. LC, sc: Emmet W. Skinner, son, 1st Dist., BVS:1885:5

SKINNER, Jane P., W, F, d. 14 Apr 1883, nr Aldie, heart disease, 75-0-0, p. unk, b. unk, unm, sc: Williamson Skinner, nephew, 1st Dist., BVS:1883:2

SKINNER, John R., W, M, d. 22 Nov 1886, nr Arcola, hemorrhage of lungs, 69-0-0, p. Peter & Sarah Skinner, b. LC, farmer, c/o: Jane Skinner, sc: Robt E. Skinner, son, 1st Dist., BVS:1886:2

SKINNER, Julia A., W, F, d. 18 Jan 1893, Aldie, paralysis, 55-0-0, p. Jonathan Nixon, b. Fauquier Co., c/o: Nathaniel Skinner, sc: J.T. Larrs, brother-in-law, 1st Dist., BVS:1893:1

SKINNER, Laura V., W, F, d. 14 Nov 1864, Bloomfield, pneumonia, 0-3-21, p. Jno T. & S. Skinner, b. Fauquier Co., sc: J.T. Skinner, father, BVS:1864:1, LC:38

SKINNER, Lucy B., W, F, d. 28 Oct 1888, Middleburg, pneumonia, 67-0-0, p. Silas & Fannie Beatie, b. Middleburg, sc: Ernest Skinner, nephew, 1st Dist., BVS:1888:4

SKINNER, Lydia, W, F, d. 18 May 1885, nr Aldie, consumption, 39-0-0, p. Nathan & Sarah Skinner, b. nr Aldie, unm, sc: Maurice McFarland, brother-in-law, 1st Dist., BVS:1885:5

SKINNER, Mary V., W, F, d. 15 Jan 1893, Aldie, typhoid fever, 61-0-0, p. Jonathan Nixon, b. Fauquier Co., c/o: Wm. Skinner, sc: J.T. Larrs, brother-in-law, 1st Dist., BVS:1893:1

SKINNER, Nancy E., W, F, d. Oct 1855, consumption, 24-0-0, p. unk, b. LC, c/o: Jno. R. Skinner, sc: J.R. Skinner, head of family, BVS:1855:8, LC:19

SKINNER, Nannie L., W, F, d. Aug 1866, Bloomfield, inflammation on brain, 0-7-0, p. J. T. & Susanna Skinner, b. Bloomfield, sc: J.B. Skinner, father, BVS:1866:2

SKINNER, Nathan, W, M, d. 20 Jan 1884, LC, consumption, 80-0-0, p. Peter & Sarah Skinner, b. LC, farmer, sc: Maurice McFarland, son-in-law, 1st Dist., BVS:1884:2

[SKINNER], no name, W, M, d. 9 Jul 1853, LC, unk, unk, p. John R. & Mary Skinner, b. LC, sc: Mary Skinner, mother, BVS:1854:2, LC:7

[SKINNER], no name, W, F, d. 12 Dec 1853, LC, unk, 0-0-1, p. A. G. & M. A. Skinner, b. LC, sc: A. G. Skinner, father, BVS:1854:2, LC:7

[SKINNER], no name, W, F, d. Jun 1855, unk, 0-3-0, p. Jno. R. & Nancy E. Skinner, b. LC, sc: J.R. Skinner, father, BVS:1855:8, LC:19

SKINNER, Peter, W, M, d. 1859/60, LC, old age, 85-9-0, p. unk, sc: John R. Skinner, son, BVS:1859:6, 1860:3, LC:36

SLACK, Ann M., W, F, d. 10 Feb 1884, LC, paralysis, 64-0-0, p. unk, b. LC, c/o: James E. Slack, sc: James E. Slack, husband, 1st Dist., BVS:1884:2

SLACK, Chas. L., W, M, d. 24 Feb 1894, nr Upperville, diphtheria, 0-10-0, p. Wm. B. & Mary E. Slack, b. nr Upperville, sc: Wm. B. Slack, father, 1st Dist., BVS:1894:1

SLACK, Elizabeth, W, F, d. 4 Nov 1859/60, Jas. Chapell's, old age, 95-0-0, p. Eveline Piot, b. nr Leesburg, c/o: Turner Slack, dec'd, sc: Jas. Chapell, son-in-law, BVS:1859:3, 1860:1, LC:34

SLACK, Fenelon, W, M, d. 4 Jan 1879, Leesburg, heart disease, 65-3-25, p. ___Slack, b. LC, mechanic, c/o: Catherine Slack, sc: Lloyd Slack, son, 2nd Dist., BVS:1879:1

SLACK, Jas. E., W, M, d. 6 May 1894, nr Upperville, diphtheria, 6-0-0, p. Wm. B. & Mary E. Slack, b. nr Upperville, sc: Wm. B. Slack, father, 1st Dist., BVS:1894:1

SLACK, Mabel E., W, F, d. 28 Feb 1894, nr Upperville, diphtheria, 5-0-0, p. Wm. B. & Mary E. Slack, b. nr Upperville, sc: Wm. B. Slack, father, 1st Dist., BVS:1894:1

SLACK, Manly, W, M, d. 16 Dec 1883, Leesburg, pneumonia, 65-0-0, p. Jos. & Mary Slack, b. LC, laborer, c/o: Mahala J. Slack, sc: Geo W. Newton, son-in-law, 2nd Dist., BVS:1883:7

[SLACK], no name, W, F, d. 30 Nov 1854, Blue Ridge, unk, p. Jas. E. & Ann M. Slack, b. Blue Ridge, sc: mother, BVS:1854:12, LC:11

[SLACK], no name, W, F, d. 30 Nov 1854, Blue Ridge, unk, p. Jas. E. & Ann M. Slack, b. Blue Ridge, sc: mother, BVS:1854:12, LC:11

[SLACK], no name, W, F, d. Oct 1855, Blue Ridge, stillborn, unk, p. Jas. & Ann Maria Slack, b. Blue Ridge, sc: James Slack, father, BVS:1855:6, LC:18

SLACK, Sigerine, W, F, d. 27 Mar 1884, LC, old age, 87-0-0, p. Thomas & Ellen Chossel, b. LC, c/o: James Slack, sc: James E. Slack, son, 1st Dist., BVS:1884:2

SLACK, Wm. B., W, M, d. 13 Apr 1894, nr Upperville, diphtheria, 4-0-0, p. Wm. B. & Mary E. Slack, b. nr Upperville, sc: Wm. B. Slack, father, 1st Dist., BVS:1894:1

SLATER, Barbaray, W, F, d. 20 Aug 1854, LC, dysentery, 46-0-19, p. Peter & Milly Myers, b. LC, c/o: Samuel Slater, sc: Samuel Slater, husband, BVS:1854:9, LC:9

SLATER, George, W, M, d. 10 Nov 1866, nr Lovettsville, cancer, 71-0-0, b. LC, farmer, c/o: Sarah Slater, sc: Sarah Slater, wife, BVS:1866:1

SLATER, Ida C., W, F, d. 20 Jun 1892, Taylorstown, dropsy, 30-0-0, p. Jonas & Mary, b. LC, unm, sc: Jonas Slater, LV Dist., BVS:1892:6

SLATER, Julia A., W, F, d. 2 Dec 1889, LC, apoplexy, 65-0-0, p. Sam. Fry, b. LC, none, c/o: Samuel Slater, sc: Sam Slater, husband, 2nd Dist., BVS:1889:4

SLATER, Mary Ann, W, F, d. 20 Nov 1875, Lovettsville Dist, 52-0-0, p. Jacob & Christine Slater, b. LC, unm, LV Dist., BVS:1875:4

SLATER, Michael, W, M, d. 20 Jun 1896, Taylorstown, heart trouble, 65-0-0, p. unk, b. Taylorstown, unm, sc: Jonas Slater, LV Dist., BVS:1896:7

SLATER, Nellie M., W, F, d. 15 Jun 1886, LC, inflammation of brain, 1-6-0, p. Wm. L. & Flora E., b. LC, sc: Wm. L. Slater, father, 2nd Dist., BVS:1886:6

SLOPER, Tracy C., W, F, d. 19 Jun 1893, Arcola, indigestion, 0-0-5, p. S. M. & Teramonia Sloper, b. Arcola, sc: D.M. Sloper, father, 1st Dist., BVS:1893:1

SMALLWOOD, James W., W, M, d. 2 Jul 1887, Unison, consumption, 31-0-0, p. Geo. W. & Eliza J. Smallwood, b. Unison, sc: Francis M. Smallwood, brother, 1st Dist., BVS:1887:1

SMALLWOOD, Jas. W., W, M, d. 26 Dec 1854, res of father, croup, 4-4-0, p. Jas. W. & Mary Smallwood, b. Landmark Farm, sc: father & mother, BVS:1854:10, LC:10

Loudoun County, Virginia, Death Register, 1853-1896   235

SMALLWOOD, John Wesley, W, M, d. 1 April 1869, Clarke Co., natural decay, unk, p. Polly Smallwood, b. LC, stonemason, married, sc: Thomas Smallwood, son, BVS:1869:1

SMALLWOOD, Martha Alice, W, F, d. 16 Sep 1856, res of parents, inflammation bowels, 1-0-5, p. Jas. W. & Mary E. Smallwood, b. on Ketoctin Mt., sc: J.W. Smallwood, father, BVS:1856:5, LC:23

SMALLWOOD, Medora, W, F, d. 3 Jun 1888, LC, dropsy, 37-0-0, p. Conard & Eliza Virts, b. LC, none, c/o: F.M. Smallwood, sc: F.M. Smallwood, husband, 2nd Dist., BVS:1888:6

SMALLWOOD, no name, W, M, d. 12 Aug 1887, Round Hill, cold, 0-4-0, p. Henry L. & Ida M. Smallwood, b. Unison, sc: Henry L. Smallwood, father, 1st Dist., BVS:1887:3

SMALLWOOD, Susanna, W, F, d. 1 Apr 1886, LC, unk, 0-9-0, p. Robert A. & Harriet, b. LC, sc: Robert A. Smallwood, father, 2nd Dist., BVS:1886:6

SMALLWOOD, William, W, M, d. 7 Nov 1876, nr Neersville, worn-out with age, 86-0-0, p. Benj & Mercilius Smallwood, b. LC, farmer, c/o: Charlotte Smallwood, sc: Charlotte Smallwood, wife, LV Dist., BVS:1876:3

SMALLWOOD, Wm. Henry, W, M, d. 7 Jul 1864, Mount Zion, wounds, 18-9-0, p. Jas W. & M.E. Smallwood, b. nr Aldie, sc: Jas W. Smallwood, father, BVS:1864:1, LC:38

SMITH, Alfred W., B, M, d. 24 Mar 1885, Purcellville, bronchitis, 0-8-0, p. Nathan & Virginia Smith, b. LC, sc: Nathan Smith, father, 3rd Dist., BVS:1885:6

SMITH, Anna M., W, F, d. 16 Dec 1887, Middleburg, pneumonia, 77-0-0, p. John & Mary Johnston, b. Alexandria, Va., c/o: Gus Smith, sc: Charles A. Smith, son, 1st Dist., BVS:1887:1

SMITH, Annie J., W, F, d. 15 Jun 1885, nr Guilford, confinement, 38-0-0, p. Alpheus & Ann E. Gustin, b. New Jersey, c/o: Henry S. Smith, sc: Henry S. Smith, husband, 1st Dist., BVS:1885:5

SMITH, Caroline, W, F, d. Jun 1877, LC, heart disease, 52-0-0, p. Adam & Christina Sanbower, b. LC, c/o: Samuel Smith, sc: Samuel Smith, husband, LV Dist., BVS:1877:4/7

SMITH, Charles, B, M, d. 8 Mar 1883, nr Leesburg, unk, 60-0-0, b. LC, laborer, unk, sc: .... Russell, friend, 2nd Dist., BVS:1883:7

SMITH, Charles, B, M, d. 30 Jul 1887, Mountville, unk, 0-6-19, p. Solomon & Jane Smith, b. Mountville, sc: Solomon Smith, father, 1st Dist., BVS:1887:1

SMITH, Charles F., W, M, d. 2 Dec 1883, Leesburg, diphtheria, 3-3-0, p. Jas. H. & Natalie Smith, b. Rockbridge Co., sc: Jas H. Smith, father, 2nd Dist., BVS:1883:7

SMITH, Chas. F., W, M, d. 17 Nov 1896, Lovettsville, consumption, 28-0-0, p. Saml & Martha, b. Lovettsville, c/o: Saml. Smith, sc: Saml. Smith, consort, LV Dist., BVS:1896:7

SMITH, Cintha B., W, F, d. 15 Jul 1855, Aldie, unk, 67-0-0, p. Jas. & Mary L. White, b. Knoxville, TN, c/o: Thos. A. Smith, sc: Wm. Berkley, son-in-law, BVS:1855:4, LC:16

SMITH, Clarence, B, M, d. 15 Mar 1894, Mountville, jaundice, 0-0-21, p. Geo. & Jinnie Smith, b. nr Mountville, sc: Jinnie Smith, mother, 1st Dist., BVS:1894:2

SMITH, Daisy Catherine, B, F, d. 21 Jul 1892, Philomont, pneumonia, 0-1-0, p. Alexander Smith, b. LC, sc: Alexander Smith, father, MT Dist., BVS:1892:8

SMITH, David, W, M, d. 5 Oct 1854, dysentery, 48-0-0, p. John J. Smith, b. New York, farmer, sc: Lewis M. Millard, friend, BVS:1854:13, LC:13

SMITH, E. H., W, M, d. 20 Dec 1880, LC, dropsy, 3-0-0, p. James M. & S. J. Smith, unm, sc: Sallie J. Smith, mother, 1st Dist., BVS:1880:3

SMITH, Edgar B., W, M, d. 24 Aug 1855, Fairfax Co., summer complaint., 0-6-13, p. Henry G. & Tingy A. Smith, b. Middleburg, sc: Henry G. Smith, father, BVS:1855:7, LC:18

SMITH, Edmonia E., W, F, d. 30 Jun 1874, Broad Run Dist.,

consumption, 60-0-0, p. Geo. H. & Susan Hancock, b. LC, c/o: P.H. Smith, sc: Patrick H. Smith, husband, BR Dist., BVS:1874:3

SMITH, Edward A., W, M, d. 2 Feb 1887, Arcola, disease of kidneys, 56-0-0, p. Aler G. & Margaret Smith, b. Arcola, farmer, c/o: Mary S. Smith, sc: Mary S. Smith, wife, 1st Dist., BVS:1887:3

SMITH, Ella C., W, F, d. 22 Apr 1888, Sterling, heart disease, 35-0-0, p. unk, b. Sterling, c/o: Henry Smith, sc: Henry Smith, husband, 1st Dist., BVS:1888:4

SMITH, Ellen, B, F, d. 20 Jan 1890, Lincoln, typhoid fever, 10-0-0, p. Nathan & Jennie Smith, b. LC, none, unm, sc: Nathan Smith, father, 3rd Dist., BVS:1890:7

SMITH, Emma, B, F, d. Feb 1892, Paxson, typhoid fever, unk, p. Nathan & Lucy Smith, b. LC, sc: Nathan Smith, father, MT Dist., BVS:1892:8

SMITH, George, W, M, d. 4 Feb 1856, LC, cancer, 78-9-5, p. George & Katharine Smith, b. LC, farmer, c/o: Eve B. Smith, sc: Job Smith, son, BVS:1856:2, LC:21

SMITH, Ginnie, B, F, d. 1 Mar 1886, nr Middleburg, burnt to death, 20-0-0, p. Mary Smith (unm), b. LC, unm, sc: Wm. Runner, brother-in-law, 1st Dist., BVS:1886:2

SMITH, Henrietta, B, F, d. 15 Nov 1896, nr Unison, consumption, 8-0-0, p. Amanda Smith, b. nr Unison, none, unm, sc: Amanda Smith, mother, MC Dist., BVS:1896:2

SMITH, Henry, B, M, d. 22 Mar 1877, Poor House, consumption, 20-0-0, b. LC, unm, sc: Wm. H. Hibbs, superintendent of poor, MC Dist., BVS:1877:5

SMITH, Henry G., W, M, d. 7 Jul 1866, nr Mount Gilead, consumption, unk, p. Hugh & Eliz. Smith, sheriff, sc: Renfro Smith, brother, BVS:1866:2

SMITH, Henry T., W, M, d. 18 Aug 1871, nr Morrisonville, thrown from a horse, 20-10-0, p. Job & Lydia Smith, b. nr Neersville, sc: Job Smith, father, JF Dist., BVS:1871:1

[SMITH], Hugh E., W, M, d. 6 Aug 1856, nr Dover, consumption, 0-0-19, p. Rufus & Mary A. Smith, b. nr Dover, sc: Rufus Smith, father, BVS:1856:4, LC:21

SMITH, Isabella, W, F, d. Jun 1877, LC, b. fever, 65-0-0, p. ....Dinges, b. West Virginia, c/o: Late Solomon Smith, sc: David A. Dinges, brother, LV Dist., BVS:1877:4/7

SMITH, J. Frank, W, M, d. 11 Jul 1886, LC, heart disease, 62-0-0, farmer, c/o: Martha Smith, sc: A.L. Smith, son, 3rd Dist., BVS:1886:4

SMITH, Jacob, W, M, d. 21 Dec 1855, LC, pneumonia, 40-2-11, p. Geo. & Eva B. Smith, b. LC, c/o: Mary Smith, sc: Mary Smith, wife, BVS:1855:2, LC:15

SMITH, James, W, M, d. 16 Nov 1871, ulcerated leg, 82-0-0, farmer, married, BR Dist., BVS:1871:3

SMITH, Jesse, B, M, d. 5 Dec 1896, nr Unison, consumption, 21-0-0, p. Amanda Smith, b. nr Unison, none, unm, sc: Amanda Smith, mother, MC Dist., BVS:1896:2

SMITH, Job T., W, M, d. 21 Jun 1879, nr Lovettsville, unk, 0-0-27, p. John L. & Mary E. Smith, b. LC, sc: John L. Smith, father, 2nd Dist., BVS:1879:1

SMITH, John N., W, M, d. 3 Jun 1887, LC, diphtheria, 8-0-0, p. John L. & Elizabeth Smith, b. LC, none, unm, sc: John L. Smith, father, 2nd Dist., BVS:1887:5

SMITH, Josephine, W, F, d. 19 Aug 1854, Middleburg, typhoid fever, 15-0-0, p. Jos. & Sallie Smith, b. Fauquier Co., sc: G. W. Adams, BVS:1854:11, LC:10

SMITH, Julia, B, F, d. 10 Jan 1891, Middleburg, dyspepsia, 7-0-0, p. W. & Harriet Smith, b. LC, laborer, unm, sc: Wm. Smith, head of family, 1st Dist., BVS:1891:1

SMITH, Katie, B, F, d. 10 Jun 1892, Mountville, pneumonia, 0-7-0, p. Solomon & Jane Smith, b. Mountville, laborer, sc: Solomon Smith, father, 1st Dist., BVS:1892:4

SMITH, Lacy V., W, F, d. 9 Dec 1874, Broad Run Dist., pneumonia, 0-10-29, p. Edward A. & Mary L. Smith, farmer, sc: Edward A. Smith, father, BR Dist., BVS:1874:3

Loudoun County, Virginia, Death Register, 1853-1896   237

SMITH, Lewis, W, M, d. 18 Apr 1890, LC, rheumatism, 19-0-0, p. William & Elizabeth Smith, b. LC, farmer, unm, sc: H.P. Kalb, brother-in-law, 2nd Dist , BVS:1890:4

SMITH, Lillian, W, F, d. 5 Nov 1886, LC, diphtheria, 12-8-0, p. Gunnell & Mary F., b. LC, sc: Gunnell Smith, father, 2nd Dist., BVS:1886:6

SMITH, Louisa, B, F, d. 26 Mar 1882, LC, consumption, 14-0-0, p. Nathan & Virga. Smith, sc: Nathan Smith, parent, 3rd Dist., BVS:1882:3

SMITH, Lucy J., W, F, d. 3 Jul 1883, nr Guilford, heart disease, 40-0-0, p. unk, b. unk, c/o: James Smith, sc: James Smith, husband, 1st Dist., BVS:1883:2

SMITH, Lula, W, F, d. 5 Feb 1878, nr Mt. Hope Church, typhoid pneumonia, 22-0-0, p. Patrick & Edmonia Smith, b. Clarke Co., unm, sc: Patrick Smith, father, BR Dist., BVS:1878:4

SMITH, Mable F., W, F, d. 5 May 1879, nr Lovettsville, bleeding, 0-5-15, p. Geo. W. & Mary E. Smith, b. LC, sc: Geo. W. Smith, father, 2nd Dist., BVS:1879:1

SMITH, Margaret, W, F, d. 10 Jul 1872, nr Gum Spring, cancer, 67-4-0, p. unk, b. Maryland, c/o: Alexander G. Smith, sc: Alexander G. Smith, BR Dist., BVS:1872:6

SMITH, Margaret Louisa, W, F, d. 8 Dec 1893, Silcott Springs, diphtheria, 9-0-0, p. Alice & Julian Smith, b. LC, c/o: daughter, sc: wife, MT Dist., BVS:1893:4

SMITH, Martha T., W, F, d. 5 Apr 1880, nr Leesburg, pneumonia, 38-0-0, p. Thomas & Theresa Vaughn, b. LC, c/o: John E. Smith, sc: John E. Smith, husband, 2nd Dist., BVS:1880:7

SMITH, Martha V., W, F, d. 25 Mar 1872, Leesburg, brain fever, 1-11-4, p. Wm. P. & Virginia Smith, b. Leesburg, sc: Wm. P. Smith, father, LE Dist., BVS:1872:4

SMITH, Mary, B, F, d. 10 Jun 1892, Unison, bronchitis & heart failure, 19-0-0, p. Jeff & Amanda Smith, b. Unison, unm, sc: Jeff Smith, father, 1st Dist., BVS:1892:4

SMITH, Matilda, B, F, d. 12 Feb 1874, Middleburg, scrofula, 11-0-0, p. Wm & Harriet Smith, b. LC, sc: Wm. Smith, father, MC Dist., BVS:1874:4

[SMITH], no name, W, M, d. 7 Dec 1854, LC, unk, 0-0-2, p. Wm. & Caroline M. Smith, b. LC, sc: Wm. Smith, father, BVS:1854:8, LC:8

[SMITH], [no name], W, F, d. 1 May 1865, nr Beaver Dam, unk, p. S.P. & M.G. Smith, sc: S.P. Smith, father, BVS:1865:1

SMITH, no name, W, F, d. Aug 1873, nr Pot House, still born, unk, p. Stephen P. & M. G. Smith, b. LC, sc: Stephen P. Smith, father, MC Dist., BVS:1873:6

[SMITH], no name, B, F, d. 10 May 1875, LC, spasms, 0-0-7, p. Milly Smith, b. Leesburg, sc: John Phillips, friend, LE Dist., BVS:1875:2

SMITH, no name, W, M, d. 12 Mar 1878, nr Lovettsville, 0-0-10, p. John L. & Mary E. Smith, b. LC, sc: John L. Smith, father, LV Dist., BVS:1878:1/5

SMITH, no name, B, M, d. 2 May 1881, LC, unk, 0-2-0, p. Thos. & Lavina Smith, b. LC, unm, sc: Thos Smith, father, 3rd Dist., BVS:1881:4

SMITH, no name, W, M, d. 2 Aug 1881, LC, dysentery, 0-10-0, p. Gunnell & Francis Smith, b. LC, sc: Gunnel Smith, father, 3rd Dist., BVS:1881:5

SMITH, no name, B, M, d. 6 Feb 1885, Philomont, unk, 0-0-1, p. Alexander & Virga Smith, b. LC, c/o: Alexander Smith, sc: Alexr Smith, father, 3rd Dist., BVS:1885:6

SMITH, no name, B, M, d. 4 Jul 1892, Unison, la grippe, 0-0-7, p. Susie Smith, b. Unison, laborer, sc: Susie Smith, mother, 1st Dist., BVS:1892:4

[SMITH], no name, B, M, d. Dec 1893, North Fork, unk, 0-0-2, p. Preston Smith, b. LC, sc: father, MT Dist., BVS:1893:4

SMITH, Olive, W, F, d. 7 Dec 1874, Middleburg, disease of heart, 34-0-0, b. Montgomery Co., VA, c/o: Chas. A. Smith, sc: Chas. A. Smith, husband, MC Dist., BVS:1874:4

SMITH, P.H., W, M, d. 12 Nov 1880, LC, tumor in stomach, 62-0-0, p.

unk, c/o: Martha Smith, sc: Martha Smith, wife, 1st Dist., BVS:1880:3

SMITH, Peter, W, M, d. 2 Jan 1892, Lenah, a falling tree, 44-0-0, p. Elias & Selina M. Smith, b. New York, farmer, c/o: Sarah E. Smith, sc: Sarah E. Smith, wife, 1st Dist., BVS:1892:2

SMITH, Ruth R., W, F, d. 2 Oct 1890, Lincoln, paralyzed, 84-0-0, p. Geo. & P. Gregg, b. LC, none, sc: Thomas R. Smith, friend, 3rd Dist., BVS:1890:7

SMITH, Sarah E., W, F, d. 8 May 1884, Hamilton, consumption, 46-11-24, p. Joshua & Sarah Hatcher, b. Virginia, c/o: Joshua Smith, sc: Joshua Smith, husband, 3rd Dist., BVS:1884:7

SMITH, Solomon, W, M, d. 9 Nov 1872, nr Lovettsville, spinal cord, 67-2-21, p. John & Eve Smith, b. LC, farmer, married, sc: Isabelle Smith, wife, LV Dist., BVS:1872:5

SMITH, Susannah, W, F, d. 21 Jun 1888, LC, dyspepsia & rheumatism, 55-0-20, p. John & Dortha Snoots, b. LC, none, c/o: Henry A. Smith, sc: Henry A. Smith, husband, 3rd Dist., BVS:1888:2

SMITH, Thomas, B, M, d. 1 Nov 1890, nr Arcola, croup, 3-0-0, p. Angie Smith (unm), b. LC, sc: Richd Jackson, brother-in-law, 1st Dist., BVS:1890:2

SMITH, Thos. Atwell, W, M, d. 29 Dec 1855, Middleburg, scrofula, 9-3-11, p. Jas. W. & Permelia Smith, b. Middleburg, sc: father, BVS:1855:3, LC:16

SMITH, Tracy Biuel, W, F, d. 14 Aug 1876, nr Bolington, croup, 0-4-0, p. Geo W. & Mary Ella Smith, b. nr Bolington, sc: Geo W. Smith, father, LV Dist., BVS:1876:3

SMITH, Virginia, B, F, d. 17 Nov 1889, LC, heart disease, 39-0-0, p. Nathan & Virginia Smith, b. LC, laborer, c/o: Nathan Smith, sc: Nathan Smith, husband, 3rd Dist., BVS:1889:5

SMITH, William, W, M, d. 24 Feb 1890, LC, rheumatism, 68-0-0, p. Jacob & Elizabeth Smith, b. LC, farmer, c/o: Elizabeth A. Smith, sc: H.P. Kalb, son-in-law, 2nd Dist., BVS:1890:4

SMITH, William A., W, M, d. 20 Jun 1856, Leesburg, dysentery, 1-7-4, p. Wm. P. & Ann V. Smith, b. Leesburg, sc: Wm. P. Smith, father, BVS:1856:1, LC:19

SMITH, William P., W, M, d. 7 Mar 1889, LC, heart trouble, 71-0-0, p. unk, b. LC, none, unm, sc: J.D. Smith, son, 2nd Dist., BVS:1889:4

SMITH, Wilson, B, M, d. 10 Jul 1883, nr Lovettsville, unk, 1-0-0, p. Susan Smith, b. LC, unm, sc: Susan Smith, mother, 2nd Dist., BVS:1883:4

SMITH, Wm., W, M, d. 20 Jun 1896, Waxpool, old age, 77-0-0, b. Ireland, farmer, c/o: Rhoda F. Smith, sc: Jos E. Smith, son, BR Dist., BVS:1896:3

SMITH, Wm., B, M, d. 3 April 1896, Middleburg, bright's disease, 79-0-0, p. unk, b. LC, laborer, consort, sc: L. Smith, wife, MC Dist., BVS:1896:2

SNEED, William, B, M, d. 5 Apr 1886, LC, frozen to death, 18-0-0, p. William & Willie A., b. LC, laborer, sc: Holman Sneed, brother, 2nd Dist., BVS:1886:6

SNIDER, Annie, W, F, d. 27 May 1896, Harpers Ferry, cancer, 11-0-0, p. unk, b. Harpers Ferry, unm, sc: Peter Snider, LV Dist., BVS:1896:7

[SNIDER], no name, B, M, d. 12 Dec 1890, nr Mountville, unk, 0-0-2, p. James & Annie Snider, b. nr Mountville, sc: James Snider, father, 1st Dist., BVS:1890:2

SNOOTS, Adie, W, F, d. 1 Dec 1887, LC, whooping cough, 1-0-0, p. Samuel & Annie Snoots, b. LC, none, unm, sc: Samuel Snoots, father, 2nd Dist., BVS:1887:5

SNOOTS, Edgar M., W, M, d. 15 Dec 1892, Leesburg, unk, 0-4-0, p. Alonzo & Nellie Snoots, b. Leesburg, unm, sc: Alonzo Snoots, LE Dist., BVS:1892:5

SNOOTS, John, W, M, d. 15 Sep 1854, LC, drowned, 16-0-20, p. John & Dorothy Snoots, b. LC, sc: John Snoots, father, BVS:1854:9, LC:9

SNOOTS, Margaret A., W, F, d. 30 Oct 1896, Morrisonville, congestion of brain, 63-0-0, p. unk, b. unk, c/o: William Snoots, sc: William Snoots, consort, LV Dist., BVS:1896:7

SNOOTS, Presley, W, M, d. 5 Aug 1890, LC, old age, 79-0-0, p. Henry

Loudoun County, Virginia, Death Register, 1853-1896 239

Snoots, b. LC, none, c/o: Sallie Snoots, sc: J.H. Shry, friend, 2nd Dist., BVS:1890:4
SNOOTS, Sallie, W, F, d. 1 Apr 1890, LC, old age, 70-0-0, p. Jacob & Betsy Fry, b. LC, none, c/o: Presley Snoots, sc: J.H. Shry, friend, 2nd Dist., BVS:1890:4
SNOOTS, Susan R., W, F, d. 25 Oct 1854, LC, dysentery, 0-11-2, p. Jonas & Ann M. Snoots, b. LC, sc: Jonas Snoots, father, BVS:1854:8, LC:7
SNOOTS, Walter M., W, M, d. 3 Sep 1872, Morrisonville, unk, 1-11-10, p. Wm. & Margaret Snoots, b. Morrisonville, shoemaker, married, sc: Wm. Snoots, father, LV Dist., BVS:1872:5
SNYDER, Jasin, W, M, d. 10 Mar 1881, LC, diphtheria, 7-0-0, p. Wm H. & Harriet Snyder, b. LC, sc: Wm H. Snyder, father, 1st Dist., BVS:1881:2
SNYDER, Maurice, W, M, d. 7 Mar 1881, LC, diphtheria, 10-0-0, p. Wm H. & Harriet Snyder, b. LC, sc: Wm H. Snyder, father, 1st Dist., BVS:1881:2
SNYDER, Sarah W., W, F, d. 16 Nov 1881, LC, malarial fever, 37-5-4, p. Wm. & C. A. Virts, b. Maryland, c/o: Peter Snyder, sc: Peter Snyder, husband, 2nd Dist., BVS:1881:7
SOLOMON, Francis, W, M, d. 15 Oct 1881, LC, cancer, 67-0-0, b. LC, sc: Geo W. Solomon, brother, 1st Dist., BVS:1881:2
SOLOMON, Jas. W., W, M, d. 14 Feb 1894, nr Farmwell, unk, 73-0-0, p. unk, b. unk, farmer, c/o: Jane Solomon, sc: H.H. Bodine, son-in-law, 1st Dist., BVS:1894:1
SOLOMON, Nancy, W, F, d. 18 May 1875, nr Belmont, cancer, 56-0-0, p. Wm. & Henrietta Soloman, b. LC, unm, sc: Jas. W. Soloman, brother, BR Dist., BVS:1875:5
SOLOMON, Thomas F., W, M, d. Feb 1857, unk, 0-0-20, p. George W. & M.A. Solomon, b. LC, sc: G.W. Solomon, father, BVS:1857:7, LC:28
SOUDER, Emily, W, F, d. 11 Oct 1887, LC, consumption, 60-0-0, p. Michael & Susan Souder, b. LC, none, unm, sc: John O. Weaning, brother-in-law, 2nd Dist., BVS:1887:5
SOUDER, M. J., W, M, d. 15 Jan 1893, Lovettsville, dyspepsia, 46-0-0, p. unk, b. Lovettsville, consort, sc: A. J. Souder, LV Dist., BVS:1893:5
SOUDER, Mary E. & Rebecca, W, F, d. 16 Jul 1866, nr Lovettsville, child bed, 0-3-0, p. Geo. P. & Rebecca Souder, b. LC, sc: G.P. Souder, father, BVS:1866:1
SOUDER, Rebecca, W, F, d. 3 May 1866, nr Lovettsville, child bed, 39-10-0, p. Mich. & Susana Fry, b. LC, c/o: G. P. Souder, sc: G. P. Souder, husband, BVS:1866:1
SOUDER, Walter H., W, M, d. 1 Nov 1886, LC, consumption, 0-4-25, p. Philip H. & Lettie, b. LC, sc: P.H. Souder, father, 2nd Dist., BVS:1886:6
[SOUELL], no name, B, F, d. 16 Oct 1866, Old Road, unk, 0-0-26, p. Saml & Louisa Souell, b. LC, sc: Samuel Souell, father, BVS:1866:3
SOWERS, Beulah, W, M, d. 10 May 1881, LC, diphtheria, 1-3-0, p. Robt L. & Harriet Sowers, b. LC, sc: H. Sowers, mother, 1st Dist., BVS:1881:2
SOWERS, Maggie H., W, F, d. 2 May 1881, LC, consumption, 28-0-0, b. LC, c/o: Jas S. Sowers, sc: J.S. Sowers, husband, 1st Dist., BVS:1881:2
[SOWERS], no name, W, F, d. 1 Jan 1874, Broad Run Dist., still born, unk, p. Robt. L. & Harriet Sowers, sc: Robt. L. Sowers, father, BR Dist., BVS:1874:3
SOWERS, Wm. C., W, M, d. 10 May 1881, LC, spasms, 0-6-0, p. Jas S. & Maggie A. Sowers, b. LC, sc: J.S. Sowers, father, 1st Dist., BVS:1881:2
SPATES, Hattie, W, F, d. 31 Jan 1886, LC, croup, 5-0-1, p. Jno T. & Sarah Spates, b. LC, sc: Jno T. Spates, father, 3rd Dist., BVS:1886:4
SPATES, Thomas, W, M, d. 27 Mar 1874, Hillsboro, 0-0-1, p. Thos. & Sarah Spates, b. Hillsboro, sc: Thomas Spates, father, JF Dist., BVS:1874:2
SPEAKS, Mary C. A., W, F, d. 20 Dec 1855, LC, unk, 0-2-21, p. Richd. J. &

Mary E. Speaks, b. LC, sc: Richd. J. Speaks, father, BVS:1855:1, LC:14

SPEAKS, Thomas J., W, M, d. 30 Oct 1886, LC, unk, unk, p. unk, b. LC, laborer, c/o: Rachael Speaks, sc: Jno. T. Shumaker, son-in-law, 2nd Dist., BVS:1886:6

SPENCER, Chas, W, M, d. May 1864, Carolina Road, dysentery, 1-0-0, p. Wm. H. & E.F. Spencer, b. LC, sc: Wm. H. Spencer, father, BVS:1864:2, LC:39

SPINKES, Lucy, W, F, d. 16 Jun 1896, nr Bloomfield, inflammation of stomach, 56-0-0, p. unk, b. nr Bloomfield, none, consort, sc: T. Pearson, head of family, MC Dist., BVS:1896:2

SPINKS, Ada, W, F, d. 25 Dec 1892, Waterford, whooping cough, 0-3-0, p. John & Nancy Spinks, b. Waterford, unm, sc: John Spinks, LE Dist., BVS:1892:5

SPINKS, David A., W, M, d. 15 Oct 1881, LC, consumption, 0-3-0, p. Jno & Mary Spinks, b. LC, sc: Mary Spinks, mother, 1st Dist., BVS:1881:2

SPINKS, H. Alexander, W, M, d. 31 Dec 1884, Leesburg, brain fever, 1-6-0, p. Alexdr. & Ada Spinks, b. LC, sc: Alexr Spinks, father, 2nd Dist., BVS:1884:5

SPINKS, Henry, W, M, d. Dec 1859/60, Union, pneumonia, 60-0-0, p. unk, b. Fairfax, laborer, c/o: Sarah Spinks, sc: Thomas Spinks, son, BVS:1859:3, 1860:1, LC:34

SPINKS, Mary, W, F, d. 28 Nov 1890, LC, croup, 4-0-0, p. Alex. Spinks, b. LC, none, c/o: Alexander Spinks, sc: Alex Spinks, father, 2nd Dist., BVS:1890:4

[SPINKS], no name, W, M, d. May 1854, unk, 0-0-1, p. Wm. F. & Sarah Spinks, b. LC, sc: Sarah Spinks, mother-in-law, BVS:1854:13, LC:13

SPINKS, Sarah, W, F, d. May 1854, consumption, 35-0-0, p. Henry & Sina Taylor, b. Fairfax, Virginia, sc: Sarah Spinks, mother-in-law, BVS:1854:13, LC:13

SPOTWOOD, Jesse, B, M, d. 23 Dec 1871, 100-0-0, sc: R.C. Littleton, MC Dist., BVS:1871:2

SPRIGG, Eva, B, F, d. 25 Aug 1893, nr Arcola, cholera infantum, 0-9-0, p. Moses & Emma Sprigg, b. nr Arcola, sc: Emily Spriggs, mother, 1st Dist., BVS:1893:2

SPRIGG, John C., W, M, d. 11 Jan 1874, Broad Run Dist., chronic rheumatism, 49-10-0, p. Benj & Fannie Sprigg, b. Dist. of Columbia, farmer, married, sc: Susan Sprigg, wife, BR Dist., BVS:1874:3

SPRIGGS, Bell, B, F, d. 20 Dec 1887, LC, hydrocephalus, 3-0-0, p. unk, b. LC, none, unm, sc: Lewis M. Shumate, friend, 2nd Dist., BVS:1887:5

[SPRIGGS], no name [2], B, M, d. 20 May 1890, nr Arcola, unk, 0-0-10, p. Bettie Spriggs (unm), b. nr Arcola, sc: Richard Overall, brother-in-law, 1st Dist., BVS:1890:2

SPRIGS, Henson, B, M, d. 25 Sep 1881, LC, old age, 80-0-0, p. unk, b. Maryland, laborer, c/o: Harriet Sprigs, sc: Lewis Harris, step-son, 2nd Dist., BVS:1881:7

SPRING, Allice L., W, F, d. 17 Apr 1890, LC, la grippe, 25-11-14, p. Thomas & Virginia Hickman, b. LC, none, c/o: D.W. Spring, sc: D.W. Spring, husband, 2nd Dist., BVS:1890:4

SPRING, Charlotte, W, F, d. 30 May 1880, nr Leesburg, old age, 80-0-0, p. --- Slater, b. LC, c/o: Henson Spring, sc: Mary Barnes, daughter, 2nd Dist., BVS:1880:7

SPRING, Henry, W, M, d. 13 Feb 1858, LC, paralyzed, 56-0-0, p. Jacob & Susan Spring, b. LC, laborer, c/o: Charlotte Spring, sc: Charlotte Spring, wife, BVS:1858:2, LC:30

SPRING, James L., W, M, d. 29 Apr 1876, LC, fever, 1-10-0, p. Jefferson & Sophia F. Spring, b. LC, sc: Jefferson Spring, father, LE Dist., BVS:1876:7

SPRING, John, W, M, d. 22 Oct 1865, res of his son William, b. colic, 70-0-0, farmer, c/o: Mary Spring, sc: Wm. Spring, son, 1st Dist., BVS:1865:3/4

SPRING, John W., W, M, d. 14 Nov 1880, nr Leesburg, diphtheria, 3-5-19, p. Jonas S. & Catharine Spring,

Loudoun County, Virginia, Death Register, 1853-1896   241

b. LC, unm, sc: Catherine Spring, mother, 2nd Dist., BVS:1880:7

SPRING, Lena M., W, F, d. 18 Sep 1886, LC, unk, 0-3-27, p. Wm. F. & Ruth N., b. LC, sc: Wm. F. Spring, father, 2nd Dist., BVS:1886:6

SPRING, Lula, W, F, d. 10 May 1875, Lovettsville Dist, 1-6-0, p. Chas & Laura Spring, b. LC, unm, LV Dist., BVS:1875:4

SPRING, Lydia A., W, F, d. 5 Oct 1883, nr Lovettsville, cancer, 60-0-0, p. Jno. & Elizth. Compher, b. LC, c/o: William Spring, sc: Wm. Spring, husband, 2nd Dist., BVS:1883:4

SPRING, Mary C., W, F, d. 4 Jun 1893, Taylorstown, tumor, 53-0-0, b. Taylorstown, unm, sc: Joseph Unger, LV Dist., BVS:1893:5

SPRING, William, W, M, d. 26 Jul 1888, LC, old age, 76-0-0, p. Casper & Eliza Spring, b. unk, farmer, unm, sc: Edward Spring, son, 2nd Dist., BVS:1888:6

SRY, Geo. H., W, M, d. 11 Dec 1854, LC, convulsions, 0-4-14, p. John & Mary M. Sry, b. LC, sc: John Sry, father, BVS:1854:8, LC:7

SRY, no name, W, F, d. 27 May 1880, nr Leesburg, unk, 0-1-0, p. John & Priscilla Sry, b. LC, unm, sc: Jno. W. Sry, father, 2nd Dist., BVS:1880:7

SRYOCK, B.F., W, F, M, d. Jan 1857, unk, 3-0-0, p. George E. & Rebecca Sryock, b. LC, sc: George E. Sryock, father, BVS:1857:7, LC:28

SRYOCK, Susan, W, F, d. 23 Dec 1856, LC, burnt, 70-0-0, p. Michael & Rosanna Sryock, b. LC, sc: George Sryock, brother, BVS:1856:7, LC:24

STANSBURY, Jesse J., W, M, d. 19 Jul 1886, LC, organic disease of liver, 57-0-0, p. --- Stansbury, b. LC, merchant, c/o: Margaret A. Stansbury, sc: M. A. Stansbury, wife, 2nd Dist., BVS:1886:6

STATLER, John, W, M, d. 31[sic] Jun 1856, LC, old age, 96-5-11, p. unk, b. LC, unm, sc: Mary J. Wenner, friend, BVS:1856:2, LC:21

STEADMAN, Charlie, W, M, d. 25 Nov 1888, LC, pneumonia, 0-7-0, p. W. P. & Mamie Steadman, b. LC, none, unm, sc: W.H. Steadman, father, 2nd Dist., BVS:1888:6

STEADMAN, Chas. M., W, M, d. 8 Jun 1888, LC, unk, 0-1-0, p. J. M. & Lillian Steadman, b. unk, teacher, unm, sc: J.M. Steadman, father, 2nd Dist., BVS:1888:6

STEADMAN, Elmo, W, M, d. 22 Jan 1893, Leesburg, diphtheria, 3-0-0, p. W. H. & Mary, b. Leesburg, unm, sc: W.H. Steadman, LE Dist., BVS:1893:6

STEADMAN, Marshall B., W, M, d. 8 May 1883, Leesburg, paralysis, 58-0-0, p. James & Alsey Steadman, b. LC, laborer, c/o: Emily Steadman, sc: Wm. H. Steadman, son, 2nd Dist., BVS:1883:7

STEADMAN, Thos. F., W, M, d. 15 Sep 1875, Leesburg, smapsma, 1-6-0, p. J. T. & Sarah R. Steadman, b. Leesburg, sc: J.T. Steadman, father, LE Dist., BVS:1875:2

STEADMAN, Thos. J., W, M, d. 30 Apr 1872, Leesburg, pneumonia, 54-0-0, p. Jas. & Alsey Steadman, b. Jefferson Co., cooper, c/o: Susan F. Steadman, sc: Susan F. Steadman, wife, LE Dist., BVS:1872:4

STEADMAN, Virginia W., W, F, d. 14 Aug 1875, Leesburg, cholera infantum, 0-10-3, p. M. B. & Emiline Steadman, b. Leesburg, sc: M.B. Steadman, father, LE Dist., BVS:1875:2

STEDMAN, Elizabeth J., W, F, d. 31 Jul 1854, Leesburg, dysentery, 34-6-2, p. James & Alice Stadman, b. Indianna, unm, sc: James Stedman, father, BVS:1854:10, LC:10

STEDMAN, James, W, M, d. 5 Apr 1857, Leesburg, gravel, 67-11-12, p. Thomas & Sina Stedman, b. Jefferson Co., cooper, c/o: Alsey Stedman, sc: Marshall B. Stedman, son, BVS:1857:2, LC:25

STEDMAN, Jenny, W, F, d. 20 Aug 1853, Leesburg, dysentery, 6-3-20, p. David & Elizth Stedman, b. unk, sc: David Stedman, father, BVS:1854:5, LC:3

STEDMAN, John, W, M, d. 28 May 1856, Leesburg, pneumonia, 70-0-0, p. Thomas & Sina Stedman, b. Jefferson, cooper, c/o: Margaret Stedman, sc: James W. Stedman, son, BVS:1856:1, LC:19

[STEDMAN], no name, W, F, d. 27 Jan 1854, LC, unk, unk, p. Jas. W. & Matilda M. Stedman, b. Leesburg, sc: James W. Stedman, father, BVS:1854:10, LC:10

STEER, James M., W, M, d. 28 Nov 1874, nr Winchester, pneumonia, 64-0-0, p. Jas. & Mary Steer, b. Waterford, mechanic, unm, sc: Frank Steer, son, JF Dist., BVS:1874:2

STEER, Joseph, W, M, d. 2 Nov 1859/60, Waterford, unk, 76-4-1, p. Isaac & Phebe Steer, b. Frederick Co. VA, miller, c/o: Sarah Steer, sc: James M. Steer, son, BVS:1859:1, 1860:3, LC:36

STEER, Leah, W, F, d. 10 Feb 1853, LC, pneumonia, 68-0-12, p. Lewis & Sarah Walker, b. Frederick, c/o: Isaac E. Steer, sc: Isaac E. Steer, husband, BVS:1854:3, LC:1

STEER, Mary E., W, F, d. 30 May 1857, Waterford, apoplexy, 42-0-0, p. Ephraim & Tacy Schooley, b. Waterford, c/o: Jonah Steer, sc: Jonah Steer, husband, BVS:1857:1, LC:24

STEER, Phebe M., W, F, d. 31 Aug 1888, LC, dysentery, 69-0-0, b. LC, sc: Frank M. Steer, son, 3rd Dist., BVS:1888:2

STEER, Samuel R., W, M, d. 15 Jul 1874, Waterford, fever, 2-3-0, p. Frank & Mary Steer, b. Waterford, sc: Frank Steer, son, JF Dist., BVS:1874:2

[STEPHENS], Hannah O., W, F, d. 1 Sep 1854, Evergreen, breast complaint, 1-3-0, p. Stephen O. & Casandra Stephens, b. Evergreen, sc: father, BVS:1854:12, LC:12

STEPHENS, Martha A.E., W, F, d. 4 Oct 1858, Wm. Fulton's Farm, pneumonia, 9-9-9, p. John & Roxanna Stevens, b. M.C. Shumate's Farm, sc: Roxanna Stevens, mother, BVS:1858:4, LC:32

STEPHENSON, Wm. H., W, M, d. 5 May 1889, Aldie, suicide, 72-0-0, p. unk, b. Fauquier Co., farmer, c/o: Catharine Stephenson, sc: Catharine Stephenson, wife, 1st Dist., BVS:1889:1

STEPTOE, Frances Ann, (f), F, d. Jun 1857, Peter Steptoe's, consumption, 37-0-0, p. Peter & Hannah Steptoe, b. nr Coe's Mill, sc: Hannah Steptoe, mother, BVS:1857:5, LC:27

STEPTOE, Lucy E., B, F, d. 15 Apr 1864, nr Coe's Mill, typhoid fever, 14-7-0, p. Phebe Parker, b. LC, sc: Phebe Parker, BVS:1864:2, LC:39

STEVENS, Cassandria, W, F, d. 20 Nov 1853, Ball's Mill, dropsy, 30-0-0, p. unk, b. Fairfax, c/o: S.O. Stevens, sc: husband, BVS:1854:6, LC:5

STEVENS, John A., W, M, d. 6 Apr 1872, LC, crushed in a well, 61-0-0, p. unk, b. Leesburg, well digger, c/o: Roxanna Stevens, sc: Roxanna Stevens, consort, LE Dist., BVS:1872:4

STEVENS, Louisa H., W, F, d. 29 Mar 1853, LC, consumption, 22-9-5, p. Enos & E. Stevens, b. LC, unm, sc: Susan A. Stevens, step-mother, BVS:1854:2, LC:7

STEVENS, Sarah, W, F, d. 2 Jul 1877, LC, dysentery, 31-0-0, p. Wm. & Hannah Otley, b. LC, c/o: Thomas Stevens, sc: Thos. Stevens, husband, JF Dist., BVS:1877:3

STEVENS, Wm. T., W, M, d. 20 Jul 1877, LC, cholera infantum, 0-2-0, p. Thos. & Sarah Stevens, b. LC, sc: Thos. Stevens, father, JF Dist., BVS:1877:3

STEWARD, Ann M., (f), F, d. 5 Apr 1859/60, LC, scarlet fever, 5-0-0, p. George & Sally A. Steward, b. LC, sc: Sally A. Steward, mother, BVS:1859:2, 1860:4, LC:37

STEWARD, Catharine, W, F, d. 18 Apr 1878, nr Taylorstown, 30-0-0, married, sc: John E. Steward, LV Dist., BVS:1878:1/5

STEWARD, Catharine E., (f), F, d. 23 Mar 1859/60, LC, unk, 1-11-2, p. George & Sally A. Steward, b. LC, sc: Sally A. Steward, mother, BVS:1859:2, 1860:4, LC:37

STEWARD, Daniel C., W, M, d. 17 Nov 1872, Ketoctin Hill, brain fever, 1-0-0, p. Jno. E. & C. Steward, b. Ko Mill, miller, married, sc: Jno E. Steward, father, LV Dist., BVS:1872:5

STEWARD, Forest, B, M, d. 15 Dec 1888, LC, consumption, 8-0-0, p.

Martin & Hannah Steward, b. LC, none, unm, sc: Armstead Hunter, friend, 3rd Dist., BVS:1888:2

STEWARD, no name, B, M, d. 1 Jul 1888, LC, bronchitis, 0-2-0, p. Jennie Steward, b. LC, none, unm, sc: Jennie Steward, mother, unm, 3rd Dist., BVS:1888:2

STEWART, Charles, B, M, d. 17 Dec 1886, nr Unison, burnt to death, 4-0-0, p. Henry & Ellen Stewart, b. nr Unison, unm, sc: Willie Carter, stepfather, 1st Dist., BVS:1886:2

STEWART, Deliah M., W, F, d. 14 Jul 1853, nr North Fork, confinement, 24-0-0, p. Dolbert & Zilpha Winston, b. unk, c/o: J.E. Stewart, sc: husband, BVS:1854:1, LC:4

STEWART, Emma J., B, F, d. 15 Dec 1880, LC, gastritis, 10-0-0, p. Alfred & Lucy Stewart, unm, sc: Lucy Stewart, mother, 1st Dist., BVS:1880:3

STEWART, Frances, B, F, d. Nov 1896, Purcellville, confinement, 39-0-0, consort, sc: husband, JF Dist., BVS:1896:10

STEWART, George, B, M, d. Aug 1869, LC, 0-0-10, b. LC, laborer, sc: Jesse Stewart, father, BVS:1869:1

STEWART, John E., W, --, d. 18 Aug 1889, LC, unk, 60-11-15, p. John & Catherine Stewart, b. LC, farmer, c/o: Rebecca Stewart, sc: J.W. Stewart, son, 2nd Dist., BVS:1889:4

STEWART, Kate, B, F, d. 6 Feb 1874, Broad Run Dist., pneumonia, 30-0-0, p. unk, unm, sc: F.W. Pleasants, employer, BR Dist., BVS:1874:3

STEWART, Nancy, B, F, d. 13 Feb 1896, LC, old age, 97-0-0, p. Andrew & Fannie Buchanan, b. Oatlands, wife, wife, sc: Elizabeth Valentine, JF Dist., BVS:1896:6

[STEWART], no name, W, F, d. 11 Jul 1853, nr North Fork, unk, 0-0-1, p. John & Sarah Stewart, b. nr North Fork, sc: father, BVS:1854:1, LC:4

[STEWART], no name, B, F, d. Dec 1896, Purcellville, 0-0-6, p. Francis & F. Stewart, b. Purcellville, sc: father, JF Dist., BVS:1896:10

STEWART, Robt, B, M, d. Dec 1873, Maxville, effects of burns, 45-0-0, b. unk, b. unk, married, sc: Sallie Stewart, wife, MC Dist., BVS:1873:5

STEWART, Robt Lewis, B, M, d. Aug 1873, Maxville, whooping cough, 1-0-0, p. Robt & Sallie Stewart, b. Middleburg, sc: Sallie Stewart, mother, MC Dist., BVS:1873:5

STILES, Columbus, B, M, d. 1 Jan 1892, Unison, unk, 1-6-0, p. Carter & Isabella Stiles, b. Unison, laborer, sc: Carter Stiles, father, 1st Dist., BVS:1892:4

STILES, no name, B, F, d. 21 Jun 1886, nr Pot House, unk, 0-0-1, p. Carter & Isabella Stiles, b. nr Pot House, sc: Carter Stiles, father, 1st Dist., BVS:1886:2

STILLIONS, Newman, W, M, d. 7 Jan 1880, LC, gravel, 87-0-0, p. unk, unm, sc: J.H. Stillions, friend, 1st Dist., BVS:1880:3

STINGER, Adolin, B, F, d. 30 Sep 1866, Washington, DC, rush blood to the head, 22-0-15, p. Joshua & Flora Stinger, b. LC, unm, sc: Joshua Stinger, father, BVS:1866:3

STINGER, Flora, B, F, d. 31 Mar 1866, nr Guilford Station, water around heart, 62-1-10, p. Chas & Flora Foster, b. Washington DC, sc: Joshua Stinger, husband, BVS:1866:3

STINGER, Matilda, B, f', d. 20 Dec 1871, unk, 20-0-0, p. Margaret Stinger, BR Dist., BVS:1871:3

STOCKS, Alpheus E., W, M, d. 24 Sep 1854, LC, dysentery, 0-6-12, p. Mahlon & Matilda J. Stocks, b. LC, sc: Matilda J. Stocks, mother, BVS:1854:9, LC:8

STOCKS, David W., W, M, d. 12 Jun 1853, LC, croup, 3-7-22, p. Mahlon & Matilda Stocks, b. LC, sc: Matilda Stocks, mother, BVS:1854:4, LC:2

STOCKS, David W., W, M, d. 12 Jan 1854, LC, croup, 3-7-22, p. Mahlon & Matilda J. Stocks, b. LC, sc: Matilda J. Stocks, mother, BVS:1854:9, LC:8

STOCKS, Elizabeth, W, F, d. 6 Jun 1866, nr Ketoctin Mountain, paralyzed, 70-0-0, p. Jacob & Esther Sands, b. LC, married, sc: Stephen Stocks, son, BVS:1866:1

STOCKS, Elizabeth E., W, F, d. 24 Sep 1879, nr Goresville, dropsy, 50-0-0, p. Saml. & Mary McCutcheon, b. LC, c/o: Joshua Stocks, sc:

Joshua Stocks, husband, 2nd Dist., BVS:1879:1

STOCKS, Marshall, W, M, d. 15 Jun 1892, Leesburg, dysentery, 0-11-0, p. Joshua & Mary Stocks, b. Leesburg, unm, sc: Joshua Stocks, LE Dist., BVS:1892:5

STOCKS, Nicholas, W, M, d. 15 Dec 1886, LC, typhoid fever, 15-0-0, p. Joshua & Catharine, b. LC, laborer, sc: Joshua Stocks, father, 2nd Dist., BVS:1886:6

STONE, Annie E., W, F, d. 1879, nr Lovettsville, dyspepsia, 45-0-0, p. Michael & Mary Fry, b. LC, c/o: William J. Stone, sc: William J. Stone, husband, 2nd Dist., BVS:1879:1

STONE, Louisa, W, F, d. 21 Oct 1855, nr Wheatland, cancer, 40-0-0, p. Francis & Susanna Stone, b. nr Leesburg, sc: Mary Grayham, sister, BVS:1855:6, LC:17

STONE, Mary, W, F, d. 14 Feb 1893, Britain, dyspepsia, 75-0-0, p. unk, b. Britain, consort, sc: Chas. L. Stone, LV Dist., BVS:1893:5

STONE, Rebecca, W, F, d. Dec 1896, Hillsboro, old age, 81-0-0, consort, JF Dist., BVS:1896:8

STONEBURNER, Christopher, W, M, d. 11 Feb 1879, LC, old age, 84-0-0, p. ___Stoneburner, b. LC, farmer, c/o: Jane A. Stoneburner, sc: James T. Stoneburner, son, 2nd Dist., BVS:1879:1

STONEBURNER, Clarence G., W, M, d. 22 Nov 1886, LC, croup, 0-1-2, p. Wm. C. & Sallie E., b. LC, sc: W. C. Stoneburner, father, 2nd Dist., BVS:1886:6

STONEBURNER, Harriet E., W, F, d. 10 Oct 1890, LC, bronchitis, 24-0-0, p. James & Mary Harper, b. LC, none, c/o: J.E. Stoneburner, sc: J.E. Stoneburner, husband, 2nd Dist., BVS:1890:4

STONEBURNER, Henry O., W, M, d. 29 Dec 1875, LC, unk, 0-0-1, p. S. G. & M. C. Stoneburner, b. Leesburg, sc: S. G. Stoneburner, father, LE Dist., BVS:1875:2

STONEBURNER, Laura J., W, F, d. 22 Sep 1854, LC, dysentery, 2-0-9, p. Peter & Catherine Stoneburner, b. LC, sc: Peter Stoneburner, father, BVS:1854:9, LC:8

STONEBURNER, Mary C., W, F, d. 8 Sep 1854, LC, dysentery, 28-0-0, p. unk, b. unk, c/o: Saml. Stoutsenberger, sc: T. M. Paxson, wife's step mother, BVS:1854:9, LC:9

STONEBURNER, Peter, W, M, d. 7 Sep 1880, nr Lovettsville, old age, 74-10-2, p. David & Mary Stoneburner, b. LC, c/o: Catherine Stoneburner, sc: Catherine Stoneburner, wife, 2nd Dist., BVS:1880:7

STONESTREET, Augustus, W, M, d. 15 Feb 1877, nr Frankville Church, old age, 88-0-0, p. unk, b. unk, farmer, married, sc: Benj. F. Fling, friend, BR Dist., BVS:1877:1

STOTT, Jane H., W, F, d. 17 Oct 1856, LC, unk, 51-0-0, p. Wm. & Jannet Ormiston, b. Pennsylvania, c/o: John E. Stott, sc: John E. Stott, head of family, BVS:1856:7, LC:23

STOTT, Margaret, W, F, d. 12 Jan 1857, bronchitis, 18-0-0, p. John E. & Jane Stott, b. New York, sc: John E. Stott, father, BVS:1857:7, LC:28

STOTT, Mary Ann, W, F, d. 14 Oct 1856, LC, unk, 18-0-0, p. John E. & Jane E. Stott, b. Pennsylvania, unm, sc: John E. Stott, father, BVS:1856:7, LC:23

STOUT, Chas. C., W, M, d. 12 Jul 1892, Lucketts, cholera infantum, 4-0-0, p. Geo. W. & Annie Stout, b. Lucketts, unm, sc: Geo W. Stout, LE Dist., BVS:1892:5

[STOUT], no name, W, M, d. 11Dec 1875, LC, unk, 0-0-1, p. Henry C. & Ann E. Stout, b. Leesburg, sc: Henry C. Stout, father, LE Dist., BVS:1875:2

STOUTS, Henry C., W, M, d. 9 Jun 1880, nr Leesburg, unk, 29-4-2, p. Jno. L. & Margaret Stouts, b. LC, laborer, c/o: Annie C. Stouts, sc: Annie C. Stouts, wife, 2nd Dist., BVS:1880:7

STOUTSENBERGER, Jacob, W, M, d. 25 Aug 1854, LC, jaundice, 56-5-7, p. John J. & Margaret M. Stoutsenberger, b. LC, farmer, c/o: Mary Stoutsenberger, sc: Margaret

A. Stoutsenberger, dau, BVS:1854:9, LC:9
STOUTSENBERGER, Mary, W, F, d. 25 Sep 1854, LC, dysentery, 54-7-19, p. Abraham & Catherine Carnes, b. LC, c/o: Jacob Stoutsenberger, sc: Margaret A. Stoutsenberger, dau, BVS:1854:9, LC:9
STOVER, Edwin A., W, F, d. Oct 1854, Aldie, consumption, 55-0-0, b. Massachusetts, painter, sc: James S. Oden, friend, BVS:1854:13, LC:13
STRATHER, Maria, B, F, d. 10 Sep 1891, Aldie, colic, 46-0-0, p. John & Rachael Davis, b. Bedford Co., laborer, c/o: John Strather, sc: John Strather, head of family, 1st Dist., BVS:1891:1
STREAM, Franklin, W, M, d. 7 Feb 1880, nr Leesburg, disease of kidney, 7-1-20, p. William & Mary A. Stream, b. LC, unm, sc: William Stream, father, 2nd Dist., BVS:1880:7
STREAM, Geo. W., W, M, d. 13 Sep 1855, LC, unk, 0-2-0, p. Wm. & Mary A. Stream, b. LC, sc: Wm. Stream, father, BVS:1855:2, LC:15
STREAM, Jacob, W, M, d. 25 Oct 1856, LC, accidental, 59-8-11, p. unk, b. LC, c/o: Susanna Stream, sc: George W. Stream, son, BVS:1856:1, LC:20
STREAM, John, W, M, d. 3 Jul 1894, Taylorstown, kidney disease, 70-0-0, p. unk, b. unk, unm, sc: Wm. L. Stream, LE Dist., BVS:1894:3
STREAM, Maud L., W, F, d. 2 Mar 1886, LC, unk, 0-10-1, p. Chas. F. & Ida V., b. LC, sc: Chas. F. Stream, father, 2nd Dist., BVS:1886:6
STRICKLER, George, W, M, d. 18 May 1857, res of Jos. Strickler, old age, 103-2-28, p. Henry & Mary Strickler, b. nr Lovettsville, farmer, c/o: Jane Strickler, decd, sc: Joseph Strickler, son, BVS:1857:4, LC:27
STRINGER, Sharper, (f), M, d. Dec 1856, Samuel Tillett's, 0-1-0, p. Alvernon Johnson, b. Samuel Tillett's, sc: Samuel Tillett, BVS:1856:5, LC:23
STRINGFELLOW, no name, B, M, d. 18 May 1884, Leesburg, unk, 0-0-3, p. Henry & Fannie Stringfellow, b.

LC, sc: Henry Stringfellow, father, 2nd Dist., BVS:1884:5
STRINGFELLOW, Susan, W, F, d. 12 Nov 1864, LC, scrofula, 68-0-0, p. ... Hamilton, b. Warren Co., c/o: B. Stringfellow, sc: Jno W. Thomas, BVS:1864:1, LC:38
STROTHER, Allen, B, M, d. 1 Dec 1886, nr Unison, pneumonia, 2-0-0, p. Laura Strother (unm), b. nr Unison, unm, sc: John H. Strother, brother, 1st Dist., BVS:1886:2
STROTHER, Harriet, B, F, d. 22 Feb 1887, Unison, unk, 4-0-0, p. Lucy Strother (unm), b. Unison, sc: Arch Strother, grandfather, 1st Dist., BVS:1887:1
STROTHER, Harriet, B, F, d. 12 Aug 1887, Unison, unk, 0-6-8, p. Harriet Strother (unm), b. Unison, sc: Arch Strother, grandfather, 1st Dist., BVS:1887:1
STROTHER, Kate/Cate S., W, F, d. 20 Jun 1859/60, Leesburg, inflammation bowel, 4-6-0, p. Henry & Mary E. Strother, b. Rappahannock, sc: Mary E. Strother, mother, BVS:1859:2, 1860:5, LC:37
STROTHER, Lucy, B, F, d. 10 May 1869, LC, consumption, 29-0-0, p. Eli & Lucinda Summers, b. LC, married, sc: Edwin Strother, husband, BVS:1869:1
STUART, Alfred, B, M, d. 30 May 1881, LC, fits, 4-0-0, p. Alfred & Lucy Stuart, b. LC, unm, sc: Alfred Stuart, father, 3rd Dist., BVS:1881:4
STUART, Alice A., B, F, d. 10 Jun 1883, Philomont, burned, 14-0-0, p. Limus & Ann Stuart, b. LC, sc: Limus Stuart, father, 3rd Dist., BVS:1883:5
STUART, Howard, B, M, d. 10 Feb 1886, LC, typhoid fever, 0-3-0, p. Jesse & Mary Stuart, b. LC, sc: Jesse Stuart, father, 3rd Dist., BVS:1886:4
SUGARS, Harry, W, M, d. 1 Jul 1889, LC, inflammation of bowels, 18-0-0, p. Jas B. & May Sugars, b. LC, none, unm, sc: Jas B. Shugars, father, 3rd Dist., BVS:1889:5
SUGARS, M., W, M, d. 10 Jul 1889, LC, unk, 4-0-0, p. Jas B. & Mary Sugars, b. LC, none, unm, sc: Jas B.

Shugars, father, 3rd Dist., BVS:1889:5

SULLIVAN, Samuel, W, M, d. 9 Feb 1853, LC, consumption, 34-0-0, p. Murtho & Elizh Sullivan, b. LC, laborer, unm, sc: Stevens T. McDaniel, head of family, BVS:1854:5, LC:3

SUMMERS, Chas. W., W, M, d. 21 Nov 1885, Bloomfield, consumption, 1-6-0, p. Armstead & Winnie Summers, b. Bloomfield, sc: Armstead Summers, father, 1st Dist., BVS:1885:5

SUMMERS, Daniel, W, M, d. 18 April 1875, nr Gum Spring, rheumatism, 75-1-0, p. Geo. & Mary Summers, b. LC, farmer, married, sc: Thos. Summers, son, BR Dist., BVS:1875:5

SURVICK, Benjamin D., W, M, d. 26 Sep 1880, Leesburg, typhoid fever, 27-8-20, p. George & Mary Survick, b. LC, butcher, c/o: Sarah H. Survick, sc: Sarah H. Survick, wife, 2nd Dist., BVS:1880:7

SURVICK, George, W, M, d. 17 Aug 1883, Leesburg, rheumatism, 72-0-0, p. Christian & Elizth Survick, b. LC, butcher, c/o: Mary A. Survick, sc: Geo W. Survick, son, 2nd Dist., BVS:1883:4

SURVICK, Jacob, W, M, d. 5 Sep 1876, Leesburg, cholera infantum, 0-0-2, p. George W. & Alice M. Survick, b. Leesburg, sc: George W. Survick, father, LE Dist., BVS:1876:7

SURVICK, Lagrand, W, M, d. Oct 1879, Leesburg, lockjaw, 0-0-6, p. Benj. & Virginia Survick, b. LC, sc: Benjamin Survick, father, 2nd Dist., BVS:1879:2

SURVICK, Mary L., W, F, d. 18 Jun 1890, LC, cholera infantum, 0-3-0, p. Boyd E. & Mollie Survick, b. LC, none, unm, sc: B.E. Survick, father, 2nd Dist., BVS:1890:4

SURVICK, Rodgers, W, M, d. 17 Aug 1883, Leesburg, measles, 0-2-0, p. Geo. W. & Alice M. Survick, b. LC, sc: Geo W. Survick, father, 2nd Dist., BVS:1883:4

SUTPHIN, no name, W, M, d. 1 Jun 1892, Mountville, cholera infantum, 0-1-0, p. Henry & Minnie Sutphin, b. Rappannoch Co., sc: Henry Sutphin, father, 1st Dist., BVS:1892:2

SUTPHIN, Phillip, W, M, d. 6 Sep 1892, Mountville, typhoid fever, 27-0-0, p. Wm. & Emily Sutphin, b. Rappahanock Co., laborer, unm, sc: Henry Sutphin, brother, 1st Dist., BVS:1892:2

SUTTEN, Geo., B, M, d. Mar 1896, Round Hill, consumption, 48-0-0, laborer, consort, sc: Mary Fitzhugh, JF Dist., BVS:1896:10

SUTTON, Willis, B, M, d. Dec 1894, Round Hill, consumption, 21-0-0, p. George & Georgiana Sutton, b. Round Hill, sc: Geo. W. Sutton, father, 3rd Dist., BVS:1894:5

SVEDBERG, Carl, W, M, d. 1 Jul 1894, nr Sterling, congestion lungs, 0-7-11, p. Jno. A. & Hedvig Svedberg, b. nr Sterling, sc: Jno A. Svedberg, father, 1st Dist., BVS:1894:1

SVEDBERG, John A., W, M, d. 18 Dec 1896, Sterling, heart failure, 59-0-0, b. Sweden, Chief Eng. U.S.N., c/o: Hedrig Svedberg, sc: Hedrig Svedberg, wife, BR Dist., BVS:1896:3

SWAIN, Elizabeth A., W, F, d. 14 Jul 1857, res of parents, unk, 14-10-0, p. John & Maria Swain, b. Maryland, sc: father, BVS:1857:3, LC:26

SWAIN, Henry H., W, M, d. 2 Aug 1878, Unison, typhoid fever, 24-8-9, p. Jno H. & Maria Swain, b. LC, merchant, unm, sc: Jno H. Swain, father, MC Dist., BVS:1878:7

SWAIN, Lucy, W, F, d. 12 Jan 1858, res of paretns, unk, 1-2-0, p. John W. & Maria Swain, b. nr Middleburg, c/o: John W. Swain, sc: John W. Swain, father, BVS:1858:4, LC:31

SWANK, Aaron, W, M, d. 16 Jun 1884, nr Lovettsville, dropsy, 69-0-0, p. Philip & Kate Swank, b. LC, farmer, c/o: Mary E. Swank, sc: Samuel Swank, brother, 2nd Dist., BVS:1884:5

SWANK, John, W, M, d. 20 Dec 1884, nr Lovettsville, paralysis, 79-0-0, p. Philip & Kate Swank, b. LC, farmer, unm, sc: Samuel Swank, brother, 2nd Dist., BVS:1884:5

SWANK, Michael, W, M, d. 5 Dec 1856, LC, consumption, 77-0-0, p. John & Catharine Swank, b. LC, unm, sc: Wm. Swank, nephew, BVS:1856:2, LC:21

SWANK, Philip, W, M, d. 8 Aug 1854, LC, dysentery, 72-1-0, p. John & Catherine Swank, b. LC, farmer, c/o: Mary Swank, sc: Wm. Swank, son, BVS:1854:9, LC:8

SWANK, Samuel P., W, M, d. 18 Jul 1883, nr Lovettsville, paralysis, 37-0-0, p. Aaron & Alcinda Swank, b. LC, farmer, c/o: Eva R. Swank, sc: Eva R. Swank, wife, 2nd Dist., BVS:1883:7

SWANK, William, W, M, d. 1 May 1880, nr Lovettsville, unk, 68-7-0, p. Philip Swank, b. LC, unm, sc: Saml P. Swank, nephew, 2nd Dist., BVS:1880:7

SWART, Adrian L., W, M, d. Dec 1856, LC, gravel, 68-0-0, p. James & Mary Swart, b. LC, sc: Robert Swart, brother, BVS:1856:7, LC:23

SWART, Ann, W, F, d. 11 Mar 1857, unk, 68-0-0, p. Henry & Constance Settle, b. LC, c/o: Adrian L. Swart, sc: M.H. Swart, son, BVS:1857:7, LC:28

SWART, Elizabeth, W, F, d. 4 Jan 1877, Goshen Farm, old age, 83-0-0, p. James Swart & wife, b. unk, unm, sc: A.L. Swart, nephew, BR Dist., BVS:1877:1

SWART, Franklin, W, M, d. 21 May 1872, nr Goose Creek, consumption, 20-0-0, p. Lafayette W. Swart & wife, b. LC, sc: L.W. Swart, BR Dist., BVS:1872:6

SWART, Martha, W, F, d. 30 Sep 1892, Lenah, deranged, 69-11-0, p. Elias & Leah Matthews, b. LC, c/o: A.L. Swart, sc: A.L. Swart, husband, 1st Dist., BVS:1892:2

SWART, no name [twin], W, F, d. 11 Feb 1891, nr Unison, premature, 0-0-1, p. W. A. & Bertie Swart, b. LC, farmer, sc: W.A. Swart, father, 1st Dist., BVS:1891:3

SWART, no name [twin], W, M, d. 11 Feb 1891, nr Unison, premature, 0-0-1, p. W. A. & Bertie Swart, b. LC, farmer, sc: W.A. Swart, father, 1st Dist., BVS:1891:3

SWART, Parmelia A., W, F, d. 4 Jan 1865, Aspen Hill, consumption, 16-0-5, p. S.W. & Huldah Swan, b. LC, servant, unm, sc: L.W. Swart, father, BVS:1865:2

SWART, Virginia K., W, F, d. 30 Jan 1891, nr Paris, membranous croup, 3-0-0, p. D. W. & Annie R. Swart, b. LC, farmer, sc: D.W. Swart, father, 1st Dist., BVS:1891:3

SWART, Wm. F., W, M, d. 27 May 1872, LC, consumption, 18-0-0, p. Lafayette & Hulda Swart, b. LC, farmer, unm, sc: Lafayette Swart, father, LE Dist., BVS:1872:4

SWOPE, Minnie A., W, F, d. 10 Nov 1891, Lovettsville, paralysis, 15-0-0, p. J.H. & Roma Swope, b. Lovettsville, farmer, unm, sc: father, LV Dist., BVS:1891:5

SYDNEY, George, B, M, d. 21 Mar 1877, LC, gastritis, 69-6-0, c/o: Louisa Sydney, sc: Thos. Sydney, son, LE Dist., BVS:1877:9

SYMONS, Martha Jane, W, F, d. 1 May 1865, Geo. B. McCarty's, 0-2-5, p. C.A. & Martha J. Symons, b. Geo B. McCarty's, sc: C.W. Symans, father, BVS:1865:1

TALBOT, Edward, B, M, d. Nov 1873, Leesburg, consumption, 32-0-0, b. LC, laborer, unm, sc: Matthew Lucket, friend, LE Dist., BVS:1873:2

TALLEY, Thomas F., W, M, d. 18 Dec 1854, LC, rheum, 12-4-7, p. John & Barbary Talley, b. LC, sc: Barbary Talley, mother, BVS:1854:8, LC:8

TATE, Guy, B, M, d. 4 Oct 1883, Silcott Springs, old age, 80-0-0, b. LC, laborer, sc: Alexander Tebbs, friend, 3rd Dist., BVS:1883:5

TATE, Juliet, B, F, d. 30 Mar 1865, Sycamore Grove, consumption, 15-0-0, p. Jerry & Hannah Tate, b. Snickersville, servant, unm, sc: Washg Beavers, head of family, BVS:1865:2

TATE, Lucy, B, F, d. 5 Apr 1889, Philomont, old age, 80-0-0, p. unk, b. LC, unk, sc: F.E. Robey, superintendent of poor, 1st Dist., BVS:1889:1

TATE, Norman, B, M, d. 29 Jun 1892, Guinea, whooping cough, unk, p. Fenton & Sophrina Tate, b. LC, sc: Fenton Tate, father, MT Dist., BVS:1892:8

TAVENER, Ann B., W, F, d. 15 May 1872, nr Broad Run, consumption, 3-0-0, p. Jas. W. & Jane Tavener, b. LC, sc: Jas. W. Tavener, BR Dist., BVS:1872:6

TAVENER, Jas. H., W, M, d. 6 Sep 1871, unk, 10-0-0, p. Jas. W. & Jane Tavener, BR Dist., BVS:1871:3

TAVENER, Jonathan, W, M, d. 24 Jun 1860, res, cancer of stomach, 50-0-0, p. Jonah & Elizabeth Tavener, b. nr Hamilton, farmer, c/o: Emma A. Tavener, sc: Jonah Tavener, brother, BVS:1860:3

TAVENER, Richard H., W, M, d. 2 Jul 1872, nr Broad Run, consumption, 0-5-0, p. Jas. W. & Jane Tavener, b. LC, sc: Jas. W. Tavener, BR Dist., BVS:1872:6

TAVENNER, Annie M., W, F, d. 19 Jun 1888, LC, diphtheria, 6-10-0, p. J. A. & Emma Tavenner, b. LC, none, unm, sc: J.W. Tavenner, father, 3rd Dist., BVS:1888:2

TAVENNER, Annie M., W, F, d. 27 Mar 1888, LC, bronchitis, 3-0-0, p. James E. & Mary Tavenner, b. LC, none, unm, sc: James E. Tavenner, father, 3rd Dist., BVS:1888:2

TAVENNER, Charles R., W, M, d. 1 Aug 1853, LC, dysentery, 3-7-25, p. Chas. H. & Marian Tavenner, b. LC, sc: Chas H. Tavenner, father, BVS:1854:5, LC:3

TAVENNER, Estelle, W, F, d. 19 Jan 1879, Hillsboro, brain fever, 30-0-0, p. Wm. & Martha Hough, b. LC, c/o: Dr. R.W. Tavenner, sc: Dr. R.W. Tavenner, husband, 3rd Dist., BVS:1879:3

TAVENNER, Fielding, W, M, d. 9 Feb 1880, Philomont, consumption, 77-0-0, p. Israel & Mary Tavenner, b. LC, farmer, c/o: Jane Tavenner, sc: Owen Tavenner, son, 3rd Dist., BVS:1880:4

TAVENNER, Frank H., W, M, d. 8 Apr 1883, Mount Gilead, consumption, 45-0-0, p. George & Hannah Tavenner, b. LC, farmer, unm, sc: Geo P. Slack, friend, 3rd Dist., BVS:1883:5

TAVENNER, Jane, W, F, d. Jan 1854, Mount Gilead, unk, 23-0-0, p. George & Sarah Tavenner, b. Mount Gilead, sc: father, BVS:1854:11, LC:11

TAVENNER, Jonathan, W, M, d. 24 Jun 1859, his res, cancer of stomach, 56-0-0, p. Jonah & Elizth Tavenner, b. nr Hamilton, farmer, c/o: Emma A. Tavenner, sc: Jonah Tavenner, brother, BVS:1859:5, LC:36

TAVENNER, Lot, W, M, d. 16 Jul 1890, Lincoln, heart disease, 83-0-0, p. J. & Elizabeth Tavenner, b. LC, farmer, c/o: Elizabeth Tavenner, sc: S.E. Tavenner, daughter, 3rd Dist., BVS:1890:7

TAVENNER, Mahlon, W, M, d. 17 Sep 1884, Hamilton, paralysis, 61-0-0, p. Joseph & Ann Tavenner, b. Virginia, farmer, c/o: Susan Tavenner, sc: Jas B. Peugh, friend, 3rd Dist., BVS:1884:7

TAVENNER, Mariam, W, F, d. 1 Sep 1854, res of parents, typhoid fever, 18-5-5, p. Fielding & Hannah Tavenner, b. parents, nr Philomont, sc: father & mother, BVS:1854:12, LC:12

TAVENNER, Mary, W, F, d. 30 Oct 1891, Mount Gilead, heart & kidney trouble, 80-0-0, p. George & Sarah Tavenner, b. Mount Gilead, wife, unm, sc: G. Phinias Slack, MT Dist., BVS:1891:6

TAVENNER, Mary T., W, M, d. 26 Dec 1892, Mountain Gap, heart failure, 47-0-0, p. unk, b. Mountain Gap, consort, LE Dist., BVS:1892:5

TAVENNER, Nannie B., W, F, d. 20 Oct 1887, Unison, pneumonia, 14-0-9, p. William & Rachel Tavenner, b. Unison, unm, sc: William Tavenner, father, 1st Dist., BVS:1887:3

TAVENNER, no name, W, M, d. 9 Aug 1880, nr Leesburg, unk, 0-0-2, p. Wm. M. & Jennie A. Tavenner, b. LC, unm, sc: Jennie A. Tavenner, mother, 2nd Dist., BVS:1880:7

TAVENNER, no name, W, M, d. 9 Aug 1880, nr Leesburg, unk, 0-0-2, p. Wm. M. & Jennie A. Tavenner, b. LC, unm, sc: Jennie A. Tavenner, mother, 2nd Dist., BVS:1880:7

TAVENNER, Richd. E., W, M, d. 10 Apr 1881, LC, consumption, 48-0-0, b. LC, sc: Wm. Torrison, brother, 1st Dist., BVS:1881:2

Loudoun County, Virginia, Death Register, 1853-1896   249

TAVENNER, Susan, W, F, d. 28 Dec 1882, LC, rheumatism of heart, 31-0-0, c/o: Henry H. Tavenner, sc: Henry H. Tavenner, husband, 3rd Dist., BVS 1882:3

TAVENNER, Susan, W, F, d. 2 Oct 1890, Hamilton, paralyzed, 80-0-0, b. LC, none, unm, sc: James Pugh, friend, 3rd Dist., BVS:1890:7

TAVENNER, Susan A., W, F, d. 20 Dec 1885, Hamilton, paralysis, 59-0-10, p. Jonah & Fanny Nichols, b. Virginia, c/o: Mahlon Tavenner, sc: J.B. Peugh, son-in-law, 3rd Dist., BVS:1885:7

TAVENNER, Sydney B., W, M, d. 19 Apr 1887, LC, pneumonia, 77-0-0, p. Richard & Lizzie Tavenner, laborer, sc: R.W. Tavenner, friend, 3rd Dist., BVS:1887:7

TAVENNER, William, W, M, d. 20 May 1882, LC, kidney disease, 72-0-0, c/o: Malinda Tavenner, sc: E.H. Tavenner, wife, 3rd Dist., BVS:1882:3

TAVENNER, Wm., W, M, d. 17 Dec 1881, LC, pneumonia, 63-0-0, b. LC, c/o: Jane Tavenner, sc: J. Tavenner, wife, 1st Dist., BVS:1881:2

TAVNER, Letta M., B, F, d. May 1871, unk, p. Frances Tavner, unm, sc: R.H. Leith, MC Dist., BVS:1871:2

TAYLOR, Albert S., W, M, d. 26 Jul 1864, Taylor's Mill, water on the brain, 1-11-0, p. C.W. & ...Taylor, b. LC, sc: C.W. Taylor, father, BVS:1864:2, LC:39

TAYLOR, Armstead, W, M, d. 2 Apr 1891, heart disease, 73-0-0, p. Charles & Nancy Taylor, b. Round Hill, farmer, husband, sc: Nancy Taylor, JF Dist., BVS:1891:7

TAYLOR, Cathn., W, F, d. 1 Mar 1855, Dover, consumption, 68-0-0, p. Danl. & Eliz. Smith, b. Newton, Frederick Co., c/o: Jesse Taylor, sc: Jesse Taylor, BVS:1855:3, LC:16

TAYLOR, Dangerfield, W, M, d. 6 Sep 1881, LC, diphtheria, 5-0-0, p. Wm. F & Ann Taylor, b. LC, sc: A. Taylor, mother, 1st Dist., BVS:1881:2

TAYLOR, Eddie, B, M, d. Aug 1877, nr Silcott Springs, dysentery, 2-0-0, p. Elijah & Julia Taylor, b. LC, sc: E. Taylor, father, MT Dist., BVS:1877:2

TAYLOR, Eppa, W, M, d. 28 Dec 1881, LC, diphtheria, 5-6-0, p. Thos E. & May Taylor, b. LC, sc: Thos E. Taylor, father, 3rd Dist., BVS:1881:5

TAYLOR, Eva, W, F, d. 13 Sep 1881, LC, diphtheria, 1-0-0, p. Wm. F & Ann Taylor, b. LC, sc: A. Taylor, mother, 1st Dist., BVS:1881:2

TAYLOR, Franklin P., W, M, d. 28 Oct 1853, LC, affection of liver, 1-6-0, p. B. F. & Sarah Taylor, b. LC, sc: --- Taylor, aunt, BVS:1854:2, LC:7

TAYLOR, Gustava E., W, F, d. 30 Aug 1888, Waxpool, consumption, 41-0-0, p. Richard & Emily Moran, b. Waxpool, c/o: William Taylor, sc: William Taylor, husband, 1st Dist., BVS:1888:4

TAYLOR, Hannah, W, F, d. 24 Feb 1879, LC, general debility, 88-0-0, b. LC, c/o: Yardley Taylor, dec'd, sc: Thomas Brown, friend, 3rd Dist., BVS:1879:3

TAYLOR, Harrison, B, M, d. 10 Oct 1888, LC, spasms, 0-0-10, p. Wm. & Mary Taylor, b. unk, none, unm, sc: William Taylor, father, 2nd Dist., BVS:1888:6

TAYLOR, Henry, B, M, d. 30 Jan 1880, LC, apoplexy, 80-0-0, p. unk, mechanic, unm, sc: Theodore Arnett, friend, 1st Dist., BVS:1880:3

TAYLOR, Henry T., W, M, d. 13 Apr 1866, nr Lincoln, 67-0-0, p. Bernard Taylor, b. nr Lincoln, farmer, married, sc: Thos E. Taylor, son, BVS:1866:2

TAYLOR, James, B, M, d. 12 Jun 1875, Leesburg, bronchitis, 1-1-0, p. Jas. & Amanda Taylor, b. Leesburg, sc: Amanda Taylor, mother, LE Dist., BVS:1875:2

TAYLOR, Kate S., B, F, d. 7 Nov 1884, LC, consumption, 9-0-0, p. Robert & Elizabeth Taylor, b. LC, unm, sc: Robt Taylor, father, 1st Dist., BVS:1884:2

TAYLOR, Lincoln, B, M, d. 12 May 1869, LC, measles, 3-0-0, p. John & Amy Taylor, b. LC, sc: Miss Birdsall, friend, BVS:1869:1

TAYLOR, Louisa, (f), F, d. May 1855, Hannah Piggott's farm, consumption, 32-0-0, p. Jno. & Sally Jackson, b. Wm. Williamson's, c/o:

Bush. Taylor, sc: Caroline Jackson, sister, BVS:1855:7, LC:18
TAYLOR, Lucy, B, f, d. 10 Sep 1872, Leesburg, diarrhea, 1-3-2, p. Matilda Taylor, b. Leesburg, sc: Daniel Paine, friend, LE Dist., BVS:1872:4
[TAYLOR], Mahlon Craven, W, M, d. 25 Mar 1854, res of father, croup, 0-2-0, p. Richard & Lydia F. Taylor, b. res of father, nr Goose Creek Meeting House, sc: father & mother, BVS:1854:12, LC:12
TAYLOR, Mary, W, F, d. 2 Oct 1876, LC, old age, 79-0-0, p. Harry & Ann Taylor, b. unk, sc: Mary Radcliff, friend, JF Dist., BVS:1876:8
TAYLOR, Nancy, W, F, d. 28 May 1854, Taylor's Mill, apoplexy, 67-0-0, b. LC, c/o: Charles Taylor, sc: Charles N. Taylor, son, BVS:1854:13, LC:12
[TAYLOR], [no name], W, M, d. Aug 1857, unk, 0-2-0, p. A.M. & Nancy J. Taylor, b. LC, sc: A.M. Taylor, father, BVS:1857:7, LC:28
TAYLOR, no name, B, F, d. Aug 1873, Middleburg, unk, 0-1-15, p. Peyton & Frances Taylor, b. Middleburg, sc: Payton Taylor, father, MC Dist., BVS:1873:6
TAYLOR, no name, B, F, d. 10 Jul 1892, nr Upperville, spasms, 0-0-14, p. Robt. & Lucinda Taylor, b. nr Upperville, sc: Robt Taylor, father, 1st Dist., BVS:1892:4
TAYLOR, Peyton, B, M, d. 20 Jun 1896, Middleburg, heart disease, 69-0-0, p. unk, b. unk, stone mason, consort, sc: Madison Taylor, son, MC Dist., BVS:1896:2
TAYLOR, Rebecca E., W, F, d. 29 Jul 1856, Yardley Taylor's, consumption, 30-0-0, p. Jonathan & Mary Hamilton, b. LC, sc: Oliver Taylor, brother-in-law, BVS:1856:4, LC:22
TAYLOR, Rebecca H., W, F, d. 5 Dec 1872, Mount Gilead Twp., unk, 60-0-0, p. Edward & Mary Walker, b. Mount Gilead Town, c/o: Bernard Taylor, sc: Bernard Taylor, husband, MT Dist., BVS:1872:2
TAYLOR, Robert, B, M, d. 7 May 1886, nr Upperville, consumption, 16-0-0, p. Robt. & Elizabeth Taylor, b. LC, unm, sc: Robt Taylor, father, 1st Dist., BVS:1886:2
TAYLOR, Ruth W., W, F, d. 8 Dec 1857, Hamilton, pneumonia, 44-10-26, p. Mary Bradfield, b. nr Chamblin's Mill, c/o: Lewis Taylor, sc: L. Taylor, widower, BVS:1857:5, LC:28
TAYLOR, Thomas E., W, M, d. 6 Jan 1893, Lincoln, congestion brain, 62-0-0, p. Henry S. & Hann J. Taylor, b. LC, farmer, husband, sc: Mary Taylor, wife, MT Dist., BVS:1893:4
TAYLOR, Thos. B., W, M, d. 13 Nov 1874, Broad Run Dist., erysipelas, 0-1-0, p. Bushrod & Sarah Taylor, b. LC, sc: B. Taylor, head of family, BR Dist., BVS:1874:3
TAYLOR, Timothy, W, M, d. 17 Jul 1869, LC, dropsy of the heart, 76-0-0, p. Timothy Taylor, b. LC, farmer, married, sc: Johnson Taylor, son, BVS:1869:1
TAYLOR, Willie N., W, M, d. 8 Sep 1866, nr Purcellville, diphtheria, 4-4-0, p. Lewis & Eliz. Taylor, b. nr Purcellville, sc: Lewis Taylor, father, BVS:1866:2
TAYLOR, Wm., W, F[sic, d. 19 Sep 1874, nr Goose Creek Bridge, unk, 0-7-0, p. Wm H & Annie Taylor, b. LC, sc: Wm. H. Taylor, father, MC Dist., BVS:1874:4
TEBBS, Annie C., W, F, d. 6 Jun 1879, Leesburg, gastritis, 22-0-0, p. Chas. B. & H. Fannie Tebbs, b. LC, unm, sc: Richd H. Tebbs, brother, 2nd Dist., BVS:1879:2
TEBBS, Clara, B, F, d. 29 Jul 1892, Trappe, cholera infantum, 0-7-21, p. Bev. & Alice Tebbs, b. Trappe, sc: Bev Tebbs, father, 1st Dist., BVS:1892:3
TEBBS, Clarence, B, M, d. 10 Jul 1892, Trappe, cholera infantum, 0-7-0, p. Bev & Alice Tebbs, b. Trappe, sc: Bev. Tebbs, father, 1st Dist., BVS:1892:4
TEBBS, Elias, B, M, d. 3 Jun 1877, Wellbourne, bronchitis, 0-13-0, p. Geo. & Ellen Tebbs, b. LC, sc: Geo. Tebbs, father, MC Dist., BVS:1877:5
TEEL, Harriet F., W, F, d. 26 Dec 1883, nr Mountville, dropsy, 38-0-0, p. Henry & Jane Teel, b. Prince

William Co., unm, sc: Geo Williams, cousin, 1st Dist., BVS:1883:2

TEPRANE, Sinah, B, F, d. 4 Sep 1872, LC, old age, 103-1-4, p. Thos. Greenage, b. Stafford Co., VA, c/o: Page Teprane, sc: Abram Wallace, friend, LE Dist., BVS:1872:4

[TERRELL], no name, W, M, d. 25 Mar 1873, Hillsboro, unk, 0-0-1, p. Frederick H. C. & Mary B. Terrill, b. LC, sc: Frederick H.C. Terrill, father, JF Dist., BVS:1874:1

THAYER, Catherine V., W, F, d. 17 Sep 1890, LC, consumption, 21-0-0, p. Geo. W. & Susan Thayer, b. LC, none, unm, sc: S.W. Thayer, father, 2nd Dist., BVS:1890:4

THOMAS, Adalaide, W, F, d. 29 May 1882, LC, consumption, 42-0-0, p. Joseph & Mary Thomas, unm, sc: Jno T. Ross, uncle, 1st Dist., BVS:1882:2

THOMAS, Armistead, B, M, d. 10 Dec 1888, Unison, consumption, 65-0-0, p. unk, b. Unison, c/o: Hulday Thomas, sc: Hulday Thomas, wife, 1st Dist., BVS:1888:4

THOMAS, Catherine S., W, F, d. 6 Dec 1878, LC, typhoid fever, 58-6-0, b. LC, unm, sc: John D. Thomas, brother, LE Dist., BVS:1878:9

THOMAS, Chandelier, (f), M, d. 25 Jan 1857, LC, consumption, 40-0-0, p. Wm. & Nancy Thomas, b. LC, laborer, c/o: Jane A. Thomas, sc: Jane A. Thomas, wife, BVS:1857:1, LC:25

THOMAS, Charles, W, M, d. 17 Dec 1865, LC, diphtheria, 0-7-0, p. Wm. H. & Alice W. Moffett, b. LC, farmer, sc: father, BVS:1865:1

THOMAS, Eli, B, M, d. 16 Mar 1884, LC, old age, 72-0-0, p. Wm. & Lucy Thomas, b. Fauquier Co., farmer, c/o: Nancy Thomas, sc: Nancy Thomas, wife, 1st Dist., BVS:1884:2

THOMAS, Elizabeth, W, F, d. 21 Apr 1858, Leesburg, unk, 26-0-0, p. Michl & Nancy Fair, b. unk, c/o: John H. Thomas, sc: John H. Thomas, husband, BVS:1858:2, LC:30

THOMAS, Elizabeth W., W, F, d. Mar 1858, Jefferson C. Thomas', 58-0-0, p. Philip & Susanna Thomas, b. LC, sc: J.C. Thomas, brother, BVS:1858:4, LC:32

THOMAS, Eveline, W, F, d. 15 Apl 1866, nr Snickersville, inflammation bowel, 53-0-0, married, sc: Wm. P. Thomas, husband, BVS:1866:2

THOMAS, Fannie, B, F, d. 31 Dec 1866, foot of mountain, dropsy, 54-0-0, p. Rich & Polly Foster, b. Fauquier Co., sc: Eli Thomas, husband, BVS:1866:3

THOMAS, Grace, W, F, d. 25 Mar 1885, nr Leesburg, child birth, unk-0-0, p. unk, b. LC, c/o: William Thomas, sc: William Thomas, husband, 2nd Dist., BVS:1885:2

THOMAS, Henry, B, M, d. 4 Jun 1884, LC, fever, 25-0-0, p. Benja. & Mary Thomas, b. LC, laborer, unm, sc: John B. Thomas, brother, 1st Dist., BVS:1884:2

THOMAS, Herod, W, M, d. 28 Jun 1873, foot of Blue Ridge, cancer of stomach, 75-0-0, p. unk, b. LC, farmer, married, sc: F.P. Thomas, son, MC Dist., BVS:1873:6

THOMAS, Hulda, B, F, d. 30 Oct 1878, nr Upperville, erysipelas, 30-0-0, c/o: Armstead Thomas, sc: Armstead Thomas, husband, MC Dist., BVS:1878:7

THOMAS, James, W, M, d. 11 Aug 1883, nr Leesburg, old age, 82-0-0, p. --- Thomas, b. LC, farmer, c/o: --- Thomas, sc: James W. Thomas, son, 2nd Dist., BVS:1883:7

THOMAS, John, B, M, d. 24 Sep 1890, nr Middleburg, la grippe, 73-0-0, p. Wm. & Susan Thomas, b. LC, unm, sc: Louis Tebbs, brother-in-law, 1st Dist., BVS:1890:2

THOMAS, Jonah, W, M, d. 1 Apr 1885, Snickersville, heart disease, 70-0-0, b. LC, farmer, unm, sc: Jesse Thomas, brother, 3rd Dist., BVS:1885:6

THOMAS, Joseph, W, M, d. 4 Jan 1882, LC, consumption, 46-0-0, p. Joseph & Mary Thomas, farmer, c/o: Vernia Thomas, sc: Vernia Thomas, wife, 1st Dist., BVS:1882:2

THOMAS, Julia B., W, F, d. 9 Dec 1873, LC, typhoid fever, 20-0-0, p. Jas. & Martha Thomas, b. LC, unm, sc: A. Thomas, brother, LE Dist., BVS:1873:2

THOMAS, Lucy, B, F, d. 10 Nov 1882, LC, malarial fever, 13-0-0, p. Ann &

H. Thomas, unm, sc: Huldah Thomas, mother, 1st Dist., BVS:1882:2

THOMAS, Mahlon, W, M, d. 8 Jan 1883, Round Hill, heart disease, 73-0-0, p. Joseph & Ruth Thomas, b. LC, farmer, c/o: Jane Thomas, sc: Wm. G. Birdsall, friend, 3rd Dist., BVS:1883:5

THOMAS, Margaret, W, F, d. 19 Aug 1883, nr Leesburg, disease of liver, 61-0-0, p. Jno. & Margaret Thomas, b. LC, sc: Jno D. Thomas, brother, 2nd Dist., BVS:1883:4

THOMAS, Margaret F., W, F, d. 11 Aug 1858, Leesburg, unk, 1-10-0, p. John H. & Elizth Thomas, b. Leesburg, sc: John H. Thomas, father, BVS:1858:2, LC:30

THOMAS, Martha, B, F, d. 25 Jun 1883, nr Leesburg, unk, 60-0-0, p. unk, b. LC, laborer, c/o: Edward Thomas, sc: Edward Thomas, husband, 2nd Dist., BVS:1883:4

THOMAS, Mary, W, F, d. 29 Nov 1857, her res, pneumonia, 67-2-10, p. James & Ruth Bradfield, b. Maryland, c/o: Jefferson C. Thomas, sc: J.C. Thomas, widower, BVS:1857:5, LC:28

THOMAS, Mary Ann, W, F, d. 11 Mar 1858, her res, consumption, 83-0-0, p. Nathaniel & Nancy Moss, b. Fauquier Co., c/o: Daniel Thomas decd, sc: Nathaniel Thomas, son, BVS:1858:4, LC:31

THOMAS, Mary Ann, W, F, d. 4 Nov 1866, nr Trappe, Blue Ridge, consumption, 65-0-0, sc: Herod Thomas, husband, BVS:1866:2

THOMAS, Mary E., W, F, d. 10 Jul 1854, Washington City, diarrhea, 31-2-6, p. unk, b. Prince William Co, c/o: John H. Thomas, sc: John H. Thomas, husband, BVS:1854:8, LC:7

THOMAS, Mary/Nancy, (f), F, d. 1 Aug 1853, LC, unk, 0-2-0, p. Saml. & Eliza Thomas, b. LC, sc: Saml Thomas, F.N., father, BVS:1854:3, LC:1

THOMAS, Moses, W, M, d. 15 Jun 1887, nr Philomont, consumption, 75-0-0, p. unk, b. LC, farmer, c/o: Elizabeth Thomas, sc: F.E. Robey, superintendent of poor, 1st Dist., BVS:1887:3

THOMAS, Nancy, W, F, d. Jun 1857, Maryland, cancer, 52-0-0, p. Daniel & Mary Thomas, b. Fauquier Co., sc: Nathaniel Thomas, brother, BVS:1857:5, LC:27

[THOMAS], no name, W, M, d. 22 Jul 1854, Leesburg, unk, 0-1-18, p. John H. & Mary E. Thomas, b. Washington City, sc: John H. Thomas, father, BVS:1854:7, LC:7

[THOMAS], no name, W, F, d. 22 Jul 1854, LC, dysentery, 0-0-18, p. John H. & Mary E. Thomas, b. LC, sc: John H. Thomas, father, BVS:1854:10, LC:10

[THOMAS], no name, W, M, d. 5 May 1869, LC, unk, 0-0-5, p. John H. & Emma Jane Thomas, b. LC, sc: John H. Thomas, father, BVS:1869:1

[THOMAS], no name, B, F, d. Oct 1873, LC, stillborn, unk, p. Wm. & Grace Thomas, b. LC, laborer, unm, sc: Wm. Thomas, father, LE Dist., BVS:1873:2

THOMAS, Randolph, B, M, d. 28 Jul 1885, Aldie, unk, 0-1-0, p. Frank & Ginnie Thompson, b. Aldie, sc: Frank Thomas, father, 1st Dist., BVS:1885:5

THOMAS, Robert, W, M, d. 15 Sep 1854, Fauquier Co, suddenly, 1-0-1, p. Alex. A. & Elizabeth Hall, b. Fauquier Co., sc: father, BVS:1854:13, LC:13

THOMAS, Salina F., B, F, d. 15 Apr 1883, nr Middleburg, unk, 10-0-0, p. Ned & Jane E. Thomas, b. nr Middleburg, unm, sc: Ned Thomas, father, 1st Dist., BVS:1883:2

THOMAS, Samuel, B, M, d. Nov 1878, Snickersville, natural causes, unk, b. Fauquier Co., c/o: Rhoda Thomas, sc: G. Anderson, friend, MT Dist., BVS:1878:2/3

THOMAS, Verlinda, W, F, d. 12 Jan 1853, Leesburg, consumption, 62-2-5, p. unk, b. unk, unk, sc: Francis M. Hole, son-in-law, BVS:1854:5, LC:3

THOMAS, Virginia A., W, F, d. 28 Jul 1854, Leesburg, diarrhea, 2-3-26, p. John H. & Mary E. Thomas, b. LC, sc: John H. Thomas, father, BVS:1854:8, LC:7

THOMAS, Wm. A., B, M, d. 1 Jul 1884, Rock Hill, consumption, 10-0-0, p. John & Susan Thomas, b. Virginia, sc: John Thomas, father, 3rd Dist., BVS:1884:7

THOMPSON, Alberta, B, M, d. 10 May 1881, LC, unk, 2-6-0, p. Dangerfield & Mary Thompson, b. LC, sc: Mary Thompson, mother, 1st Dist., BVS:1881:2

THOMPSON, B. E., W, M, d. 8 Feb 1893, nr Paris, heart failure, 52-0-0, p. unk, b. LC, farmer, c/o: Amanda V. Thompson, sc: W.J. Thompson, son, 1st Dist., BVS:1893:1

THOMPSON, C. Peyton, W, M, d. Jun 1859/60, Middleburg, consumption, 24-0-0, p. Israel B. & Frances T. Thompson, b. Prince William Co, tobacconist, sc: I. B. Thompson, father, BVS:1859:3, 1860:1, LC:34

THOMPSON, Edward, W, M, d. 7 Aug 1871, nr Woodgrove, unk, 0-11-0, p. Thomas & Ann E. Thompson, b. nr Woodgrove, sc: Thos Thompson, father, JF Dist., BVS:1871:1

THOMPSON, Edward, W, M, d. 16 Dec 1886, nr Aldie, old age, 82-0-0, p. unk, b. LC, farmer, c/o: Rebecca Thompson, sc: Maurice McFarland, son-in-law, 1st Dist., BVS:1886:2

THOMPSON, Edward M., W, M, d. 1 Mar 1888, LC, typhoid fever, 24-5-0, p. Lorenza & Ruth Thompson, b. LC, laborer, unm, sc: Ruth Thompson, mother, 3rd Dist., BVS:1888:2

THOMPSON, Eliz., (f), F, d. Nov 1855, Goose Creek Meeting House, typhoid fever, 33-0-0, p. Louisa Thompson, b. Aldie, sc: Lucius Whitenham, BVS:1855:6, LC:18

THOMPSON, Eliza R., W, F, d. 21 Jun 1853, LC, diarrhea, 1-7-11, p. T. R. & Lucinda Thompson, b. LC, sc: Lewis W. Derry, uncle, BVS:1854:4, LC:2

THOMPSON, Elizabeth, W, F, d. 31 Jul 1857, LC, old age, 87-0-0, p. Adam & Mary Vincel, b. LC, sc: Elizabeth Feagans, daughter, BVS:1857:1, LC:24

THOMPSON, Elizabeth, B, F, d. 1 Dec 1888, LC, cancer, 42-0-0, p. Caroline Jackson, b. LC, none, c/o: Samuel Thompson, sc: Samuel Jackson, husband, 3rd Dist., BVS:1888:2

THOMPSON, Emily, W, F, d. 23 Mar 1889, Philomont, paralysis, 70-0-0, p. L. R. & Emily Thompson, b. LC, unm, sc: F.E. Robey, superintendent of poor, 1st Dist., BVS:1889:1

THOMPSON, Fanny, W, F, d. 30 Sep 1889, LC, consumption, 35-0-0, p. Geo. E. & L. Gray, b. LC, none, c/o: Eli Thompson, sc: Eli Thompson, husband, 3rd Dist., BVS:1889:5

THOMPSON, Frederick, B, M, d. 19 Aug 1858, Watson's Dam, drowned, 23-0-0, p. Rosanna Thompson, b. Aldie, sc: Delia Thornton FN, aunt, BVS:1858:4, LC:32

THOMPSON, Geo R., W, M, d. 15 Jun 1888, LC, spinal affection, 9-0-0, p. Eli Thompson, b. LC, none, sc: Eli Thompson, father, 3rd Dist., BVS:1888:2

THOMPSON, Geo W., W, M, d. 5 Oct 1881, LC, fever, 35-0-0, p. Jno F. & Lucinda Thompson, b. LC, sc: Jno F. Thompson, father, 1st Dist., BVS:1881:2

THOMPSON, Harriet, W, F, d. 12 Jul 1883, Leesburg, rheumatism bowels, 65-0-0, p. unk, b. Fauquier Co., c/o: Aleanne Thompson, sc: E.E. Thompson, grand step-son, 2nd Dist., BVS:1883:7

THOMPSON, Hugh S., W, M, d. 9 Dec 1884, Hillsboro, heart disease, 61-7-0, b. Virginia, farmer, c/o: Ruth H. Thompson, sc: W.D. Thompson, son, 3rd Dist., BVS:1884:7

THOMPSON, John R., W, M, d. 2 Apr 1857, res of parents, croup, 5-6-17, p. John F. & Louisa Thompson, b. on Gray's Farm, sc: Lucinda Thompson, mother, BVS:1857:4, LC:27

THOMPSON, Lucinda, W, F, d. 20 Nov 1894, nr Arcola, bright's disease, 78-0-0, p. unk, b. unk, c/o: Jno F. Thompson, sc: Henry Thompson, son, 1st Dist., BVS:1894:1

THOMPSON, Martha, W, F, d. 9 Mar 1888, LC, consumption, 26-0-0, p. Geo. E. & Mary Gray, b. LC, none, c/o: Eli Thompson, sc: Eli Thompson, husband, 3rd Dist., BVS:1888:2

THOMPSON, Mary A., W, F, d. 2 Aug 1856, LC, neuralgia, 38-0-0, p. John & Mary Campbell, b. Fauquier Co., c/o: Elcanor Thompson, sc: Elcanor Thompson, husband, BVS:1856:2, LC:20

THOMPSON, Mary F., W, F, d. 27 Nov 1864, LC, diphtheria, 4-0-0, sc: Mary Thompson, BVS:1864:2, LC:39

THOMPSON, Milly, (f), F, d. 17 Aug 1856, Poor House, 70-0-0, b. LC, sc: steward, BVS:1856:4, LC:22

THOMPSON, Nimrod, W, M, d. 21 Feb 1855, LC, apoplexy, 55-0-0, p. Ths. & Margt. Thompson, b. LC, unm, sc: Edwd. Thompson, brother, BVS:1855:2, LC:15

[THOMPSON], no name, W, M, d. Oct 1866, Snickersville, unk, unk, p. John C. & Mary Thompson, b. Snickersville, sc: father, BVS:1866:2

THOMPSON, Orrel, W, F, d. 6 Aug 1873, Middleburg, pneumonia, 60-0-0, p. unk, b. unk, c/o: John M. Thompson, sc: John Doyle, friend, MC Dist., BVS:1873:6

THOMPSON, Pearl, W, F, d. 27 Feb 1887, Waxpool, whooping cough, 1-6-0, p. Bernard A. & Clementine Thompson, b. Waxpool, unm, sc: Bernard A. Thompson, father, 1st Dist., BVS:1887:3

THOMPSON, R. J., W, --, d. 17 Dec 1889, LC, old age, 79-0-0, p. unk, b. LC, none, c/o: Eliza Thompson, sc: Eliza Thompson, widow, 2nd Dist., BVS:1889:4

THOMPSON, Rebecca, W, F, d. 13 Jun 1855, LC, apoplexy, 47-0-0, p. Marthe & Eliz. Sullivan, b. LC, c/o: Edward Thompson, sc: Edwd. Thompson, husband, BVS:1855:2, LC:15

THOMPSON, Sarah, B, F, d. 7 May 1886, nr Middleburg, pneumonia, 3-10-0, p. John H. & Adelaide Thompson, b. Middleburg, unm, sc: John H. Thompson, father, 1st Dist., BVS:1886:2

[THOMPSON], Sarah Elizabeth, W, F, d. 1 Jan 1856, Jos. L. Hawling's farm, cramp, 1-6-0, p. Edward & Sarah E. Thompson, b. Gen. Rust's farm, sc: S.E. Thompson, mother, BVS:1856:4, LC:22

THOMPSON, Susan C., W, F, d. 19 Jul 1858, nr Mount Gilead, dysentery, 0-1-5, p. John F. & Lucinda Thompson, b. place of death, sc: Lucinda Thompson, mother, BVS:1858:4, LC:31

[THOMPSON], Thomas Richard, W, M, d. 5 Nov 1856, Short Hill, whooping cough, 3-0-0, p. Lorenzo D. & Ruth A. Thompson, b. nr Hillsboro, sc: Ruth Ann Thompson, mother, BVS:1856:5, LC:22

THOMPSON, William, B, M, d. 10 Apr 1893, nr Sterling, hiccoughs, 66-0-0, p. unk, b. Culpeper Co., laborer, c/o: Ellen Thompson, sc: Ellen Thompson, wife, 1st Dist., BVS:1893:2

THOMPSON, Wm. B., B, M, d. 8 Feb 1875, nr Guilford, pneumonia, 21-0-0, p. Wm. & Ellen Thompson, b. LC, laborer, unm, sc: Wm. Thompson, father, BR Dist., BVS:1875:5

THOMPSON, Wyatt, B, M, d. 2 Feb 1886, nr Middleburg, brain fever, 2-0-0, p. John H. & Adelaide Thompson, b. Middleburg, unm, sc: John H. Thompson, father, 1st Dist., BVS:1886:2

THOMSON, Mildred T., W, F, d. May 1854, Meadow Land, unk, b. Leesburg, c/o: Wm. M. Thomson, Decd (?), sc: R. C. Littleton, BVS:1854:11, LC:10

THORNBIRY, J. S., W, M, d. 17 Aug 1893, Kerfoots, cholera infantum, 0-6-20, p. J. T. & Lucy J. Thornbiry, b. Kerfoots, blacksmith, sc: J.T. Thornberry, father, 1st Dist., BVS:1893:1

THORNLEY, Nannie, B, F, d. 10 Apr 1886, nr Bloomfield, consumption, 22-0-0, p. Wm. & Mary Thornley, b. Fauquier Co., c/o: Joseph Thornley, sc: Joseph Thornley, husband, 1st Dist., BVS:1886:2

THORNLEY, Nelson, B, M, d. 9 May 1887, Trappe, old age, 84-0-0, p. unk, b. LC, unm, sc: Allen Davis, friend, 1st Dist., BVS:1887:3

THORNTON, Adelia, B, F, d. Dec 1865, nr Mt. Zion, unk, 25-0-0, b. unk, servant, c/o: unm, sc: Jno J. Tyler, head of family, BVS:1865:2

THORNTON, Arthur, B, M, d. 2 Jun 1892, Watson, unk, 0-2-22, p. Sam

& Emily Thornton, b. Watson, sc: Sam Thornton, father, 1st Dist., BVS:1892:4

THORNTON, Bessie, B, F, d. 1 Mar 1896, Watson, whooping cough, 0-2-0, p. Sam. & Emily Thornton, b. Watson, sc: Sam Thornton, father, BR Dist., BVS:1896:4

THORNTON, Beverly, B, M, d. 2 Aug 1872, LC, cholera infantum, 0-9-0, p. C. P. & Georgiana Thornton, b. LC, sc: Georgiana Thornton, mother, LE Dist., BVS:1872:4

THORNTON, Beverly, B, M, d. 15 Aug 1881, LC, unk, 1-0-0, p. Chas & Georgian Thornton, b. LC, sc: G. Thornton, mother, 1st Dist., BVS:1881:2

THORNTON, Chas., (f), M, d. 19 May 1853, Poor House, old age, 70-0-0, p. unk, b. unk, sc: Wm. Furr, keeper of the poor house, BVS:1854:7, LC:6

THORNTON, Chas., B, M, d. 4 Apr 1888, Aldie, spasms, 1-8-0, p. Chas. & Lucy Thornton, b. Aldie, sc: Chas Thornton, father, 1st Dist., BVS:1888:4

THORNTON, Elizabeth, B, F, d. 24 May 1877, nr Guilford Station, dropsy & heart disease, 6-0-0, p. Geo. Newman & Nellie Thornton, b. nr Guilford Station, unm, sc: S. W. Thornton, grandfather, BR Dist., BVS:1877:1

THORNTON, Ettie, B, F, d. 28 Jul 1891, Aldie, consumption, 0-14-0, p. Saml. & Emily Thornton, b. LC, laborer, unm, sc: Emily Thornton, head of family, 1st Dist., BVS:1891:1

THORNTON, Geo F., W, M, d. 10 Jul 1881, LC, unk, 0-6-0, p. Geo A & E. Thornton, b. LC, sc: E. Thornton, mother, 1st Dist., BVS:1881:2

THORNTON, Georgianne, W, F, d. 20 Apr 1881, LC, consumption, 39-0-0, p. Sanford & Elizabeth T, b. LC, sc: S. Thornton, father, 1st Dist., BVS:1881:2

THORNTON, James, B, M, d. 15 Apr 1876, Aldie, unk, 2-3-0, p. Chas & Georgianna Thornton, b. LC, sc: Chas. Thornton, father, MC Dist., BVS:1876:5

THORNTON, Laura, B, F, d. 15 Jan 1884, LC, consumption, 22-0-0, p. unk, b. LC, c/o: Sanford Thornton, sc: Sanford Thornton, husband, 1st Dist., BVS:1884:2

THORNTON, Nellie, B, F, d. 26 Jun 1877, nr Guilford Station, dropsy & cons, 24-0-0, p. S. W. & Elizabeth Thornton, b. nr Guilford Station, unm, sc: S.W. Thornton, father, BR Dist., BVS:1877:1

THORNTON, no name, B, M, d. 20 Aug 1876, Aldie, fits, 0-1-20, p. Chas & Georgianna Thornton, b. LC, sc: Chas. Thornton, father, MC Dist., BVS:1876:5

[THORNTON], no name, B, M, d. 19 Jun 1880, LC, unk, 0-0-1, p. Mary Thornton, unm, sc: Mary Thornton, mother, 1st Dist., BVS:1880:3

THORNTON, no name, B, M, d. 10 Aug 1887, Arcola, spasm, 0-3-9, p. Samuel & Emily Thornton, b. Arcola, unm, sc: Samuel Thornton, father, 1st Dist., BVS:1887:3

THORNTON, Rena, B, F, d. 10 Oct 1886, nr Unison, pneumonia, 25-0-0, p. Harriet & John W. Strother, b. nr Unison, unm, sc: John W. Strother, father, 1st Dist., BVS:1886:2

THORNTON, Rosa, B, F, d. 2 Nov 1881, LC, pneumonia, 0-11-0, p. Robt & Flora Thornton, b. LC, sc: F. Thornton, mother, 1st Dist., BVS:1881:2

THORNTON, Sanford, B, M, d. 18 Dec 1889, Sterling, paralysis, 80-0-0, p. unk, b. LC, laborer, unk, sc: Nathan Cary, son-in-law, 1st Dist., BVS:1889:1

THORNTON, Sarah E., B, F, d. 29 Mar 1877, nr Guilford Station, consumption, 0-7-0, p. Robt. Thomas & Ann M. Thornton, b. nr Guilford Station, unm, sc: S. W. Thornton, grandfather, BR Dist., BVS:1877:1

THRASHER, Elizabeth, W, F, d. 20 Feb 1889, Bloomfield, consumption, 67-0-0, p. John & Mary Hamilton, b. LC, unk, sc: Benj. F. Barton, son-in-law, 1st Dist., BVS:1889:1

THRIFT, Mary B., W, F, d. 16 Oct 1880, nr Leesburg, consumption, 54-0-0, p. Benj. & Nancy Shreve, b. LC, c/o: Sanderson Thrift, sc: T.W. Belt, son-in-law, 2nd Dist., BVS:1880:7

TIFFANY, Alma Baldwin, W, F, d. 5 Dec 1896, North Fork, exemia, 0-16-0, p. W. S. & Tacie Tiffany, b. North Fork, sc: W.S. Tiffany, father, MT Dist., BVS:1896:9

TIFFANY, no name, W, F, d. 4 Jun 1890, nr Mount Gilead, spasms, 0-0-10, p. Frank & Annie V. Tiffany, b. nr Mount Gilead, sc: Frank Tiffany, father, 1st Dist., BVS:1890:2

TIFFANY, Sarah E., W, F, d. 15 Oct 1892, Mountville, diphtheria, 6-0-0, p. F. P. & Fannie V. Tiffany, b. Mountville, sc: F.P. Tiffany, father, 1st Dist., BVS:1892:2

TILLETT, Ann, W, F, d. 19 Mar 1856, Jane Tillett's, consumption, 62-0-0, p. Giles & H. Tillett, b. nr Leesburg, sc: T.R. Tillett, nephew, BVS:1856:5, LC:23

TILLETT, C. W. F. E., W, M, d. 3 Aug 1855, LC, abscess, 21-8-17, p. Sam & Jane Tillett, b. nr Goose Creek, farmer, c/o: Harriet B. Tillett, sc: T.R. Tillett, brother, BVS:1855:4, LC:16

TILLETT, Geo. S., W, M, d. 28 Jul 1853, LC, dysentery, 1-0-28, p. Giles E. & Sarah A. Tillett, b. LC, sc: Giles E. Tillett, father, BVS:1854:3, LC:1

TILLETT, Rebanion, W, F, d. 2 Apr 1854, LC, change of life, 45-0-0, p. unk, b. LC, c/o: Giles Tillett, sc: Stevens T. McDaniel, one of the family, BVS:1854:8, LC:8

TILLETT, Thomas R., W, M, d. 8 Jan 1892, Oatlands, pneumonia, 62-0-0, p. unk, b. Oatlands, consort, LE Dist., BVS:1892:5

TIMBERS, Ellick, (f), M, d. 2 Feb 1853, LC, unk, 45-0-0, p. unk, b. unk, sc: Randolph White, head of family, BVS:1854:3, LC:1

TIMBERS, [no name], B, F, d. Dec 1876, E Side of Short Hill, 2-0-0, p. Samuel & Annie Timbers, b. E Side of Short Hill, sc: Samuel Timbers, father, LV Dist., BVS:1876:3

TIMMS, Eliza F., W, F, d. 18 Jan 1878, nr Mt. Hope Church, consumption, 25-0-0, p. Wm. L. & Susan M. Timms, b. nr Mt. Hope Church, unm, sc: Wm. L. Timms, father, BR Dist., BVS:1878:4

TIMMS, Fennell, W, M, d. 5 Apr 1877, nr Gum Spring, consumption, 26-2-9, p. Wm. S. & S, M. Timms, b. nr Gum Spring, unm, sc: Wm. S. Timms, father, BR Dist., BVS:1877:1

TINSMAN, Ann V., W, , d. 25 Sep 1853, foot of Blue Ridge, putrid sore throat, 4-0-0, p. Jno. & Susan Tinsman, b. foot of Blue Ridge, sc: father, BVS:1854:1, LC:4

TINSMAN, Carl F., W, M, d. 10 Oct 1893, nr Upperville, whooping cough, 4-0-0, p. F. M. & Sarah E. Tinsman, b. nr Upperville, farmer, sc: F.M. Tinsman, father, 1st Dist., BVS:1893:1

TINSMAN, Elizabeth E., W, F, d. 1 Mar 1877, foot of Blue Ridge, cancer in womb, 41-0-0, b. LC, c/o: Francis M. Tinsman, sc: F.M. Tinsman, husband, MC Dist., BVS:1877:6

TINSMAN, Eva, W, F, d. 21 Oct 1893, nr Upperville, whooping cough, 2-0-0, p. F. M. & Sarah E. Tinsman, b. nr Upperville, farmer, sc: F.M. Tinsman, father, 1st Dist., BVS:1893:1

TINSMAN, L. E., W, F, d. 15 Mar 1891, nr Upperville, bronchitis, 4-0-0, p. F. M. & Sarah Tinsman, b. LC, school teacher, sc: F.M. Tinsman, father, 1st Dist., BVS:1891:3

TINSMAN, Mary C., W, F, d. 13 Jan 1880, LC, scarlet fever, 9-0-0, p. George & Margaret Tinsman, unm, sc: Margaret Tinsman, mother, 1st Dist., BVS:1880:3

TINSMAN, Nancy, W, F, d. 31 Jul 1877, foot of Blue Ridge, cancer on the jaw, 73-0-0, b. LC, c/o: Henry Tinsman, sc: Francis M. Tinsman, son, MC Dist., BVS:1877:5

TINSMAN, Sarah, W, F, d. 12 Mar 1891, nr Paris, consumption, 48-0-0, p. unk, b. LC, farmer, c/o: John M. Tinsman, sc: Jno M. Tinsman, husband, 1st Dist., BVS:1891:3

TINSMAN, Susan E., W, F, d. 8 Jan 1880, LC, scarlet fever, 4-0-0, p. George & Margaret Tinsman, unm, sc: Margaret Tinsman, mother, 1st Dist., BVS:1880:3

TIPPETT, Emma J., W, F, d. 25 May 1885, nr Guilford, confinement, 21-0-0, p. John & Elvira Agur, b. Georgetown, DC, c/o: Samuel F. Tippett, sc: Samuel F. Tippett, husband, 1st Dist., BVS:1885:5

Loudoun County, Virginia, Death Register, 1853-1896   257

TIPPETT, John E., W, M, d. 25 Aug 1885, nr Guilford, croup, 0-3-0, p. Samuel & Emma J. Tippett, b. nr Guilford, sc: Samuel F. Tippett, father, 1st Dist., BVS:1885:5

TIPPETT, John H., W, M, d. 28 Oct 1877, nr Guilford Station, dysentery, 45-0-0, p. John C. Tippett & wife, b. unk, farmer, c/o: Emily E. Tippett, sc: Emily E. Tippett, wife, BR Dist., BVS:1877:1

TIPPETT, Saml H., W, M, d. 13 Jan 1864, nr Guilford Station, pneumonia, 28-0-1, p. J.C. & Leah Tippett, b. LC, farmer, sc: Leah H. Tippett, mother, BVS:1864:2, LC:39

TIPPETT, Thos E., W, M, d. 29 Jan 1864, Charlottsville, pneumonia, 22-0-11, p. J.C. & Leah Tippett, b. LC, soldier, sc: Leah H. Tippett, mother, BVS:1864:2, LC:39

TITUS, Armistead M., W, M, d. 20 Jan 1884, nr Lovettsville, consumption, 60-0-0, p. Itimus & Catharine Titus, b. LC, farmer, c/o: Amelia Titus, sc: Amelia Titus, wife, 2nd Dist., BVS:1884:5

TITUS, Emma Nora, W, F, d. 8 Aug 1877, Leesburg, typhoid fever, 24-9-0, p. Jas. A. & Sarah Anderson, c/o: Wm. T. Titus, sc: Ginnie Anderson, sister, LE Dist., BVS:1877:9

TITUS, Frances J., W, F, d. 17 Aug 1854, LC, dysentery, 10-0-17, p. Mary E. Titus, b. LC, sc: Mary E. Titus, mother, BVS:1854:8, LC:8

TITUS, Frederick, W, M, d. 30 Nov 1883, nr Leesburg, unk, 0-3-13, p. Jno. H. & Hannah Titus, b. LC, sc: Hannah Titus, mother, 2nd Dist., BVS:1883:4

TITUS, Hannah E., W, F, d. 1 Feb 1854, LC, dropsy, 5-3-11, p. Tunis & Mary A. Titus, b. LC, sc: Tunis Titus, father, BVS:1854:8, LC:8

TITUS, Jno. W. B., W, M, d. 18 Aug 1883, nr Lovettsville, summer complaint, 11-2-18, p. Jos. P. & Ann E. Titus, b. LC, sc: Jos P. Titus, father, 2nd Dist., BVS:1883:4

TITUS, John H., W, M, d. 12 Sep 1890, LC, typhoid fever, 49-0-0, p. Tunis & Mary Titus, b. LC, farmer, c/o: Hannah Titus, sc: T.S. Titus, brother, 2nd Dist., BVS:1890:4

TITUS, Laura W., W, F, d. 6 Aug 1883, nr Leesburg, cholera infantum, 0-6-14, p. Thomas S. & Laura Titus, b. LC, sc: Thomas S. Titus, father, 2nd Dist., BVS:1883:7

TITUS, Mable M., W, F, d. 17 Oct 1886, LC, diphtheria, 4-9-24, p. Chas. M. & Virginia, b. LC, sc: Chas. M. Titus, father, 2nd Dist., BVS:1886:6

TITUS, [no name], W, M, d. 28 May 1875, Leesburg, croup, 0-0-5, p. John H. & Hannah Titus, b. Leesburg, farmer, sc: John H. Titus, father, MT Dist., BVS:1875:8

[TITUS], no name, W, M, d. 15 Dec 1893, Lucketts, unk, 0-0-1, p. Burr & Virginia, b. Lucketts, unm, sc: Burr Titus, LE Dist., BVS:1893:6

TITUS, Susan R., W, F, d. 19 May 1875, Leesburg, abscess on lungs, 23-0-1, b. Leesburg, c/o: Wm. T. Titus, sc: Wm. T. Titus, husband, LE Dist., BVS:1875:2

TOLBERT, James, B, M, d. 3 Mar 1886, LC, consumption, 20-0-0, p. James & Jane, b. LC, laborer, unm, sc: James Tolbert, father, 2nd Dist., BVS:1886:6

TOLBERT, Lorenzo, B, M, d. 5 Dec 1877, nr Franklin Mills, whooping cough, 0-6-19, p. Jos. H. & Ann Tolbert, sc: Jos H. Tolbert, father, MC Dist., BVS:1877:6

TOLBERT, Lottie, B, F, d. 9 Oct 1892, Mountville, typhoid fever, 15-7-0, p. Jos. & Annetta Tolbert, b. Mountville, unm, sc: Jos Tolbert, father, 1st Dist., BVS:1892:3

TOLBERT, Lottie, B, F, d. 9 Oct 1893, nr Mountville, typhoid fever, 14-0-0, p. Jos. & Annette Tolbert, b. nr Mountville, laborer, sc: Jos Tolbert, father, 1st Dist., BVS:1893:2

TOLBERT, Wm., B, M, d. 21 Jan 1893, nr Mountville, typhoid fever, 23-0-0, p. Jos. & Annette Tolbert, b. nr Mountville, laborer, sc: Jos Tolbert, father, 1st Dist., BVS:1893:2

TOLER, Laura J., B, F, d. 15 Apr 1886, nr Guilford, kidney disease, 2-0-0, p. Turner & Emma Toler, b. Guilford, sc: Turner Toler, father, 1st Dist., BVS:1886:2

TOLIVER, Chas., W, M, d. 15 Oct 1871, unk, 2-0-0, p. Leah Toliver, BR Dist., BVS:1871:3

TOLLER, Martha Ellen, B, F, d. 12 Mar 1877, nr Guilford Station, unk, 1-8-0, p. Turner & Emma Toller, b. nr Guilford Station, unm, sc: Emma Toller, mother, BR Dist., BVS:1877:1

TOLLER, Mary C., B, F, d. 2 Jan 1877, nr Guilford Station, croup, 0-7-0, p. Turner & Emma Toller, b. nr Guilford Station, unm, sc: Emma Toller, mother, BR Dist., BVS:1877:1

TOLLIVER, Maria, B, F, d. 5 Sep 1891, nr Bolington, old age, 109-0-0, p. unk, b. unk, c/o: Joseph Tolliver, sc: grand-son, LV Dist., BVS:1891:5

TOLSON, Agnes, W, F, d. 30 Nov 1881, LC, chills, 79-1-15, p. Wm. & Mary Franklin, b. Prince William Co, c/o: Fielding Tolson, sc: Jno. W. Tolson, son, 2nd Dist., BVS:1881:7

TOLSON, Mary, W, F, d. 1 Sep 1866, nr Milltown, typhoid, 25-8-10, p. Fielding & Agnes Tolson, b. LC, unm, sc: Fielding Tolsen, father, BVS:1866:1

TOMPSON, Lydia, W, F, d. 9 Nov 1881, LC, old age, 84-0-0, b. LC, sc: G.D. Hoge, physician, 1st Dist., BVS:1881:3

TOPPINGS, Henry, W, M, d. 14 May 1881, LC, butt by a ram, 55-0-0, b. LC, sc: J. Topping, friend, 1st Dist., BVS:1881:2

TORREYSON, Maud, W, M, d. 10 Mar 1874, Hillsboro, diphtheria, 3-4-29, p. Jas. W. & Martha Torreyson, b. Hillsboro, sc: Jas. W. Torreyson, father, JF Dist., BVS:1874:2

TORRISON, Mary W., W, F, d. 13 Dec 1855, Leesburg, paralysis, 48-0-0, p. Thos. & Sarah Birkby, b. Leesburg, c/o: Wm. Torrison, sc: Wm. Torrison, husband, BVS:1855:1, LC:14

TORRISON, Samuel, W, M, d. 28 May 1854, LC, quinsy, 16-0-5, p. Lewis & Rebecca Torrison, b. LC, sc: Lewis Torrison, father, BVS:1854:10, LC:9

TORRISON, William, W, M, d. 17 Nov 1859/60, Leesburg, cancer in stomach, 54-0-0, p. unk, b. unk, c/o: Mary Torrison, sc: Mary Torrison, wife, BVS:1859:2, 1860:4, LC:37

TRACY, Ernest, W, M, d. 20 Oct 1875, Scotland, paralysis, 84-0-0, p. Jefferson James & Rachel Tracy, b. Scotland, mechanic, married, sc: Joel Tracey, son, MT Dist., BVS:1875:8

TRACY, Pearle, W, F, d. 26 Nov 1879, LC, unk, 0-0-1, p. Jas & Theadosia Tracey, b. LC, sc: Jas. H. Tracey, father, 3rd Dist., BVS:1879:3

TRACY, Tamer, W, F, d. 11 Aug 1866, Scotland, old age, 71-4-0, married, sc: Everett Tracy, husband, BVS:1866:2

TRAMEL, Joseph H., B, M, d. 18 Dec 1896, Woodburn, old age, 75-0-0, p. Henry & Tramel, b. Woodburn, laborer, sc: Henrietta Tramel, daughter-in-law, MT Dist., BVS:1896:9

TRAMIL, John, B, M, d. 15 Jan 1875, Hughesville, pneumonia, unk, p. Joseph & Henrietta Tramil, b. Hughesville, laborer, sc: Joseph Trammel, father, MT Dist., BVS:1875:8

TRAMMEL, Henry, B, M, d. 1 Jun 1880, Hughesville, croup, 0-0-10, p. Joseph & Henrietta Trammel, b. LC, sc: Jas. Trammel, father, 3rd Dist., BVS:1880:4

TRAMMELL, Elizabeth M., W, F, d. 18 Mar 1884, nr Leesburg, cancer, 70-0-0, p. --- Jenkins, b. LC, c/o: Thomas Trammell, sc: William Eagle, son-in-law, 2nd Dist., BVS:1884:5

TRAMMELL, Joseph, (f), M, d. 29 Sep 1859/60, Poor House, consumption, 50-0-0, sc: steward, BVS:1859:4, 1860:2, LC:35

TRAMMELL, Thomas, W, M, d. 24 Apr 1854, LC, dyspepsia, 40-2-17, p. unk, b. LC, farmer, c/o: Mary C. Trammell, sc: John Williams, friend, BVS:1854:9, LC:9

TRENARY, Charles Singleton, W, M, d. 20 Oct 1876, nr Scotland, pneumonia, 1-6-0, p. E. S. & Lucinda Trenary, b. LC, unm, sc: E.S. Trenary, father, MT Dist., BVS:1876:1

TRENARY, Hannah E., W, F, d. 10 Feb 1853, nr Rogers' Mill, cold, 0-5-0, p. Jas. & _____ Trenary, b. Rogers Mill, sc: father, BVS:1854:6, LC:6

Loudoun County, Virginia, Death Register, 1853-1896   259

TRENARY, Letitia M., W, F, d. 5 Dec 1873, Millville, child birth, 43-4-0, p. - Chapell, b. nr Upperville, sc: James F. Trenary, husband, MC Dist., BVS:1873:6

TRENARY, Lillian, W, F, d. 1 Oct 1880, Lincoln, colic, 21-0-0, p. Wm. H. & Hannah Trenary, b. LC, unm, sc: Wm. H. Trenary, father, 3rd Dist., BVS:1880:4

TRENARY, no name, W, M, d. 21 Oct 1869, LC, 0-0-1, b. LC, sc: James F. Trenary, father, BVS:1869:1

TRENARY, no name, W, M, d. 5 Dec 1873, Millville, stillborn, unk, p. Jas. F. & Letitia M. Trenary, b. Millsville, sc: James F. Trenary, father, MC Dist., BVS:1873:6

TRIBBEY, Effa, W, F, d. 16 Jul 1872, Between the Hills, unk, 0-1-3, p. Jno. & Sarah A. Tribbey, b. Between the Hills, laborer, married, sc: Jno T. Tribbey, father, LV Dist., BVS:1872:5

TRIBBEY, James S., W, M, d. 14 Jul 1881, LC, typhoid fever, 10-0-0, p. Saml T. & Clara Tribbey, b. LC, sc: S.T. Tribbey, father, 3rd Dist., BVS:1881:5

TRIBBY, Eliza, W, F, d. 15 Oct 1874, nr Hillsboro, heart disease, 66-0-0, p. Jas. & Ann Tribby, unm, sc: James Tribby, son, JF Dist., BVS:1874:2

TRIBBY, no name, W, M, d. 31 Jul 1874, W of Neersville, teething, 0-4-0, p. John & Sarah Tribbey, carpenter, LV Dist., BVS:1874:6

TRIBBY, Samantha J., W, F, d. 27 Dec 1883, Wheatland, measles, 7-0-0, p. Wm. F. & Emma Tribbey, b. LC, sc: Wm. F. Tribbey, father, 3rd Dist., BVS:1883:5

TRIPLETT, Margaret, W, F, d. 15 Feb 1882, LC, unk, 72-0-0, p. Wm. & Ann Triplett, unm, sc: Wm. Triplett, brother, 1st Dist., BVS:1882:2

TRIPLETT, Mary, W, F, d. 16 Sep 1858, LC, pneumonia, 59-8-5, p. unk, b. LC, c/o: Wm. Triplett, sc: Wm. Triplett, husband, BVS:1858:2, LC:30

TRIPLETT, Sarah M., W, F, d. 13 Apr 1866, nr Millville, consumption, 37-0-0, p. Elijah & Tamar Chinn, married, sc: Saml P. Triplett, husband, BVS:1866:2

TRIPLETT, Susanna E., W, F, d. 4 Dec 1858, LC, consumption, 40-0-0, p. Wm. & Susan Saffer, b. Fairfax, c/o: Nimrod Triplett, sc: Susan Saffer, mother, BVS:1858:6, LC:33

TRIPLETT, William, W, M, d. 31 Jul 1879, nr Neersville, dropsy, 84-0-0, p. unk, b. LC, laborer, sc: Jonathan Potts, friend, 2nd Dist., BVS:1879:2

TRITAPOE, Mary, W, F, d. May 1874, LC, consumption, 63-0-0, sc: Samuel Tritipoe, husband, LE Dist., BVS:1874:5

TRITAPOE, Michael, W, M, d. 4 Jul 1873, nr Short Hill, old age, 75-0-0, p. John & S. Tritapoe, b. LC, laborer, married, sc: Peter Fry, bro-in-law, LV Dist., BVS:1873:4

TRITAPOE, Nancy, W, F, d. 11 Mar 1888, LC, old age, 83-0-0, p. unk, b. unk, none, unm, sc: G.L.B. Fry, friend, 2nd Dist., BVS:1888:6

TRITAPOE, Philip B., W, M, d. 13 Jul 1890, Waterford, 50-6-0, p. Samuel & Hannah Tritapoe, b. LC, farmer, c/o: Hannah Tritapoe, sc: H.A. Tritapoe, son, 3rd Dist., BVS:1890:7

TRUMBLE, Harrison A., W, M, d. Jun 1871, unk, p. Martin & Sarah Trumble, MC Dist., BVS:1871:2

TRUSSELL, Emily, W, F, d. 6 Jan 1886, nr Aldie, consumption, 28-0-0, p. John & Margaret Thompson, b. LC, c/o: Chas Trussell, sc: John Thompson, father, 1st Dist., BVS:1886:2

TRUSSELL, Emma, W, F, d. 2 Oct 1889, LC, heart disease, 19-0-0, p. Chs. & L. A. Trussell, b. LC, none, unm, sc: Chas Trussell, father, 3rd Dist., BVS:1889:5

TRUSSELL, Jane, W, F, d. 20 Nov 1856, res, paralysis, 67-2-5, p. Archibald & Sarah Fleming, b. Berkley, c/o: Thomas Trussell, sc: T. Trussell, widower, BVS:1856:5, LC:22

TUGHMAN, Louis, B, M, d. 16 Dec 1889, Philomont, old age, 90-0-0, p. unk, b. LC, laborer, unk, sc: F.E. Robey, superintendent of poor, 1st Dist., BVS:1889:1

TURNER, Alfred, B, M, d. 1 May 1876, Middleburg, pneumonia, 53-0-0, b.

LC, laborer, c/o: Fannie Turner, sc: Fanny Turner, wife, MC Dist., BVS:1876:5

TURNER, Amanda M., W, F, d. 4 Apr 1856, Hillsboro, inflammation bowels, 45-0-0, p. Uriah & Sarah Williams, b. LC, c/o: Samuel Turner, sc: Samuel Turner, husband, BVS:1856:1, LC:20

TURNER, Carter L., W, M, d. 18 Oct 1892, Middleburg, membranous croup, 1-6-0, p. Crv. S. & L. Turner, b. Fauquier Co., sc: C. S. Turner, father, 1st Dist., BVS:1892:2

TURNER, Chas, W, M, d. Sep 1864, Middleburg, intermitting fever, 75-0-0, p. John & Jane Turner, b. Fauquier Co., Miller, c/o: Matilda Turner, sc: Matilda Turner, widow, BVS:1864:1, LC:38

TURNER, Elizabeth, W, F, d. 5 Apr 1854, Jas. Wildman's, dropsy of heart, 42-11-25, p. Robt. & Elizabeth Turner, b. Upperville, Fauquier Co., unm, sc: Jos. Wildman, bro. in law, BVS:1854:13, LC:12

TURNER, Elizabeth, W, F, d. 25 Aug 1854, Jas. Wildman's, old age, 75-0-0, p. Wm. & Mary Tumbleson, b. Pennsylvania, c/o: Robt Turner, decd, sc: Jos. Wildman, son in law, BVS:1854:13, LC:12

TURNER, Ella, B, F, d. May 1891, Woodburn, consumption, 18-0-0, p. Richard Turner, b. Woodburn, unm, sc: Richard Turner, MT Dist., BVS:1891:6

TURNER, Eva, B, F, d. 18 Jul 1890, nr Middleburg, consumption, 0-6-0, p. unm, b. nr Middleburg, sc: Logan Turner, grandfather, 1st Dist., BVS:1890:2

TURNER, Geo. N., B, M, d. 1 Mar 1889, LC, bronchitis, 20-0-0, p. Isaac & Mary Turner, b. LC, none, unm, sc: Isaac Turner, father, 3rd Dist., BVS:1889:5

TURNER, Henry, W, M, d. 18 Nov 1865, nr Leesburg, croup, 0-16-0, p. Rich & Ann E. Turner, b. Leesburg, sc: Richard Turner, father, 1st Dist., BVS:1865:3/4

TURNER, Jude, B, F, d. 15 Aug 1871, dropsy, 70-0-0, married, BR Dist., BVS:1871:3

TURNER, Maria, B, F, d. 18 Sep 1885, Mountville, cancer, 66-0-0, p. unk, b. LC, c/o: Richard Turner, sc: Nathan Henson, son-in-law, 1st Dist., BVS:1885:5

TURNER, Martha E., W, F, d. 3 Jun 1883, nr Leesburg, typhoid fever, 29-0-0, p. Wm. & Martha Burgess, b. LC, c/o: John W. Turner, sc: John W. Turner, husband, 2nd Dist., BVS:1883:7

TURNER, Mattie V., W, F, d. 20 Aug 1894, Snickersville, angina pectoris, 37-0-3, p. T. M. & Rosa Osburn, b. Snickersville, wife, sc: C. B. Turner, husb., 3rd Dist., BVS:1894:5

TURNER, Minnie, B, F, d. 18 Feb 1883, nr Middleburg, dropsy, 2-0-0, p. Kate Turner, b. nr Middleburg, unm, sc: Kate Turner, mother, 1st Dist., BVS:1883:2

TURNER, no name, B, F, d. 16 Aug 1887, Middleburg, unk, 0-0-3, p. Daniel & Ellen Turner, b. Middleburg, unm, sc: Daniel Turner, father, 1st Dist., BVS:1887:3

TURNER, Richard, B, M, d. 10 Dec 1885, Mountville, old age, 70-0-0, p. unk, b. Fauquier Co., c/o: Maria Turner, sc: Nathan Henson, son-in-law, 1st Dist., BVS:1885:5

TUTMAN, Maggie, B, F, d. 10 Mar 1876, LC, fever, 0-5-0, p. Lloyd & Nancy Tutman, b. LC, sc: Floyd Tutman, father, JF Dist., BVS:1876:8

TYLER, Mary K., W, F, d. 7 Oct 1884, LC, consumption, 81-0-0, p. James & Rebecca Smith, b. Prince William Co, c/o: John Tyler, sc: Thomas Watson, son-in-law, 1st Dist., BVS:1884:2

UMBAUGH, John W., W, M, d. Dec 1873, LC, dysentery, 14-0-0, p. M.W. & M. A. Umbauch, b. LC, farmer, unm, sc: M.W. Umbaugh, father, LE Dist., BVS:1873:2

UMBAUGH, Sallie A., W, F, d. 17 Oct 1885, nr Goresville, malarial fever, 15-0-0, p. Geo. W. & Catharine Umbaugh, b. LC, sc: Sydney Umbaugh, brother, 2nd Dist., BVS:1885:2

UMBAUGH, William T., W, M, d. 30 Aug 1888, LC, cholera infantum, 1-

Loudoun County, Virginia, Death Register, 1853-1896

2-7, p. Silas N. & Lydia Umbaugh, b. unk, none, unm, sc: Silas H. Umbaugh, father, 2nd Dist., BVS:1888:6

UNDERWOOD, Margt, W, F, d. 25 Jul 1864, Newington, accidental discharge of pistol, 26-0-0, p. Jno & Eliz Underwood, b. Maryland, sc: B. Underwood, brother, BVS:1864:1, LC:38

UNDERWOOD, Sarah V., W, F, d. 9 May 1859/60, LC, scarlet fever, 9-7-5, p. Jackson & Caroline Underwood, b. LC, sc: Caroline Underwood, mother, BVS:1859:1, 1860:4, LC:37

UTTERBACK, Amanda, W, F, d. 26 Feb 1887, LC, burned, 3-6-0, p. John G. & Mary Utterback, b. LC, none, unm, sc: John J. Utterback, father, 2nd Dist., BVS:1887:5

UTTERBACK, Mary E., W, F, d. 23 Jun 1890, LC, la grippe, 41-0-0, p. William & Mary Brown, b. LC, none, c/o: John Utterback, sc: J.E. Utterback, father, 2nd Dist., BVS:1890:4

UTTERBACK, Mary E., W, F, d. 12 Aug 1892, Leesburg, erysipelas, 15-0-0, p. John & Sarah Utterback, b. Leesburg, unm, sc: John Utterback, LE Dist., BVS:1892:5

UTTERBACK, no name, W, M, d. 16 Sep 1888, Prince William Co, unk, 0-0-8, p. Jas. L. & Frances Utterback, b. LC, sc: Jas L. Utterback, father, 1st Dist., BVS:1888:4

VALENTINE, Ada, B, F, d. 7 Mar 1888, Bloomfield, unk, 0-11-0, p. Chas. & Martha Valentine, b. Bloomfield, sc: Chas Valentine, father, 1st Dist., BVS:1888:4

VALENTINE, Agnes, B, F, d. 4 May 1884, Leesburg, unk, 49-10-0, p. Erasmus & Mary Brown, b. LC, laborer, c/o: Joseph Valentine, sc: Henry Valentine. son, 2nd Dist., BVS:1884:5

VALENTINE, Arch, B, M, d. 9 Dec 1880, nr Lincoln, unk, 0-0-2, p. Arch & Mary Valentine, b. LC, sc: Mary Valentine, mother, 3rd Dist., BVS:1880:4

VALENTINE, Armstead, B, M, d. 11 Dec 1885, nr Bloomfield, pneumonia, 55-0-0, p. Stephen & Nellie Valentine, b. nr Bloomfield, unm, sc: Elias Valentine, brother, 1st Dist., BVS:1885:5

VALENTINE, Chas. E., B, M, d. 27 Mar 1891, Bloomfield, pneumonia, 0-3-0, p. Jas. & Lettie Valentine, b. LC, laborer, unm, sc: Jas Valentine, head of family, 1st Dist., BVS:1891:1

VALENTINE, Craven, B, M, d. 25 Sep 1878, nr Bloomfield, consumption, 14-0-0, p. James & Virginia Valentine, b. LC, sc: James Valentine, father, MC Dist., BVS:1878:7

VALENTINE, Ellzey, B, M, d. 15 Jul 1876, nr Millville, consumption, 52-0-0, b. LC, laborer, c/o: Nancy Valentine, sc: Nancy Valentine, wife, MC Dist., BVS:1876:5

VALENTINE, Emily A. H., B, F, d. 7 Aug 1877, Leesburg, catarrh fever, 0-18-0, p. Hiram & Bettie Valentine, sc: Bettie Valentine, mother, LE Dist., BVS:1877:9

VALENTINE, Fenton, B, M, d. 20 Dec 1883, Leesburg, unk, 0-0-19, p. Henry C. & Nancy Valentine, b. LC, sc: Henry C. Valentine, father, 2nd Dist., BVS:1883:4

VALENTINE, Jane W., B, F, d. 15 Aug 1890, Mount Gilead, whooping cough, 1-6-0, p. Arch & L. Valentine, b. LC, none, unm, sc: Arch Valentine. father, 3rd Dist., BVS:1890:7

VALENTINE, Jennie, B, F, d. 7 May 1885, nr Bloomfield, whooping cough, 1-3-0, p. Chas. & Martha Valentine, b. nr Bloomfield, sc: Chas Valentine, father, 1st Dist., BVS:1885:5

VALENTINE, Joseph, B, M, d. 5 Nov 1884, Leesburg, paralysis, 65-0-0, p. Hiram & Mary Valentine, b. LC, laborer, c/o: Agnes Valentine, sc: Henry Valentine. son, 2nd Dist., BVS:1884:5

VALENTINE, Joseph, B, , d. 25 Jul 1877, Leesburg, consumption, 21-9-0, p. Jos. & Agnes Valentine, c/o: M.C. Valentine, sc: M.C. Valentine, wife, LE Dist., BVS:1877:9

[VALENTINE], no name, B, M, d. 2 Jun 1892, Hamilton, unk, unk, p. George & Catherine Valentine, b. LC, sc: George Valentine, father, MT Dist., BVS:1892:8

VALENTINE, Sarah F., B, F, d. 14 Mar 1856, Union, consumption, 7-0-0, p. Emory Valentine, b. New Lisbon, sc: E. Valentine, mother, BVS:1856:4, LC:22

VALENTINE, Stewart, B, M, d. 13 Aug 1879, nr Oatlands, unk, 0-3-3, p. Hiram & Bettie Valentine, b. LC, sc: Hiram Valentine, father, 2nd Dist., BVS:1879:2

VALENTINE, Vergie, B, F, d. 10 Apr 1889, LC, typhoid fever, 0-1-0, p. Geo. W. & S. R. Valentine, b. LC, none, unm, sc: Geo W. Valentine, father, 3rd Dist., BVS:1889:5

VANCE, Mary, W, F, d. 19 Apr 1854, Llangolon, pleurisy, 60-0-0, p. William A. Vance, b. Frederick, unm, sc: Dr. Jos. G. Gray, BVS:1854:12, LC:11

VANDERHOFF, William, W, M, d. 14 Jun 1883, nr Leesburg, rheumatism, 27-2-10, p. Henry & Susan A. Vanderhoff, b. LC, farmer, c/o: Lillie Vanderhoff, sc: Henry Vanderhoff, father, 2nd Dist., BVS:1883:7

VANDEVANTER, Anna, W, F, d. 22 Jan 1865, nr Woodgrove, consumption, 0-0-7, p. C.M. & Sarah Vandevanter, b. nr Woodgrove, sc: C.M. Vandevanter, father, BVS:1865:1

VANDEVANTER, Cecelia, W, F, d. 25 Aug 1853, LC, child bed, 35-4-13, p. Jno. & Mary Braden, b. LC, c/o: Washington Vandevanter, sc: Wash. Vandevanter, husband, BVS:1854:4, LC:2

VANDEVANTER, Gabriel, W, M, d. 2 Jun 1885, Clarkes Gap, natural decay, 74-0-0, b. Virginia, farmer, c/o: J.C. Vandevanter, sc: T.D. Milton, son-in-law, 3rd Dist., BVS:1885:7

VANDEVANTER, Joseph, W, M, d. 26 Sep 1886, LC, fever, 4-0-25, p. A. D. & Emma Vandevanter, sc: A.D. Vandevanter, father, 3rd Dist., BVS:1886:4

VANDEVANTER, Mary Eliza, W, F, d. 18 Oct 1858, nr Waterford, heart affection, 6-8-8, p. C.A. & Sarah J. Vandevanter, b. nr Waterford, sc: C.A. Vandevanter, BVS:1858:5, LC:33

[VANDEVANTER], no name, W, M, d. 21 Oct 1875, Hamilton, unk, 0-0-4, p. T. H. & Nannie Vandevanter, b. LC, sc: T.H. Vandevanter, father, JF Dist., BVS:1875:3

VANDEVANTER, Virginia K., W, F, d. 20 Oct 1878, nr Waterford, tumor, 30-0-0, p. Wm. & Margaret Kilgour, b. Maryland, c/o: Chas. O. Vandevanter, sc: Chas. O. Vandevanter, husband, JF Dist., BVS:1878:10

VANHORN, John, W, M, d. 15 Jun 1881, LC, dropsy, 78-0-0, b. LC, farmer, sc: Sarah Vanhorn, daughter, 1st Dist., BVS:1881:3

VANHORN, Lena V., W, F, d. 24 Feb 1884, Purcellville, bronchitis, 1-10-0, p. Edward & Lizzie Vanhorn, b. Virginia, unm, sc: Ed. O. Vanhorn, father, 3rd Dist., BVS:1884:7

VANHORN, Sarah, W, F, d. 4 Jun 1890, nr Bloomfield, la grippe, 76-0-0, p. Richd. & Deborah Carter, b. LC, c/o: Charles Vanhorn, sc: Mary Vanhorn, sister-in-law, 1st Dist., BVS:1890:2

VANRODEN, Dartha, W, F, d. 30 Oct 1853, LC, consumption, 52-0-0, p. unk, b. unk, c/o: Chas F. Vanroden, sc: Wm. Vanroden, son, BVS:1854:3, LC:2

VANSICKLER, Esther, W, F, d. 11 Nov 1854, Jas. Hampton's, old age, 89-0-0, p. James & ___ Craven, b. Pennsylvania, c/o: Philip Vansickler, decd, sc: Jas. Hampton & wife, son-in-law & dau., BVS:1854:13, LC:12

VANSICKLER, Mahala, W, F, d. 1 Apr 1891, North Fork, paralysis, 90-0-0, p. Thomas & Elizabeth Fred, b. North Fork, wife, sc: John Albert Vansickler, MT Dist., BVS:1891:6

VANSICKLER, Mahala, W, F, d. 1 Mar 1881, LC, dropsy, 77-0-0, b. LC, c/o: Philip Vansickler, sc: Philip Vansickler, husband, 3rd Dist., BVS:1881:5

VANSICKLER, Mary Ellen, W, F, d. 6 Aug 1865, 0-0-25, p. P.F. & S.P. Vansickler, b. nr Leesburg, sc: father, BVS:1865:1

VANSICKLER, Susie E. V., W, F, d. 1 Aug 1890, Philomont, typhoid fever, 17-0-0, p. J. B. & Mary Vansickler, b. LC, none, unm, sc: J.B. Vansickler, father, 3rd Dist., BVS:1890:7
VANSKIVER, Beulah, W, F, d. 14 May 1855, nr Bloomfield, typhoid fever, 65-0-0, b. LC, sc: Levin Richards, BVS:1855:5, LC:17
VARNEY, Wm., W, M, d. 6 Jan 1853, nr Purcellville, concussion brain, 49-0-0, p. unk, b. England, tailor, c/o: Mariah Varney, sc: Geo W. Noland, friend, BVS:1854:6, LC:5
VAUGHN, Anna, W, F, d. 25 Oct 1879, Round Hill, pneumonia, 2-0-0, p. Jacob & Ann Vaughn, b. LC, sc: Jacob Vaughn, father, 3rd Dist., BVS:1879:3
VEALE, Rebecca, W, F, d. 28 Dec 1892, Farmwell, heart failure, 68-0-0, p. Elijah Peacock, b. LC, c/o: Alfred Veale, sc: C.A. Arundell, son-in-law, 1st Dist., BVS:1892:2
VEANY, Thomas, (f), M, d. 1 Mar 1858, LC, pneumonia, 77-1-3, p. unk, b. LC, sc: Aaron R. Saunders, friend, BVS:1858:1, LC:29
[VENA], no name, B, , d. 13 Mar 1877, Leesburg, strangulation, 0-0-1, p. Leroy & Mary Vena, sc: Mary Vena, mother, LE Dist., BVS:1877:9
VENA, [no name], B, F, d. 4 Jul 1885, Leesburg, unk, 0-2-1, p. Leroy & Mary Vena, b. LC, sc: Leroy Vena, father, 2nd Dist., BVS:1885:2
VENAY, Armstead, B, M, d. 28 Jun 1884, LC, consumption, 54-0-0, p. Chas. & Celia Venay, b. LC, laborer, sc: Chas Venay, father, 1st Dist., BVS:1884:3
VENAY, Chas., B, M, d. 23 Oct 1892, Farmwell, asthma, 67-0-0, p. Jos. & Betsy Venay, b. Farmwell, laborer, c/o: Celia Venay, sc: Celia Venay, wife, 1st Dist., BVS:1892:3
VENAY, Francis, B, F, d. 29 May 1893, nr Sterling, unk, 21-0-0, p. Edwd. & Nancy Harris, b. nr Sterling, c/o: Richd Venay, sc: Richd Venay, husband, 1st Dist., BVS:1893:2
VENAY, Geo., B, M, d. 25 Jan 1875, nr Belmont, croup, 0-8-0, p. Chas. & Cecilia Venay, b. LC, sc: Chas. Venay, father, BR Dist., BVS:1875:5

VENAY, Louise, B, F, d. 25 Feb 1875, nr Belmont, pneumonia, 24-1-0, p. Chas. & Cecilia Venay, b. LC, laborer, unm, sc: Chas. Venay, father, BR Dist., BVS:1875:5
VENAY, Nancy, B, F, d. 15 Feb 1874, Broad Run Dist., unk, 5-0-0, p. Nancy Venay, b. LC, unm, sc: Chas. Venay, head of family, BR Dist., BVS:1874:3
VENAY, Nancy, B, F, d. 28 Feb 1875, nr Belmont, burned to death, 8-0-0, p. Chas. & Cecilia Venay, b. LC, sc: Chas. Venay, father, BR Dist., BVS:1875:5
[VENAY], no name, B, F, d. 27 Dec 1874, Broad Run Dist., unk, 0-0-3, p. Chas. & Cecila Venay, laborer, sc: Chas. Venay, father, BR Dist., BVS:1874:3
VENAY, Rose, B, F, d. 7 May 1892, Sterling, spasms, 28-0-0, p. Jno. & Margaret Williams, b. Fairfax, laborer, c/o: Saml. Venay, sc: Saml. Venay, husband, 1st Dist., BVS:1892:3
VERMILLION, Laura, W, F, d. 10 Jul 1854, cholera morbus, 1-11-0, p. John & Hannah Vermillion, sc: John Vermillion, father, BVS:1854:13, LC:13
VERMILLION, Nancy, W, F, d. 20 Apr 1876, nr Mount Gilead, pneumonia, 61-0-0, p. Thos. & Martha Caruthers, b. LC, widow, sc: Daniel White, MT Dist., BVS:1876:1
VERMILLION, Sarah, W, F, d. 28 Feb 1877, nr Round Hill, natural causes, unk, p. Caleb & _Vermillion, b. Prince Geo. Co., Md., sc: S. Osburn, relative, MT Dist., BVS:1877:2
VICKERS, Eunice A., W, F, d. 19 Dec 1879, nr Lovettsville, cold, 0-1-5, p. John T. & Rachael A.T. Vickers, b. LC, sc: John T. Vickers, father, 2nd Dist., BVS:1879:2
VICKERS, Josephine L., W, F, d. 15 May 1856, LC, whooping cough, 1-11-8, p. Wm. & Sarah A. Vickers, b. LC, sc: William Vickers, father, BVS:1856:1, LC:20
VICKERS, Rachael, W, F, d. 22 Feb 1896, Morrisonville, pneumonia, 50-0-0, p. unk, b. unk, c/o: John Vickers, sc: John Vickers, consort, LV Dist., BVS:1896:7

VICKERS, Samuel, W, M, d. 15 Apr 1891, nr Bolington, pneumonia, 1-6-0, p. John & Rachel Vickers, b. nr Bolington, farmer, unm, sc: father, LV Dist., BVS:1891:5

VICKERS, William, W, M, d. 26 Dec 1883, nr Lovettsville, bright's disease, 76-10-6, p. Catherine Vickers, b. LC, farmer, c/o: Sarah A. Vickers, sc: Julius A. Vickers, son, 2nd Dist., BVS:1883:4

VINCEL, Elizabeth, W, F, d. 26 Apr 1885, nr Lovettsville, old age, 81-0-0, p. Henry & --- Fawley, b. LC, c/o: Adam Vincel, sc: Lydia J. Hayes, daughter-in-law, 2nd Dist., BVS:1885:2

VINCEL, Elizabeth M., W, F, d. 7 Jan 1886, LC, heart disease, 67-9-0, p. John & Elizabeth, b. LC, unm, sc: John N. Vincel, brother, 2nd Dist., BVS:1886:6

VINCEL, George T., W, M, d. 5 Sep 1856, LC, affection of brain, 34-11-20, p. Adam & Elizth. Vincel, b. LC, farmer, c/o: Susan Vincel, sc: William Vincel, brother, BVS:1856:1, LC:20

VINCEL, John, W, M, d. 24 Oct 1887, LC, old age, 70-0-0, p. unk, b. LC, laborer, unm, sc: Samuel Filler, friend, 2nd Dist., BVS:1887:5

VINCEL, Louisa, W, F, d. 26 Mar 1888, LC, paralysis, 79-0-0, p. unk, b. unk, none, c/o: Geo Vincel, sc: John J. Stevens, son-in-law, 2nd Dist., BVS:1888:6

VINCEL, Louisa, W, F, d. 22 Apr 1888, LC, old age, 83-0-0, p. Philip & Charlotte Everhart, b. unk, none, c/o: Philip Vincel, sc: Wm. D. Vincel, son, 2nd Dist., BVS:1888:6

VINCEL, Mary, W, F, d. 23 Mar 1886, LC, old age, 91-9-4, p. unk, b. LC, c/o: John Vincel, sc: John N. Vincel, son, 2nd Dist., BVS:1886:6

VINCEL, Philip, W, M, d. 12 Dec 1884, nr Lovettsville, old age, 82-0-0, p. John & --- Vincel, b. LC, farmer, c/o: Louisa Vincel, sc: Wm. D. Vincel, son, 2nd Dist., BVS:1884:5

VINCEL, Soloman, W, M, d. 28 Oct 1854, LC, dysentery, 47-5-10, p. John & Mary M. Vincel, b. LC, farmer, c/o: Louisa Vincel, sc:

George Vincel, brother, BVS:1854:8, LC:7

VINCELL, Elizabeth, W, F, d. 20 Dec 1853, LC, consumption, 46-4-2, p. unk, b. unk, sc: Amanda Seitz, daughter, BVS:1854:3, LC:1

VINCELL, George, W, M, d. Oct 1876, nr Lovettsville, dyspepsia, 71-0-0, b. LC, farmer, c/o: Catherine Vincell, sc: John Vincell, son, LV Dist., BVS:1876:3

VIOLETT, Mary, W, F, d. 20 Mar 1855, LC, old age, 80-0-0, p. Jas. & Mary Lewis, b. nr Wellbourne, c/o: Jno. Violet, decd, sc: Wm. Taylor, son-in-law, BVS:1855:4, LC:16

VIRTS, Adison, W, M, d. 28 Apr 1872, nr Morrisonville, consumption, 38-2-27, p. Wm. & Mary Virts, b. LC, farmer, married, sc: Mary Virts, wife, LV Dist., BVS:1872:5

VIRTS, Annie Virginia, W, F, d. 8 Oct 1871, Waterford, diphtheria, 4-9-6, p. Chas. W. & Tacey V. Virts, b. Waterford, sc: Tacey V. Virts, mother, JF Dist., BVS:1871:1

VIRTS, Charles C., W, M, d. 23 Feb 1885, Waterford, apoplexy, 13-6-4, p. Chas. W. & Tacey Virts, b. Virginia, unm, sc: Chas W. Virts, father, 3rd Dist., BVS:1885:7

VIRTS, Chas., W, M, d. 8 Aug 1891, Oatlands, la grippe, 0-3-0, p. Chas. & Mollie Virts, b. Oatlands, laborer, unm, sc: father, LE Dist., BVS:1891:4

VIRTS, Conrad, W, M, d. 2 Dec 1881, LC, old age, 91-0-0, p. Peter & Christina Virts, b. LC, farmer, c/o: Elizabeth Virts, sc: Missouri Smallwood, daughter, 2nd Dist., BVS:1881:7

VIRTS, Cornelius O., W, M, d. 10 Apr 1881, LC, consumption, 23-6-0, p. Henry & Lydia Virts, b. LC, laborer, unm, sc: Jos J. Virts, brother, 3rd Dist., BVS:1881:5

VIRTS, Daniel L., W, M, d. 1 Aug 1891, Sandy Hook, MD, railway accident, 24-0-0, p. Mary & Isaah Virts, b. nr Bolington, laborer, unm, sc: father, LV Dist., BVS:1891:5

VIRTS, Elizabeth, W, F, d. 4 Dec 1890, LC, pneumonia, 76-0-0, p. Abram & Susan Houser, b. LC, none, c/o:

Loudoun County, Virginia, Death Register, 1853-1896 265

William Virts, sc: Samuel Tribby, nephew, 2nd Dist., BVS:1890:4

VIRTS, Elizabeth, W, F, d. 16 Dec 1886, LC, tumor on neck, 87-0-0, p. unk, b. LC, c/o: Conard Virts, sc: F. M. Smallwood, son-in-law, 2nd Dist., BVS:1886:6

VIRTS, Elizabeth C., W, F, d. 6 Jul 1872, nr Hillsboro, typhoid fever, 45-1-4, p. unk, b. unk, c/o: John M. Virts, sc: John M. Virts, husband, JF Dist., BVS:1872:1

VIRTS, Ernest E., W, M, d. 10 Dec 1873, nr Hamilton, choked with a bean, 1-0-7, p. Charles & Lucy Virts, b. LC, sc: Charles W. Virts, father, JF Dist., BVS:1874:1

VIRTS, Harriet A., W, F, d. 19 Jan 1891, Hillsboro, paralysis, 48-0-0, p. Harmon & Roseanna Reed, b. Hillsboro, wife, sc: M.M. Virts, JF Dist., BVS:1891:7

VIRTS, Henry, W, M, d. 5 Feb 1887, LC, old age, 71-0-0, p. unk, b. LC, farmer, c/o: Esther Virts, sc: John W. Virts, son, 2nd Dist., BVS:1887:5

VIRTS, Israel, W, M, d. 13 Dec 1890, Waterford, consumption, 43-0-0, p. Henry & Lydia Virts, b. LC, laborer, c/o: Annie Virts, sc: Annie Virts, wife, 3rd Dist., BVS:1890:7

VIRTS, Jacob, W, M, d. 24 Apr 1887, LC, physical weakness, 92-0-0, laborer, sc: M.M. Virts, son, 3rd Dist., BVS:1887:7

VIRTS, Jacob S., W, M, d. 19 Jul 1872, nr Hillsboro, dysentery, 0-4-26, p. Joseph & Mary Virts, b. nr Hillsboro, sc: Joseph Virts, father, JF Dist., BVS:1872:1

VIRTS, James S., W, M, d. 25 Aug 1888, LC, unk, 0-7-0, p. J. W. A. & Alverta Virts, b. LC, none, unm, sc: J.W.A. Virts, father, 3rd Dist., BVS:1888:2

VIRTS, Jno., W, M, d. 23 Jun 1872, nr Bolington, erysipelas, 74-9-28, p. Wm. & Barbary Virts, b. LC, farmer, married, sc: Jno M. Virts, son, LV Dist., BVS:1872:5

VIRTS, John A., W, M, d. 9 Nov 1874, kidney affection, 68-0-0, p. ? & Catharine Virts, tanner, LV Dist., BVS:1874:6

VIRTS, John M., W, M, d. 15 Aug 1874, bronchitis, 35-0-0, p. John &

Mary Virts, tanner, LV Dist., BVS:1874:6

VIRTS, John W., W, M, d. 20 Jan 1880, Hillsboro, consumption, 60-0-0, p. Jacob & Pleasant Virts, b. LC, c/o: Mary Virts, sc: Charles Darr, friend, 3rd Dist., BVS:1880:4

VIRTS, John W., W, M, d. 20 Jan 1879, nr Hillsboro, unk, 54-0-0, p. Jacob & Pleasant Williams [sic], b. LC, farmer, c/o: Elizabeth Virts, sc: Charles E. Darr, son-in-law, 2nd Dist., BVS:1879:2

VIRTS, Jonas S., W, M, d. 13 Apr 1859/60, LC, consumption, 34-0-0, p. Jacob & Pleasant A. Virts, b. LC, farmer, unm, sc: Jacob Virts, father, BVS:1859:1, 1860:4, LC:37

VIRTS, Malinda A. C., W, F, d. 8 Oct 1856, res of parents, typhoid fever, 5-9-8, p. Henry & Lydia A. Virts, b. nr Howser's Mill, sc: Wm. Virts, father, BVS:1856:6, LC:23

VIRTS, Mary E., W, F, d. 10 Dec 1880, Hillsboro, croup, 6-0-0, p. Abraham & Florida Virts, b. LC, farmer, sc: Abraham Virts, father, 3rd Dist., BVS:1880:4

VIRTS, Mollie, W, F, d. 27 Apr 1891, Oatlands, la grippe, 33-0-0, p. unk, b. LC, laborer, c/o: Chas. Virts, sc: husband, LE Dist., BVS:1891:4

VIRTS, no name, W, M, d. 30 Dec 1880, Morrisonville, croup, 0-0-15, p. Jas. M. & Mary Virts, b. LC, sc: Jas. M. Virts, father, 3rd Dist., BVS:1880:4

VIRTS, Oda L., W, F, d. 15 Mar 1883, nr Leesburg, croup, 14-4-4, p. Jos. L. & Eliza A. Virts, b. LC, sc: Jos L. Virts, father, 2nd Dist., BVS:1883:8

VIRTS, Orra Bell, W, F, d. 12 Oct 1871, Waterford, diphtheria, 2-9-0, p. Chas. W. & Tacey V. Virts, b. Waterford, sc: Tacey V. Virts, mother, JF Dist., BVS:1871:1

VIRTS, Peter T., W, M, d. 15 Sep 1886, LC, unk, 53-7-15, p. Adam & Susan, b. LC, laborer, c/o: Mary Virts, sc: Mary Virts, wife, 2nd Dist., BVS:1886:6

VIRTS, Pleasant A., W, F, d. 12 Mar 1854, LC, dropsy, 54-6-3, p. unk, b. LC, c/o: Jacob Virts, sc: Jonas Virts, son, BVS:1854:8, LC:7

VIRTS, Thomas B., W, M, d. 21 Jan 1884, nr Lovettsville, typhoid fever, 32-0-0, p. Henry & Esther Virts, b. LC, farmer, c/o: Delia Virts, sc: Henry Virts, father, 2nd Dist., BVS:1884:5

VIRTS, William, W, M, d. 25 Feb 1865, nr Morrisonville, consumption, 18-0-0, p. Wm. & Nancy Virts, b. LC, farmer, sc: William Virts, father, 1st Dist., BVS:1865:5

VIRTS, William, W, M, d. 2 Oct 1883, nr Lovettsville, ulcer, 62-0-0, p. --- Virts, b. LC, farmer, c/o: Catharine A. Virts, sc: M.G. Everhart, friend, 2nd Dist., BVS:1883:7

VIRTS, Wm., W, M, d. 25 Feb 1865, Morrisonville, consumption, 18-0-0, p. Wm. & Nancy Virts, b. LC, farmer, sc: Wm. Virts, father, BVS:1865:3

VIRTS, Wilbert, W, M, d. 29 Jun 1878, Neersville, 0-9-0, p. James M. & Mary E. Virts, b. LC, sc: James M. Virts, father, LV Dist., BVS:1878:1/5

WADDELL, Elizabeth, W, F, d. 16 Aug 1889, Dover, old age, 91-0-0, p. unk, b. Fauquier Co., c/o: John Waddell, sc: Jno Waddell, husband, 1st Dist., BVS:1889:2

WADELER, Emma, W, F, d. 1 Feb 1879, nr Harpers Ferry, pneumonia, 0-9-0, p. Julius & Catharine Wadeler, b. LC, sc: Catherine Wadeler, mother, 2nd Dist., BVS:1879:2

WAKE, Herewald, W, M, d. 13 Nov 1871, suicide by shooting, 20-0-0, p. B. A. & A. M. Wake, BR Dist., BVS:1871:3

WAKEHOUSE, George, W, M, d. 13 Sep 1878, LC, cholera infantum, 0-0-8, p. Wm. & Annie E. Wakehouse, b. LC, unm, sc: Wm. Wakehouse, father, LE Dist., BVS:1878:9

WALDRON, Mary J., W, F, d. 25 Jun 1890, LC, dropsy, 47-0-0, p. John & Delialah Copeland, b. LC, none, c/o: Hiram C. Waldron, sc: H.C. Waldron, husband, 2nd Dist., BVS:1890:5

WALKER, Adaline V., W, F, d. 26 Apr 1887, Arcola, consumption, 65-0-0, p. Peter 7 Sallie Skinner, b. LC, c/o: Garrett B. Walker, sc: Garrett B. Walker, husband, 1st Dist., BVS:1887:3

WALKER, Ann, W, F, d. 1 Jan 1872, nr Belmont, chronic rheumatism, 69-0-0, p. Consort of Saml Walker of Fairfax, b. Fairfax Co., c/o: Saml Walker, sc: Charles Walker, son, BR Dist., BVS:1872:6

WALKER, Jno F., W, M, d. 15 Jul 1865, Fort Delaware, measles, 24-4-0, p. Saml & Ann Walker, b. Fairfax, soldier, unm, sc: Ann Walker, mother, BVS:1865:2

WALKER, Mary J., B, F, d. 26 Feb 1884, Leesburg, measles, 0-6-0, p. Wesley & Priscilla Walker, b. LC, sc: Wesley Walker, father, 2nd Dist., BVS:1884:5

WALKER, Nathan, W, M, d. 29 Jan 1871, Waterford, pneumonia, 69-1-17, sc: Jacob R. Walker, son, JF Dist., BVS:1871:1

WALKER, Robert, B, M, d. 1 Sep 1883, nr Leesburg, unk, 0-2-15, p. John J. & Maria Walker, b. LC, sc: Wm. Simms, grandfather, 2nd Dist., BVS:1883:7

WALKER, Thomas, B, M, d. 2 Mar 1877, Poor House, kidney affection, 80-0-0, unm, sc: Wm. H. Hibbs, supt of poor, MC Dist., BVS:1877:6

WALKER, Wm. A., W, M, d. 10 Oct 1864, Skinners Mill, diphtheria, 5-0-0, p. G.B.. & W.V. Walker, b. LC, sc: G.B. Walker, father, BVS:1864:2, LC:39

WALKING, Wm., B, M, d. 11 Jun 1882, Poor House, unk, 52-0-0, p. unk, widower, sc: Jno R. Carter, superintendent, 1st Dist., BVS:1882:2

WALLACE, Christiantia, W, F, d. 11 Mar 1856, Leesburg, consumption, 22-3-7, p. J. M. & Adaline Wallace, b. Leesburg, c/o: James W. Wallace, sc: James W. Wallace, husband, BVS:1856:1, LC:19

WALLACE, Dudley, B, M, d. 20 Nov 1883, nr Farmwell, pneumonia, 1-0-0, p. Geo. & Ellen Wallace, b. nr Farmwell, unm, sc: Geo Wallace, father, 1st Dist., BVS:1883:2

WALLACE, Hezikiah, B, M, d. 18 Dec 1876, LC, measles, 5-2-0, p. Abraham & Jane Wallace, b. LC, sc:

Abraham Wallace, father, LE Dist., BVS:1876:7

WALLACE, James W., W, M, d. 23 Oct 1886, LC, paralysis, 54-0-0, p. --- Wallace, b. LC, tailor, c/o: Addie W. Wallace, sc: A. W. Wallace, wife, 2nd Dist., BVS:1886:6

WALLACE, Jane, B, F, d. 30 Aug 1883, nr Leesburg, brain fever, 49-0-0, p. David & Venus Strange, b. Alleghaney Co., laborer, c/o: Abram Wallace, sc: Abram Wallace, husband, 2nd Dist., BVS:1883:4

WALLACE, John M., W, M, d. 3 Feb 1857, Leesburg, unk, 1-4-4, p. James M. & Adelaide Wallace, b. Leesburg, sc: James M. Wallace, father, BVS:1857:2, LC:25

WALLACE, L. E., W, F, d. 21 Mar 1896, LC, pneumonia, 25-0-0, p. Wm. H. & S. Benjamin, b. LC, wife, sc: husband, LE Dist., BVS:1896:5

WALLACE, Rachel, B, F, d. Mar 1874, LC, measles, 3-0-0, p. Abrm Wallace, sc: Abram Wallace, father, LE Dist., BVS:1874:5

WALTER, Gina, W, F, d. 30 Jan 1853, LC, pneumonia, 74-6-2, p. Lewis & Sarah Walker, b. Frederick, unm, sc: Edward Mathews, friend, BVS:1854:3, LC:1

WALTER, Rheuhamah, W, F, d. Jun 1854, LC, consumption, 54-0-0, p. Amos & Sarah Veale, b. LC, sc: Elum C. Veale, brother, BVS:1854:14, LC:13

WALTON, Laura Virginia, W, F, d. 17 Sep 1896, Hamilton, peritonitis, 36-0-0, p. Robt. & Virginia Delaney Rose, b. Hamilton, sc: R.L. Walton, husband, MT Dist., BVS:1896:9

WARD, Hattie, B, F, d. 1 Aug 1872, LC, cholera infantum, 0-5-2, p. Spencer & Harriet Ward, b. Leesburg, sc: Spencer Ward, father, LE Dist., BVS:1872:4

WARD, Martha C., W, F, d. 28 Sep 1876, nr Aldie, typhoid fever, 34-0-0, b. Fairfax Co., c/o: Chas. S. Ward, sc: Chas. S. Ward, husband, MC Dist., BVS:1876:5

WARD, Mary A., W, F, d. 17 Oct 1894, nr Dover, diphtheria, 5-0-0, p. Geo. W. & Ella Ward, b. nr Aldie, sc: Geo W. Ward, father, 1st Dist., BVS:1894:1

WARFORD, Abraham, W, M, d. 21 May 1872, nr Gum Spring, pneumonia, 66-5-0, p. unk, b. LC, miller, married, sc: Abraham Warford, son, BiR Dist., BVS:1872:6

WARNER, Alcinda, W, F, d. 20 Aug 1873, nr Hamilton, consumption, 23-3-14, p. Thos. & Catherine Loveless, b. LC, c/o: George Warner, sc: George Warner, husband, JF Dist., BVS:1874:1

WARNER, Ann, B, F, d. 15 Sep 1896, nr Trappe, unk, 0-3-0, p. Robt. & Ellen Warner, b. nr Trappe, none, unm, sc: Robt Warner, father, MC Dist., BVS:1896:2

WARNER, Ann O., W, F, d. 23 Aug 1892, Morrisonville, apoplexy, 47-5-0, p. Wm. & Jane Keyes, b. LC, consort, sc: Thos. Warner, LV Dist., BVS:1892:6

WARNER, Anna, B, F, d. 10 Nov 1881, LC, unk, 0-0-14, p. Robt. & Sarah Warner, b. LC, sc: S. Warner, mother, 1st Dist., BVS:1881:3

WARNER, Bud, B, M, d. 10 Mar 1888, Bloomfield, consumption, 1-0-0, p. Thos. & Catharine Warner, b. Bloomfield, sc: Thos Warner, father, 1st Dist., BVS:1888:4

WARNER, Edward, B, M, d. 15 Nov 1892, Trappe, consumption, 21-8-0, p. Thos. & Catharine Warner, b. Trappe, laborer, unm, sc: Thos Warner, father, 1st Dist., BVS:1892:3

WARNER, Hannah E., W, F, d. 13 Feb 1875, Guilford, consumption, 47-2-0, p. John M. & Polly M. Hanford, b. New York, c/o: J.E. Warner, sc: J.E. Warner, husband, BR Dist., BVS:1875:5

WARNER, Israel, W, M, d. 15 Jun 1887, LC, old age, 91-0-0, farmer, sc: C.C. Warner, son, 3rd Dist., BVS:1887:7

WARNER, Malinda, W, F, d. 25 Oct 1883, Waterford, general debility, 83-0-0, b. LC, c/o: Israel Warner, sc: Israel Warner, husband, 3rd Dist., BVS:1883:5

WARNER, Mary P., B, F, d. 25 Jul 1886, nr Bloomfield, brain fever, 4-0-0, p. Thomas & Louisa Warner, b. nr Bloomfield, unm, sc: Thomas Warner, father, 1st Dist., BVS:1886:3

WARNER, Mollie, B, F, d. 29 Feb 1886, nr Bloomfield, measles, 8-0-0, p. Thomas & Louisa Warner, b. nr Bloomfield, unm, sc: Thomas Warner, father, 1st Dist., BVS:1886:3

[WARNER], no name, B, F, d. 28 Sep 1881, LC, unk, 0-0-10, p. Aaron & Selina Warner, b. LC, sc: S. Warner, mother, 1st Dist., BVS:1881:3

WARNER, Richard R., W, M, d. 5 Apr 1892, Morrisonville, measles, 22-3-0, p. Thos. & Ann, b. LC, unm, sc: Thos. Warner, LV Dist., BVS:1892:6

WARNER, Robert, B, M, d. 26 Mar 1887, Trappe, consumption, 5-0-0, p. Robt. & Ellen Warner, b. Trappe, sc: Robert Warner, father, 1st Dist., BVS:1887:3

WARNER, Walace, B, M, d. 13 Nov 1886, nr Trappe, spinal affection, 2-7-0, p. Robert & Ellen Warner, b. nr Trappe, unm, sc: Robt Warner, father, 1st Dist., BVS:1886:3

WASHINGTON, Arthur, B, M, d. 14 May 1886, Middleburg, unk, 1-0-0, p. Thompson & Ginnie Washington, b. Middleburg, sc: Judy Washington, grandmother, 1st Dist., BVS:1886:2

WASHINGTON, Elizabeth, W, F, d. 19 Apr 1888, LC, heart disease, 75-11-0, p. John George, b. unk, none, c/o: John Washington, sc: Geo Washington, son, 2nd Dist., BVS:1888:6

WASHINGTON, Emily, B, F, d. 30 Mar 1866, Fairfax line, consumption, 22-3-0, p. unk, unm, sc: W.A. Hutchison, head of family, BVS:1866:3

WASHINGTON, Emily, B, F, d. 26 Jun 1877, Tecumish Farm, convulsions, 0-6-0, p. Geo. & Harriet Washington, b. unk, unm, sc: Geo. Washington, father, BR Dist., BVS:1877:1

WASHINGTON, Fred, B, M, d. 15 May 1891, Sterling, consumption, 26-0-0, p. Fred & Diley Washington, b. Fauquier Co., farmer, unm, sc: Fred Washington, head of family, 1st Dist., BVS:1891:1

WASHINGTON, George, B, , d. 29 Aug 1877, LC, fever, 4-0-0, p. David & Canless [?] Washington, sc: David Washington, father, LE Dist., BVS:1877:9

WASHINGTON, John, B, M, d. 20 Feb 1886, Middleburg, unk, 3-0-0, p. Thompson & Ginnie Washington, b. Middleburg, sc: Judy Washington, grandmother, 1st Dist., BVS:1886:2

WASHINGTON, Joshua, B, M, d. 16 May 1885, nr Lovettsville, old age, 80-0-0, p. unk, b. LC, laborer, unk, sc: Emanuel Douglas, son-in-law, 2nd Dist., BVS:1885:2

WASHINGTON, Sarah, B, F, d. 12 Apr 1886, Middleburg, unk, 15-0-0, p. Thompson & Ginnie Washington, b. Middleburg, sc: Judy Washington, grandmother, 1st Dist., BVS:1886:2

WASHINGTON, Semple A., B, F, d. 9 Oct 1893, nr Sterling, spasms, 13-0-0, p. Frank & Jinnie Washington, b. nr Sterling, sc: Frank Washington, father, 1st Dist., BVS:1893:2

WASHINGTON, Thompson, B, M, d. 15 Feb 1886, Middleburg, consumption, 65-0-0, p. Thompson & Judy Wasington, b. LC, laborer, c/o: Judy Washington, sc: Judy Washington, mother, 1st Dist., BVS:1886:2

WATERS, Alphonius, W, M, d. 5 Apr 1884, nr Leesburg, unk, 0-0-25, p. Thomas W. & Roberta Waters, b. LC, sc: Thos W. Waters, father, 2nd Dist., BVS:1884:5

WATERS, Arthur G., B, M, d. 30 Dec 1881, LC, typhoid fever, 1-9-0, p. Wm. W. & Mary Waters, b. LC, sc: Wm. W. Waters, father, 2nd Dist., BVS:1881:7

WATERS, Ashby J., W, M, d. 22 Apr 1886, LC, malarial fever, 23-4-0, p. John F. & Susanna, b. LC, farmer, unm, sc: John F. Waters, father, 2nd Dist., BVS:1886:6

WATERS, Ettie May, W, F, d. 31 Aug 1878, nr Harpers Ferry, cholera infantum, 0-3-24, p. Geo. S. & Emma H. V. Waters, b. LC, sc: Geo. S. Waters, father, LV Dist., BVS:1878:1/5

WATERS, Harriet R., B, F, d. 12 Nov 1886, LC, diphtheria, 8-10-0, p. Thomas W. & Roberta, b. LC, sc: Thomas W. Waters, father, 2nd Dist., BVS:1886:6

WATERS, Hattie, B, F, d. 3 May 1872, Leesburg, whooping cough, 5-0-0, p. John & Nancy Waters, b. Leesburg,

Loudoun County, Virginia, Death Register, 1853-1896   269

sc: John Waters, father, LE Dist., BVS:1872:4

WATERS, Hattie N., B, F, d. 21 Aug 1878, LC, cholera infantum, 0-11-0, p. Wm. & Mary Waters, b. LC, unm, sc: Mary Waters, mother, LE Dist., BVS:1878:9

WATERS, Ida R., B, F, d. 2 Oct 1886, LC, diphtheria, 9-10-22, p. Thomas W. & Roberta, b. LC, sc: Thomas W. Waters, father, 2nd Dist., BVS:1886:6

WATERS, Laura, B, F, d. 1 Apr 1888, LC, diphtheria, 0-1-21, p. Thomas & Roberta Waters, b. unk, none, unm, sc: Thomas Waters, father, 2nd Dist., BVS:1888:6

WATERS, Luella Berthenia, W, F, d. 1 Nov 1878, nr Harpers Ferry, whooping cough, 2-9-4, p. Susannah C. Waters, b. LC, sc: John S. Waters, grandfather, LV Dist., BVS:1878:1/5

WATERS, Mary R., B, F, d. 15 Nov 1886, LC, diphtheria, 7-5-0, p. Thomas W. & Roberta, b. LC, sc: Thomas W. Waters, father, 2nd Dist., BVS:1886:6

WATERS, Matilda, B, F, d. 15 Mar 1892, Mountain Gap, consumption, 17-0-0, p. Robt. & Annie Waters, b. Mountain Gap, unm, sc: Robt Waters, LE Dist., BVS:1892:5

WATERS, Matilda L., B, F, d. 17 Mar 1893, Mountain Gap, consumption, 17-0-0, p. unk, b. Mountain Gap, unm, sc: father, LE Dist., BVS:1893:7

WATERS, Powell, B, M, d. 6 Sep 1878, LC, heart disease, 0-0-17, p. Joseph & Easter Waters, b. LC, unm, sc: Easter Waters, mother, LE Dist., BVS:1878:9

WATERS, Sarah, W, F, d. 9 Jan 1859/60, LC, dropsy, 61-4-7, p. Jeremiah & Susan Dutch, b. Maryland, c/o: Levi Waters, sc: John F. Waters, son, BVS:1859:1, 1860:4, LC:37

WATERS, Thomas A., W, M, d. 11 Jul 1856, LC, whooping cough, 0-1-2, p. John F. & Susan Waters, b. LC, sc: John F. Waters, father, BVS:1856:2, LC:21

WATERS, Townsend, B, M, d. 15 Jan 1886, LC, fever, 0-9-15, p. Isaac & Jennie Waters, sc: Isaac Waters, father, 3rd Dist., BVS:1886:4

WATKINS, Geo., W, M, d. 20 Aug 1853, LC, dysentery, 3-4-13, p. Geo. W. & Mary Watkins, b. LC, sc: Jno McCabe, grandfather, BVS:1854:5, LC:3

WATKINS, Geo. E., W, M, d. 2 Aug 1853, LC, unk, 3-4-13, p. Geo. W. & M. E. Watkins, b. Gum Spring, sc: Geor. W. W. Watkins, BVS:1854:2, LC:6

WATKINS, Maria, B, F, d. 21 Jun 1888, LC, pneumonia, 2-5-0, p. Nathaniel & Jennie Watkins, b. unk, none, unm, sc: Nathaniel Watkins, father, 2nd Dist., BVS:1888:6

[WATKINS], no name, B, , d. 25 Dec 1878, LC, strangulation, unk, p. Nat & Ginnie Watkins, b. LC, unm, sc: Ginnie Watkins, mother, LE Dist., BVS:1878:9

WATKINS, Walker, B, M, d. 24 Jun 1888, LC, pneumonia, 4-1-0, p. Nathaniel & Jennie Watkins, b. unk, none, unm, sc: Nathaniel Watkins, father, 2nd Dist., BVS:1888:6

WATSON, Anna M., W, F, d. 31 Jul 1881, LC, confinement, 43-0-0, b. LC, c/o: J.B. Watson, sc: J.B. Watson, husband, 1st Dist., BVS:1881:3

WATSON, Arthur, B, M, d. Oct 1872, Bull Run Mtn., kidney affect, 23-0-0, p. Frances Watson, unm, sc: George Buckhannon, MC Dist., BVS:1872:7

WATSON, Emily, B, F, d. 15 Aug 1883, nr Leesburg, typhoid fever, 26-1-2, p. Thompson & Mary Watson, b. LC, laborer, unm, sc: Mary Watson, mother, 2nd Dist., BVS:1883:7

WATSON, Emily, B, F, d. 26 Aug 1881, LC, typhoid fever, 25-2-12, p. Thompson & Mary Watson, b. LC, laborer, unm, sc: Mary Watson, mother, 2nd Dist., BVS:1881:7

WATSON, Emma Lee, W, F, d. 20 May 1876, nr Oatlands Mill, lockjaw, 0-0-8, p. J. B. & Annie M. Watson, b. LC, sc: Jacob B. Watson, father, MC Dist., BVS:1876:5

WATSON, Lemuel, W, M, d. 15 Aug 1875, Leesburg, cancer, 65-6-0, carriage maker, c/o: Lucy Watson, sc: Thos. H. Birkby, brother-in-law, LE Dist., BVS:1875:2

WATSON, Lucy, W, F, d. 1 Mar 1883, Leesburg, old age, 72-0-0, p. Thos. & Sallie Birkby, b. LC, c/o: Lemuel Watson, sc: T.W. Birkby, brother, 2nd Dist., BVS:1883:4

[WATSON], no name, W, F, d. 15 Feb 1876, nr Pleasant Valley, unk, 0-0-2, p. Taylor & Emily Watson, b. LC, unm, sc: Taylor Watson, father, BR Dist., BVS:1876:2

WATSON, Robert, B, M, d. 15 Dec 1881, LC, consumption, 23-0-0, p. Robt & Patsy Watson, b. LC, laborer, unm, sc: Robert Watson, father, 2nd Dist., BVS:1881:7

WATSON, Taylor, B, M, d. 28 Jan 1875, nr Belmont, measles, 23-4-0, p. unk, b. LC, laborer, married, sc: Chas. Venay, friend, BR Dist., BVS:1875:5

WATSON, Wm., (f), M, d. 7 Apr 1853, Leesburg, dropsy, 56-9-13, p. unk, b. LC, laborer, c/o: Emily Watson, sc: Emily Watson, wife, BVS:1854:5, LC:3

WAUGH, Mary P., W, F, d. Jun 1864, E.C.Brown's, old age, 82-0-0, b. King George Co., sc: E.C. Brown, BVS:1864:1, LC:38

WAY, Anna, W, F, d. Oct 1860, Jno Wolf's, consumption, 60-0-0, p. Wm. & Hannah Galliher, b. nr Union, farmer, c/o: Thomas Way, sc: John Wolf, son-in-law, BVS:1860:2

WEADEN, Elizabeth F., W, F, d. 19 Nov 1882, LC, diphtheria, 14-0-0, p. T. Wm. & Virginia Weaden, sc: T. Wm. Weadon, parent, 3rd Dist., BVS:1882:3

WEADON, Ann Virginia, W, F, d. Jun 1865, Purcellville, bilious fever, 18-0-0, p. Jno & Nancy Weadon, b. Purcellville, unm, sc: mother, BVS:1865:1

WEADON, Joseph V., W, M, d. 30 Mar 1830, Snickersville, consumption, 26-0-0, p. Ashford & C. Agnes Weaden, b. Bunker Hill, Clerk, sc: A. Weadon, father, MT Dist., BVS:1877:2

WEADON, Lorinda, W, F, d. 20 Mar 1872, Mount Gilead Twp., consumption, 59-0-0, p. Joseph & Elizabeth Beamersdaffer, b. Mount Gilead Town, c/o: Ashford Weadon, sc: Ashford Weadon, husband, MT Dist., BVS:1872:2

WEADON, Ruth, W, F, d. 27 Oct 1874, nr Hamilton, scalded, 3-3-3, p. Chas. & Mary Weadon, b. nr Hamilton, sc: Chas. Weadon, father, JF Dist., BVS:1874:2

WEAVER, Ann, B, F, d. Nov 1878, Guinea, heart disease, unk, p. Washington & Hannah Carter, c/o: Thos. Weaver, sc: T. Weaver, consort, MT Dist., BVS:1878:2/3

WEAVER, Delia, B, F, d. 6 Dec 1888, LC, old age, 85-0-0, p. unk, b. LC, none, unm, sc: Presly Roberts, friend, 3rd Dist., BVS:1888:2

WEAVER, Herbert, B, M, d. 2 Jun 1875, nr Snickersville, spinal disease, 2-0-0, p. Robert & Belle Weaver, b. nr Snickersville, laborer, sc: Robt Weaver, father, MT Dist., BVS:1875:8

WEAVER, Mamie, B, F, d. 10 Feb 1884, LC, pneumonia, 3-0-0, p. Frank & Nellie Weaver, b. LC, sc: Frank Weaver, father, 1st Dist., BVS:1884:3

WEAVER, Marshall, B, M, d. 1 Apr 1888, LC, brain fever, 13-0-0, p. Burr & Julia Weaver, b. LC, none, unm, sc: Burr Weaver, father, 3rd Dist., BVS:1888:2

WEAVER, Mary Magdelene, B, F, d. Feb 1894, Philomont, dropsy, 20-0-0, p. Thomas & Anna Weaver, b. Philomont, unm, sc: Thos. Weaver, father, 3rd Dist., BVS:1894:5

WEAVER, Nancy, B, F, d. 10 May 1884, LC, old age, 90-0-0, p. Frank & Nellie Weaver, b. LC, unk, sc: Frank Weaver, son, 1st Dist., BVS:1884:3

WEBB, Elizabeth, W, F, d. 15 Apr 1874, nr Harpers Ferry, infirmity, 80-0-0, p. lived with her son Joseph B. Webb, LV Dist., BVS:1874:6

WEBB, John W., W, --, d. 11 Nov 1889, LC, pneumonia, 68-0-0, p. Elisha & Eliza Webb, b. LC, laborer, c/o: Amanda Webb, sc: Amanda Webb, widow, 2nd Dist., BVS:1889:4

WEBB, Margaret, B, F, d. 12 Apr 1875, LC, dropsy, 35-6-0, c/o: Landon C. Webb, sc: L.C. Webb, husband, LE Dist., BVS:1875:2

WEBB, Margaret J., B, F, d. 15 May 1875, LC, unk, 0-1-16, p. Landon C. & Margt Webb, b. Leesburg, sc: L.C. Webb, father, LE Dist., BVS:1875:2

WEBB, Mary E., W, F, d. 7 Mar 1885, nr Lovettsville, malarial fever, 31-0-0, p. Chas. W. & Mary E. Butts, b. LC, c/o: Elisha Webb, sc: Chas W. Butts, father, 2nd Dist., BVS:1885:2

WEBB, Richard, W, M, d. 6 Feb 1887, LC, apoplexy, 68-0-0, p. unk, b. LC, none, c/o: Rebecca Webb, sc: Richard J. Webb, son, 2nd Dist., BVS:1887:5

WEBB, Robt., B, M, d. 29 May 1881, LC, unk, 0-0-1, p. Richard & Hannah W., b. LC, sc: H. Webb, mother, 1st Dist., BVS:1881:3

WEBSTER, Catharine, W, F, d. 25 May 1873, nr Cub Run, consumption, 72-0-0, p. unk, b. nr Fairfax line, married, sc: Henry A. Webster, head of family, BR Dist., BVS:1873:1

WEBSTER, Daniel, B, M, d. 20 mar 1874, nr Wheatland, dropsy, 74-0-0, p. unk, b. unk, laborer, unm, sc: Allen Webster, cousin, JF Dist., BVS:1874:2

WEBSTER, Sarah E., W, F, d. 2 May 1883, nr Guilford, pneumonia, 50-0-0, p. James & Sarah Smith, b. nr Guilford, c/o: John G. Webster, sc: John G. Webster, husband, 1st Dist., BVS:1883:2

WEEKS, John, W, M, d. 12 Mar 1887, nr Philomont, paralysis, 65-0-0, p. unk, b. LC, unm, sc: F.E. Robey, superintendent of poor, 1st Dist., BVS:1887:3

WEEKS, Sallie, W, F, d. 12 Dec 1880, LC, old age, 82-0-0, p. unk, unm, sc: J. Thomas Weeks, brother, 1st Dist., BVS:1880:2

WELLS, Danl. N., W, M, d. 25 Augt 1874, Broad Run Dist., consumption, 30-1-0, p. Danl. N. & E. R. Wells, b. Michigan, farmer, married, sc: Danl. N. Wells, Sr., father, BR Dist., BVS:1874:3

WELLS, Mary C., W, F, d. 27 Mar 1858, LC, unk, 25-0-0, p. Sanford & Ann Cockerille, b. LC, c/o: Alonzo Wells, sc: Alonzo Wells, husband, BVS:1858:6, LC:33

WELLS, Nancy, W, F, d. 21 Oct 1882, LC, consumption, 31-0-0, p. Robert & Nancy Wells, unm, sc: Robert Wells, father, 1st Dist., BVS:1882:2

WELSH, John J., W, M, d. 14 May 1890, Middleburg, hemorrhage, 21-0-0, p. J. Selden & Mary E. Welsh, b. LC, unm, sc: J. Seldon Welsh, father, 1st Dist., BVS:1890:2

WENNER, Elizabeth, W, F, d. 29 Sep 1856, LC, dysentery, 63-0-0, p. Henry & Catharine Short, b. LC, c/o: Wm. Wenner, sc: Wm. Wenner, husband, BVS:1856:2, LC:21

WENNER, Emanuel, W, M, d. 15 Jul 1887, LC, old age, 80-0-0, p. unk, b. LC, farmer, sc: Ella Wenner, daughter, 2nd Dist., BVS:1887:5

WENNER, Gertrude E., W, F, d. 15 Sep 1865, nr Hoysville, bilious dysentery, 7-6-11, p. George W. & Jane Wenner, b. nr Hoysville, farmer, sc: Geo W. Wenner, father, 1st Dist., BVS:1865:3/5

WENNER, John J., W, M, d. 1 Aug 1885, Lovettsville, unk, 46-0-0, p. Wm. W. & Susan B. Wenner, b. LC, physician, c/o: Jennie L. Wenner, sc: Jennie L. Wenner, wife, 2nd Dist., BVS:1885:2

WENNER, Mary E., W, F, d. 17 Apr 1885, nr Lovettsville, heart disease, 57-0-0, p. unk, b. LC, c/o: Emanuel Wenner, sc: Emanuel Wenner, husband, 2nd Dist., BVS:1885:2

WENNER, Mary E., W, F, d. 25 Sep 1854, LC, typhoid fever, 23-0-0, p. John & Mary Wenner, b. LC, teacher, unm, sc: Isaac S. Hough, head of family, BVS:1854:9, LC:8

WENNER, Mary Jane, W, F, d. 14 Oct 1878, nr Short Hill, heart disease, 51-0-7, p. Jacob & Margaret Smith, b. LC, c/o: John W. Wenner, sc: John W. Wenner, husband, LV Dist., BVS:1878:1/5

[WENNER], no name, W, M, d. 29 Aug 1859/60, LC, unk, 0-0-1, p. Geo W. & Mary A. Wenner, b. LC, sc: George Beamer Jr., uncle, BVS:1859:1, 1860:4, LC:37

WENNER, [no name], W, M, d. Jun 1876, nr Berlin, 0-3-0, p. A.A. & Catharine Wenner, b. LC, sc: Wm W. Wenner, grandfather, LV Dist., BVS:1876:3

WENNER, Ollie Bell, W, F, d. 27 Sep 1896, Lovettsville, typhoid fever, 19-0-0, p. Josephus & Sarah, b. Lovettsville, unm, sc: Josephine Wenner, LV Dist., BVS:1896:7

WENNER, Reginia, W, F, d. 28 Jul 1874, Berlin Ferry, teething, 0-9-7, p. Geo. J. Wenner & Martha, proprietor of Berlin Ferry, LV Dist., BVS:1874:6

WENNER, Willie, W, M, d. 1 Aug 1877, LC, dysentery, 1-6-14, p. E. C. & Leah Wenner, b. LC, sc: E.C. Wenner, father, JF Dist., BVS:1877:3

WERKING, Ann O., W, F, d. 1 May 1859/60, LC, unk, 0-1-0, p. Wm. J. & Susan Werking, b. LC, sc: Wm. J. Werking, father, BVS:1859:2, 1860:4, LC:37

WERKING, George, W, M, d. 19 May 1879, nr Lovettsville, apoplexy, 57-3-1, p. Henry & Sarah Werking, b. LC, mechanic, c/o: Catherine Werking, sc: Catherine Werking, wife, 2nd Dist., BVS:1879:2

WERKING, Henrietta E., W, F, d. 10 Oct 1856, Lovettsville, pleurisy, 4-1-9, p. Geo. & Catharine Werking, b. Lovettsville, sc: George Werking, father, BVS:1856:1, LC:20

WESSINGER, Healy G., W, F, d. 26 Sep 1857, LC, spinal affection, 63-0-0, p. unk, b. Frederick, MD, unm, sc: James W. Lakin, son-in-law, BVS:1857:1, LC:25

WEST, Hannah, W, F, d. 6 Jul 1853, Silcott Springs, dysentery, 84-0-0, p. unk, b. Lovettsville, farmer, c/o: John West, sc: Jno Orrison, son in law, BVS:1854:1, LC:4

WEY, Anna, W, F, d. Oct 1859, John Woolf's, consumption, 60-0-0, p. Wm. & Hannah Galleher, b. nr Union, c/o: Thos. A. Wey decd, sc: John Woolf, son-in-law, BVS:1859:4, LC:35

WHALAN, Minetras, W, M, d. 5 Aug 1880, LC, cholera morbus, 3-0-0, p. Minthas & Ellen Whalan, unm, sc: Ellen Whalan, mother, 1st Dist., BVS:1880:3

WHALEN, Ellen, W, F, d. 29 Mar 1884, LC, croup, 0-2-0, p. Murthas & Catharine Whalen, b. LC, sc: Murthas Whalen, father, 1st Dist., BVS:1884:3

WHALEY, Lydia, W, F, d. 12 Dec 1877, nr Gum Spring, liver disease, 62-0-0, p. Richd. & Ann Presgraves, b. LC, widow, sc: Ann Presgraves, sister, BR Dist., BVS:1877:1

WHALEY, Raymond, W, M, d. 27 Jan 1884, LC, measles, 3-0-0, p. James W. & Mary J. Whaley, b. LC, sc: James Whaley, father, 1st Dist., BVS:1884:3

WHEELER, Dennis, (f), M, d. 22 Mar 1855, old age, 75-0-0, p. unk, b. LC, sc: S.L. Hodgson, friend, BVS:1855:9, LC:19

WHITACRE, James, W, M, d. 4 Nov 1856, res, E. of Union, epilepsy, 52-0-0, p. John & Phebe Whitacre, b. his res., farmer, c/o: Margaret A. Whitacre, sc: M.A. Whitacre, widow, BVS:1856:4, LC:22

WHITACRE, Margarette, W, F, d. 20 Nov 1896, nr Unison, heart disease, 71-0-0, p. unk, b. Virginia, housekeeper, consort, sc: Jno Whitacre, son, MC Dist., BVS:1896:2

WHITACRE, Samuel J., W, M, d. 21 Oct 1881, LC, typhoid fever, 30-0-0, p. Jas. & Margaret Whitacre, b. LC, stock dealer, c/o: Margaret Whitacre, sc: Mrs. Whitacre, wife, 1st Dist., BVS:1881:3

WHITE, Agnes B., W, F, d. 4 Dec 1875, Hillsboro, heart disease, 62-0-0, b. LC, c/o: James B. White, sc: Jno. J. White, son, JF Dist., BVS:1875:3

WHITE, Alfred, B, M, d. 25 Dec 1887, Dover, pneumonia, 1-10-0, p. West & Bettie White, b. Dover, unm, sc: West White, father, 1st Dist., BVS:1887:3

WHITE, Amanda, W, F, d. 14 Jan 1865, 2 Miles S.W. of Leesburg, bilious dysentery, 47-0-0, p. unk, b. nr Leesburg, farmer, unm, sc: Chas White, brother, 1st Dist., BVS:1865:5

WHITE, Amanda, W, F, d. 14 Jan 1865, Leesburg, bilious dysentery, 47-0-0, b. nr Leesburg, farmer, unm, sc: Chas Wright, brother, BVS:1865:3

WHITE, Ann G., W, F, d. 11 Sep 1896, LC, old age, 76-0-0, p. Reed & A.

Loudoun County, Virginia, Death Register, 1853-1896

Poulton, b. LC, housekeeper, wife, sc: Wm. H. White, son, LE Dist., BVS:1896:5

WHITE, Bessie, B, F, d. 2 Aug 1892, Aldie, whooping cough, 3-0-0, p. Thos. & Salina White, b. Aldie, sc: Salina White, mother, 1st Dist., BVS:1892:3

WHITE, Cranford K., W, M, d. 4 Dec 1865, Crossroad, S. Houser's, chronic disorder of bowel, 38-0-0, p. Wm. & Manah White, b. Fairfax Co., clerk, unm, sc: Saml C. Luckett, friend, BVS:1865:3

WHITE, Crawford K., W, M, d. 4 Dec 1865, nr Cross Roade S. House, chronic disease bowel, 38-0-0, p. Wm. & Maria White, b. Fairfax Co., clerk, unm, sc: Saml C. Luckett, uncle, 1st Dist., BVS:1865:4

WHITE, Elizabet I., W, F, d. 13 Dec 1894, Leesburg, old age, 80-0-0, p. Thos. & Elizabeth, b. unk, teacher, unm, sc: Chas P. Janney, LE Dist., BVS:1894:3

WHITE, Elizabeth, W, F, d. 28 Aug 1854, LC, dysentery, 32-3-5, p. Wm & Maria White, b. Fairfax Co., unk, sc: Samuel C. Luckett, cousin, BVS:1854:9, LC:8

WHITE, Fenton, B, , d. 19 Dec 1877, LC, brain fever, 0-5-14, p. Rich. & Fannie White, sc: Fannie White, mother, LE Dist., BVS:1877:9

WHITE, Florence, B, F, d. 2 Dec 1892, Aldie, whooping cough, 0-10-0, p. Thos. & Salina White, b. Aldie, sc: Salina White, mother, 1st Dist., BVS:1892:3

WHITE, Francis, B, F, d. 10 Aug 1891, Sycolin, dysentery, 45-0-0, p. unk, b. unk, laborer, c/o: Richard White, sc: husband, LE Dist., BVS:1891:4

WHITE, Fredie, B, M, d. 10 Aug 1891, Sycolin, dysentery, 0-3-0, p. Richard & Francis White, b. Sycolin, laborer, unm, sc: father, LE Dist., BVS:1891:4

WHITE, George, B, M, d. 23 Aug 1892, Aldie, consumption, 6-0-0, p. Thos. & Salina White, b. Aldie, sc: Salina White, mother, 1st Dist., BVS:1892:3

WHITE, George E., W, M, d. 21 Sep 1856, LC, dysentery, 12-11-16, p. Wm. & Elizth. White, b. LC, sc: Elizabeth White, mother, BVS:1856:1, LC:20

WHITE, George W., W, M, d. May 1891, Hamilton, cancer, 52-0-0, p. unk, b. Hamilton, husband, sc: Mort White, MT Dist., BVS:1891:6

WHITE, Gertie, B, F, d. 23 Aug 1890, nr Aldie, dropsy, 25-0-4, p. Lisha Moten (unm), b. nr Aldie, c/o: Vince White, sc: Geo Shepphard, brother-in-law, 1st Dist., BVS:1890:2

WHITE, Hattie, B, F, d. 10 Jul 1883, Hughesville, unk, 0-8-0, p. Thomas & Sarah White, b. LC, sc: Thomas White, father, 3rd Dist., BVS:1883:5

[WHITE], Ida Bell, W, F, d. Sep 1865, nr Hughesville, lung fever, 0-6-0, p. Levi & C.A. White, b. Hughesville, sc: L. White, father, BVS:1865:1

WHITE, James W., W, M, d. 12 May 1857, LC, croup, 1-10-0, p. Joshua & Mary White, b. LC, sc: Joshua White, father, BVS:1857:1, LC:25

WHITE, Jesse, B, M, d. 19 Mar 1854, Poor House, drink, 35-0-0, p. Bob White, Laborer, sc: Wm. Furr, BVS:1854:11, LC:11

WHITE, Levi, W, M, d. 27 Jul 1857, his res, paralysis, 79-0-0, p. Daniel & Mary White, b. Ketoctin Mountain, farmer, c/o: Mary White, sc: Levi White, son, BVS:1857:4, LC:27

WHITE, Louisa, B, F, d. 14 Aug 1892, Aldie, whooping cough, 2-0-0, p. Thos. & Salina White, b. Aldie, sc: Salina White, mother, 1st Dist., BVS:1892:3

WHITE, Martha, B, F, d. 3 Jul 1892, Aldie, consumption, 14-0-0, p. Thos. & Salina White, b. Aldie, sc: Salina White, mother, 1st Dist., BVS:1892:3

WHITE, Mary C., W, F, d. 26 May 1875, Hillsboro, child birth, 29-0-0, b. Carlisle, Pa., c/o: John J. White, sc: John J. White, husband, JF Dist., BVS:1875:3

[WHITE], no name, W, M, d. 27 Feb 1859/60, LC, unk, 0-1-5, p. Burr & Cathn A. White, b. LC, sc: Burr J. White, father, BVS:1859:1, 1860:4, LC:37

[WHITE], no name, B, M, d. 10 Jan 1884, LC, unk, 0-0-1, p. Thomas & Tolina White, b. LC, sc: Thomas White, father, 1st Dist., BVS:1884:3

WHITE, Octavia, B, F, d. 14 May 1883, nr Leesburg, unk, 0-10-0, p. Richard & Fannie White, b. LC, sc: Fannie White, mother, 2nd Dist., BVS:1883:4

WHITE, Richard, W, M, d. 12 Feb 1878, Woodburn, cancer, 78-0-0, p. Benj. & Mary White, b. LC, sc: J. Laycock, friend, MT Dist., BVS:1878:2/3

WHITE, Richard, W, --, d. 27 Apr 1889, LC, catarrh, 44-0-0, p. James & Ann C. White, b. LC, farmer, unm, sc: W.H. White, brother, 2nd Dist., BVS:1889:4

WHITE, Richard, B, M, d. 12 Aug 1891, Sycolin, dysentery, 13-0-0, p. Richard & Francis White, b. Sycolin, laborer, unm, sc: father, LE Dist., BVS:1891:4

WHITE, Robt. C, W, M, d. 20 Sep 1875, Hillsboro, dysentery, 0-5-0, p. Jno. J. & Mary C. White, b. LC, sc: Jno. J. White, father, JF Dist., BVS:1875:3

WHITE, Sarah M., W, F, d. 8 Jul 1866, Hillsboro, dysentery, 6-0-0, p. Josiah R. & F. V. White, sc: J.R. White, father, BVS:1866:1

WHITE, Selina, B, F, d. 20 Dec 1896, nr Levy, unk, 0-0-5, p. Thos. & Selina White, b. nr Levy, none, unm, sc: Thos White, father, MC Dist., BVS:1896:2

WHITE, Thomas, W, M, d. 29 Dec 1857, LC, unk, 77-0-0, p. unk, b. LC, farmer, sc: Randolph White, son, BVS:1857:1, LC:25

WHITE, Thomas William, W, M, d. 30 Jun 1871, nr Hillsboro, pneumonia, unk, p. Josiah T. & Mary J. White, b. nr Hillsboro, sc: Mary White, mother, JF Dist., BVS:1871:1

WHITE, Willis, B, M, d. Aug 1873, LC, paralysis, 60-0-0, b. Leesburg, laborer, c/o: Annie White, sc: Annie White, wife, LE Dist., BVS:1873:2

WHITE, Wm. H., B, M, d. 14 Apr 1892, Mountville, whooping cough, 4-9-10, p. Henry & Rose White, b. Mountville, laborer, sc: Henry White, father, 1st Dist., BVS:1892:3

WHITING, Elizabeth V., B, , d. 2 May 1877, LC, cholera infantum, 0-9-0, p. Lydia H. Whiting, sc: Lydia H. Whiting, mother, LE Dist., BVS:1877:9

WHITING, Frances, B, F, d. 25 April 1896, nr Watson, grippe, 40-0-0, p. unk, b. nr Watson, none, consort, sc: J.J. Tyler, neighbor, MC Dist., BVS:1896:2

WHITING, James H., B, M, d. 22 Dec 1886, nr Leesburg, typhoid fever, 20-10-0, p. Peter & Mary Whiting, b. LC, unm, sc: Peter Whiting, father, 1st Dist., BVS:1886:3

WHITING, Peter, B, M, d. 5 Aug 1887, Aldie, heart disease, 70-0-0, p. unk, b. Fauquier Co., c/o: Mary Whiting, sc: Mary Whiting, wife, 1st Dist., BVS:1887:3

WHITLEY, Addison, B, M, d. 21 Apr 1892, Middleburg, whooping cough, 1-9-0, p. French & Annie Whitley, b. Middleburg, sc: French Whitley, father, 1st Dist., BVS:1892:3

WHITLOCK, Amanda B., W, F, d. 28 Jul 1883, nr Aldie, unk, 59-0-0, p. unk, b. LC, c/o: Henry Whitlock, sc: Henry Whitlock, husband, 1st Dist., BVS:1883:2

WHITLY, Estelle, B, F, d. 16 Mar 1894, Middleburg, unk, 12-6-19, p. French & Annie Whitley, b. Middleburg, sc: Annie Whitly, mother, 1st Dist., BVS:1894:2

WHITMORE, Elizabeth, W, F, d. 10 Dec 1892, Lucketts, heart failure, 67-0-0, p. John & Sarah Utterback [sic], b. Lucketts, consort, LE Dist., BVS:1892:5

WHITMORE, John W., W, M, d. 3 Aug 1856, Leesburg, dysentery, 7-0-0, p. Michael W. & Louisiana Whitmore, b. LC, sc: Harriet Duvall, grandmother, BVS:1856:1, LC:19

WHITMORE, Maud May, W, F, d. 1 Sep 1891, Pleasant Grove, unk, 0-0-12, p. Jno. C. & Ellen Virginia Whitmore, b. Pleasant Grove, sc: Jno C. Whitmore, MT Dist., BVS:1891:6

WHITMORE, no name, W, F, d. 1 Sep 1889, LC, unk, 0-0-1, p. John C. & M. V. Whitmore, b. LC, none, unm, sc: J.C. Whitmore, father, 3rd Dist., BVS:1889:5

WHITTINGTON, Mary A., W, F, d. 10 Jul 1876, Welbourne, consumption, 47-0-0, b. Page Co., c/o: Robt. W. Whittington, sc: Robt. W.

Whittington, husband, MC Dist., BVS:1876:5

WIARD, Ephraim, W, M, d. 10 Jun 1858, LC, pneumonia, 18-11-27, p. Jonathan & Maria Wiard, b. LC, sc: George Wiard, brother, BVS:1858:1, LC:30

WIARD, Michail, W, --, d. 22 Dec 1889, LC, old age, 92-7-10, p. unk, b. LC, stone mason, unm, sc: Geo C. Wire, son-in-law, 2nd Dist., BVS:1889:4

WICKS, Lilly E., B, F, d. 24 Feb 1875, Leesburg, unk, 0-7-0, p. Hannah Wicks, b. Leesburg, sc: Ann Payne, friend, LE Dist., BVS:1875:2

WIGHTMAN, Archibald J., W, M, d. 7 Aug 1883, nr Leesburg, pneumonia, 60-6-4, p. John & Sarah Wightman, b. LC, farmer, c/o: Susan Wightman, sc: Susan Wightman, wife, 2nd Dist., BVS:1883:7

WILDMAN, Elizabeth, W, F, d. 14 Sep 1854, nr Oatlands, consumption, 45-0-0, p. Wm. & Rebecca McGregin, b. nr Gum Spring, c/o: Wm. Wildman, sc: husband, BVS:1854:12, LC:12

WILDMAN, Mary Ellen, W, F, d. 13 Nov 1858, res of parents, scarlet fever, 5-3-8, p. Joseph & Ann Wildman, b. place of death, sc: Ann Wildman, mother, BVS:1858:4, LC:32

WILDMAN, Wm., W, M, d. 5 Oct 1875, Leesburg, dropsy, 84-0-0, c/o: Rebecca Wildman, sc: Rebecca Wildman, wife, LE Dist., BVS:1875:2

WILEY, Arthur H., W, M, d. 25 Aug 1878, LC, cholera infantum, 0-11-0, p. Henry & Eliza Wiley, b. LC, unm, sc: Eliza Wiley, mother, LE Dist., BVS:1878:9

WILEY, Chas. J., W, M, d. 15 Jul 1896, Waxpool, white swelling, 47-0-0, b. LC, laborer, c/o: Susan M. McNealea, sc: half-brother, BR Dist., BVS:1896:3

WILEY, Clifford C., W, M, d. Apr 1873, Hamilton, cold, 0-13-0, p. John H. & Malinda A. Wiley, b. Hamilton, sc: parents, MT Dist., BVS:1873:3

WILEY, Elizabeth S., W, F, d. 5 Sep 1857, LC, child bed, 31-0-0, p. Samuel & Cassandra Davis, b. LC, c/o: John H. Wiley, sc: John H. Wiley, husband, BVS:1857:1, LC:24

WILEY, Estella, W, F, d. Nov 1876, nr Hamilton, 0-9-0, p. W. H. & Nanie E. Wiley, b. LC, unm, sc: W.H. Wiley, father, MT Dist., BVS:1876:1

WILEY, Eva, B, F, d. 15 Dec 1883, Snickersville, unk, 7-0-7, p. Lot & Eva Wiley, b. LC, sc: Lot Wiley, father, 3rd Dist., BVS:1883:5

WILEY, Florence, W, F, d. 6 Mar 1884, nr Leesburg, heart disease, 12-10-0, p. Harrison P. & Mary E. Wiley, b. LC, sc: H.P. Wiley, father, 2nd Dist., BVS:1884:5

WILEY, Harrison, W, M, d. 25 Jun 1896, LC, paralysis, 74-0-0, b. LC, farmer, husband, sc: daughter, LE Dist., BVS:1896:5

WILEY, Laura C., W, F, d. 19 May 1879, Hamilton, consumption, 20-0-0, p. John & Malinda Wiley, b. Hamilton, sc: John H. Wiley, father, 3rd Dist., BVS:1879:3

WILEY, Mary E., W, F, d. 10 Nov 1881, LC, heart disease, 52-0-0, p. Thos. & Elizth Green, b. LC, farmer, c/o: Harrison P. Wiley, sc: Harrison P. Wiley, husband, 2nd Dist., BVS:1881:7

WILEY, Mary V., W, F, d. 25 Jul 1853, LC, dysentery, 1-8-27, p. Jno. H. & Elizth. S. Wiley, b. LC, sc: Jno H. Wiley, father, BVS:1854:4, LC:2

WILEY, Volney, W, M, d. 11 Nov 1896, LC, tumor, 19-0-0, p. Z. T. & A. E. Wiley, b. LC, unm, sc: Z.T. Wiley, father, LE Dist., BVS:1896:5

WILEY, William, W, M, d. 12 Dec 1866, Poor House, old age, 81-0-0, sc: William Furr, BVS:1866:2

WILEY, William, B, M, d. 12 Jul 1883, Leesburg, unk, 0-4-0, p. Lott & Lettie Wiley, b. LC, sc: Ginnie Neal, aunt, 2nd Dist., BVS:1883:8

WILKINSON, Evan, (f), M, d. 20 Apr 1853, on Beaverdam, pneumonia, 61-0-0, p. Wm. & Sarah Wilkinson, b. LC, farmer, c/o: Sarah Wilkinson, sc: wife, BVS:1854:6, LC:5

WILKINSON, Mary Amelia, W, F, d. Dec 1857, brain affected, 1-1-0, p. Lewis L. & Mary E. Wilkinson, b. place of death, sc: L.L. Wilkinson, father, BVS:1857:5, LC:27

WILKINSON, William, W, M, d. 11 Mar 1857, his res, old age, 90-9-0, p. Evan & Margaret Wilkinson, b.

Pennsylvania, farmer, c/o: Sarah Wilkinson, sc: Peyton Powell, son-in-law, BVS:1857:4, LC:27

WILKLOW, Mary A., W, F, d. 30 Nov 1858, LC, intermittent fever, 34-11-3, p. Peter & Nancy Cooper, b. LC, c/o: Jacob Wilklow, sc: Emily Cooper, sister, BVS:1858:1, LC:29

WILLARD, Sarah E., W, F, d. 17 Apr 1891, Lovettsville, blood poison, 43-0-0, p. Dr. Daniel & Mary Willard, b. Lovettsville, physician, unm, sc: father, LV Dist., BVS:1891:5

WILLIAMS, Alfred, B, M, d. 5 Aug 1884, LC, old age, 84-0-0, p. Alfred & Minnie Williams, b. Fairfax, laborer, unm, sc: Robt Brent, friend, 1st Dist., BVS:1884:3

WILLIAMS, Alice R., W, F, d. 20 Nov 1891, nr Unison, diphtheria, 7-10-0, p. Gus. & Annie Williams, b. LC, laborer, sc: Gus Williams, father, 1st Dist., BVS:1891:3

WILLIAMS, Ann, B, F, d. 10 Sep 1883, nr Leesburg, typhoid fever, 27-0-0, p. Jos. & Martha Ambers, b. LC, laborer, c/o: Jacob Williams, sc: Jacob Williams, husband, 2nd Dist., BVS:1883:4

WILLIAMS, Ann G., W, F, d. 22 Mar 1878, Leesburg, remitting fever, 42-0-0, b. Fauquier Co., c/o: Jno H. Williams, sc: Jno H. Williams, husband, MC Dist., BVS:1878:7

WILLIAMS, Annie, B, F, d. 4 May 1884, nr Leesburg, cease of menstruation, 15-0-0, p. Sanford & Emily Williams, b. LC, laborer, sc: Sanford Williams, father, 2nd Dist., BVS:1884:5

WILLIAMS, Benj., B, M, d. 7 Aug 1882, LC, general debility, 75-0-0, c/o: Emily Williams, sc: James Redman, friend, 3rd Dist., BVS:1882:3

WILLIAMS, Ellis, W, M, d. 21 Jan 1858, LC, dropsy, 84-3-18, p. John & Martha Williams, b. LC, farmer, c/o: Magdalina Williams, sc: Burr Williams, son, BVS:1858:1, LC:29

WILLIAMS, Frank, B, M, d. 1 Aug 1883, nr Leesburg, summer complaint, 1-1-0, p. Frank & Margaret Williams, b. LC, sc: Abram Wallace, grandfather, 2nd Dist., BVS:1883:4

WILLIAMS, Franklin Pierce, W, M, d. Oct 1876, Taylorstown, accidental shooting, 28?-0-0, p. Henry S. & Ann Mariah Williams, b. Taylorstown, unm, sc: Ann M. Williams, mother, LV Dist., BVS:1876:3

WILLIAMS, George E., B, M, d. 15 Nov 1876, LC, dropsy, 1-7-0, p. Sanford & Emily Williams, b. LC, sc: Emily Williams, mother, LE Dist., BVS:1876:7

WILLIAMS, Henry S., W, M, d. 10 May 1873, on Ketoctin Creek, unk, 53-4-10, p. Israel & A Williams, b. on Miller Creek, miller, married, sc: Mariah Williams, wife, LV Dist., BVS:1873:4

WILLIAMS, Hillary W., W, M, d. 23 Apr 1854, LC, pneumonia, 31-5-7, p. unk, b. Maryland, farmer, c/o: Mary W. Williams, sc: Mary W. Williams, wife, BVS:1854:10, LC:10

WILLIAMS, Isaac, B, M, d. 3 Jul 1882, LC, general debility, 80-0-0, sc: Wm. Jackson, friend, 3rd Dist., BVS:1882:3

WILLIAMS, James, B, M, d. 20 Jun 1880, LC, old age, 81-0-0, p. unk, unm, sc: John Thomas, friend, 1st Dist., BVS:1880:3

WILLIAMS, James E., W, M, d. 21 Aug 1856, Waterford, decline, 1-0-22, p. Wm. & Mary E. Williams, b. Waterford, sc: William Williams, father, BVS:1856:1, LC:20

WILLIAMS, Jno., B, M, d. 11 Mar 1896, LC, heart trouble, 0-5-0, p. Jo Lucy Williams, b. Leesburg, sc: Joshua Williams, father, JF Dist., BVS:1896:6

WILLIAMS, John, W, M, d. 22 Aug 1856, Waterford, croup, 3-10-7, p. Wm. & Mary E. Williams, b. Waterford, sc: William Williams, father, BVS:1856:1, LC:20

WILLIAMS, John S., W, M, d. 11 Jul 1885, nr Guilford, premature, 0-0-1, p. John H. & Mattie L. Williams, b. Guilford, sc: John H. Williams, father, 1st Dist., BVS:1885:5

WILLIAMS, Joseph, W, M, d. 3 May 1873, LC, remittent fever, 18-0-0, p. John H. Williams & wife, b. nr Middleburg, farmer, unm, sc: John

Loudoun County, Virginia, Death Register, 1853-1896   277

H. Williams, head of family, BR Dist., BVS:1873:1

WILLIAMS, Maria H., B, F, d. 16 Apr 1881, LC, consumption, 14-0-0, p. Alfred & Matilda W., b. LC, sc: ? Williams, uncle, 1st Dist., BVS:1881:3

WILLIAMS, Mary, B, F, d. 11 Aug 1879, nr Goresville, unk, 1-7-0, p. Jacob & Ann Williams, b. LC, sc: Jacob Williams, father, 2nd Dist., BVS:1879:2

WILLIAMS, Mary Conrow, W, F, d. 10 Sep 1892, Waterford, cholera infantum, 0-14-0, p. Jas. & Hannah, b. LC, unm, sc: James Williams, LV Dist., BVS:1892:6

WILLIAMS, Mary E., W, F, d. 13 Apr 1875, Waterford, dyspepsia, 62-0-0, c/o: Wm. Williams, sc: Wm. Williams, husband, JF Dist., BVS:1875:3

WILLIAMS, Matilda Ann, B, F, d. 18 May 1874, nr Ebeneezer MH, pneumonia, 30-0-0, p. Julius & Maria Mason, b. LC, c/o: Dennis Williams, sc: Dennis Williams, husband, MC Dist., BVS:1874:4

WILLIAMS, Nancy, B, F, d. 26 Mar 1887, LC, consumption, 41-0-0, p. Jane & Louisa Nichols, none, c/o: Joseph Williams, sc: Joseph Williams, husband, 3rd Dist., BVS:1887:7

WILLIAMS, Nellie M., W, F, d. 9 Jul 1889, LC, rheumatism, 11-11-21, p. C. T. & Sallie R. Williams, b. LC, none, unm, sc: C.T. Williams, father, 2nd Dist., BVS:1889:4

[WILLIAMS], no name, W, F, d. 30 May 1896, LC, unk, p. C. W. & M. E. Williams, b. LC, farmer, sc: father, LE Dist., BVS:1896:5

WILLIAMS, Sarah, W, F, d. 17 May 1890, LC, paralysis, 63-0-0, p. Samuel Eamich, b. LC, none, c/o: Tobias Williams, sc: Geo S. Williams, son, 2nd Dist., BVS:1890:5

WILLIAMS, Sarah, W, F, d. 9 Jan 1853, Bloomfield, cancer of womb, 53-1-7, p. George & Elizabeth Day, b. Frederick Co., c/o: Levi Williams, sc: husband, BVS:1854:1, LC:4

WILLIAMS, Wm., W, M, d. 23 Nov 1892, Waterford, heart trouble, 77-0-0, p. Jno. & Lydia Williams, b.

Waterford, farmer, married, sc: Jack Walker, JF Dist., BVS:1892:7

WILLIS, Arthur, B, M, d. 10 Jun 1881, LC, unk, 6-0-0, p. Danl. & Anna Willis, b. LC, sc: Danl Willis, father, 3rd Dist., BVS:1881:5

WILLIS, Henson, B, M, d. 20 Jun 1873, nr Clifton, paralysis, 51-0-0, p. Amanda Willis, b. nr Clifton, mechanic, sc: Lucinda Willis, wife, MC Dist., BVS:1873:6

WILLIS, Mittie, B, F, d. 18 Apr 1893, nr Aldie, dropsy, 45-0-0, p. John & Mary Johnson, b. nr Aldie, c/o: Albert Willis, 1st Dist., BVS:1893:2

WILLIS, no name, B, F, d. 14 Aug 1873, nr Upperville, affection of brain, 0-0-2, p. Chas. & Nancy Willis, b. nr Clifton, sc: Robert Taylor, friend, MC Dist., BVS:1873:6

WILLIS, no name, B, M, d. 15 Jul 1892, Aldie, unk, 0-1-14, p. Albert & Millie Willis, b. Aldie, sc: Albert Willis, father, 1st Dist., BVS:1892:3

WILMOUTH, Jason, W, M, d. 13 Oct 1882, LC, gravel, 78-2-7, c/o: Mary A. Wilmarth, sc: W.B. Wilmarth, son, 3rd Dist., BVS:1882:3

WILSON, Ann E., W, F, d. 10 Jun 1896, Arcola, cholera morbus, 56-0-6, b. LC, c/o: Edlott Wilson, sc: Edlott Wilson, husband, BR Dist., BVS:1896:3

WILSON, Frank, B, M, d. 30 Sep 1896, nr Welbourne, drowned, 25-0-0, p. John & Mary Wilson, b. LC, laborer, unm, sc: Mary Wilson, mother, BR Dist., BVS:1896:4

WILSON, Franklin E., W, M, d. 13 Oct 1853, LC, consumption, 14-0-0, p. John H. & Matilda Wilson, b. LC, sc: J. H. Wilson, father, BVS:1854:2, LC:6

WILSON, Frederick A., W, M, d. 1 Mar 1873, Mountain View, pneumonia, 1-6-0, p. Enoch C. & Alice L. Wilson, b. Mountain View, sc: parents, MT Dist., BVS:1873:3

WILSON, Jas. B., W, M, d. 11 Mar 1855, LC, suddenly, 53-4-10, p. Moses D. & Tama Wilson, b. nr Middleburg on Goose Creek, farmer & plasterer, c/o: Sarah C. Wilson, sc: John A. Wilson, son, BVS:1855:4, LC:16

WILSON, John M., W, M, d. 1 Mar 1854, LC, pneumonia, 71-0-0, p. Robert Wilson, b. New Jersey, sc: Wm. G. Wilson, son, BVS:1854:14, LC:13

WILSON, John W., W, M, d. 25 Jul 1885, nr Arcola, cancer, 27-0-0, p. James H. & Matilda Wilson, b. Arcola, farmer, unm, sc: James H. Wilson, father, 1st Dist., BVS:1885:5

WILSON, Luther F., W, M, d. Sep 1855, unk, 2-1-0, p. Jas. H. & M. Wilson, b. LC, sc: Jas. H. Wilson, father, BVS:1855:8, LC:19

WILSON, Moses, B, M, d. 30 Apr 1880, Lovettsville, heart disease, 47-0-0, p. unk, b. LC, laborer, c/o: Fanny Wilson, sc: Fanny Wilson, wife, 3rd Dist., BVS:1880:5

WILSON, Nelson, W, M, d. 23 Feb 1878, Poor House, brain fever, 65-0-0, b. LC, unm, sc: Wm. H. Hibbs, superintendant of poorhouse, MC Dist., BVS:1878:7

WILSON, Parel L., B, M, d. 25 Dec 1887, Trappe, spasms, 0-0-6, p. John & Mary Wilson, b. Trappe, unm, sc: John Wilson, father, 1st Dist., BVS:1887:3

WILSON, Sarah, W, F, d. 7 Jul 1890, LC, child birth, 47-0-0, p. unk, b. LC, none, c/o: William L. Wilson, sc: W.L. Wilson, husband, 2nd Dist., BVS:1890:4

WILSON, Sarah C., W, F, d. 8 Oct 1877, nr Goose Creek, whooping cough, 0-2-11, p. R.M. & Lucy E. Wilson, sc: Richd M. Wilson, father, MC Dist., BVS:1877:6

WILSON, Sarah F., W, F, d. 28 Sep 1854, dysentery, 4-6-0, p. James H. & Matilda Wilson, b. LC, sc: James H. Wilson, father, BVS:1854:13, LC:13

WILSON, Stephen H., W, M, d. 26 Jun 1894, Round Hill, dysentery, 60-0-0, p. Moses D. & Nancy Ann Wilson, b. Round Hill, husband, sc: Mrs. Wilson, wife, 3rd Dist., BVS:1894:5

WILSON, Thomas, B, M, d. 20 Aug 1880, LC, thrush, 0-2-0, p. John & Mary Wilson, unm, sc: Mary Wilson, mother, 1st Dist., BVS:1880:3

WILSON, William, W, M, d. 12 Dec 1871, Round Hill, diabetes, 76-0-0, p. not living, b. LC, farmer, c/o: Elizabeth Wilson, sc: Wm. Gregg, son-in-law, MT Dist., BVS:1871:5

WILSON, William A., W, M, d. 28 Feb 1876, Middleburg, pneumonia, 37-0-0, p. Jno. K. & Annie Wilson, b. LC, farmer, unm, sc: B.P. Noland, brother-in-law, MC Dist., BVS:1876:5

WILT, Maize, W, F, d. 16 Dec 1879, nr Leesburg, unk, 0-0-1, p. George & Annie Wilt, b. LC, sc: Annie Wilt, mother, 2nd Dist., BVS:1879:2

WINCHESTER, Mathew, W, M, d. 27 April 1883, Leesburg, pneumonia, 1-1-24, p. W. R. & Sallie Winchester, b. LC, sc: W.R. Winchester, father, 2nd Dist., BVS:1883:8

WINDSOR, Mary M., B, F, d. 5 Aug 1892, Aldie, whooping cough, 1-2-0, p. Robt. & Jinnie Windsor, b. Aldie, sc: Jinnie Windsor, mother, 1st Dist., BVS:1892:3

WINE, Jacob T., W, M, d. 19 Nov 1871, Waterford, consumption, 47-8-23, p. Daniel & Sarah Wine, b. nr Waterford, c/o: Fannie Wine, sc: David Wine, father, JF Dist., BVS:1871:1

WINE, Sarah, W, F, d. 13 Oct 1871, nr Waterford, lung disease, 73-10-29, b. nr Waterford, c/o: Daniel Wine, sc: Daniel Wine, husband, JF Dist., BVS:1871:1

WINKEY, Catharine, B, F, d. 13 Feb 1878, nr Bloomfield, scrofula, 21-0-0, b. Fauquier Co., c/o: William Winkey, sc: Henry Brent, father, MC Dist., BVS:1878:7

WINTERS, Edmond, (f), M, d. 18 Aug 1858, Leesburg, unk, 14-0-0, p. Sarah Winters, b. Leesburg, sc: Sarah Winters, mother, BVS:1858:2, LC:30

WINTERS, Issabella, (f), F, d. 10 Feb 1857, Leesburg, pneumonia, 17-10-0, p. Sarah Winters, b. Leesburg, sc: Sarah Winters, mother, BVS:1857:2, LC:25

WIRE, Geo., W, M, d. 13 Sep 1892, Lovettsville, drowned, 63-0-0, p. unk, b. LC, mechanic, consort, sc: Clayton Wire, LV Dist., BVS:1892:6

WIRE, John, W, M, d. 20 Oct 1881, LC, heart disease, 67-1-0, p. Peter & Susan Wire, b. LC, farmer, c/o:

Susan Wire, sc: Susan Wire, wife, 2nd Dist., BVS:1881:7

WIRE, Peter, W, M, d. 20 Apr 1888, LC, pneumonia, 80-0-0, p. Peter & Susan Wire, b. unk, none, c/o: Elizabeth Wire, sc: John J. Wire, son, 2nd Dist., BVS:1888:6

WIRE, Susan, W, F, d. 10 Aug 1887, LC, old age, 70-0-0, p. unk, b. LC, none, c/o: John Wire, sc: John L. Smith, son-in-law, 2nd Dist., BVS:1887:5

WISE, Mary, W, F, d. 7 Aug 1878, LC, cholera infantum, 0-5-3, p. Wm. N. & Gabriella Wise, b. LC, unm, sc: Wm. N. Wise, father, LE Dist., BVS:1878:9

WITHERS, Henria, B, F, d. 6 Aug 1876, Poor House, old age, 70-0-0, b. LC, unm, sc: Wm. H. Hibbs, superintendant of Poor, MC Dist., BVS:1876:5

WITHERS, Nancy, B, F, d. 2 Apr 1886, nr Upperville, pneumonia, 40-0-0, p. Madison & Jennie Johnson, b. Culpepper Co., c/o: Oscar Withers, sc: Oscar Withers, husband, 1st Dist., BVS:1886:3

WOLF, William, W, M, d. 11 Oct 1878, nr Neersville, paralysis, 62-0-0, p. Catherine Wolf, b. LC, farmer, c/o: Elizabeth Wolf, sc: E. Wolf, wife, LV Dist., BVS:1878:1/5

WOLFORD, Charles, W, M, d. 20 Apr 1875, nr Wheatland, consumption, 47-0-0, p. John & Jane Wolford, b. LC, sc: John Wolford, father, JF Dist., BVS:1875:3

WOLFORD, George W., W, M, d. 20 Apr 1884, nr Lovettsville, old age, 82-0-0, p. Wm. & --- Wolford, b. LC, farmer, c/o: Annie Wolford, sc: Sydney B. Wolford, son, 2nd Dist., BVS:1884:5

WOLFORD, John, W, M, d. 26 Jul 1881, LC, old age, 81-0-0, b. LC, farmer, c/o: Mary J. Wolford, sc: M.J. Wolford, wife, 3rd Dist., BVS:1881:5

WOLFORD, John W., W, M, d. 27 Apr 1888, LC, bronchitis, 34-0-0, p. Asa R. & Martha Wolford, b. unk, none, unm, sc: Asa R. Wolford, father, 2nd Dist., BVS:1888:6

WOLFORD, Roberta C., W, F, d. 11 Aug 1876, LC, brain fever, 17-0-0, p. John & Jane Wolford, b. LC, unm, sc: John Wolford, father, JF Dist., BVS:1876:8

WOOD, Mrs. Ann S., W, F, d. 16 Jul 1894, Leesburg, old age, 83-0-0, p. unk, b. unk, consort, sc: Thos. M. Wood, LE Dist., BVS:1894:3

WOOD, Charlotte, W, F, d. 1 May 1889, LC, consumption, 35-0-0, p. W. & Mary Beans, b. LC, none, c/o: Joseph Wood, sc: Josiah Wood, husband, 3rd Dist., BVS:1889:5

WOOD, Frailey, B, F, d. Aug 1894, Hamilton, consumption, 18-0-0, p. Hamilton & Mary Wood, b. Hamilton, sc: Hamilton Wood, father, 3rd Dist., BVS:1894:5

[WOOD], Isaac Edgar, W, M, d. 5 Aug 1856, res of parents, catarrh fever, 1-9-0, p. David & Susan Wood, b. nr Beans B. Shop, sc: Susan Wood, mother, BVS:1856:6, LC:23

WOOD, John W., W, M, d. 30 Jun 1883, Leesburg, old age, 79-3-21, p. Mark & Mary Wood, b. LC, teacher, c/o: Ann S. Wood, sc: Ann S. Wood, wife, 2nd Dist., BVS:1883:8

WOOD, Mary, W, F, d. 1 Dec 1889, LC, pneumonia, 40-0-0, p. W. H. & Mary Wood, b. LC, none, c/o: W.H. Wood, sc: W.H. Wood, father, 3rd Dist., BVS:1889:5

WOODEN, James, B, M, d. 9 Dec 1873, nr Guilford, brain fever, 0-4-0, p. Baker & M. Wooden, b. LC, sc: Baker Wooden, head of family, BR Dist., BVS:1873:1

WOODS, Benj, W, M, d. 21 Jul 1864, Leesburg T. Pike, spotted fever, 4-0-0, p. G.M. & W.C. Woods, b. LC, sc: Margt. C. Woods, mother, BVS:1864:2, LC:39

WOODS, Jacob F., W, M, d. Mar 1855, unk, 0-2-0, p. G. M. & Margt. E. Woods, b. LC, sc: G.M. Wood, father, BVS:1855:8, LC:19

WOODSON, Lucy, B, F, d. 9 Jun 1883, nr Oatlands, dropsy, 32-0-0, p. William & Mamie Woodson, b. LC, unm, sc: William Woodson, father, 1st Dist., BVS:1883:2

WOOLF, Jno. W., W, M, d. 17 Mar 1891, Paxson, dyspepsia, 70-0-0, p. Andrew & Sophia Woolf, b. Paxson, minister of gospel, husband, sc: Wm. A. Woolf, MT Dist., BVS:1891:6

WOOTEN, Jack, B, M, d. 31 Aug 1893, Middleburg, hemorrhages, 23-0-0, p. Jessie & Mollie Wooten, b. Middleburg, laborer, sc: Jessie Wooten, father, 1st Dist., BVS:1893:2

WORKS, Alfred W., W, M, d. 4 Sep 1882, LC, old age, 77-0-0, p. A. W. & Mary Works, farmer, widower, sc: James W. Works, son, 1st Dist., BVS:1882:2

WORNAL, Charlotte, W, F, d. 24 Mar 1858, her res, old age, 83-0-0, p. Ezekiel & Lydia Jenkins, b. on Blue Ridge, c/o: James Wornal decd, sc: Elizabeth Crane, daughter, BVS:1858:3, LC:31

WORSLEY, Virginia L., W, F, d. 3 Aug 1886, LC, unk, 67-0-0, p. Chas. G. & Debora Edwards, b. LC, c/o: William Worsley, sc: T. L. Worsley, son, 2nd Dist., BVS:1886:6

WORSLEY, Wm., W, M, d. 24 Aug 1853, LC, dysentery, 38-2-5, p. John & Elizth. Worsley, b. England, farmer, c/o: Virginia G. Worsley, sc: Virginia G. Worsley, wife, BVS:1854:4, LC:2

WORTMAN, Barnett, W, M, d. 28 Aug 1866, Goose Creek Meeting House, 0-0-24, p. G.H. & M.A. Wortman, b. Goose Creek Meeting House, sc: G.H. Wortman, tather, BVS:1866:3

WORTMAN, Bessie, W, F, d. 1 Jul 1873, Hughes Mill, measles & whooping cough, 0-11-0, p. George H. & Mary A. Wortman, b. nr Upperville, Fauquier Co, sc: parents, MT Dist., BVS:1873:3

WORTMAN, Jane E., W, F, d. 1 May 1858, LC, confined, 39-0-0, p. Peter & Sarah Snider, b. LC, c/o: George H. Wortman, sc: Geo H. Wortman, husband, BVS:1858:6, LC:33

WORTMAN, Martha A., W, F, d. 28 Jul 1874, Broad Run Dist., hernia, 49-6-4, p. Jas. & Anna Thomas, c/o: Goe. H. Wortman, sc: Geo. H. Wortman, husband, BR Dist., BVS:1874:3

[WORTMAN], [no name], W, F, d. 1 May 1858, LC, unk, p. Geo H. & Jane E. Wortman, b. LC, sc: Geo H. Wortman, father, BVS:1858:6, LC:33

WORTMAN, R. T., W, M, d. 8 May 1892, Waxpool, rupture, 50-0-0, p. Isaac & Sallie Wortman, b. Waxpool, laborer, unm, sc: A. J. Beach, bro-in-law, 1st Dist., BVS:1892:2

WORTMAN, Sarah, W, F, d. 18 May 1871, unk, 0-0-12 hours, p. John & S. A. Wortman, BR Dist., BVS:1871:3

WRENN, Marvin, W, M, d. 18 Jul 1889, Daysville, Fairfax Co., unk, 0-3-11, p. J. O. & Lula Wrenn, b. Daysville, sc: J.O. Wrenn, father, 1st Dist., BVS:1889:2

[WRENN], no name, W, M, d. 20 Mar 1875, nr Pleasant Valley, measles, 0-0-13, p. J. Oscar & Lula Wrenn, b. LC, sc: J.O. Wrenn, father, BR Dist., BVS:1875:5

WRENN, Rachael A., W, F, d. 20 Mar 1892, Waxpool, consumption, 22-0-0, p. John & Bettie Lefever, b. Waxpool, c/o: Moultrie F. Wrenn, sc: M.F. Wrenn, husband, 1st Dist., BVS:1892:2

WRIGHT, Alfred, B, M, d. 4 Sep 1875, Leesburg, heart disease, 70-0-0, minister, c/o: Hannah Wright, sc: Hannah Wright, wife, LE Dist., BVS:1875:2

WRIGHT, America, W, F, d. 14 Oct 1855, LC, bilious fever, 9-10-7, p. Saml. & Lydia Wright, b. LC, sc: Saml. Wright, father, BVS:1855:1, LC:15

WRIGHT, Charlotte, W, F, d. 18 Aug 1865, nr Waterford, bilious dysentery, 64-0-0, p. Thoms & Mary Dorrell, b. nr Waterford, farmer, c/o: Wm. Wright, sc: Chas Wright, son, 1st Dist., BVS:1865:3/5

WRIGHT, Christianna, W, F, d. 1875, nr Round Hill, unk, sc: Harriet Butts, MT Dist., BVS:1875:8

WRIGHT, Dilly A., B, F, d. 20 Jun 1878, LC, teething, 0-11-27, p. Maria Wright, b. LC, unm, sc: Maria Wright, mother, LE Dist., BVS:1878:9

WRIGHT, Ernest T., W, M, d. 16 Dec 1894, Lovettsville, heart failure, 7-0-0, p. George Wright & Mary, b. Lovettsville, unm, sc: Geo. Wright, LV Dist., BVS:1894:4

WRIGHT, Hannah, B, , d. 8 Sep 1877, LC, dropsy, 55-0-0, c/o: Alfred Wright, sc: Jesse Moton, son-in-law, LE Dist., BVS:1877:9

WRIGHT, Harriet, B, F, d. 6 Jul 1880, Hillsboro, pneumonia, 85-0-0, p. unk, b. LC, sc: Elzey Furr, friend, 3rd Dist., BVS:1880:5

WRIGHT, Henry, B, M, d. 15 May 1893, nr Sterling, ruptured blood vein, 18-0-0, p. Isaac & Sarah Wright, b. nr Sterling, laborer, sc: Sarah Wright, mother, 1st Dist., BVS:1893:2

WRIGHT, Jno. Wm., W, M, d. 1 Apr 1855, res of parents, consumption, 20-0-0, p. Wm. G. & Margt. Wright, b. nr North Fork Church, sc: Margt Wright, mother, BVS:1855:8, LC:19

WRIGHT, John, W, M, d. 31 Jul 1858, B.F. Carter's, old age, 87-0-0, blacksmith & farmer, sc: Miss Carter, Gd daughter, BVS:1858:4, LC:32

WRIGHT, John E., W, M, d. 27 Dec 1883, Leesburg, pneumonia, 57-0-0, p. --- Wright, b. LC, merchant, c/o: Henrietta V. Wright, sc: Joseph Wright, son, 2nd Dist., BVS:1883:8

WRIGHT, John T., W, M, d. 4 Oct 1854, LC, dysentery, 1-1-0, p. Chas. & Mary C. Wright, b. LC, sc: Charles Wright, father, BVS:1854:9, LC:8

WRIGHT, Joseph T., W, M, d. 8 Oct 1855, Johnson Wheeler's, typhoid fever, 22-0-0, p. Jos. & Mahala Wright, b. nr North Fork Church, carpenter, sc: Johnson Wheeler, brother-in-law, BVS:1855:7, LC:18

WRIGHT, Leonard, B, M, d. 1 Jun 1880, Hillsboro, pneumonia, 80-0-0, p. unk, b. LC, preacher, c/o: Harriet Wright, sc: Elzey Furr, friend, 3rd Dist., BVS:1880:5

WRIGHT, Lillie, W, F, d. 11 Oct 1883, Leesburg, diphtheria, 13-8-11, p. Wm. M. & Cordelia Wright, b. Albany, N.Y., sc: Edwin Wright, uncle, 2nd Dist., BVS:1883:8

WRIGHT, Lydia E., W, F, d. 5 Jun 1853, LC, typhoid fever, 3-3-13, p. Joseph L. & Margaret Wright, b. LC, sc: Joseph L. Wright, father, BVS:1854:2, LC:1

WRIGHT, Margaret, W, F, d. Fall 1857, her res, consumption, 60-0-0, p. ... Griffith, c/o: John Wright, sc: Christina Wright, BVS:1857:5, LC:28

WRIGHT, Mariah, B, F, d. 1 Jun 1872, LC, unk, 0-0-11, p. Fanny Wright, b. Leesburg, sc: Fanny Wright, mother, LE Dist., BVS:1872:4

WRIGHT, Martha, B, F, d. 24 Aug 1880, LC, unk, 14-0-0, p. John & Mary Wright, unm, sc: Mary Wright, mother, 1st Dist., BVS:1880:3

WRIGHT, Mary A., W, F, d. 1 Sep 1853, Leesburg, paralytic, 69-7-23, p. unk, b. Leesburg, c/o: Jotham Wright, sc: Washington Jarvis, son-in-law, BVS:1854:5, LC:3

WRIGHT, Ralph C., W, M, d. 24 Aug 1892, Unison, cholera infantum, 0-3-7, p. Janney & Sarah Wright, b. Unison, sc: Janney Wright, father, 1st Dist., BVS:1892:2

WRIGHT, William H., W, M, d. 13 Oct 1894, George's Mill, bright's disease, 51-0-0, p. unk, b. unk, consort, sc: Laura Wright, LV Dist., BVS:1894:4

WRIGHT, Wm. G., W, M, d. 23 May 1857, nr Wm. Wilkinson's, typhoid fever, 59-1-1, p. John & Rebecca Wright, b. nr Francis' Mill, shoemaker, c/o: Margaret Wright, sc: M. Wright, widow, BVS:1857:5, LC:27

[WYATT], no name, B, M, d. 6 Mar 1872, nr Guilford, unk, 0-0-1/2, p. Robert & Mary E. Wyatt, b. LC, sc: Mary E. Wyatt, BR Dist., BVS:1872:6

[WYCHOFF], [no name], W, M, d. Jun 1859, LC, unk, 0-5-0, p. Jonathan & Ann Wychoff, sc: Jonathan Wychoff, father, BVS:1859:6, LC:36

WYCKOFF, Ann E., W, F, d. 17 Feb 1896, Arcola, heart failure, 76-0-0, b. LC, c/o: Jonathan T. Wychoff, sc: Henrietta Wychoff, daughter, BR Dist., BVS:1896:3

WYCKOFF, Jonathan T., W, M, d. 17 Apr 1877, nr Gum Spring, unk, 65-0-0, p. Cornelius & Elizabeth Wyckoff, b. LC, carpenter, c/o: Ann Wyckoff, sc: A.O. Wyckoff, son, BR Dist., BVS:1877:1

WYCKOFF, Mary H., W, F, d. 25 Apr 1854, LC, inflam lungs, 2-6-0, p. Jonathan & A. E. Wyckoff, b. LC, sc: Jonathan Wyckoff, father, BVS:1854:13, LC:13

WYCKOFF, Nicholas, W, M, d. 20 Aug 1881, LC, dropsy of heart, 69-0-0, b.

LC, sc: B.H. Wickoff, son, 1st Dist., BVS:1881:3

[WYCKOFF], [no name], W, M, d. Jun 1860, LC, unk, 0-5-0, p. Jonathan & Ann Wyckoff, b. LC, sc: Jonathan Wyckoff, father, BVS:1860:3

WYCKOFF, Willie A., W, M, d. 27 Mar 1881, LC, bronchitis, 2-0-0, p. Jas. W. & Irene Wyckoff, b. LC, sc: Jas W. Wyckoff, father, 1st Dist., BVS:1881:3

WYNKOOP, Amanda, W, F, d. 11 Apr 1880, Woodburn, consumption, 28-0-0, p. John & Polly Wynkoop, b. LC, unm, sc: Richd Wynkoop, friend, 3rd Dist., BVS:1880:5

WYNKOOP, Catharine, W, F, d. 23 Apr 1877, Woodburn, unk, p. Geo. & Mary Carr, b. Caroline Co. Va., c/o: P. Henry Wynkoop, sc: P. Henry Wynkoop, husband, MT Dist., BVS:1877:2

WYNKOOP, Catharine, W, F, d. 18 Apr 1876, LC, hearth disease, 51-0-0, p. unk, b. LC, c/o: William B. Wynkoop, sc: William B. Wynkoop, husband, LE Dist., BVS:1876:7

WYNKOOP, Corbin, W, M, d. 11 Oct 1876, Welbourne, hip disease, 15-6-12, p. Geo. W. & Jane E. Wynkoop, b. LC, sc: Geo. W. Wynkoop, father, MC Dist., BVS:1876:5

WYNKOOP, Cornelius, W, M, d. 26 Sep 1854, LC, typhoid fever, 46-2-11, p. Cornelius & Catherine Wynkoop, b. LC, farmer, c/o: Mahala Wynkoop, sc: Mahala Wynkoop, wife, BVS:1854:10, LC:9

WYNKOOP, E. B., W, M, d. 17 Mar 1892, Mount Gilead, unk, 42-0-0, p. unk, b. LC, laborer, c/o: Catharine Wynkoop, sc: Catharine Wynkoop, wife, 1st Dist., BVS:1892:2

WYNKOOP, Elizabeth, W, F, d. 22 Nov 1866, nr Grove Church, old age, 85-0-0, p. Saml. & Rachel Cartright, sc: Cathn Bales, daughter, BVS:1866:1

WYNKOOP, Elizabeth, W, F, d. Mar 1874, LC, old age, 76-0-0, widow, sc: Saml W. Myers, friend, LE Dist., BVS:1874:5

WYNKOOP, Geo. W., W, M, d. 14 Mar 1883, nr Leesburg, dyspepsia, 48-0-0, p. William & Catherine Wynkoop, b. LC, farmer, c/o: Jane E.

Wynkoop, sc: Jane E. Wynkoop, wife, 1st Dist., BVS:1883:2

WYNKOOP, Henry, W, M, d. 25 Sep 1881, LC, pneumonia, 5-23-0, p. Albert & Nancy Wynkoop, b. LC, sc: Albert Wynkoop, father, 3rd Dist., BVS:1881:5

WYNKOOP, Henry C., W, M, d. 3 Sep 1857, Fairfax Co., dysentery, 1-0-0, p. Cornelius B. & M.F. Wynkoop, b. Fairfax, sc: Martha F. Wynkoop, mother, BVS:1857:2, LC:25

WYNKOOP, Hunter, W, M, d. 14 Aug 1888, LC, kicked by horse, 13-0-0, p. Jos. T. & Fannie Wynkoop, b. LC, none, unm, sc: Jos T. Wynkoop, father, 3rd Dist., BVS:1888:2

WYNKOOP, Joseph, W, M, d. Jul 1877, Woodburn, dropsy of heart, 0-3-0, p. P. H. & Catharine Wynkoop, b. Woodburn, sc: P. Henry Wynkoop, father, MT Dist., BVS:1877:2

WYNKOOP, Landon T., W, M, d. 25 Aug 1881, LC, diphtheria, 0-4-0, p. John & Virga. Wynkoop, b. LC, sc: John Wynkoop, father, 3rd Dist., BVS:1881:5

WYNKOOP, Laura B., W, F, d. 26 Sep 1888, LC, dyspepsia, 8-6-0, p. Samuel T. & C. Wynkoop, b. LC, none, unm, sc: Samuel T. Wynkoop, father, 3rd Dist., BVS:1888:2

WYNKOOP, Margaret E., W, F, d. 28 Aug 1857, Fairfax Co., dysentery, 3-9-0, p. Cornelius B. & M.F. Wynkoop, b. LC, sc: Martha F. Wynkoop, mother, BVS:1857:2, LC:25

WYNKOOP, Maud, W, F, d. 10 Jun 1880, LC, water on brain, 0-1-27, p. C.W. & F. M. Wynkoop, unm, sc: F.M. Wyncoop, mother, 1st Dist., BVS:1880:3

WYNKOOP, Nancy, W, F, d. 18 Jul 1856, LC, dropsy, 46-0-0, p. unk, b. LC, c/o: George Wynkoop, sc: Levi W. Nixon, friend, BVS:1856:2, LC:21

WYNKOOP, Richard S., W, M, d. 17 Nov 1882, LC, spinal meningitis, 9-0-0, p. Samuel & Catherine Wynkoop, sc: Samuel T. Wynkoop, parent, 3rd Dist., BVS:1882:3

WYNKOOP, Richd, W, M, d. 27 Mar 1865, Round Hill, consumption, 28-0-0, p. Richd & Frances Wynkoop, farmer, unm, sc: R. Wynkoop, father, BVS:1865:1

WYNKOOP, Samuel C., W, M, d. 17 Feb 1854, LC, consumption, 42-4-0, p. Philip & Elizth. Wynkoop, b. LC, Colporteur, c/o: Susanna Wynkoop, sc: Catherine A. Beales, sister, BVS:1854:9, LC:8

WYNKOOP, Susanna, W, F, d. 26 Aug 1854, LC, dysentery, 2-6-2, p. Samuel C. & Susanna Wynkoop, b. LC, sc: Henry Duncan, friend, BVS:1854:9, LC:8

WYNKOOP, Willie S., W, M, d. 15 Jan 1876, Stoke, scald, 4-10-0, p. J. Thos. & Fannie E. Wynkoop, b. LC, sc: J. Thomas Wynkoop, father, MC Dist., BVS:1876:5

YAKEY, Maud E., W, F, d. 26 Mar 1888, LC, unk, 2-0-0, p. Thomas S. & Eliza Yakey, b. unk, none, unm, sc: Thomas S. Yakey, father, 2nd Dist., BVS:1888:6

YATES, Jos. B., W, M, d. 20 Dec 1894, Washington, DC, kidney trouble, 53-0-0, p. Jos. & Elizath. Yates, b. Fauquier Co., laborer, unm, sc: V.A. Loughboro, sister, 1st Dist., BVS:1894:1

YEAMANS, Catharine, W, F, d. 27 Mar 1853, LC, dysentery, 45-0-0, p. unk, b. unk, unk, unk, sc: Geo W. Mobberly, head of family, BVS:1854:4, LC:2

YEARBY, Ann M., W, F, d. 1 Mar 1884, Leesburg, cancer, 71-0-0, p. John & Mary M. Yearby, b. LC, unm, sc: Ann S. Wood, cousin, 2nd Dist., BVS:1884:5

YOUNG, Alice, W, F, d. Jun 1858, res of parents, inflammation of brain, 0-6-0, p. Wm. & Elizabeth Young, b. place of death, sc: Wm. Young, father, BVS:1858:5, LC:32

YOUNG, David, B, M, d. 9 Aug 1888, Aldie, pneumonia, 11-0-0, p. William & Tentia Young, b. Aldie, sc: William Young, father, 1st Dist., BVS:1888:4

YOUNG, Geo., B, M, d. 29 Dec 1877, nr Aldie, pneumonia, 72-0-0, p. unk, b. unk, laborer, unm, sc: Thomas Manly, friend, BR Dist., BVS:1877:1

YOUNG, Hannah, W, F, d. 20/21 Sep 1859/60, her res, paralysis, 53-0-0, p. Abram & Martha Shoemaker, c/o:

John Young Sr., sc: J. Young, husband, BVS:1859:4, 1860:2, LC:35

YOUNG, Hannah M., W, F, d. 15 Mar 1883, nr Aldie, dropsy, 8-0-0, p. Isaiah & Fannie Young, sc: Isaiah Young, father, 1st Dist., BVS:1883:2

YOUNG, Israel, W, M, d. 10 Feb 1885, Lincoln, dropsy, 86-0-0, b. Virginia, mechanic, unm, sc: Geo W. Curl, nephew, 3rd Dist., BVS:1885:7

YOUNG, Jack, B, M, d. 20 Aug 1876, Poor House, old age, 72-0-0, b. LC, unm, sc: Wm. H. Hibbs, superintendant of poor, MC Dist., BVS:1876:5

YOUNG, John, W, M, d. 20 Nov 1880, LC, diphtheria, 2-0-0, p. Isaiah & Frances Young, unm, sc: Francis Young, mother, 1st Dist., BVS:1880:3

YOUNG, John Newton, W, M, d. 10 Aug 1872, Mount Gilead Twp., thrown from a horse, 44-0-0, p. William & Rebecca Young, b. Mount Gilead Town, farmer, unm, sc: William Young, brother, MT Dist., BVS:1872:2

YOUNG, Loas, W, F, d. 10 Jul 1858, her res, old age, 86-0-0, p. John & ...Wirt, b. German Settlement, c/o: John Young decd, sc: John Young, son, BVS:1858:5, LC:32

YOUNG, Martha, B, F, d. 15 Nov 1896, Lovettsville, heart trouble, 59-0-0, p. unk, c/o: Luther Young, sc: Luther Young, consort, LV Dist., BVS:1896:7

YOUNG, Mary, B, F, d. 16 Jan 1872, nr Bloomfield, dropsy, 30-0-0, c/o: Cyrus Young, sc: Cyrus Young, husband, MC Dist., BVS:1872:7

YOUNG, Nancy, W, F, d. 22 Jan 1856, LC, consumption, 39-0-17, p. Ebenezer & Mary E. Grubb, b. LC, c/o: Joseph A. Young, sc: Jos. A. Young, husband, BVS:1856:2, LC:21

YOUNG, no name, B, M, d. 21 May 1889, LC, unk, 0-0-1, p. Henson & M. Young, b. LC, none, unm, sc: Henson Young, father, 3rd Dist., BVS:1889:5

YOUNG, Sylvester, B, , d. 3 Aug 1877, LC, dropsy, 72-0-0, sc: Henry Calley, friend, LE Dist., BVS:1877:9

YOUNG, Thomas, W, M, d. 20 Aug 1887, LC, congestion of lungs, 72-0-0, p. Geo. & Catharine Young, farmer, c/o: Catharine Young, sc: C.F. Otley, friend, 3rd Dist., BVS:1887:7

YOWELL, Rodney, W, M, d. 29 Jul 1888, LC, consumption, 3-1-20, p. A. J. & Sallie C. Yowell, b. LC, none, unm, sc: A.J. Yowell, father, 3rd Dist., BVS:1888:2

ZIMMERMAN, Saml., W, M, d. 21 Aug 1855, LC, typhoid fever, 65-0-0, p. unk, b. Alexandria, farmer, unm, sc: Hugh Thompson, friend, BVS:1855:2, LC:15

Loudoun County, Virginia, Death Register, 1853-1896   285

Index

This index includes only those persons included in a listing whose surname differs from the deceased. Slaves are indexed both under "Slaves" and if they had a surname, under that surname.

A

Abell
  John   62
  Sarah   62
Adams
  Adaline   209
  Charles   47, 165
  Charles B.   1
  Chas.   209
  David E.   112
  G.W.   236
  Henry   148
  Mary   47, 148
  Noble   50, 156
  Rebecca   232
  Rich.   232
Adrain
  E.   78
  Jas E.   78
Agur
  Elvira   256
  John   256
Alder
  George F.   160
Alexander   232
  James   42
  Jane   42
Allen
  Arch   44
  Jacob   65
  Jake   155
  Jno. F.   36
  Wilson   155
Ambers
  Jos.   276
  Martha   276
Ambler
  Susan   142, 211
  Wm.   142
Anderson
  C.F.   19
  Eli   107
  G.   252
  J.A.   129
  Jas. A.   257
  Jno.   84
  Sarah   107, 257
  Spencer   115
  Susanna   115
Ankers
  Arthur   207
  Jane   207
  S.W.   48
Armes
  Millie   48
Armstead
  Addison B.   212
  Mary   212
Arnett
  Lucy   224
  Moses   3
  Ruth   112
  Theodore   249
  Wm.   224
Arnold
  Adam   50
Arundell
  C.A.   263
  J.   96
Ashby
  Barbry   161
  Robert   161
Austin
  Wm.   109
Axline
  David   105
  Eve   105
Ayers
  Mary   134
  Samuel   134
Ayles
  Millie   211

B

Bailey	
Henry	22
Baker	
Cyrus	138
Baldwin	
Eliza	2
Bales	
Cathn	282
Thos.	177
Ball	
C.B.	27
Chas.	159
John	102
John T.	166
Sarah	102
Wm.	112
Bank	
Eliza	145
Bantz	
Jacob	216
Barker	
Letitia	50
Nathaniel	50
Barnes	
Mary	240
Barnett	
Charity	109
Henry	109
Barnhouse	
J.R.	76
Barrett	
Wilson	223
Bartlett	
Julia	2
N.H.	158
Barton	
Benj. F.	255
Bassell	
Rebecca	44
Batson	
Elizth	109
John	109
Bayly	
Mary	113
Pierce	113
Beach	
A.J.	280
Andrew	71
Beales	
Anne J.	222
Catherine A.	283
Beall	
L.L.	192
Lemuel L.	21
Beamer	
George	271
Beamersdaffer	
Elizabeth	270
Joseph	270
Beans	
J.B.	20
Mary	279
W.	279
William	118
Beatie	
Fannie	233
Silas	233
Beatty	
Ann	211
David	225
Hester	225
Landon	211
Wm.	114
Beavers	
Delilah	193, 205
James	2
Jno. A.	1
John	164
Mary	164
Thomas	193
Thos.	205
W.	1
Washg	247
Bell	
Ann	213
Thomas	228
Belt	
Alfred C.	6, 8, 13
T.W.	255
Benjamin	
S.	267
Sarah	35
W.H.	45
Wm. H.	267
Bennett	
Geo. W.	2
Sydney	231
Sydnor	24, 109
Benteley	
Kitty	116
Robert	116

Loudoun County, Virginia, Death Register, 1853-1896

Bentley
  R.M.   1
Benton
  James R.   233
Berkley
  Chas   166
  Chas.   165
  Maria   165
  Wm.   3, 27, 235
Berry
  Anica   5
  Sandy   14
Berryman
  Jeffrey   8
Best
  James   128
  Martha   128
Beverley
  J.B.   116
Beverly
  Robert   217
Bias
  Benj.   146
Binns
  Geo.   84
Birdsall
  Miss   249
  Wm. G.   252
Birkby
  Chas T.   46, 208
  Sallie   270
  Sarah   258
  Thos.   258, 270
  Thos. H.   270
Bladen
  Betsy   102
  Wesley   102
Blakely
  Letticia   113
  Wm.   113
Blandon
  Thomas   217
Bleakley
  Emily   149
  Wm.   149
Blundell
  Daniel   214
  Eliza   214
Bodine
  H.H.   210, 239
  Isaiah   202
  Jane   210

  Mary   202
Boger
  Mary A.   163
Bogue
  John   89
  Judith   89
Bolen
  Joseph   62
Boley
  John   180
Bolon
  Ellen   215
  Ezra   215
Booker
  Dinah   4
  Jas   4
Booth
  Robert   125 / 105
Boss
  Elizabeth   69
  Elizth F.   132
  Matilda   25
  S.M.   69
  Saml M.   132
Bowman
  G.W.   3
  Jas.   23
Boyle
  T.M.   50
Braden
  Jno.   262
  Mary   204, 262
  Noble   204
  Noble S.   19
  Oscar   51
Bradfield
  F.M.   231
  James   252
  John   90
  Mary   250
  Ruth   252
Bradford
  Webster   146, 151
Bramhall
  Nancy   137
Branhall
  Blanco   111
Breckenridge
  Nancy   229
  Samuel   229
Brent

Henry	278	Ariss	210
Robt	276	Lucy	210
Brewer		**Budd**	
H.R.	68	Alice	109
Brickner		Mana	109
S.A.	79	**Burgess**	
Briscoe		Martha	260
Adam	14	Wm.	260
John	14	**Burrows**	153
Winney	14	**Burson**	
Bronaugh		W.G.	83
Geo. W.	15	**Buskirk**	
Brooken		Abram	43
Elizabeth	81	Ann	43
Brooks	174	**Bussard**	
Lucy	58	O.M.	210
Brown		**Butcher**	
Ann	47, 172	Jno. B.	1
Benjamin	194	**Butler**	
E.C.	270	James	166
Erasmus	261	**Butts**	
Helen	212	Chas. W.	271
Isaac	37	Harriet	280
John	47	Mary E.	271
Joseph	153	William	189
M.F.	203	**Byrne**	
Mary	20, 261	Charles	181, 212
Newman	132		
Sarah	37, 194		
Thomas	193, 249	**C**	
William	261		
Bruce		**Calley**	
Alexr	112	Henry	283
Martha	112	**Campbell**	
Bryant		Geo. W.	75
Peggy	58	John	254
Peter	58	Mary	254
Buchanan	191	**Carey**	
Andrew	243	James	80
Fannie	243	Mary	80
Buchannan		**Carner**	
M.	113	A.E.	105
Robt.	113	**Carnes**	
Buckhannon		Abraham	245
George	269	Catherine	245
Robert	145	Loretta	60
Buckhanon		**Carpenter**	
Mahala	110	Marshall	180
Buckman		**Carr**	
Bushrod	57	Geo.	282
Buckner		Isaac	158
		Mary	121, 282

Loudoun County, Virginia, Death Register, 1853-1896

Roberta E.	95	Chamblin	
Saml	27	A.G.	141
Thos.	121	Henry W.	116
Carrington		Jno M.	37
Hilleary	216	Lydia V.	211
Carter		Wm.	165
A.B.	4	Champ	
Ada	72	Hannah	71
Amanda	7	Samuel	71
Chas.	72	Chancellor	
Deborah	262	E.	96
Edward L.	1, 33	Lorman	7, 22
Fannie	93	Chapell	259
Fanny	13	Jas.	234
Francis	111	Cheek	
Geo	210	Samuel	55
George	181	Chichester	
Hannah	270	A.M.	116
Jno R.	27, 162, 175, 184, 186, 206, 266	Chinn	
		Elijah	259
John	171	Francis	1
Lucy	171	R.S.	6
Martha	170, 209	Tamar	259
Miss	281	Chossel	
Richd.	262	Ellen	234
Saml J.	36	Thomas	234
Washington	54, 270	Clapham	
Willie	243	Hannah M.	133
Wm.	67	Clark	
Cartright		Eliza	15
Rachel	282	Mrs. E.J.T.	228
Saml.	282	S.J.	142
Caruthers		Clarke	
Martha	263	George	114
Thos.	263	Clayton	
Cary		Catharine	170
Nathan	255	Wm.	170
Oscar	38	Clems	
Case		Nimrod	62
Christina	33	Clendening	
John	33	Saml	132
Casey		Cline	
Abner	173	C.	94
Cassaday		John	94
Mary J.	5	Coats	
Cassady		Calvin	190
Mary J.	93	Jane	190
Castleman	90	Cochran	
Cattleman		Edwd	69
Alfred	101	Ellen	48
S.	101	Emily	69

Fanny	92	Elizabeth	70
John	48	John	206, 266
Wm. B.	92	Rebecca	206
Cocke		Samuel	70
Washington	45	Copen	
Cockerille		Cecil	62
Ann	271	Wm.	62
Jane	63	Corder	
John	63, 206	A.B.	77
Sanford	271	May	77
Cockrell		Cornwell	
Jno.	211	Jno. S.	59
Rebecca A.	211	Corum	
Cockrille		Waren	202
Fanny	67	Cost	
Coe		Jonathan	224
Duane	136	M.	224
Sarah P.	136	Costelloe	
Cole		Mary	89
Emily	130	Robert	89
Peter	130	Cox	
Coleman		Elizabeth	204
John J.	157	John	7
Collins		Joseph	56
Margaret	76	Mrs.	106
Combs		Sarah	56
John	23	Craig	93
Compher		Crain	
Catherine	138	Chas	79
Elizth.	241	Elizabeth	40
Jno.	241	Jno	149
Mary A.	183	John	40
Peter	138	Mary	149
Wm.	183	Crane	
Conard		Elizabeth	280
Amanda	100	P.B.	161
David	120	Phila B.	7
Joseph	100	Crankins	
Mary	74	Mary	34
Connard		Thos	34
Joseph	180	Craven	
Cook		Alfred	135, 153
Emly	55	Henry	31
Cooper		James	262
Adam	72	Mary	171
Emily	276	William	171
Nancy	276	Wm.	171
P.W.	35	Crawford	
Peter	276	Danl	76
Copeland		Margt	76
Delialah	266	Cridler	

Richard M.	114	Allen	254
Crim		Ann	117
Elias	76	Betsy	45
Rosanna	76	Cassandra	275
Susan	216	Elizabeth	49
Crissey		John	107, 245
F.J.	160	John W.	49
F.P.	52	Lafayette	12
Crooks	73	Martha	107
Crosburry		Mary	78
M.	201	Maurice	78
Sam	201	Rachael	245
Crosen		Robt.	162
Laurie	186	Samuel	275
Pierson	186	Sherlock	45
Cross		Wm.	117
Jane	94	Day	
Jas.	70	Dr.	48
Manly	94	Elizabeth	277
Nancy	70	George	277
Richard	55	Ginnie	72
Cully		Jennie	191
Henry	141, 211	Julius	191
Cummins		Sarah	23
Angie	88	Daymoode	
Harrison	88	Alfred	81
Curl		Dean	
Geo W.	283	Chas	227
Curry		George	47
Ann	190	Jesse	13
John	190	Demory	
Mary	75	Mary	208
Robt	75	Peter	208
		Dennis	
D		Wm A.	158
		Derry	
Dailey		Lewis W.	253
Frances J.	145	Detrol	133
Daily		Dibrill	
John Z.	117	A.	65
Daniel		Dier	
Frances	113	Annacretis	27
Jos.	150	Annacretus	27
Tacy	150	Ellen	27
Darne		Diggs	
Jas. W.	192	N.	202
Darr		Dinges	236
Charles	88, 265	Elizabeth	111
Charles E.	265	Frederick	111
Davis		Dishman	
A.G.	52	Elizabeth	233

Samuel	233	
Dixon	42	
Joseph	105	
Sarah	105	
Dodd		
Elizabeth	102	
George	102	
Mary	169	
Donaldson		
Elizabeth	190	
Thomas	190	
Donohoe		
Lewis	43	
Dorrell		
G.W.	189	
Mary	280	
Thoms	280	
Dorsett		
Mary	192	
Samuel	192	
Douglas		
David	56	
Emanuel	268	
Francis	56	
William	56	
Dove		
John	207	
Dowell		
John	7	
Malinda	124	
Mrs.	224	
R.	124	
Downs		
John W.	35	
Doyle		
John	254	
Drish		
Eleanor	114	
John	114	
Dulin		
Edward	184	
John	157	
Mary	184	
Rebecca	157	
Duncan		
Henry	283	
Dutch		
Jeremiah	269	
Susan	269	
Duvall		
Harriet	274	

E

Eagle	
William	258
Eamich	
Samuel	277
Eaton	
Isaac	85
Martina	85
Edwards	
Abner	88
Ann	160
Chas. G.	280
Debora	280
N.	183
R.H.	191
Richard H.	154
S.M.	183
Sarah	88
Wesley	160
Elgin	
Annett	54, 56
Charles	153
Daniel	56
Elizabeth	122
Gustavus	122
Thos. G.	61
Walter	230
Elzey	
Frances	116
Wm.	116
Emerson	
Thos.	166
Emery	
Catharine	208, 230
Jacob	208, 230
Eskridge	
Chas G.	13
Ethern	
Joseph	34
Mary	34
Evard	
Mary	150
Everhart	
Charlotte	264
M.G.	266
Philip	264
Ewers	
Phebe	58
Ruth	214
Wm.	214

F

- Fair
  - Michl — 251
  - Nancy — 251
- Farr
  - Jane — 59
  - Nicholas — 59
- Fauntleroy
  - John — 174
- Fawley
  - Elizabeth — 73
  - Eve — 114
  - Henry — 73, 264
  - John — 106, 114
  - Margaret A. — 106
  - Wm. — 73
- Feagans
  - Elizabeth — 253
  - Elizth — 228
  - Wilford — 228
- Figgins
  - Enoch — 100
  - S. — 100
- Filler
  - Catherine — 230
  - Frederick — 230
  - Samuel — 264
- Fillers
  - Wm. H. — 76
- Fitzhugh
  - Mary — 246
  - Matilda — 188
  - Wm. — 188
- Fleming
  - Archibald — 259
  - Sarah — 259
- Fling
  - Benj. F. — 244
- Florrey
  - Edith — 226
  - John — 226
- Ford
  - Sarah — 23
- Foster
  - Chas — 243
  - Flora — 243
  - Polly — 251
  - Rich — 251
- Fox
  - Annie — 154
  - Harriett — 13
  - Jacob — 86
- Frame
  - Jane — 58
  - Jas W. — 58
- Franklin — 175
  - A.T. — 58
  - Mary — 258
  - Wm. — 258
- Fred
  - Elizabeth — 262
  - Thomas — 262
- Freeman
  - L.H. — 155, 156
  - Lewis H. — 71
- French
  - Ann — 51
  - Eliz. — 87
  - Louis — 51
- Fritts
  - Geo. — 148
- Fry
  - Betsy — 239
  - Elizabeth — 89
  - Elizth — 89
  - G.L.B. — 259
  - Jacob — 239
  - M. — 183
  - Mary — 244
  - Mich. — 239
  - Michael — 244
  - Nicholas — 183
  - Peter — 259
  - Sam. — 234
  - Susana — 239
- Fulton
  - Susan — 75
- Furr
  - Edward — 174
  - Elzey — 116, 281
  - F.E. — 79
  - Gill — 65
  - Henry — 151
  - Mary A. — 65
  - Rachel — 174
  - W. — 87, 102, 150, 212
  - William — 275
  - Wm. — 3, 37, 58, 60, 61, 84, 151, 153, 165, 176, 195, 255, 273

G

Galliher	
Hannah	270
Wm.	270
Gant	
A.C.	125
Ann	17
Gardner	
Ann	197
Lois	197
Garner	
Catharine	213
Garrison	
Ellen	137
Nelson	137
Gaskins	
Harrison	10
Nelson	112, 200
Sarah	9
Violet	4
William H.	77
Gassway	
Catharine B.	174
Gayner	
Ann E.	175
Geaslin	
George A.	103
George	
John	268
John, Jr.	8
Samuel W.	10
Ghaskins	
Judith	10
Gheen	
Nancy	210
Thos	210
Gibson	
Alice	198
Alpheus	44
Frank	153
Israel	198
John M.	158
Joseph	10
Solomon	33
Giddings	
G.	129
Gillham	
John	107
Mary	107
Gist	
Rector	143
Glascock	
Edith	191
Hesekiah	191
Thomas	102
Glasscock	
Hezekiah	59
Mrs. Thos	206
Sarah	59
Gochnauer	
Joseph	85
Golden	
John W.	177
Goodchilds	
R.	159
Goode	
Ellen	84
Geo.	84
Goodhart	
Elizabeth	42
Henry	42
J.W.	75
Sophia	75
Goodin	
R.F.	118
Goodwin	
Anna	43
David	43
Goorelin	
Elizabeth	146
Wm.	146
Gott	
Ellen	32
Richard	32
Gover	
C.C.	70
Grady	
Dr. Ewell B.	209
F.T.	3
Sarah	209
Graham	
Mary	82
Gray	
Dr. Jos. G.	262
Frances	46
Geo. E.	253
Harriet	68
Jane	160
Jno.	160
John	46, 68
L.	253

Loudoun County, Virginia, Death Register, 1853-1896   295

Mary		253	Hall		
William H.		46	Alex. A.		252
Grayham			Elizabeth		252
Mary		244	Jno.		122
Grayson			John W.		214
Alexr L.		11	Louis		198
Miss		5	Mary		122
Green		144	Sarah E.		214
Alverda		126	Halley		
Chancy		123	Bolling		194
Elizth		275	Hamer		
Flora		154	John		83
Gilbert		123	Mary		83
J.P.H.		126	Hamilton		245
Margaret		63	Jack		6
Thomas		63	James		59
Thos.		275	Jno.		170
W.S.		214	John		255
Greenage			Jonathan		250
Thos.		251	Mary	6, 23, 250, 255
Gregg			Sarah		59
Emily J.		11	Winifred		170
Geo.		238	Hammerley		
John		176	Mandly		91
P.		238	Hammerly		
Sally		176	J.W.		89
Wm.		278	Hampton		
Griffith		281	Caroline		193
Grooms			Jas.		262
Sanford		217	Marcus		155
Grubb			Hancock		
Curtis		117	Geo. H.		236
Ebenezer		74, 283	Jane		166
John		137	Susan		236
Mary E.		74, 283	Haneback		
Rachel A.		117	Jane		166
Gulick			Hanes		
Geo.		79	Jos. A.		123
Sarah		79	Margaret		197
Gustin			Thomas		197
Alpheus		235	Hanford		
Ann E.		235	John M.		267
			Polly M.		267
	H		Haris		
			Harriet		9
Haines			Harns		
Ed		190	Richd		39
Edward		81	Harper		
Mary		81	Catharine		37
Sarah		190	James		244
William		191	Julius		152

Mary	244	Geo. R.	154
W.H.H.	188	Virginia	154

Harris
- Charles 153
- Edgar 155
- Edwd/ 263
- Eli 56
- John 66
- Lewis 240
- Lucinda 28
- Malinda 66
- Mary 47, 218
- Moton 156
- Nancy 263
- William H. 185

Harrison
- Burr W. 194
- H. 201
- Janet K. 99
- Sallie 194
- Samuel 20
- Sarah 105
- Sarah A. 216
- Thomas 105

Harvy
- Mahala 14

Hatcher
- Joshua 238
- Saml 206
- Sarah 206, 238

Havener
- Bassill 30
- Joseph 181
- Rachel 30
- Sallie 181
- Thos. A. 185
- Wm. 181

Hawkins
- Mary 190

Hawley
- E. 194

Hawling
- Jemima 12
- Sidney 24

Hawlings
- Joseph L. 81

Hayes
- Lydia J. 264

Head
- Christopher 35
- Emily 35

Healey
- Jonathan 211
- Patience 211

Heater
- Nancy 71

Heaton
- N.R. 3

Hefling
- Elizabeth 32
- James 32

Hefner 105

Heilbach
- Sebastian 32

Helm
- Jos. 1
- Lewis C. 68

Henderson
- Chas. 102
- Delia 102
- F.M. 163
- Mollie 119
- Samuel 119

Hensey
- Thomas 126

Henson
- Nathan 260

Herdle
- Nancy 88
- Niland 88

Hern
- Eliza 39
- Wm. 39

Heskett
- James 40

Hibbs
- Benj. F. 52, 82, 145, 155, 188, 214
- Catharine A. 113
- Henry 39, 207
- Mary 203
- W.H. 70, 207
- Wm. 203
- Wm. H. 53, 58, 107, 115, 132, 169, 206, 207, 236, 266, 278, 279, 283

Hickman
- Eleanora 39
- Thomas 240
- Virginia 240

Loudoun County, Virginia, Death Register, 1853-1896 297

Higgins
  Harriet 138
  Hugh 138
Hipkins
  Elizabeth 148
Hirst
  E.S. 1, 11
Hixon
  Isabella 121
  Jas 121
Hixson
  A. 219
  Jas 219
Hodge
  Hannah W. 68
  Robert H. 68
Hodgson
  S.L. 122, 272
Hoffman
  Jno 160
  Mary 162
  Peter 162
  Sally 12
Hogans
  S.H. 187
Hoge
  G.D. 258
  Isaac 226
  L.D. 131
  Rachel N. 225
  Thomas 232
Hole
  Francis M. 252
Hollingsworth
  C.L. 173
Holmes
  Abigail 79
  Wm. 79
Holtzclaw
  Martha V. 123
Hooe
  Bernard 58
  Eliza J. 73
  Howson 73
  Margt. 58
Hoskinson
  Robt J. 157
Hough
  Elizth. 87
  Hannah 202
  Harriet 120, 219

  Isaac S. 271
  Jacob 87
  John 177
  L.W.S. 145, 228
  Martha 248
  Mary *See*
  Mary A. 201
  May 177
  R.R.S. 145
  Sarah A. 78. 106
  Wm. 106, 201, 202, 219, 248
  Wm. H. 174, 201
Householder
  Dr. A.B. 225
  Gideon 122
  Julia A. 122
Houser
  Abram 264
  Saml H. 151
  Susan 264
Howard
  Julian 115
  Luke 64
Howell
  Jos. 148
Howser
  R.S. 162
  Sarah 162
Hughes
  Amos 150
  Isaac 117
  Sally 117
Humphrey
  Abner 133
  Mary 133
  Wm. 51
Hunt
  Hannah 112
  Harry 53
  John L. 112
Hunter
  Allice 18
  Armstead 243
  Hannah 78
  Sarah 18
Hurst
  James 160
  Sarah 160
Hutchins
  Betsey 183
  Francis 183

Hutchison			W.B.	34
Eliz	133, 149		Wm.	276
H.B.	36		Jacobs	
John	113, 145		J.R.	207
John W.	175		R.B.	108
Jos. A.	13		Susan B.	108
Julia	197		W.L.	70
Llewellyn	197		James	
M. B.	13		Levi	6, 7, 22
W.A.	268		Madison	7
Wm A.	156		Janney	
Wm. A.	231		Abijah	152
Hyde			Asa	6
Daniel	45		Blexton	193
Sarah	45		Chas P.	273
Hyott			Hannah	193
Anna	43		Jonas	178
Jas	43		Mary	193
			Mary A.	152
I			Pleasant	178
			Stacy	193
Iden			Jared	
Douglas	126		John	65
Ish			Jarvis	
Jacob	211		Washington	281
Susan	211		Jenkins	258
			Delilah	19
			Ellen	111
J			Ezekiel	280
			Jno.	215
Jackson	111		Lydia	280
Addison	16		Margt.	215
Caroline	253		Mary	70
Ellen	47		Reuben	111
Fannie	148		Westly	70
Francis	110		Jett	
Geo	110		Ann	79
Henry	148		Lucky	9
Jane	173		Peter	79
Jno H.	120		Johnson	
Jno.	249		A.W.	18, 142
John	151		Aaron	109
Julia	116		Absalom	58
Lee	165		Aleck	68
Leven	152		Alice	229
Luise	165		Alvernon	245
Mary	16, 151		Belle	68
Richd	238		Catharine	118
S.E.	13		Denis	146
Sally	249		Ellen	22
Samuel	173			

Fanney A.	138	Mary	51
G.	229	Kendrick	
James	206	Wm. L.H.	15
Jennie	279	Kettle	
John	118, 277	Jas M.	61
Louise	58	Keyes	
Madison	279	Jane	267
Malinda	109	Wm.	267
Margaret	57	Kid	
Martha Jane	22	Henly	194
Mary	277	Kidd	
Matilda	146	Joseph S.	213
Robert	109	Martha S.	213
Sally	147	Kidwell	
Thos.	138	Henry	186
Johnston		Kilby	
George	108	S.	208
John	235	W.	208
Mary	235	Kilgour	
Jones		Margaret	262
Agie	18	Wm.	262
Burr	84	King	
Ellen	68	Craven A.	20
Henry	94, 171, 215	Thomas	93
James W.	48	Kinsolving	
Jane	48	A.O.	20
John	85, 112, 163	Klein	
Leven T.	184	Sarah A.D.	83
Lydia H.	173		
Mary	112		**L**
Millen	84		
Milly	14	Lacock	
Presley	125	Emily	210
Priscilla	165	Joseph	210
Priscilla A.	108	Lakin	
Sarah	163	James W.	272
Thomas	165	Lanham	
Thos. A.	108	Wm. A.	136
Virginia	42	Larrs	
Wm.	18	J.T.	233
Wm. A.	33, 48	Lawrence	
		John W.	222
	K	Mary K.	222
		Lawson	
Kalb		Jno. W.	181
H.P.	237, 238	Leazer	
Keen		Daniel	227
H.L.	184	L.	227
James	51	Lee	38
John	61	A.D.	53
		Alice	53
		Arch	158

Flora	68	J.S.		27
Henry	68	Loughboro		
John	127	VA.		283
Joshua	95	Love		
Louis W.	44	Mary H.		45
Maria	11	Rebecca		137
Shadrac	11	Samuel		137
Theodocia	95	Loveless		
Lefever		Catherine		267
Bettie	280	Thos.		267
John	280	Low		
William	34	Wm.		100
Leith		Lowe		
Dr.	59	Miss		208
Fanny	215	Lucas		
R.H.	249	Charles		177
Wm. G.	207	Charlotte		193
Lemon		Fenton		204
Jane	49	Millie		154
Leonard		Peyton		154
Mary	218	Lucius		
Robt	218	Charles		13
Lewis		Lucket		
Addison	14	Matthew		63, 247
Elizabeth	123	Luckett		
Fanny	20	F.F.		84
Jas.	123, 264	G.F.		53
Jon	146	Kate		224
Jonathan	211	Lucinda		113
Mariah	14	Saml C.		115, 273
Martha J.	14	Samuel C.		273
Mary	264	William		113
Welby	14	Lumbaugh		
Lightfoot		John		216
G.L.	96	Mary		216
Lindsey		Lumm		
Hannah E.	14	John		209
Littleton		Nancy		209
Edgar	103	Lutz		
Hannah	104	Lutz		84
John R.	104	Lynch		
R.C.	240, 254	Jno H.		65
Thos J.	62	Lynn		
Lloyd		J.		15, 119
Ann	206	Jno A.		38
Geo. E.	206	Joseph		133
Lodge		Sarah		133
Harmon	117	Lyon		
Long		Alex		201
John	97	Alexander		102
Look		Jane		102

Loudoun County, Virginia, Death Register, 1853-1896

Virginia		201	Mavin		
			Mary		135
M			Robt.		135
			McArter		
Maffett			Robert		111
C.J.C.		79	McCabe		
Chas E.		79	Jno		269
Jas.		48	John		115
Major			McCarty		
John		47	Billington		16
Mary		47	Geo.		135
Mankin			L.W.		13
Chas. C.		70	McCray		
Manly			Edgar		104
Caroline		53	Wm.		48
Elizabeth		96	McCutcheon		
Thomas		283	Mary		243
Thos.		53	Saml		243
Marlow			McDaniel		
Jas.		45	Ann		192
Phebe		45	Edwd.		192
Marshal			Stevens T.		246, 256
Ellen		29	McDonald		
Ruel		29	James W.		160
Martin			John		170
B.B.		41	Nancy		170
Catharine		188	McFarland		
Nicholas		188	A.		176
Mason			Bethanie		162
Betsey		96	M.		176
Geo W.		34	Maurice		233, 253
George		96	McGarvick		
Julius		277	James Henry		197
Levinia		15	Pleasant		197
Maria		277	McGavack		
Wm.		57	John		177
Massey			Sarah		177
Julus		15	McGregin		
Matheis			Rebecca		275
Mary E.		95	Wm.		275
Mathers			McIlhollen		
B.F.		54	Charlotte		65
Mathews			Henry		65
Edward		267	McIntosh		
Mathias			Jesse		128
M.		162	McKendra		
Maria		162	Phebe		173
Matthews			Wm.		173
Elias		143, 247	McKimmey		
Leah		247	Wm. F.		42
Nancy		143	McNealea		

Susan M.	275	Elizabeth	229
McOldrick		Ellen Mead	30
Jno.	187	Jno.	229
Susan	187	Robert	30
McPherson		Wm. H.	251
Daniel	193	Monroe	
Lucinda	118	Madison	207
Susan	193	Ulysses	27
Wm. E.	164	Moore	
McVeigh		A.M.	170
Elizabeth	219	Alex G.	91
Jessie	219	Alexander B.	91
Milton	17, 60	Geo S.	53
Mead		George S.	27
Aquila	38	Hannah	33
Joseph	11, 19	James W.	71
Melville		Mary	172
Maria	24	Peter	33
Mercer		Wm.	172
Richard S.	23	Moraity	
Mershon		Michael	159
Huldah	82	Moran	
Milburn		Catharine B.	127
Sarah	211	Emily	163, 249
Zenith	211	J.M.	15, 16, 17
Millard		John M.	16
Lewis M.	235	Josh G.	201
Mills		Mary J.	201
Harrison	91	Richard	249
Mary	95, 96	Richd Y.	163
Michael	180	Morris	
Rosanna	180	Mahlon	196
Sally	181	Morrison	
Wm.	95	Arch.	179
Milne		Cornelia	83
Mary	161	Jane	179
Wm.	161	John	83
Milton		Morton	
T.D.	262	Cornelia	22
Minor		Margaret	128
Mary E.	228	Richard	128
Mitchell		Moss	217
Sarah	174	Emily	42
Mobberly		Frances	107
Geo W.	283	John	107
John	36	Nancy	252
Maria	36	Nathaniel	252
Mock		Thos	42
Wm.	102	Wm.	85
Moffett		Moten	
Alice W.	251	Lisha	273

Loudoun County, Virginia, Death Register, 1853-1896

Philip	211	Newlon		
Moton		Margaret	62	
Edward	110, 111, 140	Wm.	62	
Jesse	280	Newman		
Mott		Frances	54	
A.R.	2, 13, 45, 91	George	14	
Mount		Mary	44	
James	185	T.W.	212	
Mulhen		Newton		
Bridget	133	Alex.	177	
James	133	Geo W.	234	
Mullen		Nichols	114	
Michael	152	Fanny	249	
Murphee		Isaac G.	14	
Delia	44	Jane	29, 277	
John	44	Jonah	249	
Murray		Joshua	55	
Catharine	60	Louisa	277	
Lee	58	Martha	191	
Ralph	60	Miss	9	
Murry		Naoma	55	
Alfred	218	Nathan	29	
Elizabeth	218	Rebecca	122	
Muse		Sarah	205	
Frances	181	Swithen	122	
Myers		Thos.	150	
Fenton	124	Wm.	191, 205	
Israel	29, 159	Nickens		
Mary	29, 159	Nickens	154	
Milly	234	Nixon		
Peter	234	Casandra	221	
Saml W.	230, 282	J.B.	55	
Susan	124	J.L.	232	
		J.W.	18	
N		John	221	
		Jonathan	233	
Nalls		Levi W.	14, 20, 282	
Carr B.	217	M.F.	220	
Sarah A.	217	Noble		
Neal		George	166	
Enoch	155, 156	Nancy	166	
Ginnie	275	Noland		
Neil		B.P.	278	
Ida	14	Catharine	45	
Nelson	18	Geo W.	263	
Elizabeth	152	Mary	174	
Richard	25	Philip	174	
Nesmith		Wm.	45	
Oscar	184	Wm. B.	67	
Neuman		Norris		
Mary	115	Elizth	90	

Nourse
  Milly 4

O

Oden
  James S. 245
Offutt
  Sarah 192
Ogden
  Leven 187
  Levin 205
  Robert 186
Ormiston
  Jannet 244
  Wm. 244
Orr
  Jno M. 139
  John M. 217
Orrison
  A. 100
  Annanias 230
  Charles W. 18
  David 137
  Jas A. 142
  Jno 272
  M. 93
  Mary 100, 137, 230
  Nancy 152
Orshman
  Hadley 29
  Henson 29
Osburn
  Abner 129
  Bushrod 18
  Jonah 1
  Octavius 149
  Patience 129
  Richard 116
  Rosa 260
  S. 263
  T.M. 260
Oswald
  Martha 34
Otley
  C.F. 284
  Charles F. 186
  Hannah 242
  Wm. 242
Overall
  Richard 240

Owens
  Mary 72

P

Page
  Laura 181
Paine
  Daniel 250
Palmer
  Abraham 159
  Daniel T. 163
  Jas H. 134
  Leah 163
  Priscilla 132
  R.H. 90
  Richard 90
  S.E. 38
  Wm 42
Pancoast
  Jane A. 116
  Joseph 116
Parke
  Edmund 221
Parker
  Henry 1
  Phebe 242
Parkinson
  Amanda 44
  Frank 44
Paxson
  F.M. 129
  T.M. 244
Paxton
  C.R. 67
Payne
  Ann 275
  Harriet 66
  Nancy 21
Peacock
  Elijah 263
Pearson
  T. 226, 240
Perry
  Sarah 104
Peterson
  Richard 14
Peugh
  J.B. 249
  Jas B. 248
Peyton

Loudoun County, Virginia, Death Register, 1853-1896

John	175	Powell		
Philips		Maria	115	
Isabell	125	Pamela	133	
Phillips		Peyton	5, 133, 276	
John	237	Power		
Pierce		Margaret A.	101	
Franklin	13	Robert	49	
Pierpoint		Robt	101	
Eli	138	Pratt		
Hannah	138	J.D.	37	
Piersall		Presgraves		
Thomas	199	Ann	143, 272	
Pierson		R.H.	6	
Alexander	85	Richd	143	
Craven	70	Richd.	272	
Grace	113	Prichard		
Mary E.	131	Benj.	183	
Piggott		Elizth	183	
Mary	56	Pugh		
Wm.	56	James	249	
Piles		Purcell		
Delilah	85	E.R.	150	
Jos.	95	Jonah	18	
Pinkett		Putnam		
Jane	5	Betsey	101	
Pinkit		Martin	101	
Chloe	202			
Piot				
Eveline	234	**Q**		
Plaster				
Frances	164	Quin		
Henry	164	John	174	
Jane	148			
Michael	148	**R**		
Mrs. Michael	104			
Pleasants		Radcliff		
F.W.	243	Mary	250	
Polk		Raidan		
James	13	L.	123	
Poole		Lebberton	123	
Louisa	214	Ramey		
Wm. H.	214	Sewell	78	
Potterfield		Ramsey		
L.H.	180	Betsy	120	
Luther H.	120	John	120	
Potts		Randal		
E.D.	215	Rachel	17	
Jonas	191	Randolph		
Jonathan	259	James J.	226	
Patsie	191	Susan	226	
Powel		Rawlings		
Wm. A.	4	Nancy	220	

Rhodes	220	Richard	76
Redman		Robb	
James	276	Annie	136
Reed		John P.	136
Charlotte	135	Roberson	
Harmon	265	Alfred	122
James	135	Eliza	122
Roseanna	265	Roberts	
Smith	217	Ann	187
Reeder		Presly	270
Wm. A.	1, 135	Robey	
Rees		Andrew	213
Cyrus B.	130	F.E.	30, 41, 56, 60, 63, 68, 77,
Reeves			80, 83, 91, 94, 104, 117, 141,
Mary	202		147, 178, 182, 189, 204, 229,
Walter	202		231, 247, 252, 253, 259, 271
Relerani		Frank	108
Philo	78	Wm.	125, 131
Renolds		Robinson	
Elizabeth	176	Chas	206
Thos.	176	Lydia	206
Rex		Roby	
Eliza B.	180	Andrew	217
Enoch G.	180	B.W.	94
Reynolds		Roderick	
J.K.	88	John J.	222
Rice		Rogers	
Isaac M.	3	Dinah	135
Richard		Hamilton	135
John T.	210	Richard L.	179
Richards		S.P.	8
B.H.	179	Roller	
Elizabeth	162	Frederick	171
Jesse	161	Rollins	
Levin	167, 263	Emma	219
Samuel	162	Jas. A.	133
Riley		Philip	219
Ann R.	80	Wm.	81
Annie	93	Rolls	
John	6	Mrs.	71
Riney		Rose	
Sarah A.	120	Robt.	267
Rinker		Virginia Delaney	267
Ann	136, 197	Ross	
C.W.	197	Jno	206
Thos.	136	Jno T.	251
Riticor		Wm Stephin	218
Elija V.	36	Roszel	
John	221	Sarah	90
Sallie	221	Stephen	90
Roach		Roy	

Bettie	77	Harriett	146
Joseph	77	James	177
Runner		Kate	177
Wm.	236	Mary	128
Rupp		Wm H.	128
Geo W.	213	Wm.	146
Ruse		Schneider	
Jacob	81	John	160
Mary	81	Schooley	
Russ	5	Eli S.	16
Geo H.	57	Ephraim	242
George	5	Jonas	45
Russeau		Sarah A.	45
Henry	179	Tacy	242
Sarah	179	Seaten	
Russell	227, 235	William	139
H.H.	171	Seeders	
Harriet	49	Sarah	189
Henry	184	Wm.	189
Jas. W.	119	Seitz	
Mary	48	Amanda	264
Matilda	184	Selma	
Robt E.	212	Esther	15
Robt.	48	Settle	
T.E.A.	213	Constance	247
Rust		Henry	247
Geo T.	2	Shaffner	
Ryan		Peter R.	109
John F.	163, 177	Shelton	
Margaret A.	177	Lydia	187
		Shepherd	
S		Frances	221
		Martha	198
Saffer		Thos	198
B.F.	135	Shepphard	
Susan	259	Geo	273
Wm.	259	Shillions	
Sanbower		Susan	112
Adam	235	Shiner	
Christina	235	Catharine	228
Elizabeth	222	Shipman	
Michael	222	Saml	106, 222
Sanders		Shoars	
Wilson C.	14	Priscilla	83
Sands		Shoemaker	
Esther	243	Abram	283
Jacob	243	Martha	283
Saunders		Shorb	
Aaron R.	263	Townsend	197
Al	83	Short	
Danl	217	Catharine	271
		Henry	271

Townsend	197
Shreve	
Benj.	255
Daniel	181
Francis	163
Nancy	255
Shriver	
Susanah	120
Shry	
J.H.	239
Shryock	
George	185
Polly	185
Saml	74
Shugers	
John	100
Shumaker	
Catherine	80
Jno. T.	240
Shumate	
Diadama	113
L.M.	129
Lewis M.	240
Murphy	113
Signey	
W.	231
Silcott	
Jacob	93
Jeane	93
Kate	168
Washington	168
Simmons	
Maria	184
Mary	183
Simms	
Wm.	266
Simpson	115, 175
Catharine	158
Henson	59
John	149
M. A.	59
Nancy	149
Saml	158
Sinclair	
George	120
John W.	112
Skillman	
B.W.	63
Skinner	15
Mary J.	199
N.J.	1

Peter	266
Sallie	266
Slack	
G. Phinias	248
Geo P.	248
James R.	8
Slater	240
Cathn.	77
Jacob	77
Slaves	
A. Washington	16
Abby	5
Abby Russ	5
Abraham	12
Adaline	3
Adam	20
Adam Briscoe	14
Addison Jackson	16
Addison Lewis	14
Agie Jones	18
Agnes	12
Albert	4, 6, 21
Alcinda	22, 23
Alfred	3, 6, 10, 23
Alice	4, 6, 14, 22
Alla	9
Allice	14
Allice Hunter	18
Alsey	1, 21
Amanda	9, 10, 14, 15, 17, 19, 20
Amanda Carter	7
Amanda R.	25
Amelia	3, 10
Amey	21
Amos	13
Amy	8
Amy Ann	22
Andrew	9
Angelina	6, 13, 15
Anica Berry	5
Ann	9, 11, 14, 23, 25
Ann Gant	17
Anna	9, 12
Annabella	19
Annett	5
Annie	8
Arcaner Turner	25
Arch	17
Arianna	7

Loudoun County, Virginia, Death Register, 1853-1896

Armena	19	Dundinah	15
Armistead	3, 10	Easther	15
Arthur	3, 19	Edgar	15
Ary Sweney	1	Edith	10, 18, 22
Bartley	22	Edward	24
Becca	21	Eli	1
Bella	5	Eliz. Thornton	17
Ben	18	Eliza	2, 3, 4, 5, 8, 11, 12, 14, 21
Benjamin	2, 21, 22	Eliza Ann	17
Bet Tilman	1	Eliza Clark	15
Betsy	3, 15	Eliza Jane	13
Bettie	21	Eliza Maria	9
Betty	2, 5, 7, 12, 25	Elizabeth	2, 3, 6, 7, 8, 16, 17, 22
Billy	4, 15		
Bob	3, 17, 18	Elizabeth Florence	9
Burr	9, 16	Ellen	1, 2, 6, 8, 9, 16, 18, 19, 22, 25
Bushrod	5, 22		
C. H. Smith	7	Ellen Johnson	22
Caroline	6, 8, 10, 13, 17, 23	Ely	22
Catharine	6, 12, 18	Emanuel	5
Catharine Dorcas	12	Emily	3, 6, 7, 9, 12, 14, 15, 17, 19, 22
Catherine	18		
Cela	5, 11, 16, 20	Emma	1, 6
Charity	21, 23	Esther	4, 15, 17
Charles	4, 5, 6, 10, 17, 20, 22	Eugene Washington	16
Charles Edwin	18	Eve	4, 15, 19
Charles Henry	2	Fanny	1, 2, 4, 7, 21
Charlotte	1, 18	Fanny Carter	13
Chloe	19	Fanny Lewis	20
Cidnah	4	Flavius	7
Cidney	4, 9	Flora	12, 18
Cinthia	24	Florabell	20
Clara	4, 11, 18, 25	Florinda	23
Clarissa	9	Frances	5, 6, 10, 12, 16, 20, 22, 24
Clinton	13		
Cordelia	9, 10	Frank	1, 17, 20, 24
Cornelia	10	Frankey	3
Cornelia Morton	22	Franklin	17
Craven A. King	20	Franklin Pierce	13
Cyrus	24	Gabriel	20
Daniel	12, 20	Geo	6
Delila	4, 10	Geo. Stewart	23
Delilah	9	George	2, 4, 5, 6, 8, 9, 11, 12, 17, 24
Delilah Jenkins	19		
Delpha	2	George Newman	14
Dinah	2, 5, 15	George Russ	5
Dinah Booker	4	George Thompson	8
Dink	16	George Turner	25
Dolly	19	Gooley	19
Dorothy	10	Hager	6

Hagerty	22	John Combs	23
Hanna P.	20	John Henry	9
Hannah	3, 10, 11, 12, 18, 19, 25	John Richard	20
Hannah Elizabeth	22	John Riley	6
Harriet	1, 4, 9, 11, 12, 14, 15, 16, 18, 24	John Walker	14
		Jonah	6, 9
Harriet Ann	8, 15	Jonathan	6
Harriet Haris	9	Joseph	3, 6
Harriett	13, 15	Josephine	8, 14
Harriett Fox	13	Joshua	11
Harriett or Hammat	2	Judith	10, 17, 19, 22
Harrison	8, 11	Judith Ghaskins	10
Harrison Gaskins	10	Judith Nelson	18
Harry	11	Julia	8, 17, 19
Helen	20, 22	Julia Ann	3
Henrietta	6, 8, 19	Juliet	18
Henry	13, 16, 17, 22, 23, 25	Julus Massey	15
Henry Bailey	22	Juno	3
Henry Parker	1	Jupitor	12
Henson	2	Kesiah	15
Herbert	22	Kitty	3, 13, 14, 19, 20, 24, 25
Hester	20	Lafayette Davis	12
Hiram	11	Laura	4, 12, 25
Howard	10	Laura Virginia	21
Huldah	18, 19	Lavenia	3
Ida Neil	14	Letitia	20
Irena	11	Letty	11, 12
Isaac Turner	25	Levina	4
Jack Hamilton	6	Levinia Mason	15
Jackson	3	Lewis	12
James	7, 11, 16, 20, 25	Lewis Thomas	13
James Polk	13	Lewis Warner	7
Jane	1, 2, 3, 5, 6, 11, 15, 18, 19, 27	Lina	7, 11
		Lititia	16
Jane Pinkett	5	Littitia	16
Jane Susan	9	Livenia	17
Jas Booker	4	Livinia	3
Jas.	23	Lizzie	5
Jemima	8, 17	Lizzy	16
Jennie	15	Logan	18
Jenny	11, 21	Lot	3
Jenny Linn	25	Louis	5
Jerry	2	Louisa	3, 5, 10, 15, 20
Jesse	11	Lucinda	1, 17, 20, 21, 25
Jesse Dean	13	Lucinda Summers	1
Jno	23	Luckey	17
Joanna	25	Lucky Jett	9
John	1, 3, 7, 9, 10, 11, 13, 14, 23, 24, 25	Lucy	2, 7, 9, 11, 13, 17, 19, 20, 22
John Briscoe	14	Luticia	20

Loudoun County, Virginia, Death Register, 1853-1896

Lutitia	16	Monarchy	9
Lydia	21	Moses Arnett	3
Madison James	7	Nace Tilman	1
Mahala	8, 14, 15, 20	Nancy	3, 6, 7, 14, 15, 16, 18, 19, 21, 22, 23, 24
Mahala Harvy	14	Nancy Payne	21
Malinda	20	Nannie	2
Malinda Walker	14	Nat	1
Mana	20	Nelly	2, 3, 10, 24
Mann	20	Nelson	3
Marcus	16	Newman	12
Margaret	1, 2, 8, 16, 18, 23, 24	Noah	12
Maria	3, 4, 5, 6, 7, 8, 9, 11, 12, 15, 19, 20, 21, 22, 23, 24	Olivia	19
Maria Lee	11	Oscar	24
Maria Melville	24	Parris	2
Mariah	15, 19	Patience	18
Mariah Lewis	14	Patsey	8
Marietta	9	Patsy	23
Mars	12	Patsy Russ	5
Martena	2, 10	Patty Web	1
Martha	1, 5, 17, 19, 25	Peggy	6, 25
Martha Jane	4	Percella	16, 22
Martha Jane Johnson	22	Permelia	8
Martha Washington	16	Peter	4, 18
Martin	1, 22	Phebe	5
Mary	1, 2, 4, 5, 6, 7, 10, 11, 12, 16, 19, 20, 21, 22, 23, 24	Philip	5
Mary Ann	4, 24	Pompy	8
Mary Brown	20	Priscilla	16
Mary Catharine	15	Rachel	1, 16, 21
Mary Ellen	8	Rachel Randal	17
Mary Frances	16	Ralph	25
Mary Hamilton	6, 23	Ralphney	23
Mary Jackson	16	Randolph	11
Mary Jane	7, 8, 10, 11, 13	Rebecca	1, 11, 14, 21
Mary Virginia	12	Richard	4, 11, 16
Mary West	6, 19	Richard Henry	17
Matilda	1, 7, 8, 13, 18, 24	Richard Nelson	25
Matilda Boss	25	Richard Peterson	14
Mensor	3, 24	Robert	10, 17
Meshack	12	Rocksalina	24
Mike	3	Rocksaline	24
Mildred	8	Rosanna	22
Millie Parker	1	Rose Ellen	22
Milly	2, 11, 12, 13, 20, 23, 25	Rosetta	19
Milly Jones	14	Ruth	21
Milly Nourse	4	Ruth Arnett	3
Mima	3	Sally	1, 4, 13, 20
Mitty	7	Samuel	6, 8, 15, 17, 19, 21
Molly	3	Sandy	25
		Sandy Berry	14

Sanford	21	Wm Jones	18
Sarah	2, 4, 5, 10, 11, 13, 16, 17, 20, 21, 24	Wm West	6
		Zina	10
Sarah Day	23	**Smallwood**	
Sarah Ford	23	F.M.	265
Sarah Gaskins	9	Missouri	264
Sarah Hunter	18	**Smith**	
Sarah Margaret	2	A.G.	154
Scott	5	Alexander	89
Shadrac Lee	11	C.H.	7
Shem	9	Caroline M.	204
Sidney	9	Danl.	249
Silas	24	Delight	61
Silvy	22	Eliz.	249
Simon	3	Emeline	47
Solomon	5	Fannie	228
Sophia	5	Geo. W.	61
Squire	3	H.M.	199
Stephen	4, 10, 12	Jacob	34, 271
Stephen Parker	1	James	260, 271
Susan	5, 7, 8, 9, 11, 14	Jno T.	88
Susan Steward	14	Jno.	139
Sylvia	5, 7	John L.	279
Tascar	5	Margaret	271
Tena	10	Mark	179
Tera	3	Mary	174
Theadosia	6, 7	P.A.L.	209
Thomas	1, 9, 13, 22, 24	R.	4
Thornton	12	Rebecca	260
Tilly	16	Rose	95
Toby	20	Rufus	12
Toney	14	Samuel	215
Tyna	22	Sarah	139, 271
Vermelia	2, 4	Thomas	47
Violet	3, 17, 25	Thos.	228
Violet Gaskins	4	Wm	204
Violett	25	Wm.	95, 151
Virginia	7	**Smoot**	
Walter	5	Geo.	95
Washington	17	Nancy	95
Welby Lewis	14	**Snider**	
Wesley	19	Peter	280
Westwood	6	Sarah	280
William	17	**Snoots**	
William Stringer	24	Dortha	238
Winefred	13	Henry	28
Winney	14	John	238
Winney Briscoe	14	Jonas	103
Winny	14, 18, 20	Margaret A.	183
Wm	9	Susan	77

Solomon	223	Harriet		255
Elizth.	227	John W.		255
James	227	Reuben		213
Spriggs		Sullivan		
Harriet	47	Eliz.		254
Hester	47	Marthe		254
Spring		Summers		
Cathn	61	Eli		245
Henry	61	Lucinda	1,	245
Stansbury		Surghnour		
J.J.	81	Harriet		230
Steadman		James		230
David	190	Sutton		
Elizabeth	190	Mary		76
Steer		Swan		
Wm. B.	55	Huldah		247
Stephens		Nancy		53
Jno. J.	212	S.W.		247
Stevens		Thomas		53
Elizabeth	36	Swart		
Henry	103	C.F.		24
Jas	36	Swarts		
John	242	Adrian		167
John J.	264	Ann		167
Roxanna	242	Sweney		
Steward		Ary		1
Susan	14	Sythe		
Stewart		S.P.		134
Geo.	23			
Martha	119	**T**		
Wm.	119			
Stiles		Tarleton		
Burr	139	Burr		196
Stoneburner		Mary R.		196
Stoneburner	188	Tate		
Stout		William		172
John L.	77	Tavenner		
Stoutsenberger		F.L.		50
Jacob	126	Fielding		223
Saml	244	H.		223
Strange		Henry		113
David	267	Jno.		122
Venus	267	Jonathan		12
Stream		Taylor		
Jacob H.	196	A.M.		40
Pleasant	53	Ann		212
Wm.	53	Elizabeth		102
Stringer		Frank		84
William	24	Geo. W.		156
Stringfellow		Hannah J.		134
Henry	147	Harriett		79
Strother				

Henry	212, 240	Albert	173
Henry H.	148	Elkanah	61
Henry S.	134	George	8
Jos	92	Hugh	284
LWm.	264	Hugh S.	12
Mahlon	168	Isabella	154
Manly	115	John	259
Mary S.	168	John C.	23
Robert	277	L.D.	87
Robt C.	102	Margaret	259
Robt. S.	102	Sally	61
Sarah	115	Susan	177
Sina	240	Wm. B.	177
Timothy	79	Thomson	
Tebbs		John M.	17
Alexander	247	Thorndley	
Louis	251	Mary	184
Richard	74	Wm.	184
Tennyson		Thornton	
James W.	149	Delia	253
Sarah	149	Eliz.	17
Thatcher		Humphrey	52
J.H.	117	Samuel	57
Thayer		Thrift	
Frances	30	Chas	37
G.W.	30	Nancy	37
Thomas		Throckmorton	
Ann	130	Eliza J.	135
Anna	280	Jas. B.	135
Catharine	166	Tillett	146
Catherine	79	Caroline	232
George T.	130	Honor	146
Hannah	100, 150	Samuel	232, 245
Henry	78	Tilman	
Herrod	220	Bet	1
Isaac	150	Nace	1
J.C.	4	Timbers	
Jas.	280	Margaret	84
John	276	Timms	
Jonah	149	Chloe	103
Jos.	155	Wm.	103
Lettie	168	Tippett	
Lewis	13	John	140
Malinda	169	John C.	15
Mary A.	220	Leah H.	140
Moses	168	Titus	75, 99
Peter	100	Mary A.	141
Ruth	155	T.S.	146
Sarah	78	Tolbert	
Thompson		H.H.	90
		Toliver	

Mary	163		**V**	
Wm.	163			
Torreysen		Valentine		
Catherine	175	Elizabeth	243	
Lewis	175	Jos.	84	
Torrison		Vandevanter		
Amy	103	C. M.	19	
John	103	Elizabeth	68	
Wm.	248	Jos.	68	
Tribby		Vaughn		
Samuel	265	Theresa	237	
Triplett	10	Thomas	237	
Ebenzer	157	Veale		
Simon	157	Amos	267	
Thos M.	109	Sarah	267	
Trundle		Veirs		
E.A.	128	Leroy	28	
Tumbleson		Vena		
Mary	260	Leroy	28	
Wm.	260	Mary	28	
Turner		Venay		
A.	152	Celia	29	
Arcaner	25	Chas.	29, 270	
Armistead	166	Vincel		
George	25	Adam	253	
Isaac	25	Louisa	157	
Mary	2	Mary	253	
Mary P.	112	Philip	157	
R.H.	22, 232	W.D.	127	
Tyler		Vincell		
J.J.	232, 274	Philip	7	
Jno J.	27, 254	Virts		
John J.	160	C. A.	239	
John T.	232	Conard	235	
		Eliza	235	
U		Isaac	33	
		Jno.	83	
Underwood		John	182	
Caroline	42	Lizzie	83	
Unger		M.M.	70	
Joseph	241	Michael	142	
Upson		Peter	74	
Amos	157	Sarah	142	
K.	157	Wm.	239	
Utterback				
Alias	114	**W**		
Geo. G.	56			
John	135, 274	Wadell		
Margaret	114	Eliza	207	
Sarah	135, 274	James	207	
		Waldron		

Ann	208	Weadon		
Carlisle	208	Wm.		168
Mollie J.	97	Weaning		
Walker		John O.		239
Edward	250	Web		
Jack	277	Patty		1
John	14	Wells		
Lewis	242	Elizabeth		60
Malinda	14	Isaac B.		60
Mary	250	Joseph		55
Sarah	242	Welsh		
Walkman		Frances		99
Jno F.	50	Sylvester		99
Wallace		Wenner		
Abram	251, 276	Alice		59
Waltman		Mary J.		241
M.	2	West		
M.V.	43	Hannah		197
Milton B.	206	Jno		197
Ward		Mary		6, 19
Eli	177	Wm		6
Millie	177	Whaley		
Warfield		Amelia M.		140
J.S.	229	Charles A.		25
Matilda	229	Chas W.		91
Warner		James		91
Dr.	43	Jas		29
Lewis	7	Jas.		140
Washington		Mary		29, 91
A.	16	Wheeler		
Albert	16	Johnson		281
David	206	Whitacre		
Eugene	16	Catharine		114
John E.	68	Michael		114
Maria	158	T.		50
Martha	16	White		
Robt	158	Alfred		78
Sarah	212	Daniel		263
Waters		Jas.		208, 235
Catherine	80	Joshua		17, 181
Dyer	80	Levi		193
E.H.	182	Mary		193, 208
Joseph	125	Mrs.		3
Roberta	217	Mary L.		235
Thos.	217	Nancy		85
Watson		Randolph		256
Emily	219	Rebecca		56
Mary	91	Richard		56
Shirley	91	Wm.		85
Thomas	260	Whitenham		
Wm.	219	Lucius		253

Loudoun County, Virginia, Death Register, 1853-1896

Whitmore	
Louisiana	93
Wiard	
Mary	208
Wildman	
Elizabeth	187
John W.	25
Jos.	260
Wm.	187
Wiley	
Chas.	178
Hesikiah	173
Kitty	173
Wilhelm	81
Wilkins	
Jas J.	24
Wilkinson	
Mrs. Wm.	112
Williams	8
Addison	112
C.T.	227
Chas F.	227
Chas T.	32
Chas.	8
Cornelius	181
Eliza	181
Geo	251
Israel	73
Jacob	265
James	191
Jas.	181
Jno.	263
John	258
Lucy	191
Margaret	263
Mary	72, 73
Pleasant	265
Sarah	260
Uriah	260
William	153
Wm.	55
Williamson	
Thos	204
Wilson	
Sarah	145
Wily	
John	232
Nannie	232
Windsor	
Robt	57
Winslow	
Jno.	200
Winston	
Dolbert	243
Zilpha	243
Winters	
Dennis	19
James	81
Wire	
David	34
Elizbt	34
Geo C.	275
Peter	120
Susannah	120
Wirt	
John	283
Withers	
Emily	97
Wolf	
John	148, 270
Sarah	148
Wolford	
Ann	87
Wood	
Ann W.	283
Ham	66
Thos M.	183
Woodson	
Charlotte	103
Woody	
Sarah E.	116
William	116
Woolf	
John	272
Worley	
Hannah M.	150
Worthington	
Jas	17
Joe	122
Joseph	151
Sallie	151
Wren	
Joanna	28
Thos.	28
Wrenn	
C.B.	143
Julia Ann	32
Wright	
George	186
Harriet	4
J.	97
Jonathan	150

Margt.	185		
Mary A.	97, 150	**Y**	
Nancy	187	Yakey	
Paterson	187	T.S.	149
Wm.	185	Young	
Wrightman		Cyrus	179
G.M.	38	Geo	156
Wynkoop		Henson	31
Elizabeth	41		
Thomas	41	**Z**	
		Zellers	
		Jas.	180

Other Heritage Books by Elizabeth R. Frain:

Fairfax County, Virginia Death Register, 1853-1896

Loudoun County, Virginia Death Register, 1853-1896
Elizabeth R. Frain and Marty Hiatt

Loudoun County, Virginia Marriages After 1850: Volume 1, 1851-1880
Patricia B. Duncan and Elizabeth R. Frain

Union Cemetery, Leesburg, Loudoun County, Virginia: Plats A and B, 1784-1995

Union Cemetery, Leesburg, Loudoun County, Virginia: The Later Plats, 1880-1995

Other Heritage Books by Marty Hiatt:

Early Church Records of Loudoun County, Virginia, 1745-1800

Northern Virginia Genealogy: Volume 1 Numbers 1-4 1996

Northern Virginia Genealogy: Volume 1 Number 2 April 1996

Northern Virginia Genealogy: Volume 1 Number 3 July 1996

Northern Virginia Genealogy: Volume 1 Number 4 October 1996

Northern Virginia Genealogy: Volume 2 Number 1 January 1997

Northern Virginia Genealogy: Volume 2 Number 2 April 1997

Northern Virginia Genealogy: Volume 2 Number 3 July 1997

Northern Virginia Genealogy: Volume 2 Number 4 October 1997

Northern Virginia Genealogy: Volume 3 Number 1 January 1998

Northern Virginia Genealogy: Volume 3 Number 2 April 1998

Northern Virginia Genealogy: Volume 3 Number 3 July 1998

Northern Virginia Genealogy: Volume 3 Number 4 October 1998

Northern Virginia Genealogy: Volume 4 Number 1 Winter 1999

Northern Virginia Genealogy: Volume 4 Number 2 Spring 1999

Northern Virginia Genealogy: Volume 4 Number 3 Summer 1999

Northern Virginia Genealogy: Volume 4 Number 4 Fall 1999

Northern Virginia Genealogy: Volume 5 Numbers 1-4

Northern Virginia Genealogy: Volume 6 Numbers 1-4

Northern Virginia Genealogy: Volume 7 Numbers 1-4 2002

Northern Virginia Genealogy: Volume 8, 2003

Northern Virginia Genealogy: Volume 9

Those at Rest: Lovettsville Union Cemetery, Loudoun County, Virginia, 1879-1999

Claims Presented to the Court of Augusta [Virginia], 1782-1785
Transcribed by Clay Hamilton and Marty Hiatt

Loudoun County, Virginia Death Register, 1853-1896
Elizabeth R. Frain and Marty Hiatt

Marriage and Death Notices from the Genius of Liberty, 1817-1843
Marty Hiatt, Ann Hennings and Patricia B. Duncan

Other books by Marty Hiatt and Craig Roberts Scott:

Implied Marriages of Fairfax County, Virginia
Loudoun County, Virginia Chancery Suits, 1759-1915
Loudoun County, Virginia Tithables, 1758-1786
Loudoun County, Virginia Tithables, 1758-1786
Louisa County, Virginia 1850 Federal Census
New Jerusalem Lutheran Church Cemetery
Washington County, Virginia Marriages: Minister's Returns, 1776-1855

www.ingramcontent.com/pod-product-compliance
Lightning Source LLC
Chambersburg PA
CBHW071956220426
43662CB00009B/1151